European Labour Law

54—

European Labour Law

by
Roger Blanpain
and
Chris Engels

This book was originally published as a monograph in the International Encyclopaedia of Laws / Labour Law

Fifth and revised edition
1998

Kluwer Law International
The Hague • London • Boston

Published by Kluwer Law International
P.O. Box 85889
2508 CN The Hague, The Netherlands

Sold and distributed in the USA and Canada by
Kluwer Law International
675 Massachusetts Avenue
Cambridge, MA 02139, USA

Sold and distributed in all other countries by
Kluwer Law International
Distribution Centre
P.O. Box 322
3300 AH Dordrecht, The Netherlands

A C.I.P. Catalogue record for this book is available from the Library of Congress

Printed on acid-free paper

Cover design: Louis Rinck

ISBN 90 411 0587 5 (Kluwer)

© 1998 Kluwer Law International

Kluwer Law International incorporates the publishing programmes of Graham & Trotman Ltd, Kluwer Law and Taxation Publishers and Martinus Nijhoff Publishers

The Authors

Professor Dr. R. Blanpain is professor at the Faculty of Law of the Catholic University of Leuven where he teaches both Belgian Labour Law and Comparative Labour Law. He has been Dean of the Law Faculty (1984–1988), and a Past-President of the International Industrial Relations Association (1986–1989).

At present Roger Blanpain is Director of the Institute for Labour Relations of the University of Leuven, Honorary President of the Belgian Association of Industrial Relations, Director of the Euro-Japan Institute for Law and Business and Member of the Executive Committee and Vice-President of the International Society for Labour Law and Social Security. He is also the editor of the International Encyclopaedia of Laws, the International Encyclopaedia for Labour Law and Industrial Relations, the Bulletin of Comparative Labour Law and of the book on Comparative Labour Law and Industrial Relations (6th ed. 1997). He is a *doctor honoris causa* of the University of Szeged, Hungary (1997). He is a member of the Belgian Royal Academy of Sciences (1992).

Professor Dr. Chris Engels studied law at the Catholic University of Leuven in Belgium (1979–1984). He obtained his Ph.D. at the Catholic University of Leuven in Belgium and got his Masters Degree (LL.M.) at the University of California, Los Angeles (USA).

At present Chris Engels is a Professor at the Faculty of Law of the Catholic University of Leuven, where he teaches courses in European and Comparative Labour Law, and Procedural Social Law. He is also a member of the Brussels bar.

The Authors

4

Table of Contents

Table of Contents

Table of Contents

Table of Contents

Table of Contents

Table of Contents

Table of Contents

Epilogue: In Search of . . .

Appendices

Table of Contents

List of Abbreviations

Art.	Article
CBI	Confederation of British Industry
CEEP	Centre Européen des Entreprises Publiques
COJ	Court of Justice
COPA	Comité des Organisations Agricoles
EC	European Communities
EEA	European Economic Area
EFTA	Economic Free Trade Association
ESC	Economic and Social Committee
ECSC	European Coal and Steel Community
ed.	Editor
EMF	European Metal Workers Federation
EP	European Parliament
ETUC	European Trade Union Confederation
Euratom	European Atomic Energy Community
EWC	European Works Council
ICFTU	International Confederation of Free Trade Unions
IELL	International Encyclopedia for Labour Law and Industrial Relations
IGC	Intergovernmental Conference
ILO	International Labour Organisation
OECD	Organisation for Economic Cooperation and Development
O.J.	Official Journal
SE	Societas Europaea
SEA	Single European Act
TEU	Treaty of the European Union
T.P.R.	Tijdschrift voor Privaat Recht
T.S.R.	Tijdschrift voor Sociaal Recht
UNICE	Union of Industrial and Employers Confederation of Europe
v.	versus
VAT	Value added tax
WCL	World Confederation of Labour

List of Abbreviations

Prologue

1. Writing about European labour law in 1998 and beyond conjures up feelings of *distress* about record high unemployment figures, a growing dual society and the inability to effectively tackle the challenge we are faced with.

Indeed, *unemployment*[1] has reached such levels that one can readily talk about a kind of social harassment in the European work places: more than 50 per cent of employees in the Community at present are either unemployed or afraid of becoming idle. The pace with which our industrialised countries are thrown into post industrial communication societies is so swift that their very social fabric and cohesion is threatened. The speed of the economic and technological change and its profound nature are so dramatic that social measures aiming at reintegrating those who are being pushed out from their present jobs are often more than inadequate.

It is equally evident that only within larger frameworks, surpassing the nation-States, like the European Union, that appropriate solutions can be elaborated. Indeed, our economics are becoming more and more international, our enterprises more and more part of international networks, producing international products or rendering such services. Repetitive jobs in industry and services alike, some management jobs included, are exportable and exported to low wage countries or wiped out by new technologies. Only *creative work* can bring about the high added economic value which is necessary to support our ailing societies and finance adequately appropriate social policies. Creative work needs creative minds and a supportive infrastructure. Creativity presupposes a mental revolution where learning and training of young and adults is focused on abstraction, analyzing and solving problems rather than on the intake of rules to be repetitively applied in any circumstances.

It was therefore laudable that the European Union under the Maastricht Treaty, got extended competence regarding the development of quality education (Art. 126 EC) and vocational training Art. 127 EC), while fully respecting the responsibility of the Member States for the content and organisation of *vocational training*. This allows for a European strategy and effort to engage and involve national decision makers in a mental reconversion leaving repetition training and heading towards more creative education. Not much progress was made in this area. The mental revolution has not yet taken place, despite the Commission's White Paper on Education, Training, Teaching and Learning; 'Towards the Learning Society'[2] and the EP's Resolution on this White Paper.[3]

It is especially in the area of employment that results are really disappointing. The hope which was given impetus by the Delors White Paper (1993) on 'growth, competitiveness and employment,' partly sustained by the White Paper (1994) on

Social Policy, has disappeared as the Council has not really answered the call for a Confidence Pact on Employment (1996) in the rush toward the EMU, which is undoubtedly necessary, but insufficient to deal with the problems of exclusion and poverty, which result from unemployment. Europe does not address the issues of the day. The plan adopted at the 1994 Council in Essen is insufficient and inappropriate, as most unemployment policies are geared to restore the industrial society of yesterday, which we are leaving at an increasing speed, catapulted as we are into an information-network society, which is characterised by out-sourcing, decentralisation, team- and networking over the boundaries of enterprises and countries.[4]

The Treaty of Amsterdam, negotiated at the summit meeting of the European Council of Ministers, 16 and 17 June 1997, did not add anything significantly new regarding employment. The EMU received all the focus. The basic question remains; what will the impact be of the European Monetary Union on jobs, on wages and employment conditions and on collective bargaining?[5]

Few would contest the necessity and utility of a single European currency. That is beyond discussion. But the EMU is more than that. It is an ironclad arrangement, aiming at low inflation, limited public deficits and establishing a politically independent Central European Bank, which will govern on a purely monetary basis. Prices and interest rates are permanent. The EMU goes along and fortifies the pure market ideology of the globalised, digital driven world economy, where only the best, preferably new products and services at the lowest possible price, are winners.

The point is that, when all those (financial) elements are fixed, labour costs across national boundaries are transparent and totally comparable. More importantly, however, reducing labour costs (productivity included) becomes for the enterprises one of the, if not the, most important factor(s) in the competitive battle on European and foreign markets.

Labour costs (direct and indirect) become the flexible, adaptable element *par excellence*.

Labour costs will have to be controlled by companies. This will lead to an increase in restructuring, more machines to replace human labour, more relocations and more redundancies. More unemployment is in the air and taken for granted (the so-called natural rate of unemployment). Minimum wages will be more and more questioned as the cause of unemployment for the lower skilled workers. The dual society and inequalities will continue to grow at exasperating rate.[6]

Labour costs will be manipulated because, as already indicated earlier, they are an important element in the competition to attract foreign investment. It is no wonder that the bulk of foreign direct investment in Europe goes to Great Britain,[7] where wage costs are 30–40–50 per cent cheaper than in quite a number of EU Member States.[8] Siemens of Germany has calculated that wage costs in Scotland constitute only 33 per cent of costs in Berlin. 'The financing of the welfare system means that Germany's non-wage labour costs exceed their US equivalent by 175 per cent and those in Japan by 140 per cent'.[9]

It must be explicitly stated that labour costs and related issues like social security expenditures, remain exclusively within the national sphere of competence even after the Treaty of Amsterdam and the new social chapters. The same is true for employment policies. Indeed, the new employment chapter in the Treaty of the EC deals mainly with the co-ordination of national policies. The off-shoot is that **there**

are no social countervailing mechanisms counter the EMU. In other words, Europe will remain, what it is at present; a paradise for **social dumping**.

Labour costs issues remain a national issue. European decisions on these issues require a unanimous decision at European level, also for the harmonization of direct and indirect taxes at European level. The more Member States there are, the more difficult it will be to reach a unanimous decision on these very important issues.

The EU, as it currently stands, is becoming more of a free trade zone, instead of a real social Union. In other words, Europe needs a full, fledged social policy at European level.

But we are not there yet. The consequence is that social policies, including collective bargaining, will undergo the full weight of the globalisation of the economy, fortified by the EMU, concentrating on low inflation and consequently accepting a high degree of unemployment.[10] The focus is on increased flexibility as, according to leading EMU and OECD ideology, unemployment is caused largely by labour market rigidities, which have to be removed in order to promote employment.

It is true that unnecessary rigidities on the labour markets exist, but it is clear that the market mechanisms have to be socially corrected in order to be acceptable from the human point of view.

In other words, there is asymmetric development between globalisation of the economy, global economic decisions and local social systems and taxation. 'Thus, the asymmetric patterns of globalisation mean that the benefits of free trade will not be shared equally. It is not the globalisation itself but its asymmetric development which will ensure harmonisation downwards of labour, social and environment conditions'.[11] The Economic and Social Council concludes rightly 'that basic minimum global standards must be established in respect of human, workers and environmental rights'. It underlines that 'the current mood of powerlessness in the face of the problems needing to be solved, e.g., unemployment, results in part from the fact that at present the worldwide process of globalisation is being met by isolated national or regional strategies'.[12]

But even at the regional level, this strategy is not forthcoming in Europe. The highly praised 'European social model' is at stake. The idea that 'social protection', set out in Article 2 of the Treaty, must be seen 'as a productive factor facilitating change and progress rather than a burden on the economy or an obstacle to growth,[13] is becoming more and more of a chimera.

The special jobs summit of the European Council in Amsterdam (16–17 June 1997) was important, not only for the decisions that were taken, but also for those that were postponed. The non-adjustment of the composition of the European Commission and the European Parliament, as well as the decision-making process (more majority voting was necessary, in order to prevent ongoing veto's) in view of the enlargement of the European Union to 20 or more Member States, belong to the later category.

Developments in the European Union are also important for the situation in Eastern and Central Europe, which is far from being rosy. Since the fall of the Berlin wall, countries in Eastern and Central Europe have been struck by deregulated labour markets, high unemployment, weak trade unions and employers' associations, token tripartitism and a growing decentralisation in (weak) bargaining. Guy

Standing of the ILO reports, 'plant and enterprise bargaining is becoming the norm in many countries. Often there has been a two-tier process with national framework agreements setting minima and general directions . . . while enterprise management's and unions negotiate annual or, less often, bi-annual agreements on actual wages, working conditions and various other issues'.[14]

Minimum wages have become meaningless in many countries. Eastern Europe, as well as other regions, lives in the grip of pure market mechanisms. *De facto*, 'corporate governance' prevails: unilateral managerial decision-making is the rule. The future for substantive collective bargaining providing for a balance between economic and social policies seems very bleak.

This does not take away from the fact that a more social Europe, providing for minimum conditions and setting rules for a social playing field, putting an end to social dumping and asymmetric developments, is a 'must'.

So this is a book for a social Europe. It is indeed clear that the individual must occupy a central place in the vast common European market, governed by the economic rules for free and creative enterprise. There is a need for socially inspired measures, which monitor and guide the economic development in such a way that justice and freedom foster well-being for all. The term 'social' means that Europe, in the framework of social and economic cohesion and genuine solidarity, guarantees fundamental human rights to employers, workers, the self-employed, handicapped persons and pensioners, in line with a humanistic and personalised vision, which should make Europe the shining corner of the world.

We study the European labour law covering the 15 Member States of the EU. This law also applies to the EEA, which means also to Iceland, Norway and Switzerland.

According to the 1995 Labour Force Survey of Eurostat the Member States have:

- a *total population* of 365,000,000;
- *people in employment*: 148,000,000;
- 124,000,000 (84 per cent) full-time;
- 82 per cent employees;
- 89 per cent: in permanent jobs;
- 11 per cent: in temporary jobs;
- 16 per cent: self-employed;
- 24,000,000 (16 per cent) worked part-time (80 per cent women);
- 65 per cent in the services sector;
- 30 per cent in industry;
- 5 per cent in agriculture;
- women: 41 per cent;
- less than 25 of age: 12 per cent;
- *unemployment*: 18,000,000 (11 per cent);
- 49 per cent for a year or more;
- 20 per cent looking for a first job.

1. The Commission uses a definition of unemployment, which is in accordance with the recommendations of the ILO and is generally suitable for international comparisons. According to this definition, all persons above 15 years of age, who are art of work (i.e., have not done a single hour of paid work during the week, who are actively looking for a job and who are

available (ready to start work within two weeks) are considered 'unemployed' (Question EP 1746/96, C. Cedershiöld), 15 July 1996).

2. (COM) (95)0590-C4-0597/95).
3. *O.J.*, 14 April 1997, No. C 115/85-92.
4. 'Work in the XXIst Century,' in: *Comparative Labour Law and Industrial Relations* (ed. R. Blanpain-C. Engels), Deventer, 1997.
5. Compare Mahnkopf, Birgit and Altvater, Elmar, Transmission Belts of Transnational Competition? Trade Unions and Collective Bargaining in the Context of European Integration, *European Journal of Industrial Relations*, 1995, No. 1, 101–118.
6. 'The UK has experienced an unprecedented rise in inequality over the past 20 years. The richest 10 per cent of the population has now as much income as all the households in the bottom 50 per cent, and also all of measures poverty has increased. This change is here to stay. The large rise in unemployment explains the trend of growing inequality. As unemployment grew during the 1980s and 1990s, there has been an increase in both no-earner and two-earner households. By 1993, more than 70 per cent of income in the bottom 10 per cent of households came from means-tested benefits such as income support and housing benefit (Andrew Balls study points to 'unprecedented rise in inequality', *Financial Times*, 28 July 1997.

    The same can be noted for the USA. Laura Tyson D'Andrea writes as follows: 'Unfortunately, the economy's expansion has failed to reverse two disturbing long-run trends: stagnant or falling real earnings for the majority of workers and increasing income-inequality among workers and households. In addition, the gap between rich and poor households is much larger than it was 20 years ago'. (Inequality amid prosperity, *International Herald Tribune*, 12–13 July 1997.)
7. 'The UK's main attraction is low-cost flexible labour'. Graham Bowley, There's no place like overseas, *Financial Times*, 24 July 1997.
8. The recent rise in the value of the pound, could, if permanent, offset this partly or totally.
9. Peter Norman, Germany in a frail condition, *Financial Times*, 28 July 1997.
10. Cross-border labour mobility is relatively low in the Community, in particular in comparison to mobility within the United States. However, data from the Organization for economic cooperation and development show that in Australia and Canada, which are monetary unions one may compare with a future economic and monetary union (EMU), inter-regional mobility is not considerably higher than in many European countries and is significantly lower than in the United States. The comparison with the United States that is frequently used to show that the Community is not an optimal currency area is thus perhaps not such a convincing argument. The examples of Australia and Canada provide another argument showing that the role of labour mobility may not be as important as may be suggested in the literature. In EMU, Member States will no longer be able to use their exchange rate as an instrument to deal with country-specific economic shocks. However, a fundamental issue is whether the non-availability of the exchange rate instrument in EMU actually is such a big loss. First of all, it may be argued that – given the economic convergence in the Community – the likelihood of shocks just hitting one Member State is rather small. Studies have found that in the Community a large proportion of employment shocks are region and not country-specific. Furthermore, exchange rate adjustments are not appropriate when dealing with industry specific shocks. Neither are they appropriate in case of long lasting shocks because they would hinder necessary structural adjustments. Finally, studies show that interregional migration even within Member States is not substantial in response to shocks. Therefore, one may argue that the present currency areas in Europe are not substantially superior to a future EMU' (Written Question E-0552/97 by Ulf Holm (V), O.J., 1888 October 1997, C 319/111).
11. Economic and Social Committee, Opinion on 'Employment, Competitiveness and Economic Globalisation', 19 March 1997, *O.J.*, 26 May 1997, No. C 158/17-18.
12. *Idem*, p. 19.
13. European Commission, *Progress report on the implementation of the medium-term social action programme 1995–1997, Social Europe*, Supplement 4/96, 1.
14. Guy Standing, Labour Market Governance in Eastern Europe, *European Journal of Industrial Relations*, 1977, p. 151.

2.   These fundamental social rights can *in abstracto* be promulgated either by the International Labour Organisation (ILO), by the European Institutions, by national

States or by regions. It seems to me, however, that specific European measures are needed and indicated, and this for various reasons.

a. The international standards laid down by the ILO are enormously important as world-wide rules of behaviour, but for evident reasons they need coaching and adaptation in order to respond to Europe's social side and to the more advanced European level of development. European norms have still, of course, where possible and appropriate, to build further on the ILO conventions and recommendations.
b. National rules are not always sufficient: the extent of national instruments stops at the national borders. When issues and realities transcend national frontiers, such as the free movement of labour in the EC or the restructuring of enterprises, which affect workers in different countries and thus take a European dimension, rules are needed at the appropriate level so that economy and justice go hand in hand and the standards, as well as the issues at stake, have a transnational or supranational character.

In short, Europe must have its own specific social policy and, consequently, its own full-fledged labour law.

3. This book deals with *European Law*: Europe on the one hand and labour law on the other. Europe covers *in casu* the territory for which the EC is competent. Europe also needs a Community law. This concept is reasonably simple. However, the nation of *labour law* is more difficult. Although the expression 'labour law' is used in Article 118 of the EC Treaty, where the promotion of close cooperation between Member States in the social field is addressed, it is clear that an explicit and generally accepted definition of European labour law is at present nonexistent. This is even more noticeable since 'provisions relating to the rights and interests of employed persons' are considered, in conformity with the European Single Act of 1986, to be of national – and not European – jurisdiction (Art. 100A, §2 of the EC Treaty); indeed, measures relating to these rights and interests are subject to a unanimous decision by the Council so that each Member State enjoys a right of veto, as will be explained in much more detail later. However, since the (1989) Social Charter and the Agreement on Social Policy, concluded between 11 Member States (Maastricht 1991), a rather broad notion of labour law prevails within that framework. Indeed, Article 1 of the Agreement reads:

> 'the Community and the Member States shall have as their objectives the promotion of employment, improved living and working conditions, proper social protection, dialogue between management and labour, the development of human resources with a view to lasting high employment and the combating of exclusion. To this end the Community and the Member States shall implement measures which take account of the diverse forms of national practices, in particular in the field of contractual relations, and the need to maintain the competitiveness of the Community economy.'

It is nevertheless possible to advance a European definition of labour law since the worker is the main focus on labour law and there is a European definition of a worker. This European definition was formulated by the Court during the settlement of disputes concerning the implementation of free movement for workers, and appears in Article 48 of the EC Treaty.

> 'Since freedom of movement for workers constitutes one of the fundamental principles of the Community, the term "worker" in Article 48 may not be interpreted differently according to the law of each Member State but must have a Community meaning. Since it defines the scope of that fundamental freedom, the Community concept of a "worker" must be interpreted broadly. That concept must be defined in accordance with objective criteria which distinguish the employment relationship by reference to the rights and duties of the persons concerned. *The essential feature of an employment relationship, however, is that for a certain period of time a person performs services for and under the direction of another person in return for which he receives remuneration.*'[1]

In giving this interpretation, the European Court associates itself with the definition of the term 'worker', which is accepted in the Member States in general.[2] Labour law relates thus to employees, who work in subordination. Workers presuppose employers, namely those for which the services in subordination are rendered against pay. European labour law, consequently, like national labour law in the Member States, deals with the relations between employers and workers.

1. COJ, 3 July 1986, *Lawrie-Blum* v. *Land Baden-Württemberg*, No. 66/85, IELL, *Case Law* No. 98, 1196–1197. This does not diminish the fact that, for certain European instruments, reference is made to the national definitions. This is the case with the directive of 14 February 1997 concerning the transfer of enterprises (*Foreningen of Arbejdsledere i Danmark* v. *A/S Danmols Invenar*, No. 105/85, IELL, *Case Law* No. 77).
2. 'Employed or Self-employed,' Special Issue, *Bulletin of Comparative Labour Relations*, Brooks, B. and Engels, C. (Guest Editors), No. 24, 1992, p. 175.

4.   National labour law usually limits itself to regulating employment in the private sector. European labour law, however, also covers employment in the public sector. This is the case for the regulation of equal treatment of men and women regarding pay and working conditions or of the free movement of workers. The scope of European labour law has consequently to be defined accordingly, case by case.

European labour law, taking into account the fact that European rules, which relate to workers, deals with both individual (e.g., concerning the free movement of workers or the equal treatment of men and women) and collective labour relations (e.g., information and consultation of workers' representatives in the case of collective redundancies or workers' participation in the Societas Europaea (SE)), can be defined as 'the body of European legal rules that govern the individual and collective labour relations between employers and workers, namely those who perform work in subordination.'

5.   Our book on European labour law is *de facto* the result of the revision and integration of two earlier studies, namely *Labour Law and Industrial Relations of the European Community* (1991) and *Labour Law and Industrial relations of the European Union. Maastricht and beyond: from a Community to a Union* (1992) both published by Kluwer and since then updated (1993). It was indeed an obvious step to amalgamate both books, since the European regulations emanate from the same institutions and affect largely the same groups of employers and employees, especially since the Maastricht Treaty came into force on 1 November 1993.

6. The Maastricht Top of 9–10 December 1991 was an important event, also for those interested in what direction the Europe of the Twelve, as a social Community of some 150,000,000 managers and employees, would go. The debate in Maastricht was dominated by the battle between the United Kingdom and the European continental Member States concerning a more progressive profile for the European Community regarding social matters. The outcome was painful as well as historic. Painful in the sense that the United Kingdom opted out and is going its own way, at least for the moment; historic as the 12 Member States, the United Kingdom included, not only agreed to confirm the '*acquis communautaire*' reached in the social field, but also, in a *Protocol on Social Policy*, that the other 11 Member States could equally do their own thing and launch more progressive social policies. Thus a *new social European dimension* came into being.

7. The 11 Member States committed themselves in Maastricht to the promotion of employment, improved living and working conditions, proper social protection, dialogue between management and labour, the development of human resources with a view to lasting high employment and the combating of exclusion.

The Maastricht Protocol on Social Policy and the consecutive Agreement on Social Policy include an extension of the social competence of the 11 Member States as well as of qualified majority voting and the possibility of collective labour agreements to be concluded at Community level with, under certain conditions, binding effect *erga omnes*.

8. Not only the British had difficulties with a more progressive social Europe. Also the Greek, the Irish, the Portuguese and the Spanish had their problems and asked for and obtained more financial help to pay among other things for a higher social protection through a strengthening of the economic and social cohesion of the Community, including the setting up of a *Cohesion Fund* to promote projects in the field of environment and infrastructure.

9. The importance of the Maastricht Protocol and Agreement on Social Policy between the eleven Member States is also to be evaluated in the light of the imperative economic convergence, agreed upon in Maastricht, in the framework of the Economic and Monetary Union at the earliest by 1 January 1997 or at the latest by 1 January 1999: namely the danger than in one or more Member States an eventually impossible monetary devaluation would be compensated by a social devaluation. The Maastricht Protocol and Agreement on Social Policy will hopefully contribute to check and contain that threat.

10. Hopefully, as the Maastricht outcome on social policy constituted indeed a compromise, formulated by the Dutch Presidency, trying to win the agreement of the United Kingdom. The text, which was finally adopted by 11 Member States, is thus not as far-reaching as some, like the Commission or some Governments, had hoped for. But at least important progress for 11 Member States could be reported.

Since then, Austria, Finland and Sweden have joined the EU, so that the Maastricht Agreement applies to 14 Member States.

11. Anyway, the Maastricht Protocol means that there is a *two-track social Europe*: one for the Community as a whole and one for the Community minus the United Kingdom. For the 14 Member States an economic and a social Europe constitutes indeed two sides of the same coin and should develop harmoniously and together, as both condition each other. For the United Kingdom, represented by the Conservative John Major, on the contrary an extension of the Community's social role would add more rigidities to the labour market and thus decrease the much needed flexibility and increase unemployment. The British Prime Minister was, as he put it, 'not prepared to put British jobs on the line.' Major reported a victory at Maastricht. Time will however show whether this was indeed a British victory ('game, set, match'), how long Great Britain will be isolated as far as social policies are concerned and when it will again join the Community on these issues.

12. All this also means that there are two possible ways for the 14 Member States to develop social policies: one within the framework of the EC Treaty, which remained, regarding social policies, largely unchanged after Maastricht and one within the framework of the agreement concluded between the Member States of the European Community with the exception of the United Kingdom.

To this has to be added that the Maastricht Protocol and Agreement on Social Policy is considered to constitute a part of the *'acquis communautaire'* which means that they will also apply to those countries which accede to the EEA.

13. Obviously, mention has to be made of the Treaty of Amsterdam (16–17 June 1997), which contains no less than VI Sections. Above all, there is an inflation of protocols and declarations: 14 protocols and 46 declarations.

Quite a number of issues dealt with by the European Council, relate directly to employment, industrial relations and labour law. As far as 'social Europe' is concerned, the playing field is clear. Some capital steps were taken with the introduction of new chapters in the Treaty of the European Community concerning employment (Chapter III) and social policy (Chapter IV), a general principle of non-discrimination, references to the Social Charter of the Council of Europe etc.

The new Chapter IV incorporates the Social Agreement of Maastricht. This is quite important. The two track social Europe due to the British opt-out, will come to an end once the treaty is ratified. There is a possibility to do something more at the European level in the social field.

The Treaty does not provide for new, directly enforceable individual or collective social rights. But it does give a legal basis for action by the appropriate institutions of the EU in certain areas, non-discrimination or employment policies, for example. So, a dynamic process can be launched, if the political will is there and subsidiarity rules permit fully fledged European action.

Special mention must be made to the following:

– fundamental rights, with reference to the European Convention for the Protection of Human Rights, the European Social Charter, issues like the principle of non-discrimination, disability, equality of men and women and protection of data;

- the Employment Chapter (III): co-ordinating national strategies, as employment policies are clearly left to the competence of the Member States;
- the Chapter on Social Policy (IV), integrating the Maastricht Agreement on Social Policy; and also providing for the possibility of positive discrimination;
- the environment: looking for a balance between the environment and high employment;
- culture and non-professional sport;
- a Protocol on the application of the principles of subsidiarity and proportionality, clearly indicating that regarding matters of mixed competence, the EU can only intervene when there is additional (European) value and only as far as necessary, leaving maximum authority to Member States and consequently to the Social Partners;
- the Presidency Conclusions regarding employment, competitiveness and growth. In that framework mention has to be made of the Commission's Action Plan for the Single Market submitted to the Amsterdam Summit.

It will take some time, before the Treaty of Amsterdam will be ratified. Therefore, the Treaty is included here by way of an Annex. Once the Treaty has been ratified and it enters into force, the relevant provisions will be integrated into the main text of this book.

14. This book contains a General Introduction and two Parts: one devoted to individual labour law (I) and a second that deals with collective labour law (II). The book ends with an epilogue, an annex, appendices a short bibliography, an alphabetical list of cited cases from the European Court of Justice and an index.

In the General Introduction, attention is paid to the *institutional framework* leading to European Community law (§1). Here, the three European Treaties (ECSC, Euratom and the EC) are examined, as well as the Institutions of the Community (the EP, the Council, the Commission and the Court) and other organs, such as the ESC, the European Social Fund, certain advisory bodies, etc. Then follows the legislative process in the Communities and the relationship of the EC to other international organisations, especially the ILO, the EEA and the Europa Agreements concluded with some Central and Eastern European States. §2 is devoted to the European social partners, especially UNICE and ETUC. §3 deals with the jurisdiction of the EC, namely the ECSC, Euratom and the EEC with regard to labour law matters. The final section (§4) of the General Introduction examines the genesis and the development of European labour law. Special attention is paid to the relationship between the economic and social aspects of Community affairs and due regard is given to the solemn declaration of the basic social rights for workers (1989) and the social action programme, whose purpose is to implement that declaration. We self-evidently pay adequate attention to the remarkable progress, at least legally speaking, which was reached during the Maastricht top of December 1991 where the already mentioned Protocol and Agreement on Social Policy were concluded, as well as to the Delors White Paper (December 1993), indicating measures to foster growth and combat unemployment and exclusion, the White Paper on European Social Policy (July 1994), the measures to combat unemployment as agreed upon by the Council at the European top in Essen (December 1994), the

Confidence Pact for Employment (1996) and self-evidently the IGC, which started in 1996. In this framework the question is raised whether we do need to include fundamental social rights in the Treaty of the European Union. The answer is 'yes.'

The Treaty of Amsterdam (1997) did not follow that road. But the Treaty does contain, as already indicated earlier, quite a number of stipulations relating to fundamental rights, labour law and industrial relations.

It will take some time before the Treaty of Amsterdam is ratified by the Member States and integrated in Community Law. As long as this has not happened, the Treaty of Maastricht (1991) and the Social Protocol and Agreement are still in force. The two systems, the prevailing and the coming one – before and after Amsterdam – have to be dealt with separately.

For those reasons, we will expand on the Treaty of Amsterdam in the annex.

Following this order of ideas, speculation concerning and discussion of the question regarding the convergence or divergence of labour law systems in the Member States of the Community is of course a 'must.' This discussion concludes the General Introduction.

15. The first Part is devoted to *individual labour law*. Here, important developments have taken place, especially due to the crucial role of the Court. We discuss the free movement of workers (Chapter 1), the equal treatment of men and women (Chapter 5) and the restructuring of enterprises (Chapter 10) in relation to collective redundancies, the transfer of enterprises and the insolvency of the employer. A theme that recently made rather technical but nevertheless important headway is the health and safety of workers in the working environment (Chapter 8). Another far-reaching subject is the European Treaty of June 1980 relating to elements of international private labour law (Chapter 2). In other fields developments can be noted, and this is so in the area of working time (Chapter 4 and 7), the protection of motherhood (Chapter 6) and individual employment contracts (Chapter 3). Regarding the latter point some concrete measures were taken, namely regarding part-time employment and temporary work and the employer's obligation to inform employees of the conditions applicable to the contract of employment relationship.

16. The second Part deals with *collective labour law*. Here the possibilities for European-wide collective agreements are evaluated against the background of European social realities (Chapter 1) including the Maastricht Agreement on Social Policy. In Chapter 2 we examine the proposals of the Commission regarding worker's participation in the public limited liability company and the SE, as well as the very important directive on EWCs and transnational information and consultation procedures.

17. There is no doubt that both the Protocol and the Agreement belong to Community Law. The Protocol is annexed to the Maastricht Treaty and forms an integral part thereof (Art. 239). The wording of the Protocol is such that it includes the Agreement.

'The fact that the Agreement operates between eleven Member States is of no importance: all twelve Member States have agreed to this arrangement and, therefore, by virtue of Article 236 of the EC Treaty . . . it is valid.'[1]

The first chapter of Part II provides *a general framework for the European collective agreements*, which may be concluded under the Maastricht Protocol and Agreement on Social Policy between the eleven Member States. Indeed, *the possible venue* of European collective agreements leads to a number of complicated problems, also legal ones, which can only be tackled if one has a better insight into the complex and delicate set of relationships which constitute the collective bargaining process and which may eventually lead to collective agreements. Two of the more difficult points concern self-evidently the scope and the binding effect of those agreements. It is interesting to note that the social partners failed to agree on issues like the EWC and the shift of the burden of proof regarding equal treatment, but succeeded in concluding a first European collective agreement on Parental Leave on 14 December 1995, which was promulgated by a Council Directive and a Second one on Part-time work on 6 June 1997.

1. P. Watson, 'Social Policy after Maastricht,' *Common Market Law Review*, 1993. 489–490.

18.   I would like to add a word about the language and terminology used. I am obviously writing in a foreign language, which, despite the best efforts of the best rewriter, remains an awkward exercise. The language and terminology used by the European Communities do not simplify the task. A sentence such as 'the rights conferring immediate or prospective entitlement to old age benefits, including survivors benefits, under supplementary company or inter-company pension schemes outside the national statutory social security schemes' may illustrate the point, certainly for non-native English speakers. Many European texts have been drafted in French and one is acutely aware of this fact when reading the translation. This is certainly the case for the smaller Community languages like Dutch, my mother tongue, which is practically never used as an original language for writing and formulating Community instruments. This deeply influences the language used in this book, because, for reasons of legal security, we wish to stick as closely as possible to the wording of Community law. Moreover, the terms used in the different Community languages to convey the same message do not always have the same meaning. A typical example can be found in the directive concerning the transfer of enterprises (1977); here the terms: *bedrijfstak*, company or intercompany, *professionel ou interprofessionel, betrieblichen oder überbetrieblichen, professionali o interprofessionali, faglige eller fvaerfagliche*, should have the same meaning, *quod non*! Rightly the European Commission indicated that a Community instrument cannot be interpreted on the basis of one, isolated, linguistic version, but must be explained in accordance with the goals of the instrument and its direction in close relation with the versions in the other Community languages.[1]

The same problem was illustrated by the *Rockfon* case (Denmark),[2] where the meaning of the word 'establishment,' used in the Directive on collective redundancies (1975), was discussed. Indeed, the term 'establishment' is not defined in the Directive. Rockfon maintained that it was not an establishment, since it has no management which can independently effect large-scale dismissals.

The Court observed that the term 'establishment' is a term of Community law and cannot be defined by reference to the laws of the Member States.

The various language versions of the Directive use somewhat different terms to convey the concept in question:

'the Danish version has "virksomhed", the Dutch version "plaatselijke eenheid", the English version "establishment", the Finnish version "yritys", the French version "établissement", the German version "Betrieb", the Greek version επιχείρηση", the Italian version "stabilimento", the Portuguese version "estabelecimento", the Spanish version "centro de trabajo" and the Swedish version "arbetsplats".'

A comparison of the terms used show that they have different connotations signifying, according to the version in question, establishment, undertaking, work centre, local unit or place of work. As was held in *Bouchereau*, the different language versions of a Community text must be given a uniform interpretation and in case of divergence between the versions the provision in question must therefore be interpreted by reference to the purpose and general scheme of the rules of which it forms a part.[3]

The Summit of Edinburgh (11–12 December 1992) addressed the issue under the heading 'SIMPLIFICATION OF AND EASIER ACCESS TO COMMUNITY LEGISLATION.' The Summit led to the following declaration:

'Making new Community legislation clearer and simpler.
While the technical nature of most texts and the need to compromise among the various national positions often complicate the drafting process, practical steps should nevertheless be taken to improve the quality of Community legislation, such as the following:
(a) guidelines for the drafting of Community legislation should be agreed upon, containing criteria against which the quality of drafting of legislation would have to be checked;
(b) delegations of Member States should endeavour, at all levels of the Council proceedings, to check more thoroughly the quality of legislation;
(c) the Council Legal Service should be requested to review draft legislative acts on a regular basis before they are adopted by the Council and make suggestions where necessary for appropriate redrafting in order to make such acts as simple and clear as possible;
(d) the jurist-linguist group, which does the final legal editing of all legislation before it is adopted by the Council (with the participation of national legal experts), should give suggestions for simplifying and clarifying the language of the texts without changing their substance.'

In this context, one should note that the Treaty of Amsterdam (1997) contains a chapter 10, under the heading '**transparency**'. The second paragraph of Article A of the TEU is amended, stating that 'decisions are taken as openly as possible and as close as possible to the citizen'. A new Article 191 a is introduced in the TEC, namely that 'any citizen of the Union . . . shall have a right of access to European parliament, Council and Commission documents . . .'.

1. *Commission* v. *Denmark*, 11 April 1990, No. C 100/90, O.J., 2 June 1990, C. 135/6. Action brought on 11 April 1990 by the Commission of the European Communities against the Kingdom of Denmark, Case No. C-100/90, O.J., 2 June 1990, No. C 135/6.
2. COJ, 7 December 1995, Case C-449/93, *JUR.*, 1995, 4291.
3. *See further* No. 442b.

19. To conclude this prologue, a word of sincere thanks is more than due. For the writing of this book a great deal of material, especially of legal and judicial nature, has been used. It was collected and will be published as a *Codex of European Labour Law* in the IELL, with Prof. Dr. Chris Engels as co-author. As always, we were able to count on the excellent logistic services of the members of our fine Leuven Institute of Labour Law and on the faithful services of Sonja Honsia, Tecy Theuwissen and Josephine Van Rijmenant. And last but not least a sincere word of thanks to Mrs. Lisa Engels-Salas, who kindly agreed to rewrite our English writing. It is unnecessary to say that the mistakes and failures in this book are our own. The buck stops here.

Leuven, 31 January 1998

Roger Blanpain
Chris Engels

General Introduction

§1. The Institutional Framework

I. THE TREATIES

A. From a Community to a Union

20. Since Maastricht there are not less than four Treaties: The Treaty on the European Union (1991), the European Coal and Steel Community (1951), the European Economic Community and the European Atomic Energy Community (1957). The Treaty on the European Union has two elements: the first stands alone, separate from the existing Community legal order, whereas the second effects a substantial amendment of the Treaty of Rome and in so doing alters its name from the EEC Treaty to the EC Treaty – officially, the Treaty establishing the European Community. There are all too many potential sources of confusion, but one such source is removed by the expedient of identifying the provisions of the Treaty on European Union by the letters A-S. Numbers are preserved for the other three treaties.[1]

The three European Communities, namely the European Coal and Steel Community (1951), the European Economic Community and the European Atomic Energy Community (1957) were established by an equal number of treaties concluded among the Member States as independent bodies with a legal personality.

The ECSC and Euratom aim at a rather limited sectorial integration. The EC, on the other hand, envisages much wider economic integration with a common market. This follows from Article 2 of the EC Treaty which will be mentioned later.

---

1. S. Weatherill and P. Beaumont, *EC Law – The essential Guide to the legal Workings of the European Community*, London, 1993, 9.

21. By the Maastricht Treaty (December 1991) on the Political Union, the then 12 Member States established amongst themselves a European Union. That Treaty marked a new stage in the process of creating an 'ever closer union among the peoples of Europe, where decisions are taken as closely as possible to the citizen.' The phrase 'ever closer union' replaces the words 'Union with a federal goal,' which were part of the last draft of the Treaty by the Dutch Presidency and to which the British had fundamental objections. Indeed, for many British the word 'federalism' means bureaucratic centralism from Brussels, which they refuse.

The change in name of the new European construction: from a Community to a Union, gives however an important signal. A Union constitutes a closer, a more intense relationship than a mere Community: a community relates to people with the same characteristics or interests; a union means a far-reaching involvement, an intimate working together towards a common goal. It is like the difference between acquainted people and a (successful) marriage. Of course, we are still on our way and quite a number of further steps toward a real union have to be taken. It is a little awkward that the most integrated part of the new European Union is the (European) Community.

The Maastricht agreements can be seen as a very important event in post-war European history. Indeed, this Treaty will irreversibly, progressively and following a rigorous timetable, lead to an Economic Monetary Union with a single European currency (ECU), at the latest by 1 January 1999, to an independent Central Bank, German style, as well as to the gradual development of a common foreign and defence policy and ultimately to a European federation, notwithstanding the right of the British to opt out of the EMU and the British exemption from the extension of Community competence in the social sphere.

The EMU calls for strict economic discipline by the Member States, among others regarding inflation and public debt (maximum 60 per cent of GNP).

    1. Since there is no generalised 'opting out' possibility.

22. The European Union can be described as a Greek temple with a common front and three different pillars: the first pillar being composed of the '*acquis communautaire*,' contained in the Treaties of Paris and Rome, as amended among others by the Single European Act and the Treaty on the European Union, with fully fledged European legislation and jurisdiction by the Court of Justice; the two other pillars refer to forms of mere co-operation between full sovereign States, without real integration into the EC framework. Some label this construction as a 'legal monster' (*un monstre juridique*): very heavy, complex and difficult to handle.

The European Union is thus founded on the European Communities, supplemented by the policies and forms of co-operation established by the Maastricht Treaty, namely through the implementation of a common foreign and security policy, which includes the eventual framing of a common defence policy as well as of a common policy in the area of justice and home affairs (Art. A).

23. The Union has the following objectives:

– to promote economic and social progress which is balanced and sustainable, in particular through the creation of an area without internal frontiers, through the strengthening of economic and social cohesion and through the establishment of an economic and monetary union, ultimately including a single currency;
– to assert its identity on the international scene, in particular through the implementation of a common foreign and security policy including the eventual framing of a common defence policy which might in time lead to a common defence;
– to strengthen the protection of the rights and interests of the nationals of its Member States through the introduction of a citizenship of the Union;
– to develop a close co-operation on justice and home affairs;
– to maintain in full the *acquis communautaire* and build on it (Art. B).

36

The objectives of the Union shall be achieved while respecting the principle of sub-sidiarity as defined in Article 3b of the Treaty establishing the European Community.

The European Union shall provide itself with the resources necessary to attain its objectives and carry through its policies, but with two specific limitations: the Union shall have due regard to the national identity of its Member States, whose systems of government are based on democracy; the Union shall respect the rights and freedoms as guaranteed by the European Convention for the Protection of Human Rights and Fundamental Freedoms, and as they result from the constitutional traditions common to Member States as general principles of Community Law (Art. F).

In this context, it is interesting to note the opinion[1] of the Court of Justice on a request from the Council of the European Union on the following question:

'Would the accession of the European Community to the Convention for the Protection of Human Rights and Fundamental Freedoms of 4 November 1950 be compatible with the Treaty establishing the European Community?'

The Court gave the following opinion:

'It follows from Article 3b of the Treaty, which states that the Community is to act within the limits of the powers conferred upon it by the Treaty and of the objectives assigned to it therein, that it has only those powers which have been conferred upon it.

No Treaty provision confers on the Community institutions any general power to enact rules on human rights or to conclude international conventions in this field.

In the absence of express or implied powers for this purpose, it is necessary to consider whether Article 235 of the Treaty may constitute a legal basis for accession.

That provision, being an integral part of an institutional system based on the principle of conferred powers, cannot serve as a basis for widening the scope of Community powers beyond the general framework created by the provisions of the Treaty as a whole and, in particular, by those that define the tasks and the activities of the Community.

It is in the light of those considerations that the question whether accession by the Community to the Convention may be based on Article 235 must be examined.

It should first be noted that the importance of respect for human rights has been emphasised in various declarations of the Member States and of the Community institutions. Reference is also made to respect for human rights in the preamble to the Single European Act and in the preamble to, and in Article F(2), the fifth indent of Article J.1(2) and Article K2(1) of, the Treaty on European Union.

It is well settled that fundamental rights form an integral part of the general principles of law whose observance the Court ensures. Respect for human rights is therefore a condition of the lawfulness of Community acts. Accession to the Convention would, however, entail a substantial change in the present Community system for the protection of human rights in that it would entail the entry of the Community into a distinct international institutional system as well as integration of all the provisions of the Convention into the Community legal order.

Such a modification of the system for the protection of human rights in the Community, with equally fundamental institutional implications for the Community and for the Member States, would be of constitutional significance and would therefore be such as to go beyond the scope of Article 235. It could be brought about only by way of Treaty amendment.'

Concluding, the Court stated that 'As Community law now stands, the Community has no competence to accede to the European Convention for the Protection of Human Rights and Fundamental Freedoms.'

1. Opinion 2/94 of 28 March 1996, issued under Article 228(b) of the EC Treaty, not yet published.

B. The European Community

24.   The Treaty establishing the European Economic Community was amended in Maastricht and the EEC renamed as European Community.

1. Objectives

25.   The Maastricht Treaty sets out the objectives of the Community as follows:

'The Community shall have as its task, by establishing a common market and an economic and monetary union and by implementing the common policies or activities referred to in Articles 3 and 3A, to promote throughout the Community an harmonious and balanced development of economic activities, sustainable and non-inflationary growth respecting the environment, a high degree of convergence of economic performance, a high level of employment and of social protection, the raising of the standard of living and quality of life, and economic and social cohesion and solidarity among Member States' (Art. 2).

This competence relates, according to Article 3, among others to:

- measures concerning the entry and movement of persons in the internal market (d);
- a policy in the social sphere comprising a European Social Fund (i);
- the strengthening of economic and social cohesion (j);
- a policy in the sphere of the environment (k);
- a contribution to the attainment of a high level of health protection (o);
- a contribution to education and training of high quality and to the flowering of the cultures of the Member States (p).

The Community shall act within the limits of the powers conferred upon it by the Treaty and of the objectives assigned to it therein (3b).

2. Subsidiarity

26.   In the areas which do not fall within its exclusive jurisdiction, the Community shall take action, in accordance with the principle of subsidiarity. Defining subsidiarity for the first time, Article 3b states that the Community shall take action '. . . only if and insofar as the objectives of the proposed action cannot be sufficiently achieved by the Member States and can therefore, by reason of the scale or effects of the proposed action, be better achieved by the Community. Any action of the Community shall not go beyond what is necessary to achieve the objectives of this Treaty' (Art. 3b).

27.   The question is twofold. First, at what level should decisions be taken: at EC level, at national level, or at more local levels: regional, at the level of a district or of a township or at sectorial, enterprise or plant level? Secondly, as far as labour law and industrial relations are concerned, the question is, who should take the decisions: the State, or any other Governmental institution, public authorities therefore, or the social partners; namely management and labour, by way of e.g., collective agreements, in the framework of pluralistic societies, leaving room for autonomous norm setting by the representatives of employers and employees in the area of labour and working conditions. Subsidiarity may also embrace unilateral decision-making by management, in the framework of 'managerial prerogatives' in the economic area, which constitute a recognised right in societies with free market economics.

Subsidiarity means first that one should not do at EC level what can be done equally well or better at some other level. It contains, as far as the competence of the EC is concerned, a restrictive meaning, both for the implied and the external powers of the EC. Thus, in order to constitute the appropriate level, the EC has to deliver 'better results' than at the other levels. As Article 3b states, the EC can only take action if and insofar as the objectives of the proposed action cannot be sufficiently achieved by the Member States. The better results will be achieved by reason of scale or effects of the proposed action. Scale refers undoubtedly to action which transcends national borders, like freedom of movement of workers, exchange of students, of migrant labour and the like, and should not be so difficult to determine.

28.   The same reasoning applies, secondly, to the relations between the public authorities and the social partners. With equal results the autonomy of the social partners should prevail. This, however, presupposes that the social partners are really representative of the employers and the employees they are supposed to represent. This undoubtedly creates problems in countries, where unions have less than let's say 20 per cent of workers organised, as is e.g., the case in France; the same applies *ceteris paribus* to the employers' associations. Self-evidently national criteria for 'representativity' apply, as well as the ILO standards, especially for those EC Member States which have ratified Conventions Nos. 87 and 98 of the International Labour Organisation.

29.   Once the level of action and (or) the competent actors are defined, the effect of the subsidiarity rule stops in this sense, that subsidiarity does indeed not

contain a principle following which recognised competences have to be interpreted restrictively. Once a competence is placed at the appropriate level it has to be interpreted on its own merits, as words mean what they mean.

It will not be easy to determine the appropriate level and the competent actors in a number of situations, especially in those areas where, pursuant to Article 2 (Maastricht) 'the Community shall support and complement the "activities" of the Member States,' given the fundamental differences in approach to these matters in the various Member States. This is, in the framework of the social *acquis communautaire* especially the case in the United Kingdom which adheres to legal non-interventionism, versus most continental European Member States which are legal interventionists, like Belgium, Germany, France, and others.

A lot of compromises will made as the Community proceeds and a different approach regarding social policies is not excluded between the two Europes, the Europe of the 15 and the Europe of the (Maastricht) 14.

30. Subsidiarity is both a legal and a political notion. It is for the political institutions of the Common Market, first of all the Commission, the EP and the Council to decide upon the scope and the application of the subsidiarity rule in gauging the objectives of proposed actions, their scale and their effects. It is questionable whether the European Court should intervene in this area by interpreting the meaning of subsidiarity, as defined in Article 3b of the EC Treaty, although this possibility cannot be excluded.

On the European summit in Edinburgh (11 and 12 December 1992), the European Council determined 'the overall approach to the application by the Council of the subsidiarity principle and Article 3B of the Treaty on European Union.'

According to the Council Article 3B mainly covers three elements:

1. *The principle of attribution of powers.* The principle that the Community can only act where given the power to do so – implying that national powers are the rule and the Community's the exception – has always been a basic feature of the Community legal order.
2. *The principle of subsidiarity in the strict legal sense.* The principle that the Community should only take action where an objective can better be achieved at the level of the Community than at the level of the individual Member States is present in embryonic or implicit form in some provisions of ECSC Treaty and the EEC Treaty. The principle holds for matters that do not fall within the exclusive powers of Community.
3. *The principle of proportionality or intensity.* The principle that the means to be employed by the Community should be proportional to the objective pursued, applies to all Community action, whether outside or within exclusive powers.

3. 'The acquis communautaire'

31. The Treaty of Maastricht confirmed the *acquis communautaire* (EC Treaty as amended by the Single Act) regarding social policies, which remain thus unchanged, except for some modifications like the one of Article 119 of the EC

Treaty concerning equal pay for men and women in order to cope with the consequences of the *Barber* case, as will be explained later.

Let us however repeat again that in Maastricht a Separate Protocol on Social Policy was agreed which authorises 14 Member States besides the United Kingdom 'to have recourse to the Institutions, procedures and mechanisms of the Treaty for the purposes of taking among themselves and applying as far as they are concerned the acts and decisions required for giving effect to the [above-mentioned] Agreement.'

C. Integration

32.   There is no doubt that the three Communities and the legal acts which emanate from them constitute one integrated and cohesive body. Obviously Article 232 of the EC Treaty indicates that the provisions of the EC Treaty will not affect the provisions of the other treaties; however, given the general scope *ratione materiae* of the EC Treaty, this Article is interpreted in the sense that the provisions of the EC Treaty (as well as the secondary law, which is derived from it) are also binding for the sector of coal, steel and atomic energy, provided that issues which are not or not exhaustively regulated by those treaties are at stake. In other words, the EC Treaty, as *lex generalis*, will only yield when the issues are dealt with in one of the two sectorial treaties, as *leges speciales*.

To give one example, Article 69 of the ECSC Treaty regulates only the free movement of workers, who have recognised qualifications in coal mining or steel-making occupations. Consequently, Articles 48 and following of the EC Treaty concerning free movement for workers are applicable to the other workers who are occupied in these sectors. The same is true, *ceteris paribus*, for workers employed in the atomic energy sector.

> 1. P. Eeckman, *Inleiding tot het institutioneel recht van de Europese Gemeenschap*, Antwerp, 1990, 8.

33.   Attempts to amalgamate the three Communities into one have up to now failed. A Treaty establishing a single Council and a single Commission of the European Communities was however signed in Brussels on 8 April 1965, namely the so-called Merger Treaty. Consequently, the three Communities have the same administrative infrastructure. Moreover, the text of the Treaties has been changed a number of times, e.g., on the occasion of the acceptance of 1986 of the so-called 'European Single Act,' which entered into force in 1987. In the then newly introduced Article 8A of the EEC Treaty, the Community received the mission to adopt measures with the aim progressively to establish the internal market over a period ending on 31 December 1992. At the same time, the European Parliament received a greater, although still modest, say in the elaboration of European legislation, while a (limited) replacement of the rule of unanimous voting in the Council was replaced by qualified majority voting.[1] Important to mention also were the Articles 118A and 118B of the EC Treaty. Article 118A concerns the improvement, especially in the working environment, of the health and the safety of workers, while Article 118B invites the Commission to develop the dialogue between management and labour at a European level. A new Article 130A puts 'economic and social cohesion' as a Community priority in the forefront.

  1. *See further* P.J.G. Kapteyn and P. VerLoren van Themaat, *Introduction to the Law of the European Communities*, 2nd ed., Deventer, 1989, 27.

34.   Undoubtedly, in the Maastricht Treaty the EC Treaty was amended on a number of important points especially as far as the institutional framework is concerned. Some of the most important changes are:

- the President of the Commission will be nominated by the Government by common accord, after consulting the EP, and once nominated, the entire Commission will be subject to a vote of approval from the Parliament;
- the EP will have, under a very cumbersome procedure, involving among others a Commission for Conciliation, new powers to amend and veto certain Council acts, thus acquiring a power of co-decision;
- the EP will be allowed to set up committees of inquiry to investigate alleged contraventions or maladministration in the implementation of Community law, except where the case is already *sub judice*, and it will also have extra powers to scrutinise Community finances;
- the European Court will have the competence to impose financial penalties on Member States which do not live up to their legal obligations under Community legislation;
- a new Community institution, the Committee of the Regions, will comprise representatives of regional and local bodies. It will have an advisory role and members will be appointed for four-year terms.

35.   The 15 Member States of the European Communities are: Austria, Belgium, Denmark, Finland, France, Germany, Greece, Ireland, Italy, Luxembourg, the Netherlands, Portugal, Spain, Sweden and the United Kingdom.

II. THE INSTITUTIONS AND THEIR COMPETENCES

36.   The European Communities have a number of common institutions, namely: the European Parliament (EP), the Council, the Commission and the Court of Justice. In addition, there are subsidiary bodies like the Consultative Committee of the ECSC, the ESC of the EC and of Euratom and the already mentioned Committee of the Regions, which has a consultative competence (Art. 198c EC Treaty).

A. The European Parliament

37.   The EP consists of 626 'representatives of the peoples of the States brought together in the Community' (Art. 137 EC Treaty). The members of the EP are elected by direct universal suffrage. Their mandate last 5 years. The number of representatives elected in each Member State is as follows:

Austria:	21	France:	87	the Netherlands:	31
Belgium:	25	Greece:	25	Portugal:	25
Denmark:	16	Ireland:	15	Spain:	64
Germany:	99	Italy:	87	Sweden:	22
Finland:	16	Luxembourg:	6	United Kingdom:	87

The total number therefore is 626.

38. The EP is a very special Parliament. First, there is in the European construction no real Government which, like national Governments, would need the confidence of Parliament. For the EP to exercise a certain control over the Commission and for it to censure the activities of the Commission, such a motion has to be carried by a two-thirds majority of the votes cast, representing a majority of the full Parliament. In fact, however, this procedure constitutes such a huge task that it has no real significance in practice. The legislative role of the EP is slowly expanding. It has a supervisory and consultative role. More important powers are to be found in the cooperation procedure and the conciliation and veto procedures. Except where otherwise provided in the Treaty, the EP acts by an absolute majority of votes.

39. In quite a number of cases, the EC and Euratom treaties provide that the Council has to consult the EP. Thus, the very important Article 100 of the EC Treaty reads:

> 'the Council shall, acting unanimously on a proposal from the Commission, and after consulting the European Parliament and the Economic and Social Committee, issue directives for the approximation of such laws, regulations or administrative provisions of the Member States as directly affect the establishment or functioning of the common market.'

This consultation is asked on behalf of the Council. The advisory competence, however, relates to proposals emanating from the Commission, which may alter its proposal at any time, e.g., to take into account the resolutions of the EP, until and at such time as the Council comes to a decision. This way the interplay between these three main actors is clearly demonstrated. Since the Maastricht Treaty of 1991, however, the EP may, acting by a majority of its members, request the Commission to submit any appropriate proposal on matters on which it considers that 'a Community act is required for the purpose of implementing this Treaty' (Art. 138b EC Treaty). This gives a right of initiative to the EP.

40. Supervision by the EP in essence concerns the working of the Commission (not of the Council, although the Council answers written and oral questions from the members of the EP). Regarding the budget, however, the EP enjoys a codecision-making competence. The EP approves the budget. It may, acting on the majority of its members and two-thirds of the votes cast, if there are important reasons, reject the draft budget and ask for a new draft to be submitted to it (Art. 203, §8 EC Treaty). The EP also has the right to amend the draft budget and to propose to the Council modifications relating to necessary expenditures of the EC. If the modification proposed by the EP has the effect of increasing the total amount, then the Council has to approve it.

The EP also has a decisive voice regarding the requests of European States to become a member of the Community. In this case the EP must give its assent. The same competence exists in the case where the Community concludes an association agreement (Art. O of the EU Treaty). Under the Maastricht Treaty, the power of blocking legislation by not giving assent has been extended to among others the functioning of the Structural Funds (Art. 130 (I) EC Treaty).

41. Article 6 of the Single Act establishes a cooperation procedure by which the role of the EP concerning legislation is enhanced in a positive way. This procedure is laid down in Article 149 of the EC Treaty. Even more important, at Maastricht new conciliation and veto procedures were adopted (Art. 189b of the EC Treaty). Both procedures will be examined later.[1]

1. Part I, Chapter, 1, IV.

B. The Council

42. The Council of the European Communities, established by Article 1 of the Merger Treaty of 1965, is undoubtedly the most important European institution, since the Council is the principal European legislator.

In conformity with Article 2 of that Treaty, the Council 'consists of representatives of Member States. Each Government shall delegate to it one of its members.' Which member assists at a given meeting depends on the agenda. If the Social Council meets, the Ministers competent for these affairs, e.g., the Ministers of Employment, will attend. The Social Council belongs to the so-called sectorial or specialised councils. If general points are on the agenda the Ministers of Foreign Affairs will meet in the General Council. The European Council is the Council of Heads of Governments and Prime Ministers, which meets three times a year together with the Ministers of Foreign Affairs.

43. The Council is an institution of the Community. This means that, although national interests are defended in the Council and the Ministers defend the point of view of their respective Governments, Member States are bound to take all necessary measures to realise the objectives of the Communities. This follows clearly from Article 5 of the EC Treaty:

> 'Member States shall take all appropriate measures, whether general or particular, to ensure fulfilment of the obligations arising out of this Treaty or resulting from action taken by the institutions of the Community. They shall facilitate the achievement of the Community's task. They shall abstain from any measure which could jeopardise the attainment of the objectives of this Treaty.'

44. The Council exercises only the powers which are conferred upon it by the Treaties; the Council thus does not enjoy a general competence, except in what will be discussed later on in relation to Article 235 of the EC Treaty. Its Article 145 points out that the Council, in order to attain the objectives set out in the Treaty, shall 'ensure coordination of the general economic policies of the Member States [and] have power to take decisions.' The Council therefore has the power to take decisions which are binding *erga omnes*.

45. As the most important tasks of the Council relating to labour law, one can mention:

- the organisation of the free movement for workers (Art. 48–51 EC Treaty);
- the approximation of (labour) laws (Art. 100–102 EC Treaty);
- the elaboration of a social policy (Art. 117–122 EC Treaty);
- the implementation of decisions regarding the Social Fund (Art. 125 EC Treaty);
- the development of quality education and vocational training (Art. 126–127 EC Treaty);
- the promotion of a stronger economic and social cohesion (Art. 130A–E);
- the implementation of the Social Charter and the Maastricht Agreement on Social Policy.

46. If action by the Community should prove necessary in order to attain one of the objectives of the Community and the Treaty does not provide the necessary powers, the Council can, acting unanimously on a proposal from the Commission and after consultation with the EP, take the appropriate measures.

47. The Council acts by absolute majority, qualified majority or unanimity. Absolute majority is the general rule. Article 148, §1 of the EC Treaty provides: 'unless otherwise provided in this Treaty, the Council shall act by a majority of its members.' In practice, however, this general rule is the exception.

48. In most cases, voting with a qualified majority is practised. Where the Council is required to act by a qualified majority, the votes of its members are weighted as follows:

Austria	4	Germany	10	the Netherlands	5
Belgium	5	Greece	5	Portugal	5
Denmark	3	Ireland	3	Spain	8
Finland	3	Italy	10	Sweden	4
France	10	Luxembourg	2	United Kingdom	10

Sixty-two (out of the total of 87) votes in favour are sufficient for a decision on a proposal from the Commission. If this is not the case, 64 votes, cast by at least ten members, are necessary (Art. 148, §2, EC Treaty). This rule is made in order to protect the smaller Member States: the idea is that the Commission in formulating its proposals will take the interests of the smaller Member States into account. Moreover, Article 189a(1) of the EC Treaty requires unanimity for the Council to amend the proposal.

In regard to labour law, a qualified majority is needed for the following issues:

- *free movement of workers* (Art. 49 EC Treaty);
- the establishment of the internal market (100A EC Treaty);
- *the improvement of the working environment, health and safety of workers* (Art. 118A EEC Treaty);
- economic and social cohesion (Art. 130E EC Treaty);
- the environment (Art. 130R EC Treaty);
- the European Social Fund (Art. 125 EC Treaty);
- the implementation of the Maastricht Agreement on Social Policy (partly) (1991).

49.   The requirement of unanimity remains extremely important, however, for labour law matters in general for the 15. An explicit condition was even proposed by the British delegation that each Member State should enjoy the right to veto in these matters. In essence, one can state that labour law, also according to the European Single Act, has remained *de facto* subject to national competence.

Unanimity is required for decisions regarding:

- *the rights and interests of employed persons* (Art. 100A, §2 EC Treaty);
- economic and social cohesion (Art. 130D EC Treaty).

The 'blocking minority' is the minimum number of votes required to prevent decision by qualified majority; at present it is 26.

C. The Commission

50.   The Commission of the European Communities replaces the High Authority of the ECSC and the Commission of the EEC and Euratom (Art. 9 Merger Treaty). The Commission consists of 20 members 'chosen on the grounds of their general competence and whose independence is beyond doubt' (Art. 157, §1 EC Treaty). Smaller countries have one national as a member, larger countries two. Their term of office is 5 years and is renewable (Art. 158 EC Treaty). The Commission acts by majority vote (11 votes).

The Maastricht Treaty gives Parliament a say in the appointment of the Commission. This procedure goes as follows. The Governments of the Member States nominate by common accord, after consulting the European Parliament, the person they intend to appoint as President of the Commission. They then nominate in consultation with the nominee for President the other members whom they intend to appoint as members of the Commission. The President and the other nominees are subject to a vote of approval by the European Parliament. After approval by the European Parliament, the President and the other members of the Commission are appointed by common accord of the governments of the Member States.

This procedure will be applied for the first time to the President and the other members of the Commission whose term of office begins on 7 January 1995.

51.   The Commission is, in contrast to the Council, European *par excellence*: in conformity with Article 157 §2 of the EC Treaty 'the members must, in the general interest of the Communities, be completely independent in the performance of their duties.' They may neither seek nor take instructions from any Government or from any other body. Each Member State has the obligation not to influence the members of the Commission. The Commission is, however, as already indicated, accountable to and can be dismissed collectively by the EP. Indeed, the Commission is a collegium: each commissioner is accountable to the EP for all decisions taken by the Commission. Nevertheless, there is a division of labour, which takes place under the form of a distribution of portfolios; each commissioner is thus competent for a number of directorates-general. This means, for example, that the Social Commissioner is responsible for 'employment, industrial relations and social affairs, education and training.' Administratively speaking, the Commission is divided in various directorates-general and some general services, such as the legal department. Directorate-general V is competent for employment, industrial relations and social affairs.

52.   The most important task of the Commission is undoubtedly its participation in the *European legislative process* (Art. 155, 3 EC Treaty). In quite a number of cases, the Treaties indicate that the Council can only act on proposal from the Commission. In other words, the Commission enjoys the right of initiative regarding European legislation and without its proposal nothing can happen. We repeat that the Council can only act with unanimity if it amends the proposal of the Commission, while the Commission is entitled to change its proposals as long as the Council has not made a decision, either on its own initiative, or at the request of the Council itself, of the EP or of the ESC.

53.   Another important task of the Commission is to ensure that 'the provisions of this Treaty and the measures taken by the institutions pursuant thereto are applied' (Art. 155, EC Treaty). It is in this context that the Commission will see to it that the Member States live up to their obligations under the Treaty. If the Commission considers that a Member State has failed to fulfil an obligation under the Treaty and does not comply with its opinion, the Commission may bring the matter before the Court of Justice (Art. 169, EC Treaty). The Commission likewise exercises the competences conferred to it by the Council (Art. 145, 3, EC Treaty). The Commission also has a decision-making power of its own. Moreover, it is competent to conduct the negotiations that may lead to the conclusion of international agreements and to maintain such relations as are appropriate with all international organisations (Arts. 228, 229 and 238, EC Treaty).

D. The Court of Justice

54.   The Court 'ensures that in the interpretation and application of this Treaty the law is observed' (Art. 164, EC Treaty). The Member States undertake to respect the competence of the Court regarding disputes concerning the interpretation or application of the Treaty (Art. 219, EC Treaty).

The Court consists of fifteen judges and is assisted by nine Advocates-General. It is the duty of the Advocate-General, acting with complete impartiality and independence in an open court, to make reasoned submissions on cases brought before him in order to assist the Court in the performance of its task (Art. 166, EC Treaty).

'The Judges and Advocates-General are chosen from persons whose independence is beyond doubt and who possess the qualifications required for appointment to the highest judicial offices in their respective countries or who are jurisconsults of recognised competence; they are appointed by the common accord of the Governments of the Member States for a term of six years' (Art. 167, EC Treaty).

Their term of office is renewable.

55.   The Court is competent to judge whether Member States live up to their duties under the Treaties (Art. 169–170, EC Treaty) and to review the legality of the acts of the Council and of the Commission and whether they need to be declared void (Arts. 173–174, EC Treaty). The Court is likewise competent regarding preliminary rulings concerning the interpretation of Community law at the request of courts or judges of Member States (Art. 177, EC Treaty). This means, for example, that when a national judge is confronted in a case with Community law the meaning of which is not clear to him, he can ask the European Court one or more questions regarding the meaning of the Community law involved. The Court will eventually make a preliminary ruling which is binding for the national judge.

The judgments of the Court are made in last resort and are consequently not susceptible to appeal. They are enforceable in all Member States of the Community. Enforcement is governed by the rules of civil procedure in force in the State in whose territory it is carried out. The courts of the country concerned have jurisdiction over complaints that enforcement is being carried out in an irregular manner (Art. 192, EC Treaty). In addition, natural and private persons also have access to the Court.

56.   In conformity with Article 168A of the EC Treaty, a Court of First Instance was attached to the Court of Justice, in order to ease the case load of the latter. The Court of First Instance is not a new institution; it has its seat with the Court of Justice. It consists of fifteen members who are chosen from persons whose independence is beyond doubt and who possess the ability required for appointment to judicial office. They are appointed by the common accord of the Governments of the Member States for a term of six years.

57.   The Court of First Instance is competent for:

– disputes regarding the Communities and their staff;
– appeals by enterprises concerning ECSC levies, production quotas, prices and competition;
– certain appeals relating to compensation concerning the points raised above.

Right of appeal to the Court of Justice is possible on points of law (incompetence of the Court of First Instance, irregularities of procedure and violation of Community law) (Art. 168A, EC Treaty).

For the years 1991–1994 the activity of the Court of Justice can be summarised as follows: 150 cases were dealt with by judgment and 324 by order terminating the proceedings.

III. OTHER ORGANS

58. Besides the four above-mentioned institutions, there is in the framework of the Communities, even if one limits oneself to social affairs, an important number of other organs, with which representatives of employers and workers are associated. Some of these organs were explicitly established by the Treaties themselves, such as the Consultative Committee of the ECSC, the ESC of the EC or the European Social Fund. Others were created in the course of time to assist the Council and/ or the Commission in the execution of their tasks.

A. The Economic and Social Committee (EC-Euratom)

59. The ESC consists 'of representatives of the various categories of economic and social activity, in particular, representatives of producers, farmers, carriers, workers, dealers, craftsmen, professional occupations and representatives of the general public' (Art. 193, EC Treaty). The members of the Committee are appointed by the Council for four years. Their appointments are renewable. They 'may not be bound by any mandatory instructions' and 'have to be completely independent in the performance of their duties, in the general interest of the Community' (Art. 194, 3° EC Treaty). Out of each of the larger Member States, 24 members are appointed; 21 for Spain, 12 for Austria, Belgium, Greece, the Netherlands, Portugal and Sweden, 9 for Denmark, Finland and Ireland and 6 for Luxembourg. The 222 members are divided in three groups: employers' and employee representatives and the so-called rest group (diverse interests).

The ESC is consulted by the Council or by the Commission where the Treaties so provide and may be consulted when these institutions consider it appropriate. Since the Paris Summit of 1972, the Committee is entitled to give advice on its own initiative regarding Community matters.

B. The Consultative Committee (ECSC)

60. This Committee is composed of an equal number of producers, workers, consumers and dealers (Art. 18, §1 ECSC Treaty). The Committee is consulted by the Commission whenever this is prescribed by the Treaty or when the Commission considers it appropriate. The Committee has the right to give advice on its own initiative regarding Community matters.

C. The European Social Fund

61. The Fund was established by Article 123 of the EC Treaty:

'In order to improve employment opportunities for workers in the internal market and to contribute thereby to raising the standard of living, a European Social Fund is hereby established . . . ; it shall aim to render the employment of workers easier and to increase their geographical and occupational mobility within the Community, and to facilitate their adaptation to industrial changes and to changes in production systems, in particular through vocational training and retraining.'

The Council, acting in the framework of the cooperation procedure and after consulting the Economic and Social Committee, adopts implementing decisions relating to the European Social Fund (Art. 125 EC Treaty).

Pursuant to Article 130D of the EC Treaty, the Council is obliged to define the tasks, priority objectives and the organisation of the structural Funds, which may involve the grouping of the Funds (European Agricultural Guidance and Guarantee Fund, European Social Fund, European Regional Development Fund).

For the Fund these tasks are:

1. combating long-term unemployment and facilitating the integration into working life of young people and of persons exposed to exclusion from the labour market (referred to as 'Objective 3'),
2. facilitating the adaptation of workers of either sex to industrial changes and to changes in production systems (referred to as 'Objective 4').

For this purpose, the Council Regulation of 24 June 1988 was adopted.[1] Assistance from the funds in general will be concentrated on five priority objectives, to be discussed later.[2] The aim is to focus Community structural action both on these regions and on areas experiencing the greatest difficulties.

1. No. 2052/88 on the tasks of the Structural Funds and their effectiveness, on the coordination of their own activities and those with the operations of the European Investment Bank and other existing financial instruments. O.J., 15 July 1988. No. L 185/9; amended by Regulation (EC) 2081/93 of the Council, 20 July 1993, O.J., No. 193, 31 July 1993, 56.
2. General Introduction, §4, II.

62. The Fund is administered by the Commission. The Commission is assisted in this task by a committee presided over by a member of the Commission and composed of representatives of Governments, trade unions and employers' organisations (Art. 124, EC Treaty).

D. European Centre for the Development of Vocational Training

63. The Centre (CEDOFOP) was established in 1975.[1] The aim of the Centre is to assist the Commission in encouraging the promotion and development of vocational training and in-service training at Community level. The Centre is located in Thessaloniki (Greece). It is administered by a management board comprising representatives from Governments, the Commission and the social partners. The Centre assists the Commission through the organisation of scientific and technical documentation, information and research activities.

1. Regulation No. 337/75 of 10 February 1975, O.J., 13 February 1975, No. L 39; as amended by Regulation No. 1946/93, 30 June 1993, O.J., No. L 181, 23 July 1993, 13.

E. European Foundation for the Improvement of Living and Working Conditions

64. The Foundation, established in 1975,[1] has the aim 'to contribute to the planning and establishment of better living and working conditions through action designed to increase the disseminate knowledge likely to assist this development.' It priorities are the following:

- man at work;
- the organisation of work and particularly job design; problems peculiar to categories of workers;
- long-term aspects of improvement of the environment;
- the distribution of human activities in space and in time.

The seat of the Foundation is located in Dublin. It is governed by an Administrative Board, composed of representatives of Governments, the Commission and both sides of industry. A Committee of Experts helps the Foundation in an advisory capacity.

1. Regulation No. 1365/75 of 26 May 1975, O.J., 30 May 1975, No. L. 139 as amended by Regulation No. 1947/73, 30 June 1993, O.J., No. L 181, 23 July 1993, 13.

F. The Standing Committee on Employment

65. The Standing Committee was established in 1970.[1] It aims at setting up permanent dialogue, concertation and consultation between the Council, the Commission and the social partners in order to facilitate the coordination of the labour market policies of the Member States. The Committee intervenes before the competent Community institutions take decisions. The Committee offers a permanent possibility for confrontation of points of view from all partners involved in the shaping of social policies. It is however not a forum for negotiation. In practice, a lot of talk takes place, but there is no real exchange of viewpoints nor are decisions reached.

1. Decision No. 70/532 of 14 December 1970, as amended by Decision No. 75/62 of 20 January 1975, O.J., 28 January 1975, No. L 21.

G. The Employment and Labour Market Committee[1]

65bis. This Committee (1997) will assist the Council in the field of employment and labour market policy, fighting unemployment as agreed at the meeting of the European Council in Essen (1994). The Committee will be responsible for monitoring employment trends, following national employment policies, providing reports, recommendations and exchange of information. The Committee is composed of two representatives from each Member State, in addition to two representatives from the Commission.

1. Council Decision, 2 December 1996, O.J., . . .

H. The European Agency for Safety and Health at Work

66. A European Agency for Safety and Health at Work was established by a regulation of 18 July 1994.[1] Bilbao (Spain) was designated as its seat. The aim of the Agency is to provide the Community bodies, the Member States and those involved in the field with the technical scientific and economic information of use in the field of safety and health at work in order to encourage improvements, especially in the working environment, as regards the protection of the safety and health of workers as provided for in the Treaty and successive action programmes concerning health and safety at the workplace (Art. 2).

For the purpose of achieving this aim the Agency's role shall be to:

(a) collect and disseminate technical, scientific and economic information;
(b) collect technical, scientific and economic information on research into safety and health at work and on other research activities;
(c) promote and support cooperation and exchange of information and experience amongst the Member States including information on training programmes;
(d) organise conferences and seminars and exchanges of experts from the Member States;
(e) supply the Community bodies and the Member States with the objective available technical, scientific and economic information they require to formulate and implement judicious and effective policies;
(f) establish, in cooperation with the Member States, and coordinate a network;
(g) collect and make available information on safety and health matters from and to third countries and international organisations (WHO, ILO, PAHO IMO, etc.);
(h) provide technical, scientific and economic information on methods and tools for implementing preventive activities;
(i) contribute to the development of future Community action programmes.

1. No. 2062/94, O.J., 20 August 1994, No. L 216/1.

I. Other Advisory Committees

67. Quite a number of other consultative bodies in which representatives of business and labour are represented may be mentioned:

- the Advisory Committee on Safety, Hygiene and Health Protection at Work;
- the Advisory Committee on Equal Opportunities for Women and Men;
- the Advisory Committee on Free Movement of Workers;
- the Advisory Committee on Vocational Training.

J. Sectorial Joint Committees and Informal Groups

68. A number of joint and informal groups committees, composed of representatives of employers and workers' organisations have been set up and function at sectorial level, namely in the following sectors:

European Joint Committees and Working Groups (1996)

Joint Committees (JC)	Informal Working Parties
Agriculture (1963)	Hotel and catering (1984)
	Sugar (1984)
Road Transport (1965)	Commerce and retail (1985)
	Insurance (1987)
Inland waterways (1967)	Banking (1990)
Rail transport (1972)	Furniture (1991)
	Footwear (1977)
Fishing (1974)	Construction (1991)
	Cleaning industry (1992)
Sea transport (1987)	Textiles and clothing (1992)
Civil aviation (1990)	Wood (1994)
Telecommunications (1990)	Private security (1994)
Postal services (1994)	

The most important task of these joint committees lies in the assistance of the Commission in formulating and executing social policies. They are moreover *fora for dialogue, the exchange of information* and the *promotion of consultation between management and labour.* They give advice to the Commission upon request or on their own initiative.

In 1996, some 30 common opinions, recommendations and resolutions were adopted on various issues in the framework of the sectoral social dialogue. Very few binding agreements are concluded.

On 24 July 1997, the European social partners from the agriculture sector signed a framework agreement aimed at improving paid employment in the sector in the European Union.

This agreement provides a basis for negotiations for national social partners. It deals with issues concerning the adaptation of working time and working conditions, flexibility and new ways of organising work. It recommends, more particularly, a reduction in working hours from the current 40 to 39 hours a week, and the introduction of the notion of flexibility, both internally (variations in normal working hours, training and parental leave) and externally, as regards the possibility of drawing up new forms of contracts such as fixed-time contracts and part-time, seasonal and temporary work. The partners will also combat illegal work.

IV. THE LEGISLATIVE PROCESS

A. Community Law

69.   Community law embraces the body of legal norms that prevail in the framework of the three European Communities: the EC, the ECSC and Euratom. We distinguish between *primary law* on the one hand and *secondary law* on the other. Primary law consists of the legal norms that are contained in the three Treaties and accessory documents such as the protocols and accession treaties. Secondary law concerns the legal norms that derive from the above-mentioned documents and which are contained in the decisions taken by the European institutions pursuant to the powers that the Treaties have conferred upon them.

Also part of Community law are the norms that are made by the legal subjects of the Communities themselves pursuant to the EC Treaty. Collective agreements are one example of norms that can be concluded in execution of Article 118B of the EC Treaty, which reads as follows: 'the Commission shall endeavour to develop the dialogue between management and labour at a European level which could, if the two sides consider it desirable, lead to relations based on agreement.'

To this has to be added, as we will *see* further, the possibility of collective labour agreements to be concluded at Community level which under certain conditions are binding *erga omnes*, pursuant to the Maastricht Agreement on Social Policy (1991).[1]

It is undoubtedly so that the power relations between the social partners at a European level are presently such that European collective agreements still belong to the category of Eurodreams: nevertheless one cannot exclude the possibility of 'home-made law' by the social partners.

Also part of Community law are the general principles common to the laws of the Member States (compare Art. 215, EC Treaty). These are principles relating to equal treatment, respect for acquired rights and the like. It is also through this channel that fundamental human rights prevail in Community law.'

In this context Art. F of the EU-Treaty is of the greatest importance. It reads:

'2. The Union shall respect fundamental rights, as guaranteed by the European Convention for the Protection of Human Rights and Fundamental Freedoms signed in Rome on 4 November 1950 and as they result from the constitutional traditions common to the Member States, as general principles of Community law.'

1. *See* Part II.

B. Secondary Law

1. EC and Euratom

70.   In order to carry out this task, the Council and the Commission can, in accordance with the provisions of the Treaties, take five kinds of measures.
Three of them are legally binding, namely:

– the regulation;
– the directive;
– the decision.

Not legally binding are:

– the recommendation and
– the opinion.

a. Regulations

71.   The regulation 'shall have general application. It shall be binding in its entirety and directly applicable in all Member States' (Art. 189, 2, EC Treaty). The regulation is clearly a generally binding norm, like an act of Parliament. It is immediately and directly binding without any specific intervention of the national authorities. The regulation is also directly binding for citizens, who may invoke it before the national judge. Consequently, the regulation supersedes national law; and national law which is contrary to regulations is null and void and may not be applied. Regulations state the reasons on which they are based and refer to any proposals and opinions, which are required to be obtained pursuant to the Treaties (Art. 190). Regulations are published in the *Official Journal* and enter into force on the date specified or, in the absence thereof, on the twentieth day following their publication (Art. 191, 1).

b. Directives

72.   A directive is binding as to the result to be achieved, upon each Member State to which it is addressed, but leaves to the national authorities the choice of form and method (Art. 189, 3, EC Treaty). A directive is thus, in comparison to a regulation, a much more flexible measure, which leaves it up to the national authorities to translate it into national law in the most appropriate way. It is only the result which counts. Compliance can be obtained by an act of Parliament, but other ways are also possible. Thus, collective agreements are rendered obligatory by a governmental decree and may cover the private sector of the economy as a whole. The extension of collective agreements is possible in quite a number of Member States, namely, Belgium, France, Germany and the Netherlands, to give only a few examples. In Belgium, Directive No. 77/187 of 14 February 1977 regarding the transfer of

enterprises was subject to a nation-wide collective agreement, No. 32 *bis*, which was concluded in the National Labour Council in June 1985, and extended by Royal Decree. This extension has, according to Belgian law, the consequence that the normative part of the collective agreement becomes legally binding for all private employers and their employees and becomes a part of imperative law, which is penally sanctioned. In a case brought before it the Court decreed, in relation to an Italian affair, that where it is true that the Member States may leave the implementation of the social policy objectives pursued by a directive in the first instance to management and labour, this possibility does not, however, discharge them from the obligation of ensuring that all workers in the Community are afforded the full protection provided for in the directive. The State guarantee must cover all cases where effective protection is not ensured by other means. This is certainly the case when collective agreements only cover specific economic sectors and, owing to their contractual nature, create obligations only between members of the trade union in question and employers or undertakings bound by the agreements.[1]

Recently, the Directive on EWCs of 22 September 1994 was partly transposed into the national laws of Belgium and Norway by way of collective agreement as is explained later. Whether that, rather transnational directive, could be transposed by way of a collective agreement, in lieu of an act of Parliament, is a matter for discussion, to which we return later.

1. COJ, 10 July 1986, No. 235/84, IELL, *Case Law*, No. 99.

73. Directives state the reasons on which they are based and refer to the proposals or opinions that were required to be obtained (Art. 190, EC Treaty). Directives are made known to the parties to whom they are addressed and take effect upon such notification (Art. 191, 2 EC Treaty). In fact, directives are, for reasons that are self-evident, also published in the *Official Journal*. The directive indicates the date by which Member States must implement the measures necessary to comply with its provisions. The Member States shall inform the Commission that they have done so. If a Member State does not comply in due time, the Commission may bring the matter before the Court. The Court can declare by judgment that, by failing to adopt within the prescribed time period the measures necessary to comply with a directive, a Member State has not fulfilled its obligations under the Treaty.

If the Court of Justice finds that a Member State has failed to fulfil an obligation under the EC Treaty, the State shall be required to take the necessary measures to comply with the judgment of the Court of Justice.

If the Commission considers that the Member State concerned has not taken such measures it shall, after giving that State the opportunity to submit its observations, issue a reasoned opinion specifying the points on which the Member State concerned has not complied with the judgment of the Court of Justice.

If the Member State concerned fails to take the necessary measures to comply with the Court's judgment within the time-limit laid down by the Commission, the latter may bring the case before the Court of Justice. In so doing it shall specify the amount of the lump-sum or penalty payment to be paid by the Member State concerned which it considers appropriate in the circumstances.

If the Court of Justice finds that the Member State concerned has not complied with its judgment it may impose a lump-sum or penalty payment on it (Art. 171 EC Treaty).

Directives that contain clear obligations have a direct, binding effect and can be invoked by a citizen against a Member State that does not sufficiently comply by adopting the necessary measures. In this case a citizen may invoke a directive before a national judge.

The Court decided in a landmark judgment that in case of failure of a Member State to transpose a directive, *in casu* relating to the protection of employees in the event of the insolvency of the employer, 'interested parties may not assert those rights against the State in proceedings before the national court in the absence of implementing measures adopted within the prescribed period.' A Member State is, however, obliged to make good the damage suffered by individuals as a result of the failure to implement the directive.[1]

1. COJ, 19 November 1991, *A. Francovich and D. Others* v. *Italian Republic*, No. C-6/90 and C-9/90; IELL, *Case Law*, No. 174; *Jur.*, 1991.

c. Decisions

74. Like the regulation, a decision is binding in its entirety upon those to whom it is addressed (Art. 189, 4 EC Treaty). Decisions can be addressed to natural persons or to legal persons. A decision is not a general norm, but is directed to certain specific persons. Decisions, which are addressed to Member States, can have a binding effect on the individual, who can invoke the decision before the judge. Decisions are notified to those to whom they are addressed and take effect upon such notification. Some decisions are also published in the *Official Journal*, although this is not legally obligatory.

d. Recommendations and Opinions

75. Opinions and recommendations have no binding force (Art. 189, last para. EC Treaty). Likewise, resolutions and solemn declarations, like that of the Basic Social Rights of Workers, adopted on 8–9 December 1989 in Strasbourg by eleven Member States, are not legally binding. They only contain political engagements.

However, since recommendations cannot be regarded as having no legal effect at all, the national courts are bound to take them into consideration in order to decide disputes submitted to them, in particular where they cast light on the interpretation of national measures adopted in order to implement them or when they are designed to supplement binding Community decisions.[1]

1. COJ, 13 December 1989, *S. Grimaldi* v. *Fonds des Maladies Professionnelles*, No. C-332/88, *Jur.*, 1989, 4407.

e. International Agreements

76. Also part of Community law are the international agreements concluded by the Communities; these agreements are binding on the institutions of the Community and on Member States (Art. 228, 7 EC Treaty). Mention should also be made of international agreements that are concluded by the Member States at the occasion of a meeting of the Council. *De facto* these do not belong to Community law.

2. *The ECSC*

77.   The terminology used in the ECSC Treaty is different from that used in the EC and Euratom Treaties. In order to carry out the tasks assigned to it, the High Authority (read the Commission) can take decisions, make recommendations and deliver opinions (Art. 14, §1). General decisions are equal to (EC) regulations; individual decisions are addressed to individuals; while ECSC recommendations are equivalent to EC directives. Opinions have the same meaning in the three Treaties.

V. THE DECISION-MAKING PROCESS

78.   The decision-making process leading to European legislation clearly demonstrates the underlying relations between the institutions involved, especially the Commission, the Council and the EP.

79.   First, the position of the Commission should be repeated. The Commission enjoys the right of initiative: it has a monopoly in initiating Community legislation. In general, the Council may not make a decision without a proposal from the Commission. This right of initiative has however been eroded by the fact that the Council can invite the Commission to make a proposal and the Commission usually accepts to do so. Since the Maastricht Treaty of 1991, however, the EP may, acting by a majority of its members, request the Commission to submit any appropriate proposal on matters on which it considers that 'a Community act is required for the purpose of implementing this Treaty' (Art. 138b EC Treaty). This gives a right of initiative to the EP. It should be added that the Commission can always amend its proposal as long as the Council has not made a decision. This should allow the Commission to adapt its proposals to the resolutions or opinions from the EP or the ESC. Furthermore, where the Council, in pursuance of the Treaty, acts on a proposal from the Commission, unanimity is required for an act constituting an amendment to that proposal (Art. 189, A, 1 EC Treaty).

80.   The Council, as indicated earlier, is not obliged to follow the opinion of either the Commission or the EP. If the Council does not follow the Commission, then decisions by the Council must be taken by unanimity. It should be added that the European Single Act introduced a procedure aimed at strengthening the role of the EP regarding the shaping of European legislation within the framework of a so-called cooperation procedure: this procedure prevails when the Council takes decisions by a qualified majority (Art. 189c, EC Treaty).

The very intricate cooperation mechanism leads to the following decision-making procedure:

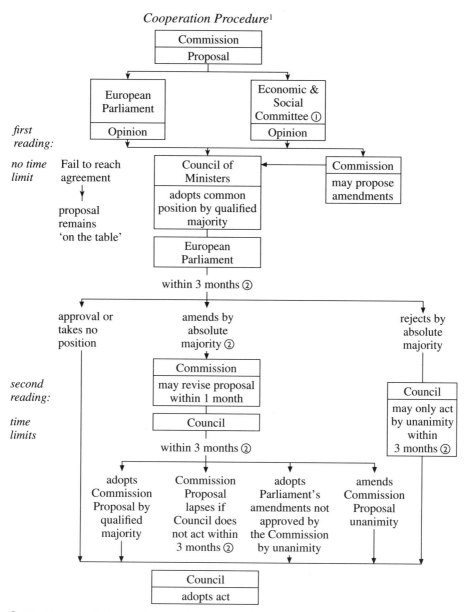

Cooperation Procedure[1]

① Must be consulted on agriculture. Movement of labour. Right of establishment. Transport. Approximation of laws. Social policy. European Social Fund. Vocational training.
② Maximum 4 months.
③ May only restore Parliament's position as expressed in first reading or deal with passages not considered in first reading

　　1. C.D. Ehlerman, 'Commission Lacks Power in 1992 Process,' *European Affairs*, 1990, No. 1, 69.

1. the Commission makes a proposal to the Council;
2. the Council forwards that proposal to the EP and the ESC for their opinions;
3. the EP and the ESC give their advice;
4. the Commission can amend its proposal taking the advice of the EP and the ESC into account;
5. the Council discusses the proposal from the Commission as well as the opinions of the EP and the ESC and adopts a common position by qualified majority if that position corresponds with the proposal of the Commission; if not, a unanimous vote is required;
6. the Council forwards its common position to the EP;
7. if the EP approves the common position within a period of three months or takes no decision within that period, the Council adopts definitively the act in question in accordance with the common position;
8. if the EP rejects the common position of the Council within a period of three months, unanimity is required for the Council to take a decision;
9. if the EP amends the common position, these amendments will be forwarded to the Council and to the Commission. The Commission makes a new proposal. The Council can accept that proposal by a qualified majority or amend it by unanimity. The amendments of the EP that were not retained by the Commission can be accepted by the Council by unanimous vote.

81.   At Maastricht (1991) a new procedure was introduced: the conciliation and veto procedure (Art. 189b). It increases the power of Parliament, which can reject a common position of the Council.

To that end a Conciliation Committee, composed of the members of the Council or their representative and an equal number of representatives of the European Parliament, will function.

The new procedure applies among others to the following matters:

– freedom of movement for workers (Art. 49 EC Treaty);
– freedom of establishment (Art. 54, 2 EC Treaty);
– approximation of laws (Art. 54, 2 EC Treaty);
– education (Art. 126, 4 EC Treaty);
– public health (Art. 129, 4 EC Treaty).

The procedure runs as follows:

1. The Commission submits a proposal to the European Parliament and the Council.

   The Council, acting by a qualified majority after obtaining the opinion of the European Parliament, adopts a common position. That common position is communicated to the European Parliament together with the reasons which led the Council to adopt its common position. The Commission equally informs the European Parliament fully of its position.

2. If, within three months of such communication, the European Parliament:
   (a) approves the common position, the Council definitively adopts the act in question in accordance with that common position;
   (b) has not taken a decision, the Council adopts the act in question in accordance with its common position;
   (c) indicates by an absolute majority that it intends to reject the common position, it has immediately to inform the Council.
   The Council may then convene a meeting of the Conciliation Committee to explain further its position. The European Parliament can thereafter either confirm, by an absolute majority its rejection of the common position, in which event the proposed act is not adopted, or propose amendments;
   (d) proposes amendments to the common position by an absolute majority; the amended text is forwarded to the Council and to the Commission, which deliver an opinion on those amendments.
3. If, within three months of the matter being referred to it, the Council, acting by a qualified majority, approves all the amendments of the European Parliament, it shall amend its common position accordingly and adopt the act in question; however, the Council shall act unanimously on the amendments on which the Commission has delivered a negative opinion. If the Council does not approve the act in question, the President of the Council, in agreement with the President of the European Parliament, shall forthwith convene a meeting of the Conciliation Committee.
4. The Conciliation Committee has the task of reaching agreement on a joint text, by a qualified majority of the members of the Council or their representatives and by a majority of the representatives of the European Parliament. The Commission takes part in the Committee's proceedings and takes all the necessary initiatives with a view to reconciling the positions of the European Parliament and the Council.
5. If, within six weeks of its being convened, the Conciliation Committee approves a joint text, the European Parliament, acting by an absolute majority of the votes cast, and the Council, acting by a qualified majority, have a period of six weeks from that approval in which to adopt the act in question in accordance with the joint text. If one of the two institutions fails to approve the proposed act, it shall be deemed not to have been adopted.
6. Where the Conciliation Committee does not approve a joint text, the proposed act is not adopted unless the Council, acting by a qualified majority within six weeks of expiry of the period granted to the Conciliation Committee, confirms the common position to which it agreed before the conciliation procedure was initiated, possibly with amendments proposed by the European Parliament. In this case, the act in question will be finally adopted unless the European Parliament, within six weeks of the date of confirmation by the Council, rejects the text by an absolute majority of its component members, in which case the proposed act shall be deemed not to have been adopted.
7. The periods of three months and six weeks may be extended by a maximum of one month and two weeks respectively by common accord of the European Parliament and the Council. The period of three months referred to in paragraph 2 shall be automatically extended by two months where paragraph 2(c) applies.

Conciliation and Veto Procedure

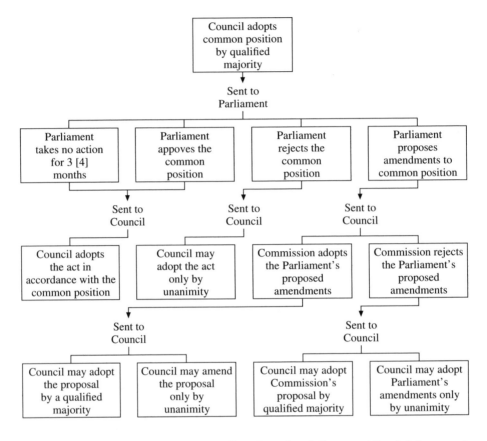

82. It is convenient here to underline the role of Coreper (*Comité des repré-sentants permanents*). This committee, composed of the Permanent Representatives of the Member States, prepares the meetings of the Council. *De facto*, Coreper is doing part of the Council's job by dealing with the proposals, opinions, amendments, etc. from the Commission. If agreement is reached within Coreper on a decision that must be taken by the Council, that point is placed in part A of the agenda of the Council and is automatically adopted. Coreper thus exercises significant influence. The Council itself negotiates the controversial issues that are eventually settled during (nightly) marathon sessions.

VI. Relations with Other International Organisations

A. General

83. The relation of the EC to other international organisations is dealt with in Articles 229–231 of the EC Treaty. It is 'for the Commission to ensure the

maintenance of all appropriate relations with the organs of the United Nations, of its specialised agencies and of the General Agreement on Tariffs and Trade. The Commission shall also maintain such relations as are appropriate with all international organisations' (Art. 229). 'The Community, shall establish all appropriate forms of cooperation with the Council of Europe' (Art. 230), and 'close cooperation with the Organisation of Economic Cooperation and Development – OECD, the details of which shall be determined by common accord' (Art. 231).

When agreements between the Community and one or more States or international organisations are to be concluded, the Commission will make recommendations to the Council, which will authorise the Commission to open the necessary negotiations. The Commission conducts these negotiations in consultation with special committees appointed by the Council to assist it in this task and within the framework of such directive as the Council may issue to it. According to Article 228 EC Treaty, the EP is involved in various ways, namely by way of consultation, cooperation or following the conciliation and veto method, discussed earlier depending on the issues at stake.

Whether the Community is competent to contract legal obligations in regard to other international organisations depends on its competence regarding the issues at stake. This competence can follow explicitly from the Treaty or can be implicitly deduced from the internal competence conferred by the Treaties. The question then is whether conferred internal competence contains the possibility to contract international obligations. This is possible if the external competence is needed to exercise the internal competence fully. Subsequently, the question must be examined whether the conferred competence is exclusively an EC one or whether the competence is shared with the Member States. Finally, one must underline that within this framework one is talking not only about negotiation and the conclusion of international agreements but also about the competence to take part in the activities of other international organisations.

B. The International Labour Organisation

84.   The question arises whether the EC as such has the competence to participate in the activities of the ILO, more specifically in the legislative activities of the ILO which lead to the adoption of international conventions and recommendations. This problem recently cropped up again at the occasion of the discussion of the night-work convention, which was recently adopted. This is a simple matter as the following illustrates.

85.   First one has to examine whether the EC has the necessary external competence for the points under discussion and whether that competence is exclusive or not. In general, one can say that the Community, when Community law confers internal competence to Community institutions, is competent to contract international obligations that are necessary to achieve the Community objectives.[1] This point is consequently to be examined case by case. The Community, to give an example, seems not to have external competence for 'the rights and interests of employed persons,' which are, pursuant to Article 100A of the EC Treaty, dealt with by the unanimous vote of the Council. The Community, on the contrary, seems to have external competence regarding matters of safety and health of the workers on which, pursuant to Article 118A of the EC Treaty, a decision can be taken by qualified majority. That competence, however, is not exclusive to the Community, but is rather shared with the Member States. First, the Member States remain competent regarding health and safety, as Member States can maintain or introduce more stringent matters for the protection of working conditions (Art. 118A, §3, EC Treaty). Moreover, Member States also remain competent to take measures regarding health and safety issues that are not dealt with by the Community. It is thus clearly a shared competence.

1. H. Verschueren, *Internationale arbeidsmigratie. De toegang tot de arbeidsmarkt voor vreemdelingen naar Belgisch, internationaal en Europees Gemeenschapsrecht*, Bruges, 1990, Deel III, 2.1.

86. The Court of Justice delivered an opinion regarding the relationship with the ILO, on 19 March 1993, pursuant to Article 228(1) of the EC Treaty.

In its request, the Commission sought the Court's opinion on the compatibility with the EC Treaty of Convention No. 170 of the International Labour Organisation concerning safety in the use of chemicals at work and, in particular, on the Community's competence to conclude that Convention and the consequences which this would have for the Member States.

In its opinion the Court estimated that it was necessary to examine the question whether Convention No. 170 came within the Community's sphere of competence and, if so, whether the competence was exclusive in nature.

Convention No. 170 concerned safety in the use of chemicals at work. The field covered by Convention No. 170 falls within the 'social provisions' of the EC Treaty which constitute Chapter 1 of Title III on Social Policy.

It appears from Article 118A of the Treaty that the Community enjoys an internal legislative competence in the area of social policy. Consequently, Convention No. 170, whose subject-matter coincides, moreover, with that of several directives adopted under Article 118A, falls within the Community's areas of competence.

In order to determine whether that competence is exclusive it was relevant to note that the provisions of Convention No. 170 are not of such a kind as to affect rules adopted pursuant to Article 118A.

However, any difficulties which might arise for the legislative function of the Community could not constitute the basis for exclusive Community competence. For the same reasons, exclusive competence could not be founded on the Community provisions adopted on the basis of Article 100 of the Treaty, such as, in particular, Council Directive 80/1107/EC of 27 November 1980 on the protection of workers from the risks related to exposure to chemical, physical and biological agents at work and individual directives adopted pursuant to Article 8 of Directive 80/1107, all of which laid down minimum requirements.

A number of directives adopted in the areas covered by Part III of Convention No. 170 do, however, contain rules, which were more than minimum requirements. This was the case, for instance, with regard to those on the classification, packaging and labelling of dangerous substances.

Those directives contain provisions which in certain respects constitute measures conferring on workers, in their conditions of work, more extensive protection than that accorded under the provisions contained in Part III of Convention No. 170.

The scope of Convention No. 170, however, is wider than that of the directives mentioned. The definition of chemicals, for instance, is broader than that of the products covered by the directives. In addition (and in contrast to the provisions contained in the directives), the Convention regulated the transport of chemicals.

While there is no contradiction between these provisions of the Convention and those of the directives mentioned, it must nevertheless be accepted that Part III of Convention No. 170 is concerned with an area which is already covered to a large extent by Community rules.

In those circumstances, it must be considered that the commitments arising from Part III of Convention No. 170, falling within the areas covered by the directives mentioned above, are of such a kind as to affect the Community rules laid down in those directives and that consequently Member States could not undertake such commitments outside the framework of the Community institutions.

In so far as it had been established that the substantive provisions of Convention No. 170 come within the Community sphere of competence, the Community is also competent to undertake commitments for putting those provisions into effect.

Article 3 requires that the most representative organisations of employers and workers should be consulted on the measures to be taken to give effect to the provisions of Convention No. 170.

As Community law stood, social policy and in particular cooperation between both sides of industry, were matters which fell predominantly within the competence of the Member States.

This matter has not, however, been withdrawn entirely from the competence of the Community. According to Article 118B of the Treaty, the Commission is required to endeavour to develop the dialogue between management and labour at European level.

Consequently, the question whether international commitments, whose purpose is consultation with representative organisations of employers and workers, falls within the competence of the Member States or of the Community can not be separated from the objective pursued by such consultations.

Article 5 of Convention No. 170 requires that the competent authority was to have the power, if justified on safety and health grounds, to prohibit or restrict the use of certain hazardous chemicals, or to require advance notification and authorisation before such chemicals are used.

Even if the competent authority referred to in that article is an authority of one of the Member States, the Community might nevertheless assume the aforementioned obligation for external purposes. Just as, for internal purposes, the Community might provide, in an area covered by Community rules, that national authorities are to be given certain supervisory powers, it might also, for external purposes, undertake commitments designed to ensure compliance with substantive provisions which fall within its competence and imply the attribution of certain supervisory powers to national authorities.

In Ruling 1/7 of 14 November 1978, the Court pointed out that when it appears that the subject-matter of an agreement or contract falls in part within the competence of the Community and in part within that of the Member States, it is important to ensure that there is a close association between the institutions of the Community and the Member States both in the process of negotiation and conclusion and in the fulfilment of the obligations entered into. This duty of cooperation, to which attention was drawn in the context of the EAEC Treaty, must also apply in the context of the EC Treaty since it results from the requirement of unity in the international representation of the Community.

In this case, cooperation between the Community and the Member States was all the more necessary in view of the fact that the former could not, as international law then stood, itself conclude an ILO convention and must do so through the medium of the Member States.

It was therefore for the Community institutions and the Member States to take all the measures necessary so as to best ensure such cooperation both in the procedure of submission to the competent authority and ratification of Convention No. 170 and in the implementation of commitments resulting from that Convention.

In consequence the Court concluded that the ILO Convention No. 170 is a matter which falls within the joint competence of the Member States and the Community.

87.   Subsequently one must consider the ILO procedures regarding the rights and obligations of regional groupings under the constitution of the ILO. *Grosso modo*, one can say that the EC as such can at present participate in the meetings set up by the ILO, is entitled to speak in the capacity of observer, but has neither the right to submit amendments, nor the right to vote. The centre of gravity consequently lies with the Member States. One must, however, distinguish different aspects.

> 'The preparation of international labour standards is governed by Article 14, §2 of the ILO Constitution and Articles 38 and 39 of the Standing Orders of the Conference. For countries that have ratified it, Article 5 §1(a) of Convention No. 144 is also relevant. The Constitution requires consultation of Member States. The question arises whether in certain circumstances the organs of a regional organisation can reply in place of or in addition to the Member States. On the occasion of the preparatory work for the Hours of Work and Rest Periods (Road Transport) Convention 1979 (No. 153), it appeared to the Office that there was nothing in the standing orders to prevent a group of governments from giving a body such as the Commission of the European Communities the authority to reply on their joint behalf; the reply was treated for ILO purposes as a reply from the governments. Where the Member States reply themselves, an additional reply from such a body can be taken into account in the reports to the Conference in the same manner as a reply from any other international organisation having by virtue of its functions an interest in the subject matter of the proposed international standards.'

It is ILO constitutional practice for the most representative national organisations of employers and workers to be consulted in connection with the preparation of government replies. For States that are parties to Convention No. 144 such consultation is a legal obligation. However, nothing stands in the way for the Commission, when formulating its opinion, to seek the advice of the European social partners and pass that advice on to the ILO.[1]

1. ILO, Governing Body, *The Relationship of Rights and Obligations under the Constitution of the ILO to Rights and Obligations under Treaties establishing regional Groupings*, 215th session. Fourth item on the agenda. February–March 1981.

88. The consideration and adoption of international labour standards is governed by Article 19, §1 to §3 of the Constitution and Article 40 of the Standing Orders of the Conference. Under these provisions, the respective positions of the delegates of Member States belonging to a regional grouping and the representatives of any such grouping attending the Conference may be summarised as follows:

– both delegates and representatives are entitled to speak in committee and plenary sittings. There is nothing to prevent the delegates of a number of member governments from agreeing to have one spokesman, who could be one of these delegates or the representative of the regional grouping as such. Under ILO rules, no regional agreement may take away the right of the delegate of a Member State to speak in addition to the spokesman;
– the right to submit amendments to proposed texts is normally limited to delegates; however, on the occasion of consideration of Convention No. 153, it appeared to the Office that there was nothing in the Standing Orders to prevent a group of government delegates from authorising a representative of a regional body to hand in amendments on their joint behalf; such amendments were treated as submitted by the government delegates in question;
– only the delegates may vote. Article 4, §1 of the Constitution seems to imply that their right to vote must be exercised individually.

89. Article 19, §5(b) and (c), §6(b) and §7(b)(i) and (ii) of the Constitution deals with the submission of Conventions and Recommendations to the competent authority. The competent authority is the one that has the power to legislate or to take action in order to implement the Convention of the Recommendation concerned. Convention No. 144 requires consultation of the most representative national organisations of employers and of workers on the proposals to be made to the competent authority in connection with the submission of Conventions and Recommendations. Where these proposals emanate from a body other than the Governments of the Member States that are parties to that Convention, ways and means of satisfying that obligation will have to be found. Member States have a constitutional obligation to inform the Director-General of the measures taken to bring instruments before the competent authority, and of the action taken by that authority. It would seem to be possible for a group of Member States to authorise an organ of a regional grouping to inform the Director-General on their joint behalf. In any case, copies of such information must be communicated to the most representative organisations of employers and workers.

90. Ratification of international labour conventions is dealt with in Article 19, §5(d) of the ILO Constitution. The consistent interpretation of that provision has been that only ILO members may ratify such conventions. The responsibility for application and follow-up (making reports) of international labour standards also belongs to the Member States.

91. Finally, we must point out that the national organisations of workers and employers take the view that regional arrangements must not be such that they interfere with the performance by States of their obligations under the ILO Constitution.[1] This is easy to understand: the ILO is really tripartite and national delegations to the ILO Conference are equally tripartite, composed of representatives of the Government and of both sides of industry. The same is not true at the European level. Within the framework of the European Community, the social partners have at most an advisory status and have often only a very marginal input.

1. ILO, Governing Body, *Report of the Committee on Standing Orders and the Application of Conventions and Recommendations*, 215th session. Twelfth item on the agenda. 3–6 March 1981.

92. The entering into force of the Single European Act and other developments in relations between the EC and the ILO make it necessary to update the understanding of their mutual relations, in particular with a view to strengthening the scope and procedures for cooperation and consultation in a spirit of reciprocity between the two institutions. This was done by an exchange of letters on 21 December 1989.[1] It was agreed that cooperation between the two organisations could be expanded, particularly with regard to:

– development;
– employment policies;
– working conditions;
– health and safety;
– industrial relations;
– social security and social protection;
– the proportion of equal opportunities and equal treatment;
– the social policies of sectorial policies, particularly in the sphere of maritime transport and ports;
– freedom of movement and migration policies;
– vocational training.

To this end, it has been agreed that the former arrangements should be refined and extended as follows:

– the Community represented by the Commission, shall attend the meetings of the International Labour Conference and the Governing Body, to which it will continue to be regularly invited;
– the Commission, for its part, shall ensure that where appropriate, representatives of the ILO are invited to attend meetings of bodies depending on the Commission that deal with social and labour issues, which by their nature are of interest to the ILO;
– the President of the Commission and the Director-General of the ILO or their representatives shall consult each other at the appropriate stage on any development

within their organisation that might have a bearing on the cooperation between the two parties;
– a high-level meeting shall be held once a year, alternately in Brussels and Geneva, in order to review cooperation during the year and to determine the direction of future activities.

1. Exchange of Letters with the Commission of the European Communities, 245th Session, Sixth item on the agenda, February-March 1990.

C. The European Economic Area

93. On 2 May 1992, the agreements concerning the European Economic Area between the European Communities and EFTA were signed at Porto, Portugal.[1] The agreement came into force on 1 January 1994 and established an economic area of 17 Member States with some 372,000,000 inhabitants. The main part of the agreement, some 129 articles, is very close to the corresponding provisions of the Treaty of Rome. The agreement is followed by 47 protocols and 22 annexes. The annexes provide for the integration into the agreement of around 1,700 legal EC acts, which form the '*acquis communautaire.*' In total some 12,000 pages, including European labour law, as well legislation and case law.

It is very interesting to note that the European Commission considers the Maastricht agreements to constitute an integral part of the '*acquis communautaire,*' which means that the Protocol and the Agreement on Social Policy would also apply to the EFTA countries which ratified the EEA agreement.

Developments within the EEA are meant to be dynamic and homogeneous. Chapter 1 of Part V of the EEA Agreement (horizontal provisions relevant to the four freedoms) deals with social policy (Arts. 66 to 71). Article 66 states that the Contracting Parties agree upon the need to promote an improved standard of living and improved working conditions, while Article 71 says that all parties shall endeavour to promote the dialogue between management and labour at European level.

The EEA-EFTA countries are involved in the decision-making process leading to European legislation but have no voting rights. After a Community instrument is adopted by the Council of Ministers it then goes to the Joint Committee of the EEA which will decide whether the instrument will be translated into the national laws of the EEA-EFTA countries. Every EFTA country has to agree. So formally there is a kind of opting in the EU legislation by those Member States. If they opt in, the annex to the EEA Treaty, which contains the list of applicable Community texts, is amended. The Annexes contain a list of the applicable Community legislation. Whenever a new instrument is adopted, a corresponding amendment will be made to the Annex of the EEA Agreement.

This applies also to European measures taken in conformity with the Maastricht Agreement on Social Policy. So the Directive on information and consultation of employees will have to be formally inserted into the law of the EEA-EFTA countries and, theoretically at least, the opting in can be rejected. In practical terms, however, one is talking about an opting out since the EEA-EFTA countries are involved in the negotiations on the Directive. The text which comes thus on the desk of the Council of Ministers is also the result of their input. Indeed, from the beginning it has been the intention that there should be one legal-economic-social area (with some exceptions) among the EEA Members. According to Article 102 of the EEA agreement, the Joint Committee should take a decision concerning an amendment of an Annex to the EEA Agreement as soon as possible after the adoption by the Community of the corresponding new Community legislation with a view to permitting a simultaneous application of the latter and of the amendment of the Annex.

The Contracting Parties have the obligation to make all efforts to arrive at an agreement on matters relevant to the EEA Agreement. If an agreement on an amendment of an Annex still cannot be reached, the EEA Joint Committee is to examine all further possibilities to maintain the good functioning of the Agreement and may also take any decision necessary to this effect (Art. 102(4) EEA). Among such decisions the possibility of taking notice of the equivalence of legislation is specially mentioned. The EEA Joint Committee could also, for example, provide for transitional periods. In order to not extend the discussion in the Joint Committee unreasonably it is further required that a decision must be taken at the latest at the expiry of a period of six months from the date of referral to the EEA Joint Committee of a decision by the EC Council or, if that date is later, on the date of entry into force of the corresponding Community legislation.[2]

European labour law covers 17 countries, as Switzerland rejected the Treaty by referendum, which has also consequences for Liechtenstein, so that only the 15 and Iceland and Norway are members of the club.

1. Peter Laurijssens, 'De Europese Economische Ruimte: Model voor de relaties met Centraal- en Oost-Europa,' *Jura Falconis*, 1992–1993, 343–367.
2. Norberg S., Hökberg K., and others, *The European Economic Area. EEA Law*, Deventer, 1993, 143.

D. Europe Agreements with Central and Eastern European Countries

94.   The first Europe Agreements, concluded with Hungary, Poland and the Czech and Slovak Federal Republic on 16 December 1991, and later on with Bulgaria, Estonia, Latvia, Lithuania, Romania and Slovenia, contain some important articles, giving an even wider scope to European labour law. Let us take the Czech and Slovak Agreement as an example. In this agreement we first find stipulations concerning employment of workers:

> 'the treatment accorded to workers of the CSFR nationality, legally employed in the territory of a Member State shall be free from any discrimination based on nationality, as regards working conditions, remuneration or dismissal, as compared to its own nationals. The legally resident spouse and children of a worker legally employed in the territory of a Member State, with the exception of seasonal workers, shall have access to the labour market of that Member State, during the period of that workers' authorized stay of employment.'

The CSFR shall accord the same treatment to Community workers, spouses and children. Of self-evident importance are the provisions concerning the approximation of laws. The Contracting Parties recognise that an important condition for the CSFR's economic integration into the Community is the approximation of the CSFR's existing and future legislation to that of the Community. The CSFR shall endeavour to ensure that its legislation will be gradually made compatible with that of the Community. The approximation shall extend to the following areas in particular: customs law, company law, banking law, company accounts and taxes, intellectual property, protection of workers at the workplace, financial services, rules on competition, protection of health and life of humans, animals and plants, consumer protection, indirect taxation, technical rules and standards, nuclear law and regulation, transport and the environment. Lastly, the agreement contains provisions concerning social cooperation concerning the protection of health and safety of workers, taking as a reference the level of protection existing in the Community.

> 'With regard to employment, cooperation between the parties shall focus notably on upgrading job-finding and careers-advice services, providing backup measures and promoting local development to assist industrial restructuring. It shall also include measures such as the performance of studies, provision of the services of experts and information and training.'

With regard to social security, cooperation between the parties shall seek to adapt the social security systems to the new economic and social situation, primarily by providing the services of experts and information and training.

Following the disintegration of the CSFR, the agreement came to apply to the Czech Republic and the Slovak Republic.

In 1997, a partnership and cooperation agreement was concluded between the European Communities and their Member States and the Russian Federation.[1] Article 74 of the cooperation agreement deals with Social cooperation and reads as follows:

1. With regard to health and safety, the Parties shall develop cooperation between them with the aim of improving the level of protection of the health and safety of workers.

   The cooperation shall include notably:

   – education and training on health and safety issues with specific attention to high risk sectors of activity;
   – development and promotion of preventive measures to combat work related diseases and other work related ailments;
   – prevention of major accident hazards and the management of toxic chemicals;
   – research to develop the knowledge base in relation to working environment and the health and safety of workers.

2. With regard to employment, the cooperation shall include notably technical assistance relating to:

   – optimization of the labour market;
   – modernization of the job-finding and consulting services;

- planning and management of the restructuring programmes;
- encouragement of local employment development;
- exchange of information on the programmes of flexible employment, including those stimulating self-employment and promoting entrepreneurship.

3. The Parties shall pay special attention to cooperation in the sphere of social protection which, *inter alia*, shall include cooperation in planing and implementing social protection reforms in Russia.

These reforms shall aim to develop in Russia methods of protection intrinsic to market economies and shall comprise all directions of social security activities.

The cooperation shall also include technical assistance to the development of social insurance institutions with the aim of promoting gradual transition to a system consisting of a combination of contributory and social assistance forms of protection, as well as respective non-governmental organizations providing social services.

1. O.J., L-327, 28 November 1997, 97/800 ECSC, EC, Euratom, p. 1.

§2. The Social Partners

I. THE EMPLOYERS' ORGANISATIONS

95.   At the European level, various employers' organisations are active. Beside UNICE (Union of Industrial and Employers' Confederations of Europe), which organises 32 central federations of industry from 22 countries and thus groups national confederations of employers' organisations, like the British CBI or the French CNPF, there are specific organisations for agriculture, namely COPA (*Comité des Organisations Agricoles*), and for enterprises that are active in the public sector, namely CEEP (*Centre Européen des Entreprises Publiques*).

UNICE has largely coordinating competences. 'However Unice's statutes do not require unanimity. For matters of policy, all federations from a minimum of three countries voting together are able to block a proposal. However in practice, voting is very seldom used.'[1]

> 1. Z. Tyszkiewicz, 'Unice: the Voice of European Business and Industry in Brussels – A Programmatic Self-Presentation' in: *Employers' Associations in Europe: Policy and Organisation*, D. Sadowski & O. Jacobi (eds.), Baden, 1991, 92; J.J. Oechslin, 'Employers' Organizations,' in: R. Blanpain-C. Engels (eds.), *Comparative Labour Law and Industrial Relations in Industrialized Market Economies*, VIth and revised edition, The Hague, Kluwer Law International, 1997.

96.   UNICE is headed by a President chosen by the Council of Presidents (of the member-associations), by an Executive Committee, composed of the managing directors of the member associations, as well as by a Committee of Permanent Delegates and by a Secretary-General.

One can say that UNICE, which also groups employers' organisations from non Member States of the EC, is one of the most important social partners at the European level. UNICE is represented in the different European organs wherein both sides of industry are members. It monitors the activities of the members from the employers' side of the ESC notwithstanding the fact that these are appointed on an individual basis. Other fora for UNICE are the European Social Fund, CEDEFOP, the European Foundation for the Improvement of Living and Working Conditions, etc. Moreover, UNICE negotiates on behalf of employers within the framework of the social dialogue set up by the Commission in cooperation with the European social partners.[1]

> 1. J.J. Oechslin and J.F. Retournard, 'International Employers' Organisation,' IELL, Nos. 91–124.

97.   Regarding the social policy of the EC, UNICE self-evidently supports the idea of a social dimension of the internal market '1992.' It believes in the social

dialogue and states that it is the duty of the participants to search for the right balance in three main areas:

– between workers' aspirations and the economics constraints and imperatives imposed by competition;
– between managements' need to preserve the right to manage, and the workers' desire to be involved in corporate decision-making;
– between centralisation and decentralisation: i.e., what must be done at Community level and what is best left to other levels, according to the principle of subsidiarity.

The 'right point of balance,' for UNICE, is that point at which no harm is done to the ability of Europe's companies to compete successfully in a free, open and global market. Europe must give itself the same ability to respond rapidly and flexibly to changes in the world market as that enjoyed by its main competitors. Not only must new rigidities and constraints be avoided, but also quite a few of the existing ones must be reduced or eliminated since they bear, according to UNICE, a large share of the responsibility for our loss of competitiveness. Regarding workers' participation, UNICE is of the opinion that there is no need for European legislation. The Community institutions should not impose on all European Member States a method of industrial relations that companies in many of these States would view as alien to their traditions and as a serious handicap to their operation.

98.   Despite all this, UNICE believes that it is quite possible for employers and the ETUC to find common ground and to support the Commission's work in a number of areas in the social field where Community action can bring added value to business, benefit the workers, improve competitiveness and thus help create jobs.
These areas fall into five main categories:

– increase mobility;
– encourage and improve education and training;
– improve health and safety in the workplace;
– guarantee equal opportunities;
– promote the social and economic cohesion of the EC, especially through a more efficient use of the structural funds.

The proposals from the Commission in implementing the Social Charter of Strasbourg are submitted by UNICE to a test of relevance, based on the following six criteria:

– a demonstrated, genuine need for the proposed legislation;
– subsidiarity;
– impact on the competitiveness of companies;
– effect on national industrial relations traditions, and on the balance of forces established in each country;
– contribution to the creation of the internal market, to growth and to job creation;
– the balance of new rights by new obligations.

Measures that pass this test will have UNICE's full support.[1]

1. Z.J.A. Tyskiewicz, 'European Social Policy. Striking the Right Balance.' June 1988 (mimeo).

99.   UNICE is rather critical of the Community's past performance regarding social policy. The criticism is voiced as follows:

1. *Divorce from reality*: many of the proposals, discussed at present in the Commission were devised in the 1970s and early 1980s;
2. *Brussels knows best*;
3. *Legislation too detailed*: the tendency of the Commission to produce social legislation which is far too detailed and prescriptive; the directives look more like regulations, which leave no choice as to methods and procedures. A directive should lay down what must be done, while leaving others free to decide how to do it;
4. *Poor quality of many of the social-policy directives*, e.g., the 'so-called subcontracting directives';
5. *High cost*, e.g., the recently resurrected proposed directive on parental leave;
6. *Unnecessary legislative measures*, e.g., the VDU directive, which contrary to evidence suggests that working with VDU's presents a special danger;
7. *The principle of subsidiarity*: 'this illustrates a lack of respect not only for the principle of subsidiarity but also for the very important element of proportionality contained in that principle. In other words, the Commission should be more careful not to legislate in areas best left to Member States or to the social partners; and when it does decide to legislate, it should not go into more detail than is strictly necessary to achieve the minimum objectives';
8. *Legal acrobatics*: this means shoe-horning legislation which should normally require unanimity, into the health and safety Article 118A, which requires only a qualified majority vote. Good examples of this are the directives on Working Time and on Pregnant Women.

100.   UNICE's messages to the European Community have been the following:

1. *Anticipate the needs of the 21st century* by acknowledging that the world of work has changed and continues to change. There are new sources of competition, new technologies, new market conditions, profound demographic and political changes – the latter especially in Eastern and Central Europe. Therefore social policy must anticipate the needs of the 21st century and not – as happened in 1989 over the Social Charter – hark back to the 1950s and 1960s.
2. *Social and economic policies should go hand in hand*: the only sure way to fight unemployment and pay for social progress is through improved competitiveness leading to investment and economic growth. In the past there has been too wide a gulf between DG V, responsible for social policy and DG II which is responsible for economic policy.
3. *Respect for European diversity*: European diversity must be respected and preserved. If convergence is necessary, let it evolve naturally. Subsidiarity and proportionality must be respected and over-harmonisation avoided.

4. *Balanced support to the social partners*: the Commission should observe strict neutrality in dealing with the social partners. The 11–Agreement obliges the Commission to 'ensure balanced support for the parties' to the Social Dialogue. That is very important for UNICE, in view of the large sums of money now made available to the trade unions from the Community budget.

5. *Measures in two categories are supported*: Community legislative measures will be supported by employers in two main categories: first, all measures needed to ensure the smooth functioning of the Single Market (for example: mobility, language-training, cross border education and training, mutual recognition of qualifications, internationalisation of employment services and so on); secondly, all measures needed to prevent unacceptable forms of competition (for example: competition based on health and safety, equality, treatment of young people and so on).

6. *No EC legislation in socio-cultural matters*: UNICE will strongly resist Community legislation in those areas of social policy which are deeply socio-cultural. This covers collective labour laws and industrial relations systems, including procedures for worker information and consultation, which have developed over many years and in a variety of ways in the 15 Member States. Each meets the specific needs of local culture and tradition and should not be destroyed through harmonisation.

7. *Individual and collective bargaining*: the legislator should stay away from matters normally settled through individual or collective negotiations. These are matters which concern the direct relations between employed people and their employers, for instance: job content, employment contracts, remuneration, working hours, leave, training leave and so on. Social policy is unique because, in contrast to most, if not all, other policy areas, at national level the social partners and not the legislators are the main players. The 11–Agreement in the Maastricht Treaty now also fully recognises the role of the social partners at Community level. It gives them a statutory right to consultation and, if they so decide, to negotiation. Thus, in certain cir-cumstances, they can act in place of the legislator. Experience will show whether they succeed in this new role. They will need to respect their own precepts as regards subsidiarity and proportionality, and deal only with those matters which cannot be handled at other levels. However, if handled correctly, this new process could put a check on the legislator and produce framework agreements better adapted than directives to the realities of the work place.

8. *Impact assessment and cost-benefit analysis*: improved impact assessment procedures and full cost benefit analysis should be applied, which is not the case at present. However, the Commission lacks the resources for this and in any case, it should be carried out by an independent and impartial body.

9. *Return to the correct form of directives*: a return to the form of directives foreseen in the Treaty. These should be binding as to the results to be achieved, while leaving ample freedom of choice regarding the methods of implementation best suited to local circumstances.

10. *Priority of the Treaty of Rome*: we must live with two treaties dealing with social policy: the Treaty of Rome and Single Act alongside the 11–Agreement

in the Maastricht Treaty. There are contradictions and incompatibilities between these two documents. UNICE asks the Commission to give priority to the Treaty of Rome. We should try to make progress as 12, and not as 11 versus 1.

11. *Create 'win-win' situations*: UNICE calls on the Commission to create 'win-win' situations and avoid 'win-lose' confrontations such as the current one over the Works Councils. With good will on all sides it should be quite possible to devise ways and means of achieving basic social policy objectives, which meet the needs of all parties. UNICE is ready at any time to sit down with the European Trade Union Confederation, to work out a mutually satisfactory framework for the information and consultation of workers in transnational companies. That really could create a 'win-win' situation and pave the way for a more practical and satisfactory approach to the definition of Community social policy in the future.[1]

According to UNICE, the revision of the treaties in the framework of the IGC (1996) has to be achieved in the light of precise objectives: return to competitiveness and employment; re-establishment of citizens' confidence in the Union, which presupposes a dual approach:

1. Clarifying and reaffirming the strategic options of the Union:
   (a) UNICE raises to the rank of absolute priority the restoration of European competitiveness, which, it claims, is an essential precondition for growth and job-creation. UNICE is against including a chapter on employment in the Treaty, or the Social Chapter or even a package of fundamental social rights considering that this would lead to 'counterproductive legal uncertainty.' UNICE considers that 'Social Europe has to be achieved at the rhythm of its economic means; first public opinion has to be convinced of the structural reforms required to create favourable conditions for employment.'
   (b) UNICE, moreover, sets out the need:
      i. to complete the Internal Market and to this end setting a new deadline of 1 January 1999. The employers reaffirm the attachment to achieving economic and monetary union, under the conditions provided by the Treaty;
      ii. to reaffirm the logic of the market economy and free competition;
      iii. to enhance the authority of the EU on the international scene.
2. The EU must give itself the capacity to take and implement decisions. This, according to UNICE, presupposes:
   (a) a stronger role for the Commission, both by keeping its right of initiative and with greater responsibility for implementing decisions;
   (b) greater transparency in the work of the Council and strict limitation of decisions taken through unanimity;
   (c) increased powers for the EP over budget control and fraud prevention, and this with simple procedures;

(d) total revision of the regulatory framework, especially with a view to its simplification through rigorous implementation of the principle of subsidiarity and proportionality.

The Confidence Pact for Employment proposed by the Commission may, according to UNICE (May 1996), play a useful role if everyone is aware of its possibilities and limits, if it does not contribute to making Europe a scapegoat for employment problems and if it does not serve as a pretext for lifting the responsibility of fighting against unemployment from Member States.

It is mainly the Member States that must act to increase the flexibility of labour markets, reform social protection systems, simplify the legislation and achieve better budgetary and financial discipline. Despite its reservation on the efficacy of the Confidence Pact UNICE is willing to work with trade unions. Some discussion themes have already been identified by UNICE and the European trade unions, for example, the problem of integrating young people in the labour market. UNICE wants the trade unions also to address matters like the flexibility of the labour system.

   1. Z.J.A. Tyskiewicz, 'European Social Policy; the Employers' View' (mimeo, November 1993).

Federations – Members of UNICE from EC countries

Austria	VÖI	Vereinigung Österreichischer Industrieller
Belgium	VBO-FEB	Verbond van Belgische Ondernemingen – Fédération des Entreprises de Belgique
Denmark	CDI	Confederation of Danish Industries
	DA	Danish Employers' Confederation
Finland	TT	Confederation of Finnish Industry and Employers
France	CNFP	Conseil National du Patronat Français
Germany	BDI	Bundesverband der Deutschen Industrie
	BDA	Bundesvereinigung der Deutschen Arbeitgeberverbände
Great Britain	CBI	Confederation of British Industries
Greece	FIG	Fédération des Industries Grècques
Ireland	IBEC	Irish Business and Employers' Confederation
Italy	Confindustria	Confederazione Generale dell' Industria Italiana
Luxembourg	Fedil	Fédération des Industriels Luxembourgeois
The Netherlands	VNO	Verbond van Nederlandse Ondernemingen
	NCW	Nederlands Christelijk Werkgeversverbond
Portugal	AIP	Associaçao Industrial Portuguesa
	CIP	Confederaçao da Industria Portuguesa
Spain	CEOE	Confederación Española de Organizaciones Empresarioles
Sweden	SI	Federation of Swedish Industries
	SAF	Swedish Employers' Confederation

Federations – Member of UNICE from EFTA countries

Iceland	CIE	Confederation of Icelandic Employers
	FII	Federation of Icelandic Employers
Norway	NHO	Confederation of Norwegian Business and Industry
Switzerland	VORORT	Union Suisse du Commerce et de l'Industrie
	ZVSAO	Union Centrale des Associations Patronales Suisses

Federations – Member of UNICE from other countries

Cyprus	OEB	Employers & Industrialists Federation Cyprus
Malta	MFOI	Malta Federation of Industry
San Marino	ANIS	Associazione Nazionale dell' Industria Sammarinese
Turkey	TUSIAD	Turkish Industrialists' and Businessmen's Association
	TISK	Turkish Confederation of Employer Associations

II. THE TRADE UNIONS[1]

101. The most important European trade union is undoubtedly the European Trade Union Confederation (ETUC). The ETUC has its headquarters in Brussels near most European institutions, which it tries to influence to the utmost. In the same building, one finds the International Confederation of Free Trade Unions (ICFTU), with which the ETUC, whose group is also affiliated to the World Confederation of Labour (WCL), has close ties. The ETUC was created in 1973 and presently represents some 45 million members, who belong to 40 national trade unions from 21 countries including:

Trade union confederations from EC countries

Austria	ÖGB	Österreichischer Gewerkschaftsbund
Belgium	CSC	Confédération des Syndicats Chrétiens
	FGTB	Fédération Générale du Travail de Belgique
Denmark	LO	Landsorganisationen i Danmark
	FTF	Funktionaerernes og Tjenestemaendenes Faellesraad
Finland	SAK	Suomen Ammattiliittojen Keskusjärjestö
	TVK	Toimihenkilö-ja Virkämiesjarjestöjen Keskus liitto
France	CFDT	Confédération Française Démocratique du Travail
	CGT-FO	Confédération Générale du Travail – Force ouvrière
	CFTC	Confédération Française des Travailleurs Chréiens

79

Germany	DGB	Deutscher Gewerkschaftsbund
	DAG	Deutsche Angestelltengewerkschaft
Great Britain	TUC	Trade Union Congress
Greece	GSEE	Geniki synomospondia ergaton ellados
	ADEDY	Anotati Diikisis Enoseon Dimision Ypallilon
Ireland	ICTU	Irish Congress of Trade Unions
Italy	CGIL	Confederazione Generale Italiana del Lavoro
	CISL	Confederazione Italiana Sindacati Lavoratori
	UIL	Unione Italiana del Lavoro
Luxembourg	CGT-L	Confédération Générale du Travail du Luxembourg
	LCGB	Lëtzebuerger Chrëschtleche Gewerkschafts-Bond
The Netherlands	FNV	Federatie Nederlandse Vakbeweging
	CNV	Christelijk Nationaal Vakverbond
Portugal	UGT	Uniao Geral de Trabalhadores
Spain	UGT	Union General de Trabajadores
	CSCO	Confederacion Sindical de Comisiones Obreras
	ELA/STV	Solidaridad de Trabajadores Vascos
Sweden	LO	Landsorganisationen i Sverige
	TCO	Tjänstemännens Centralorganisation

Trade union confederations from EFTA countries

Iceland	ASI	Althysdusamband Islands
	BSRB	Bandaleg Starfsmanna Rikis of Baeja
Norway	LO	Landsorganisasjonen i Norge
Switzerland	SGB	Schweizerischer Gewerkschaftsbund
	CNG	Christlichnationaler Gewerkschaftsbund der Schweiz

Trade union confederations from other countries

Cyprus	SEK	Synomospondia Ergaton Kypro
	Türk-Sen	Kibris Türk Isçi Sendikalari Federasyonu
Malta	GWU	General Workers Union
	CMTU	Confederation of Trade Unions
Turkey	DISK	Türkiye Devrimci Isçi Sendikalari Konfederasyonu
	Türk-Is	Türkiye Isçi Sendikalari Konfederasyonu

The European industry committees

European Metalworker's Federation in the Community (EMF)
European Federation of Agricultural Worker's Unions in the European Community (EFA)
European Regional Organisation of the International Federation of Commercial. Clerical and Technical Employees (EURO–FIET)

Postal, Telegraph and Telephone International – European Committee
European Secretariat of Entertainment Trade Unions (EGAKU)
Contact Office of Miners' and Metalworkers' Free Trade Unions in the European
    Communities
European Committee of Food, Catering and Allied Workers' Unions within the IUF
    (ECF–IUF)
European Public Services Industry Committee (PSI)
Committee of Transport Workers' Unions in the European Community
European Teachers' Trade Union Committee (ETTUC)
European Federation of Building and Woodworkers in the EEC
European Graphical Federation
European Federation of Chemical and General Workers' Unions (EFCGU)
European Group of the International Federation of Journalists
European Trade Union Committee: Textiles, Clothing, Leather

More than 80 per cent of the individual members are nationals of EC Member
States. It is also important to note that the French, Portuguese and Spanish com-
munist trade unions are not affiliated to the ETUC, which is not the case for the
Italian Communists.

> 1. J.P. Windmuller and S.K. Pursey, 'The International Trade Union Movement,' in: R. Blanpain
> and C. Engels (eds.), *Comparative Labour Law and Industrial Relations in Industrialized Market
> Economies*, VIth and revised edition, The Hague, Kluwer Law International, 1997.

102.   The ETUC is the most important, if not the only, partner representing the
workers at European level. It monitors the workers' group in the ESC, is represented in the various advisory committees in which the social actors operate and is
the workers' partner *par excellence* in the conduct of the social dialogue. Outside
the Community, the ETUC maintains contacts with the Council of Europe, the
European Free Trade Association and the OECD.

103.   Organs of the ETUC are: the Congress, the Executive Committee, the
Steering Committee and the Secretariat. The structure of the ETUC was strengthened at the occasion of its 1991 Congress, held in Luxembourg. Pursuant to Article
11 of the ETUC Constitution, the Executive Committee decides on policies needed
to implement the general strategy adopted by the Congress; draws up the negotiatory
mandate to be used by the ETUC in its dealings with European employers' organisations and its relations with the European institutions and evaluates their outcomes and decides on trade union action to be taken in support of joint trade union
demands and positions. The ETUC has promoted the establishment of various
European sectorial organisations like the European Metal Workers Federation. The
sectorial committees try in their turn to lobby the European institutions, to coordinate (national) collective bargaining by formulating common demands concerning
e.g., working time, equal treatment of men and women and others, and seek to
organise contacts with multinational enterprises. They are still, however, rather
weak organisations lacking sufficient means and power to force the multinational
enterprises to a European bargaining table.

104.   Ever since it was founded, the ETUC[1] has always defended a concept of Europe based on solidarity, justice, peace, full employment and the well-being of working men and women irrespective of their branch of activity in both the public and private sectors. The resolve to build up Europe on the basis of these objectives has always been a motivating factor behind the ETUC's action to promote the EC, the enlargement of the Community and the close cooperation which must be developed between the EC and EFTA countries in both economic and social fields.

The ETUC considers that the completion of the internal market is not only a matter of eliminating physical, technical and fiscal barriers in order to create a large liberal market; it is also, and indeed primarily, one of the means of returning to job-creation growth and to the road to economic and social progress bringing full employment and well-being to European workers. Completion of the internal market must go hand in hand with the improvement of social protection for workers. Regional disparities and imbalances must not become worse nor must social rights be reduced and undermined to the detriment of working people under pressure from international and national undertakings and from the accelerated concentration of enterprise. The form, content and social consequences of the European internal market must therefore be subject to negotiation. In the context of the completion of the internal market, the adjustment and modernisation of industry and services must be backed up with measures to develop economic democracy. This means the essential right for workers and their trade unions to negotiate and be informed and consulted. This right must also guarantee workers and their unions genuine influence on company decisions.

> 1. ETUC, 'Creating the European Social Dimension in the Internal Market,' adopted by the Executive Committee on 11 February 1988 (mimeo).

105.   According to the ETUC there are four levels on which the social dimension must be promoted: the sectorial level, the national level, the regional level and the Community level. There are two channels for creating the social dimension of the Common Market: European social legislation on the one hand and European collective bargaining on the other.

The Council and the Governments carry fundamental responsibility for adopting social legislation that should establish fundamental social rights. The rights must cover:

– industrial relations between employers and trade unions and economic democracy (information, consultation, negotiation, participation);
– protection for all workers irrespective of the size of the firm they are employed in or of the nature of their employment contract, particularly in the case of insecure employment conditions;
– social protection (sickness, accidents, retirement, unemployment);
– the right to safety and health;
– the right to initial training and to further vocational training;
– the right to occupational equality.

106.   The ETUC wants binding Community instruments (directives) governing the social programme and more especially regarding:

- *The free movement of persons*: recognition of vocational qualifications (vocational training pass); status of frontier workers and simplification of administrative procedures for migrant workers; simplification of the rules for transferring social insurance entitlements from several Member States – measures to speed up payments; abolition of the discrimination of workers' incomes from several Member States in the taxation field; the right to vote in local elections for the citizens of a Community Member State residing in any other Member State; the right to initiate and further training; establishment of European educational leave.
- *Freedom of movement of goods*: creation of a tripartite standardisation body; framework directive on safety and health at the workplace; technical directives laying down the instruments of worker protection and limit values of dangerous substances; directive on consumer goods, safety and measures to protect consumers against dangerous substances.
- *Economic democracy*: framework directive on information, consultation and negotiation on the conduct of companies in the Common Market; participation rights for workers in the context of the harmonisation of company law (Vth Directive – SE); protection of all acquired rights and agreements concluded irrespective of the legal form of European cooperation of enterprises; directive on European social reporting; implementation of fundamental trade union rights and extension to all companies in the Common Market (trade union freedom, right of assembly, protection of trade union representatives, recognition of European bargaining delegations).
- *Industrial integration*: environmental protection directives (polluter pays principle, prevention principle, transborder rights of appeal, application of the state of the arts); directives in the sectorial development field (integration of industrial and social measures); directives controlling competition and preventing the formation of monopolies.
- *Social cohesion*: framework directives on working time and work organisation (maximum weekly/annual working time, minimum rest periods, overtime, nightwork, shiftwork); extension and full enforcement of the directives on equal opportunities for men and women; directive on parental leave; framework directives incorporating all forms of work into social legislation and social insurance schemes; workers' rights regarding hiring and dismissal (further development of the directive on collective redundancies); minimum rights for all regarding access to health services and public institutions; minimum rights providing every citizen with a guaranteed subsistence basis (especially in the event of unemployment and old age).

107. In addition to legislative intervention, which is essential, the development of a social dimension must, according to the ETUC, be based on *collective bargaining*. The social dialogue must be developed and stimulated at the European, regional and sectorial level within the meaning of Article 118B of the EC Treaty:

> 'the Commission shall endeavour to develop the dialogue between management and labour at the European level which could, if the two sides consider it desirable, lead to relations based on agreement.'

The European level could be a new level for negotiations particularly for multinationals and the sectors. The Community should create the legal framework to facilitate these negotiations and ensure that any results obtained are duly applied. In this line of thought,

– the social dialogue could lead to real commitments on problems arising at the European level. These framework agreements must be given concrete form, implemented and articulated at the national, sectoral and company level depending on the circumstances and on any agreements which are already in effect;
– the social dialogue could serve as a point of reference for legislative initiatives by the Commission, prompted either by the social partners' wish to have their agreements extended into legislation or as a means of overcoming disagreement so that there is no 'social vacuum' on an element of the internal market.

108.   At its seventh Statutory Congress, held in Luxembourg, 13 to 17 May 1991, the ETUC approved the following resolution concerning: Policies for Social Progress and Solidarity. We limit ourselves to the most interesting paragraphs:

'1. At the level of Community legislation, the ETUC will take action to achieve progress with regard to the *fundamental social rights provided for in the Commission's Social Act Programme.*
    This action programme needs to be implemented in a rapid and progressive manner.

2. Social rights must be promoted equally vigorously in the European Economic Area, established by the EC and EFTA.

3. However the ETUC is not content with the Social Action Programme as it stands, and wants, amongst other things, the following provisions to be added:
– *the right to a guaranteed minimum wage, determined by law and/or collective agreement; the right to a guaranteed minimum income;*
– *the right for groups of people such as pensioners, the sick, the unemployed and disabled persons, to receive benefits which are linked to the purchasing power of working people;*
– *protection of workers against individual or collective dismissals;*
– *equal treatment for non-Community workers.*
. . .

5. *Atypical* work and insecure work contracts are developing in an uncontrolled fashion and this is contrary to the trade union objective of better employment.
    The ETUC demands that this type of work should be limited (strict limits should be set on the use of this type of contract, on the number of employees concerned, on the length of contracts and on how often the latter are renewed), and that it should be monitored within firms by workers' representation bodies. The ETUC further demands equal treatment (in areas such as social welfare, wages, training, working conditions and health and safety) for workers involved in forms of atypical work.

The ETUC seeks the adoption of concrete measures to reduce substantially the percentage of workers involved in insecure employment.

6. The *organisation of working time* and its reduction continue to be fundamental concerns of European trade union policy, since the have a bearing on job creation and the improvement of living and working conditions. The ETUC demands that support measures be implemented by the Community authorities to make working time into one of the primary concerns of the Social Dialogue at all levels.

The affiliated organisations remain committed to achieving the objective of a 35-hour week through collective bargaining.

7. Forms of working time organisation are becoming increasingly diverse without any real bargaining taking place prior to the introduction of these changes. This sometimes leads to a deterioration in the working conditions of the employees concerned. The ETUC considers that any reorganisation of working time must:
- take account of the precise nature of the working environment (organisation, ergonomic aspects and working conditions, training, etc.);
- take account of the effects of these changes on working conditions and more particularly on women's employment possibilities;
- entail procedures for information, consultation and negotiation with workers and their representatives;
- guarantee compensation for the workers concerned in the form of a reduction of working time without loss of earnings. This reduction may take a number of forms and should have positive effects on employment.

Precise rules must be devised for the conduct of night work on account of the particular problems associated with the latter, and these rules should be based on the ILO conventions and recommendations of June 1990.

8. *Training* in general and vocational training in particular have a vital, ongoing role to play in future forms of employment and skilled work, as well as in individual people's personal, social and career development. With that in mind:
- the right to life-long training and paid educational leave during normal working hours should be guaranteed for all workers throughout their working lives;
- vocational training standards and certificates should be recognised throughout the European labour market;
- the social partners should be given a greater say on education and training policies. The authorities should assume responsibility for training wherever it takes place;
- the social partners should be allowed equal participation in the implementation of Community programmes such as FORCE, COMETT, EUROTECNE and IRIS.
- employers should be obliged to provide training in accordance with the needs of their employees as well as their own needs.
  . . .

10. The ETUC intends to promote strong action by the trade union movement to change thinking and make real progress in the area of *equal rights for men and women*.

The principle of equal opportunities in the labour market first requires that of equal pay for work of equal value. Nowadays differences in wages for men and women have increased in certain countries and sectors. An appropriate starting point would be to apply and revise legislation more efficiently. However, it is the responsibility of trade union organisations to incorporate this demand to a greater extent in collective bargaining by demanding that the work done by men and women should be evaluated and remunerated more equitably. It also means that women must be able to obtain skilled posts and have equal access to vocational training and all levels of qualification and of company hierarchy. There must also be respect for the dignity of women at their place of work.

Equal opportunities for men and women requires a fairer allocation of professional and household responsibilities, which in turn means there should be:
– the right of people to assume paternal or maternal responsibilities having had access to relevant information and education and to the means needed to exercise these rights;
– protection of the jobs of pregnant and nursing women, and of their health at their place of work;
– guaranteed provision of 16 weeks' maternity leave with no loss of earnings;
– the extension of adequate and sufficient local authority provision of crèches, day nurseries, canteens, etc.;
– the right to parental leave and to leave for family reasons, organised in such a way as to encourage both men and women to use it.

11. The ETUC demands humanised working conditions, with effective policies on *health and safety* and prevention of occupational hazards, and work being organised in such a way as to allow working people and their representatives the opportunity to gain expertise in new technology and new products and help with their introduction and development.

Preventative measures must be aimed at ensuring that all workers enjoy a high level of health protection and safety, regardless of the size of the company and the type of contract they hold. To that end, specific representation measures will be needed in small and medium-sized companies, together with additional measures for the effective application of directives in this type of enterprise.

With that end in mind, the ETUC intends to build up its competence and powers of influence, particularly with regard to problems associated with European technical standardisation, through the work of the European Trade Union Technical Bureau for Health and Safety, which it set up recently.

The ETUC will demand that a complaints and redress procedure be introduced to combat all failures to apply Community directives. The ETUC demands that the Commission draw up a proposal for a Directive on the Labour Inspectorate, with a view to extending its powers to monitor and enforce compliance.

. . .

14. As far as *migrant workers from third countries* are concerned, the ETUC demands:
– the right to equal treatment and equal opportunities for workers from third countries who are residing legally in a Member State;
– that the Treaty be amended to include a clear stipulation that immigration is one of the EC's competencies;
– that effective measures are taken to protect all working people residing in a country against discrimination on the grounds of race, sex, age, religion, or ethnic or national origin;
– that EC instruments are adopted to eliminate discrimination against black and other ethnic minority residents regardless of national status.

15. With regard to working people with disabilities, action must be taken to integrate them fully into society and the labour market at national and European level. The ETUC demands immediate action in order to obtain:
– the right to ergonomic equipment and buildings which make jobs more readily available to disabled people; the right to improved protection against dismissal;
– the setting aside by companies of a fixed quota of jobs specifically for disabled people.

16. With regard to working people with particular problems policies should be introduced to combat discrimination against workers with special difficulties such as alcoholism or drug dependency, and there should be help with rehabilitation for them; working people who are seropositive and sufferers from Aids must not be subjected to any form of discrimination at work. If any person's ability to work is restricted on account of an HIV-related illness, appropriate, reasonable measures should be taken to change his or her working conditions.'

109.   Regarding the Social Dialogue the following resolutions were adopted:

'. . .

2. The role, responsibility and autonomy of the social partners within the process of European integration should be clearly defined and recognised. The success of the social dimension of the internal market depends upon open acceptance of this role and it must be given expression both through Community legislation and by means of a social dialogue leading to common provisions, framework agreements and *Europe-wide collective agreements.*

3. To that end, the reform of the Treaty of the European Community should guarantee fundamental social rights such as those of association, negotiation and collective action at cross border level, including the right to strike, for both public and private sector workers.

4. The reform of the Treaty should include provisions for prior *consultation* of the social partners on all legislative initiative from the Commission which concern them.

The ETUC demands, moreover, that Treaty Article 118b give a *legal framework to European level industrial relations*. It should ratify and guarantee the implementation of negotiations taking place at that level, and that it provide for the creation of a structural instrument for the Social Dialogue.

5. The ETUC demands an immediate strengthening of the *European Social Dialogue*: both through a qualitative improvement of its content, and through full commitment on the part of the negotiating parties to act on its results. The ETUC is ready to be a party to European collective agreements along the lines of the framework agreement concluded with CEEP; and through developing consultation and negotiations within four Social Dialogue areas:
a. The *inter professional* level, where ETUC will work with UNICE and CEEP to define European social policy priorities;
b. The *level of the sectors and branches* (public and private), in order to determine objectives and priorities in the framework of the completion of the internal market, to anticipate possible adverse effects from the latter and eliminate them through forward-looking management of the labour market, and to make the most of the internal market's positive potential, particularly as regards job creation;
c. The *level of multinational companies*, in which restructuring and mergers are increasingly common and workers need transnational representative bodies for information, consultation and negotiation on transnational issues which concern them;
d. The *level of crossborder regions*, which constitutes a new economic, social and cultural area. Dialogue should be developed between the social partners from the countries concerned. Instruments for dialogue should be set up to deal with transfrontier social problems, and if necessary these bodies should include representatives from the authorities.

6. In order to promote social objectives and upward convergence, the ETUC will coordinate collective bargaining policies by publishing an annual statement recommending collective bargaining priorities which could be addressed by negotiators at both national and sectoral level.'

110. Regarding Economic Democracy, the ETUC adopted the following resolutions:

'1. At a time when economic integration is intensifying restructuring, mergers and takeovers of enterprises, and more and more decisions are bypassing local and national levels, it is vital that working people should be guaranteed:
– the rights to *information, consultation, negotiation, participation and verification* within European companies and transnational companies operating within Europe, above all on problems relating to employment and the introduction of new technology;
– regulations for control of mergers, including information and consultation and protection of rights which have been acquired, together with the right to *transnational collective action* including strike action;

– protection of workers and their rights, particularly in their *wages, in the event of insolvency*;
– the introduction of annual *social audits* in all European-scale companies;
– the right to *vocational training and paid educational leave* during normal working hours for all workers throughout their working lives.

2. As far as European-scale multinational companies are concerned, the ETUC supports the adoption soon of the proposal for a directive on the establishment of *European Company Councils* in enterprises with branches operating in several Member States, though it would like to see improvements to the scheme. The Community norm must introduce guarantees and sufficient means (the costs will be borne by the enterprise) allowing effective development of the rights to information, consultation and participation.

3. The ETUC further wants the *European Company Statute* to be adopted rapidly and insists that it should include unconditional provisions for company and group level worker participation.'

The ETUC is, as far the IGC (1996) is concerned, of the opinion that there is no incompatibility between employment and the single currency. According to the ETUC, the European construction has to be given back its credibility, and the concerns of workers and citizens alike over the needs currently confronting them are to be responded to. ETUC defends the need to place the EU's social content on the IGC's agenda, i.e., 'employment and social rights'; recommending three things: building a Europe of jobs, building a social Europe and building a democratic Europe.

It remains to be proved that there is no incompatibility between the single currency and employment; on the contrary, the two need to be attained at the same time. However, despite the fact that the 'social' issue has progressed with the Social Protocol 'social measures are less binding than monetary ones: for an economic or monetary move, there is an instrument or a binding decision, which is not the case for social issues.'

The EU cannot alone resolve the problem of 20 million unemployed but it 'has the responsibility to create added value to employment.'

Concluding, ETUC does not want to resume discussion on the criteria or modalities of Monetary Union but expects the EU and Governments to invest themselves as much in fighting unemployment and in favour of social rights as in the realisation of the Euro.

In their dialogue with the employers ETUC (May 1996) proposed convening:

'(a) a common procedure with the Commission concerning the reorientation of the Structural Funds according to employment and the development of the "social partnership";
(b) the feasibility of a European Framework agreement concerning new forms of employment following consultation of the Commission on the flexibility of labour and the security of workers;
(c) the possibility of negotiating a European framework agreement on access to training throughout working life;

(d) examination of the prospects of transposing the Directive on working time
and its extension to the sectors currently excluded and the appropriateness of
establishing a European framework of reference that could guide negotiations
at the appropriate levels in the different countries with regard to planning,
the reduction of working time and the organisation of labour favourable to
employment;
(e) the possibility of arriving at an initiative of social partners for the integration of young people at work that could lead, *inter alia*, to a Commission
recommendation with regard to programmes for young people under way or
in preparation.'

111.   Mention should also be made of a newcomer on the European scene,
namely CESI. The European Confederation of Independent Trade Unions, CESI, is
an autonomous umbrella organisation made up of trade unions with no party-
political, philosophical or organisational affiliations and with members drawn from
17 European countries. CESI claims to have more than 7 million members.
CESI was founded in April 1990, with headquarters based in Brussels.
The member organisations of CESI are:

– European umbrella organisations,
– national trade union associations,
– individual national trade unions.

CESI accepts as its own the principles of democracy, social solidarity and trade
union pluralism.
CESI wants:

– the Political Union of the European Community;
– the Economic and Monetary Union of the European Community;
– a strong European Parliament;
– the strengthening of the Economic and Social Committee;
– participation of the social partners in European legislative procedures;
– participation of the social partners in European measures against unemployment;
– employees' co-determination and participation in decisions of importance to them;
– equal treatment of men and women at the work place;
– greater freedom of movement for employees in the private and public sectors;
– a strong and independent public service and improved cooperation between civil
  services in Europe;
– proper training and safety standards at the work place;
– minimum social security standards (retirement, unemployment, sickness, accident,
  care, maternity, etc.);
– the financing of old-age pensions to be guaranteed.

The Europa Academy, CESI's Research and Further Education Institute, was founded
in 1990 to support employees in the private and public sectors in Europe, their representatives and all interested parties through the provision of information, advice,
and vocational, political and cultural education and training.

Organisations-members

Akademikernes Pellesorganisasjon, Norway;
Algemene Vakcentrale, The Netherlands;
Autonome Lakomotivfuhrergewerkschaften Europa, Germany;
Bandalag Haskolamenntadra Rikisstarfsmanna, Iceland;
Christlicher Gewerkschaftsbund Deutschland, Germany;
Confédération Internationale des Fonctionnaires, Brussles;
Conféderazione Italiana Sindacati Autonomi Lavoratori, Italy;
Convençăo Sindical Independente, Portugal;
Confederacion de Sindicatos Independientes y Sindical de Funcionarios, Spain;
Council of Managerial and Professional Staffs, UK;
Deutscher Beamtenbund, Germany;
Electrical Electronic Telecommunication & Plumbing Union, UK;
Fédération de la Fonction Publique Européenne, Brussels;
Federazione Italiana dei Medici Pediatri, Italy;
Svaz Ceskych Lekaru, Czech Republic;
Sveriges Akademikers Centralorganisation, SACO, Sweden.

§3. Competences of the EC Regarding Labour Law

112. One can state quite categorically that the protection of workers as an explicit objective of the EC has been controversial from the very beginning and has been subordinate to the economic aims of the Community. The reasoning that the social caboose would be pulled by the economic locomotive has clearly prevailed.

The majority of the group of experts asked by the Governments in 1955 to look into the question was of the opinion that there was no need for specific social clauses in the EC Treaty. It was only the French Government which underlined that the difference in wages and working conditions among the Member States could influence competition in the Common Market. Consequently, the European Treaties contain few concrete competences allowing for a genuine social and labour law policy. The EC boat, in relation to social policy, is a small vessel with very short paddles. Once more, we repeat that the European institutions have only that power conferred upon them (explicitly or implicitly) by the Treaties. For other matters the national Governments remain sovereign.

I. THE ECSC

113. The fact that economics prevail over social matters already appears in the ECSC Treaty of 1951, although we can read in Articles 2 and 3 that the ECSC aims at the growth and continuity of employment,

> 'improved working conditions and a rising standard of living for the workers in each of the industries for which it is responsible, so as to make their harmonisation possible while maintaining their improvement.'

These objectives are however subordinate to the promotion of economic development. The removal of restrictions on the free movement of labour is only a means to an economic end (Art. 69). Article 68 allows the High Authority to take wage protection measures: if it

> 'finds that wage reduction entails a lowering of the standard of living of workers and at the same time is being used as a means for the permanent economic adjustment of undertakings or as a means of competition between them, it shall, after consulting the Consultative Committee, make a recommendation to the undertaking or Government concerned with a view to securing,

at the expense of the undertakings, benefits for the workers in order to compensate for the reductions.'

Again, these measures are clearly economically inspired.

II. EURATOM

114. Euratom aims to contribute to the raising of the standard of living (Art. 1) and must, in order to perform its task, 'establish uniform safety standards to protect the health of workers and of the general public and ensure that they are applied' (Art. 2B); it must also 'ensure . . . freedom of employment for specialists within the Community' (Art. 2G). The protection of health and safety of the workers and of the general public against the dangers arising from radiation is dealt with in Articles 30–39 of the Treaty.

III. THE EC

A. The 15

115. Title VIII of the EC Treaty deals with 'social policy, education, vocational training and youth.' The three last items were added by the Maastricht Treaty (1991). The underlying philosophy appears quite clearly when one reads Articles 117 and 118.

> 'Member States agree upon the need to promote improved working conditions and an improved standard of living for the workers, so as to make their harmonisation possible while maintaining improvement. They believe that such a development will ensue not only from the functioning of the common market, which will favour the harmonisation of social systems, but also from the procedures provided for in this Treaty and from the approximation of provisions laid down by law, regulation or administrative action' (Art. 117).

The Commission has been given the task of promoting close cooperation between Member States in the social field, in particular in matters relating to:

- employment;[1]
- labour law and working conditions;
- basic and advanced vocational training;
- social security;
- the prevention of occupational accidents and diseases;
- occupational hygiene;
- the right of association and collective bargaining between employers and workers.

1. COJ, 9 July 1987, *Germany and Others* v. *Commission*, No. 281/285, IELL, *Case Law*, No. 107. The promotion of the integration into the work force of workers from non-member countries must be held to be within the social field and within the meaning of Article 188, insofar as it

is closely linked to employment. This also applies to their integration into society. With regard to the cultural integration of immigrant communities from non-member countries, whilst this may be linked, to an extent, with the effects of migration policy, it is aimed at immigrant communities in general without distinction between migrant workers and other foreigners, and its link with problems relating to employment and working conditions is therefore extremely tenuous.

116.   This important task will be accomplished in close contact with Member States by making studies, delivering opinions and arranging consultations both on problems arising at national level and on those of concern to international organisations. In summary, Articles 117 and 118 embrace broad objectives but do not contain sufficient measures.

117.   A Spanish citizen, Fernando Roberto Gimenez Zaera, civil servant of His Majesty, wanted to gauge the effectiveness of both articles; he was prompted to do so by the rather unfriendly decision to suspend payment of his retirement pension provided for by the general social security scheme which Fernando, who is employed in the public service, received in respect of his previous employment in the private sector.[1] The decision was taken in application of a Spanish Act of 1983, which provided that the receipt of a retirement pension covered by the social security scheme was incompatible with the exercise of any remunerated function, profession or activity in any public administration. For Gimenez Zaera this was not 'the promotion of improved conditions and standard of living for workers' Article 117 had promised, on the contrary, and Fernando wanted to find out whether Article 117 was more than a mere scrap of wasted paper. More precisely, the referring Spanish judge, before whom Giminez Zaera had brought the case, wanted to know whether Articles 2, 117 and 118 of the EC Treaty were compatible with the decision to suspend the payment of a (private sector) retirement pension, while the employee was working and receiving pay from the public sector.

     1. COJ, 29 September 1987, *Giminez Zaera* v. *Instituto de la Seguridad Social y Tesoria General de la Seguridad Social*, No. 126/86, IELL, *Case Law*, No. 108.

118.   In formulating its answer to the Spanish judge, the Court took a deep breath and started from Article 2 of the EC Treaty. This article indeed describes the objectives of the EC. The aims laid down in that provision are concerned with the existence and functioning of the Community; they are to be achieved through the establishment of the Common Market and an economic and monetary union and by implementing the common policies or activities, to promote throughout the Community a harmonious and balanced development of economic activities, sustainable and non-inflationary growth respecting the environment, a high degree of convergence of economic performance, a high level of employment and of social protection, the raising of the standard of living and quality of life, and economic and social cohesion and solidarity among Member States. The implementation of those aims is the essential object of the Treaty. With regard to the promotion, the Court concluded, of an accelerated raising of the standard of living, in particular, it should therefore be stated that this was one of the aims that inspired the creation of the EC and which, owing to its general terms and its systematic dependence on the

establishment of the Common Market and the progressive approximation of economic policies, cannot impose legal obligations on Member States or confer rights
on individuals.

119. The Court has consistently held that Article 117 is essentially in the nature
of a programme. However, this does not mean that Article 117 is deprived of any
legal effect. It constitutes an important aid, in particular for the interpretation of
other provisions of the Treaty and of secondary Community legislation in the social
field. The attainment of those objectives must nevertheless be the result of a social
policy to be defined by the competent authorities.[1]

Article 118 does not encroach upon the Member States' power in the social field
insofar as the latter is not covered by other provisions of the Treaty, such as, for
example, the free movement of workers, the common agricultural policy or the
common transport policy. It nevertheless provides that those powers must be exercised within the framework of cooperation between Member States which is to be
organised by the Commission. In this connection, it must be emphasised that where
an article of the EC Treaty – in this case Article 118 – confers a specific task on
the Commission, it must be accepted, if that provision is not to be rendered wholly
ineffective, that it confers on the Commission necessarily and *per se* the powers
that are indispensable in order to carry out that task. Accordingly, the second
paragraph of Article 118 must be interpreted as conferring on the Commission all
the powers that are necessary to arrange the consultations. In order to perform the
task of arranging consultations, the Commission must necessarily be able to require
the Member States to notify essential information, in the first place to identify the
problems and in the second place to pinpoint the possible guidelines for any future
joint action on the part of the Member States; likewise it must be able to require
them to take part in the consultations. Since the Commission has a power of a
purely procedural nature to initiate consultation, it cannot determine the result of
that consultation and cannot prevent the Member States from implementing drafts,
agreements and measures which it might consider not in conformity with Community policies and actions.[2]

1. This was confirmed in: *Sloman Neptun Schiffarts AG* v. *Seebetriebsrat Bodo Ziesemer der
   Sloman Schiffarts AG*, No. C-72/91 and C-73/91, 17 March 1993, not yet published.
2. COJ, 9 July 1987, *Germany and Others*, No. 281/285, IELL, *Case Law*, No. 107.

120. In the meantime, we have not forgotten Fernando Roberto Gimenez Zaera.
The outcome of the story is that national Governments remain sovereign regarding
social matters and the EC has no message to deliver as far as the cumulation of a
private pension and public pay are concerned. Giminez Zaera was in the wrong
place at the wrong time!

121. In other words, the policies the Commission may launch regarding labour
law matters consist of studies, reflection and consultation; the EC has no power to
make decisions regarding the content of labour law. This has beyond doubt been
reinforced by Article 100A, §2 of the EC Treaty, as amended by the Single European Act, according to which 'provisions relating to the rights and the interests of
employed persons' must be taken unanimously by the Council, which confers upon

every Member State a right to veto. This has also as a consequence that the specific competences of the EC regarding labour law matters are exceptional and must be interpreted restrictively. These competences concern:

- the free movement for workers, to be voted upon by qualified majority but nevertheless situated in an economic context, namely the establishment and functioning of the common economic market (Arts. 48–51);
- the health and safety of workers (Art. 118);
- the promotion of social dialogue (Art. 118B);
- equal pay for equal work for men and women (Art. 119);
- paid holiday schemes (Art. 120);
- the creation of a European Social Fund in order to improve employment opportunities for workers and to contribute to the raising of their standard of living (Arts. 123–128) with the aim of promoting social cohesion (Art. 130A–D);
- education, vocational training and youth (Arts. 126–127).

Less specific (labour law) possibilities toward carrying out the mandatory objectives of Article 117 can be found in Articles 100 and 235 of the EC Treaty. Article 100 provides that:

> 'the Council shall, acting unanimously on a proposal from the Commission, issue directives for the approximation of such provisions laid down by law, regulation or administrative action in Member States as directly affect the establishment or functioning of the common market.'

Article 235 provides that, if action by the Community should prove necessary for the attainment of one of the Community objectives and the EC Treaty has not provided the necessary powers, the Council may act unanimously to take the appropriate measures. As indicated above, unanimity in the Council is also needed for labour law matters (Art. 100A, §2).

It is on the basis of Article 100 of the EC Treaty that the directives relating to collective redundancies (1975), transfer of enterprises (1977) and the insolvability of the employer (1980) have been accepted. In other words not only the direct effect on the establishment or the functioning of the Common Market was to be indicated but a unanimous vote was needed as well.

122.   So much to say yet much-a-do about nothing. The Treaty brags a great deal, but does little. The cornerstone is clearly the rule of unanimity and we have sufficiently underlined the democratic deficit.

B. The New Social Dimension after Maastricht (1991) for the 14

1. The Protocol on Social Policy

123.   In Maastricht the then 12 Member States could not agree on an extension of common social policies, which would apply to all Member States. The United

Kingdom had, for reason of pure local politics, decided to 'opt out' but agreed that the other eleven countries could go ahead. The High Contracting Parties made a Protocol on Social Policy noting 'that eleven Member States wish to continue along the path laid down in the 1989 Social Charter; that they have adopted among themselves an agreement to this end; that this Agreement is annexed to this Protocol; that this Protocol and the said Agreement are without prejudice to the provisions of this Treaty, particularly those which relate to social policy which constitute an integral part of the *'acquis communautaire'*:

1. 'Agree to authorise those 11 Member States to have recourse to the institutions, procedures and mechanisms of the Treaty for the purposes of taking among themselves and applying as far as they are concerned the acts and decisions required to give effect to the above-mentioned Agreement.' This means that the usual (legislative) procedures, involving the Commission, the EP, the ESC and the Council will be followed with full competence of the European Court and that eventual decisions, e.g., directives, will be binding according to Community law.
2. 'The United Kingdom of Great Britain and Northern Ireland shall not take part in the deliberation and the adoption by the Council of Commission proposals made on the basis of this Protocol and the above-mentioned Agreement.' This seems to indicate that the full Commission, British Commissioners included, will elaborate the proposals leading to European labour and social security legislation; that the full EP, British MP's included, will function, as well as the ESC. It is only in the Council that the United Kingdom shall not participate in the deliberation and adoption of the proposals. It is self-evident that special problems will arise when the United Kingdom will act as President of the Council. Under the Protocol 'Acts adopted by the Council and any financial consequences other than the administrative costs entailed for the institutions shall not be applicable to the United Kingdom of Great Britain and Northern Ireland' (Protocol 2). 'This Protocol is annexed to the Treaty establishing the European Community' (Protocol 3).

124. The 11 Member States, wishing to implement the 1989 Social Charter on the basis of the *acquis communautaire* (1) extended the social competence of the Community, (2) enlarged the possibilities for decision-making with qualified majority and (3) laid a stronger legal basis for European collective agreements. The Maastricht Protocol and Agreement do not constitute a part of the EC Treaty and have as such no relation with e.g., Article 100A2 of that Treaty, which stipulates that rights and interests of employed persons should be decided on a unanimous basis and thus forms a kind of a general rule in the EC Treaty, restrictively keeping labour law in the national sphere. This is, under the Protocol and the Agreement, no longer the case. Pursuant to (the new) Articles 1 and 2, especially 2,1 and 2 of the Agreement an important part of labour law is now also subject to European competence, implied and external competences included, given the fact that the Protocol authorises the eleven Member States to have full recourse to Community institutions, procedures and mechanisms. One thing and another means that the social competences laid down in the agreement, in our view, have to be interpreted in their own right and on their own merits; and not restrictively as is the case in the labour law provisions of the Treaty, due to the pervasive impact of Article 100A2, as mentioned earlier.

125.   In a Communication of 14 December 1993 the Commission indicated how it sees the application of the Agreement on Social Policy especially regarding the consultation of the social partners and then negotiation of European collective agreements and their implementations, as well as concerning the implementation of directives by way of collective agreement.[1] We extensively refer to this document as we analyse the meaning and significance of the Protocol and the Agreement.

> 'The aim of this communication is to set out the Commission's approach to the implementation of the Protocol and Agreement taking into account past experience in this field. The Commission will of course be prepared to review and amend these procedures in the light of experience gained and of the debate it expects to stimulate with the other Community institutions, the Member States and the organisations of social partners at Community level. This will be a dynamic process which will grow and develop over time. The Commission firmly believes therefore that it will only be possible to determine the changes and adjustments required through practical experience in applying the Agreement. The opportunity for such revision will be provided by the report on progress in achieving the objectives of Article 1 of the Agreement which the Commission is required to draw up each year under Article 7 of the Agreement. This latter report will, for practical purposes, be merged with the Report on the application of the Community Charter of the Fundamental Social Rights of Workers.'

Regarding the scope of the Agreement on Social Policy the Communication (1993) indicates that

> 'the Agreement is soundly based in law given that the Protocol on Social Policy, which was adopted by the Twelve and thus ranks as a treaty, allows for measures to be taken by eleven Member States.
>
> Thus the Community nature of measures taken under the Agreement is beyond doubt, which means that the Court of Justice will be empowered to rule on the legality of directives adopted by the Eleven and to interpret them. The scope of these directives will comply with the territoriality principle; in other words, such directives will not apply on the territory of the United Kingdom, but a UK national – or the subsidiary of a UK-registered group – resident on the territory of each of the other eleven Member States will be subject to the (harmonised) legislation of the Member State in question. Finally, the Protocol forms part of the *acquis communautaire* like any other provision of the EC Treaty.
>
> It is important to stress, though, that the Treaty on European Union does not preclude institutions having recourse in the social field to the provisions of the EC Treaty pursuant to procedures governing the twelve Member States.

Social policy is therefore governed:

- by the provisions of the EC Treaty as amended by the Treaty on European Union; and
- by the provisions introduced by the Agreement, which will form a new basis for Community action, including the possible adoption of legislative measures by the eleven Member States which signed the Agreement.'

Social policy is thus subject to two freestanding but complementary legal frames of reference.

'The Commission's principal objective is to promote the development of a European social policy which will benefit all the citizens of the Union and will therefore enjoy, as far as is possible, the support of all the Member States.

The Commission hopes, therefore, that Community social policy action will once again be founded on a single legal basis. A major opportunity to achieve this will be the conference of representatives of Member States governments in 1996.'

126. 'The main considerations,' the Communication (1993) continues,

'to be taken into account when deciding which procedure to opt for i.e., EC Treaty or Agreement of the Eleven – are:

- the nature of the proposal;
- the attitudes of the social partners to it;
- the need to ensure that the social dimension progresses at the same pace as other Community policies, and hence the possibility for the Council to reach decisions by qualified majority;
- the desire to ensure that all workers throughout the Community benefit from the proposed measure;
- the possibility for all twelve Member States to move forward together.

As far as future proposals are concerned, the Commission will decide on a case by case basis, in the light of the above criteria, whether or not to make use of the Protocol. However, for proposals concerning health and safety at work, the Commission will give priority to instruments which enable a decision to be taken by all twelve Member States.

As regards the proposals presented under the social action programme and still pending at the Council, the Commission will decide on a case by case basis whether or not to make use of the Agreement in order to progress the proposals, should there be an impasse at the Council. In cases where it opts for using the Agreement, the Commission will do everything possible – in agreement with the social partners concerned, where appropriate – to ensure that work which has already been done is taken into account and thus to speed up the consultative process.'

Overview of the Main Legal Bases for Social Policy Measures

MAASTRICHT PROTOCOL

Qualified Majority Possible (Art. 2(1))

improvement in particular of the working environment to protect workers' health and safety
working conditions
the information and consultation of workers
equality between men and women with regard to labour market
opportunities and treatment at work the integration of persons excluded from the labour market

Unanimity (11) Required (Art. 2(3))

social security and social protection of workers
protection of workers where their employment contract is terminated representation and effective defence of the interests of workers and employers, including co-determination
conditions of employment for third-country nationals legally residing in Community territory
financial contributions for promotion of employment and job creation

Explicitly excluded from Community jurisdiction (Art. 2(6))

pay
right of association, the right to strike, the right to impose lock-outs

EC TREATY

Qualified Majority Possible

Article 49: free movement of workers
Article 54: freedom of establishment
Article 57: mutual recognition of diplomas
Article 125 (new): ES (application decision)
Article 127 (new): vocational training
Article 118a: health and safety at work
Article 11a, Article 43: agriculture;
Article 76: transport

Unanimity 12 Required

Article 51: social security (measures necessary for freedom of movement)
Article 100: internal market
Article 130d: tasks, priority objectives and organisation of the Structural Funds
Article 235

*Operational Chart Showing the Implementation
of the Agreement on Social Policy*

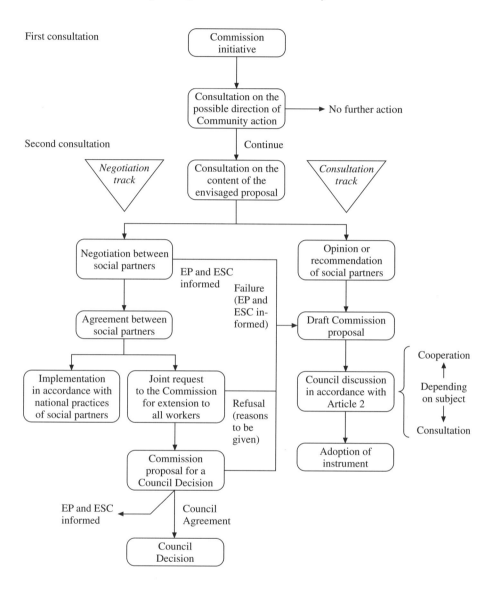

2. Extension of Social Competence

127. Article 1 of the Agreement broadens the scope of Community action in the social sphere. The text of Article 1, however, indicates that this competence is shared with the Member States as it expressly refers to 'the Community and the Member States.' The Community and its Member States have now as their objectives:

- the promotion of employment;
- improved living and working conditions;
- proper social protection;
- dialogue between management and labour;
- the development of human resources with a view to lasting high employment; and
- the combating of exclusion.

To this end the Community and its Member States shall implement measures which take account of the diverse forms of national practices, in particular in the field of contractual relations, and the need to maintain the competitiveness of the Community economy.

Pursuant to Article . . . the Commission shall draw up a report each year on progress in achieving the objectives of Article 1, including the demographic situation in the Community. It shall forward the report to the EP, the Council and the ECS. The EP may invite the Commission to draw up reports on particular problems concerning the social situation.

128. The Community thus received a broad mandate in the social sphere. Only two restrictions apply, which are self-evident, namely national diversity and the need to maintain competitiveness. Both restrictions are of a rather programmatic, not of a legal, nature and are not further qualified except in the case of national diversity, where Article 1 adds 'in particular in the field of contractual relations.' These relations refer especially, it seems, to collective labour relations, which are largely excluded from the scope of application of Article 2, as we will see later. Contractual relations may include areas like collective bargaining and forms of employee participation, like co-determination.

Both restrictions seem, in view of the diversity of national labour relations systems and the necessity for lasting high employment, at present surely appropriate.

IV. ANALYSIS OF THE NEW SOCIAL DIMENSION

A. Legislation (Art. 2)

129. Article 2 allows the Community to formulate regulations, directives or recommendations with either qualified majority or unanimity with a view of achieving the objectives of Article 1 in quite a number of fields, with the exclusion however of 'pay, the right of association, the right to strike or the right to impose lock-outs.'

The 'provisions adopted pursuant to this article shall not prevent any Member State from maintaining or introducing more (stringent) protective measures compatible with the Treaty' (Art. 2,5).

130. It seems to me that there is a delicate relationship between issues which can be dealt with by qualified majority and those for which unanimity is needed. It is e.g., possible that in the area of equal treatment between men and women, for which there is qualified majority, measures are put forward which would include an element of job protection, saying e.g., that a discriminated worker, who makes a complaint to the labour inspection, cannot be dismissed for the reason of doing so. The last point concerning job security belongs self-evidently to the group of issues to be dealt with on a basis of unanimity. Nevertheless, in accordance with the adagium: '*accessorium sequitur principale*,' the issue as a whole falling under the scope of equal treatment can be dealt with on the basis of qualified majority. One could draw an argument to arrive at an opposite conclusion from the wording of the last sentence of Article 4,2 (concerning the implementation of European collective agreements by way of a Council decision) where it reads 'that the Council shall act by qualified majority, except where the agreement in question contains one or more provisions relating to one of the areas referred to in Article 2,3, in which case it shall act unanimously.' This argument however is not decisive. Article 4,2 constitutes a deviation from a general principle of law. If the eleven Member States had wanted to depart from that general principle also regarding Community legislation, pursuant to the Articles 1 and 2, 1–3, they should have done so *expressis verbis*.

Another problem rises if on the basis of objective elements, like the goal and the content of a Community act, different legal bases in the Treaty both qualify to found the given act. In that case the act should be taken on the bases of the different articles on which Community competence rests. This is, however, not the case when, due to a double legal base, at the same time qualified majority rule, involving the cooperation of the EP on the one hand and unanimity voting in the Council on the other hand are required. In that case, the Court ruled, preference has to be given to qualified majority voting involving the cooperation of the EP since the participation of the EP reflects at the level of the Community a fundamental democratic principle, namely the involvement of the Peoples of Europe through the intermediary of a representative assembly.[1]

1. *See* COJ, 19 June 1991, Dioxyde directive (Arts. 100A and 130S) *Commission* v. *Council*, C 300/89, *Jur.*, 1991, 851.

1. Qualified Majority Voting

a. Procedure

131. Article 2,1 provides that the Community shall with a view to achieving the objectives of Article 1, support and complement Member States' activities in a number of fields, which we will enumerate later.

'To this end, the Council may adopt, by means of directives adopted by qualified majority, minimum requirements for gradual implementation, having, regard to the conditions and technical rules obtaining in each of the Member States. Such directives shall avoid imposing administrative, financial and legal restraints in a way which would hold back the creation of small and medium-sized undertakings' (Art. 2,2).

Through the reference in the last sentence of Article 2,2 to Article 189c of the Treaty, those directives can be taken with a qualified majority, after consulting the ESC.

132. By way of derogation from Article 148,2 of the Treaty establishing the European Community, acts of the Council which must be adopted by a qualified majority shall be deemed to be adopted if they have received at least 44 votes in favour.[1] The unanimity of the Members of the Council, with the exception of the United Kingdom of Great Britain and Northern Ireland is necessary for acts of the Council which must be adopted unanimously and for those amending the Commission proposal (Protocol, 2).

    1. Protocol on Social Policy, 2, 2nd para.

b. Areas

(1) HEALTH AND SAFETY
133. Directives with qualified majority can be taken in order to improve in particular the working environment to protect workers' health and safety. For the sense of the phrase 'working environment to protect worker's health and safety' we refer to what we said about Article 118A of the EC Treaty.[1]

    1. *See*: Part. I, Chapter 7, §2, A. 'The eleven High Contracting Parties note that in the discussions on Article 2(2) of the Agreement it was agreed that the Community does not intend, in laying down minimum requirements for the protection of safety and health of the employees, to discriminate in a manner unjustified by the circumstances against employees in small and medium-sized undertakings' (Declaration on Article 2(2)).

(2) WORKING CONDITIONS
134. 'Working conditions' is a notion with a rather broad content and relates to all the conditions under which work in subordination by an employee is performed for the benefit of an employer, such as:

– the *different categories of workers*: blue-collar, white collar, commercial travellers, seamen, student-workers . . .;
– the individual labour contracts, including contracts for an indefinite period, fixed term contracts, temporary work, the trial clause as well as the form and the content of the contracts; also the ability to conclude a labour contract (for e.g., minors and migrant workers);
– *rights and duties of the parties during the employment contract*, thus the duties of the worker, like the execution of orders, the responsibility for damages etc.

Equally the duties of the employer: the obligation to provide the employee with work in accordance with the individual agreement, the responsibility of the employer for the belongings of the worker, the ability to change the conditions of work . . .;

– *working time*, including hours of work, part-time, overtime, night-, shift- and Sunday work; as well as *annual vacation and holidays*;
– *incapacity to work* in case of illness, of an accident at work, of military service, of an act of God. This includes the consequences as to the obligation to work and whether the execution of the (individual labour) contract is suspended or not in case of incapacity to work;
– *protection of certain categories of workers, protection against discrimination in employment*: this refers to young, elderly, handicapped and female workers, mothers, to measures to promote equal treatment regarding jobs, promotion and vocational training . . .;
– *covenants of non-competition*: this contract clause relates to the stipulation preventing the employee to engage in a business or an employment contract competing with his employer also when the individual labour contract has been terminated or has come to an end;
– *conditions regarding the inventions by employees*.

(3) Information and Consultation

135. The meaning of the word '*information*' seems rather simple: it is the communication of knowledge. Disclosure of information to workers means that the employer provides information of which explanation may be sought and questions can be raised. The meaning of the word '*consultation*' is, however, less clear and much more ambiguous. One may define consultation from a number of perspectives. In the British context consultation 'refers to subjects within the scope of managerial prerogative' while negotiation 'refers to matters within the power of joint regulation by management and trade unions.'[1] It thus refers to (a) the object of consultation, as well as (b) to the dimension of the influence of labour on management decision making. Others lay emphasis on (c) the nature of the exercise: consultation would then concern questions of common interests, whereas negotiation would relate to problems where management and labour have adversary relationships.[2] A. Marsh indicates that

> 'theoretically the distinction between consultation and negotiation depends on the proposition that consultation is non-competitive and integrative in nature, whereas negotiation is competitive and concerned with temporary and unsatisfying compromises, consultation therefore being equipped to resolve conflict and negotiation merely to contain it.'[3]

Personally, we would like to define consultation from the point of view of influence by labour on management decision making. Consultation then means that advice is given to the employer, leaving the decision making of the employer intact. It implies that the employer retains the power to make decisions, after having listened to the views of the employee representatives. This advice does not require either unanimity nor a majority, unless required, and can take place either at the request of the employer or at the request of labour or may be mandatory by law. Consultation includes an exchange of views, even of proposals and counter proposals, in short, a discussion in depth.

1. IELL, *Great Britain*, 1992, para. 42.
2. *See*: *La participation des travailleurs aux décisions dans l'entreprise*, Genève, ILO, 1981, 22 and ILO Recommendation No. 94 of 1952.
3. *Concise Encyclopaedia of Industrial Relations*, Oxford, 1979, 100.

136.   Between consultation and negotiation, which are difficult to distinguish in practice, stands the expression used in quite a number of EC directives: 'consultation with a view to reaching agreement.'[1] It seems to me that this expression goes further than consultation in the strict sense, where the employer asks for the benefit of the ideas of the employees on the matter. Here more is required: the parties are also asked to try to reach an agreement, which actually means that one leaves the area of consultation and lands in fact in the area of negotiation.

1. Directive of February 1975 on Collective Redundancies or the 1977 Directive on Acquired Rights.

137.   The putting into effect of information and consultation rights involves a number of questions, which will have to be resolved by the Community legislator or by the social partners through a European collective agreement, although the last is not likely, as employers do not favour these developments.

The most important concern:

– the subject matter; what kind of information; topics of consultations;
– the involved entity in the enterprise (plant or group) and access to decision-makers;
– when information has to be given or consultations held;
– to whom information has to be given or who should be consulted;
– the obligation of headquarters to help subsidiaries in providing required information and engage in meaningful consultation;
– the problems concerning confidentiality regarding the shared information, and the consultation process.[1]

1. *See*: R. Blanpain, *Comparative Labour Law and Industrial Relations*, 1st ed., 1982, 208–219.

138.   The competence of the Community to deal with 'information and consultation' does, it seems to me, include the powers to establish mechanisms and structures through which and to which information can be given or through which consultation can be organised, e.g., the setting up of a European Works Council, although the establishment of a EWC undoubtedly belongs to the sphere of 'representation of workers,' for which, according to Article 2,3 unanimity is needed. Also here the adagium: *accessorium sequitur principale* should play in full.

(4) EQUAL TREATMENT

139.   Another field which can be dealt with by qualified majority voting is the 'equality between men and women with regard to labour market opportunities and treatment at work.' This competence belongs self-evidently also to the *acquis communautaire* and we refer for its meaning to what we said about Article 119 of the EC Treaty and the relevant directives concerning equal treatment of men and women,[1] taking the Maastricht changes to Article 119 and others regarding the *Barber* Case into account.

1. *See* Part I, Chapter 4.

(5) INTEGRATION OF EXCLUDED PERSONS

140.   This competence relates to the integration of persons excluded from the labour market, without prejudice to Article 127 of the Treaty. This article belongs to Chapter III (dealing with education, vocational training and youth) which is part of (the new) Title VIII of the EC Treaty dealing with social policy, education, vocational training and youth.

2. Unanimous Voting

a. Procedure

141.   According to Article 2,3 of the Maastricht Agreement between the then 11 Member States, the Council shall act unanimously on a proposal from the Commission, after consulting the EP and the ESC, in a number of areas, which are enumerated immediately hereafter.

> '*Unanimity* of all members of the Council, with the exception of the United Kingdom, shall be necessary for the acts of the Council which must be adopted unanimously and for those amending the Commission proposal' (Protocol, 2).

b. Areas

(1) SOCIAL SECURITY AND SOCIAL PROTECTION OF WORKERS

142.   Unanimous voting is required in the field of social security and social protection of workers.

(2) JOB SECURITY

143.   Unanimous voting is also required in the case of *protection of workers where their employment contract is terminated*. This relates to the different methods of terminating the employment relationship, e.g., by consent, by way of notice, immediate dismissal, through judicial dissolution and the like. It covers also the term of notice, the reason(s) for dismissals, reinstatement, special protection for shop stewards, members of works councils, supervisory boards, pregnant women workers and the like, all forms of compensation, redundancy payments and the like included. Job security covers, in our opinion, individual as well as collective dismissals.

(3) Representation and Collective Defence Including Co-Determination

144. Representation and collective defence of the interests of workers and employers, including co-determination, has to be read together with paragraph 6 of Article 2. That paragraph indicates that the provisions of Article 2 do not apply to 'pay, the right of association, the right to strike and the right to impose lock-outs.'

145. Representation of workers relates to e.g., works councils, shop stewards, committees of health and safety, staff associations and the like as well as to representation through trade unions and at different levels: plant, enterprise, group of enterprises, multinational enterprises included, sectorial, national and European. *Co-determination*[1] also covers all forms of worker's participation, where an (elected) employee, a trade union representative, or someone whom the employees confide in (the so-called Dutch model) sits on the supervisory board or the management of a company. Needless to say employers are mainly represented by employer's associations.

> 1. *See* Part II, Chapter 2, §3, II. 'In Britain used almost exclusively to describe the West German form of industrial democracy' (M. Terry and L. Dickens, *European Employment and Industrial Relations Glossary*, London, 1991, 48).

146. Collective defence of the interest of workers and employers involves, taking paragraph 6 of Article 2 and representation of employers and workers into account, mainly collective bargaining. This relates to the indication of the parties, competent to conclude a collective agreement, to the content and to the form of the agreement, to the level of bargaining, to the binding effect of the agreement, to the extension procedures and the like. One can also add the settlement of industrial disputes, by way of mediation, conciliation or arbitration.

(4) Third Country Nationals

*147. This competence relates to conditions of employment for third-country nationals legally residing in Community territory. These nationals, when they are workers, do not enjoy among others the right of free movement in the Community and undoubtedly improvement in this field is called for.

(5) Financial Contributions for Promotion of Employment

*148. A final competence, to be voted upon unanimously, concerns financial contributions for promotion of employment and job-creation, without prejudice to the provisions relating to the Social Fund.

3. Excluded Areas

*149. The provisions of Article 2 do, as already mentioned, not apply to 'pay, the right of association, the right to strike or the right to impose lock-outs' (Art. 2,6).
    The rights of association, collective bargaining and to strike or to impose lock-outs are self-evidently completely interlinked and have no full-fledged and adequate meaning in themselves. Indeed, workers unite in order to be able to collectively defend their interests by way of collective bargaining on the basis of market strength,

by the use of the ultimate weapon, the strike. The same is *ceteris paribus* true for the employers. For the ILO, freedom of association includes the right to strike.[1] As we have said earlier, 'collective bargaining without the right to strike amounts to collective begging.' It will therefore not be easy to clearly define each of these rights separately.

    1. W.B. Creighton, 'Freedom of Association' in: *Comparative Labour Law and Industrial Relations in Industrialised Market Economies*, 4th ed., Deventer, Vol. II. 39.

150.   Pay, freedom of association, strike and lock-out remain thus a purely national affair. The different notions: the right of association, the right to strike and the right to impose lock-outs have however a Community meaning in law. It will indeed in time be essential to know exactly what they signify in order to judge whether the European Community in dealing with a given issue acted within the limits of its powers or not. In the light of the fact that the Maastricht Protocol on Social Policy aims at the construction of a social Europe, Article 2,6 must be seen as an exception to the general rule and has thus to be interpreted restrictively. It is at the same time interesting to note that the High Contracting Parties in Maastricht put the right to strike and the right to impose lock-outs on an equal footing, which is e.g., not the case in a number of Member States, e.g., France and Italy.

a. Pay

151.   For the notion of pay, we can, I assume, refer to what was said in relation to Article 119 of the Treaty, which deals with equal pay for male and female workers.[1] There are still important differences between the labour costs in various member countries. These differences, however, are matched by equivalent variations in the level of productivity in the countries concerned.

    1. *See* Part I, Chapter 4.

b. Right of Association

152.   The right of association contains the right to form and to join or not to join trade unions, staff associations or employers' associations, the right of those organisations to draw up their own constitutions and rules, to elect their representatives and to formulate their programs. It includes the right to form and to join national federations and confederations of employers' associations and of trade unions, as well as European or international organisations. It also embraces the acquisition of legal personality and the right to own property, to conclude contracts and the like.

c. Right to Strike or to Impose Lock-outs

153.   The right to strike 'concerns the (collective) refusal by workers, usually but not always organised in a trade union, to continue working, in order to put pressure on employers or on the government.'[1] The lock-out is 'the employer practice of denying the possibility of work to employees in connection with an industrial dispute.'[2]

1. Terry and L. Dickens, *idem*, 188.
2. *Idem*, 126.

B. The Role of the Commission

154. The Maastricht Agreement on Social Policy awarded the Commission a very dynamic task, confirming its role of initiator and animator at European level. First, the Commission shall, with a view to achieving the objectives of Article 1 and without prejudice to other provisions of the EC Treaty, *encourage cooperation* between the Member States and *facilitate the coordination* of their action in all social policy fields under this Agreement (Art. 5).

Secondly, the Commission shall have the task of *promoting the consultation* of management and labour at Community level and shall take any relevant measure *to facilitate their dialogue* by ensuring balanced support for the parties (Art. 3,1).

155. These last tasks are very important ones. Promotion of consultation is dealt with immediately hereafter. Facilitating the social dialogue relates not only to the interaction between the European Confederations like UNICE, CEEP and the ETUC, but also to relations at European sectorial or enterprise level. Support may mean financial or logistic support to trade union meetings across boundaries, to the functioning of European works councils, to the organisation of management training e.g., in the conduct of a social dialogue at European level and the like. The support, Article 3,1 reads, certainly at the demand of UNICE which was complaining about earlier unbalanced support, should be balanced and equally divided between management and labour.

C. Involvement of the Social Partners

156. The role of the social partners has been dramatically enhanced at the occasion of the Maastricht summit: from consultation with the European Community regarding the implementation of Community directives to collective bargaining at European level. In consequence the social partners are, since the coming into effect of the Maastricht Treaty, Protocols and Agreement included, entitled to real involvement in the shaping of European labour law from the initial stages, as well as, for certain countries where this is legally possible,[1] in the implementation of Council directives. At the same time a stronger legal basis has been laid for European-wide collective bargaining and mechanisms were introduced, ensuring a binding effect of European collective agreements *erga omnes*. Nonetheless, especially regarding these agreements quite a number of extremely complex problems of a legal nature arise, for the solution of which ultimately further Community legislation may be needed.

1. These are countries where there exists a so-called extension procedure by which through a (Governmental) measure the collective agreements are made binding on all employers and employees, which fall within the territorial and professional scope of the agreement, whether they are a member of one of the contracting parties or not.

1. Consultation at Community Level (Art. 3)

157. The Commission has the task of promoting the consultation of management and labour at Community level (Art. 3,1). To this end, before submitting proposals in the social field, the Commission must consult management and labour on the possible direction of Community action (Art. 3,2). This means that the social partners are involved *ab initio*, before the decision is taken to do something or not. If, after such consultation, the Commission considers Community action advisable, it shall consult management and labour on the envisaged proposal. Management and labour shall forward to the Commission an opinion, or where appropriate, a recommendation (Art. 3,3). Management and labour can thus formulate either their own opinion or a joint recommendation, which the Commission self-evidently is free to incorporate or not.

To our mind, this consultation constitutes an essential element of the European legislative process and a possible ground for the annulment of a Community decision by the Court of Justice if that part of the legislative procedure has not been properly respected.

a. Procedure

158. In this context the Communication (1993) of the Commission describes the Agreement as containing two stages:

Stage 1:
Article 3(2) specifies that 'before submitting proposals in the social policy field, the Commission shall consult management and labour on the possible direction of Community action.'

Stage 2:
> 'If, after such consultation, the Commission considers Community action advisable, it shall consult management and labour on the content of the envisaged proposal. Management and labour shall forward to the Commission an opinion or, where appropriate, a recommendation (Article 3(3) of the Agreement).
>
> In the light of the experience already acquired, the Commission proposes to proceed as follows:
> – the first consultation of the social partners would take place on receipt of the letter from the Commission. The requested consultation may be by letter or, if the social partners so desire, by the convening of an *ad hoc* meeting. The consultation period should not exceed six weeks;
> – the Commission will decide its position in the light of comments received during the first round of consultations, and will decide whether to proceed to the second phase;
> – the second consultation phase will be initiated with the receipt of the second letter sent by the Commission, setting out the content of the planned proposal together with indication of the possible legal basis;

On the occasion of this second consultation, the social partners should deliver to the Commission in writing and, where the social partners so wish
through an *ad hoc* meeting, an opinion setting out the points of agreement
and disagreement in their respective positions on the draft text. Where
appropriate, they should deliver a recommendation setting out their joint
positions on the draft text. The duration of this second phase shall also not
exceed 6 weeks.

The new consultative procedures will not be a complete substitute for the old,
especially where these involve the use of well established tripartite consultative committees. In particular, the following committees would be the mechanism for consultation of the social partners, including where appropriate
consultation under the terms of Article 3: the Advisory Committee on Safety,
Hygiene and Health Protection at work and the Advisory Committee on the
Free Movement of Workers. The two procedures may, on occasion, therefore
operate in a parallel way depending on the subject matters of the specific
proposal. The Commission will ensure, however, that duplication is avoided
and that there is the maximum of transparency at all stages of the different
procedures.

The Commission thinks it expedient to re-examine the way the social dialogue works at present with a view to promoting dialogue under the Agreement. To this end, it intends to take the appropriate steps to rationalise the
various consultation processes, including such processes at sectoral level.'

b. Social Partners

159.   One of the important questions to be solved concerns self-evidently the
problem which organisations qualify to be consulted.

This very delicate question is in the Communication (1993) dealt with as follows:

'As a matter of general principle the Commission believes that organisations
should be consulted within the terms of Article 3 of the Agreement in so far
as they meet the following criteria.
The organisations should:
– be cross industry or relate to specific sectors or categories and be organised
at European level;
– consist of organisations which are themselves an integral and recognised
part of Member State social partner structures and with the capacity to
negotiate agreements, and which are representative of all Member States, as
far as possible;
– have adequate structures to ensure their effective participation in the consultation process.'

At the same time, the Commission recognises that there is a substantial body of
experience behind the social dialogue established between the UNICE, CEEP and
ETUC. It has also taken note of their joint position regarding the implementation
of the new procedures introduced by the Agreement.

There are a number of organisations which meet the criteria set out and which are thus potential candidates for involvement in the consultation process. The Commission does not wish to take a restrictive view of this issue, but is at the same time conscious of the practical problems posed by a multiplicity of potential actors. Only the organisations themselves are in a position to develop their own dialogue and negotiating structures. The Commission will endeavour to promote the development of new linking structures between all the social partners so as to help rationalise and improve the process. Special attention will be paid here to the due representation of small and medium-sized undertakings.

This raises the question of whether or not it is necessary in the first phase to create some form of consultation body or 'umbrella liaison' committee for the purposes of the procedure foreseen under Article 3 of the Agreement. Having carefully considered the matter, the Commission considers that at this initial stage this is not the best way forward, though this question will undoubtedly need to be re-examined in the light of experience as the process develops.

160. The situation regarding consultation of the social partners on social policy matters is now as follows:

– The Commission will continue its policy of wide-ranging consultation to ensure that its policy relates as closely as possible to economic and social realities. Such consultation will cover all European or, where appropriate, national, organisations which might be affected by the Community's social policy.
– Within the framework of Article 3 of the Agreement it will undertake formal consultations with the European social partners' organisations.
– The Commission feels that these specific consultation procedures under the terms of Article 5 of the Agreement should apply to all social policy proposals, whatever legal basis is eventually decided on. The Commission also reserves the right to engage in specific consultations on any other horizontal or sectoral-based relations (including agreements) within the social partners' sphere of competence.

List of European social partner organisations consulted in accordance with Article 3 of the Agreement on Social Policy (1996)

1. *General cross-industry organisations:**
– Union of Industrial and Employers' Confederations of Europe (UNICE);
– European Centre of Enterprises with Public Participation (CEEP);
– European Trade Union Confederation (ETUC).

2. *Cross-industry organisations representing certain categories of workers or undertakings*:
– European Association of Craft, Small and Medium-Sized Enterprises (UEAPME – 'Joint Committee of Social Dialogue');
– Confédération européenne des cadres (CEC);
– Eurocadres.

3. *Specific organisations*:
– EUROCHAMBRES.

4. *Sectoral organisations with no cross-industry affiliation*
– Eurocommerce;
– COPA/COGECA;
– EUROPECHE;
– Association of European Cooperative Insurers, AECI;
– International Association of Insurance and Reinsurance Intermediaries, BIPAR;
– European Insurance Committee, CEA;
– Banking Federation of the European Community;
– Savings Banks Group of the European Community, GCECEE;
– Association of Cooperative Banks of the EC;
– European Confederation of woodworking industries, CEI-bois;
– Confederation of the National Hotel and Restaurant Associations in the EC, HOTREC;
– European Construction Industry Federation;
– European Regional Airlines Association, ERA;
– Airports Council International – European Region, ACI-Europe;
– Association des Transports aériens à la demande;
– Association of European Community Airlines, AECI;
– Association of European Airlines, AEA;
– Organisation européenne des bateliers;
– International Union for Inland Navigation;
– European Community Shipowners Association, ECSA;
– Community of European Railways, CER;
– International Road Transport Union, IRU.

> * Sectoral organisations of UNICE and committees of the ETUC also consulted as required.

The Communication (1993) by the Commission has been widely criticised, in the EP as well as in the ESC.[1] Both institutions are of the opinion that the list of representative organisations has to be reviewed. The ESC[1] feels that a representative organization should satisfy the following four criteria:

1. A European representative organization must be widely spread over the EU. This means that it must have member organizations at the appropriate relevant negotiation level in at least three-quarters of the EU Member States and be seeking to be represented in the others;
2. the European organization must have a mandate from its member organizations to negotiate at European level;
3. all the organizations affiliated to the European organization, either in their own name or through their member organizations, must be entitled to negotiate in the Member States and must be able to implement conventions concluded at European level in accordance with national practices and usage;

4. the European organization must be made up of organizations that are considered in their Member States as representative.

Alongside this form of representativeness there is another matter to consider: If the social partners offer an agreement to the Commission and request that it be submitted to the Council for a decision, has the agreement concluded been reached by organizations which represent a sufficient quantity of employers and employees, on the understanding that the social partners have autonomy in their choice of negotiating partners? This question should not be answered using criteria based on figures. What is essential when answering this question is that every representative organization which fulfills the criteria set out above should be admitted to the talks if it so wishes, at the appropriate relevant negotiation level.

This criticism has been repeated at the occasion of the conclusion of the European Collective Agreements on Parental Leave of 14 December 1995 and of 6 June 1997 on part-time. Also organisations like UEAPME (the European Union of Crafts and SME's) or CESI repeated their objections concerning the representative nature of the social partners in negotiations in the framework of the social dialogue. UEAPME indicated that in the absence of a solution, a legal conflict with the Commission seemed inevitable. On 6 September 1996, UEAPME, which claims to represent 6 million SME's, employing 27,000,000 workers, introduced a claim with the Court of First Instance to annul the Directive of 3 June 1996, which rendered binding the Collective Agreement on Parental leave, as UEAPME considers that it should have been a party to the negotiations.[2]

The Commission's position remains unchanged. In a written question[3] regarding the fact in the EU Member States, SMEs account for more than 60 per cent of jobs in the private sector, that the organization representing such undertakings should take part in the talks, given its important expertise in connection with private sector jobs; and that employers' associations from a number of countries are currently involved in Europe-wide efforts to set up a joint umbrella organization, the Commission was asked how to ensure that the current tripartite talks become official quadripartite talks, so that the interests of SMEs, the undertakings which actually create jobs, are better represented?

The Commission answered as follows:

> 'In a recent Communication, the Commission points out that the social dialogue is a key element of the European social model.[4] The economic and political integration of Europe, as well as its social stability, would have been unthinkable without the involvement and active support of the social partners. This Communication presents all the aspects of the social dialogue, the issues it deals with and the way it operates, and raises questions concerning the effectiveness of certain of its aspects, the transparency and profile of its results, and the problem of representativeness.
>
> The social dialogue covers different situations and practices. The Agreement on Social Policy annexed to the EC Treaty makes a very clear distinction between the consultation of the social partners, on the one hand, and the dialogue between them, which may lead to negotiations and the conclusion of agreements at Community level, on the other.

The Commission regularly informs a large number of trade union and employers' organizations of the main lines and content of its social initiatives. In a Communication of 14 December 1993 it gave a list of organizations to be consulted formally under Article 3 of the Agreement on Social Policy, which includes organizations representing small and medium-sized enterprises (SMEs).

As regards negotiations proper, the Commission sees a need to ensure that the principle of the independence of employers' and workers' organizations is preserved, which means that they must recognize each other as partners authorized to negotiate at European level. It follows that the Commission does not have the power to impose the participation of a particular trade union or employers' organization at the negotiating table.

The Commission would remind that the development of the dialogue and the negotiating structures is the exclusive responsibility of the social partners. It encourages the partners to promote a dialogue which is as open and representative as possible by showing openness and flexibility in order to ensure appropriate participation in the negotiations. The Commission is ready to support all positive measures adopted by the partners in this area'.

Indeed, the notion of 'social partner,' as used in Article 118B of the EC-Treaty and in the Maastricht Agreement, is a legal concept the European Court of Justice may have to interpret. It is self-evident that the meaning which is given to the notion of social partner has to be appropriate in view of the tasks which have been given to the social partners in the relevant Community texts. Indeed, the notion has not been defined in the EC texts.

It follows, however, as well from the texts as from the missions which have been given to the social partners, that there are two levels on which they have to act, namely:

a. *The level of the Member States regarding*:
   – implementation of Directives by the social partners (Art. 2,4 of the Maastricht Agreement 1991));
   – implementation of agreements, concluded at Community level (Art. 4,2 of the Maastricht Agreement).
b. *At Community level regarding*:
   – consultation of management and labour at Community level (Art. 3,1 of the Maastricht Agreement);
   – the dialogue between management and labour at European level which could lead to relations based on agreements (Art. 118B of the EC Treaty).

Both levels are self-evidently intimately intertwined. Indeed, they concern first the establishment of European legislation, which then has to be transposed into national rule-setting, and secondly European collective agreements, which may, according to national procedures and practices, be implemented at national level. In other words, the notion social partners needs to take both levels into account and not only a single one.

Self-evidently, the criteria which have been elaborated by the International Labour Organisation in its case law concerning the 87 and 98 Conventions on trade union freedom and collective bargaining have to be taken into account, as all the EU Member States are members of the ILO and the above-mentioned Conventions have been ratified by most if not all of them. Trade union freedom moreover, is retained as such in the Constitution of the ILO.

According to the ILO, employers' associations and trade unions need to be representative. Repeatedly, the ILO's Committee on Freedom of Association has underlined that the determination of the most representative trade union organisation has to be made in an *objective* and *independent* manner, that it can be reconsidered

1. Opinion of the ESC on the 'Commission communication concerning the development of the social dialogue at Community level', *O.J.*, 19 March 1997, No. C 89/28.
2. The claim is based on Article 173 of the EC Treaty which allows to challenge the legality of acts of the Council by individuals or organisations which have an interest.
3. E-0447/97 by Kirsi Piha, *O.J.*, 18 October 1997, C 319/87. *See also* EP: 'Resolution on the Commission communication concerning the development of the social dialogue at Community level', *O.J.*, 22 September 1997, C 286/338. (The EP asks to be granted a power of co-decision within the framework of the legislative procedure, in the form of rejection or approval).
4. Doc. COM(96) 448.

2. Implementation of Directives

161. According to Article 2,4 a Member State may entrust management and labour, at their joint request, with the implementation of directives adapted pursuant to paragraphs 2 and 3 of Article 2.

In this case, the Member State must ensure that, no later than the date on which a directive must be transposed, 'management and labour have introduced the necessary measures by agreement, the Member State being required to take any measure enabling it at any time to be in a position to guarantee the results imposed by that directive' (Art. 2,4.2).

162. For practical purposes this means that directives can be transposed into national law by way of collective bargaining between management and labour at national, inter-industry, level. It presupposes that such collective agreements can have, through one mechanism or another, an effect *erga omnes*, namely become legally binding upon all employers and workers who are meant to be covered by the collective agreement. It also means that the binding effect of the collective agreement should be such, that private parties (employer-employees) cannot deviate from them; and also that there is a mechanism through which the directive continues to have effect, even when contracting parties to the collective agreement would have denounced the collective agreement until a new act implementing the directive has been enacted.

163. Article 2,4 does in fact not add anything new. Implementation of directives by way of collective bargaining was already a current and by the EC accepted practice in such countries as Belgium, where collective agreements, concluded at national inter-industry level, can be extended to the private sector as a whole by a Royal Decree, which means Government involvement. These extended agreements are penally sanctioned and have, once announced, at least for the individual normative part of the agreement, a prolonged binding effect, as the individual obligations between employer and employee, under the collective agreement, are legally supposed to have been incorporated in the individual agreements of workers covered by the (extended) collective agreement.

In Belgium, this has been, as said, standing practice. Directives such as the ones on collective redundancies (1975), on acquired rights in case of transfer of enterprises (1977) and on information and consultation (EWC's 1994), have been transposed into Belgian law, totally or partially, by way of extended collective agreements. It has been a way for the Belgian social partners to demonstrate, with subdued acquiescence by the Belgian Parliament, their social autonomy. It is in this context interesting to note that the Ghent Labour Court of Appeal (Belgium)[1] accepted that an extended collective agreement transposing a directive of which the objective has a binding effect, *in casu* the transfer of enterprises directive of 1977, can change imperatively binding civil law, in this case concerning the transfer of obligations.

In Belgium, governmental intervention may, however, be needed in order to fully implement the directives, as even extended collective agreements do not necessarily cover public companies, which effect the functioning of the Common Market.

1. 11 October 1989, *Journal des Tribunaux de Travail*, 1989, 489.

164.   This is to say that only some of the industrial relations systems in the Member States of the Community qualify, unless dramatic changes would occur in those countries, *quod non*, to have their collective bargaining systems act as a conveyer belt of directives into national law. Belgium, Germany, France, the Netherlands, to give some examples, may, under certain conditions, be in that league as they have extension procedures in one form or another.

165.   Regarding this matter the Communication (1993) of the Commission reads as follows:

> 'Article 2(4) of the Agreement states that a signatory Member State "may entrust management and labour, at their joint request, with the implementation of directives adopted pursuant to paragraphs 2 and 3". However, the Member State remains responsible for ensuring that "management and labour have introduced the necessary measures by agreement" and for taking "any necessary measures enabling it at any time to be a position to guarantee the results imposed by that directive". This implementation of a directive by agreement must take place "no later than the date on which a directive must be transposed in accordance with Article 189".'

This provision establishes, in the context of the Agreement, the general principle that directives may be implemented by collective agreement. This principle has been recognised in the case law of the Court of Justice.[1] It is also in line with the implementation requirements of the International Labour Organisation[2] and the Council of Europe.[3]

Article 2(4) does not require the Member States to introduce any particular or special procedures or that any explicit formal terms of reference be given to the social partners; nor is there any need for them to submit a joint request prior to negotiations between them on an agreement for implementation of the directive. The actual conclusion of an agreement and its forwarding to the competent authority of the Member State should be regarded as a tacit joint request within the meaning of the first paragraph of Article 2(4).

1. Case 91/81 (1982) ECR 2133; Case 193/83 (1985) ECR 427.
2. ILO Conventions Nos. 100, 101, 106, 111, 171, 172, etc.
3. Article 35 (1) of the European Social Charter.

166. The Communication continues:

'Under the second subparagraph of Article 2(4) the Member State concerned remains responsible for ensuring that, no later than the date on which a directive must be transposed in accordance with Article 189, the social partners have introduced the necessary measures by agreement and for taking "any necessary measure enabling it at any time to be in a position to guarantee the results imposed by that directive". This wording is a slightly amended version of corresponding provisions in certain directives.[1]

Under Article 2(4), the Member State must "guarantee the results imposed by that directive", although it may entrust management and labour with its implementation. In this connection the reference in Article 1 of the Agreement to measures which "take account of the diverse forms of national practices, in particular in the field of contractual relations" is relevant.'

1. Article 2(1) of Council Directive 92/56/EEC of 24 June 1992; Article 9(1) of Council Directive 91/533/EEC of 14 October 1991.

3. Social Dialogue (Arts. 3–4)

167. The social dialogue, in the sense of meetings and exchange of views between management and labour at Community level, which may eventually lead to contractual relations, including collective agreements, has become, since Maastricht, an outspoken and expressly foreseen priority of the European Community. The Commission, it is stated in Article 3,1, 'shall take any relevant measure to facilitate their dialogue by ensuring balanced support for the parties.' This language and approach underline the voluntarism of the industrial relation system the eleven founding fathers in their Maastricht Agreement wanted to develop at Community level. This tendency is reinforced by the possibility to conclude European collective agreements and by giving the social partners the right of the firstborn to create European law as will be described in the following paragraphs.

4. Community-wide Agreements (Art. 4)

a. The Agreement of 31 October 1991

168. On the occasion of the Maastricht summit sufficient legitimacy has finally been given to European collective bargaining. This was made possible by an historic agreement between UNICE, CEEP and the ETUC, concluded in Brussels on 31 October 1991, which paved the way for Maastricht – just in time for the summit. That agreement (*see* Annex 3) was elaborated with the dynamic support and under the competent guidance of the Commission and especially of the then Director-General of DG V, Mr. J. Degimbe.[1]

1. R. Delarue, 'Europees collectief overleg: tussen euforie en eurofobie.' *De Gids op Maats-chappelijk Gebied*, 1991, 1083–1094.

169.   An agreement was possible due to different factors, in particular to the divergent interests of the parties involved, namely of the Commission, of the employers' association and of the trade unions.

The Commission had indeed to conclude that the Community approach to social policy, through the Community Social Charter of 1989 and the Action Programme, had not been successful and was looking for other ways to provide the Community with a fair social face.

The social partners, employers as well as trade union representatives, had to face the fact that their input in the Community legislative process, also due to the well-known democratic deficit, was rather minimal.

The employers were moreover in a sense afraid of Community legislation, especially labour law directives which might impose undue restrictive obligations on business; at the same time UNICE's representatives got a little bit tired of formulating polite no's to proposals in the social field.

Trade unions, on the other hand, were eagerly looking forward to play a more effective role at a European level in the furthering of the interests of their members and the workers, as the ETUC's Luxemburg Congress had clearly indicated.

Mr. Z.J.A. Tyskiewicz, Secretary General of UNICE, explains as follows:[1]

'Why did UNICE accept the idea of European-level negotiations? Why did we go down that road? Why in a Europe where collective bargaining tends to move away from the centre as far down as the plant level are we recentralising bargaining and bringing it up to the European level? The reason is that the employers were convinced that Maastricht would result in much wider powers for the Commission and the Council in the social field: a great extension of qualified majority voting, and therefore a greater number of legislative acts in the social field. Experience so far in EC social legislation is that the legislator is getting it wrong.

The legislator is being too detailed, too prescriptive, is trying to fix everything from Brussels. We became convinced that the only way to stop him or her would be by negotiating some of these issues ourselves. We felt we would be better custodians of subsidiarity than the legislator. We were also quite convinced the unions would be too. The reason is that our members and theirs will be breathing down our necks because they do not want to lose national sovereignty. Naturally they do not want the European level organisations treading on their territory. That is very healthy. They will allow us to go along only with broad framework type agreements, rather than the prescriptive and detailed type of legislation that we are getting from the Commission.

That was our reason for agreeing to negotiate. The unions' reason was different. Of course they can get more out of the European legislator than they can out of European employers. But for them it was very important to consolidate their role at European level because in many cases they are losing power and influence at national level and this was a way of regaining a part of that power at European level. Although their motivation and ours was not the same, we reached the same destination point.'

De facto quite an evolution took place as well in the ETUC as in UNICE. Until the 7th Congress (1991) the ETUC was mainly a coordinating body of the 44 associated national confederations. The 15 sectorial committees were not integrated in the decision-making structure. The British TUC and the Scandinavian unions wanted to continue this way. Others, like the Belgian unions, wanted to go a step further and build a supranational structure. This was done at the Luxemburg Congress of May 1991. The sectorial committees became integrated in the ETUC, the financial means of the European union increased and the decision-making structure strengthened. Without those changes the Agreement of 31 October 1991 would for mere organisational purposes practically not have been possible.

Until recently UNICE was opposed to European bargaining. The official credo was that aside from some specific fields like health and safety, free movement of labour, vocational training and the like, labour matters were to be dealt with at a national level. Within UNICE however the mentality slowly changed as some European labour law seemed to be unavoidable in the long run. Better to join. The British CBI was however resolutely opposed to eventual European bargaining: consultation yes, negotiation no. The British employers feared that European agreements might lead to mandatory national negotiations in Britain. Needless to say the Conservative Government was not too happy either. Other confederations, like the Greek and the Portuguese ones, also had doubts. The majority however, led by the Belgians, the French and the Italians, was of the opinion that UNICE should play a constructive role. It was that group that finally won.

The social partners, the ETUC included, will have to further supra-nationalise their decision-making structure. It is impossible to continue to work on a basis of unanimous decision-making: also here majority decisions are called for.

1. 'Social Policy after Maastricht. The point of view of the employers,' November 1992 (mimeo).

170. These divergent interests paved the way for an agreement whereby the Commission and the social partners (gladly) accepted to increase the role of the Commission and the consultative role of the partners, to promote their dialogue and to give management and labour the right for a first try to elaborate European social minimum standards by way of agreements, thus getting in a sense pre-eminence over the EP, which is not involved in that part of the legislative process. Only if the social partners would not succeed and/or their proposal not be implemented by a Council decision, would the legislative process resume its normal course. One of the great technical difficulties was self-evidently the question how to arrive at a procedure whereby those collective agreements would become binding *erga omnes*, namely for all concerned employers and employees, throughout the Community.

This Brussels agreement between the social partners of 31 October 1991 paved, as said, the way for the acceptance at the Maastricht summit of Articles 3,4 and 4 which contain the legal basis for collective bargaining at European level. This does however not take away that, as already indicated above, enormous complex legal problems remain to be solved as the collective agreements themselves are a complex institution, even more so at a European level.

b. The Maastricht Deal

171. The Maastricht Agreement concerning the Community's future social policy on the basis of a reinforced dialogue between the social partners reads as follows:

> 'if at the occasion of consultations between the Commission and the Social Partners on the possible direction of Community action or advisable Community action, the partners express the feeling that they would like to deal themselves with the involved problem, they can express to the Commission their wish to do so and initiate the procedure provided for in Article 4. The duration of the procedure shall not exceed *nine months*, unless the management and labour concerned and the Commission decide jointly to extend it' (Art. 3,3–4).

172. Article 4 thus lays down the groundwork for European collective agreements. 'Should management and labour so desire,' it reads, 'the dialogue between them at Community level may lead to contractual relations including agreements,' thus expanding on Article 118B of the EC Treaty.

Two ways are foreseen to implement these agreements concluded at Community level: they

> 'shall be implemented either:
> 1. in accordance with the procedures and practices specific to management and labour and the Member States or,
> 2. in matters covered by Article 2, at the joint request of the signatory parties, by a Council decision on a proposal from the Commission' (Art. 4,2).

It should be underlined again that the EP does not intervene in this procedure at all; and that the Council self-evidently always has the last word and can at any time take measures which would abolish or amend an agreement, which has been implemented by a Council decision, or simply withdraw the implementation decision.

(1) IMPLEMENTATION IN ACCORDANCE WITH NATIONAL PRACTICE

173. Implementing European agreements between the social partners in accordance with national practice does not imply any obligation on the Member States to apply the agreements directly or to work out rules for their transposition, nor any obligation to amend national legislation in force to facilitate their implementation. This means that the European agreements will have to be implemented in the Member States through the collective bargaining system which is prevalent in each country.[1] It signifies also clearly that the Member States at this stage do not want to change the national systems of bargaining in any way.

This way of doing things engages self-evidently a number of intricate problems to which we will come back later in section IV of this General Introduction.

1. Declaration on Article 4,2.

(2) IMPLEMENTATION BY A COUNCIL DECISION

174. The Council can, at the joint request of the signatory parties and on a proposal from the Commission, implement an agreement by a decision, whether this is a regulation, a directive or even, theoretically at least, a recommendation. The Council shall act by qualified majority, except where the agreement in question contains one or more provisions relating to one of the areas referred to in Article 2,3, in which case it will act unanimously (Art. 4,2). Quite a number of problems arise here too, which we will discuss in section IV. In order to do so the 'Community agreements' have to be put in a more general perspective and some explanatory remarks are due.

c. The Communication of the Commission (1993)

(1) CONCLUDING AN AGREEMENT

175. According to the Communication (1993),

'the social partners consulted by the Commission on the content of a proposal for Community action may deliver an opinion or, where appropriate, a recommendation to the Commission. Alternatively, they may also, as stated in Article 3(4), "inform the Commission of their wish to initiate the process provided for in Article 4". Should they decide on this latter course of action, they may embark, independently, upon a process of negotiation which could lead to the establishment of a direct agreement between the parties. The negotiation process may take up to nine months and may be extended with the agreement of the Commission.

The question of whether an agreement between social partners representing certain occupational categories or sectors constitutes a sufficient basis for the Commission to suspend its legislative action will have to be examined on a case-by-case basis with particular regard to the nature and scope of the proposal and the potential impact of any agreement between the social partners concerned on the issue which the proposals seek to address.

In their independent negotiations, the social partners are in no way required to restrict themselves to the content of the proposal in preparation within the Commission or merely to making amendments to it, bearing in mind, however, that Community action can clearly not go beyond the areas covered by the Commission's proposal. The social partners concerned will be those who agree to negotiate with each other. Such agreement is entirely in the hands of the different organisations. However, the Commission takes the view that the provisions regarding small and medium-sized undertakings referred to in Article 2(2) of the Agreement should be borne in mind by organisations which are signatory to an agreement.

The negotiations may not exceed nine months, unless the social partners concerned and the Commission decide jointly to extend them. The Agreement between the Eleven has associated the Commission in this decision on extension and empowered it to assess the two parties' chances of arriving at an agreement within the period set. This will prevent any prolongation of fruitless negotiations which would ultimately block the Commission's ability to regulate. In making such an assessment, the Commission will respect fully the social partners' independence.'

176.   The Communication continues:

'At or before the end of this nine-month period, therefore, the social partners have to submit to the Commission a report taking stock of the negotiations. This report may inform the Commission that:
a. they concluded an agreement and jointly request the Commission to propose that the Council adopt a decision on implementation, or
b. having concluded an agreement between themselves, they prefer to implement it in accordance with the procedures and practices specific to management and labour and to the Member States, or
c. they envisage pursuing the negotiations beyond the nine months and accordingly request the Commission to decide with them upon a new deadline, or
d. they are unable to reach an agreement.
Where point d) applies, the Commission will look into the possibility of proposing, in the light of the work already done, a legislative instrument in the field in question and will forward the result of its deliberations to the Council. The Economic and Social Committee and the European Parliament will also be consulted in accordance with the procedures laid down in the Treaty.
   At any event, and without prejudicing the principe of the autonomy of the social partners (a principle which underlies Articles 3 and 4 of the Agreement), the Commission feels that the European Parliament must be fully informed at all stages of any consultation or negotiation procedure involving the social partners.'

177.   Consultation of the Member States will take place as in the past. As regards the situation in the EFTA countries, the point has already been made that the Protocol forms parts of the *acquis communautaire* like any other provision of the EC Treaty. Thus, a decision taken on the basis of Article 4 may be extended to the EFTA countries too. In practice, the social partners' organisations normally cover the EFTA countries, so that they are *de facto* integrated at all stages of the consultation procedure, with negotiation being a matter for the social partners.

(2) The Implementation of the Agreements
   178.   Agreements concluded at Community level are to be implemented:

   'a. either in accordance with the procedures and practices specific to management and labour and the Member States; this provision is subject to the following declaration:

"The 11 High Contracting Parties declare that the first of the arrangements for application of the agreements between management and labour at Community level – referred to in Article 4(2) – will consist in developing, by collective bargaining according to the rules of each Member State, the content of the agreements, and that consequently this arrangement implies no obligation on the Member States to apply the agreements directly or to work out rules for their transposition, nor any obligation to amend national legislation in force to facilitate their implementation";

b. or, in matters covered by Article 2, at the joint request of the signatory parties, by a Council decision on a proposal from the Commission;

c. the Council is to act by qualified majority, except where the agreement in question contains one or more provisions relating to one of the areas referred to in Article 2(3), in which case it is to act unanimously.

In the event of negotiations resulting in an agreement that the social partners decide to implement via the voluntary route, the terms of this agreement will bind their members and will affect only them and only in accordance with the practices and procedures specific to them in their respective Member States.'

(3) THE COUNCIL

179. The Commission's view is that implementing an agreement concluded at Community level by means of a Council decision on a proposal from the Commission at the joint request of the social partners, leads to the adoption of a decision on the agreement as concluded.

'By virtue of its role as guardian of the Treaties, the Commission will prepare proposals for decisions to the Council following consideration of the representative status of the contracting parties, their mandate and the "legality" of each clause in the collective agreement in relation to Community law, and the provisions regarding small and medium-sized undertakings set out in Article 2(2). At all events, the Commission intends to provide an explanatory memorandum on any proposal presented to the Council in this area, giving its comments and assessment of the agreement concluded by the social partners.

Where it considers that it should not present a proposal for a decision to implement an agreement to the Council, the Commission will immediately inform the signatory parties of the reasons for its decision.'

180. The Communication of 1993 states:

'Under Article 4(2) of the Agreement, the Commission is not legally required to consult the European Parliament on requests made to it by the social partners concerning implementation of an agreement by means of a Council decision. However, the Commission does intend to inform Parliament and to send it the text of the agreement, together with its proposal for a decision and the explanatory memorandum, so that Parliament may, should it consider it advisable, deliver its opinion to the Commission and to the Council.

125

The Council decision must be limited to making binding the provisions of the agreement concluded between the social partners, so the text of the agreement would not form part of the decision, but would be annexed thereto.

If the Council decides, in accordance with the procedures set out in the last subparagraph of Article 4(2), not to implement the agreement as concluded by the social partners, the Commission will withdraw its proposal for a decision and will examine, in the light of the work done, whether a legislative instrument in the area in question would be appropriate.'

d. The Collective Agreement on Parental Leave of 14 December 1995

181.   The foundations and steps leading to the conclusion of this agreement and its implementation by way of a Directive were as follows:

– management and labour may, as said, in accordance with Article 4(2) of the Agreement on social policy, request jointly that agreements at Community level be implemented by a Council decision on a proposal from the Commission;
– paragraph 16 of the Community Charter of the Fundamental Social Rights of Workers on equal treatment for men and women provides, *inter alia*, that 'measures should also be developed enabling men and women to reconcile their occupational and family obligations';
– the Council, despite the existence of a broad consensus, had not been able to act on the proposal for a directive on parental leave for family reasons, as amended on 15 November 1984;
– the Commission, in accordance with Article 3(2) of the Agreement on social policy, consulted management and labour on the possible direction of Community action with regard to reconciling working and family life;
– the Commission, considering after such consultation that Community action was desirable, once again consulted management and labour on the substance of the envisaged proposal in accordance with Article 3(3) of the said Agreement;
– the general cross-industry organisations (UNICE, CEEP and the ETUC) informed the Commission in their joint letter of 5 July 1995 of their desire to initiate the procedure provided for by Article 4 of the said Agreement;
– the said cross-industry organisations concluded on their own, on 14 December 1995, a framework agreement on parental leave and they have forwarded to the Commission their joint request to implement this framework agreement by a Council Decision on a proposal from the Commission in accordance with Article 4(2) of the said Agreement;
– the Commission then drafted its proposal for a Directive, taking into account the representative status of the signatory parties, their mandate and the legality of the clauses of the framework agreement and compliance with the relevant provisions concerning small and medium-sized undertakings;
– the Commission, in accordance with its Communication of 14 December 1993 concerning the implementation of the Protocol on social policy, informed the European Parliament by sending it the text of the framework agreement, accompanied by its proposal for a Directive and the explanatory memorandum;

- the Commission also informed the Economic and Social Committee by sending it the text of the framework agreement, accompanied by its proposal for a Directive and the explanatory memorandum.
- The Council implemented the Agreement on Parental Leave by way of a Directive of 3 June 1996.

e. The Agreement on Part-time Work of 6 June 1997

181bis. Negotiations between the social partners started on 21 October 1996, when the Commission decided to involve the social partners on this issue as the adoption of a Directive on 'atypical work' did not seem possible.

The agreement does not cover all atypical workers which the ETUC would have liked (e.g., also temporary workers, contracts of a short duration, seasonal work, homework, telework), but only part-time work.

The purpose of the agreement is two-fold:

a. To provide for the removal of discrimination against part-time workers and to improve the quality of part-time work; and
b. to facilitate the development of part-time work on a voluntary basis and to contribute to the flexible organization of working time in a manner which takes into account the needs of employers and workers.

The agreement was implemented by Council Directive 97/81 EC of 15 December 1997.[1]

> 1. Concerning the framework Agreement on part-time work concluded by UNICE, CEEP and the ETUC, O.J., 20 January 1998, L14/9.

D. Economic and Social Cohesion

182. At the Maastricht Top, especially at the request of Spain, special attention was given to the strengthening of the economic and social cohesion of the Community, already recognised in Articles 2 and 3 of the EC Treaty, as vital to the full development and enduring success of the Community. To this end a special Protocol on Economic and Social Cohesion was concluded. More funds are made available and a *Cohesion Fund* was set up that provides Community financial contributions to projects in the field of environment and trans-European networks (infrastructure) in Member States with a GNP per capita of less than 90 per cent of the Community average which have a programme leading to the fulfilment of the conditions of economic convergence as set out in Article 104C of the Treaty.

E. Vocational Training

183. The third Chapter of Title VIII of the EC Treaty deals with education, vocational training and youth. Pursuant to that Chapter, the Community will encourage co-operation on education policy between Member States, supplementing their action, while respecting the responsibility of the Member States for the content of teaching, the organisation of education and their cultural and linguistic diversity (Art. 127,1).

Community action shall aim to:

- facilitate adaptation to industrial changes, in particular through vocational training and retraining;
- improve initial and continuing vocational training in order to facilitate vocational integration and reintegration into the labour market;
- facilitate access to vocational training and encourage mobility of instructors and trainees and particularly young people;
- stimulate cooperation on training between educational or training establishments and firms;
- develop exchanges of information and experience on issues common to the training systems of the Member States.

The Community and the Member States shall foster cooperation with third countries and the competent international organisations in the sphere of vocational training. The Council, acting with qualified majority and after consulting the Economic and Social Committee, shall adopt measures to contribute to the achievement of the objectives, excluding any harmonisation of the laws and regulations of the Member States (Art. 127,2–4).

F. Equal Pay, Article 119 EC Treaty, The Barber Case

184.   Article 6 of the Maastricht Agreement relates to equal pay and is in fact a redrafted copy of Article 119 EC Treaty to which a new paragraph is added, which reads as follows:

> 'this Article shall not prevent any Member State from maintaining or adopting measures providing for specific advantages in order to make it easier for women to pursue vocational activity or to prevent or compensate for disadvantages in their professional careers.'

185.   An additional Protocol was also concluded concerning the *Barber* Case.[1] In the *Barber* Case the European Court decided that a pension paid under a contracted-out pension scheme constitutes consideration paid by the employer to the workers in respect of his employment and therefore falls within the scope of Article 119 of the EC Treaty.[2] The question arose whether this applied to those pension schemes which were engaged before the judgment on the *Barber* Case was made (17 May 1990). It was feared by some that the European Court might give a retroactive effect to its decision. The Maastricht summit, however, put the pension community at ease by deciding in its Protocol concerning Article 119 of the Treaty establishing the European Community on the following provision, which shall be annexed to the Treaty:

'for the purposes of Article 119 of this Treaty, benefits under occupational social security schemes shall not be considered as remuneration if and in so far as they are attributable to periods of employment prior to 17 May 1990, except in the case of workers or those claiming under them who have before that date initiated legal proceedings or introduced an equivalent claim under the applicable national law.'

1. *See* Part I, Chapter 4.
2. *Barber Douglas Harvey* v. *Guardian Royal Exchange Assurance Group*, 17 May 1990, No. 262/88, IELL, *Case Law*, No. 146.

§4. European Labour Law: Trailer or Locomotive?

186. The previous section leaves no doubt regarding the answer to our title. However, this does not diminish from the fact that certain important social steps were taken. Let us first take a look at the accomplishments of the ECSC, as an example of social progress in two sectors of industry, and thereupon examine the EC record.

I. THE ECSC

187. The ECSC[1] constituted a first attempt toward a common policy, not only at economic, but also at social and regional levels, encroaching in an important way upon the far-reaching restructurings that have been carried out in the coal and steel sectors over the years. Between 1960 and 1980, coal production decreased in the Community from about 450 million tons to 21 million tons. One million jobs were lost. Between 1984 and 1988, 40,000 jobs disappeared very year. In Belgium the number of workers diminished by 68 per cent. The steel sector was also harshly hit. In 10 years during the 1970s, out of 800,000 jobs, 300,000 were lost. Jobs continue to go.

Article 56 of the ECSC Treaty offers the Community the possibility of promoting the creation of new and economically sound activities capable of reabsorbing redundant workers into productive employment by way of granting subventions. Pursuant to this article, non-repayable restructuring loans permitted the creation of new jobs in other sectors of industry. In the steel sector, important vocational retraining programmes were set up. One should also mention the housing programme for coal and steel workers, whereby[2] houses (with cheap rent facilities) were built.

1. EC, *A Social Europe*, 4th ed., Brussels, 1990, 49–51.
2. European Commission, *Social Policy of the Community*, Brussels, 1996.

II. THE EC

188. As far as social development in the EC is concerned, we shall distinguish between three periods: the first, 1957 to 1974, was characterised by a rather cautious approach; the second, 1974 to 1990, was at first a golden period for labour law until 1980, at which time it witnessed an abrupt breakdown. The third period, which started in 1990, has been marked for the adoption of the Community Charter for basic social rights for workers.

A. 1957–1974

189. During this first period, the economic credo of the EC was clearly adhered to. Nevertheless, some steps were taken regarding social security for workers within the framework of free movement for workers and by the launching of the European Social Fund. A new climate, however, came about through the adoption of 'preliminary guidelines for a Community social policy programme,'[1] drafted by the Commission in 1971, which led to the important declaration of Heads of States and Prime Ministers at the occasion of the 1972 Paris Summit that: 'they attach as much importance to vigorous action in the social field as to the achievement of the monetary and economic union.'[2]

   1. 'Preliminary Guidelines for a Community Social Programme,' *Bulletin of Comparative Labour Relations*, No. 3, 1972, 81–149 (out of print).
   2. Ph. Van Praag, 'Trends and Achievements in the Field of Social Policy in the European Communities,' *Idem*, No. 4, 1973, 150 (out of print).

190. Little by little the way was paved toward the Social Action Programme, which was adopted by the Council in a resolution of 21 January 1974.[1] The Council underlined the necessity to take measures toward realising the following priorities:

– *attainment of full and better employment in the Community*
   1. the establishment of appropriate consultation between Member States on their employment policies and the promotion of better cooperation by national employment services;
   2. the establishment of an action programme for migrant workers who are nationals of Member States of third countries;
   3. the implementation of a common vocational training policy and the setting up of a European Vocational Training Centre;
   4. the undertaking of action to achieve equality between men and women with regard to access to employment and vocational training and advancement with regard to working conditions, including pay.
– *the improvement of living and working conditions so as to make their harmonisation possible while maintaining their improvement*
   5. the establishment of appropriate consultation among Member States on their social protection policies;
   6. the establishment of an initial action programme, relating in particular to health and safety at work, the health of workers and improved organisation of tasks, beginning in those economic sectors where working conditions appear to be the most difficult;
   7. the implementation, in cooperation with the Member States, of specific measures to combat poverty by drafting pilot schemes.
– *increased involvement of management and labour in the economic and social decisions of the Community and of workers in the life of undertakings*

8. the progressive involvement of workers or their representatives in the life of undertakings in the Community;
9. the promotion of the involvement of management and labour in the economic and social decisions of the Community.

It is beyond doubt that the action programme was only partly implemented when the 1976 deadline expired. A partial success cannot, however, be denied.

1. Social Action Programme. Resolution of the Council of 21 January 1974, *Bulletin of Comparative Labour Relations*, No. 5, 1974, 135–187 (out of print).

B. 1974–1989

191. This period can be divided into two parts; the first, from 1974 to 1980 and the second from 1980 to approximately 1989, which has been marked by the movement toward deregulation, headed by Mrs. Thatcher.

192. The first part of this period has been labelled by some as 'the golden period of harmonisation.'[1] Various labour law directives were adopted, namely:

– 1975: the directives relating to equal pay on the one hand and to collective redundancies on the other;
– 1976: the directive concerning equal treatment of men and women with regard to working conditions;
– 1977: the directive concerning the transfer of enterprises and acquired rights for workers;
– 1978, the directive relating to equality between men and women with regard to social security;
– 1980: the directive relating to the insolvability of the employer.

The 1970s also saw the beginning of the publication of a series of directives concerning health and safety.

1. F. Blanquet, *1992: l'Europe: vers l'harmonisation des législations sociales*, 1987, not yet published (l'âge d'or de l'harmonisation).

193. New winds started to blow in the 1980s. Deregulation and in particular flexibility became the holy slogans in the battle against the economic and social crisis, against sluggish economic growth and massive unemployment and toward the successful conquering of domestic and foreign markets. The vision of Mrs. Thatcher and of employers prevailed: more regulations led to greater unemployment and produced counter-productive effects for the workers. Many proposals for directives failed to obtain approval in the Council: the notorious Vredeling proposals regarding the information and consultation of workers in undertakings with a complex structure (1980–1983); the proposal on part-time work (1982); the proposal concerning temporary work (1982–1984); as well as the proposed recommendation in relation to the reduction and reorganisation of working time. The revised proposal of 1972 concerning the Fifth Directive which related to limited liability companies and forms of workers' participation (1983), was likewise unsuccessful, while the proposal regarding the SE, already initiated in 1970, was a dead duck. No wonder then that the new social action programme of 22 June 1984 was less ambitious.[1] It addressed 5 points:

– unemployment, especially of young people;
– the introduction of new technologies;
– industrial safety;
– the cost of social security and its influence on the competitiveness of undertakings and on the living standards of workers;
– a more intense dialogue between the employers' and workers' representatives at a European level.

Much attention was also paid to safety at work and many directives toward that goal were adopted: the protection of workers from risks related to exposure to chemical, physical and biological agents at work (1980); the major accidents hazards of certain industrial activities (1982); the protection of workers against metallic lead (1982), asbestos (1983) and noise at work (1986).

1. O.J., 1984. No. C 175/1.

194.   Nonetheless, it is the Single European Act of 1986, aiming at the establishment of the internal market, in particular, that attracted most of the attention in the second half of the 1980s. The White Paper of 1985 concerning the internal market does not contain a single word on the harmonisation of labour law. On top of that, the Single Act confirmed, as indicated earlier, the national sovereignty of Member States over 'rights and interests of employed persons' which requires, in the case of Community decisions, unanimous voting by the Council. In so doing it gives each Member State the right to veto those proposals from the Commission which regard labour law. Under these circumstances, it was difficult to maintain that social policies were as important as economic and monetary matters. Undoubtedly, Article 118A allows qualified majority voting concerning health and safety for workers. This gave birth to the framework directive of 12 June 1989 concerning measures to encourage the safety and health of workers at work. This directive contains a number of minimum requirements and general principles relating to the prevention of industrial risks, vocational training, information, consultation and participation of workers, and should be looked upon as the basis for a number of specific directives relating to the workplace, machinery, personal protective equipment and display of screen equipment.

195.   A new article, Article 130A, insists on the necessity of economic and social cohesion in the Community, meaning that the differences between regions should be done away with through a dynamic action of the structural funds (the social fund, the regional fund and the agricultural fund) in favour of less-developed regions. Here important decisions have already been taken. From 1993 on, the funds will dispose of no less than 15 billion ECU yearly. Five objectives guiding future structural policies were retained:

– aid will be granted to regions with a gross national product per inhabitant of less than 75 per cent of the European average;
– aid will be granted to regions that are undergoing industrial deterioration with the aim to contribute to the restructuring of enterprises, to combat unemployment and to create new jobs in new economic sectors;
– the long-standing fight against unemployment will be continued;
– the insertion of young people into the work process will be promoted;
– structural problems, especially in the agricultural sector, will be fought.

196.   These measures notwithstanding, the criticism remained that the White Paper of 1985 concerning the 1992 internal market was *one-sided, liberal (conservative) and purely economic* and that there was a social vacuum. Voices were raised to plead again for a social dimension of the internal market. These voices were heard and the Commission created an interdepartmental working party, whose mission was to draft a report concerning the social dimension of the Common Market. This was published as a separate number of 'Social Europe' in 1988. The European Council also intervened; at the 1989 Madrid Summit, the 1972 catch phrase that as much importance must be given to the social dimension as to economic and monetary policies was repeated.

These developments, under the dynamic leadership of the President of the Commission, the French socialist Jacques Delors, led to a *Community Charter of Basic Social Rights for Workers*, which was solemnly approved and promulgated at the occasion of the meeting of Heads of State and Prime Ministers, with the exception of Great Britain, in Strasbourg on 9 December 1989, exactly 20 years after the 1789 French Universal Declaration of Human Rights. The idea is that future social policies in general and those regarding labour law in particular will be inspired by this Community Charter in the years to come.

C. 1990 and Beyond: The Community Charter and the Social Action Programme – The Maastricht Agreement on Social Policy

1. The Community Charter of Basic Social Rights

a. Foundation

197.   The basic social rights for workers are founded upon the firm will to promote the standard of living on the one hand and social consensus on the other. The Charter is based in the first place on Article 117 of the EC Treaty under the terms of which the Member States have agreed on the need to promote improved living and working conditions for workers so as to make their harmonisation possible while maintaining their improvement. The preamble to the Charter indicates that one of the priority objectives in the economic and social field is to promote employment; to this end the completion of the internal market presents major opportunities for growth and for job creation. Social consensus contributes to the strengthening of the competitiveness of undertakings, of the economy as a whole and of the creation of employment; thus it is an essential condition for ensuring sustained economic development.

b. Objectives

198. The Charter should, drawing upon the Conventions of the ILO and the European Social Charter of the Council of Europe, guarantee social improvements especially regarding:

- the freedom of movement;
- living and working conditions;
- health and safety in the work place;
- social protection;
- education and training;
- equal treatment combating every form of social exclusion and discrimination, including discrimination on grounds of sex, race, colour, opinion and religion;
- equal treatment of migrant workers and nationals of third countries.

c. Scope

199. With regard to the scope of the Charter, different points must be made. First, the solemn declaration has only political consequences and no legally binding effect. It is an expression of the political will of the eleven Governments who supported the Charter, nothing more, nothing less. Departing from the fact that the Charter is not legally binding, one can ask whether the Court could describe the stipulations of the Charter as being 'general principles of Community law.' The answer is no. After all, for the Court to conform to a consistent opinion, there must be a treaty signed by all Member States, and this is not the case here, because the British opted out. In summary, one can say that the Charter is not an instrument of Community law, nor is it a treaty signed by all Member States in relation to which Community law could be examined by the Court for its compatibility with the principles contained in the Charter.[1] The Charter must still be implemented by policy decisions made by the Community institutions. The decisions that the Community intends to take are contained in the Action Programme put forward by the Commission on 29 November 1989.

1. L. Betten, 'EG Handvest van sociale grondrechten een hol vat?,' *Sociaal Maandblad Arbeid*, 1990, 127.

200. It should be underlined that the preamble leaves no doubt that the implementation of the Charter cannot lead to an extension of the competences of the Community, as they are conferred on the institutions by the Treaties. Of equal importance is the principle of subsidiarity: responsibility for the initiatives to be taken with regard to the implementation of basic social rights, which must be applied according to the principle of subsidiarity, lies, according to the circumstances, with the Member States or their constituent parts or with the European Community. The implementation may take the form of laws, collective agreements or existing practices, and requires, where appropriate, the active involvement of both sides of industry at the various levels concerned. In summary, the respective roles of the Community, national Governments and the social partners are to be respected. Finally, we read in the preamble that the Charter tries to consolidate what has already been achieved at a social level through the actions of Member States, the social partners and the Community and that the solemn declaration of basic social rights at the Community level must not, when implemented, provide grounds for any retrogression compared with the situation currently existing in each Member State. Let it be added that the Charter not only addresses employees, but also self-employed workers and on certain points European citizens in general.

d. Content

201. The Charter consists of a preamble, which we have just analysed, and two titles: the first title contains the basic social rights for workers; the second deals with the implementation of the Charter.

(1) THE TWELVE COMMANDMENTS
202. Title I contains 12 headings, which are further detailed in 26 points. These headings relate to:

– the right to freedom of movement;
– employment and remuneration;
– the improvement of living and working conditions;
– the right to social protection;
– the right to freedom of association and collective bargaining;
– the right to vocational training;
– the right of men and women to equal treatment;
– the right of workers to information, consultation and participation;
– the right to health protection and safety at the workplace;
– the protection of children and adolescents;
– the protection of elderly persons; and
– the protection of disabled persons.

203. This enumeration clearly shows that most of the social rights contained in the Charter are already provided for by other Conventions or EC instruments and consequently do not contain much added social value. The right of *free movement for workers* is already foreseen in Articles 48 to 51 of the EC Treaty. *Vocational training* is dealt with in Article 127 of the EC Treaty; *equal treatment* is widely covered by the existing directives, with the exception of the provision that measures should also be developed enabling men and women to reconcile their occupational and family obligations (point 16). *Health protection and safety* at the workplace is already dealt with in Article 118A of the EC Treaty.

204. Other headings do however contain new elements. Under the heading *employment and remuneration*, the following rights are guaranteed: freedom of occupation (point 4); an equitable wage, sufficient to enable a decent standard of living, also in the case of atypical employment contracts as for instance when wages are withheld, seized or transferred (point 5), as well as access to public placement services free of charge (point 6). The *improvement of living and working conditions* must result from an approximation of these conditions, while improvement is being maintained in regard particularly to the duration and organisation of working time and forms of employment other than open-ended contracts, such as fixed term contracts, part-time, temporary work and seasonal work. The improvement must cover, where necessary, the development of certain aspects of employment regulations such as procedures for collective redundancies and those regarding bankruptcies (point 7). A right to a weekly rest and to annual paid leave is likewise guaranteed (point 8). The conditions of employment must be stipulated in laws, a collective agreement or a contract of employment (point 9). *Social protection* embraces an adequate level of social security benefits, sufficient resources and social assistance (point 10).

205.   Under *freedom of association and collective bargaining*, trade union (both positive and negative) freedom is guaranteed (point 11), as well as the right to negotiate and conclude collective agreements, not only at a European level in particular but also at inter-occupational and sectoral levels (point 12). The right to strike is explicitly recognised as well as the necessity to encourage the settlement of industrial disputes through the establishment and utilisation of conciliation, mediation and arbitration procedures (point 13). Internal legal order will determine under which conditions and to what extent such rights apply to the armed forces, the police and the civil service (point 14).

206.   *Information, consultation and participation of workers* must be especially developed in companies or groups of companies having establishments or companies in more than one Member State. Such information, consultation and participation must be implemented in due time and particularly when technological changes are introduced; in the case of restructuring or mergers of undertakings, of collective redundancies and when transborder workers in particular are affected by employment policies pursued by the undertaking where they are employed (points 17–18). In view of the *protection of children and adolescents*, the employment age must not be lower than 15 years (point 20); these workers must receive equitable remuneration (point 21); measures should be taken to guarantee specific development, vocational training and access to employment; yet at the same time the duration of work must be limited (no overtime) and night work prohibited in the case of workers under 18 years of age (point 22), while vocational training should take place during working hours (point 23). *Elderly persons* are entitled at the time of retirement to enjoy resources affording a decent standard of living (point 24), as well as medical and social assistance specifically suited to their needs (point 25). Finally, all *disabled persons* must be entitled to additional concrete measures aimed at improving their social and professional integration. These measures must concern vocational training, ergonomics, accessibility, mobility, means of transport and housing (point 26).

In most cases it is provided that measures must be taken 'in accordance with arrangements applying in each country,' 'in accordance with national law,' 'in accordance with national practices,' 'under the conditions laid down by national legislation and practice,' or (once) 'the internal legal order.' Another expression used is: 'taking account of the practices in force in the various Member Countries,' namely, regarding 'information, consultation and participation of workers.' These different formulations are absolutely not accidental and co-determine who is competent to enact the measures: the EC, the Member States or their constituent parts, the social partners or the individual natural or legal person.

(2) IMPLEMENTATION

207.   Title II (points 27–30) deals with the implementation of the Charter. It is more particularly the responsibility of the Member States, in accordance with national practices, notably by means of legislative measures or collective agreement (which is however the job of the social partners), to guarantee the fundamental social rights and to implement the social measures indispensable to the smooth operation of the internal market as part of a strategy of economic and social cohesion. Thus, and this is important, it is the Member States that are in the front line to implement the Charter. Then comes the Commission. The European Council invites the Commission to submit initiatives that fall within its powers, as provided for in the Treaties, with a view to adopting legal instruments for an effective implementation. During the last three months of every year, the Commission shall establish a report on the application of the Charter by the Member States and by the EC. The report shall be forwarded to the European Council, the EP and the ESC.

2. The Action Programme

208.   The Commission communicated its *Action Programme relating to the implementation of the Community Charter of Basic Social Rights for Workers* on 29 November 1989.[1] The action programme contains a number of measures which, according to the Commission, need to be developed in order to implement the most urgent aspects of the principles of the Charter. In accordance with the already referred to principle of subsidiarity whereby the Community acts when the set objectives can be reached more effectively at its level than at that of the Member States, the Commission's proposals relate to only part of the issues raised in certain articles of the Charter. The Commission indeed takes the view that responsibility for the initiatives to be taken, as regards the implementation of social rights, lies with the Member States, their constituent parts or the two sides of industry as well as, within the limits of its powers, the European Community.

In most cases, the Commission has indicated the nature of the proposals to be presented: proposals for a directive, regulation, decision, recommendation or communication or again opinions within the meaning of Article 118 of the EC Treaty. The first set of proposals, representing the most urgent priorities were put forward in the Commission's 1990 programme. A second set were included in the 1991 work programme. Further proposals were presented in 1992. The Commission asked the Council to undertake to adopt a decision concerning the Commission proposals within a period of 18 months, but in any case within two years at the outside, after transmission of the proposals to the EP, the ESC and the two sides of industry. The overall outcome has not been unsuccessful, as we will see later, when the different proposals and or directives are examined.

1. Com (89) 568 final.

3. The Maastricht Agreement on Social Policy (1991), the Green and the White Papers (1993)

209. The Maastricht Agreement entered into force on 1 November 1993. So it is too early to evaluate its implementation. One can however already note that on the social front, not much has happened since Maastricht approved – *grosso modo* – the Agreement of 31 October 1991, concluded by the social partners. The Commission has started the consultation procedure on information and consultation of employees, after the failure to agree on the proposal for a EWC in the framework of the 12.

At the end of 1993, Commissioner Flynn presented his Green Paper on 'European Social Policy. Options for the Future.'

According to the Green Paper, European social policy is entering into a critical phase. This is due to three main factors:

(i) the present Social action program is reaching its natural end. The Commission has presented all of the 47 proposals involved and, while some of the most important proposals are still pending before the Council, the majority have been adopted;

(ii) the entry into force of the Treaty on European Union has opened up new possibilities for Community action in the social field, particularly by giving a stronger role to the social partners; and

(iii) the changing socio-economic situation, reflected notably in the serious levels of unemployment, is requiring a new look at the link between economic and social policies, both at national and Community level. The Commission considers that this situation requires the launching of a wide-ranging debate about the future direction of social policy, before it proceeds to put forward specific proposals.

To prepare this Green Paper, the Commission issued a public appeal for contributions and comments.

The intention was to stimulate a wide-ranging debate within all Member States about the future lines of social policy in the European Union. The Commission will follow these discussions carefully and seek to draw from them the major themes of the future White Paper. This Green Paper does not deal with the procedural implications of the new Maastricht provisions as these will be the subject of a separate Communication.

Of course, this process will be taking place at a moment when the attention of the Community is focused on the whole issue of how to reconcile economic and social objectives in the face of rising unemployment and growing concern about Europe's ability to remain competitive into the 21st century.

There is much debate in all Member States about how to tackle employment, much of which is now recognised as being structural in character. The issues under discussion include the need for greater labour market adaptability, the suggestion that wage differentials should be widened and that wages should vary more in function of economic conditions, and questions about whether social benefits should be reduced or targeted so as to provide greater incentives to seek work. This is linked to the problems which all Member States are having in funding the growing demand on social protection systems and the search for greater efficiency in the operation of these as one means of making savings.

At the same time, there exists a growing degree of public concern that, contrary to the objective of ensuring that economic and social progress should go hand in hand as clearly stated in both the Treaties of Rome and Maastricht, the net impact of the integration process could be a levelling down of social standards. This is reflected in the fear that the creation of a single market could open the way to a form of social dumping, that is the gaining of unfair competitive advantage within the Community through unacceptably low social standards. But there is also a concern that, somehow, the imperative of action at European level can become a pretext for changes in social standards at national level.

In this context, this Green Paper, and the process of debate which it is designed to trigger, will be interactive with the discussions around the White Paper on growth, competitiveness and employment, adopted at the European Council on 10 December 1993.

The premise at the heart of this Green Paper is that the next phase in the development of European social policy cannot be based on the idea that social progress must go into retreat in order for economic competitiveness to recover. On the contrary, as has been stated on many occasions by the European Council, the Community is fully committed to ensuring that economic and social progress go hand in hand. Indeed, much of Europe's influence and power has come precisely from its capacity to combine wealth creation with enhanced benefits and freedoms for its people.

In current conditions this will not be easy, the Green Paper admits. But Europe's continuing contribution to the search for a model of sustainable development which combines economic dynamism with social progress can only be made if the issues are openly debated and a consensus arrived at. The rich diversity of the cultures and social systems within the European Union is a competitive advantage in a fast changing world. All societies are in the same process of learning. But diversity may deteriorate into disorder if the common goals, which embody the distinctive values of European society and are set out in the Treaty on European Union, are not defended by the efforts of Member States and by people themselves.

Part I of the Green Paper sets out what the Community has already achieved in the social sphere. Part II looks at the social challenges now facing us all. It examines the risks of declining social cohesion in Europe and the threats to important common goals such as social protection, solidarity and high levels of employment. A new medium-term strategy is needed which will draw together economic and social policies in partnership rather than in conflict with each other. Only in this way will sustainable growth, social solidarity and public confidence be restored. It is acknowledged that European production systems need to be based on the new technologies. There can be no social progress without wealth creation. But it should also be recognised that the consequent structural changes will have considerable impact on other important areas, such as employment intensity, working and living conditions, the quality of life and the development of industrial relations. Part III discusses the possible responses of the Union to these challenges, both in terms of what Member States want and of what the Community is trying to achieve. Part IV provides a brief conclusion. Part V brings together the questions raised in different parts of the Green Paper. These will be focus of the debate to follow.

Europe is at a turning point, the Green papers concludes. Decisions taken in the coming period will set the direction of social policy for many years to come. Now is the time for all sections of opinion to make their views known.

D. The White Paper on Growth, Competitiveness and Employment (1993)

210. At the Brussels summit, 10 and 11 December 1993, the European Council focused on the examination of the economic situation and measures to combat unemployment in the light of the White Paper on the medium-term strategy for growth, competitiveness and employment, prepared by the Commission. It adopted a short- and medium-term action plan whose implementation it will itself monitor: based on specific measures at the levels of the Union and of the Member States directed at, in the short term, reversing the trend and then, by the end of the century, significantly reducing the number of unemployed.

The action plan consists of:

– a general framework for the policies to be pursued at Member State level to promote employment;
– specific accompanying measures to be conducted at Community level;
– a monitoring procedure.

The primary purpose of the action plan is to reinforce the competitiveness of the European economy. The economy must respond to new requirements. It must also adapt to a world undergoing unprecedented change in production systems, organisation of work and modes of consumption. The action plan rests on four prerequisites:

(i) a healthy economy;
(ii) an open economy;
(iii) an economy geared to solidarity:

'The necessary adjustments must not call into question the model of our society, which is founded on economic and social progress, a high level of social protection and continuous improvement in the quality of life. Solidarity must first be shown between those with jobs and those without; one expression of such solidarity is to allocate part of productivity gains on a priority basis to investment and job creation, in particular through a policy of wage moderation. In addition, solidarity must contribute, by means of a comprehensive policy covering both prevention and reintegration, to the fight against social exclusion. Solidarity must also be shown between regions in the context of economic and social cohesion';

(iv) a more decentralised economy, given the growing importance of the local level; the economy needs to be geared to the possibilities offered by the new technologies and to mobilise to a greater extent than hitherto the job-creation potential available within small and medium-sized enterprises.

Because of the institutional, legislative and contractual peculiarities of each Member State, the Community's action must focus on defining objectives, while leaving Member States free to choose the means appropriate to their situation within a general framework defined in common. *Member States* should pay particular attention to the following measures:

- improving education and training systems. Continuing training is, in particular, to be facilitated so as to ensure ongoing adjustment of skills to the needs of competitiveness and to combating unemployment;
- improving flexibility within enterprises and on the labour market by removing excessive rigidities resulting from regulation as well as through greater mobility;
- examination, at enterprise level, of economically sound formulas for the reorganisation of work; such measures must not be directed towards a general redistribution of work, but towards internal adjustments compatible with improved productivity;
- targeted reductions in the indirect cost of labour (statutory contributions), and particularly of less-skilled work, in order to achieve a better balance between the costs of the various factors of production; fiscal measures possibly relating, *inter alia*, to the environment could be one of the means of offsetting a drop in social contributions, within a general context of stabilising all statutory contributions and reducing the tax burden;
- better use of public funds set aside for combating unemployment by means of a more active policy of information, motivation and guidance of job-seekers through specialised agencies, whether public or private;
- specific measures concerning young people who leave the education system without adequate training;
- developing employment in connection with meeting new requirements linked to the quality of life and protection of the environment.

The common framework thus defined will serve as a reference for Member States' policies. These policies will be periodically reviewed within the Council in order to analyse the results and learn from experience how future action should be conducted.
    Specific action at Community level exists of:

1. full use of the single market;
2. trans-European networks in transport and energy;
3. infrastructures in the sphere of information;
4. funding of the energy, transport and environment networks and infrastructures in the sphere of information;

5. research (framework programme for 1994–1998) (especially in information technology) and lastly;
6. the social dialogue.

The success of the action plan presupposes the commitment of all those involved to preserving social cohesion; this will be easier to achieve if a dialogue is established at all appropriate levels on the objectives to be pursued and the means to be employed. In this connection the European Council invites the Commission to continue its efforts to lead the social dialogue and to make full use, subject to the provisions of the Protocol on Social Policy of the new possibilities and calls upon both sides of industry to respond constructively.

Each year, beginning in December 1994, the European Council will take stock of the results of the action plan and will at the same time take any measure it deems necessary to achieve the objectives it has set itself.

The European Council's discussions will among others be based on:

– a summary report from the Commission, accompanied by any new suggestions; in this context the European Council in particular requests the Commission to study the question of new sources of jobs;
– a report from the Council on the lessons to be drawn from national employment policies.

E. The White Paper on European Social Policy (1994)

211. On 27 July 1994 the Commission adopted a White Paper on European Social Policy. The White Paper sets out the Commission's approach to the next phase of social policy development (1995–1999) and follows the wide ranging debate which was initiated by the Green Paper on Social Policy – 'Options for the Union.' In all, more than 500 reactions have been received from a wide variety of sources. The Commission's White Paper on Growth, Competitiveness and Employment also provided a valuable complementary focus in the debate about the need to create more jobs and at the same time preserve the basis of social protection which the people of Europe have come to prize.

The White Paper makes a number of proposals which are intended to form the basis for discussing on a new social action programme – to be agreed by the next Commission in 1995.

The White Paper stresses that European social policy must serve the interests of the Union as a whole and of all its people, both those in employment and those who are not: the Union's social policy cannot be secondary to economic development or to the functioning of the internal market. Europe needs to look for new ways to reconcile the twin objectives of economic growth and social progress.

Key features of the social policy White Paper are:

1. *The need for a new mix between economic and social policies.* The paper emphasises the need to take a broader view of social policy particularly in the current climate of major socio-economic upheaval. Social policy should not simply be

focused on the labour market and labour law, but on integrating all people into the economy and society as a whole, particularly by widening access to paid employment.

2. *Jobs – Top Priority*. The central message of the paper is that the pursuit of better, stable jobs is both a central objective of the Union and the means of addressing more effectively many of the Union's widest social objectives. The White Paper contributed to the process already mapped out by the White Paper on 'Growth, Competitiveness and Employment' leading to the adoption of a new action plan at the Essen Summit in December 1994.

The White Paper stresses two other important issues in relation to employment:

- there is a separate chapter on the specific issue of skills and the need for a massive effort of investment in training particularly trough the European Social Fund;
- a series of actions aimed at promoting the development of a real European labour market.

3. *Developing and consolidating the legislative base*. The White Paper does not propose a lengthy new legislative agenda. However, it focuses on two main themes:

(i) compelling the existing legislative programme:

'Progress made over the last eighteen months with the adoption of the Directives on Working Time and Young People and the adoption of a common position on the Directive on Information and Consultation, means that the existing legislative corpus covers the main preoccupations addressed in the previous action programme. The White Paper stresses the Commission's determination to see progress made between now and the end of the year on the pending Directives concerning:

- the posting of workers
- non standard work.
If progress cannot be made, the Commission will reopen discussions with the social partners on the issues addressed in these proposals.'

(ii) application of European law
The White Paper stresses the Commission's determination to pursue vigorously the implementation of existing legislation. For example, in the field of Health and Safety, only one Member State has transposed all the adopted Directives.

4. *Strengthening cooperation and action*. The White Paper sets out specific proposals and suggestions for future action across a whole range of related themes. Some of the key elements are:

- establishment of a high level panel to review the operation of the single market with regard to the free movement of people;

- a new action programme on equal opportunities between men and women announced for next year;
- renewed emphasis on the role of the social dialogue between management and labour at European level as well as on increased cooperation with voluntary and other non-governmental bodies.

The White Paper also calls for a longer term perspective with regard to the development of social policy. In particular it suggested that the following matters should be seriously considered at the next Intergovernmental Conference, due to be held in 1996:

- the need to ensure that European social policy is once again founded on one legal framework. This is vital if the integrity of the law and the principle of the equal treatment of all are to be respected;
- the fact that the Treaties as they stand do not give the Commission any explicit competence to combat racial discrimination. If the revision of the Treaty gives the Union competence in this field, consideration will be given to legislation combating all kinds of discrimination including those on the grounds of race, religion, age and disability;
- whether the time is now ripe for the Union to move towards a Citizens' Charter of Social Rights, taking forward the Community Charter of the Fundamental Social Rights of Workers and defining the social rights of all citizens of the Union.

F. 1996 and Beyond: Unemployment – the IGC and Social Rights

1. Unemployment[1]

a. The European Council in Essen (1994)

212. In line with the strategy of the (1993) White Paper to consolidate growth, improve the competitiveness of the European economy and the need to create more jobs, the European Council in Essen (9–10 December 1994) decided to take measures in the following five key areas:

1. Improving employment opportunities for the labour force by promoting investment in *vocational training*. To that end a key role falls to the acquisition of vocational qualifications, particularly by young people. As many people as possible must receive initial and further training which enables them through life-long learning to adapt to changes brought about by technological progress, in order to reduce the risk of losing their employment.
2. Increasing the employment-intensiveness of growth, in particular by:
   - more *flexible organisation* of work in a way which fulfils both the wishes of employees and the requirements of competition;
   - a wage policy which encourages job-creating investments and in the present situation *requires moderate wage agreements* below increases in productivity, and finally;

- the promotion of initiatives, particularly at regional and local level, that create jobs which take account of new requirements, e.g., in the *environmental and social-services spheres.*

3. Reducing *non-wage labour costs* extensively enough to ensure that there is a noticeable effect on decisions concerning the taking on of employees and in particular of unqualified employees. The problem of non-wage labour costs can only be resolved through a joint effort by the economic sector, trade unions and the political sphere.

4. Improving the *effectiveness of labour-market policy*: the effectiveness of employment policy must be increased by avoiding practices which are detrimental to readiness to work, and by moving from a passive to an active labour market policy. The individual incentive to continue seeking employment on the general labour market must remain. Particular account must be taken of this, when working out income-support measures.

   The need for and efficiency of the instruments of labour-market policy must be assessed at regular intervals.

5. Improving measures to help *groups which are particularly hard hit* by unemployment: particular efforts are necessary to help young people, especially school leavers, who have virtually no qualifications, by offering them either employment or training.

   The fight against long-term unemployment must be a major aspect of labour-market policy. Varying labour-market policy measures are necessary according to the very varied groups and requirements of the long-term unemployed.

   Special attention should be paid to the difficult situation of unemployed women and older employees.

The European Council urged the Member States to transpose these recommendations in their individual policies into a multi-annual programme having regard to the specific features of their economic and social situation. It requests the Labour and Social Affairs and Economic and Financial Affairs Councils and the Commission to keep close track of employment trends, monitor the relevant policies of the Member States and report annually to the European Council on further progress on the employment market starting in December 1995.

Thus, each year the European Council will take stock of the results of the action plan and will at the same time take any measure it deems necessary to achieve the objectives it has set itself.

The European Council's discussions will be based on:

- summary reports from the Commission, accompanied by any new suggestions; in this context, the European Council, in particular, requests the Commission to study the question of new sources of jobs;
- reports from the Council on the lessons to be drawn from national employment policies.

1. *See*: Blanpain R., 'Work in the XXIst Century,' in: *Comparative Labour Law and Industrial Relations*, 6th ed. (ed. R. Blanpain-C. Engels), Kluwer, The Hague, forthcoming.

b. The Confidence Pact for Employment (1996)

213.   In the meantime, the President of the European Commission has bravely fought to engage all European and national actors in a *European Confidence Pact for Employment* (1996). However, much more than grandiose statements have not been obtained. National Governments have no money to invest in European (information) infrastructure, however necessary they may be. The European Union indeed fails to put its ambitious plans into deeds. The employment conditions continue to deteriorate.

c. Diminishing Labour Costs. Financing Social Security by Increasing VAT[1]

214.   Social security contributions represent a significant element of labour costs. Expenditure on social security in the private sector (employees) amounts in Belgium to more than 1,250 billion BEF; and some 80 per cent of this huge sum comes from levies on pay (employer's contribution of 53 per cent and employee's contribution of 27 per cent). The situation has become untenable. The system as it exists at present carries within itself the seeds of *its own destruction*. The cost of labour is no longer competitive and the social security burden on those who are in jobs (with an economically active population of some 37 per cent) has become correspondingly heavier. Social security simply cannot continue to be financed on this basis. Radical action is called for, to relieve labour of a significant proportion of the burden of social security contributions. At the same time, we have to maintain social security provisions and, consequently, continue to finance them. Which means that we need to devise an alternative method of financing for a significant proportion of social security.

Needless to say, so radical a change should preferably be implemented on a European-wide level, in the context of whatever form of social convergence.

What we are proposing is that the social security objectives should be achieved by introducing a social security tax (SST) which would be financed from a supplementary levy on value added, to be additional to VAT as it exists at present. The idea is to abolish social security contributions altogether, and replace them with the SST. This is a generalisation of the system in Denmark where VAT is 25 per cent. That an increased VAT is socially regressive, as the poor would pay relatively more than the rich, is a persistent leftist taboo which is absolutely unfounded. On the contrary, a social VAT can be socially progressive, if well designed.

The idea of a social security tax derived from an increase in VAT should, as said earlier, be examined in the context of the single market.

The European Union aims to establish a single market inside which the *same rules of the game* would apply, more particularly as regards *competition*. Nowadays, whether deliberately or not, social security contributions represent a factor that is distorting competition in favour of systems where the level of contributions is lower, which amounts to a (hidden) form of internal social dumping. Consequently, it will be necessary to strengthen not only economic convergence in Europe, but also *social convergence*. The introduction of a more 'level playing field' in terms of the levy of social security contributions would be one of the instruments of such an operation.

It is encouraging to see that the European Commission engages itself along those lines. In its paper on 'Taxation in the European Union'[2] it says, under the heading 'Promoting employment':

> 'In subscribing to the objectives of the White Paper on Growth, Competitiveness and Employment, the Member States underlined the need to put an end to the relative over taxation of labour in order to promote employment within the EU . . . Clearly, reversing this trend should be a priority. The effect on the promotion of employment will depend on the possibility of changing permanently and significantly the relative gross prices of labour and non-labour factors of production. Reversing the tax burden on labour could, to some degree, be self-financing. But to avoid increasing budget deficits, Member States have rightly subordinated fiscal restructuring to the need to fund the net costs of reducing labour taxation, either through alternative sources of revenue or from expenditure cuts. Public expenditure cuts may contribute, but are unlikely on their own to be able to fund a sufficiently significant tax reduction on labour. *The choice for alternative funding includes indirect taxation* (VAT and excise duties); capital and real property taxation; and new or increased environmental or energy taxes. In that context, it might be considered to what extent a more comprehensive approach to the taxation of energy products would contribute to providing Member States with alternatives for the reduction of labour costs, while at the same time contributing to the fulfilment of Community environmental objectives. It is also important to examine the relationship between taxation and the financing of social protection systems to ensure that systems promote employment and avoid disincentives to work.'

1. EEC Regulation 1408/71 of 14 June 1971 on the application of social security schemes to employees and their families moving within the Community applies, in substantive terms, to all legal systems concerning the following branches of social security:
   (a) sickness and maternity benefits;
   (b) disability benefits, including the maintenance or improvement of earning capacity;
   (c) old-age benefits;
   (d) benefits for rightful claimants;
   (e) benefits for accidents at work and occupational illnesses;
   (f) benefits in the event of death;
   (g) unemployment benefits;
   (h) family allowances.
2. 20 March 1996.

2. The IGC and Social Rights[1]

a. Social Rights in the Treaty?

215. The 1996 Intergovernmental Conference on the Treaty of European Union (TEU) will have to consider three models for the future of European social law and policy.

The first is *Europe à la carte*, i.e., Member States are free to pick and choose which Union policies to accept. This is currently the position with the Maastricht Social Protocol and Agreement of 14 Member States, from which the UK was allowed to opt out. This approach undermines the EU as a constitutional order of States, and is at variance with the objectives of Article B of the TEU, in particular 'to maintain in full the *acquis communautaire*.' Practical experience with the Social Agreement shows that *de facto* Member States cannot avoid the consequences of measures adopted under the Agreement. For example, despite the exclusion of the UK from Council Directive 94/45/EC on European works councils, all companies with UK employees that have set up works councils to date have included British workers in their agreements, and an increasing number of UK companies are signing agreements, although not legally required to do so. However, *de jure*, there is unnecessary complexity and divisiveness. This model is dangerous and should not be totally accepted.

The second model is a *multi-speed Europe*. Member Stares pursue the same social objectives, but some move faster than others. This has been used in the Accession Treaties to allow new Members a longer period of adaptation. It will certainly have to be used when the Union is enlarged to include some Central and Eastern European States, Cyprus, and Malta. It is also a technique which has been used in some employment directives (e.g., on working time and young persons), and it may become more common in the future.

The third model is *Europe with variable geometry*. This would allow non-participation in certain social policies as a limited exception, but subject to certain rules. This differs from *Europe à la carte* because all Member States accept the same limitations on their sovereignty in certain 'core' policy areas, there is a single institutional framework, and there is the same set of social objectives and respect for certain fundamental rights applicable to all EU activities.

The second and third models can work only if there is a clear definition of specific social objectives, and a statement of fundamental social rights. Measures in the social field, whether at Community level or on the basis of subsidiarity at the national or regional level, must not be allowed to violate these objectives and fundamental rights.

Fundamental rights must also be distinguished from those 'instrumental' rights by which they are achieved. While fundamental rights must be prescribed for the whole Community, and must be applied at all levels and by all institutions and persons, the specific policies and instrumental rights by which they are achieved are best formulated in accordance with the principles of subsidiarity and proportionality (Article 3B of the Treaty).

1. *See*: Blanpain R., Hepple B., Sciarra S., and Weiss M., *Fundamental Social Rights: Proposals for the European Union*, Leuven, Peeters, 1996.

216. Our proposal is to include fundamental social rights in the Treaty of the European Union, as follows.

In Title I (Common Provisions), Article F.2, add the italicised words:

'The Union shall respect fundamental rights, as guaranteed by the European Convention for the Protection of Human Rights and Fundamental Freedoms signed in Rome on 4 November 1950, *the European Social Charter signed at Turin on 18 October 1961, and the Protocols thereto. and the Community Charter of Fundamental Social Rights of Workers adopted at Strasbourg on 9 December 1989*, and as they result from the constitutional traditions common to the Member States, as general principles of Community law.'

In Title II, Part One (Principles), Article 3, add the italicised words:

'For the purposes set out in Article 2, the activities of the Community shall include, as provided in this Treaty and in accordance with the timetable set out therein:
. . .

(*u*) *a contribution to the promotion of employment, improved living and working conditions, proper social protection, dialogue between management and labour, the development of human resources with a view to high employment and the combating of exclusion, and the promotion of equal opportunities and equal treatment for all persons.*

In Title VIII (Social Policy, Education, Vocational training and Youth), Chapter 1: Social Provisions, replace Article 117 with the following new Article on Fundamental Social Rights:

'*Article 117 [Fundamental Social Rights]*
The Member States agree that labour is not a commodity, and that everyone has the right to lead a life in accordance with human dignity and with adequate social protection.
    To this end, the European Institutions and the Member States, having due regard to the reciprocal obligations of all those concerned, shall take appropriate measures, whether general or specific, to guarantee economic and social rights.
    They shall abstain from any measure which could jeopardise their realisation.
    These rights include specifically:
1. The right to work, and to earn a living in an occupation freely entered upon;
2. The right to life-long education, vocational guidance and training;
3. The right to equitable remuneration, to just terms and conditions of work, and to protection against unjustifiable termination of employment;
4. The right to equality of opportunity and equality of treatment, without distinction of any kind, such as race, colour, ethic, national or social origin, culture or language, religion, conscience, belief, political opinion, sex or gender, marital status, family responsibilities, sexual orientation, age, or disability;
5. The right to health and safety in the working environment;
6. The right of children and young persons, pregnant women and those who have recently given birth, and the elderly to protection;
7. The right to protection of health, to social security, to social and medical care, and to benefit from social welfare services;

8. The right to personal privacy in respect of employment and occupation;
9. The right to associate, to organise, to bargain collectively, and to resort to collective action in the event of a conflict of interests;
10. The right to information, consultation and participation, in respect of decisions affecting the interests of workers.'

b. The *Comité des Sages* (23 March 1996)

217. The next Treaty on the European Union should immediately stipulate the content of a 'minimum threshold of fundamental social rights,' then, at a later stage, engage in a consultation process leading in five years to a comprehensive and modern list of civic and social rights and duties. These are the two main proposals to emerge from the *Comité de Sages* set up by the European Commission in October 1995, in anticipation of the revision of the Maastricht Treaty.

The Committee considers that the Intergovernmental Conference should decide to:

1. consolidate in a single Treaty the provisions which are currently dispersed throughout the fifteen treaties, with the articles continuously numbered;
2. create a sounder legal basis for the work of the Court of Justice of the European Community to ensure that fundamental rights are applied in practice. A catalogue of these rights to which the Court could refer to control Community acts, would contribute to the Court's effectiveness.
3. integrate immediately into the Treaty an initial list of fundamental rights. The following rights would be recognised:
– equality before the law;
– ban on any form of discrimination;
– equality between men and women;
– freedom of movement within the Union;
– right to choose one's occupation of profession and educational system throughout the territory of the Union,
– right of association, and
– the right to defend one's rights of collective bargaining and action.

Another list of rights to be recognised are:

– to education,
– to work,
– to social security,
– to protection for the family, etc.

A 'minimum clause' would be included in the Treaty, according to which each Member State must set in place a minimum income for persons who are unable to find paid employment.

The Union should engage in broad consultation, not only with the traditional social partners, but also with the EP, citizens' representations, non-governmental organisations, etc., in order to draw up a list of modern fundamental rights.

In order to clarify the situation, the seven members of the group also suggest that the powers of the Union and those of Member States be clarified. If wage levels, social provisions, modes for funding social systems remain in the hands of the States in the framework of the principle of subsidiarity, then a threshold of common fundamental social rights needs to be defined, consequences drawn of the rights of citizens to move freely in the EU, common approaches for problems such as unemployment, immigration, drugs, cancer and AIDS, etc., should be encouraged.

c. A Social Clause in International Trade

218. Time and again, it has been underlined that international competition and commerce accept differences on the labour market and in remuneration, but have to take into account the respect of fundamental human rights, e.g.,

– the prohibition of child labour and of forced labour;
– trade union freedom and free collective bargaining;
– equal treatment.

Europe and the US have repeatedly expressed their wish to include 'a social clause' in international trade agreements, to be discussed within in the framework of the World Trade Organisation. This idea is not welcomed everywhere, especially not in Asia, where many proclaim the social clause to be a protectionist move and imposing Western cultural standards. To this is rightly objected that these fundamental rights are laid down in ILO conventions, which have been negotiated and should apply worldwide.

It will take time and tenacious political will to find a consensus on this issue, on the exact content and formulation of the social clause, on its possible binding effect and the monitoring mechanism, which may accompany these human rights standards in the follow-up of their implementation.

G. The Treaty of Amsterdam (1997) – Employment

218bis. The Treaty of Amsterdam contains some capital improvements with the introduction of new chapters concerning employment (Chapter III) and social policy (Chapter IV), a general principle of non-discrimination, and references to the Social Charter of the Council of Europe.

The new Chapter IV incorporates the Social Agreement of Maastricht, which is quite important. Once the Treaty of Amsterdam is ratified, the two-track social Europe, brought about by the British opt-out, will come to an end. There will be the possibility to do something more at the European level in the social field.

The Treaty does not provide for new, directly enforceable individual or collective social rights. But it does gives a legal basis for action by the appropriate institutions of the EU in certain areas, such as regarding non-discrimination or employment policies. Thus, a dynamic process can be launched, if the political will is there and subsidiarity rules, allowing fully fledged European action.

The following topics merit special mention:

- fundamental rights, with reference to the European Convention for the Protection of Human Rights, the European Social Charter, issues like the principle of non-discrimination, disability, equality of men and women and protection of data;
- the Employment Chapter (III): coordinating national strategies, since employment policies are clearly left to the competence of the Member States;
- the Chapter on Social Policy (IV), integrating the Maastricht Agreement on Social Policy; and also providing for the possibility of positive discrimination;
- environment: looking for a balance between environment and high employment;
- culture and non-professional sport;
- a Protocol on the application of the principles of subsidiarity and proportionality, clearly indicating that regarding matters of mixed competence, the EU can only intervene when there is additional (European) value and only as far as necessary, leaving maximum authority to Member States and consequently to the Social Partners;
- the **Presidency Conclusions** regarding employment, competitiveness and growth. In that framework mention has to be made of the Commission's Action Plan for the Single Market submitted to the Amsterdam Summit. Below are some of the more important conclusions:

1. In order to maintain momentum in fostering economic growth and fighting unemployment, **an extraordinary meeting of the European Council** under the Luxembourg Presidency will review progress in the implementation of, among others, the initiatives concerning job creating potentials for small and medium-sized enterprises, a new Competitiveness Advisory Group, the study of good practices on employment policies of the Member States, and the initiatives of the EIB in creating employment opportunities, as referred to in the European Council Resolution on Growth and Employment. The European Council invites the Commission and the Council, in co-operation with the EIB, to prepare a progress report to this European Council.
2. The Council reiterates the need for a positive and coherent approach to job creation, encompassing a stable **macroeconomics framework**, completion of the Single Market, active employment policies and the modernization of labour markets to bring Member States further towards the goal of full employment.
3. The European Council welcomed the interim joint report on employment prepared by ECOFIN, the Labour and Social Affairs Council and the Commission and the progress report on the **Confidence Pact** on Action for Employment in Europe, presented by the President of the Commission.
4. Restoring a sustained, high rate of **non-inflationary growth** is necessary to achieve a long-lasting solution to the Community's unemployment problem and to make further headway towards sound public finances. Structural deficiencies continue to restrain both growth and the degree to which growth can be translated into additional employment.
5. The European Council attaches paramount importance to creating conditions in the Member States that would **promote a skilled and adaptable workforce**

and flexible labour markets responsive to economic change. This requires active intervention by the Member States in the labour market to help people develop their employability. Such action is important if the European Union is to remain globally competitive, and in order to tackle the scourge of unemployment.

6. A reduction in the overall tax burden is desirable in most Member States, in particular the **tax burden on labour**. Also, a restrictive restructuring of public expenditure is called for to encourage investment in human capital, research and development, innovation and the infrastructure essential to competitiveness.

7. Furthermore, the employment relevance of **training and lifelong learning** should be strengthened, tax and social welfare systems should be further reviewed in order to enhance employment opportunities, and more active labour market policy measures should be implemented. Efficiency and equity gains are to be improved by using social transfers in a more active way and by transforming benefit systems into proactive systems which improve the employability of workers.

8. The European Council notes with satisfaction the work done on indicators that will allow **bench-marking** of the measures and policies pursued by the Member States under their multi-annual employment programmes. The European Council invites the Employment and Labour Market Committee and the Economic Policy Committee to discuss these issues with a view to enabling Member States to identify particularly good performance and effective practices and to take them into account in the formulation of their policies.

9. Efforts made by social partners on **wage moderation** were acknowledged and should be pursued. Furthermore, wage agreements should take more account of differences in qualifications and between regions in order to facilitate job creation.

10. The European Council strongly welcomes the agreement concluded by the Social Partners on part-time working and calls on them to bear in mind in their discussions the need to strike a **balance between labour market adaptability and social security, in order to enhance employability**.

11. The European Council notes with satisfaction the overwhelmingly positive reaction of Member States to its invitation made in Florence to select regions or cities which could act as candidates for **pilot projects** on territorial and local employment pacts. As a result, around 90 such pacts have been established that will be launched at a conference in Brussels in November this year.

12. The European Council reaffirms the importance it attaches to a well functioning internal market as an essential element of the overall strategy to promote competitiveness, economic growth and employment throughout the Union. It welcomes the **Commission's 'Action Plan** for the Single Market'[1] and endorses its overall objective. The four strategic targets in the Action Plan should form the basis for a renewed political effort to remove remaining obstacles so as to ensure that the full potential benefit of the Single Market is realized'.

It will take some time, before the Treaty of Amsterdam will be ratified. Therefore, we will deal with the Treaty by way of an Annex, and will duly integrate its provisions in the main text of the book, once ratification has taken place and the Treaty enters into force.

1. The Action Plan follows the Commission's report on the Impact and Effectiveness of the Single Market. It sets priorities to give a clear and strategic vision of what now is needed.

Four Strategic Targets have been set. They are of equal importance and must be pursued in parallel.

1. **Making the rules more effective**: The Single Market is based on confidence. Proper enforcement of common rules is the only way to achieve this goal. Simplification of rules at Community and national level is also essential to reduce the burden on business and create more jobs.

2. **Dealing with key market distortions**: There is general agreement that tax barriers and anti-competitive behaviour constitutes distortions that need to be tackled.

3. **Removing sectoral obstacles to market integration**: The Single Market will only deliver its full potential if barriers that remain – and of course, any new ones that emerge – are removed. This may require legislative action to fill gaps in the Single Market framework, but it also calls for a significant change in national administrations' attitudes towards the Single Market.

4. **Delivering a Single Market for the benefit of all citizens**: The Single Market generates employment, increases personal freedom and benefits consumers, while ensuring high levels of both health and safety and environmental protection. But further steps are needed, including steps to enhance the social dimension of the Single Market. And to enjoy their Single Market's rights to the full, citizens must be aware of them and be able to obtain speedy redress.

Within each of these Strategic Targets, the Commission has identified a limited number of important specific actions aimed at improving the functioning the Single Market by 1 January 1999. (E.C., *Forum. Special Jobs Summit*, Brussels, 1997, 11 p.).

218ter.   The fact that an Employment Chapter was introduced by the Treaty of Amsterdam underlines the fact that **unemployment** is considered to be the number one social enemy.

The Chapter is part of an ongoing effort by Governments and Social partners, laid down at the Council meeting in Essen and stated in the 'Recommendation on the broad guidelines of the economic policies of the Member States and of the Community' of 2 July 1997. The guidelines are not a binding set of rules, but references for national governments. They aim to promote sustainable, non-inflationary growth and a high level of employment through sound public finances; a macro-economic policy mix conducive to growth, employment and convergence; price and exchange-rate stability; better functioning of product and service markets; and fostering employment and labour market reforms. The Council wants Member States to intensify their efforts to implement the Essen strategy.

The Recommendation calls for:

– More efforts to eliminate labour market rigidities and ensure more efficient operation while 'ensuring both equity and efficiency in the social protection system'.

The occupational and regional mobility of labour should be improved and the efficiency of employment services enhanced to 'reduce bottlenecks which could lead to an early end to the growth process';

– the whole educational system – including vocational training – should be adapted both to the needs of markets and to 'the improvement of human capital'. Priority should be given to improving the employability of unemployed people, especially low-skilled, inexperienced labour, and to reducing skill mismatches on the labour market.

Attention should also be given to improving the employment prospects of young people and women;

– higher employment growth should be fostered through 'the maintenance of appropriate wage trends and in some cases by wages that better reflect productivity differentials'. Where possible, non-wage labour costs should be cut to encourage employment, and attention should be given to incentives to employ disadvantaged groups. Adaptation of working time and work organization 'in the mutual interest of firms and work forces' will also encourage employment; and
– local and regional initiatives in the field of new labour-intensive services should be encouraged'.[1]

On 29 November 1996, the social partners, CEEP, ETUC and UNICE adopted a joint statement calling for a co-ordinated strategy on employment at EU level.

All these efforts, however, did not seem to succeed in solving the unemployment problem. The European monetary strategy, coupled with an increasing insistence on more flexibility of the labour markets, seems to be insufficient to cope with the massive problem of millions of unemployed.

     1. *European Industrial relations Review*, September 1996, No. 272, 2.

1. European Jobs Summit, Luxembourg, November 1997

a. Commission's proposals

The extraordinary Council meeting in Luxembourg on Employment, 20–21 November 1997, was preceded by a document of the Commission containing various proposals.[1]

The European Commission, in drafting European Employment Guidelines, suggested that an integrated strategy must be built on four priorities or pillars; **entrepreneurship, employability, adaptability and equal opportunities.**

     1. *Forum special. Jobs summit*, 1997.

A new culture of Entrepreneurship in the EU

The idea is to engender a new climate and spirit to stimulate the creation of more jobs and better jobs. We must make it easier to start-up and run businesses by providing a clear, stable and predictable set of rules. Member States should review and simplify the administrative burdens on small and medium-size enterprises.

- Reduce significantly the overhead costs for enterprises of hiring an additional worker.
- Adapt existing regulations to facilitate easier transition to self-employment.

Obstacles, especially those within existing social security regimes, for people moving from employment to self-employment and setting up micro-enterprises need to be tackled.

Develop the markets for venture capital, thereby mobilizing Europe's wealth behind entrepreneurs and innovators. Member States should examine the specific needs of small and medium enterprises as regards financing, principally in the form of equity or guarantee capital.

Establish a pan-European secondary market for trading in less important stocks and shares, particularly designed for small and medium enterprises (secondary capital market) by the year 2000.

Make the taxation system more employment friendly. In order to encourage enterprises to create new jobs, Member States must reverse the average long-term trend towards higher taxes and charges on labour (which have increased from 35 per cent in 1980 to over 42 per cent in 1995).

Set a target for reducing the tax burden on labour, while maintaining budget neutrality, with a view to achieving substantial progress by the year 2000.

A new culture of employability in the EU

The idea is to tackle the skills gap, by modernizing education and training systems, and by strengthening their link to the workplace, so that all workers, especially jobseekers, are equipped to take new employment opportunities. Currently, over 20 per cent of young people in the Union leave education and training without recognized qualifications. Only 10 per cent of those adults who are formally unemployed are getting any training at all. It means that jobs are often vacant because no one with adequate skills can be recruited. To improve the employability of people we must:

- Tackle long-term and youth unemployment.

Member States should seek early identification of individual needs and early action to ensure that every unemployed adult is offered a new start – in the form of a job, training, retraining, work placement or other employability measure – before reaching twelve months of unemployment. Every unemployed young person is given such a new start before reaching six months of unemployment.

- Ease the transition from school to work. Employment prospects are poor for the 10 per cent of young people who drop out of the school system early and many of the 45 per cent who do not complete upper secondary education. Member States must seek to reduce the numbers dropping out of the education system early by 50 per cent within five years and progressively reduce the share who do not complete upper secondary level.

Improve the apprenticeship systems and increase participation in apprenticeship training in line with the best performing Member States.

– Move from passive to active measures. Benefit and training systems should ensure that they actively support employability and provide clear incentives for the unemployed to seek and take up work or training opportunities. Each Member State should set a target for the number of people to be transferred from passive income support to active workers.

– Develop a partnership approach. Both enterprises and the social partners should be involved in joint efforts to invest Europe's wealth in its future by offering the necessary work experience/training positions. The Social Partners are urged to decide on a framework agreement as soon as possible on how to open workplaces across Europe for training, work practice, traineeships and other forms of employability measures and to agree on the terms and conditions.

Continue the impressive contribution which has been made over the past five years to the wage moderation which has contributed so much to the improved economic outlook and the improved prospects for new job creation.

A new culture of adaptability in the EU
The idea behind this pillar is to equip enterprises and the workforce to embrace new technologies and new market conditions.
   To promote and encourage adaptability we must:

– Modernize work organization. Social partners and Member States should rethink existing working patterns. It is suggested that Social partners negotiate, at the appropriate levels, agreements on work organization and flexible working arrangements, including reductions in working time.
   Member States should put in place a framework for more adaptable forms of contracts. Those in non-standard work should be given greater security and occupational status. Those who opt to work reduced hours should not be penalized in terms of career progression or in terms of maintaining social security protection.

– Support adaptability in enterprises. In order to renew skill levels within enterprises, Member States should remove fiscal and other obstacles for the promotion of investment in human resources and offer tax incentives for the development of in-house training. Incentives to workers to avail of training opportunities should also be encouraged.
   Re-focus their State Aid policies on upgrading the labour force, the creation of sustainable jobs and efficiently functioning labour markets.

A new culture of equal opportunities in the EU
The idea is to modernize societies so that men and women can work on equal terms, with equal responsibilities, to develop the full growth capacity of our economies. To strengthen Equal Opportunities we must:

- Tackle gender gaps: Member States should translate their commitment to equality of opportunity and breaking down gender segregation, and make consistent efforts to reduce the gap in unemployment rates between women and men by actively supporting the increased employment of women.
- Reconcile work and family life: Policies on career breaks, parental leave and part-time work are of particular importance to women. As are adequate provision of good quality care for children and other dependents. Member States should seek to raise levels of care provision, using the standards of the best performing Member States as a benchmark.
- Facilitate return to work: Specific attention should be given to women considering a return to the paid workforce after an absence. They may face problems of poor employability due to outdated skills and may have difficulty in accessing training opportunities if they have not been registered as 'jobseekers'. Moreover, negative taxation and benefit systems may reduce financial incentives to seek work. Member States should address these and other obstacles.

These four pillars represent the European Commission's view of the priorities for action. They represent priorities for a Europe in transition. These guidelines refer to Member States employment policy, not to new initiatives at European level. The guidelines represent a challenge to traditional thinking by declaring long-term objectives.

Europe can change its employment situation by working together to ensure that employers and employees are equipped to engage fully in the new, more diverse, skill and process driven European economy.

b. Social partners

The social partners (CEEP, UNICE, ETUC) were fully involved in the preparation of the summit meeting and were regularly consulted. They broadly subscribed to the strategy and the four pillars put forward by the commission. The employers obviously were reluctant to accept specific employment targets. Needless to say that the social partners remained miles away from each other regarding reorganization of working time, especially the 35 hour week and the issue of information and consultation at national level, as suggested by the Commission.

c. Jobs Summit: Conclusions Luxembourg

The European Council decided that the relevant provisions of the new Title on employment in the Treaty of Amsterdam are to be put into effect immediately. This decision makes it possible in practice to implement the provisions on co-ordination of Member States' employment policies in advance, as of 1998. Such co-ordination will be based on common lines of approach for both objectives and means, the 'employment guidelines', drawing directly on the experience built up in the multilateral surveillance of economic policies, with success observed in the case of convergence. The idea is, while respecting the differences between the two areas and between the situations of individual Member States, to create for employment, as for economic policy, the same resolve to converge towards jointly set, verifiable, regularly updated targets.

The implementation of the 'guidelines' may vary according to their nature, their impact on Member States and the parties to whom they are addressed. They must respect the principle of subsidiarity and Member States' responsibilities with regard to employment and must be compatible with the broad economic policy guidelines.

After being adopted by the Council on the basis of a proposal from the Commission, the 'guidelines' will have to be incorporated into national employment action plans drawn up by the Member States in a multi-annual perspective. This is how they will be given practical effect, in the form of national objectives which are quantified wherever possible and appropriate, followed by their transposition into national regulatory, administrative or other measures. The differing situations of the Member States in relation to the problems addressed by the 'guidelines' will result in differing solutions and emphases, in line with individual situations. Member States will set themselves deadlines for achieving the desired result in the light, *inter alia*, of the administrative and financial resources which can be drawn upon. However, it is crucial for the coherence and effectiveness of the approach as a whole that all Member States make use of the 'guidelines' in analyzing their own situation and framing their policy and that they establish their attitude to each of them in their national employment action plan.

In a similar way to the multilateral surveillance principle applied in the economic convergence process, Member States will each year send the Council and the Commission their national employment action plan, together with a report on the manner of its implementation. On that basis, the Council will hold an annual review of the way in which Member States have put the 'guidelines' into practice in their national policies and will submit a report to the European Council, which will establish the approach required in laying down the 'guidelines' for the following year.

Regular contact with the Council will properly pave the way for the six-monthly meeting of the social partners with a *troika* at the level of Heads of State or Government and the Commission before the European Council meeting. In the course of such contacts between the Council and the social partners, a detailed exchange of views will in particular be held on the implementation of the 1989 Community Charter of the Fundamental Social Rights of Workers.

d. The 'guidelines' for 1998

The European Council has adopted the conclusions below, which centre on four main lines of action; improving employability, developing entrepreneurship, encouraging adaptability in businesses and their employees to enable the labour market to react to economic changes, and strengthening equal opportunities policy. The objective of these measures, which are to form part of the overall strategy for employment, is to arrive at a significant increase in the employment rate in Europe on a lasting basis. The European Council calls upon the Commission to submit every three years a report on the evolution of employment rates in Europe.

e. Improving employability

i. Tackling youth unemployment and preventing long-term unemployment   In order to influence the trend in youth and long-term unemployment the Member States will develop preventive and employability-oriented strategies, building on the early identification of individual needs; within a period to be determined by each Member State which may not exceed five years and which may be longer in Member States with particularly high unemployment. Member States will ensure that;

– every unemployed young person is offered a new start before reaching six months of unemployment, in the form of training, retraining, work practice, a job or other employability measure;
– unemployed adults are also offered a fresh start before reaching twelve months of unemployment by one of the aforementioned means or, more generally, by accompanying individual vocational guidance.

These preventive and employability measures should be combined with measures to promote the re-employment of the long-term unemployed.

ii. Transition from passive measures to active measures   Benefit and training systems where that proves necessary must be reviewed and adapted to ensure that they actively support employability and provide real incentives for the unemployed to seek and take up work or training opportunities.
Each Member State:

– will endeavour to increase significantly the number of persons benefiting from active measures to improve their employability. In order to increase the numbers of unemployed who are offered training or any similar measure, it will in particular fix a target, in the light of its starting situation, of gradually achieving the average of the three most successful Member States, and at least 20 per cent.

iii. Encouraging a partnership approach   The actions of the Member States alone will not suffice to achieve the desired results in promoting employability. Consequently;

– the social partners are urged, at their various levels of responsibility and action, to conclude as soon as possible agreements with a view to increasing the possibilities for training, work experience, traineeships or other measures likely to promote employability;
– the Member States and the social partners will endeavour to develop possibilities for lifelong training.

iv. Easing the transition from school to work   Employment prospects are poor for young people who leave the school system without having acquired the aptitudes required for entering the job market. Member States will therefore;

– improve the quality of their school systems in order to substantially reduce the number of young people who drop out of the school system early; and
– make sure they equip young people with greater ability to adapt to technological and economic changes and with skills relevant to the labour market where appropriate, by implementing or developing apprenticeship training.

f. Developing entrepreneurship

Making it easier to start up and run businesses by providing a clear, stable and predictable set of rules and by improving the conditions for the development of risk capital markets. The new facilities offered by the EIB combined with the Member States' efforts will enable new businesses to be set up more easily. The Member States should also reduce and simplify the administrative and tax burdens on small and medium-sized enterprises. To that end the Member States will;

– give particular attention to significantly reducing the overhead costs and administrative burdens for businesses, and especially small and medium-sized enterprises, in particular when hiring additional workers; and
– encourage the development of self-employment by examining, with the aim of reducing, any obstacles which may exist, especially those within tax and social security regimes, to moving to self-employment and the setting up of small businesses, in particular for employed persons.

i. *Exploiting the opportunities for job creation*   If the European Union wants to deal successfully with the employment challenge, all possible sources of jobs and new technologies and innovations must be exploited effectively. To that end the Member States will;

– investigate measures to exploit fully the possibilities offered by job creation at local level in the social economy and in new activities linked to needs not yet satisfied by the market, and examine, with the aim of reducing, any obstacles in the way of such measures.

Making the taxation system more employment friendly and reversing the long-term trend towards higher taxes and charges on labour (which have increased from 35 per cent in 1980 to more than 42 per cent in 1995). Each Member State will;

– set a target, if necessary and taking account of its present level, for gradually reducing the overall tax burden and, where appropriate, a target for gradually reducing the fiscal pressure on labour and non-wage labour costs, in particular on relatively unskilled and low paid labour, without jeopardizing the recovery of public finances or the financial equilibrium of social security schemes. It will examine, if appropriate, the desirability of introducing a tax on energy or on pollutant emissions or any other tax measure; and
– examine, without obligation, the advisability of reducing the rate of VAT on labor-intensive services not exposed to crossborder competition.

g. Encouraging adaptability in businesses and their employees

i. Modernizing work organization   In order to promote the modernization of work organization and forms of work;

– the social partners are invited to negotiate, at the appropriate levels, in particular at sectoral and enterprise levels, agreements to modernize the organization of work, including flexible working arrangements, with the aim of making undertakings productive and competitive and achieving the required balance between flexibility and security. Such agreements may, for example, cover the expression of working time as an annual figure, the reduction of working hours, the reduction of overtime, the development of part-time working, lifelong training and career breaks;
– for its part, each Member State will examine the possibility of incorporating in its law more adaptable types of contract, taking into account the fact that forms of employment are increasingly diverse. Those working under contracts of this kind should at the same time enjoy adequate security and higher occupational status, compatible with the needs of business.

ii. Support adaptability in enterprises   In order to renew skill levels within enterprises Member States will;

– re-examine the obstacles, in particular tax obstacles, to investment in human resources and possibly provide for tax or other incentives for the development of in-house training; they will also examine any new regulations to make sure they will contribute to reducing barriers to employment and helping the labour market adapt to structural change in the economy.

h. Strengthening the policies for equal opportunities

i. Tackling gender gaps   Member States should translate their desire to promote equality of opportunity into increased employment rates for women. They should also pay attention to the imbalance in the representation of women or men in certain economic sectors and occupations. Member States will;

– attempt to reduce the gap in unemployment rates between women and men by actively supporting the increased employment of women and will act to reverse the under-representation of women in certain economic sectors and occupations and their over-representation in others.

ii. Reconciling work and family life   Policies on career breaks, parental leave and part-time work are of particular importance to women and men. Implementation of the various Directives and social partner agreements in this area should be accelerated and monitored regularly. There must be an adequate provision of good quality care for children and other dependents in order to support women's and men's entry and continued participation in the labour market. The Member States will;

– strive to raise levels of care provision where some needs are not met.

iii. Facilitating return to work   The Member States will;

– give specific attention to women, and men, considering a return to the paid workforce after an absence and, to that end, they will examine the means of gradually eliminating the obstacles in the way of such return.

iv. Promoting the integration of people with disabilities into working life   The Member States will;

– give special attention to the problems people with disabilities may encounter in participating in working life.

All these efforts, however, do not seem to succeed in solving the unemployment problem. The European monetary strategy, coupled with an increasing insistence on more flexibility of the labour markets, seems to be insufficient to cope with the massive problem of millions of unemployed.

H. Implementation of Directives by Member States

European Labour Law deals only with certain aspects of wages and working conditions, industrial relations and human resources management. Directives relate to:

a. Labour and working conditions
   – collective redundancies;
   – transfer of undertakings;
   – insolvency of the employer;
   – information on individual working conditions;
   – EWC's;
   – posting of workers.
b. Equality of treatment for men and women
c. Free movement of workers
d. Health and Safety at Work (33 directives)
e. Public Health

As of June 1997, only 65 per cent of single market directives are fully operational in all Member States.[1] The picture for the implementation of the 54 labour law directives by the Member States seems to be somewhat better. In January 1997, the picture of implementation was as follows:

Austria	90%
Belgium	82%
Denmark	96%
Finland	100%
France	87%
Germany	96%
Greece	82%
Ireland	89%
Italy	78%
Luxembourg	94%
Netherlands	94%
Portugal	81%
Spain	72%
Sweden	96%
UK	96%.

This means that much still has to be done to make European labour law effective.

1. Action Plan for the Single Market. The 'New 1999 Objective' (12 June 1997).

III. CONVERGENCE OR DIVERGENCE?

219.   The question is asked whether the accomplishment of a real internal market will bring the different national systems of labour law and of industrial relations closer together, and eventually make them more harmonised or even uniform. One could indeed be of the opinion that the fact that our different national systems within that one large market will be confronted with the same challenges, such as ever-growing (international) economic competition, the continuous introduction of new technologies, with the new worker – more educated, more creative and more participatory (the knowledge worker) –, with the same urbanisation of our societies, with similar environmental problems, will have a convergent influence. The fact is that similar problems tend to be solved by the same solutions. One could also advance the argument that the labour law rules of the game – like many other rules for that matter – should be the same in order so that fair competition between countries does not have an adverse effect. The fact that it is easier to dismiss a worker in Great Britain than in the Netherlands disturbs the market. Investors may be attracted by cheaper conditions in those countries where there are the least 'social constraints.' Thus, in order to combat eventual competition falsification we need at least to harmonise or, if possible, make uniform labour law rules. It then becomes a duty for the European authorities to see to it that the rules of the game are the same for all or at least equivalent. A convergent movement, i.e., getting closer together, would first be brought about by the natural functioning of the invisible hand, the market, and subsequently through a pointed policy of the authorities.

220.   One could also argue that the existent divergence between the national systems of labour law and of industrial relations will continue and even persist further and that Governments should not intervene in that process, but let them go their natural (or national?) course. This attitude is based first in the enormous variety of solutions that currently characterise the labour law systems of the 15 Member States and which will probably persist. Before answering the question *divergence or convergence?*, let us look into this diversity, which is greater than is usually realised. It is said with reason that this diversity is not accidental, but rather the result of our own proper social, cultural, political, historical and societal developments, which must be respected in their individuality. Some examples may suffice to illustrate the point.

221.   A first distinction regarding labour between the Member States is undoubtedly the fact that some systems are very *formal* while others are very informal. One of the most formal systems of the EC countries is undoubtedly the German system in which most matters are dealt with by law, in which judges intervene with authority and efficiency and where every German seems to be a born lawyer, believing in the rule of law and approaching societal problems from the legal angle. Workers' participation, to give one example, is meticulously detailed and the legal rules are lived up to in practice; in Germany a strike is not only legally but also *de facto* governed by the peace obligation between the social partners and so on. In other words, the German system is legally predictable and probably a little bit boring. In Belgium, on the other hand, one might say that law and strikes have almost nothing to do with each other. Strikes in Belgium are a matter of pure power relations in the field.

Germany is at one end of the spectrum, Italy is at the other: the formal elements in Italy are less important. Informality carries the day. Labour relations develop in relation to individual and collective emotions, which themselves are carried by the moods of the time, thus making Italy a paradise of immense creativity, and bringing a lot of – not always pleasant – surprises, such as was the case in the Coba wildcat strikes. It is only in Italy that the notion '*statu d'agitatione*' as an element of industrial warfare is known.

222.   A second distinction can be found in the *organisation of workers*, more precisely the degree of unionisation, trade union structures and trade union ideology.

The *degree of unionisation* differs enormously from country to country. Belgium and Denmark score rather high: some 50 per cent or more of workers are organised (there are no really controlled and certified figures available); France and Spain are at a much lower level with less then 10 per cent of the work force organised. Lately, the number of trade union members has diminished dramatically in certain countries. In a space of 10 years, the French unions lost 50 per cent of their membership. At present only 2 per cent of French young people between the ages of 18 and 24 are members of a union. Other countries lie between the two extremes.

One can find the same diversity in the *trade union structures*: on the one hand, Germany has a streamlined trade union organisation per sector of industry, on the other, Great Britain still has craft unions, which are organised in certain sectors on the basis of craft or trade; then there are the demarcation lines between the trade unions themselves running along different patterns in the Member States, whereby, for example, workers organised by the French metal workers' union are members of the Belgian textile organisation.

The same is true for the trade union ideology: one distinguishes between unions from the North, which are more or less integrated in the neo-capitalist system, and the more contesting organisations from the South; while British unions are characterised by their approach of adverseness with, as it is called, some touches of 'new realism' shown by certain organisations which are convinced that they can only adequately defend the interests of their members when they accept the reality of the market economy and the profit motive. Diametrically opposed to this is the still communist French *Confédération Générale du Travail*, which has the greatest number of members in France, but still is denied membership of the ETUC.

223. A third example of diversity can be found in the structure and the role of the *employers' associations*. Some organisations are more centralised than others, pursuant to the proper character of their own labour relations system. The *Deutsche Arbeitgebersbund* is more centralised in its organisation and decision-making structure than, say, the British Confederation of Industries. Another point: all employers' organisations self-evidently engage in wide-ranging political lobbying, giving advice to their members on tax and related matters, exports, etc. There is nevertheless an important difference depending on the question whether the employers' organisations also engage in collective bargaining and are parties to a collective agreement or not. Thus, we cite the French *Confédération Nationale du Patronat Français* which has a clear profile as the employers' negotiator for the French private sector as a whole. It is clear that the British organisation does not play such a role. This is again a very important point of diversity between the Member States regarding industrial relations.

224. Still another, and probably the most important distinction can be found in the difference in *legal culture* between Great Britain on the one hand and continental Europe (minus Denmark) at the other. It is indeed a fact that 'it is not in the tradition of Her Majesty's Government to regulate conditions of work by Acts of Parliament.' Working conditions in Great Britain are not regulated by acts. This is a job for the social partners. And if the Government feels that one of the partners has too much power, there may be legal intervention, such as Mrs Thatcher instigated,

to curb trade union power and in so doing increase the power of the employers to make their points more easily accepted at the bargaining table, if there is bargaining at all. This could be looked upon as one pointed form of legal interventionism. This characteristic of the British legal system is of the utmost importance for Community developments regarding labour law. Indeed, Mrs Thatcher was consequent with herself when she underlined in her famous speech in Bruges in 1988 that she was not going to accept labour law rules from Brussels, where she had prevented them successfully in London. That is why she refused to sign the Social Charter and why John Major did not accept the Maastricht Agreement on Social Policy. The European continent on the contrary is generally more legally interventionist: our labour law codes are more than full of texts, even in a period of so-called deregulation.

225.   An equally striking difference concerns the *legally binding effect of collective agreements*. It is unthinkable for continental lawyers that a collective agreement in Great Britain is not legally binding and constitutes only a 'gentlemen's agreement,' that it cannot lead to legal obligations because 'parties do not have the intention to create such obligations.' A collective agreement is only binding in law if the parties expressly declare this in their agreement. In continental Europe, on the contrary, there is, in accordance with the Roman adagium *pacta sunt servanda*, a clear legal binding effect of the obligations created by the agreement. Just as important is the possibility in certain Member States to give the collective agreement a general binding effect by which the normative part of the collective agreement, which is, say, concluded at sectorial level, becomes legally binding for all employers and all workers of that sector, whether they are members of the contracting parties or not. If the agreement is concluded at inter-industry level all employers and all workers of the private sector may fall within the scope of the legally binding agreement. Such a procedure by which agreements can be extended exists in Belgium, France, Germany and the Netherlands, to give a few examples. The impact of this extension procedure on a national system of industrial relations is enormous. One example may suffice. In Great Britain where extension of agreements is not a given practice, Ford Motor Co. conducts negotiations with its some 30,000 employees on its own, without being for that matter a very active member of the employers' association. In Belgium, on the contrary, where extension of agreements is standard practice, Ford Motor Co. is a very active member of Fabrimetal, the employers' organisation of the metal working trades. The reason is self-evident: Ford wants maximum influence over the outcome of the collective agreement that will be negotiated by Fabrimetal, an agreement which Ford would be involved in, even if it were not a member of the organisation. In summary, the extension of agreements leads to stronger employers' associations and more centralised labour relations and therefore has a basic influence over labour law and industrial relations.

226.   The role of *Governments* in industrial relations, particularly in the area of income policies, is another topical example. In certain Member States, Governments play the role of third parties in the industrial relations scene, sometimes that of the most important actor, and do not hesitate to intervene in wage policies when it becomes necessary to protect the competitiveness of the undertakings. Over the

last few years, such interventions have taken place in Belgium, France, Greece and Spain, not to mention other countries. In Germany, such an intervention is unheard of and almost constitutionally impossible. In Germany, the holy principle of 'tariff' autonomy of the social partners prevails, meaning that the Government cannot interfere directly in the setting of wages, as this belongs to the autonomy and prerogative of the social partners. The most the German Government can do is bring the parties together within the framework of what is called 'concerted action' in order to give, on the basis of an experts' report on the economic situation in Germany, some guidelines concerning pay, which one hopes the social partners will respect. This situation in Germany is easily understandable when one realises that it is the outcome of a reaction against Nazi Germany, where a dictatorship controlled almost every aspect of life; in the Federal Republic the power of the Government has been confined within the framework of a pluralistic democracy in favour of the social partners. This is just another large difference between the systems of the Member States.

227. One could go on for ever citing examples regarding workers' participation, the way strikes are allowed and regulated and so on. *Diversity is the general rule.* In other words, there is no European system of industrial relations. The systems are mainly national and will remain so for a long time to come. Therefore one has to give a very nuanced answer to the question: convergence or divergence of labour law in Europe? First, it is clear that diversity will continue, not only because this lies in the nature of things: Germans are not Italians and *vice versa* and it is best that it stays this way. As important is the fact that the national systems constitute a delicate balance between social factors and actors, which has come about over the years and evolves in its own rhythm and tempo. Harmonisation over the boundaries jeopardises those balances and has a strong chance of being rejected. This certainly is the case in relation to everything in labour relations to do with *power*, namely collective bargaining, workers' participation, strikes, lockouts, etc. It is no accident that the European proposals concerning workers' participation have already been on the table for more than 20 years without any real prospect of being adopted. These proposals encroach too much upon the existing balance of power. Moreover, collective labour relations are bedeviled by ideology and mask societal options: pro market or pro Government intervention. Moreover, quite a number of voices quickly point out that our labour relations should become more *decentralised* and that problems regarding e.g., working time, except for very general framework (national or sectoral) agreements, must be dealt with at the level of the undertaking, thus taking into account that it is the enterprises that have to do battle on the markets and that the great diversity in goods and services prevalent today make simple, uniform formulas that are valid for all enterprises and situations, totally inadequate.

On the other hand, it is likewise clear that the market comes into play and that it will push the national systems together from the point of view of cost, while a certain harmonisation 'while improvement is being maintained' (Art. 117, EC Treaty) is also indicated. European measures, for that matter, can perfectly respect the diversity between the Member States. But here one should also be cautious. Lower unit labour costs and longer working hours may constitute, for example for Portugal, a winning card in the attraction of foreign investment and thus jobs, which would disappear if one started to equalise wages over the boundaries and make working time more uniform.

228. In a nutshell, one can say that there will be a convergence of systems and a certain harmonisation of labour law as far as the result and the cost of the systems are concerned: the market will come into play and lead, together with the common challenges that confront all Member States, to an unavoidable convergence which, supported by political and trade union pressure, will bring the systems closer to each other. This convergence will however go hand in hand with a continuous divergence as far the content of labour relations and labour law is concerned: the way people are hired and fired, the way strikes are organised and so on. These will mainly be determined at a national level. Summing up: *convergence of costs versus divergence of content.* The danger is that convergence of costs goes together with an ongoing process of **social dumping**.[1] There is asymmetry between an economic monetary Europe and a social Europe, which remains mainly national. Competing on labour costs in a free market without a social counter balance, leads to social dumping and diminishing working conditions.

1. The granting of benefits to undertakings (reduction of social security contributions) that are most exposed to international competition, in order to promote job creation is an advantage constituting State aid caught by Article 92(1) of the EC Treaty. It is therefore incompatible with the common market (Belgium, Maribel case, Decision of the Commission, 4 December 1996.)

229. Consequently it becomes self-evident that the establishment of the internal market calls more now than ever for an intensive comparison of legal systems. We not only need to know each other's systems better than before; the harmonisation process presupposes that one starts with an examination of the national systems, of what they have in common and how they differ from each other in order, if necessary, to develop Community law which has most of its roots in national practices and experiences. It was with this preoccupation in mind, and one that supersedes the EC anyway, that in 1975 we started the publication of an *International Encyclopedia of Labour Law and Industrial Relations*, which consists at present of some 60 international and national monographs and that in 1991 the *International Encyclopedia of Laws* was launched. This project will also contain international and national monographs of about 60 countries in diverse fields of law such as civil procedure, commercial and economic law, constitutional law, contracts, corporations and partnerships, criminal law, environmental law, insurance law, medical law, social security law, family and succession law, intellectual property, tax law, private international law, intergovernmental organizations and transport law.

Part I. Individual Labour Law

230.   Individual labour law consists of the body of rules that relate to the individual relations between the employer and the worker. In this study of European individual labour law we concentrate on not only the laws in force but also the most important proposals made by the Commission which did not yet reach their finishing point. Consecutively we deal with:

– free movement of workers;
– international private labour law;
– individual employment contracts;
– child care and the protection of young people at work;
– the equal treatment of men and women;
– protection of motherhood;
– working time, Sunday rest, night work and parental leave;
– health and safety at the workplace;
– employee participation in profits and enterprise results;
– restructuring of enterprises: collective redundancies, transfer of enterprises and the insolvability of the employer.

Chapter 1. The Free Movement of Workers

231. The free movement of persons in general and for workers in particular is one of the cornerstones of the EC. Pursuant to Article 3C of the EC Treaty, the activities of the Community include: 'an internal market characterised by the abolition, as between Member States, of obstacles to the free movement of goods, persons, services and capital' (the so-called four fundamental freedoms).

232. With the three directives, all passed on 28 June 1990, concerning the right of residence, this free movement for persons was opened widely to European citizens, nationals of Member States, in general,[1] for employees and self-employed persons who have ceased their occupational activity,[2] and for students.[3] The right of residence for students is now regulated by Directive 93/96 of 29 October 1993.[4] The Member States are thus obliged to grant the right of residence to nationals of Member States, who do not enjoy this right under other provisions of Community law and to members of their families, provided that they themselves and the members of their families are covered by sickness insurance in respect of the risks of the host Member State and have sufficient resources to avoid becoming a burden on the social assistance system of the host Member State during their period of residence. These resources are sufficient when they are higher than the level of resources below which the host Member State may grant social assistance to its nationals. Students must also prove that they have sufficient resources to avoid becoming a burden on the social assistance system of the host Member State during their period of residence. For students the right of residence is restricted to the duration of the course of studies in question. The right of residence is evidenced by means of the issue of a document known as a 'Residence permit for a national of a Member State of the Community.'

The provisions of Community law governing the free movement of workers do not apply to purely internal situations of a Member State.[5] A national of a Member State who has never exercised the right of freedom of movement within the Community cannot rely on Article 48 of the EC Treaty in circumstances wholly within the domestic sphere of that Member State.[6]

1. 90/361, O.J., 13 July 1990. No. L 180/26.
2. 90/365, O.J., 13 July 1990, No. L 180/28.
3. 90/366, O.J., 13 July 1990, No. L 180/28.
4. O.J., 18 December 1993, No. L 317, 59.
5. COJ, 18 October 1990, *Massam Dzodzi* v. *Belgian State*, Joined Cases Nos. 297/88 and 197/89, IELL, *Case Law*, No. 151.
6. COJ, 28 January 1992, *V. Steen* v. *Deutsche Bundespost*, C-332/90, IELL. *Case Law*; COJ, 16 June 1996, *V. Steen* v. *Deutsche Bundespost*, C-132/93, not yet published.

233. Freedom of movement constitutes a fundamental right of workers and their families. It is however not an autonomous, but a purposeful right within the framework of the economic objectives of the Community; this right is only conferred for reasons of the performing of an economic activity. It is a contribution to the economic needs of the Member States.

> 'Mobility of labour is looked upon as one of the means by which the worker is guaranteed the possibility of improving his living and working conditions and promoting his social advancement, while helping to satisfy the requirements of the economies of the Member States.'[1]

It should be underlined that Article 48 concerning the free movement of workers has a *direct effect* on the legal orders of the Member States and confers on individuals rights which national courts must protect.[2] Article 48, however, does not aim to restrict the power of the Member States to lay down restrictions within their own territory on the freedom of movement of all persons subject to their jurisdiction in the implementation of domestic criminal law.[3]

1. Considering of Regulation No. 1612/68 of 15 October 1968 on freedom of movement for workers within the Community.
2. COJ, 14 July 1974, *G. Dona* v. *M. Mantero*, No. 13/76, IELL, *Case Law*, No. 25.
3. COJ, 28 March 1979, *Regina* v. *V.A. Saunders*, No. 175/78, IELL, *Case Law*, No. 31.

234. Free movement of workers entails the right to work in another Member State under the same conditions as national workers; it includes the right to move freely within the territory of Member States for this purpose and the right to stay in a Member State. The expression 'free movement for workers' was first used in the EC Treaty. In the case of the ECSC, one could not really talk of free movement for workers. It is indeed characteristic for the ECSC rules that access to the labour market was restricted to specific sectors of the economy and to specific groups of workers within those sectors who have special qualifications. It was also restricted in time and regarding the possibility to search freely for work. Free movement was only possible in the ECSC when there is an offer of employment actually made.[1] Pursuant to Articles 2G and 96 of the Euratom Treaty there is in the sector of atomic energy free movement for skilled workers. In this study we limit ourselves, for obvious reasons, to the free movement for workers in the EC.

1. H. Verschueren, *Internationale arbeidsmigratie. De toegang tot de arbeidsmarkt voor vreemdelingen naar Belgisch, internationaal en Europees Gemeenschapsrecht*, Bruges, 1990, 207–208.

§1. FREE MOVEMENT

I. Right to Leave

235. The right to move freely within the territory of the Member States is laid down in Article 48, §3(b) of the EC Treaty. In implementation thereof, Member States have, in accordance with Directive No. 68/360 of 15 October 1968,[1] the obligation to abolish restrictions on the movement and the residence of nationals of the said States and of the members of their families (Art. 1) and to grant them the right to leave their territory in order to take up activities as employed persons (Art. 2, §1). Member States in particular may not demand from their nationals any exit visa or equivalent document (Art. 2, §4). For the execution of this right, the simple production of a valid identity card or passport is sufficient (Art 2, §1). Member States are obliged to issue or renew an identity card or passport which states the holder's nationality (Art. 2, §2). The passport must be valid for all Member States and for countries through which the holder must pass when travelling between Member States. When a passport is the only document on which the holder may lawfully leave the country, its period of validity shall not be less than five years (Art. 2, §3).

1. Directive on the abolition of restrictions on movement and residence within the Community for Workers of Member States and their families (O.J., 19 October 1968, No. L 257).

236.   The right to move freely as well as the right to entry and residence is, pursuant to Article 48 of the EC Treaty, linked to 'an offer of employment actually made.' In accordance with this text, there must be in the person of the worker a concrete offer of employment as a precondition for the right to move and residence. However, the Court is of the opinion that free movement for workers also entails the right to look for work when one wishes to pursue an effective and genuine activity.[1] From its side, the Council made on the occasion of the adoption of the directive in 1968 a declaration stating that a national of a Member State has the right to look for work on the territory of another Member State during a period of three months, and this right becomes defunct if the national concerned becomes dependant on the social assistance of the host Member Country. This last restriction is, according to some, unjustified.[2]

A national of another Member State who entered a State in order to seek employment may be required to leave the territory of that State (subject to appeal) if he has not found employment there after six months, unless the person concerned provides evidence that he is continuing to seek employment and he has genuine chances of being engaged.[3] Requiring nationals of other Member States, who are seeking employment in Belgium to leave its territory after a period of three months, is contrary to Article 48 of the EC Treaty.[4]

1. 23 March 1982, *D.M. Levin* v. *Staatssecretaris van Justitie*, No. 53/81, IELL, *Case Law*, No. 45.
2. H. Verschueren, *op. cit.*, 339.
3. 26 February 1991, *The Queen* v. *the Immigration Appeal Tribunal, ex parte Gustaff Desiderius Antonissen*, No. C-292/89, IELL, *Case Law*, No. 159.
4. COJ., 20 February 1997, *Commission* v. *Belgium*, C-344/95, not yet published.

II. Access and Residence

A. Access

237.   The Member States must to those who have a valid identity card or a valid passport grant access to their territory, even if the identity card does not allow its

holder to leave the territory of the Member State in which it was issued.[1] Community law does not however stand in the way of a Member State, in one ECJ case Belgium, controlling its territory as to whether those who have the right of residence carry their residence permit on them, as is done for Belgian nationals, who are required to carry their identity card. This control at entry into the country would however be contrary to Community policy if it appeared that the controls are systematic, arbitrary or unnecessarily annoying.[2] The Member States are moreover entitled to take necessary measures to ensure that they have sufficient information concerning migration within their territory. Nationals of other Member States can thus be obliged to make a declaration of residence, provided however that a reasonable period of time is granted; this is not the case with a term of three days from arrival on the territory of the Member State. Sanctions taken to implement this obligation are acceptable but need, qua character and weight, to be comparable with a sanction taken against nationals who have committed minor offences. Imprisonment is in no way acceptable.[3] No entry visa or equivalent document may be demanded except from members of the family who are not nationals of a Member State. Member States shall accord to such persons every facility for obtaining any necessary visas (Art. 3, §2).

In the case of Mrs Danielle Roux[4] the Court ruled that prior registration of a national of a Member State of the Community with a social security scheme established by the legislation of the host State cannot be required as a condition for obtaining the right of residence or the delivery of a corresponding residence permit. The case was as follow: Mrs. Roux, a French national had applied to the Liège municipal authorities for a residence permit, declaring her profession as that of self-employed waitress. The aliens department rejected that application on the ground that the applicants' profession was not that of self-employed waitress, since she worked for an employer. As the activity of the employed person was not carried on in compliance with the employment and social security legislation in force in Belgium, the authorities ordered Mrs. Roux to leave the country. In this case, the Court said that registration with one social security scheme rather than another cannot justify a refusal to issue a residence permit or a decision ordering expulsion from the territory. Articles 4 of Directive 68/360 and 6 of Directive 73/148 preclude Member States from accepting only prior registration with a social security scheme as evidence that the person concerned falls within one of the categories enjoying freedom of movement of persons and must thus be issued with a residence permit. Member States are obliged to issue a residence permit to a national of another Member States if it is not disputed that the person is engaged in economic activity, without it being necessary in that regard to classify the activity as that of an employed or self-employed person. Therefore Member States may not, on the basis of Community rules concerning freedom of movement for persons, refuse to issue a residence permit on the ground that the Community citizen does not exercise his activity in accordance with the social security legislation in force.

Nationals of a Member State may not be required to answer questions put by border officials regarding the purpose and duration of their journey and the financial means at their disposal for it before they are permitted to enter the country.[5]

1. 5 March 1991, *Panagiotis Giagounidis* v. *City of Reutlingen*, No. C-376/89, IELL. *Case Law*, No. 162.

2. COJ, 27 April 1989, *Commission* v. *Belgium*, No. 321/87, IELL, *Case Law*, No. 134.
3. COJ, 12 December 1989, *Criminal Proceedings* v. *Lothar Mesnner*, No. C 265/88, IELL, *Case Law*, No. 140.
4. 5 February 1991, *Danielle Roux* v. *Belgian State*, No. C-363/89, IELL, *Case Law*, No. 157.
5. COJ, 30 May 1991, *Commission* v. *Netherlands*, No. C-68/89, IELL, *Case Law*, No. 165.

B. Residence

1. In the Case of Employment

238.   The right of residence for workers of Member States and for their families is dealt with in the above-mentioned Directive No. 68/360 of 15 October 1968. The right to reside, which follows directly from the EC Treaty, is proved by a document entitled 'Residence Permit for a National of a Member State of the EC'[1] (Art. 4, §2), and is to be delivered by the Member States. Completion of the formalities for obtaining a residence permit cannot hinder the immediate beginning of employment under a contract concluded by the applicants (Art. 5). The Residence Permit has a compulsory content.[2] Residence documents and eventual visas are issued and renewed free of charge (Art. 9, §1–2).[3] Moreover, Member States have the obligation to take the necessary steps to simplify as much as possible the formalities and procedure for obtaining the documents (Art. 9, §3).

1. Community law has not deprived Member States of the power to adopt measures to enable the national authorities to have precise information about population movements within its territory (COJ, 14 July 1977, *Concetta Sagulo et al.* No. 8/77, IELL, *Case Law*, No. 27).
2. The text of this statement is given in the annex to the directive and reads as follows:
    'This permit is issued pursuant to Regulation (EEC) No. 1612/68 of the Council of the European Communities of 15 October 1968 and to the measures taken in implementation of the Council Directive of 15 October 1968.
    In accordance with the provisions of the above-mentioned Regulation, the holder of this permit has the right to take up and pursue an activity as an employed person in * territory under the same conditions as * workers.'
    * Belgium, German, French, Greek, Irish, Italian, Luxembourg, Netherlands, Portuguese, Spanish and United Kingdom, according to the country using the permit. (Amended by the Act of Accession of Spain and Portugal (O.J. No. L 302, 15 November 1985, p. 208).)
3. For residence documents a payment may be asked of an amount not exceeding the dues and the taxes charged for the issue of identity cards to nationals (Art. 9, §1, Directive No. 68/360).

239.   For the issue of a residence permit, Member States may require only the production of the following documents:

– by the worker:
   a. the document with which he entered their country;
   b. a confirmation of engagement from the employer or a certificate of employment;

– by the members of the worker's family:
   c. the document with which they entered the territory;
   d. a document issued by the competent authority of the State of origin or the State from which they have come, proving their relationship (Art. 4, §3).

A member of the family who is not a national of a Member State shall be issued with a residence document which shall have the same validity as that issued to the worker upon whom he is dependent (Art. 4, §4).

A Member State may not require from a person enjoying the protection of Community law that he should possess a general residence permit instead of the document provided for in Article 4, §2 of Directive No. 68/360, nor may it impose penalties for the failure to possess such a permit.[1]

1. *Sagulo* Case, *op. cit.*

240. The residence permit must be valid throughout the territory of the Member State which issued it for at least five years from the date of issue and be automatically renewable (Art. 6 §1). Breaks in residence not exceeding six consecutive months and absence for military service do not affect the validity of a residence permit (Art. 6 §2). Where a worker is employed for a period exceeding three months but not exceeding one year in the service of the employer in the host State or in the employment of a person providing services, the host Member State is obliged to issue him a temporary permit, the validity of which may be limited to the expected period of employment (Art. 6, §3).

A Member State is required to recognise the right of residence within its territory of the workers who are in possession of a valid identity card, even if that card does not allow its holder to leave the territory of the Member State in which it was issued. It is herein of no importance to know whether the card was issued prior to the accession of the issuing Member State to the Communities, that the card does not mention that its validity is limited to the national territory or that the holder of the card was admitted to the host Member State solely on the basis of his passport.[1]

1. COJ, 5 March 1991, *P. Giagounidis* v. *City of Reutlingen*, No C-376/89, IELL, *Case Law*, No. 162.

241. The residence permit is a really powerful document: it is definitely acquired; a valid permit may not be withdrawn from a worker solely on the grounds that he is no longer in employment, either because he is temporarily incapable of work as a result of illness or accident, or because he is involuntarily unemployed, this being duly confirmed by the competent employment office (Art. 8, §1), except on grounds of public policy, public security or public health (Art. 10). The period of residence may however be restricted, but by no less than twelve months if the worker has been involuntary unemployed in the Member State for more than twelve consecutive months (Art. 7, §2).

242. In the case of employment for a short period of less than three months, a residence permit is not necessary. The document with which the person concerned entered the country and a statement by the employer on the expected duration of employment shall be sufficient to cover his stay (Art. 8, §1, a). The same applies in the case of a worker who, while having his residence in the territory of the Member State to which he returns as a rule each day or at least once a week, is employed in the territory of another Member State. The competent authority of the State where he is employed may issue such worker with a special permit valid for five years and automatically renewable (Art. 8, §1, b). It also applies for a seasonal worker who holds a contract of employment stamped by the competent authority of the Member State on whose territory he has come to pursue his activity (Art. 8, §1, c). In all these cases the competent authorities of the host Member State may require the worker to report his presence in the territory (Art. 8, §2).

2. In the Case of Ceased Occupational Activity

243. The right of a worker and the members of his family to remain in the territory of a Member State after having been employed in that State follows from Article 48, §3(d) of the EC Treaty and is further laid down in Regulation No. 1251/70 of 29 June 1970.[1] In contrast to the right of workers in general to remain in another Member State, these workers do not need to prove that they have sufficient resources not to become dependent on the social assistance of the host Member State. The right of equal treatment established by Regulation No. 1612/68 applies to the persons concerned (Art. 7).

   1. O.J., 30 June 1970, No. L 142/30.

244. The right to remain permanently in the territory of a Member State belongs to:

a. a worker who at the time of termination of his activity has reached the age laid down by the law of that Member State for entitlement to an old age pension and who has been employed in that State for at least the last twelve months and has resided there continuously for more than three years;
b. a worker, who having resided continuously in the territory of that State for more than two years, ceases to work there as an employed person as a result of permanent incapacity to work. If such incapacity is a result of an accident at work or an occupational disease entitling him to a pension for which an institution of that State is entirely or partially responsible, no condition shall be imposed on the length of service;
c. a worker who, after three years' continuous employment and residence in the territory of that State, works as an employed person in the territory of another Member State, while retaining his residence in the territory of the first State, to which he returns, as a rule each day or at least once a week.

The condition as to length of residence and employment shall not apply if the worker's spouse is a national of the Member State concerned or has lost the nationality of that State by marriage to that worker (Art. 2).

245. The members of a worker's family who are residing with him enjoy the same right, even after the worker's death. If, however, the worker dies during his working life before having acquired the right to remain in the territory of the State concerned, members of his family shall be entitled to remain there permanently on the condition that:

- the worker, on the day of his decease, had resided continuously in the territory of that Member State for at least two years;
- his death resulted from an accident at work or an occupational disease; or
- the surviving spouse is a national of the State of residence or lost the nationality of that State by marriage to that worker (Art. 3).

Community legislation does however not confer a right of residence in the territory of another Member State on a national of a Member State who on the accession of his country to the Community was unemployed in that other Member State after having been employed there for a number of years, who remained unemployed after the date of accession and for whom it is objectively impossible to find employment.

This was the fate of Mr. Tsiotras who had been resident in Germany since 1960 where, until October 1978, he pursued various occupations as an employee. He had been unemployed since then and from September 1981 has been paid allowances by the social services.

At the time of the accession of the Hellenic Republic to the European Community, Mr. Tsiotras was a German residence permit holder which allowed him to work. In December 1981 he applied for an extension of that permit, which was refused on the ground that the applicant was not unfit to work.

It appears from the provisions of Directive 68/360 that the right of residence conferred by Community law on workers of Member States who are unemployed in the host Member State presupposes that those workers, exercising the right of freedom of movement, have previously been employed in the host Member State.

The Court added that no provision of the Act of Accession of the Hellenic Republic to the Community or of secondary legislation assimilates the post occupied by a national of that Member State before its accession to the Community to that occupied by a national of a Member State under provisions of Community law relating to the freedom of movement for workers. It follows that a Greek national who finds himself in the circumstances described by the national court does not enjoy a right of residence under Article 48(3)(c) of the Treaty or Article 7 of Directive 68/360.

As regards right of residence in order to find employment, the Court noted that the actual effect of Article 48 is guaranteed in so far as Community law or, failing that, the law of a Member State, allows the person concerned a reasonable time in which to learn of offers of employment on the territory of the Member State in question suited to their professional qualifications and to take, as appropriate, the necessary measures to take up employment.

It followed from the foregoing that, even if it were established that a person in Mr. Tsiotras' situation was, after the accession of the Hellenic Republic to the Community, looking for employment in another Member State, he would no longer enjoy a right of residence to that end under Community law in so far as several years had passed since accession and, according to the national court, it was objectively impossible for him to obtain employment.

As regards right of residence in cases of unemployment, the right to remain within the territory of the host Member State presupposes that the person concerned has been previously employed there in the context of freedom of movement for workers. That is not the case of a person who finds himself in the circumstances described.[1]

1. COJ, *Tsiotras D. v. Landeshauptstadt Stuttgart*, No. C–171/19, 26 May 1993, not yet published.

246.   Continuity of residence may be attested by any means of proof in use in the country of residence. This continuity is not affected by temporary absences not exceeding a total of three months per year, nor by longer absences due to the compliance with the obligations of military service. Periods of involuntary unemployment, duly recorded, and absences due to illness or accident are considered as periods of employment (Art. 4).

247.   The person entitled to the right to remain shall be allowed to exercise it within two years from the time of becoming entitled to such right, even if he leaves the territory of that Member State during that period (Art. 5).

248.   The permit:

a. shall be issued and renewed free of charge;[1]
b. must be valid throughout the territory of the Member State;
c. must be valid for at least five years and be automatically renewable.

Periods of non-residence not exceeding six consecutive months shall not affect the validity of the residence permit (Art. 6). Member States shall facilitate re-admission to their territories of workers who have left those territories after having resided there permanently for a long period and have been employed there and who wish to return there when they have reached retirement age or are permanently incapacitated for work (Art. 8, §2). Regulation No. 1251/70 does not affect national provisions which are more favourable (Art. 8, §1).

1. Or on payment of a sum not exceeding the dues and the taxes payable by nationals for the issue of renewal of identity documents (Art. 6, §1, a).

III. Equal Treatment

249.   Freedom of movement entails the abolition of any discrimination based on nationality between workers of the Member States as regards employment, remuneration and other conditions of work and employment (Art. 48, §2, EC Treaty); it also implies the right to stay in a Member State for the purpose of employment in accordance with the provisions governing the employment of nationals (Art. 48, §3c). These provisions regarding equal treatment are a specification of the more general principle of equality, which is laid down in Article 6 of the EC Treaty and following which:

> 'within the scope of application of this Treaty, and without prejudice to any special provisions contained therein, any discrimination on grounds of nationality shall be prohibited.[1]

1. The Council, acting in accordance with the procedure referred to in Article 189c, may adopt rules designed to prohibit such discrimination (Art. 6,2, EC Treaty, amended by the TEU).

250.   Equal treatment regarding free movement for workers is further elaborated in Regulation No. 1612/68 of 15 October 1968 on freedom for workers within the Community.[1] The regulation is to be interpreted in the light of the requirement that family life be respected, as referred to in Article 8 of the Convention for the Protection of Human Rights and Fundamental Freedoms. Compliance with that requirement constitutes one of the fundamental rights recognised, as the Court has consistently held, in Community law.[2] The Court judged rightly that equal treatment:

> 'plays an important role in the integration of a migrant worker and his family into the host country, and thus in achieving the objective of free movement of workers.'[3]

1. O.J., 19 October 1968, No. L 257 amended by Regulation No. 312/76 of 9 February 1976, O.J., 14 February 1976, No. L 39 and Regulation 2434/92 of 27 July 1992, O.J., 26 August 1992, No. L 245, 1.
2. COJ, 18 May 1989, *Commission* v. *Germany*, 18 May 1989, No. 249/86, IELL, *Case Law*, No. 134 *bis*.
3. 11 July 1985, *Ministère Public* v. *R.H.M. Mutsch*, No. 137/84, IELL, *Case Law*, No. 79.

A. *National Law*

251.   In Articles 3, 4 and 8 respectively of the regulation, the impact of the equality principle on certain national provisions is laid down. National provisions or practices, where they limit application for an offer of employment, or the right of foreign nationals to take up and pursue employment or subject these to conditions not applicable in respect of their own nationals, are null and void.[1] The rules regarding equality of treatment forbid not only overt discrimination by reason of nationality but also all covert forms of discrimination which, by the application of other criteria of differentiation, lead to the same result. This interpretation, which is necessary to ensure the effective working of one of the fundamental principles of the Community, is explicitly recognised by the fifth recital of the preamble to Regulation No. 1612/68 which requires that equality of treatment of workers shall be ensured 'in fact and by law.'[2] Inasmuch as the object of the provisions of the Treaty and of secondary law is to regulate the situation of individuals and to ensure their protection, it is also for national courts to examine whether individual decisions are compatible with the relevant provisions of Community law.[3]

1. 'There shall be included in particular among those provisions or practices those which:
   a. prescribe a special recruitment procedure for foreign nationals;
   b. limit or restrict the advertising of vacancies in the press or through any other medium or subject it to conditions other than those applicable in respect of employers pursuing their activities in the territory of that Member State;
   c. subject eligibility for employment to conditions of registration with employment offices or impede recruitment of individual workers, where persons who do not reside in the territory of that State, are concerned (Art. 3, §2).'
   Provisions or practices which restrict by number or percentage the employment of foreign nationals in any undertaking, branch of activity or region, or at a national level, do not apply to nationals of the other Member States. When in a Member State the granting of any benefit to undertakings is subject to a minimum percentage of national workers being employed, nationals of the other Member States shall be counted as national workers (Art. 4); *see also* COJ, *Commission* v. *Spain*, 22 March 1993, C-375/92, not yet published.

2. Taking into consideration, as a criterion for the grant of a separation allowance, the fact that a worker has his residence in the territory of another Member State may, according to the circumstances, constitute discrimination forbidden by Article 7, §1 and §4 of Regulation No. 1612/28 (COJ, 12 February 1974, *Sotgia* v. *Deutsche Bundespost*, No. 152/73, IELL, *Case Law*, No. 9b.) 'Where a public body of a Member State, in recruiting staff for posts which do not fall within the scope of Article 48(4) of the Treaty, provides for account to be taken of candidates' previous employment in the public service, that body may not, in relation to Community nationals, make a distinction according to whether such employment was in the public service of that particular State or in the public service of another Member State' (COJ, 23 February 1994, *Scholz I.* v. *Opera Universitaria di Cagliari and Others*, No. C-419/92, *Jur.*, 1994, 505.
3. COJ, 28 October 1974, *Rutilli* v. *Minister of the Interior*, No. 35/75, IELL, *Case Law*, No. 19.

252.   One can of course require that the worker concerned has the linguistic knowledge required by reason of the nature of the post to be fulfilled (Art. 3, §1). This requirement is however, as an exception to the general rule of free movement for workers, to be interpreted restrictively.[1] The post of full-time teacher, whatever the subject taught, is one of those posts. In order to foster one of its national languages, a Member State may therefore rely on that provision when laying down the requirement that any candidate for such a post should possess a sufficient knowledge of the language concerned. This must be interpreted as not precluding national provisions making access to a post subject to the requirement that candidates should have a sufficient knowledge of one of the official languages of a Member State, provided that the conditions in which that requirement is declared satisfied are not more favourable to persons who have pursued their linguistic studies in the Member State concerned than to persons who possess diplomas recognised as equivalent by that State but who pursued the same studies in another Member State.[2]

Article 48, 2 of the EC Treaty precludes the legislation of a Member States from limiting to one year, with the possibility of renewal, the duration of contracts of employment for foreign language assistants at a university where no such limitation existed in principle in relation to other teachers;[3] as well as the application of national law according to which posts for foreign-language assistants must or may be the subject of employment contracts of limited duration, whereas, for other teaching staff performing special duties, recourse to such contracts must be individually justified by an objective reason.[4]

1. H. Verschueren, *op. cit.*, 304.
2. COJ, 28 November 1989, *A. Groener* v. *Minister for Education and the City of Dublin Vocational Educational Committee*, No. 379/87, IELL, *Case Law*, No. 139.
3. COJ, *Allué P. and Others* v. *Università degli Studi di Venzia and Others*, 2 August 1993, No. C-259/91, C-331/991 and C-332/91, not yet published.
4. COJ, *Spotti M.C.*, v. *Freistant Bayern*, 20 October 1993, not yet published.

B. Collective and Individual Agreements

253.   Pursuant to Article 7, §4 of Regulation No. 1612/68, any clause of a collective agreement or any other collective regulation concerning eligibility for employment, remuneration and other conditions of work or dismissal is null and void insofar as it lays down or authorises discriminatory conditions in respect to workers who are nationals of other Member States. The same applies to individual employment contracts.

C. Work

254.   Activities are subject to Community law regarding equal treatment within the framework of the EC only insofar as they constitute an economic activity within the meaning of Article 2 of the Treaty.[1] The rule of non-discrimination applied in judging all legal relationships, by reason either of the place where they are entered into or the place where they take effect, can be located within the territory of the Community.[2] It follows that activities temporarily carried on outside the territory of the Community are not sufficient to exclude the application of that principle, as long as the employment relationship retains a sufficiently close link with that territory.[3] In the absence of any distinction, in Article 48 of the EC Treaty:

> 'it is of interest whether a worker is engaged as a workman, a clerk of an official or even whether the terms on which he is employed come under public or private law. So the public sector as well as the private sector is involved. The exception contained in Article 48, §4 regarding employment in the public service is to be interpreted as meaning that this exception to the free movement concerns only access to a post forming part of the public service. Once the worker is employed in the public sector the equality principle prevails in full. The nature of the legal relationship between the employee and the employing administration is of no consequence in this respect.'[4]

1. COJ, 12 December 1974, *B.N.O. Walrave, L.N.J. Koch* v. *Association Union Cycliste Internationale*, No. 36/74, IELL, *Case Law*, No. 12.
2. *Idem.*
3. COJ, 12 July 1984, *Sàrl Prodest* v. *Caisse Primaire d'assurance maladie de Paris*, No. 237/87, IELL, *Case Law*, No. 61. The case concerned the question whether a Belgian temporary worker sent by a French undertaking to Nigeria remained covered by the French social security system. The answer was yes.
4. COJ, 12 Feb. 1974, *Giovanni Maria Sotgiu* v. *Deutsche Bundespost*, No. 152/73; *see also: Commission* v. *Italian Republic*, 16 June 1987, No. 225/85, IELL, *Case Law*, No. 104.

255.   The free movement of workers self-evidently concerns persons in employment, namely employment in subordination. Articles 6, 48 (free movement of workers) and 56 (right of establishment for self-employed persons) of the EC Treaty have in common the prohibition, in their respective spheres of application, of any discrimination on the grounds of nationality.[1]

1. *Walrave/Koch* Case, *op. cit.*

256.   Equal treatment for workers entails the right to take up an activity as an employed person, to exchange applications for and offers of employment, and to conclude and perform contracts of employment (Art. 1–2 of the regulation).[1] Medical, vocational and other criteria should not be discriminatory, although a vocational test is not excluded (Art. 6). The employment offices should provide the same assistance to nationals of other Member States as to their own nationals (Art. 5).

1. Community law does not prevent a Member State from requiring as a condition for permitting a vessel to participate under its catch quorum that 75 per cent of the crew should be nationals

of the EC Member States; it does prevent the requirement that 75 per cent of the crew should have their domicile in the harbour of the State concerned (COJ, 14 December 1989, *The Queen* v. *Ministry of Agriculture, Fisheries and Food, ex Parte Agegate Ltd.*, No. C-3/87, IELL, *Case Law*, No. 141. *See also*: COJ, 19 January 1988, *Pesca Valentia Limited* v. *Minister for Fisheries and Forestry, Ireland and the Attorney General*, No. 223/86, IELL, *Case Law*, No. 115.)

D. *Performance of Work*

257.   The right to equal treatment with regard to social and tax advantages (Art. 7, §2 of the regulation) operates only for the benefit of workers and does not apply to nationals of Member States who move in search of employment. Those who move in search of employment qualify for equal treatment only as regards access to employment.[1] There is a basis in Community law for the view that the rights guaranteed to migrant workers do not necessarily depend on the actual or continuing existence of the employment relationship. Persons who have previously pursued an effective and genuine activity as an employed person in the host Member State but who are no longer employed are nevertheless considered to be workers under certain provisions of Community law.[2]

  1. COJ, 18 June 1987, *Centre public d'aide sociale de Courcelles* v. *M.C. Lebon*, No. 316/85, IELL, *Case Law*, No. 105.
  2. COJ, 21 June 1988, *Sylvie Lair* v. *Universität Hannover*, No. 39/86, IELL, *Case Law*, No. 124. The case concerned a national of a Member State who had taken up employment in another Member State and there, after giving up her employment, commenced a course of higher education leading to a professional qualification. The question was whether Community law entitles that national to claim a training grant on the same basis as a national from the host Member State. The Court said yes, provided there is a link between the previous occupational activity and the studies in question.

258.   Likewise, no discrimination may take place regarding working conditions on the basis of nationality (Art. 7, §1–3 of the Regulation No. 1612/68), namely regarding:

– remuneration, dismissal and, if the worker becomes unemployed, reinstatement or re-employment;
– social and tax advantages;
– training in vocational schools[1] and retraining centres.

The notion 'social advantage' receives a rather extensive interpretation by the Court. The Court judged that:

> 'in view of the equality of treatment which the provision seeks to achieve, the substantive area of application must be delineated so as to include all social and tax advantages, whether or not attached to the contract of employment'[2]

and that the concept of social advantage encompasses 'not only the benefits accorded by virtue of a right but also those granted on a discretionary basis.'[3]

> 'As the Court has repeatedly held, the purpose of Article 7, §2 of Regulation No. 1612/68 is to achieve equal treatment, and therefore the concept social

advantage, extended by that provision to workers who are nationals of other Member States, must include all advantages which, whether or not linked to a contract of employment, are generally granted to national workers primarily because of their objective status as workers or by virtue of the mere fact of their residence on the national territory and the extension of which to workers who are nationals of other Member Countries therefore seems suitable to facilitate their mobility within the Community.'[4]

One must recognise that the Court, in its interpretation of the concept social advantages as working conditions, has gone beyond the widest meaning of the concepts. This is not a criticism from an ideological point of view, but a mere legal ascertainment. It does not seem necessary, in order to obtain the Community objectives, to qualify the right to live together with a non-married partner as a social advantage of a worker. It might have sufficed to invoke the right of equal treatment under Article 6 of the EC Treaty.

1. It should be noted that in order for an educational institution to be regarded as a vocational school for the purposes of that provision, the fact that some vocational training is provided is not sufficient. The concepts of a vocational school is a more limited one and refers exclusively to institutions which provide only instruction either alternating with or closely linked to an occupational activity, particularly during apprenticeship. This is not true of universities (*idem*).
2. 30 September 1975, *A. Christie* v. *Société Nationale des Chemins de Fer Français*, No. 32/75, IELL, *Case Law*, No. 20.
3. 12 January 1982, *F. Reina and L. Reina* v. *Landeskreditbank Baden-Württemberg*, No. 65/81, IELL, *Case Law*, No. 42.
4. 17 April 1986, *State of the Netherlands* v. *A. F. Reed*, No. 59/85, IELL, *Case Law*, No. 90.

259.   The Court of Justice seems to accept the following as 'social advantages':

– measures with a view to allowing the rehabilitation of the handicapped, insofar as such measures concern workers themselves;[1]
– the suspension of the execution of the employment contract in order to fulfil the obligations of military service, also when the military service is performed in another Member State;[2]
– a separation allowance;[3]
– a special protection against dismissal;[4]
– fare reduction cards issued by a national railway authority to large families;[5]
– allowances for a handicapped adult of another Member State who has never worked in the State, but who resides there and is dependent upon his father who is employed there as a worker.[6]

The Court ruled that the advantages that this regulation extends to workers who are nationals of other Member States, are all those which, whether or not linked to a contract of employment, are generally granted to national workers primarily because of their objective status as workers or by virtue of the mere fact of their residence on the national territory. Therefore, a benefit to certain categories of national workers, who have rendered services in wartime to their own country and whose essential objective is to give those nationals an advantage by reason of the hardships suffered for their country, does not fulfil the essential characteristics of the 'social advantages' referred to in Article 7, §2.

The Court ruled likewise that the Community does not exceed the limits of its jurisdiction because the exercise of its jurisdiction affects measures adopted in the field of demographic policy for which the EC is not competent. Moreover, the concept of 'social advantage' encompasses interest-free loans granted at childbirth by a credit institution incorporated under public law, on the basis and guidelines and with the financial assistance from the State, to families with a low income with a view to stimulating the birthrate.[7]

Other social advantages are:

- guaranteed income for old persons;[8] a minimum income[9] and a special old-age allowance guaranteeing a minimum income;[10]
- the right to a worker to use his own language in proceedings before the courts of the Member State in which the worker resides, under the same conditions as national workers;[11]
- job security and the lack of career structure which makes it impossible for the workers to move to higher grades and has an impact on their pay and retirement pensions;[12]
- the assistance for maintenance and training with a view to the pursuit of university studies leading to a professional qualification;[13]
- a fellowship in the framework of a cultural agreement;[14]
- study funding granted by a Member State to the children of workers;[15]
- childbirth and maternity allowances;[16]
- tide-over allowances;[17]
- tide-over allowances;
- a funeral payment.[18]

1. 11 April 1973, *Michel* v. *Fonds national de reclassements des handicapés*, No. 76/72, IELL, *Case Law*, No. 8.
2. 15 October 1969, *S. Ugliola* v. *Württembergische Milchverwertung Südmilch A.G.*, No. 15/69, IELL, *Case Law*, No. 3.
3. *Sotgiu, op. cit.*
4. In the case of an industrial accident resulting in a loss of earning capacity of more than 50 per cent (13 December 1972, *P. Marsman* v. *M. Rosskamp*, No. 44/72, IELL, *Case Law*, No. 7).
5. COJ, 30 Sept. 1975, *Anita Cristini* v. *Société National des Chemins de Fer Français*, No. 32/75.
6. 16 December 1976, *V. Inzirillo* v. *Caisse d'Allocations Familiales de l'Arrondissement de Lyon*, No. 63/76, IELL, *Case Law*, No. 26. *See also*: COJ, 27 May 1993, *Hugo Schmid* v. *Belgian State*, No. C-310/91, not yet published.
7. *Reina* Case, *op. cit.*
8. *C. Castelli* v. *Office National des Pensions pour Travailleurs Salariés*, No. 261/83, IELL, *Case Law*, No. 62.
9. *Courcelles* Case, *op. cit.*
10. 9 July 1987, *M. Frascogna* v. *Caisse de dépots et consignations*, No. 256/86, IELL, *Case Law*, No. 106.
11. *Mutsch* Case, *op. cit.*
12. *Commission* v. *Italy*, No. 225/85, *op. cit.*
13. *Lair* Case, *op. cit. See also* COJ, 15 March 1989, *G.B.C. Echternach and A. Moritz* v. *Dutch Minister of Education and Sciences*, No. 389 and 390/87, IELL, *Case Law*, No. 133.
14. COJ, 27 September 1988, *A. Matteuci* v. *Communauté Française de Belgique*, No. 235/87, IELL, *Case Law*, No. 128.

15. COJ, 26 February 1992, *M.J.E. Bernini* v. *Netherlands Ministry of Education and Science*, No. C-3/90, IELL, *Case Law*, No. 185.
16. COJ, 19 March 1993, *Commission of the European Communities* v. *Grand Duchy of Luxembourg*, No. C–111/91, IELL, *Case Law*, No. 202.
17. COJ, 12 September 1996, *Commission* v. *Belgium*, Case C-278/98, not yet published.
18. COJ, 23 May 1996, *John O'Flynn* v. *Adjudication Officer*, C-237/94, not yet published.

260.   Not only benefits fall within that category. In *Peter de Vos* v. *Stadt Bielefeld*,[1] the question arose of the qualification of advantages accorded at the occasion of the military service. Pater de Vos was a senior doctor at the city of Bielefeld.

A collective labour agreement (1966) applicable to employees of the Federal Republic of Germany and the *Länder* and to employees of municipal authorities and undertakings ('the CLA'), envisages supplementary old-age and survivors' insurance with the Pension Institution of the Federal Republic and the *Länder* ('the VBL'). The employer pays monthly contributions to that body for the person insured.

The plaintiff performed military service in the Belgian army from 29 March 1993 to 1 March 1994. During that period, the defendant did not contribute to the VBL on behalf of the plaintiff. The VBL therefore suspended the plaintiff's membership from 28 March 1993 to 2 March 1994.

In the action brought before the Labour Court of Bielefeld, the plaintiff claimed that the defendant was required to pay contributions to the VBL during the period of his military service in the Belgian army, by virtue of Articles 48 of the Treaty and 7 of Regulation No. 1612/68.

The obligation on the part of the employer to contribute is, however, not linked to the employment contract. It should therefore be held, so ruled the Court of Justice, 'that the continued payment of supplementary old-age and survivors' pension insurance contributions, as provided for by the German legislation, is not made by virtue of a statutory or contractual obligation incumbent on the employer as conditions of employment and work within the meaning of Article 7(1), but is an advantage granted by the State itself to those called upon as partial compensation for the consequences of their obligation to perform military service.

Such an advantage cannot therefore, the Court concluded, be considered to be granted to national workers because of their objective status as workers or by virtue of the mere fact of their residence on the national territory and it thus does not have the essential characteristics of social advantages referred to in Article 7(2) of Regulation No. 1612/68.

One wonders about the outcome of this case and is a little puzzled about the conclusion of the Court that the obligation on the part of the employer is not linked to the employment contract when one sees that the advantage is provided for by a collective labour agreement, negotiated for the benefit of employees.

1. COJ, 14 March 1996. Case C-315/94, *Jur.*, 1996, 1417.

E. Trade Union Freedom, Workers' Participation, Management of Public Bodies

261.   Equal treatment in the framework of free movement of labour also encompasses *collective labour relations*, namely the right of employees to become a member of a trade union, including the right to vote and to be eligible for the administration or management posts of a trade union. Likewise, the worker has the right of eligibility for workers' representative bodies in the undertaking. The worker who is a national of another Member State may, however, be excluded from taking part in the management of bodies governed by public law and from holding an office governed by public law (Art. 8).

Concerning the question whether certain jobs in the Belgian Railroads could be reserved for Belgians only and answering a point made by the Belgian Government, the Court ruled relating to the meaning of Article 8 of the regulation:

> 'indeed as the Belgian Government itself admits, Article 8 of Regulation No. 1612/68 is not intended to debar workers from other Member States from certain posts, but simply permits them to be debarred in some circumstances from certain activities which involve their participation in the exercise of powers conferred by public law, such as – to use the examples given by the Belgian Government itself – those involving the presence of trade-union representatives on the board of administration of many bodies governed by public law with powers in the economic sphere.'[1]

Freedom of movement prohibits national legislation from denying foreign workers the right to vote in elections for members of a professional institute (in case of occupational guild) for which they are required to be affiliated and to which they must pay contributions, and which is responsible for defending the interests of the affiliated workers and exercises a consultative role with regard to legislation.[2]

1. 17 December 1980, *Commission* v. *Belgium*, No. 149/79, IELL, *Case Law*, No. 39.
2. COJ, 4 July 1991, *ASTI Association de Soutien aux Travailleurs Immigrés* v. *Chambre des Employés Privés*, No. C-213/90, IELL, *Case Law*, No. 166.

F. Housing

262. Equal treatment furthermore encompasses all the rights and benefits accorded to national workers in matters of housing, including ownership of the housing he needs.[1] A worker from another Member State may, with the same rights as nationals, put his name down on the housing lists in the region in which he is employed, where such lists exist; he enjoys the resulting benefits and priorities. If his family has remained in the country from which he came, they are considered for this purpose as residing in the said region where national workers benefit from a similar presumption (Art. 9).

1. *See also* COJ, 30 May 1989, *Commission* v. *Hellas*, No. 305/87, No. 305/87, IELL, *Case Law*, No. 135*ter*.

IV. Workers' Families

263. Family members have, in accordance with Articles 10 to 12 of Regulation No. 1612/68 of 15 October 1968, the right to settle (Art. 10), the right to take up

an activity as an employed person (Art. 11) and to be admitted to the general educational, apprenticeship and vocational training courses (Art. 12). These rights follow directly from the EC Treaty.[1] The Court is of the opinion that these rights are linked to those rights that the migrant worker enjoys under Article 48 of the EC Treaty and Articles 1 *et seq.* of the regulation.[2] The regulation obliges the national authorities of the host Member State to treat the concerned workers and related persons equally. The Court ruled in the case *Centre Public d'Aide sociale de Courcelles* v. *Marie-Christine Lebon* that:

> 'the members of the worker's family within the meaning of Article 10 of Regulation No. 1612/68 qualify only indirectly for the equal treatment accorded to the worker himself by Article 7 of the regulation. Social benefits guaranteeing the minimum means of subsistence in general terms operate in favour of the members of the worker's family only if such benefits may be regarded as a social advantage within the meaning of Article 7, §2 of the regulation regarding the worker himself.'[3]

However, the provisions of Community law on the free movement of workers do not apply to purely internal situations of a Member State, such as the situation of a national of a non-member country, who, solely in the capacity as a spouse of a national of a Member State, claims a right to reside or to remain in the territory of that Member State. This holds e.g. for the following provisions: Regulation (EC) No. 1612/68 of the Council of 15 October 1968, Regulation (EC) No. 1251/70 of the Commission of 29 June 1970 and the Council Directive 68/360/ EC of 15 October 1968.[4]

1. COJ. 15 March 1989, *G.B.C. Echternach and A. Moritz* v. *Dutch Minister for Education and Sciences*, Joined Cases No. 389–390/87, IELL, *Case Law*, No. 133.
2. 7 May 1986, *E. Gül* v. *Regierungspräsident Düsseldorf*, No. 131/85, IELL, *Case Law*, No. 92.
3. *Op. cit.*
4. COJ, 18 October 1990, *Massam Dzodzi* v. *Belgian State*, Joined Cases Nos. 297/88 and 197/89, IELL, *Case Law*, No. 151. *See also*: COJ, 22 July 1992, *Camille Petit* v. *Office National des pensions (ONP)*, No. C-153/91, IELL, *Case Law*, No. 193.

A. Right to Settle

264. Irrespective of nationality, the right to settle with a worker who is a national of one Member State and who is employed in the territory of another Member State belongs to:

a. his spouse and any of their descendants who are under the age of 21 years or are dependents;
b. dependent relatives in the ascending line of this worker and his spouse (Art. 10, §1).

The Member States facilitate the admission of any member of the family not falling with the provisions of paragraph 1 if he is dependent on the migrant worker or living under his roof in the country from which he comes (Art. 10, §2). This right must be interpreted widely since it is the objective of the free movement for workers to integrate the migrant worker and his family as well as possible. If the objective is to be reached, the worker must have available for his family housing that is considered normal for national workers in the region where he is employed (Art. 10, §3). It is however not conditional on any requirement that the family must live under the same roof permanently;[1] such an interpretation is in accordance with Article 11 of the regulation. Pursuant to this article, the members of the family are also entitled to take up an activity as employed persons throughout the territory of that same State when work is performed in a place that is remote from that in which the migrant worker lives. The condition of having appropriate housing available is only required for the settling of each member of the family; once the family is reunited, no other conditions can be imposed upon the migrant worker than those which also apply to national workers.[2] A provision in the national legislation which makes renewal of the residence permit of members of the family of Community migrant workers conditional on their living in appropriate housing, not only at the time when they settle with the migrant worker concerned but for the entire duration of their residence, is contrary to Community law.

1. COJ, 13 February 1985, *Aissatou Diatte* v. *Land Berlin*, No. 267/83, IELL, *Case Law*, No. 70.
2. COJ, 18 May 1989, *Commission* v. *Germany*, No. 249/86, IELL, *Case Law*, No. 134 *bis*.

B. Right to Work

265.   The spouse and any of the worker's children who are under the age of 21 years or dependent on the migrant worker have, pursuant to Article 11 of Regulation No. 1612/68, the right, even if they are not members of any Member State, to take up any activity as an employed person throughout the territory of the host State. This is not the case for a national of a non-member country married to a worker having the nationality of a Member State, when that worker has never exercised the right of freedom of movement within the Community. Any discrimination which nationals of a Member State and their spouses from non-member countries may suffer under the law of that State falls within the scope of that law and must therefore be dealt with within the framework of the internal legal system of that State.[1]

This is the case with any activity; therefore the same rules with regard to access to and the practice of a profession apply in the same way as to nationals of the host State.[2] Article 11 confers on the members of a migrant worker's family only the right to exercise any activity in the host Member State: it does not constitute the legal basis for a right of residence in the Community as a whole. It cannot be read without a reference to Article 10 of the regulation.[3]

1. COJ, 5 June 1997, *Land Nordrhein Westfalen* v. *Kari Uecker; Vera Jacquet* v. *Land Nordrhein Westfalen*, Joined Cases C- 64/96 and C-65/96, not yet published.
2. *Gül* Case, *op. cit.* The case concerned a medical doctor of Cypriot nationality married to a British national.
3. COJ, 13 February 1985, *Aisatou Diatta* v. *Land of Berlin*, No. 267/83, IELL, *Case Law*, No. 70.

C. Training of Children

266.   Finally, again in view of promoting the social integration of the Community migrant worker and his family, Regulation No. 1612/68 provides that the children of a migrant worker are admitted to the host State's *general educational, apprenticeship and vocational training* courses under the same conditions as the nationals of that State, if such children are residing in its territory (Art. 12). Although the national authorities retain full jurisdiction regarding education and the determination of the conditions referred to in Article 12, these conditions must however be applied without discrimination between the children of national workers and those of workers who are nationals of another Member State and who reside in the territory.[1]

In the case of *Carmina Di Leo* (an Italian national, and a child of a Community worker) v. *Land Berlin*, the question was raised whether the German authorities could refuse her the benefit of educational or training grants for studies completed outside the territory of Germany provided by the German law on individual inducement to enter training, on the ground that Miss Di Leo was registered as a medical student at the University of Sienna in Italy and that the nationals of a Member State of the EC are excluded from the benefit of the aid when the training is given in a State of which they are nationals. The Court ruled that according to Article 12, when a Member State offered its nationals the possibility of receiving a grant for education or training given abroad, the child of a Community worker had to be able to receive the same benefit if it decided to pursue its studies outside the host Member State. That interpretation could not be invalidated by the fact that the prospective recipient of the education or training decided to follow courses in the Member State of which that person was a national. Neither the residence notice laid down in Article 12 nor the objective pursued by the Regulation justified such a restriction which, moreover would give rise to another form of discrimination against children of Community workers in comparison with nationals of the host Member State. Therefore children of Community workers are to be treated as nationals for the purpose of awarding educational or training grants, not only when the education or training takes place in the host State but also when it is provided in a State of which those children are nationals.[2]

This right of the children to training encompasses any form of education, including courses provided at a university,[3] and the guidance, training and vocational rehabilitation of the handicapped.[4] Article 12 refers not only to rules relating to admission; aid for maintenance and training with the view to following (middle and higher) education constitutes a social advantage in the sense of Article 2, §7 of the regulation to which migrant workers are entitled under the same conditions as national workers. The regulation aims again at the social integration of the Community foreign worker and his family in the host Member State.[5]

Since study funding granted by a Member State to the children of workers constitutes, for a migrant worker, a social advantage within the meaning of Article 7(2) of Regulation (EC) No. 1612/68 when the worker continues to provide for the maintenance of the child, no further requirements may be imposed such as conditions relating to residence.[6]

1. COJ, 3 July 1974, *Donata Cassagrande* v. *Landeshaupstad München*, No. 9/74, IELL, *Case Law*, No. 11.

2. 13 November 1990, *Carmina Di Leo* v. *Land Berlin*, No. C-308/89, IELL, *Case Law*, No. 155.
3. *Echternach* Case, *op. cit.*
4. COJ, 11 April 1973, *S. Michel* v. *Fonds national de reclassement social des handicapés*, No. 76/72, IELL, *Case Law*, No. 8.
5. *Idem.*
6. COJ, 26 February 1992, *M.J.E. Bernini* v. *Netherlands Ministry of Education and Science*, No. C-3/90, IELL, *Case Law*, No. 185.

§2. SCOPE OF APPLICATION

I. Workers

A. *In General*

267.   The Court has ruled consistently that the notion 'worker' in Article 48 of the EC Treaty has a Community meaning in law. The term 'worker' and 'an activity as an employed person' may not be defined by reference to the national laws of the Member States. If that were the case, the Community rules on free movement for workers would be frustrated, as the meanings of those terms could be fixed and modified unilaterally, without any control by the Community institutions, by national laws which would thus be able to exclude at will certain categories of persons from the benefit of the Treaty.

268.   It is appropriate therefore, in order to determine their meaning, to have recourse to the generally recognised principles of interpretation, beginning with the ordinary meaning to be attributed to those terms in their context and in light of the objectives of the Treaty.[1] In this respect, it must be stressed that the terms 'worker' and 'activity as an employed person' define the field of application of one of the fundamental freedoms guaranteed by the Treaty and, as such, may not be interpreted restrictively.

Nevertheless, a person who has worked only as a self-employed person before becoming unemployed cannot be classified as a 'worker' within the meaning of Article 48 of the Treaty, not even when the person concerned previously worked as an employed person.[2]

1. *Idem.*
2. COJ, 4 October 1991, *D. Maxwell Middleburgh* v. *Chief Adjudication Officer*, No. C-15/90, IELL, *Case Law*, No. 174.

260.   The concept of 'worker' must, the Court rightly ruled, be defined in accordance with objective criteria which distinguish the employment relationship by reference to the rights and duties of the persons concerned. The essential feature of an employment relation, however, is the fact that for a certain period of time a person performs services for and under the direction of another person in return for which he receives remuneration.[1] The Court therefore retained three criteria: (1) performance of services (2) in subordination for (3) remuneration.

1. *Lawrie-Blum* Case, *op. cit.*

269.   Performance of services means the pursuit of effective and genuine activities, part-time included, with the exclusion of activities of such a small scale as to be regarded as purely marginal and ancillary. It follows both from the statement of the principle of freedom of movement for workers and from the place occupied by the rules related to that principle that they only guarantee the free movement for workers who pursue or are desirous of pursuing an economic activity.[1] A worker employed under an *'oproepcontract'* (on call contract) under which the person concerned performed sixty hours of work, is a worker within the meaning of Article 48 of the Treaty.[2] The motives that may have prompted a worker to seek employment in another Member State are of no account in regard to his right to enter and reside in the territory of the latter, provided that he pursues or wishes to pursue an effective and genuine activity.[3] The fact that teachers' preparatory service, like apprenticeships in other occupations, may be regarded as practical preparation directly related to the actual pursuit of the occupation in point is not a bar to the application of Article 48 of the EC Treaty if the service is performed under the conditions of an activity as an employed person.[4] Equally a national of a Member State who has worked in another Member State within the framework of a course of vocational training must be regarded as a worker within the meaning of Article 48 of the EC Treaty, at least if he has provided services for which he has received payment and provided his activities were effective and genuine.[5]

The duration of the activities pursued by the person concerned is a factor which may be taken into account by the national court when assessing whether they are effective and genuine or whether they are so limited as to be merely marginal and ancillary.[6] In assessing whether a person is a worker, account should be taken of all the occupational activities which the person concerned has pursued within the host Member State, but not the activities which he has pursued elsewhere within the Community.[7]

A migrant worker who voluntarily leaves his employment in order to take up, after a certain lapse of time, a course of full-time study in the country of which he is a national retains his status as a worker provided that there is a link between the previous occupational activity and the studies in question.[8] However, a migrant worker who leaves his employment and begins a course of full-time study unconnected with the previous occupational activities, will not retain his status as a migrant worker for the purposes of Article 48 of the EC Treaty, except in the case he becomes involuntarily unemployed.[9]

1. *Levin Case, op. cit.*
2. COJ, 26 February 1992, *V.J.M. Raulin* v. *Netherlands Ministry of Education and Science*, No. C-357/89, IELL, *Case Law*, No. 184.
3. *Levin* Case, *op. cit.*
4. *Lawrie-Blum* Case, *op. cit.*
5. COJ, 26 February 1992, *M.J.E. Bernini* v. *Netherlands Ministry of Education and Science*, No. C-3/90, IELL, *Case Law*, No. 185.
6. COJ, 26 February, 1992, *V.J.M. Raulin* v. *Netherlands Ministry of Education and Science*, No. C-357/89, IELL, *Case Law*, No. 184.
7. *Idem.*
8. COJ, 26 February 1992, *M.J.E. Bernini* v. *Netherlands Ministry of Education and Science*, No. C-3/90, IELL, *Case Law*, No. 185.
9. COJ, 26 February 1992, *V.J.M. Raulin* v. *Netherlands Ministry of Education and Science*, No. C-357/89, IELL, *Case Law*, No. 184.

B. Sports – The Bosman Case

270.   The job has to have an economic nature within the meaning of Article 2 of the EC Treaty. Consequently, the Court ruled that the practice of sport is subject to Community law only insofar as it constitutes an economic activity in the meaning of Article 2.[1]

> 'This applies to the activities of professional or semi-professional football players, who are in the nature of gainful employment or remunerated service';

it follows logically that:

> 'where such players are nationals of a Member State they benefit in all the other Member States from the provisions of Community law concerning free-dom of movement of persons and of provision of services. However, those provisions do not prevent the adoption of rules or of a practice excluding foreign players from participation in certain matches for reasons which are not of an economic nature, which relate to the particular nature and context of such matches and are thus of sporting interest only, such as, for example, matches between national teams from different countries.'[2]

Community law is also applicable to football trainers.[3] There is no need to under-line that the free movement of professional soccer players is *de facto* not respected given the restrictions imposed upon players for reasons of nationality on one hand and the systems of blockade which operate in the case of a transfer of players from one club to another, at international as well as national level on the other hand. Fifa and Uefa, which have set up international cartels to monopolise professional soccer on a world-wide basis, are violating Community law relating to competition in general and to Articles 85 and 86 of the EC Treaty in particular.

1. *Walrave/Koch Case, op. cit.*
2. COJ, 14 July 1976, *G. Dona* v. *M. Mantero*, No. 13/76, IELL, *Case Law*, No. 25.
3. COJ, 15 October 1987, *Unectef* v. *G. Heylens*, No. 222/86, IELL, *Case Law*, No. 111.

271.   This was more than confirmed in the *Bosman* Case,[1] where the Court of Justice did justice, which was more than overdue in sports, especially regarding the transfer system in which sportsmen, especially soccer players were – and still are outside the EU – treated like cattle which can be sold and bought. The Court reaffirmed that free movement of workers applies to professional sports and that it constitutes a fundamental right. Transfer systems designed to block players and nationality clauses limiting EU players to be lined up are contrary to Article 48. This landmark decision is a marvellous example of the contribution of European law to human rights and human dignity. Let us consider the facts, the arguments and the Court's ruling.

Mr. Bosman, a professional footballer of Belgian nationality, was employed from 1988 by RC Liège, a Belgian first division club, under a contract expiring on 30 June 1990, which assured him an average monthly salary of BEF 120,000, includ-ing bonuses. On 21 April 1990, RC Liège offered Mr. Bosman a new contract for one season, reducing his pay to BEF 30,000, the minimum permitted by the URBSFA (Belgian Soccer Federation) federal rules. Mr. Bosman refused to sign and was put on the transfer list. The compensation fee for training was set, in accordance with the said rules, at BEF 11,743,000.

Since no club showed an interest in a compulsory transfer, Mr. Bosman contacted with US Dunkerque, a club in the French second division, which led to his being signed.

On 27 July 1990, a contract was also concluded between RC Liège and US Dunkerque for the temporary transfer of Mr. Bosman for one year, against payment by US Dunkerque to RC Liège of a compensation fee of BEF 1,200,000 payable on receipt by the Fédération Française de Football (FFF) of the transfer certificate issued by URBSFA.

However, RC Liège did not ask URBSFA to send the said certificate to FFF. As a result, neither contract took effect. On 31 July 1990, RC Liège also suspended Mr. Bosman, thereby preventing him from playing for the entire season.

– *Interpretation of Article 48 of the Treaty with regard to the transfer rules*
The first question was to ascertain whether Article 48 precludes the application of rules laid down by sporting associations, under which a professional footballer who is a national of one Member State may not, on the expiry of his contract with a club, be employed by a club of another Member State unless the latter club has paid to the former a transfer, training or development fee.

> Application of Article 48 to rules laid down by sporting associations
> It is to be remembered that, having regard to the objectives of the Community, sport is subject of Community law only in so far as it constitutes an economic activity within the meaning of Article 2 of the Treaty. This applies to the activities of professional or semi-professional footballers, where they are in gainful employment or provide a remunerated service.
>
> It is not necessary, for the purposes of the application of the Community provisions on freedom of movement for workers, for the employer to be an undertaking; all that is required is the existence of, or the intention to create, an employment relationship.
>
> Furthermore, application of Article 48 is not precluded by the fact that the transfer rules govern the business relationships between clubs rather than the employment relationships between clubs and players.
>
> The argument based on points of alleged similarity between aport and culture cannot be accepted, since the question relates to the scope of the freedom of movement of workers, which is a fundamental freedom in the Community system.
>
> As regards the arguments based on the principle of freedom of association, it must be recognised that this principle, enshrined in Article 11 of the European Convention for the Protection of Human Rights and Fundamental Freedoms and resulting from the constitutional traditions common to the Member States, is one of the fundamental rights which, as the Court has consistently held and as is reaffirmed in the preamble to the Single European Act and in Article F(2) of the Treaty on European Union, are protected in the Community legal order.

However, the rules laid down by sporting associations to which the national court refers cannot be seen as necessary to ensure enjoyment of that freedom by those associations, by the clubs or by their players, nor can they be seen as an inevitable result thereof.

Finally, the principle of subsidiarity, as interpreted to the effect that intervention by public authorities, and particularly Community authorities, in the area in question must be confined to what is strictly necessary, cannot lead to a situation in which the freedom of private associations to adopt sporting rules restricts the exercise of rights conferred on individuals by the Treaty.

Existence of an obstacle to freedom of movement for workers
It is true that the transfer rules in issue in the main proceedings apply also to transfers of players between clubs belonging to different national associations within the same Member State and that similar rules govern transfers between clubs belonging to the same national association.

However, those rules are likely to restrict the freedom of movement of players who wish to pursue their activity in another Member State by preventing or deterring them from leaving the clubs to which they belong even after the expiry of their contracts of employment with those clubs.

Since they provide that a professional footballer may not pursue his activity with a new club established in another Member State unless it has paid his former club a transfer fee agreed upon between the two clubs or determined in accordance with the regulations of the sporting associations, the said rules constitute an obstacle to the freedom of movement for workers.

Consequently, the transfer rules constitute an obstacle to freedom of movement for workers prohibited in principle by Article 48 of the Treaty. It could only be otherwise if those rules pursued a legitimate aim compatible with the Treaty and were justified by pressing reasons of public interest. But even if that were so, application of those rules would still have to be such as to ensure achievement of the aim in question and not go beyond what is necessary for that purpose.

Existence of justifications
First, it was argued that the transfer rules are justified by the need to maintain a financial and competitive balance between clubs and to support the search for talent and the training of young players.

In view of the considerable social importance of sporting activities and in particular football in the Community, the aims of maintaining a balance between clubs by preserving a certain degree of equality and uncertainty as to results and of encouraging the recruitment and training of young players must be accepted as legitimate.

As regards the first of those aims, Mr. Bosman has rightly pointed out that the application of the transfer rules is not an adequate means of maintaining a financial and competitive balance in the world of football. Those rules neither preclude the richest clubs from securing the services of the best players nor prevent the availability of financial resources from being a decisive factor in competitive sport, thus considerably altering the balance between clubs.

As regards the second aim, it must be accepted that the prospect of receiving transfer, development or training fees is indeed likely to encourage football clubs to seek new talent and train young players.

However, because it is impossible to predict the sporting future of young players with any certainty and because only a limited number of such players go on to play professionally, those fees are by nature contingent and uncertain and are in any event unrelated to the actual cost borne by clubs of training both future professional players and those who will never play professionally. The prospect of receiving such fees cannot, therefore, be either a decisive factor in encouraging recruitment and training of young players or an adequate means of financing such activities, particularly in the case of smaller clubs.

It has also been argued that the transfer rules are necessary to safeguard the world-wide organisation of football.

However, the present proceedings concern application of those rules within the Community and not the relations between the national associations of the Member States and those of non-member countries.

– Interpretation of Article 48 of the Treaty with regard to the nationality clauses
By its second question, the national court seeks in substance to ascertain whether Article 48 of the Treaty precludes the application of rules laid down by sporting associations, under which, in matches in competitions which they organise, football clubs may field only a limited number of professional players who are nationals of other Member States.

Existence of an obstacle to freedom of movement for workers
Article 48(2) expressly provides that freedom of movement for workers entails the abolition of any discrimination based on nationality between workers of the Member States as regards employment, remuneration and conditions of work and employment.

That principle precludes the application of clauses contained in the regulations of sporting associations which restrict the right of nationals of other Member States to take part, as professional players, in football matches.

Existence of justifications
It was argued that the nationality clauses are justified on non-economic grounds, concerning only the sport as such.

Here, the nationality clauses do not concern specific matches between teams representing their countries but apply to all official matches between clubs and thus to the essence of the activity of professional players.

In those circumstances, the nationality clauses cannot be deemed to be in accordance with Article 48, otherwise it would be deprived of its practical effect and the fundamental right of free access to employment which the Treaty confers individually on each worker in the Community would be rendered nugatory.

None of the arguments submitted detracts from that conclusion.

– The temporal effects of this judgment

In the present case, the specific features of the rules laid down by the sporting associations for transfers of players between clubs of different Member States, together with the fact that the same or similar rules applied to transfers both between clubs belonging to the same national association and between clubs belonging to different national associations within the same Member State, may have caused uncertainty as to whether those rules were compatible with Community law.

In such circumstances, overriding considerations of legal certainty militate against calling in question legal situations whose effects have already been exhausted. An exception must, however, be made in favour of persons who may have taken timely steps to safeguard their rights.

These arguments induced the Court to decide that:

'Article 48 precludes the application of rules laid down by sporting associations, under which a professional footballer who is a national of one Member State may not, on the expiry of his contract with a club, be employed by a club of another Member State unless the latter club has paid to the former club a transfer, training or development fee.

Article 48 precludes the application of rules laid down by sporting associations under which, in matches in competitions which they organise, football clubs may field only a limited number of professional players who are nationals of other Member States.

The direct effect of Article 48 cannot be relied upon in support of claims relating to a fee in respect of transfer, training or development which has already been paid on, or is still payable under an obligation which arose before, the date of this judgement, except by those who have brought court proceedings or raised an equivalent claim under the applicable national law before that date.'

1. COJ, 15 December 1995, *Union Royale Belge des Sociétés de Football Association ASBL and Others* v. *Jean-Marc Bosman and Others*, Case C-415/93, *Jur.*, 1995, 4921.

C. Others

272. According to the Court of Justice, the following activities have an economic character; the membership of a religious community, provided that for effective and genuine activities there is a certain counterpart; the apprenticeship of a teacher, when lessons are given to the school's pupils and thus provide a service of some economic value to the school.[1] Activities are not considered economic if they constitute employment in the framework of therapy – because here the social element supersedes the economic one, again showing that in the EC the economic prevails over the social.[2]

1. *Lawrie-Blum* Case, *op. cit.*
2. COJ, 31 May 1989, *J. Bettray* v. *Staatssecretaris van Justitie*, No. 344/87, IELL, *Case Law*, No. 135.

273.   Freedom of movement also applies to activities in the *public sector* (as well as to public international organisations)[1] and to activities in the private sector that take place on the territory of the EC, or even outside the Community, provided there are enough close links, as indicated above.[2]

1. *Echternach* Case, *op. cit.*
2. *See* No. 153.

274.   The decision of the Court in the *Rush Portuguese* Case concerning free movement of workers is remarkable. The Court recognised the right of undertakings who are performing activities in another Member State, on the basis of the free movement of services, to perform them with their own workers, even if those workers themselves – as was the case with Portuguese workers until 1992 – do not benefit from the right of free movement on the basis of Article 48 of the EC Treaty.[1] This could mean that workers from third countries, non Member States, who are already present and employed in a given Member State might, through the channel of rendering of services under Articles 59–60 of the EC Treaty, be employed in other Member States.

1. COJ, 27 March 1990, *Rush Portuguesa LDA* v. *Office National d' Immigration*, No. 113/89, IELL, *Case Law*, No. 143. *See also*: COJ, 9 August 1994, *R. van der Elst* v. *Office des Migrations Internationales*, C-43/93, *Jur.*, 1994, 3803.

275.   Work *in subordination* means to perform services for and under the direction and supervision of another person. In *Lawrie-Blum*, the Court ruled that:

'in the present case, it is clear that during the entire period of preparatory service the trainee teacher is under the direction and supervision of the school to which he is assigned. It is the school that determines the services to be performed by him and his working hours and it is the school's instructions that he must carry out and that he must observe.'

276.   To this needs to be added that he migrant worker should be a *national* of a Member State (Art. 1, Regulation No. 1612/68). Each Member State determines who are and who are not its nationals. The Community has however the jurisdiction to indicate the consequences of the nationality in relation to the free movement of workers.[1] Moreover there must be intra-Community movement. Community law regarding free movement for workers is not applicable on a purely domestic relation within a Member State, as in the case of workers who have never taken advantage of free movement within the Community.[2]

1. H. Verschueren, *op. cit.*, 273.
2. *Idem. See also*: COJ, 28 January 1992, *Volker Steen* v. *Deutsche Bundespost*, No. C-332/90, IELL, *Case Law*, No. 182.

277.   Finally, there must be *remuneration*. This income may be lower than what, in the host State, is considered as the minimum required for subsistence, whether that person supplements the income from his activity as an employed person with other income so as to arrive at that minimum or is satisfied with the means of support that is lower than the said minimum, provided that he pursues an activity as an employed person that is effective and genuine;[1] the fact that he claims financial assistance out of the public funds of the latter in order to supplement the income he receives from those activities does not exclude him from the provisions of Community law relating to freedom of movement for workers.[2]

1. *Levin* Case, *op. cit.*
2. COJ, 3 June 1986, *R.H. Kempf* v. *Staatssecretaris van Justitie*, No. 139/85, IELL, *Case Law*, No. 96.

II. Family Members

278.   The provisions of the Treaty concerning free movement for workers and the rules adopted to implement them cannot be applied to cases which have no factor linking them with any of the situations governed by Community law. For instance, Dutch authorities were allowed to refuse permission to nationals of Surinam to reside in the Netherlands with their daughter and son who are Netherlands nationals of whom the Surinam nationals are dependents. Since neither the daughter nor the son were migrant workers there was no factor linking their case with any of the situations governed by Community law.[1] That interpretation of Community law has as a consequence, however, that a national of a Member State may be treated less favourably than a national of a non Member State who has taken advantage of the right to move freely, so that there is a factor linking this case to a Community situation. Some qualify this as 'reverse discrimination.'[2]

The status of a *dependent member of a worker's family*, as stated by Regulation No. 1612/68, is the result of a factual situation. The person having that status is a member of the family who is supported by the worker and there is no need to determine the reasons for recourse to the worker's support or to raise the question whether the person is able to support himself by taking up paid employment. A claim for the grant of a minimex submitted by a member of a migrant worker's family who is dependent on the worker cannot affect the claimant's status as a dependent member. To decide otherwise would amount to accepting that the grant of the minimex could result in the claimant forfeiting the status of dependent member and consequently justify either the withdrawal of the minimex itself or even the loss of the right of residence. Such a solution would in practice undermine the equal treatment accorded to the migrant worker. The status of dependent worker should therefore be considered independently from the grant of the minimex. It must also be pointed out that the status of dependent member does not presuppose the existence of a right to maintenance either. If that were the case, the composition of the family would depend on national legislation, which varies from one State to another, and that would lead to the application of Community law in a nonuniform manner.[3]

1. COJ, 27 Oct. 1982, *Elestina Christina Esselina Morson* v. *State of the Netherlands and Head of the Plaatselijke Politie within the meaning of the Vreemdelingenwet; Sewradjie Thanjan* v. *State of the Netherlands*, Joined Cases Nos. 35 and 36/82 (herein referred to as 'Morson').
2. H. Verschueren, *op. cit.*
3. *Centre public d'aide sociale de Courcelles* Case, *op. cit.*

279. A number of cases deal with the notion of 'spouse.' The Court ruled in this connection that the marital relationship cannot be regarded as dissolved as long as it has not been terminated by the competent authority. It is not dissolved merely because the spouses live separately, even where they intend to divorce at a later date.[1] In the absence of any indication to the contrary in the regulation, it must be held that the term spouse in Article 10 refers to a marital relationship only. Therefore, the companion, in a stable relationship, of a migrant worker cannot be treated as his spouse. It must however, the Court ruled, be recognised that the possibility of a migrant worker of obtaining permission for his unmarried companion to reside with him, can assist his integration in the host country and thus contribute to the achievement of free movement of workers. Consequently, this possibility must also be regarded as falling within the concept of a social advantage, for the purposes of Article 7, §2 of Regulation No. 1612/68,[2] so it must be accorded to a migrant worker as it is to the national worker.

1. *Diatta* Case, *op. cit.*
2. *Read* Case, *op. cit.*

280. The right to equal treatment related to training, provided for in Article 12 of the regulation, also benefits the children of a migrant worker who is deceased.[1] In *Brown* v. *the Secretary of State of Scotland*, the case concerned a child who was born after his parents had ceased to work and reside in the United Kingdom. As a result, he never had the status of a member of a worker's family in the United Kingdom. The Court ruled that the fifth recital in the preamble to Regulation No. 1612/68 indicates that that regulation is intended to establish freedom of movement for workers by, *inter alia*, eliminating obstacles to the mobility of workers, in particular as regards the worker's right to be joined by his family and the condition for the integration of his family into the host country. It follows that Article 12 of the regulation must be interpreted as meaning that it grants rights only to a child who has lived with his parents or one of them in a Member State whilst at least one of his parents resided there as a worker. It cannot therefore create rights for the benefit of worker's child who was born after the worker ceased to work and reside in the host State.[2] Article 12 does not apply either in the case of children of migrant workers residing in another State, or to the State in which the children go to school. Article 12 does not preclude a Member State from imposing a fee as a condition for admission to ordinary schooling within its territory on those children, even though it does not impose it on nationals.[3] On the other hand, a child of a migrant worker retains his status as a member of the family when that family returns to the Member State of origin and the child, even after a period of interruption, stays in the host State to pursue an education which he could not continue in the country of origin.[4]

As the Court of Justice has consistently held,[5] the principle of equal treatment set out in Article 12 of the Regulation extends to all forms of education, whether vocational or general, including university courses. The same principle requires that the child of a migrant worker be able to continue his studies in order to complete his education successfully.

Consequently, Article 12 of the Regulation also encompasses financial assistance for those students who are already at an advanced stage in their education, even if they are already 21 years of age or older and are no longer dependants of their parents. Accordingly, to make the application of Article 12 subject to an age-limit or to the status of dependent child would conflict not only with the letter of that provision, but also with its spirit.

1. COJ, 27 September 1988, *Commission v. Belgium*, No. 42/87, IELL, *Case Law*, No. 129.
2. COJ, 17 Sept. 1987, *Steven Malcom Brown v. Secretary of State for Scotland*, No. 197/86.
3. COJ, 27 September 1988, *Belgium v. R. Humbel and M.T. Edel*, No. 263/86, IELL, *Case Law*, No. 130.
4. COJ, 15 March 1989, *G.B.C. Echternach and A. Moritz v. Dutch Minister of Education and Sciences*, Joined Case Nos. 389–390/87, IELL, *Case Law*, No.133.
5. COJ, 4 May 1995, *Landesambt für Ausbildungsförderung Nordrhein-Westfalen v. Lubor Gaal*, C-7/94, *Jur.*, 1995, 1031.

III. Exceptions

A. *Employment in the Public Sector*

281.   Pursuant to Article 48, §4 of the EC Treaty, the provisions of free movement for workers do not apply to employment in the public sector. This provision has given cause to a great deal of controversy. The Court is, for evident reasons, of the opinion that the term 'employment in the public sector' requires uniform interpretation and application throughout the Community. It should indeed be recalled, as the Court has constantly emphasised in its case-law, that recourse to the provisions of the domestic legal system to restrict the scope of the provisions of Community law would have the effect of impairing the unity and efficacy of that law and consequently cannot be accepted.[1] Moreover, it must be borne in mind that, as a derogation from the fundamental principle that workers in the Community should enjoy freedom of movement and not suffer discrimination, Article 48, §4 must be construed in such a way that it limits its scope to what is strictly necessary for safeguarding the interests which that provision allows the Member States to protect.[2] The Court comes to the conclusion that 'employment in the public sector' must be understood as meaning those posts which involve direct or indirect participation in the exercise of powers conferred by public law in the discharge of functions whose purpose is to safeguard the general interests of the State or of other public authorities. In order to carry out these functions, a special relationship of allegiance to the State on the part of persons occupying them and the reciprocity of rights and duties which form the foundation of the bond of nationality is needed.[3] Thus the Court retains the content of the function and not the legal qualification of the employment relationship as a criterion:

> 'in the absence of any distinction in the provision Article 48, §4, it is of no interest whether a worker is engaged as a blue-collar worker (*ouvrier*), a white-collar worker (*employé*) or an official (*fonctionnaire*) or even whether the terms on which he is employed come under public or private law.'

Finally, it should be indicated that Article 48, §4 only relates to the access to public employment. It cannot justify discriminatory measures with regard to remuneration or other conditions of employment once they have been admitted to the public sector.[4]

1. COJ, 17 December 1980, *Commission v. Belgium*, No. 149/79, IELL, *Case Law*, No. 39.
2. *Lawrie-Blum* Case, *op. cit.*
3. *Idem.*
4. *Sotgiu* Case, *op. cit.*

282.   The following jobs are not considered to be public functions: post office workers;[1] trainee locomotive drivers, loaders, plate-layers, shunters and signallers with the national railways and unskilled workers with the local railways as well as posts for hospital nurses, children's nurses, night-watch men, plumbers, carpenters, electricians, garden hands, architects and supervisors with a municipality;[2] permanent employment as a nurse in a public hospital;[3] a trainee teacher;[4] a researcher;[5] a foreign-language teacher at a university[6] and a secondary school teacher.[7] The same goes for posts in the public sectors of research, teaching, health, transport, ports and telecommunications, and in the water, gas and electricity distribution services.[8] On the other hand, duties of managing or advising the State on scientific questions could be described as employment in the public sector within the meaning of Article 48, §4.[9] Finally, one should note that a Member State may reserve the promotion to certain public functions that involve participation in the exercise of power to its own nationals.[10]

Article 90(1) of the EC Treaty, in conjunction with Articles 30, 48 and 86, precludes rules of a Member State which confer on an undertaking established in that State the exclusive right to organise dock work and requires it for that purpose to have recourse to a dock-work company whose workforce is composed exclusively of nationals.[11]

1. *Sotgiu* Case, *op. cit.*
2. *Commission v. Belgium*, No. 149/79.
3. COJ, 3 June 1986, *Commission v. France*, No. 307/84, IELL, *Case Law*, No. 95.
4. *Lawrie-Blum* Case, *op. cit.*
5. COJ, 16 June 1987, *Commission v. Italy*, No. 225/85, IELL, *Case Law*, No. 104.
6. COJ, 30 May 1989, *P. Allué and C.M. Coonan v. Università degli Studi di Venezia*, No. 33/88, IELL, *Case Law*, No. 136.
7. 27 November 1991, *A. Bleis v. Ministère de l' Education Nationale*, No. C-4/91, IELL, *Case Law*, No. 177.
8. COJ, 2 July 1996, *Commission v. Luxemburg*, Case C-473/93, not yet published; *see also* COJ 2 July 1996, *Commission v. Belgium* (distribution of water, gas and electricity), Case C-173/94; 2 July 1996, *Commission v. Hellas*, Case C-290/94, not yet published.
9. *Commission v. Italy*, No. 225/85.
10. *Commission v. Belgium*, No. 149/79.
11. COJ, 10 December 1991, *Merci Convenzionali Porto di Genova v. Siderurgica Gabrielli SpA*, No. C-179/90, IELL, *Case Law*, No. 178.

B. Public Policy, Security and Public Health

283.   Pursuant to Article 48, §3 of the EC Treaty, free movement for workers entails the right:

a. to accept offers of employment actually made;
b. to move freely within the territory of Member States for this purpose;
c. to stay in a Member State for the purpose of employment in accordance with the provisions governing the employment of nationals of that State laid down by law, regulation or administrative action;
d. to remain in the territory of a Member State after having been employed in that State, subject to conditions which shall be embodied in implementing regulations to be drawn up by the Commission.

These rights are however subject to limitations justified on grounds of public policy, public security or public health. These limitations were more precisely defined in Directive No. 64/221 of 25 February 1964,[1] which aims at protecting the nationals of other Member States against possible abuse of these limitations regarding the free movement of workers.

1. Directive on the coordination of special measures concerning the movement and residence of foreign nationals that are justified on the grounds of public policy, public security or public health, O.J., No. L 56, 4 April 1964.

284. Taken as a whole, these limitations, placed on the powers of Member States in respect of the control of aliens, are a specific manifestation of the more general principle enshrined in Articles 8, 9, 10 and 11 of the Convention for the Protection of Human Rights and Fundamental Freedoms, signed in Rome on 4 November 1950 and ratified by all the Member States, and in Article 2 of Protocol No. 4 of the same Convention, signed in Strasbourg on 16 September 1963. These provide in identical terms that no restrictions in the interests of national security or public safety shall be placed on the rights secured by the above quoted Articles other than such as are necessary for the protection of those interests in a democratic society.[1] There are moreover procedural safeguards:

'any person enjoying the protection of the provisions of Directive No. 64/221 must be entitled to a double safeguard comprising notification to him of the grounds on which any restrictive measure has been adopted in his case and the availability of a right of appeal.'[2]

1. COJ, 28 October 1975, *Roland Rutilly* v. *Minister for the Interior*, No. 36/75, IELL, *Case Law*, No. 19.
2. *Idem.*

1. Scope of Application

285. Directive No. 64/221 applies, *ratione personae*, to any national of a Member State who resides in or travels to another Member State, either in order to pursue an activity as an employed or self-employed person, or as a recipient of services (Art. 1, §1), e.g., tourists. The directive applies also to the spouse and the members of the family, who enjoy freedom of movement (Art. 1, §2).

Ratione materiae, the directive relates to all measures concerning the entry into their territory, the issue and renewal of residence permits, or exclusion from their territory, taken by Member States on grounds of public policy, public security or public health. Such grounds cannot be invoked to service economic grounds (Art. 2).

The expression 'subject to limitations justified on the grounds of public policy' concerns not only the legislative provisions which each Member State has adopted to limit freedom of movement and residence for nationals of other Member States within its territory but also concerns individual decisions taken in application of such legislative provisions.[1] Prohibition on residence may be imposed only in respect of the whole of the national territory; in the case of partial prohibitions on residence, limited to certain areas of the territory; persons covered by Community law must, under Article 6 of the EC Treaty, be treated on equal footing with the nationals of the Member States concerned.[2]

1. *Rutilly* Case, *op. cit.*
2. *Idem.*

2. Grounds of Public Policy or Security

286. It should be emphasised that the concept of public policy, in the context of the Community and where, in particular, it is used as a justification for derogating from the fundamental principle of freedom of movement for workers, must be interpreted strictly so that its scope cannot be determined unilaterally by each Member State without being subject to control by the institutions of the Community. Nevertheless, the particular circumstances justifying recourse to the concept of public policy may vary from one country to another country and from one period to another, and it is therefore necessary in this matter to allow the competent national authorities an area of discretion within the limits imposed by the EC Treaty.[1] In any event, the concept of 'public policy' presupposes the existence, in addition to the perturbation to the social order which any infringement of the law involves, of a genuine and sufficiently serious threat affecting one of the fundamental interests of society.[2]

1. COJ, 4 December 1974, *Y. van Duyn* v. *Home Office*, No. 41/74, IELL, *Case Law*, No. 13; 27 October 1997, *Regina* v. *P. Boucherau*, No. 30/77, IELL, *Case Law*, No. 28.
2. 'It follows that a Member State, for reasons of public policy can, where it seems necessary, refuse a national of another Member State the benefit of the freedom of movement for workers in a case where such a national proposes to take up a particular offer of employment even though the Member State does not place a similar restriction upon its own nationals. It is a principle of international law, which the EC Treaty cannot be assumed to disregard in the relations between Member States, that a State is precluded from refusing its own national the right of residence' (*Van Duyn* Case, *op. cit.*). *See also: Regina* Case, *op. cit.*

287. Measures taken on grounds of public policy or of public security must be based exclusively on the *personal conduct* of the individual concerned (Art. 3, §1).[1] This provision of the directive confers on individuals the rights that are enforceable by them in the national courts of a Member State and which the national courts must protect.[2]

Article 3 of Directive No. 64/221 imposes on Member States the duty to base their decision on the individual circumstances of any person under the protection of Community law and not on general considerations.[3]

The association with a body or an organisation involving participation in its activities, as well as the identification with its aims and its designs, may be considered a voluntary act of the person concerned and, consequently, as part of his personal conduct.[4]

1. The term 'measures' in Article 2 relates only to provisions laid down by law, regulations or administrative action, to the exclusion of the action of the judiciary. The term 'measures' in Article 3 includes the action of a court which is required by the law to recommend in certain cases the deportation of a national of a another Member State (*op. cit.*).
2. *Van Duyn* Case, *op. cit.*
3. *Rutilly* Case, *op. cit.*
4. *Van Duyn* Case, *op. cit.*

288.   Previous criminal convictions do not in themselves constitute grounds for taking measures to limit the free movement for workers and their dependents (Art. 3, §2). These convictions are relevant only insofar as the circumstances which gave rise to them are evidence of personal conduct constituting a present threat to the requirements of public policy.[1] The directive therefore prevents the deportation of a national of a Member State who is unlawfully in possession of arms and who causes the death of his brother by negligence, if such a deportation is ordered for the purpose of deterring other aliens, that is, if it is based on reasons of a general preventive nature.[2] The mere failure by a national of a Member State to comply with the formalities concerning entry, movement and residence of aliens is not of such a nature as to constitute in itself conduct threatening public policy and public security and cannot therefore by itself justify a measure ordering expulsion or temporary imprisonment for that purpose.[3] Likewise, a Member State may not, by virtue of the reservation relating to public policy, expel a national of another Member State from its territory or refuse him access to its territory by reason of conduct which, when attributable to the former State's own nationals, does not give rise to repressive measures or other genuine and effective measures intended to combat such conduct.[4]

Expiry of the identity card or passport used by the person concerned to enter the host country and to obtain a residence permit does not justify expulsion from the country (Art. 3, §3). The State that issued the identity card or passport must allow the holder of such document to re-enter its territory without any formality even if the document is no longer valid or the nationality of the holder is in dispute (Art. 3, §4).

1. *Regina* Case, *op. cit.*
2. COJ, 26 February 1975, *C.A. Bonsignore* v. *Oberstadtdirektor Köln*, No. 67/74, IELL, *Case Law*, No. 17.
3. COJ, 8 April 1976, *J.N. Royer*, No. 48/75, IELL, *Case Law*, No. 23.
4. COJ, 18 May 1982, *Rezguia Adoui* v. *Belgian State and City of Liège; Dominique Cornuaille* v. *Belgian State*, Joined Cases Nos. 115 and 116/81. The case related to prostitution in Belgium.

3. Public Health

289.   The only diseases or disabilities justifying refusal of entry into a territory or refusal to issue a first residence permit are those listed in the annex to the directive

(Art. 4, §1). Diseases or disabilities occurring after a first residence permit has been issued do not justify refusal to renew the residence permit or expulsion from the territory (Art. 4, §2).

4. Procedural Safeguards

290.   A decision to grant or refuse a first residence permit must be taken as soon as possible and in any event not later than six months from the date of application for the permit. The person concerned is allowed to remain temporarily in the territory pending a decision. The host country may, if necessary, request the Member State of origin of the applicant and other Member States to provide information concerning any previous police record. Such enquiries cannot be made as a matter of routine. The Member State consulted must give its reply within two months (Art. 4, §5). In the case of expulsion, a reapplication for a residence permit may be lodged after a reasonable period has elapsed. Such an application must be examined by the appropriate administrative authority in the host State, which must take into account, in particular, the arguments put forward in order to establish that there has been a material change in the circumstances justifying the first expulsion measure.[1]

   1. *Adoui* Case, *op. cit.*

291.   An important safeguard is self-evidently the fact that one knows the reasons for limiting the right of free movement. These reasons must be made known unless this is contrary to the interests of the security of the State involved (Art. 6). It is clear from the purpose of the directive that the notification of the grounds must be sufficiently detailed and precise to enable the person concerned to defend his interests. It is sufficient in any event that the notification be made in such a way as to enable the person concerned to comprehend the content and the effect thereof.[1] The person concerned must be officially notified of any decision to refuse the issue or renewal of a residence permit or to expel him from the territory. The period allowed for leaving the country must be stated in this notification. Except in cases of urgency, this period may not be less than fifteen days if the person concerned has not yet been granted a residence permit and not less than one month in all other cases (Art. 7).

   1. *Adoui* Case, *op. cit.*

292.   Against decisions limiting the freedom of movement, the same legal remedies as those open to nationals of the host State must be made available (Art. 8). In this connection, it should be emphasised that Article 9 is complementary to Article 8. Article 9 imposes obligations on Member States which may be relied upon by the persons concerned before national courts. Article 9 provides that where there is no right of appeal to a court of law, or where such an appeal may only be in respect of the legal validity of the decision, or where the appeal cannot have suspensory effect, a decision cannot, except in cases of urgency, be taken by the administrative authority until an opinion has been obtained from a competent authority of the host country. The directive leaves a margin of discretion to Member

States for defining 'the competent' authority. Any public authority independent of the administrative authority, which is so constituted that the person concerned enjoys the right of representation and of defence to it, as the domestic law of that country provides for, may be considered as such an authority.[1] These conditions may not be less favourable to the person concerned than those applicable to proceedings before other national authorities of the same type.[2] The directive does not require the authority to be a court or to be composed of members of the judiciary.[3] Any decision refusing the issue of a first residence permit or ordering the expulsion of the person concerned before the issue of the permit must, where that person so requests, be referred for consideration to the authority whose prior opinion is required. The person concerned is then entitled to submit his defence in person, except where this would be contrary to the interests of national security (Art. 9, §2). A decision ordering expulsion cannot be executed, except in cases of urgency that have been properly justified, against a person protected by Community law until the party concerned has been able to exhaust the remedies guaranteed by Articles 8 and 9 of Directive No. 64/221.[4] However, it cannot be inferred from that provision that the person concerned is entitled to remain on the territory of the State concerned throughout the proceedings initiated by him. Such an interpretation, which would unilaterally enable the person to suspend the measure affecting him by lodging an application, is incompatible with the objective of the directive. This objective is to reconcile the requirements of public policy, public security and public health with the guarantees that must be provided for the persons affected by such measures as long as the person concerned is able to obtain a fair hearing and to present his defence in full.[5]

Finally, it should be pointed out that Directive No. 64/221 also applies to workers with the right to be employed in the territory of a Member State after having been employed in that State,[6] to students,[7] to employees and self-employed persons who have ceased their occupational activity[8] and in the case of right of residence in general.[9]

1. COJ, 22 May 1980, *Regina* v. *Secretary of State for Home Affairs ex parte M. Santillo*, No. 131/79, IELL, *Case Law*, No. 37.
2. *Adoui* Case, *op. cit.*
3. *Idem.*
4. *Royer* Case, *op. cit.*
5. COJ, 5 March 1980, *Josette Pescastaign* v. *Belgian State*, No. 98/79, IELL, *Case Law*, No. 34.
6. Directive of 18 May 1972, No. 72/194, O.J., 26 May 1972, No. L 121/26.
7. Directive of 29 October 1993, No. 93/96, *op. cit.*
8. Directive of 28 June 1990, No. 90/365, O.J., 13 July 1990, No. L 180/28.
9. Directive of 28 June 1990, No. 90/364, O.J., 13 July 1990, No. L 180/26.

§3. PROMOTION

I. Employment Services

293.   Free movement for workers in a single market demands the development of a direct cooperation between the central and regional employment services. This cooperation was established by Regulation No. 1612/68 of 15 October 1968 regarding the clearing of vacancies and applications for employment and the resulting placing of workers in employment along with the exchange of information and the making of studies of employment and unemployment with the view to securing freedom of movement for workers within the Community (Arts. 13–14). The specialist service of each Member State shall regularly send to the specialist services of the other Member States and to the European Co-ordination Office:

a. details of vacancies which could be filled by nationals of other Member States;
b. details of vacancies addressed to non-Member States;
c. details of applications for employment by those who have formally expressed a wish to work in another Member State;
d. information, region and by branch of activity, on applicants who have declared themselves actually willing to accept employment in another country.

The specialist service of each Member State shall forward this information to the appropriate employment services and agencies as soon as possible.

The details of vacancies and applications will be circulated according to a uniform system to be established by the European Coordination Office in collaboration with the Technical Committee.

If necessary, the European Coordination Office may adapt this system in collaboration with the Technical Committee (Art. 15).

Any vacancy communicated to the employment services of a Member State shall be notified to and processed by the competent employment services of the other Member State concerned.

Such services shall forward to the services of the first Member State the details of suitable applications.

The applications for employment shall be responded to by the relevant services of the Member States within a reasonable period, not exceeding one month.

The employment services shall grant workers who are nationals of the Member States the same priority as the relevant measures grant to nationals *vis-à-vis* workers from non-Member States.[1]

  1. Amended by Regulation 2434/92 of 27 July 1992.

294. The regulation also contains measures for controlling the balance of the labour market. On the basis of a report from the Commission, drawn up from the information supplied by the Member States, the latter and the Commission shall at least once a year analyse jointly the results of Community arrangements regarding vacancies and applications.[1]

The Commission and the Member States will also examine the possibilities of giving priority to nationals of Member States when filing employment vacancies in order to achieve a balance between vacancies and applications for employment within the Community (Art. 19.2).

Regulation No. 1612/68 established a European Coordination Office with the task of promoting vacancy clearance at Community level (Art. 21), as well as an Advisory Committee responsible for studies and advice (Arts. 24–31) and a Technical Committee charged with the mission to assist the Commission (Arts. 32–37).

  1. As amended by Council Regulation (EEC) No. 2434/92 of 27 July 1992 amending Part II of Regulation (EEC) No. 1612/68 on freedom of movement for workers within the Community, O.J., 26 August 1992, No. L 245.

II. Vocational Training

295. The Commission has the task of promoting close cooperation between Member States regarding basic and advanced vocational training (Art. 118, EEC Treaty). Article 128 of the EC Treaty was replaced by Article 127 introduced by the Maastricht Treaty (1991).

Article 127, underlining the principle of subsidiarity, reads as follows:

'1. The Community shall implement a vocational training policy which shall support and supplement the action of the Member States, while fully respecting the responsibility of the Member States for the content and organisation of vocational training.

2. Community action shall aim to:
– facilitate adaptation to industrial changes, in particular through vocational training and retraining;
– improve initial and continuing vocational training in order to facilitate vocational integration and reintegration into the labour market;
– facilitate access to vocational training and encourage mobility of instructors and trainees and particularly young people;
– stimulate cooperation on training between educational or training establishments and firms;
– develop exchanges of information and experience on issues common to the training systems of the Member States.

3. The Community and the Member States shall foster cooperation with third countries and the competent international organisations in the sphere of vocational training.'

To implement these goals, the European Centre for the Development of Vocational Training was established in 1975. Mention should be made of Article 50 of the EC Treaty which provides for the exchange of young workers between Member States within the framework of a joint programme, as well as of Council Recommendation of 30 June 1993 on access to continuing vocational training.[1]

1. O.J., 23 July 1993, No. 181, 37.

296. By a decision of 2 April 1963, the Council laid down the general principles for implementing a common vocational training policy (No. 63/266).[1] These general principles must enable every person to receive adequate training with due regard to freedom of choice of occupation, place of training and place of work. The common vocational training policy should enable every person to acquire the technical knowledge and skills necessary to pursue a given occupation and to reach the highest possible level of training, whilst encouraging, particularly in regard to young persons, intellectual and physical advancement, civic education and physical development. The general guidelines laid down by the Council in 1971 state that:

'in view of the constantly changing needs of the economy, the aim of vocational training should be to offer the opportunity of basic and advanced training and a continuity of in-service training designed, from a general and vocational point of view, to enable the individual to develop his personality and to take up a career.'

This led the Court to rule in the *Gravier* Case:

'that any form of education which prepares for a qualification of a particular profession, trade or employment or which provides the necessary training and skills for such a profession, trade or employment, is vocational training whatever the age and the level of training of the pupils or students, even if the training programme includes an element of general education.'[2]

1. O.J. No. 63, 20 April 1963, 1338/63.
2. COJ, 13 February 1985, *Françoise Gravier* v. *City of Liège*, No. 293/83, IELL, *Case Law*, No. 71.

297.   With regard to the issue whether university studies prepare for a qualification for a particular profession, trade or employment or provide the necessary training and skills for these, it must be emphasised that this is the case not only where the final academic examination directly provides the required qualification for a particular profession, trade or employment, but also insofar as the studies in question provide specific training and skills, even if no legislative or administrative provisions make acquisition of that knowledge a prerequisite for that purpose. In general, therefore, university studies fulfil these criteria. The only exceptions are certain courses of study which, because of their particular nature, are intended for persons wishing to improve their general knowledge rather than prepare themselves for an occupation.[1]

1. COJ, 2 February 1988, *Vincent Blaizot* v. *Université de Liège*, No. 24/86, IELL, *Case Law*, No. 118.

298.   The meaning of the term 'vocational training' is somewhat restricted by Article 57 of the EC Treaty. This article relates to the directives for the mutual recognition of diplomas, certificates and other evidence of formal qualifications. Consequently, these directives, even when they relate to vocational training, are not covered by Article 127 of the EC Treaty.[1]

1. COJ, 30 May 1989, *Commission* v. *Council*, No. 242/87, IELL, *Case Law*, No. 135 *bis*, Jur. 1989, 1925.

299.   In the above-mentioned *Gravier* Case,[1] the Court was of the opinion that the common vocational policy referred to in Article 127 of the Treaty is gradually being established and that it constitutes an indispensable element of the free movement of persons. Access to vocational training is in particular likely to promote free movement of persons throughout the Community by enabling them to obtain a qualification in the Member State where they intend to work and to complete their training and develop their particular talents in the Member State whose vocational training programmes include the special subject desired. It follows from all the foregoing that the conditions of access to vocational training fall within the scope

of the Treaty and that the imposition on students who are nationals of other Member States of a charge, a registration fee or the so-called 'minerval' as a condition of access to vocational training, where the same fee is not imposed on students who are nationals of the host Member State, constitutes discrimination on grounds of nationality contrary to Article 6 of the Treaty.

Article 6 of the Treaty therefore applies to financial aid granted by a Member State to its own nationals in order to allow them to follow a course of vocational training in so far as that aid is intended to cover the costs of access to the courses.

A national of a Member State who has been admitted to a course of vocational training in another Member State derives from Community law a right of residence in the second Member State for the purpose of following that course and for the duration thereof. That right may be exercised regardless of whether the host Member State has issued a residence permit. The right of residence in question may nevertheless be made subject to certain conditions to which the prohibition of discrimination with regard to access to vocational training does not apply.[2]

1. *Gravier* Case, *op. cit.; see also* COJ, 3 May 1994, *Commission* v. *Belgium*, No. C-47/93, *Jur.*, 1994, 1593.
2. COJ, 26 February 1992, *V.J.M. Raulin* v. *Netherlands Ministry of Education and Science*, No. C-357/89, IELL, *Case Law*, No. 184.

300. Whilst it is true that the conditions for access to vocational training, including university studies in general, fall within the scope of the Treaty for the purposes of Article 6 thereof, assistance given by a Member State to its nationals when they undertake such studies nevertheless fall outside the Treaty, at the present stage of development of Community law, except to the extent to which such assistance is intended to cover registration and other fees, in particular tuition fees, charged for access to education.[1]

Article 6 of the EC Treaty, the Court furthermore states, precludes a Member State from requiring a student who is a national of another Member State and who enjoys, under Community law, a right of residence in the host Member State, to possess a residence permit in order to be entitled to benefit under the system of funding study costs.[2]

1. COJ, 21 June 1988, *Sylvie Lair* v. *Universität Hannover*, No. 39/86, IELL, *Case Law*, No. 124.
2. COJ, 26 February 1992, *V.J.M. Raulin* v. *Netherlands Ministry of Education and Science*, No. C-357/89, IELL, *Case Law*, No. 184.

III. Recognition of Qualifications and Diplomas

301. It is self-evident that, given the ever-increasing education of Europeans and advanced training, there can only be full-fledged free movement for workers once diplomas obtained in one Member State are valid in the other Member States.[1] With this aim in view, the Council adopted a number of directives concerning the mutual recognition of diplomas, certificates and other evidence of formal qualifications (Art. 57, EC Treaty). Notwithstanding the fact that Article 57 relates to self-employed persons only, one must ascertain that some of those directives, such as those concerning medical doctors, pharmacists and others, contain a clause making those directives also applicable to the workers and their dependents as stated in Directive No. 1612/68.

1. However, Article 48 of the EC Treaty does not preclude a Member State from prohibiting one of its own nationals who holds an academic title acquired through postgraduate studies and awarded in another Member State from using that title in its territory without obtaining administrative authorisation for that purpose. The authorisation procedure must be intended solely to verify whether the academic title acquired through postgraduate studies was duly awarded, must be easily accessible and is not subject to the payment of excessive administrative charges. Furthermore, the decision that is taken must be open to judicial review, the person concerned must be able to ascertain the grounds for that decision and the penalties prescribed for non-observance of the authorisation procedure may not be disproportionate to the seriousness of the offense. *See*: COJ, 31 March 1993, *Dieter Kraus* v. *Land Baden Württemberg*, No. C-19/92, not yet published.

302. It soon became clear, however, that it is impossible to make individual directives for each profession, a training programme of its own included, and that more general measures are indicated. Such a general measure is Council Decision No. 85/368 of 16 July 1985 on the comparability of vocational training qualifications between the Member States of the European Community.[1] The Commission establishes this comparability in close cooperation with the Member States and the organisations of workers and employers at Community level. To that end:

– the relevant occupations or groups of occupations are selected on a proposal from the Member States or the competent employer or worker organisations at Community level;
– mutually agreed job descriptions for the occupations are drawn up;
– the vocational training qualifications recognised in the various Member States are matched with the job descriptions.

Finally, tables incorporating information are established on the level of vocational training, the vocational titles and the corresponding vocational training qualifications, the organisations and institutions responsible for dispensing vocational training and the organisations competent to issue or to validate diplomas, certificates or other documents certifying that vocational training has been acquired (Art. 3).

1. O.J., 31 July 1985, No. L 199/29.

303. Of capital importance is Directive No. 89/48 of 21 December 1988 on a general system for the recognition of higher-education diplomas awarded on completion of professional education and training of at least three years' duration.[1] This directive applies to any national of a Member State wishing to pursue a regulated profession in a host Member State in a self-employed capacity or as an employed person (Art. 2, §1). In a nutshell, the directive provides that the holder of a diploma of a post-secondary course of at least three years' duration can take up or pursue that profession in any Member State. The same applies if the applicant has pursued the profession in question full-time for two years during the previous ten years in another Member State which does not regulate that profession (Arts. 1 and 3).

Notwithstanding this, the host Member State may under certain conditions require the applicant to provide evidence of professional experience or to complete an adaptation period not exceeding three years or to take an aptitude test (Art. 4). The host State may allow the applicant to undergo there, on the basis of equivalence, that part of his professional education and training that is required and which he has not undergone in his Member State of origin (Art. 5). The directive contains further rules concerning the eventual proof of good character, whether the applicants have been declared bankrupt or not as well as concerning the suspension or prohibition of the pursuit of the profession (Art. 6); it also regulates the use of professional titles of the host State corresponding to that profession (Art. 7). Finally, attention must be drawn to the *Heylens* Case in which the Court ruled that:

> 'where in a Member State access to an occupation [in this case football trainer] as an employed person is dependent upon the possession of a national certificate or a foreign diploma recognised as equivalent, the principle of free movement of workers laid down in Article 48 of the EC Treaty requires that it must be possible for a decision refusing to recognise the equivalence of a diploma granted to a worker who is a national of another Member State by the Member State to be made the subject of judicial proceedings in which its legality under Community law can be reviewed, and for the person concerned to ascertain the reasons for the decision.'[2]

The Council Directive 89/48 limits itself to the recognition of higher education diplomas awarded on completion of professional education and training of at least three years' duration. Other forms of professional education fall outside the scope of Directive No. 89/48. In order to also cover these, a new directive was passed, Directive No. 92/51 on a second general system for the recognition of professional education and training to supplement Directive 89/48.[3] This complementary general system is based on the same principles and contains the same rules as the initial general system. This complementary system covers levels of education and training not covered by the initial general system, namely that corresponding to other post-secondary education and training courses, and that corresponding to long or short secondary courses, possibly complemented by professional training or experience.

Since the complementary system covers occupations the pursuit of which is dependent on the possession of professional or vocational education and training qualifications of secondary level and generally requires manual skills, the complementary system must also provide for the recognition of such qualifications even when they have been acquired solely through professional experience in a Member State which does not regulate such professions. The Directive 92/51 contains several systems of recognition, namely the system where a host Member State requires possession of a diploma (Arts. 3 and 4); the system where a host Member State requires possession of a diploma and the applicant is the holder of a certificate or has received corresponding education and training (Art. 5); and the system of recognition where a host Member State requires possession of a certificate (Arts. 6 and 7). Articles 8 and 9 of the Directive 92/51 deal with special systems for the recognition of other qualifications.

Mention should also be made of the Resolution of 3 December 1992 concerning transparency of qualifications[4] and the Joint Opinion of the Social Partners of 3 July 1992 on vocational qualifications and certification.

1. O.J., 24 January 1989, No. L 19/16. A profession cannot be described as regulated when there are in the host Member State no laws, regulations or administrative provisions governing the taking up or pursuit of that profession or of one of its modes or pursuit, even though the only education and training leading to it consists of at least four and a half years of higher-education studies on completion of which a diploma is awarded and, consequently, only persons possessing that higher-education diploma as a rule seek employment in and pursue that profession (COJ, 1 February 1996, *Georgios Aranitis* v. *Land Berlin*, Case C-164/94, *Jur.*, 1996, 135).
2. 15 October 1987, No. 226/86, IELL, *Case Law*, No. 111.
3. O.J., 24 July 1992, No. L 209/25.
4. O.J., 19 February 1993, No. C 49/1.

Chapter 2. International Private Labour Law

304. International private labour law deals with the question: which judge has jurisdiction and which legal system is applicable in the case where a labour contract is based on various legal systems and consequently more than one judge and more than one legal system could be competent to solve a given legal conflict. In this case, two European conventions should be mentioned, namely: the Convention on Jurisdiction and the Enforcement of Judgments in Civil and Commercial Matters of 27 September 1968, on the one hand, and the Convention on the Law applicable to Contractual Obligations of 19 June 1980, on the other.[1]
A Directive of 16 December 1996 concerns the posting of workers.

1. *See* the consolidated versions and the protocols on the interpretation by the Court of Justice, O.J., 26 January 1998, C 27/1.

§1. THE COMPETENT JUDGE

305. The Convention of 1968 lays down the rules to indicate which judge is competent in the case of a labour contract with international aspects, when e.g., a French worker is employed by an American undertaking in Germany.[1] Article 1 of the Convention states that the Convention shall apply in civil and commercial matters whatever the nature of the court or tribunal. It is generally accepted that labour law conflicts are civil law matters and that the Convention is thus applicable in regard to questions of labour law.[2] The Convention, however, does not apply to social security (Art. 1, §3). Yet this does not diminish the fact that the Convention applies when a case relates at the same time to labour law and to social security law, provided that the labour law aspect is predominant. The Convention is not applicable in cases of arbitration (Art. 1, §4).

1. *See*: B. Massant and F. Tilleman, 'Grensoverschrijdende arbeidsrelaties in het internationaal arbeidsrecht,' in: *Werken zonder Grenzen, Fiscale en juridische aspecten van grensoverschrijdende tewerkstelling*, H. van Hoogenbemt (ed.), Kalmthout, 1990, 13–26.
2. COJ, 13 November 1979, No. 25/79, *Sanicentral GmbH* v. *R. Collin*, IELL, *Case Law*, No. 33*bis*; 26 May 1982, Case No. 133/81, *Ivenel* v. *Schwab*, IELL, *Case Law*, No. 47*bis*.

306. Persons domiciled in a Contracting State[1] shall, whatever their nationality, be sued in the courts of that State. Persons who are not nationals of the State in which they are domiciled shall be governed by the rules of jurisdiction applicable to nationals of that State (Art. 2). The notions of domicile and jurisdiction of the courts of each Contracting State are determined by the law of that State. The Convention also contains rules providing for special jurisdiction:

– a person domiciled in a Contracting State may, in another Contracting State, be sued:
  1. in matters relating to a contract, in the courts for the place of performance of the obligation in question (Art. 5, §1); this is, as far as an employment contract is concerned, the place where the employee habitually carries out his work. If the employee does not habitually carry out his work in any one country, the employer may be sued in the courts for the place where the business which engaged the employee was or is now situated;[2]

     The interpretation of Article 5,1 was raised concerning an employment contract which was performed in various States in connection with a dispute between Mulox IBC Limited, an English company with its registered office in London, and a former employee, Hendrick Geels, a Netherlands national resident in Aix-les-Bains (France), following termination of his employment contract by his employer.

     Mr. Geels brought an action against his former employer before the Counseil des Prud'hommes, Aix-les-Bains, for compensation in lieu of notice plus damages.

     Mulox appealed against that judgment to the Cour d'Appel, Chambéry, arguing that the French courts had no jurisdiction because the place of performance of the employment contract in question was not restricted to France and that Mulox was established in the United Kingdom.

     In the matter of employment contracts, the Court of Justice ruled, the concept of 'place of performance of the relevant obligation' must be interpreted as referring, for the purposes of applying in Article 5(1) of the Convention, to the place where the employee actually carried out the activities agreed with his employer.

     Where the work which the employee is to carry out is performed in the territory of several Contracting States, the place where the contractual obligation is performed, within the meaning of Article 5(1) of the Convention, should be identified rather as the place where or from where the employee principally discharges his obligations on behalf of his employer. In order to determine that place, which is a matter for the national court, account should be taken of the fact, referred to in the main proceedings, that the performance of the duties entrusted to the employee was carried out from an office situated in a Contracting State where the employee had established his residence, from where he carried out his activities and to which he returned after each business trip. Moreover, the national court could take into account the fact that when the dispute was brought before it, the employee was carrying out his work exclusively within that Contracting State. In the absence of other connecting factors, that place must be deemed to be, for the purposes of Article 5(1) of the Convention, the place of performance of the obligation on which is grounded a complaint on the basis of an employment contract.[3] In *Rutten v. Cross Medical Ltd*, the Court ruled that Article 5(1) must be interpreted as meaning that where, in the performance of a contract of employment, an employee carries out his work in several Contracting States, the place where he habitually carries out his work, within the meaning of that provision, is the place where he has established the effective centre of his working activities. When identifying that place, it is necessary to take into account the fact that the employee spends most of his working time in one of the Contracting States in which he has an office where he organizes his activities for his employer and to which he returns after each business trip abroad.[4]

2. in matters relating to tort,[5] delict or quasi-delict in the courts for the place where the harmful event has occurred (Art. 5,3);

3. as regards a civil claim for damages or restitution based on an act giving rise to criminal procedures, in the court of those proceedings, to the extent that the court has jurisdiction under its own law to carry out civil proceedings (Art. 5, §4);

4. as regards a dispute arising out of the operations of a branch, agency or other establishment, in the courts for the place in which the branch, the agency or other establishment is situated (Art. 5, §5). The dispute may relate 'to the local hiring of the staff to work there';[6]

- a person domiciled in a Contracting State may also be sued:
1. where he is one of a number of defendants, in the courts of the place where any of them is domiciled (Art. 6, §1).
2. . . .

1. Namely Belgium, Denmark, France, Germany, Greece, Ireland, Italy, Luxembourg, the Netherlands, Portugal, Spain and the United Kingdom.
2. *See also*: COJ, 15 February 1989, Case No. 32/88, *Six Constructions Ltd* v. *P. Humbert*, IELL, *Case Law*, No. 132*bis*.
3. COJ, *Mulox IBC Limited* v. *H. Geels*, 13 July 1993, No, C–125/92, not yet published.
4. 9 January 1997, C-383/95, not yet published.
5. As e.g., in the case of the non-payment of minimum wages which are mandatory and sanctioned by penal law.
6. COJ, 22 November 1978, *Somafer SA* v. *Saar-Ferngas AG*, No. 33/79, IELL, *Case Law*, No. 29*bis*.

307. If the parties, one or more of whom is domiciled in a Contracting State, have agreed that a court of a Contracting State is to have jurisdiction to settle any disputes, that court shall have exclusive jurisdiction. This agreement must be in writing. National law cannot impose additional validity conditions.[1] The choice of the parties supersedes any other jurisdictional rule. When a defendant does not contest the jurisdiction of the court, it is considered that he accepts it except where he appears solely to contest the jurisdiction (Art. 18).

Finally, Article 21 should be mentioned: when a case is introduced before different courts and relates to the same parties, object and cause, the court before which the case was last introduced, must refer it to the court where the case was first introduced.

1. COJ, 13 November 1979, *Sanicentral GmbH* v. *R. Collin, op. cit.*; 24 June 1981, *Elefanten Schuh* v. *P. Jacqmain*, IELL, *Case Law*, No. 41*bis*: 'the legislation of a Contracting State may not allow the validity of an agreement conferring jurisdiction to be called into question solely on the ground that the language used is not that prescribed by the legislation.'

§2. The Applicable Law

308.   The Convention on the Law applicable to Contractual Obligations of 19 June 1980 applies to contractual obligations, and therefore also to individual employment contracts, in any situation involving a choice between the laws of different countries.[1] Jurisdiction to interpret the Convention rests with the Court of Justice.

> 1. C. Salaert, 'Krachtlijnen van het internationaal privaat arbeidsrecht,' *Tijdschrift voor Sociaal Recht*, 1990, 101–127. The Convention of 19 June 1980 entered into force on 1 April 1991.

309.   Pursuant to Article 3 of the Convention, a contract is governed by the law chosen by the parties. The choice must be expressed or demonstrated with reasonable certainty by the terms of the contract or the circumstances of the case. By their choice, the parties can select the law applicable to the whole or to a part only of the contract (§1). The fact that the parties have chosen a foreign law does not, where all the other elements relevant to the situation at the time of the choice are connected with one country only, prejudice the application of the rules of the law of that country which cannot be derogated from by contract (mandatory rules) (Art. 3, §3). To the extent that the law applicable to the contract has not been chosen, the contract is governed by the law of the country with which it is most closely connected (Art. 4, §1).

310.   The choice for the parties of an individual employment contract is not completely free. Indeed, Article 6 of the Convention provides that: 'notwithstanding the provisions of Article 3, in a contract of employment a choice of law made by the parties shall not have the result of depriving the employee of the protection afforded to him by the mandatory rules of the law which would be applicable in the absence of a choice' (§1). Where there is an absence of choice, a contract of employment is governed:

a. by the law of the country in which the employee habitually carries out his work in performance of the contract, even if he is temporarily employed in another country; or
b. if the employee does not habitually carry out his work in any country, by the law of the country in which the place of business through which he was engaged is situated;

unless it appears from the circumstances as a whole that the contract is more closely connected with another country, in which case the contract will be governed by the law of that country.

311.   This does not mean that the law chosen must yield in its totality; only the least favourable conditions must be let go. Mandatory rules from which the parties cannot deviate concern, for instance, those relating to the health and safety of workers, which can be looked upon as of public order, and those relating to collective labour agreements, which are binding for the employer. The choice of laws regarding the individual employment contract by the Convention clearly indicates the will of the Contracting Parties to limit the freedom of choice of the employer and the employee and to make the law, with which the contract is most closely connected, applicable in most cases.

§3. POSTING OF WORKERS

I. The Proposed Directive of 1991

312. The proposal for a Directive (91/C 225/05) of the Council concerning the posting of workers in the framework of the provision of services was introduced by the Commission on 28 June 1991.[1]

This proposal rightly addresses the question which national labour legislation should be applied to undertakings which post a worker to carry out *temporary work in another Member State.* The solution to this question depends on which criteria are laid down by the conflict of law rules of the Member States for determining the applicable labour law. As the application of these criteria varies under the existing rules of Member States, the outcome may be that the determination of the applicable law gives rise to legal uncertainty, and may give rise to distortions of competition between national and foreign undertakings, making it *difficult to anticipate the working conditions applicable to the undertaking involved.*

To increase legal certainty, the Commission argued, to ascertain in advance the working conditions and to eradicate practices which may be both detrimental to fair competition between undertakings and prejudicial to the interests of the workers concerned, *a coordination of the law of the Member States is needed.* In so doing the Commission is in effect reaffirming its commitment to the principle of *subsidiarity* for, given the dimension, nature and effects of the task involved, the objectives can be undertaken more effectively in common than by the Member States acting separately.

It is self-evident that it is difficult to achieve the completion of the internal market without unifying the conflict of law rules. The disparities of national systems may in fact prove to be an obstacle to the economic freedom envisaged by the Treaty.

Freedom to provide services is one of the fundamental principles of the Treaty and may be restricted only by provisions which are justified by the general good and imposed on all persons operating in the Member States in which the service is to be provided.

Community law does not preclude Member States from applying their legislation or collective labour agreements relating to wages, working time and other matters to any person who is employed albeit temporarily, within their territory, even though his or her employer is established in another State.

With respect to labour law, *the Convention of Rome of 19 June 1980 on the law applicable to contractual obligations* should be mentioned. That Convention came into force on 1 April 1991. It now governs relations between Belgium, Denmark, France, Germany, Greece, Italy, Luxembourg, the United Kingdom, Ireland, Portugal, Spain and the Netherlands.

The Convention lays down general criteria to determining the applicable law and – more importantly – enables the judge to make the contract subject to mandatory rules, sometimes referred to as 'directly applicable rules' applying at the place where the work is carried out (Art. 7). Such immediately applicable rules are not identified by the Convention of Rome. The proposal for a directive sets out to clarify this point by stipulating the body of rules covered by Article 7 of the Convention, i.e., 'public order rules' which constitute a hard core of minimum protection for workers on secondment, collective agreements containing mandatory provisions included.

It is clear from the last recital to the proposed directive that 'this directive is *without prejudice to national laws relative to the hiring out of workers, notably to the functioning of temporary employment business*, as well as to the entry, residence and employment of third country workers.'

1. O.J., 30 August 1991, No. C 225/6. *See also*: Amended proposal for a Council Directive concerning the posting of workers in the framework of the provisions of services, 16 June 1993, O.J., 9 July 1993, No. C 187/5.

A. *Scope*

313. The proposal applies to undertakings which post a worker to carry out temporary work in a Member State other than the State, whether a Member State or otherwise, whose law governs the employment relationship.

According to Article 2 of the proposal, the undertakings must fall in one of the following three categories:

- main contractors or subcontractors which, in the course of carrying out a contract for services, within the meaning of Article 60 of the Treaty, post a worker to carry out temporary work in the territory of a Member State on behalf and under the direction of the undertaking (*subcontracting*, the 'Rush Portuguesa' situation);
- *temporary employment businesses* which place a worker with a user undertaking operating in a Member State to carry out temporary work in so far as there is an employment relationship between the temporary work firm and the employee (the 'Seco' situation);
- undertakings which place a worker with one of their establishments or with another undertaking whether an associated undertaking or not, established in another Member State to carry out temporary work (*intra-firm* or *intra-group mobility*).

No distinction is made between workers posted by a main contractor or by a subcontractor; nor is there a difference of treatment between undertakings posting workers in the framework of a *public contract* or a *private one*.

'The combination and interdependence of Articles 1 and 2 make it unnecessary to incorporate a list of exclusions such as commercial travellers, members of the travelling personnel of an undertaking which operates international transport services for passengers or goods by rail, road, air, internal waterway or by sea, and civil servants and equivalent personnel employed by administrative bodies.'

B. Material Content

314. Article 3, which is the proposal's central provision, does not intend to harmonise the material rules of the Member States concerning labour law and working conditions, but rather to coordinate their conflicts of law rules in order to designate which mandatory rules in force in the host country must be respected by an undertaking posting workers to carry out temporary work in that country. In that sense, 'this is not a labour law instrument,' but a proposal concerning international private law closely related to the freedom to provide services.

In drawing up the list of 'hard core' protective working conditions, the Commission considered that a threefold requirement should be met:

– the rules ought to be mandatory or compulsory in all or the majority of the Member States. That is the case with the provisions concerning the matter refereed to in Article 3(b);
– the rules ought to apply to all employees habitually employed in the same place, occupation and industry. It would not be in conformity with Community law to oblige a foreign provider of services to respect certain working conditions that are not binding on national or local undertakings;
– the designation and application of the envisaged mandatory rules should be compatible with the temporary nature of the performance of work in the host country and consistent with the proposal's stated aims and objectives. In the light of this condition mandatory *rules concerning the form, suspension, alteration and termination of the contract of employment and workers' rights on information, consultation and participation are not dealt with.*

That is also the reason why the proposal excludes undertakings from the observance of *rates of pay and paid leave* in so far as the length of the posting of the employees is *less than three months within a period of reference of one year.* The marginal nature and number of such postings, as well as their limited relevance with respect to practices amounting to the distortion of competition, justify the aforementioned exclusion.

This leads us to the wording of Article 3, which reads as follows:

'Member States shall see to it that, whatever the law applicable to the employment relationship, the undertaking does not deprive the worker of the terms and conditions of employment that apply for work of the same character at the place where the work is temporarily carried out, provided that:
(a) they are laid down by laws, regulations and administrative provisions, collective agreements or arbitration awards, covering the whole of the occupation and industry concerned having an '*erga omnes*' effect and/or being made legally binding in the occupation and industry concerned and

  (b) they concern the following matters:
   (I) maximum daily and weekly hours of work, rest periods, work on Sundays and night work;
   (II) minimum paid holidays;
   (III) the minimum rates of pay, including overtime rates and allowances, but excluding benefits provided for by private occupational schemes;
   (IV) the conditions of hiring out of workers, in particular the supply of workers by temporary employment businesses;
   (V) health, safety and hygiene at work;
   (VI) protective measures with regard to the working conditions of pregnant women or women who have recently given birth, children, young people and other groups enjoying special protection;
   (VII) equality of treatment between man and women and prohibition of discrimination on the grounds of colour, race, religion, opinions, national origin or social background.'

Paragraphs 1(b)(II) and (III) would not apply to employment relationship when the length of the posting of workers is *less than three months*, within a reference period of one year from the beginning of the posting. In calculating the three-month period, account should be taken of any previous periods for which the post has been filled by a posted worker.

II. Directive 96/71 of 16 December 1996[1]

315.   Although the Directive (96/71) merits applause, it should be clearly stated that this measure combats social dumping only to a certain extent, as not all working conditions are covered, neither does it contribute to greater convergence of working conditions in the Common Market, not does it make things simpler.[2]

There is no convergence, since the variety of systems remains as it is; which does not make matters easier, since one will have to be well informed not only about Governmental rules and their interpretation, but also about collective agreements. In practical terms this means that these agreements should be available in official languages of the Members States. Whether this is really feasible is another matter.

---

  1. O.J., C-018, 21 January 1997, p. 1.
  2. 'National legislation which requires an employer, as a person providing a service within the meaning of the Treaty, to pay employer's contributions to the social security fund of the host Member State in addition to the contributions already paid by him to the social security fund of the State where he is established places an additional financial burden on him, so that he is not, so far as competition is concerned, on an equal footing with employers established in the host State.
     The public interest relating to the social protection of workers in the construction industry may however, because of conditions specific to that sector, constitute an overriding requirement justifying such a restriction on the freedom to provide services. However, that is not the case where the workers in question enjoy the same protection, or essentially similar protection, by virtue of employer's contributions already paid by the employer in the Member State of establishment,' and is contrary to Articles 59 and 60 of the EC-Treaty (COJ, 28 March 1996, *Michel Guiot and Climatec SA*, Case C-272/94, not yet published).

A. Legal Base

316.   The legal base of this Directive is Article 57,2 EC Treaty, relating to the freedom of services, which allows for a majority vote. Great-Britain and Portugal voted against the majority.

B. Scope of Application

317.   The Directive applies to undertakings, established in a Member State, which post workers for a limited period (Art. 2,1) in the framework of transnational services to the territory of a Member State (Art. 1,1), other than the Member State in which the worker works normally (Art. 2,1) in the framework of either:

– subcontracting;[1]
– a group;[2]
– temporary work for a user (Art. 1,3).[3]

The notion of worker is that which applies in the law of the Member State to whose territory the worker is posted (Art. 2,2).

The merchant navy undertakings are excluded as regards seagoing personnel (Art. 1,2).

  1. '. . . post workers to the territory of a Member State on their account and under their direction under a contract concluded between the undertaking making the posting and the party for whom the services are intended, operating in that Member State, provided there is an employment relationship between the undertaking of origin and the worker during the period of posting' (Art. 1,3,a).
  2. '. . . post workers to an establishment or to an undertaking owned by the group in the territory of a Member State, provided there is an employment relationship between the undertaking of origin and he worker during the period of posting' (Art. 1,3,b).
  3. '. . . being a temporary employment undertaking or placement agency, hire out a worker to a user undertaking established or operating in the territory of a Member State, provided there is an employment relationship between the temporary employment undertaking or placement agency and the worker during the period of posting' (Art. 1,3,c).
     Member States can provide that temporary workers get equal treatment compared to temporary workers active on their territory (Art. 3,9).

C. Terms and Conditions of Employment

1. Minimum Conditions

318.   Working conditions, which apply and have to be guaranteed to posted workers, are those laid down by:

– governmental rules;
– collective agreements or arbitration awards, generally binding,[1] concerning building work,[2] and

– other collective agreements or arbitration awards, generally binding, for *other activities* indicated by the Member State (Art. 3,10) concerning:
  (a) working time (maximum work and minimum rest periods);
  (b) minimum paid annual vacation;
  (c) minimum wage (including overtime);[3]
  (d) rules concerning temporary work;
  (e) safety, health and hygiene at work;
  (f) protection of motherhood, children and youngsters;
  (g) equal treatment for men and women and other matters relating to non-discrimination (Art. 3,1).

There are minimum conditions. They can obviously be improved upon (Art. 3,7, 1st para.).

1. These are agreements or awards which must be observed by all undertakings in the geographical area and in the profession or industry concerned. In the absence of a system for declaring collective agreements or arbitration awards to be of universal application, Member States may, if they so decide, base themselves on:
   – collective agreements or arbitration awards which are generally applicable to all similar undertakings in the geographical area and in the profession or industry concerned, and/or
   – collective agreements which have been concluded by the most representative employers' and labour organisations at national level and which are applied throughout the national territory, provided that their application to the undertakings referred to in Article 1(1) ensures equality of treatment on matters listed in the first subparagraph of paragraph 1 of this Article between those undertakings and the other undertakings referred to in this subparagraph which are in a similar position.
     Equality of treatment, within the meaning of this Article, shall be deemed to exist where national undertakings in a similar position:
   – are subject, in the place in question or in the sector concerned, to the same obligations as posting undertakings as regards the matters listed in the first subparagraph of paragraph 1, and
   – are required to fulfil such obligations with the same effects (Art. 3,8).
2. All building work relating to the construction, repair, upkeep, alteration or demolition of buildings, and in particular the following work: 1) excavation, 2) earthmoving, 3) actual building work, 4) assembly and dismantling of prefabricated elements, 5) fitting out or installation, 6) alterations, 7) renovation, 8) repairs, 9) dismantling, 10) demolition, 11) maintenance, 12) upkeep, painting and cleaning work, 13) improvements.
3. This doe snot apply to complementary pension schemes (Art. 3,1, iii). The notion of minimum wage is the wage as defined by law or practice of the posted Member State (Art. 3,1, last para.). Allocations which go along with the posting are considered to be pay, except when they concern the payment of expenses made, such as for travel, housing and catering (Art. 3,7, 2nd para.).

2. Other Conditions

319. Member States can impose:

– working conditions relating to public order;[1]
– working conditions contained in generally binding collective agreements, other than construction, as indicated above (Art. 3,10).

Undertakings of the Member States should be treated equally (Art. 3,10).

Undertakings from non Member States cannot have a more favourable treatment than enterprises located in Member States (Art. 1,4).

1. E.g. forced labour or labour inspection.

3. Exceptions[1]

320.   Possible exceptions are foreseen as follows.

a. In the case of *initial assembly and/or first installation of goods where this is an integral part of a contract* for the supply of goods necessary for taking the goods supplied into use and carried out by the skilled and/or specialist workers of the supplying undertaking, the first subparagraph of paragraph 1(b) (*annual holidays*) and (c) (*minimum pay*) shall no apply, if the period of posting *does not exceed 8 days.*

   This exception does not apply to activities in the field of building work.

b. Member States may, after consulting employers and labour, in accordance with the traditions and practices of each Member State, decide not to apply the first subparagraph of paragraph 1(c) (*minimum pay*) in the cases referred to in Article 1(3)(a) (*subcontracting*) and (b) (*group*) when the length of the posting *does not exceed one month.*

c. Member States may, in accordance with national laws and/or practices, provide that exemptions may be made from the first subparagraph of paragraph 1(c) (*minimum pay*) in the cases referred to in Article 1(3)(a) (*subcontracting*) and (b) (*temporary work*) and from a decision by a Member State regarding b. above, by means of generally binding collective agreements concerning one or more sectors of activity, where the length of the posting *does not exceed one month.*

d. Member States may provide for exemptions to be granted from the first subparagraph of paragraph 1(b) (*annual holidays*) and (c) (*minimum pay*) in the cases referred to in Article 1(3)(a) (*subcontracting*) and (b) (*group*) on the grounds that the amount of *work to be done is not significant.*

1. The duration of the posting is done over a period of one year after its commencement. The duration of the posting effectuated by a replaced worker is taken into consideration (Art. 3,6).

D. Co-operation and Transparency (Art. 4)

321.   This covers the following points:

– Member States indicate one or more liaison offices and inform the other Member States and the Commission;

– Member States provide for co-operation between the administration competent for the surveillance of the working conditions stated in Article 3, especially regarding information on the transnational supply of workers including manifest abuses or possible cases of unlawful transnational activities;

– Member States and the Commission look closely at the equal treatment of enterprises;
– Member States must see to it that the information concerning working conditions is 'generally available.'

E. Enforcement (Art. 5)

322.   Member States take appropriate measures in the event of failure to comply with this Directive.

They shall in particular ensure that adequate procedures are available to workers and/or the representatives for the enforcement of obligations under this Directive.

F. Jurisdiction (Art. 6)

323.   In order to enforce the right to the terms and conditions of employment guaranteed in Article 3, judicial proceedings may be instituted in the Member State in whose territory the worker is or was posted, without prejudice, where applicable, to the right, under existing international conventions on jurisdiction, to institute proceedings in another State.

G. Implementation (Art. 7) – Review (Art. 8)

324.   Member States shall bring into force the laws, regulations and administrative provisions necessary to comply with this Directive within a period of three years. They shall forthwith inform the Commission thereof.

When Member States adopt these provisions, they shall contain a reference to this Directive or shall be accompanied by such reference on the occasion of their official publication. The methods of making such reference shall be laid down by Member States.

The Commission will review the operation of the Directive with a view to propose the necessary amendments to the Council where appropriate 5 years after adoption.

Chapter 3. Individual Employment Contracts

325. Earlier proposals of the Commission concerning certain aspects of individual employment contracts, like the amended proposal for a directive on voluntary part-time work (5 January 1983), on the one hand, and on the supply of workers by temporary employment businesses and fixed-duration contracts of employment (6 April 1984), on the other, have been lost in the trenches of the EC labyrinths as they were countered by a veto from one or another Member State. The proposals of the Commission were taken in order to implement the Community Charter of the Fundamental Social Rights of Workers, adopted in Strasbourg in December 1989. Whether those proposals will have more success that their predecessors is doubtful. Three proposals for directives concern the approximation of the law of the Member States of 29 June 1990 relating to certain employment relationships (1) with regard to working conditions;[1] (2) with regard to distortions of competition;[2] and (3) supplementing the introduction of measures to encourage improvements in the safety and health at work of temporary workers.[3] A fourth proposal concerns 'a form of proof of an employment relationship.'

Of these proposals only two have up to now been adopted, be it in an amended form, namely concerning the safety and health of workers with a fixed-duration employment relationship or a temporary employment relationship (25 June 1991) and concerning the employer's obligation to inform employees of the conditions applicable to the contract or employment relationship (14 October 1991).

1. O.J., 8 September 1990, No. C 224/4.
2. O.J., 8 September 1990, No. C 224/6.
3. O.J., 8 September 1990, No. C 224/8.

§1. Part-Time – Fixed Duration – Temporary Work

I. The Proposals of 29 June 1990

326. Three proposals for a directive date from, as indicated, 29 June 1990. The first proposal is based on Articles 100 and 117 of the EC Treaty and point 7 of the Community Charter, namely that:

'the completion of the internal market must lead to an improvement in the living and working conditions of workers in the European Community. This process must result from an approximation of these conditions while the improvement is being maintained, as regards in particular . . . forms of employment other than open-ended contracts, such as fixed-term contracts, part-time work, temporary work and seasonal work.'

Based on Article 100, the proposal must be adopted by a unanimous vote in the Council.

327. The second proposal concerning the distortion of competition is based on Article 100A of the EC Treaty (completion of the internal market) and could thus be adopted by the Council by a qualified majority of votes. The third proposal for a directive relating to the health and safety of workers is based on Article 118A of the EC Treaty and could also be adopted by qualified majority. However, it is beyond doubt that the legal grounds for both proposals will be contested and eventually, if adopted by the Council, be brought before the Court. The three proposals can be summarised as follows:

A. Part-Time Employment

328. Regarding part-time work (at least 8 hours a week), the following rules are proposed:

- access to vocational training operations initiated by the undertaking under conditions comparable to those enjoyed by workers employed full-time for an indefinite duration;
- part-time workers will be taken into account on the same footing as other employees (and in proportion to the duration of their work) for the calculation of the threshold that is required for the setting up of worker's representative bodies within the undertaking;
- where the employer intends to use part-time workers he must inform the workers' representative bodies existing within the undertaking in good time. In undertakings with more than 1,000 employees, a regular report concerning part-time work must be drawn up;
- right to equal treatment for workers employed full-time and for an indefinite duration in regard to benefits in cash and in kind granted under social assistance schemes or under non-contributory social security schemes;
- equal treatment regarding access to the social services in the undertaking;
- information of part-time workers when full-time workers for an indefinite period are recruited;
- equal treatment regarding social protection under statutory and occupational social security schemes;
- equal (proportional) treatment as full-time workers for an indefinite duration regarding annual holidays, dismissal allowances and seniority allowances.

B. Employment Contracts for a Fixed Duration

329. The fixed duration contract includes seasonal work and is concluded directly between the employer and the employee, where the end of the contract is established by objective conditions, such as: reaching a specific date, completing a specific task or the occurrence of a specific event.

The following rules are proposed:

- access to vocational training operations initiated by the undertaking under conditions comparable to those enjoyed by the workers employed full-time for an indefinite duration;
- employees with a fixed duration contract are taken into account (in proportion to the duration of their work) for the calculation of the threshold at which, within the undertaking, national provisions require the setting up of workers' representatives bodies within the undertaking;
- workers' representative bodies in the undertaking must be informed in good time; if there are more than 1,000 employees, a regular report shall be drawn up;
- the contract must contain the grounds for recourse to this type of employment relationship;
- equal treatment as full-time workers for an indefinite duration regarding benefits in cash and in kind granted under social assistance schemes or under non-contributory social security schemes;
- equal access to social services within the undertaking;
- information when full-time workers for an indefinite duration are recruited;
- equal treatment regarding social protection under statutory and occupational security schemes;
- a limit on the renewal of temporary employment relationships of a duration of 12 months or less for a given job so that the total period of employment does not exceed 36 months;
- a provision for a form of equitable allowance in the event of an unjustified break in the employment relationship before the end of the fixed term;
- as regards health and safety at work, the same conditions as those of other workers in the user undertaking with full application of Directive No. 89/391 on the introduction of measures to encourage improvements in the safety and health of workers at work and the individual directives covering the risks of health and safety of workers at the workplace;
- no employment for work requiring special medical supervision over a long period, except in certain cases in which medical supervision is provided beyond the term of the contract.

C. Temporary Work

330. Temporary employment covers any relationship between the temporary employment business which is the employer and its employee, where the latter has no contract with the user undertaking where he preforms his activities.

Regarding temporary workers, the following rules are proposed:

- temporary workers are proportionally taken into account for the calculation of the threshold at which, within the undertaking, national provisions require the setting up of workers' representative bodies within the undertaking;

- workers' representatives must be informed in good time about this type of employment;
- the contract must contain the grounds for recourse to this type of employment relationship;
- equal treatment as full-time workers for an indefinite duration regarding benefits in cash and in kind granted under social assistance schemes or under non-contributory social security schemes;
- equal access to social services within the undertaking;
- clauses preventing or prohibiting the conclusion of a contract of employment between the user undertaking and the employee of a temporary employment business are null and void;
- appropriate measures to ensure that the contractual obligations of the temporary employment business towards its temporary employees are fulfilled, notably with respect to the payment of remuneration and social security contributions;
- a limit on the renewal of temporary employment relationships of a duration of 12 months or less so that the total period of employment does not exceed 36 months;
- a provision for a form of equitable allowance in the event of an unjustified break in the employment relationship before the end of the fixed term;
- as regards health and safety at work, the same conditions as those for workers in the user undertaking with full application of Directive No. 89/391 on the introduction of measures to encourage the improvements in the safety and health of workers at work and individual directives covering the risks of health and safety of workers at the workplace;
- the temporary employment contract must specify the occupational qualification required, the place of work, the working times, the specific features of the job to be filled and, in particular, whether the job falls within the category of major risks as defined in the national legislation; all these facts must be brought to the knowledge of the workers concerned;
- without prejudice to the liability of the temporary employment business, the user will be responsible for the safety, health and hygiene at the workplace;
- before a temporary worker takes up any activity requiring special occupational qualifications or skills or special medical supervision, he must be informed by the user employer of the risks he faces and, if necessary, receive the appropriate training;
- no employment for work requiring special medical supervision over a long period, except for certain cases in which medical supervision is provided beyond the term of the contract.

II. Directive: Health and Safety

331. On 25 June 1991 the Council adopted a Directive (91/383) supplementing the measures to encourage improvements in the safety and health at work of workers with a fixed-duration employment relationship or a temporary employment relationship.[1] The directive is based on Article 118A of the EC Treaty. The motivation of the directive reads that 'recourse to forms of employment such as fixed-duration employment and temporary employment has increased enormously' and 'that research has shown that in general workers with a fixed-duration employment relationship or temporary employment relationship are, in certain sectors, more exposed to the risk of accidents at work and occupational diseases than other workers.' These additional risks are linked to certain peculiar modes of integrating new workers into the under-taking and can be reduced through adequate provision of information and training from the beginning of the employment. The specific situation of these workers and the risks they face call for special rules, supplementing the directives on health and safety, notably Directive 89/391 of 12 June 1989, particularly as regards the provision of information, the training and the medical surveillance of the workers concerned.

1. O.J., 29 July 1991, No. L 206/19.

A. Scope

332. The directive applies to:

1. *fixed-duration contracts of employment*: 'concluded directly between the em-ployer and the worker, where the end of the contract is established by objective conditions such as: reaching a specific date, completing a specific task or the occurrence of a specific event' (Art. 1(1));
2. *temporary employment*: 'relationships between a temporary employment busi-ness which is the employer and the worker, where the latter is assigned to work for and under the control of an undertaking and/or establishment making use of his services' (Art. 1(2)).

These definitions are rather broad. In certain legal systems fixed duration contracts exclusively relate to contracts which specify their duration, and thus are e.g., dis-tinguished from seasonal contracts or contracts for a specific task to be performed. Also the definition of temporary work may differ from what is prevalent in some Member States as certain definitions relate only to certain types of work, e.g., of a limited temporary nature and the like. This means that the implementation of the directive into national law may be broader than the topics covered suggest.

B. Object: Equal Treatment

333. The purpose of the directive is to ensure that the concerned workers are afforded, as regards safety and health at work, the same level of protection as that of other workers in the user undertaking and/or establishment (Art. 2(1)), namely workers engaged for an indefinite period.

Article 2(2) affirms this abundantly: 'the existence of an employment relation-ship as referred to in Article 1 shall not justify different treatment with respect to working conditions inasmuch as the protection of safety and health at work are invol-ved, especially as regards access to personal protective equipment.' Self-evidently, Directive 89/391 of 12 June 1989 and the individual directives concerning health and safety apply in full without prejudice to more binding and/or more specific provisions set out in this directive (Art. 2(3)).

C. Provision of Information to Workers

334. Before a worker takes up any activity he is informed by the undertaking (and/or establishment) making use of his services of the risks he faces.
Such information covers:

1. any special occupational qualifications or skills or special medical surveillance required, as defined in national legislation;
2. clear indications of increased specific risks, as defined in national legislation, that the job may entail (Art. 3).

Regarding *temporary employment* Member States shall take the necessary steps to ensure that before workers are supplied, a user undertaking shall specify to the temporary employment business, *inter alia*, the occupational qualifications required and the specific features of the job to be filled; the temporary employment business shall bring all these facts to the attention of the workers concerned. The Member States may provide that the details of the information shall appear in a contract of assignment (Art. 7).

D. Worker's Training

335. Member States shall take the necessary measures to ensure that each worker receives sufficient training appropriate to the particular characteristics of the job, account being taken of his qualifications and experience (Art. 4).

E. Use of Worker's Services and Medical Surveillance of Workers

336. Member States have the option of prohibiting workers from being used for certain work which would be particularly dangerous to their safety and health, and to ensure that they are provided with appropriate special medical surveillance, also beyond the end of the employment relationship of the worker concerned (Art. 5).

F. Protection and Prevention Services

337. Member States shall take the necessary measures to ensure that protection and prevention agencies[1] are informed of the assignment of concerned workers to the extent necessary to be able to carry out adequately their activities for all the workers of the undertaking (Art. 6).

1. *See*: Article 7 of Directive 89/391 EC.

G. Temporary Employment: Responsibility

338. Member States shall take the necessary measures to ensure that, without prejudice to the responsibility to the temporary employment business as laid down in national legislation, the user undertaking and/or establishment is/are responsible, for the duration of the assignment for the conditions governing performance of the work. These conditions are limited to those connected with 'safety, hygiene and health at work' (Art. 8).

H. Reporting

339.   Member States shall report to the Commission every five years on the practical implementation of the directive, setting out the points of view of workers and employers. The Commission shall bring the report to the attention of the EP, the Council, the ESC, the Advisory Committee on Safety, Hygiene and Health Protection at Work. The Commission shall submit to the EP, the Council and the ESC a regular report on the implementation of this directive (Art. 10).

III. Part-time Work: The Collective Agreement of 6 June 1997[1]

A. Developments

339bis.   The Commission made unsuccessful preliminary proposals, which tried to regulate and restrict the use of 'atypical work'. It later changed its attitude, as these forms of employment were increasingly perceived as opportunities for the creation of employment. At the same time they were seen as responding to both the need of employers for greater flexibility and the desire of employees to reconcile work and family life while retaining employment security.

In 1995, the Commission started consultations on 'flexibility in working time and security for workers', within the framework of the Maastricht Agreement on Social Policy. After these consultations, some social partners decided to try to negotiate an agreement on these issues, which was reached in June 1996.

The negotiation process was not easy. The ETUC wanted to have a deal on all forms of atypical work, while UNICE said that there were different forms of work at stake, which deserved appropriate consideration. After difficult negotiations an agreement was reached and finally signed on 6 June 1997.

It is the intention of the parties to consider the need for similar agreements relating to other forms of flexible work.

The agreement will be rendered binding by a Council Directive.

1. The agreement was implemented by Council Directive 97/81 EC of 15 December 1997 concerning the Framework Agreement on part-time work concluded by UNICE, CEEP and the ETUC, O.J., 20 January 1998, L 14/9.

B. Purpose

339ter.   The purpose of the agreement is:

a. The removal of discrimination against part-time workers and the improvement of the quality of part-time work; and

b. to facilitate the development of part-time work on a voluntary basis and to contribute to the flexible organization of working time in a manner which takes into account the needs of employers and workers (Clause 1).

C. Scope

339quater.   This agreement applies to part-time workers, who have an employment contract or employment relationship as defined by the law, collective agreements or practice, in force in each Member State.

Member states may[1] for objective reasons, exclude wholly or partly from the terms of this agreement part-time workers, who work on a casual basis[2] (Clause 2).

1. 'After consultation with the social partners in accordance with national law, collective agreements or practice, and/or the social partners at the appropriate level in conformity with national industrial relations practice'.
2. 'Such exclusions should be reviewed periodically to establish if the objective reasons for making them remain valid.'

D. Definitions

339quinquies.   *Part-time worker* refers to an employee, whose normal hours of work, calculated on a weekly basis or on average over a period of employment of up to one year, are less than the normal hours of work of a comparable full-time worker.

Comparable full-time worker means a full-time employee in the same establishment having the same type of employment contract or relationship, who is engaged in the same or similar work/occupation, due regard being given to other considerations which may include seniority, qualifications/skills.

Where there is no comparable full-time worker in the same establishment, the comparison shall be made by reference to the applicable collective agreement or, where there is no applicable collective agreement, in accordance with national law, collective agreements or practice (Clause 3).

E. Principle of Non-discrimination

339sexies.   In respect of employment and conditions, part-time workers shall not be treated in a less favourable manner than comparable full-time workers solely because they work part time, unless different treatment is justified on objective grounds.

Where appropriate, the principle of *pro rata temporis* shall apply.

The modalities of application of this clause shall be defined by the Member States and/or the social partners, having regard to European legislation, national law, collective agreements and practice.

When justified by objective reasons, Member States, after consultation of the social partners in accordance with national law or practice and/or social partners may, where appropriate, make access to particular conditions of employment subject to conditions such as a period of service, time worked or earnings qualification. Qualifications relating to access by part-time workers to particular conditions of employment should be reviewed periodically having regard to the principle of non-discrimination (Clause 4).

F. Opportunities for Part-time Work

339septies.   Member States[1] and the social partners[2] should identify and review obstacles of a legal or administrative nature which may limit the opportunities for part-time work and, where appropriate, eliminate them.

A worker's refusal to transfer from full-time to part-time work or vice versa should not in itself constitute a valid reason for termination of employment, without prejudice to termination in accordance with national law, collective agreements and practice, for other reasons such as may arise from the operational requirements of the establishment concerned.

As far as possible, employers should give consideration to:

(a) requests by workers to transfer from full-time to part-time work that become available in the establishment;
(b) requests by workers to transfer from part-time to full-time work or to increase their working time should the opportunity arise;
(c) the provision of timely information on the availability of part-time and full-time positions in the establishment in order to facilitate transfers from full-time to part-time or vice versa;
(d) measures to facilitate access to part-time work at all levels of the enterprise, including skilled and managerial positions and, where appropriate, to facilitate access by part-time workers to vocational training to enhance career opportunities and occupational mobility;
(e) the provision of appropriate information to existing bodies representing workers about part-time working in the enterprise (Clause 5).

  1. 'Following consultations with the social partners in accordance with national law or practice'.
  2. 'Acting within their sphere of competence and through the procedures set out in collective agreements'.

G. Provisions on Implementation

339octies.   Member States and/or social partners can maintain or introduce more favourable provisions than set out in this agreement.

Implementation shall not constitute valid grounds for reducing the general level of protection. This does not prejudice the right of Member States and/or social partners to develop different provisions, in the light of changing circumstances.

The social partners retain the right to conclude, at the appropriate level, including European level, agreements adapting and/or complementing the provisions of this agreement.

The signatory parties will review this agreement, five years after the date of the Council decision, if requested by one of the parties to this agreement (Clause 6).

§2. Conditions Applicable to the Contract of Employment:
Information

340. The Council adopted on 14 October 1991, Directive (91/553 EEC) on an employer's obligation to inform employees of the conditions applicable to the contract of employment relationship.[1] This directive was adopted pursuant to point 9 of the Community Charter of Fundamental Social Rights for Workers, which states: 'the conditions of employment of every worker of the European Community shall be stipulated in laws, a collective agreement or a contract of employment, according to arrangements applying in each country.' 'The development in the Member States,' the consideration reads, 'of new forms of work has led to an increase in the number of types of employment' and led certain Member States to consider it necessary to subject employment relationships to formal requirements, designed to provide employees with improved protection against possible infringements of their rights and to create greater transparency in the labour market. This legislation of the Member States differs considerably on such fundamental points as the requirement to inform employees in writing of the main terms of the contract or employment relationship, which may have a direct effect on the operation of the Common Market.

It is therefore necessary to establish at Community level the general requirement that every employee must be provided with a document containing information on the essential elements of his contract or employment relationship. This directive is without prejudice to national law and practice concerning: 'the form of the contract or employment relationship, proof as regards the existence and content of a contract or employment relationship, and the relevant procedural rules' (Art. 6).

1. O.J. 18 October 1991, No. L 288/32.

I. Scope

341. The directive applies to every paid employee having a contract or employment relationship defined by the law in force in a Member State and/or governed by the law in force in a Member State (Art. 1(1)). In view of the need to maintain a certain degree of flexibility in employment relationships, Member States should be able to exclude certain limited cases of employment relationships from the scope of application, namely: 'with a total duration not exceeding one month and/or with a working week not exceeding eight hours or, of a casual and/or specific nature provided, in these cases, that its non-application is justified by objective considerations' (Art. 1(2)).

II. Obligation to Provide Information

A. *In General*

342. An employer is obliged to notify the employee of the essential aspects of the contract or employment relationship.

This information covers at least the following:

(a) the identities of the parties;
(b) the place of work; where there is no fixed or main place of work, the principle that the employee is employed at various places and the registered place of business or, where appropriate, the domicile of the employer;
(c) (i) the title, grade, nature or category of the worker for which the employee is employed; or
    (ii) a brief specification or description of the work;
(d) the date of commencement of the contract or employment relationship;
(e) in the case of a temporary contract or employment relationship, the expected duration thereof;
(f) the amount of a temporary contract or employment relationship, the expected duration thereof;
(g) the amount of paid leave to which the employee is entitled, or where this cannot be indicated when the information is given, the procedures for allocating and determining such leave;
(h) the length of the periods of notice to be observed by the employer and the employee should their contract or employment relationship be terminated or, where this cannot be indicated when the information is given, the method for determining such periods of notice;
(i) the initial basic amount, the other component elements and the frequency of payment of the remuneration to which the employee is entitled;
(j) the length of the employee's normal working day or week;
(k) where appropriate:
    (i) the collective agreements governing the employee's conditions of work; or
    (ii) in the case of collective agreements concluded outside the business by special joint bodies or institutions, the name of the competent body or joint institution within which the agreements were concluded (Art. 2(2)).

Information concerning paid leave, periods of notice, remuneration and working time may, where appropriate, be given in a form of reference to the laws, regulations and administrative or statutory provisions or collective agreements governing those particular points (Art. 2(3)).

B. Expatriate Employees

343. Where an employee is required to work in a country other than the Member State whose law and or practice governs the contract, the duration of which is more than one month, the documents must be in his position before departure and must include at least the following additional information:

(a) the duration of employment abroad;
(b) the currency to be used for the payment of remuneration;
(c) where appropriate, the benefits in cash or kind attendant on the employment abroad;
(d) where appropriate, the conditions governing the employee's repatriation.

The information concerning currency and remuneration may 'where appropriate, be given in the form of a reference to the laws, regulations and administrative or statutory provisions or collective agreements governing those particular points' (Art. 4).

C. Modifications

344.   Any change in the conditions must be the subject of a written document to be given by the employer to the employee at the earliest opportunity and not later than one month after the date of entry into effect of the change in question. This is not compulsory in the event of a change in the laws, regulations, etc. (Art. 5).

D. Term and Form of Information

345.   The (general) information

'may be given to the employee, not later than two months after the commencement of the employment, in the form of:
(a) a written contract of employment; and/or
(b) a letter of engagement; and/or
(c) one or more other written documents, where one of these documents contains at least all the information referred to in Article 2(2)(a), (b), (c), (d), (h) and (i).'

Where no or only partial information has been given, the employer is obliged to give to the employee, not later than two months after the commencement of the employment, a written declaration signed by the employer and containing at least the (general) information.

When the contract or the employment relationship comes to an end before expiry of a period of two months from the date of the start of work, the information must be made available to the employee by the end of this period at the latest (Art. 3).

In case of employment relationships in existence upon entry into force of the directive (30 June 1993), the employer must give the employee, on request, the necessary documents within two months of receiving that request (Art. 9(2)).

III. Defence of Rights

346.   The employees, who consider themselves wronged by failure to comply with the obligations arising from this directive, have the right to pursue their claims by judicial process after possible recourse to other competent authorities (Art. 8(1)).

Member States may, however, provide that access to the means of redress are subject to the notification of the employer by the employee and the failure by the employer to reply within 15 days of notification. The formality of prior notification may in no case be required in the cases of expatriates, referred to in Article 4 of the directive, nor for workers with a temporary contract or employment relationship, nor for employees not covered by a collective agreement or by collective agreements relating to the employment relationship (Art. 8(2)).

IV. Implementation

347.   The directive had to be transposed into national law, not later than 30 June 1993. Member States could also entrust employer's and worker's representatives with the task of introducing the required provisions into national law by way of agreements, being, however, obliged to take the necessary steps enabling them at all times to guarantee the results imposed by the directive (Art. 9(2)).

§3. RECRUITMENT AND PLACEMENT: MONOPOLY OF THE PUBLIC EMPLOYMENT OFFICE?

348.   In a landmark decision the Court challenged the monopoly of public employment offices in the activity of finding work for persons seeking employment.[1] The case concerned the putting in contact with employers of persons seeking work, which in Germany is, on the basis of the *Arbeitsförderungsgesetz* (Law on the Promotion of Employment – 'the AGF'), the exclusive right of the *Bundesanstalt für Arbeit* (Federal Employment Office – 'the BA'). Notwithstanding that exclusive right, a specific recruitment and placement business has developed for business executives. It is carried on by recruitment consultants which are to some extent tolerated by the BA. The fact nevertheless remains that any legal measure which contravenes a legal prohibitions is void by virtue of Article 134 of the German Civil Code and that, according to decisions of the German courts, that prohibition applies to recruitment activities carried on in breach of the AFG. In the case under review the recruitment consultants presented a candidate to a client, who the client decided not to recruit while refusing at the same time to pay the consultants' fees, on the basis that his contract with them was void. In the case which was ultimately submitted to the Court in Luxemburg, the Court was asked whether the provisions of the Treaty on the freedom to provide services precluded a legal provision prohibiting private recruitment consultants from finding placements for business executives and whether the monopoly on the placement of executives vested in a public employment office constituted an abuse of a dominant position.
The Court ruled as follows:

> 'A public employment office engaged in the activity of finding work for persons seeking employment is subject to the prohibition in Article 86 of the Treaty, provided the application of that provision does not defeat the specific task entrusted to it. A Member State which has conferred an exclusive right to carry on that activity upon that public employment office is in breach of Article 90(1) of the Treaty where it creates a situation in which that office is obliged to infringe the terms of Article 86 of the Treaty. That is the case, in particular, where the following conditions are met:

- the exclusive right extends to finding employment for business executives;
- the public employment office is manifestly incapable of satisfying demand on the market for such activity;
- the actual pursuit of that activity by private personnel consultants is rendered impossible by the maintenance in force of a statutory provision prohibiting it, with the annulment of the corresponding contracts as a penalty for contravention;
- the activity in question may extend to nationals or to the territory of other Member States.'

1. COJ, 23 April 1991, *K. Höfner and F. Elser* v. *Macroton GmbH*, No. C-41/90, IELL, *Case Law*, No. 164.

A second case (1997)[1] concerns the Italian Law of 23 October 1960 which lays down a prohibition on acting as an intermediary in employment relationships, whether as an employment agency or as an employment business. Failure to comply with the statute gives rise to penal sanctions.

The question which was asked is essentially, whether the provisions of the Treaty preclude national legislation under which any activity as an intermediary between supply and demand in employment relationships is prohibited unless carried on by public employment agencies.

The Court decided in a landmark decision that:

1. Placement of employees is an economic activity, even if entrusted to public offices;
2. a body such as a public placement office may therefore be classed as an undertaking for the purposes of the Community competition rules;
3. public placement offices remain subject to competition rules unless, and to the extent to which it is shown that their application is incompatible with discharge of their duties;
4. it must be stated that the application of Article 86 of the Treaty cannot obstruct the performance of the particular task assigned to those offices that they are manifestly not in a position to satisfy demand in that area of the market;
5. pursuant to Article 86(b) of the Treaty, such abuse may in particular consist in limiting the provision of a service, to the prejudice of those seeking to avail themselves of it;
6. as the Commission has rightly pointed out, the market in the provision of services relating to the placement of employees is both very extensive and extremely diverse. Supply and demand on that market covers all sectors of production and relate to a range of jobs requiring anything from unskilled labour to the scarcest and most specialised professional qualifications;
7. on such an extensive and differentiated market, which is, moreover, subject to enormous changes as a result of economic and social developments, public placement offices may well be unable to satisfy a significant portion of all requests for services;
8. by prohibiting, on pain of penal and administrative sanctions, any activity as an intermediary between supply and demand on the employment market unless

carried on by public placement offices, a Member State creates a situation in which the provision of a service is limited, contrary to Article 86(b) of the Treaty, if those offices are manifestly unable to satisfy demand on the employment market for all types of activity;

9. a potential effect of abusive conduct on trade between Member States is sufficient and arises in particular where the placement of employees by private companies may extend to the nationals or to the territory of other Member States.

The conclusion of the Court is straightforward and clear. A monopoly on the labour market violates European competition law:

- As public placement offices are manifestly unable to satisfy demand on the market of all types of activity;
- the actual placement of employees by private companies is rendered impossible by the maintenance in force of statutory provisions under which such activities are prohibited and non-observance of that prohibition gives rise to penal and administrative sanctions; and
- the placement activities in question could extend to the nationals or to the territory of other Member States.

In many countries placement of workers was still by and large a monopoly of the Public Employment Offices. The general rules, with some exceptions were still that:

1. Placement by fee charging private employment agencies; and
2. that the putting of a worker at the disposal of a user-enterprise is forbidden, except, e.g., in the case of temporary work.

It is clear that this situation is both illegal and obsolete.

First of all, the monopoly of the Public Employment Office is contrary to the letter and the spirit of Convention No. 181 of the ILO (1997) and with European competition law. It is evident that the Official Employment Offices can no longer satisfy the demand on the market for all types of activity in a *de facto* manner. The national Public Employment Offices cannot cope with the diversity of the modern labour markets at European level.

In conclusion one can say that:

1. the monopoly of the Public Employment Offices has to be abolished;
2. enterprises must be able to propose a total package of services on the labour market, vocational training included;
3. the scope of possibilities to put workers at the disposal of users-enterprises must be widened.

Other issues, such as serving the needs of job seekers, also have to be addressed

First, in general the present set of rules governing private employment agencies responds to the needs and the leverage of the employers. It is completely supply oriented. The employee has no input. He can mostly only react, not pro-act, as a full-fledged actor on the labour market. He undergoes developments. Indeed, search, selection and outplacement activities can in many countries only be undertaken on the initiative and at the expense of the employer.

All the individual jobseeker can do is pass on his name and CV to advertisement agencies, temporary work agencies and job placement agencies, hoping they may do something. He cannot, however, ask them to provide him with a service of, e.g., looking for a job, in accordance with his talents and experience, since these agencies cannot ask him any fee.

The individual job seeker is left with the services of the Official Employment Office, which despite all its good will, cannot fulfil the requests it might be confronted with. This is certainly the case if someone is looking for work abroad. For practical purposes, the job seeker will have to continue to have to rely on informal amateurism, all jobseekers writing the same letters to the same well-known companies, asking friends of friends, readings newspapers etc. Professional help seems to be excluded.

We all want, rightly, to protect the job seekers and the unemployed by preventing their exploitation, but we should not do more in order to see to it that they effectively get the professional services of the same quality as the employers' may get.

We should be more creative than to say that job seekers are not entitled to professional help outside the Public Employment Office as no fees can be asked. Maybe a kind of insurance system should be set up, like in the case of health services, when one can go to the doctor and get the fee refunded, totally or partially.

1. COJ, 11 December 1997, Job Centre Coop. arl, Case No. C-55/96, not yet published.

I. Contract Labour

We should also address the issue of contract labour as more and more agencies are becoming talent banks where the self-employed plug in their names and talents and the agencies provide them with self-employed job offers. The agencies match the demand and the supply of self-employed services. They are in a sense placement agencies for the self-employed. There is obviously plenty of room for this labour market service, which is growing in importance as the distinction between employee and self-employed in this outsourced and information society becomes in itself more and more obsolete. The only question is, how to organise this. Certainly, in a more relaxed and flexible way. Moreover, there is a bridge to be built between the employee and the self-employed world. The only (organised) service on the labour market for which the official regulation spells out that the service can lead to self-employment, is outplacement.

II. Vocational Training

A last point concerns vocational training, of which all agree that there should be more training, permanent and open to all; also focusing on the 'social skills', needed to operate in this world of increasing teamwork.

In conclusion, it is obvious that we need a new and fresh look at the modern labour markets, at the way to really match demand and supply for both sides; employment seekers and those who employ in a fair way, where the idea of co-investment could be retained. Permanent and adequate vocational training remains an essential feature of any labour market policy.

Chapter 4. Child Care and the Protection of Young People at Work

349. Children should be at the forefront of social consideration and precaution, as they are particularly vulnerable. Some of the problems this involves are addressed in a recommendation and in a directive.

§1. CHILD CARE

350. In each of the Community's Member States, without exception, the demand for reasonably priced child-care services exceeds the supply. The lack of adequate child-care services and initiatives to reconcile family responsibilities with employment or work-related training constitutes a major barrier to women's access to, and more widespread participation in, the labour market. This situation is, of course, at odds with the principle of equal opportunities for men and women. This problem was addressed in point 16 of the Community Charter of the Fundamental Social Rights of Workers under the heading of equal treatment for men and women: measures should also be developed enabling men and women to reconcile their occupational and family obligations.

The *Recommendation on Child Care* which was adopted on 31 March 1992,[1] outlines various courses of action designed to remedy this situation. In practical terms, the Member States are invited to take and/or progressively encourage initiatives in four areas, so as to enable women and men to reconcile more effectively their occupational, family and upbringing responsibilities.

The first area concerns child-care services as such. It is recommended that all the competent authorities should enable parents to have as much access as possible to these services, with particular endeavours being made to ensure, for example, through adequate financial contributions, that the services are offered at affordable prices and are available in all areas and regions, both urban and rural. Such services should, moreover, be flexible and diverse, so as to be fully responsive to the needs of the children and their parents. The recommendation also points to the need for child-care workers to be given training, both initial and continuing, which is commensurate with the importance and the social and educative value of their work.

The other three areas are more general in nature, the intention being to shape certain aspects of society in such a way that having children will no longer constitute an insurmountable obstacle to pursuing a career.

Firstly, the recommendation calls on the Member States to take and/or encourage initiatives so that arrangements for special leave enabling employed parents, both men and women, to properly discharge their occupational, family and upbringing responsibilities, take realistic account of women's increased participation in the labour force. Priority should be given to ensuring that leave arrangements are flexibly organised.

Secondly, it is recommended that the Member States should support action to create an environment, structure and organisation at work which take into account the needs of working parents with responsibility for the care and upbringing of children.

Finally, Member States are asked to promote and encourage, with due freedom of the individual, a more equal sharing of parental responsibilities between men and women since the latter still tend to assume the full burden of the 'house wife,' with the result that their career prospects are less secure.

    1. 92/24, O.J., 8 May 1992, L 123.

§2. PROTECTION OF YOUNG PEOPLE AT WORK (DIRECTIVE OF 22 JUNE 1994)

I. Introductory Remarks

351.   The Directive of 22 June 1994 on the protection of young people at work[1] was adopted pursuant to points 20 and 22 of the Community Charter of the Fundamental Social Rights of Workers (1989) which state that:

> 'Without prejudice to such rules as may be more favourable to young people, in particular those ensuring their preparation for work through vocational training, and subject to derogations limited to certain light work, the minimum employment age must not be lower than the minimum school-leaving age and, in any case, not lower than 15 years' (point 20);

> 'Appropriate measures must be taken to adjust labour regulations applicable to young workers so that their specific development and vocational training and access to employment needs are met' (point 22).

> 'The duration of work must, in particular, be limited – without it being possible to circumvent this limitation through recourse to overtime – and night work prohibited in the case of workers of under eighteen years of age, save in the case of certain jobs laid down in national legislation or regulations.'

In its Resolution on Child Labour of 1987, the EP summarised the various aspects of work by young people and stressed its effects on their health, safety and physical and intellectual development, and pointed to the need to adopt a directive harmonising national legislation in the field.

The directive rightly stresses that children and adolescents must be considered specific risk groups, and measures must be taken with regard to their safety and health; and that the vulnerability of children calls for Member States to prohibit their employment and ensure that the minimum working or employment age is not lower than the minimum age at which compulsory schooling as imposed by national law ends or 15 years in any event. Derogations from the prohibition on child labour may be admitted only in special cases and under specific conditions but, under no circumstances, may such derogations be detrimental to regular school attendance or prevent children from benefiting fully from their education. In view of the nature of the transition from childhood to adult life, work by adolescents should be strictly regulated and protected.

It is consequently mandatory that every employer should guarantee young people working conditions appropriate to their age and that he should implement the measures necessary to protect the safety and health of young people on the basis of an assessment of work-related hazards to the young. Young people should in particular be protected against any specific risks arising from their lack of experience, absence of awareness of existing or potential risk, or from their immaturity.

Quite a number of specific measures are retained:

- the prohibition of the employment of young people for dangerous tasks;
- the adoption of specific minimal requirements in respect of the organisation of working time;
- the maximum working time of young people should be strictly limited;
- night work by young people should be prohibited, with the exception of certain jobs;
- young people should be granted minimum daily, weekly and annual periods of rest and adequate breaks.

With respect to the weekly rest period, due account should be taken of the diversity of cultural, ethnic, religious and other factors prevailing in the Member States; it is ultimately for each Member State to decide whether Sunday should be included in the weekly rest period, and if so to what extent.

The directive was adopted pursuant to Article 118A of the EC Treaty which provides that the Council shall adopt, by means of directives, minimum requirements to encourage improvements, especially in the working environment, as regards the health and safety of workers, and in doing so avoid imposing administrative, financial and legal constraints in a way which would be detrimental to the creation and development of small- and medium-sized undertakings. This means that the directive has been adopted with a qualified majority. It is also important to note that account has been taken of the principles of the ILO regarding the protection of young people at work, including those relating to the minimum age for access to employment or work.

The UK had problems with this directive and was granted the right to refrain from implementing certain provisions for given period of time.[2]

1. O.J., 20 August 1994, No. L 216/12.
2. Article 17,1(b).

II. Purpose and Scope

A. *Purpose*

352. The aim of the directive is to ensure that young people are protected against economic exploitation and against any work likely to harm their safety, health or physical, mental, moral or social development or to jeopardise their education.

Member States shall take the necessary measures:

– to prohibit work by children;
– to ensure that work by adolescents is strictly regulated and
– to see to it that employers guarantee that young people have working conditions which suit their age.

Regarding work of young people, the minimum working or employment age should not be lower than the minimum age at which compulsory full-time schooling as imposed by national law ends or 15 years in any event (Art. 1).

B. Scope

353. This Directive applies to any person under 18 years of age having an employment contract or an employment relationship defined by the law in force in a Member State and/or governed by the law in force in a Member State.[1]

Member States may make legislative or regulatory provision for this Directive not to apply to occasional work or short-term work involving:

(a) domestic service in a private household,[2] or
(b) work regarded as not being harmful, damaging or dangerous to young people in a family undertaking (Art. 2).

> 1. 'Contracts for services are not covered' (statement of the Council and the Commission).
> 2. This includes activities such as babysitting (statement by the Council and the Commission).

III. Definitions

354. For the purposes of this directive definitions are as follows:

(a) 'young person': any person under 18 years of age having an employment contract/relationship;
(b) 'child': any young person of less than 15 years of age or who is still subject to compulsory full-time schooling under national law;
(c) 'adolescent': any young person of at least 15 years of age but less than 18 years of age who is no longer subject to compulsory full-time schooling;
(d) 'light work': all work which, on account of the inherent nature of the tasks which it involves and the particular conditions under which they are performed:
   (i) is not likely to be harmful to the safety, health or development of children, and
   (ii) is not such as to be harmful to their attendance at school, their participation in vocational guidance or training programmes approved by the competent authority or their capacity to benefit from the instruction received:
(e) 'working time': any period during which the young person is at work, at the employer's disposal and carrying out his activity or duties in accordance with national legislation and/or practice:
(f) 'rest period': any period which is not working time (Art. 3).

IV. Prohibition of Work by Children

355.   Member States shall adopt the measures necessary to prohibit work by children.

They may make provision for the prohibition of work by children not to apply to:

(a) children pursuing cultural or similar activities;
(b) children of at least 14 years of age working under a combined work/training scheme or an in-plant work-experience scheme;
(c) children of at least 14 years of age performing light work other than cultural or similar; light work other than that may, however, be performed by children of 13 years of age for a limited number of hours per week in the case of categories of work determined by national legislation. In such a case, the working conditions relating to the light work in question must be determined (Art. 4).

V. Cultural or Similar Activities

356.   The employment of children for the purposes of performance in cultural, artistic, sports or advertising activities shall be subject to prior authorisation to be given by the competent authority in individual cases.[1]

Member States shall lay down the working conditions for children and the details of the prior authorisation procedure, on condition that the activities:

(i) are not likely to be harmful to the safety, health or development of children, and
(ii) are not such as to be harmful to their attendance at school, their participation in vocational guidance or training programmes approved by the competent authority or their capacity to benefit from the instruction received.

In the case of children of at least 13 years of age, Member States may authorise the employment of children for the purposes of performance in cultural, artistic, sports or advertising activities.

The Member States which have a specific authorisation system for modelling agencies with regard to the activities of children may retain that system (Art. 5).

1. The phrase 'in individual cases' does not mean that, where the activities of a number of children are involved, prior authorisation is required for each individual child (statement by the Council and the Commission).

VI. General Obligations on Employers

357.   The employer shall adopt the measures necessary to protect the safety and health of young people, taking particular account of the specific risks to their safety, health and development which are a consequence of their lack of experience, of absence of awareness of existing or potential risks or of the fact that young people have not yet fully matured (Art. 6,1).

The employer shall implement these measures on the basis of an assessment of the hazards to young people in connection with their work. The assessment must be made before young people begin work and when there is any major change in working conditions and must pay particular attention to the following points:

(a) the fitting-out and layout of the workplace and the workstation;
(b) the nature, degree and duration of exposure to physical, biological and chemical agents;
(c) the form, range and use of work equipment, in particular agents, machines, apparatus and devices, and the way in which they are handled;
(d) the arrangement of work processes and operations and the way in which these are combined (organisation of work);
(e) the level of training and instruction given to young people.

When this assessment shows that there is a risk to the safety, the physical or mental health or development of young people, an appropriate free assessment and monitoring of their health shall be provided at regular intervals.[1] The free health assessment and monitoring may form part of a national health system (Art. 6,2).

Moreover, the employer shall inform young people of possible risks and of all measures adopted concerning their safety and health. Furthermore, he shall inform the legal representatives of children of possible risks and of all measures adopted concerning children's safety and health (Art. 6,3).

The employer shall involve the protective and preventive agencies[2] in the planning, implementation and monitoring of the safety and health conditions applicable to young people (Art. 6,4).

1. Without prejudice to Directive 89/391/EC.
2. Referred to in Article 7 of Directive 89/391/EC.

VII. Vulnerability of Young People – Prohibition of Work

358. Member States must ensure that young people are protected from any specific risks to their safety, health and development which are a consequence of their lack of experience, of absence of awareness of existing or potential risks or of the fact that young people have not yet fully matured. To this end they must prohibit the employment of young people for:

(a) work which is objectively beyond their physical or psychological capacity;
(b) work involving harmful exposure to agents which are toxic, carcinogenic, cause heritable genetic damage or harm to the unborn child or which in any other way chronically affect human health;
(c) work involving harmful exposure to radiation;
(d) work involving the risk of accidents which it may be assumed cannot be recognised or avoided by young persons owing to their insufficient attention to safety or lack of experience or training; or
(e) work in which there is a risk to health from extreme cold or heat, or from noise or vibration.

Work which is likely to entail specific risks for young people includes:

– work involving harmful exposure to the physical, biological and chemical agents referred to in point I of the Annex, and
– processes and work referred to in point II of the Annex to the directive.

Member States may authorise derogations in the case of adolescents where such derogations are indispensable for their vocational training, provided that protection of their safety and health is ensured by the fact that the work is performed under the supervision of a competent person[1] (Art. 7).

> 1. Within the meaning of Article 7 of Directive 89/391/EEC and provided that the protection afforded by that Directive is guaranteed. Member States may, by legislative or regulatory provision, authorise derogations from Article 8(2), Article 9(1)(b), Article 10(1)(b) and, in the case of adolescents, Article 12, for work in the circumstances referred to in Article 5(4) of Directive 89/391/EEC, provided that such work is of a temporary nature and must be performed immediately, that adult workers are not available and that the adolescents are allowed equivalent compensatory rest time within the following three weeks (work by adolescents in the event of *force majeure*).

VIII. Working Time

359. In case of permitted child labour the working time of children must be limited to:

(a) 8 hours a day and 40 hours a week for work performed under a combined work/training scheme or an in-plant work-experience scheme;[1]
(b) 2 hours on a school day and 12 hours a week for work performed in term-time outside the hours fixed for school attendance, provided that this is not prohibited by national legislation and/or practice; in no circumstances may the daily working time exceed 7 hours; this limit may be raised to 8 hours in the case of children who have reached the age of 15;
(c) 7 hours a day and 35 hours a week for work performed during a period of at least a week when school is not operating; these limits may be raised to 8 hours a day and 40 hours a week in the case of children who have reached the age of 15;
(d) 7 hours a day and 35 hours a week for light work performed by children no longer subject to compulsory full-time schooling under national law.

Member States shall adopt the measures necessary to limit the working time of adolescents to 8 hours a day and 40 hours a week (Art. 8,1).

Where a young person is employed by more than one employer, working days and working time shall be cumulative.

Member States may authorise derogations either by way of exception or where there are objective grounds for so doing and determine the conditions, limits and procedure for implementing such derogations (Art. 8,5).

Where daily working time is more than four and a half hours, young people are entitled to a break of at least 30 minutes, which shall be consecutive if possible[2] (Art. 12).

1. The time spent on training by a young person working under a theoretical and/or practical combined work/training scheme or an in-plant work-experience scheme shall be counted as working time (Art. 8,3).
2. Article 12 does not specify at what point during the daily working time a break must be allowed (statement by the Council and the Commission).

IX. Night Work

360. Permitted work by children cannot take place between 20.00 hours and 06.00 hours. Work by adolescents either between 22.00 hours and 06.00 hours or between 23.00 hours and 07.00 hours is prohibited (Art. 9,1).

Member States may authorise work by adolescents in specific areas of activity during the period in which night work is prohibited but in no case between 00.00 hours and 04.00 hours. In that event, Member States shall take appropriate measures to ensure that the adolescent is supervised by an adult where such supervision is necessary for the adolescent's protection.

However, Member States may authorise work by adolescents during the period in which night work is prohibited in the following cases, where there are objective grounds for so doing and provided that adolescents are allowed suitable compensatory rest time and that the objectives of the directive are not called into question:

– work performed in the shipping or fisheries sectors;
– work performed in the context of the armed forces or the police;
– work performed in hospitals or similar establishments;
– cultural, artistic, sports or advertising activities (Art. 9,2).

Prior to any assignment to night work and at regular intervals thereafter, adolescents shall be entitled to a free assessment of their health and capacities, unless the work they do during the period during which work is prohibited is of an exceptional nature (Art. 9,3).

X. Rest Period

361. In case of permitted child work, for each 24 hour period, children are entitled to a minimum rest period of 14 consecutive hours; adolescents are entitled to a minimum rest period of 12 consecutive hours (Art. 10,1).

For each 7 day period, in case of permitted child labour, adolescents are entitled to a minimum rest period of 2 days, which shall be consecutive if possible. Where justified by technical or organisation reasons, the minimum rest period may be reduced, but may in no circumstances be less than 36 consecutive hours. The minimum rest period shall in principle include Sunday (Art. 10,2).

These minimum rest periods may be interrupted in the case of activities involving periods of work that are split up over the day or are of short duration (Art. 10,3).

Member States may make provision for derogations in respect of adolescents in the following cases, where there are objective grounds for so doing and provided that they are granted appropriate compensatory rest time:

(a) work performed in the shipping or fisheries sectors;
(b) work performed in the context of the armed forces or the police;
(c) work performed in hospitals or similar establishments;
(d) work performed in agriculture;
(e) work performed in the tourist industry or in the hotel, restaurant and café sector;
(f) activities involving periods of work split up over the day (Art. 10).

In case of permitted child labour there must be a period free of any work including, as far as possible, the school holidays of children subject to compulsory full-time schooling under national law (Art. 11).

XI. Measures. Non-reducing Clause. Final Provisions

362.   Each Member State shall lay down any necessary measures to be applied in the event of failure to comply with the provisions adopted in order to implement this Directive; such measures must be effective and proportionate (Art. 14).

Without prejudice to the right of Member States to develop, in the light of changing circumstances, different provisions on the protection of young people, as long as the minimum requirements provided for by this Directive are complied with, the implementation of this Directive shall not constitute valid grounds for reducing the general level of protection afforded to young people (Art. 16).

The directive must enter in force not later then two years after its adoption or ensure. The directive can also be implemented by means of collective agreements.

Member States shall report to the Commission every five years on the practical implementation of the provisions of this directive, indicating the viewpoints of the two sides of industry. The Commission shall inform the European Parliament, the Council and the Economic and Social Committee thereof (Art. 17).

Chapter 5. Equal Treatment for Men and Women

363. Few principles received such an important and frequent backing in international legal instruments as the principle of equal treatment of men and women, and this is also true in the field of employment. All international organisations took initiatives in this area: the United Nations, the ILO especially, the Council of Europe and the EC.

The EC played an important role, first by adopting Article 119 in the EC Treaty, which contains the principle of equal pay for equal work, and consequently by adopting several directives:

- 1975: relating to the application of equal pay for men and women;[1]
- 1976: relating to the implementation of the principle of equal treatment for men and women as regards access to employment, vocational training and promotion, and working conditions;[2]
- 1978: concerning the progressive implementation of the principle of equal treatment for men and women in matters of social security;[3]
- 1986: on the implementation of the principle of equal treatment for men and women in occupational social security schemes.[4]

Equal treatment was of course also retained as a fundamental social right in the Community Charter:

> 'Whereas, in order to ensure equal treatment, it is important to combat every form of discrimination, including disscrimination on grounds of sex, colour, race, opinions and beliefs, and whereas, in a spirit of solidarity, it is important to combat social exclusion.'

Therefore principle 16 of the Charter was adopted, which reads as follows:

> 'Equal treatment for men and women must be assured. Equal opportunities for men and women must be developed. To this end, action should be intensified to ensure the implementation to the principle of equality between men and women as regards in particular access to employment, remuneration, working conditions, social protection, education, vocational training and career development. Measures should also be developed enabling men and women to reconcile their occupational and family obligations.'

1. 10 February 1975, No. 75/111, O.J., 19 February 1975, No. L 45/19.
2. 9 February 1976, No. 76/207, O.J., 14 February 1976, No. L 39/40.

3. 19 December 1978, No. 79/7, O.J., 10 February 1979, No. L 6/24.
4. 24 July 1986, No. 86/378, O.J., 12 August 1986, No. L 45/40, amended by Directive 96/97 of 2 December 1996.

§1. PRINCIPLE AND SCOPE

364.   Contrary to Articles 117 and 118, which are limited to fixing in social matters the general objectives for an approximation of the laws and cooperation between Member States, Article 119 of the EC Treaty creates an obligation for the Member States to realise equal pay for men and women for work of equal value.[1]

Article 119, which was the outcome of a French initiative, has a double objective:

– a social objective: to lay down the principle of equal treatment, which was already embodied in Convention No. 100 of the ILO, into Community law;
– an economic objective: 'for in creating an obstacle to any attempt at "social dumping" by means of the use of female labour less well paid than male labour, it helped to achieve one of the fundamental objectives of the common market, the establishment of a system of ensuring that competition is not distorted.'[2]

1. Adv. Gen. Dutheillet de Lamothe, COJ, 25 May 1971, *G. Defrenne* v. *Belgium*, No. 80/70, IELL, *Case Law*, No. 4.
2. COJ, 15 May 1986, *M. Johnston* v. *Chief Constable of the Royal Ulster Constabulary*, No. 222/84, IELL, *Case Law*, No. 94.

365.   Article 119 is part of the social objectives of the Community aimed at social progress, as laid down in the preamble preceding the Treaty. The Court has repeatedly stated that the respect for fundamental personal human rights is one of the general principles of Community law, the observance of which it has a duty to ensure. There can be no doubt that the elimination of discrimination based on sex forms part of those fundamental rights.[1] It is part of the foundation of the Community. In particular, since Article 119 appears in the context of the harmonisation of working conditions while improvement is being maintained, the objection that the terms of this article may be observed in no other way than by raising the lowest salaries must be set aside.[2] It is clear that the 5 instruments, namely, Article 119 and the 4 directives, form one body of rules that are complementary to each other and fortify each other.

1. 15 June 1978, *G. Defrenne* v. *Sabena*, No. 149/77, IELL, *Case Law*, No. 29.
2. COJ, *G. Defrenne* v. *Sabena*, 8 April 1976, No. 43/75, IELL, *Case Law*, No. 22.

366.   Article 119 and the directives have a general scope of application, which follows from the nature of the principle of equal treatment, and thus apply to the private sector as well as to the public sector,[1] and to the self-employed.[2]

1. COJ, *G. Defrenne* v. *Sabena*, 8 April 1976, No. 43/75, IELL, *Case Law*, No. 22. ECJ., *Hellen Gester* v. *Freistaat Bayern*, 2 October 1997, C-1/95, not yet published.
2. COJ, 8 November 1983, *Commission* v. *U.K. of Great Britain and Northern Ireland*, No. 165/82, IELL, *Case Law*, No. 54.

§2. Definition

367. The notion 'equal treatment' is defined differently in the various Community instruments. In the 1975 directive, equal treatment is defined as 'the elimination of all discrimination on grounds of sex' (Art. 1), while the 1976 directive provides that 'the principle of equal treatment shall mean that there shall be no discrimination whatsoever on grounds of sex either directly or indirectly by reference in particular to marital or family status' (Art. 2, §1). It covers all forms of distinction or unequal treatment. What is meant is 'objective' discrimination: the existence of discrimination does not require a specific intention to discriminate.

> 'The Directive precludes provisions of domestic law, which make reparation of damage suffered as a result of discrimination on grounds of sex in the making of an appointment subject to the requirement of fault'.[1]

> 1. COJ, 22 April 1997, *Nils Draehmpaehl* v. *Urania Immobilienreserve OHG*, C-180/95, not yet published.

I. Equality of Opportunity or of Outcome

368. The question arises whether Community law aims at equality of opportunity (at the start) or at equality of outcome (at the finish). In the case of equal pay, equality of outcome is what is really meant. This is, however, not so for all provisions of the directive of 1976. Article 4, §2 speaks of 'equal opportunity' regarding access to employment,[1] including promotion; no actual job is thus guaranteed. In the case, however, of working conditions, including dismissal, equality of outcome is meant.

> 1. COJ, 10 April 1983, *Colson and Kamann*, No. 14/83, IELL, *Case Law*, No. 57.

II. Direct and Indirect Discrimination

369. Community law prohibits direct and indirect discrimination: direct on grounds of sex, indirect when other criteria are used, which are *prima facie* objective and acceptable, but *de facto* lead to a discriminatory treatment of one sex. This we find expressed in Article 2, §1 of the 1976 directive regarding equal treatment: '. . . either directly or indirectly by reference in particular to marital or family status.' This applies in the case of Article 119 as well as for the 1975 directive on equal pay. In *Jeanette Jenkins* v. *Kingsgate* the Court ruled in that sense in relation of part-time work. Ms. Jenkins was a female part-time employee who received an hourly rate that was 10 per cent lower than the hourly rate of pay for full-time work. The Court ruled that a difference in pay between full-time and part-time workers does not amount to discrimination as prohibited by Article 119 of the Treaty unless it is in reality merely an indirect way of reducing the pay of part-time workers on the ground that the group of workers is composed exclusively or predominantly of women.[1] The same problem was dealt with in *Karin von Weber*

Hartz v. *Bilka-Kaufhaus* since part-time employees working for Bilka could obtain a pension under the company scheme only if they had worked full-time for at least 15 years over a total period of 20 years. Again the Court ruled that Article 119 is infringed when part-time employees are excluded from its occupational pension scheme, where that exclusion affects a far greater number of women than men, unless the undertaking shows that the exclusion is based on objectively justified factors unrelated to any discrimination on grounds of sex.[2]

This ruling was confirmed in *Helga Nimz* v. *Hamburg* which involved a dispute between Mrs. Nimz and her employer Hamburg Stadt over the latter's refusal, based on the provisions of a collective wage agreement entered into with the national public service, to grant her passage to a higher salary bracket on the ground that Mrs. Nimz worked less than three quarters of the normal working hours. The Court indicated that this constitutes discrimination unless the employer can prove that there are factors which depend for their objectivity in particular on the relationship between the nature of the duties performed and the experience afforded by the performance of those duties after a certain number of working hours have been worked.

In case of indirect discrimination in a provision of a collective agreement, the national court is required to disapply that provision, without requesting or awaiting its prior removal by collective negotiations or any other procedure and to apply the same arrangements as are applied to other employees.[3]

It is also unlawful for national legislation applicable to many more women than men to limit, on the basis of their individual timetables, the compensation that members of staff committees employed on a part-time basis are to receive from their employer – in the form of paid holidays or overtime pay – in respect of their participation in training courses relating to the activities of staff committees. The training courses concerned were organised within the full-time work timetable in force in an undertaking. The therefore exceeded the individual work timetables of the part-time employees. Nevertheless compensation for the part-time employees was restricted to overtime pay or paid holidays, in accordance only with their part-time timetable, while full-time employees were compensated for their participation in the same training courses on the basis of their full-time work timetable. Only objective factors unrelated to any discrimination on the basis of sex can justify such difference in treatment.[4]

1. 31 March 1981, No. 96/80, IELL, *Case Law*, No. 41. In this case, the employer explained that he paid part-time workers less in order to encourage them to become full-time. *See also*: COJ, 13 July 1989, *Ingrid Rinner-Kühn* v. *FWW Spezial-Gebäude-reinigung GmbH & Co. KG*, No. 171/88, IELL, *Case Law*, No. 136*ter*.
2. COJ, 13 May 1986, No. 170/84, IELL, *Case Law*, No. 93; *see also*: COJ, 27 June 1990, *M. Kowalska* v. *Freie und Hansestadt Hamburg*, No. C-33/89, temporary severance grant provided for by collective agreement only for part-time workers.
3. 7 February 1991, *Helga Nimz* v. *Freie und Hansestadt Hamburg*, C-184/89, IELL, *Case Law*, No. 158.
4. COJ, 4 June 1992, *Arbeitswohlfart des Stadt Berlin e. V (AWSB)* v. *M. Bötel*, No. C-360/90, IELL, *Case Law*, No. 188.

370.   In *Stadt Lengerich* v. *Angelika Helmig*,[1] the Court ruled on *overtime pay for part-time employees*. The questions were raised in the course of proceedings between women working part-time and their employers. The women claimed that they were entitled to overtime supplements for hours worked in addition to their individual working hours at the same rate as that applicable for overtime worked by full-time employees in addition to normal working hours. Under the relevant collective agreements, full-time or part-time employees were entitled to overtime supplements only for time worked in addition to the ordinary working hours laid down by those agreements, but part-time employees were not entitled to the supplements for hours they worked over and above their individual working hours.

The applicants considered that the relevant provisions of the collective agreements discriminated against them in breach of Article 119 of the EEC Treaty and the 1975 directive by restricting overtime supplements to overtime worked in excess of the normal working hours.

The Court raised the question

'whether these provisions may constitute indirect discrimination incompatible with Article 119 of the Treaty. To that end it must be determined whether they establish different treatment for full-time and part-time employees and whether that difference affects considerably more women than men.

There is unequal treatment wherever the overall pay of full-time employees is higher than that of part-time employees for the same number of hours worked on the basis of an employment relationship.

In the circumstances considered, part-time employees do receive the same overall pay as full-time employees for the same number of hours worked. Part-time employees also receive the same overall pay as full-time employees if they work more than the normal working hours fixed by the collective agreements because on doing so they become entitled to overtime supplements.

Consequently, the provisions at issue do not give rise to different treatment as between part-time and full-time employees and there is therefore no discrimination incompatible with Article 119 of the Treaty and Article 1 of the Directive.'

1. 15 December 1994, Case C-399/92, C-409/92, C-425/92, C-34/93, C-50/93 and C-78/93, *Jur.*, 1994, 5727.

371. Jennifer Meyers[1] and an Adjudication Officer (UK) had a disagreement concerning her right to deduct child-care costs from her gross income in order to obtain family credit. Family credit is an income-related benefit which is awarded in order to supplement the income of low-paid workers who have the care of a child.

Meyers, being a single parent, made an application for family credit in respect of herself and her daughter, then aged three. The application was rejected by the Adjudication Officer on the ground that her income, as calculated for the purposes of that benefit, was greater than the level conferring entitlement.

In her appeal to the Social Security Appeal Tribunal, Meyers submitted that the non-deduction of child-care costs for the purposes of calculating her net income discriminated against single parents, since it is much easier for couples to arrange their working hours so that any children can be looked after by one of them. As most single parents are women, it also constitutes indirect discrimination against women.

One of the conditions for the award of family credit is that the claimant should be engaged in remunerative work. The aim of the benefit is to ensure that families do not find themselves worse off in work than they would be if they were not working. It is therefore intended to keep poorly paid workers in employment. That being so, family credit is concerned with access to employment, as referred to in Article 3 of the directive.

Furthermore, it is not only the conditions obtaining before an employment relationship comes into being which are involved in the concept of access to employment. The prospect of receiving family credit if he accepts low-paid work encourages an unemployed worker to accept such work, with the result that the benefit is related to considerations governing access to employment.

That finding was not invalidated by the UK's arguments which sought to show that there was no link with an employment relationship. It is precisely the existence of an employment relationship which confers entitlement to the benefit, even though the worker is not the direct recipient of that benefit, as in the case of a woman who is married or cohabiting and is unemployed, but who receives the benefit by virtue of her husband's or partner's work.

Furthermore, compliance with the fundamental principle of equal treatment presupposes that a benefit such as family credit, which is necessarily linked to an employment relationship, constitutes a working condition within the meaning of Article 5 of the directive. To confine the latter concept solely to those working conditions which are set out in the contract of employment or applied by the employer in respect of a worker's employment would remove situations directly covered by an employment relationship from the scope of the directive.

1. COJ, 13 July 1995, Case C-116/94, *Jur.*, 1995, 2131.

372.   Another interesting case related to compensation for attendance at training courses providing staff council members with the necessary knowledge for performing their functions.[1]

That question was raised in proceedings between *Johanna Lewark*, the plaintiff, and the *Kuratorium*, the defendant, concerning the latter's failure to compensate the plaintiff for the time spent on a training course which was necessary for the performance of her staff council functions but which took place outside her individual working hours.

The plaintiff was employed for 30.8 hours a week in the care unit. She was also on the local staff council, which consisted of three members.

The dialysis centre employed twenty-one employees in the care unit, seven men and fourteen women. Of the men, six worked full-time and one part-time. Of the women, four worked full-time and ten part-time. The plaintiff was the only member of the staff council to work part-time.

From 12 to 16 November 1990, the plaintiff, on the basis of a decision of the staff council and with the defendant's consent, attended a full-time training course in order to obtain the knowledge that was necessary for performing her staff council functions. The training course on 13 November 1990 lasted for 7.5 hours. If she had not been on the course, the plaintiff would not have worked on that day, because of her being employed part-time. However, the defendant paid her on the basis of her contractual working hours of 30.8 hours a week, without compensation for the time she had spent on that course.

According to the Industrial Relations Law, the staff council members attending such courses are to be released by their employer from the obligations arising from their employment, without loss of pay.

The plaintiff sought compensation for the 7.5 hours she spent on the course. In her opinion, staff council members who work part-time could not be required to make special sacrifices compared with those who work full-time. She considered that the defendant's refusal constituted discrimination incompatible with both Article 119 of the Treaty and the Directive (1975).

It followed that compensation received for losses of earnings due to attendance at training courses imparting the information necessary for performing staff council functions must be regarded as pay within the meaning of Article 119, since it constituted a benefit paid indirectly by the employer by reason of the existence of an employment relationship.

It is indisputable, the Court said, that where training courses, necessary for performing staff council functions, are organised during the full-time working hours in force in the undertaking but outside the individual working hours of part-time workers serving on those councils, the overall pay received by the latter is, for the same number of hours worked, lower than that received by the full-time workers serving on the same staff councils.

Since a difference in treatment was found to exist, it followed from settled case-law that, if it were the case that a much lower proportion of women than men worked full-time, the exclusion of part-time workers from certain benefits would be contrary to Article 119 where, taking into account the difficulties encountered by women workers working full-time, that measure could not be explained by factors excluding any discrimination on grounds of sex.

According to the order for reference, the official employment and social statistics showed that at the end of June 1991, 93.4 per cent of all part-time workers were women and 6.6 per cent were men.

As those figures were not disputed, it was considered that the application of legislative provisions such as those at issue in the main proceedings in principle caused indirect discrimination against women workers. It would be otherwise only if the different treatment found to exist was justified by objective factors unrelated to any discrimination based on sex.

If a Member State is able to show that measures chosen reflect a legitimate aim of its social policy, are appropriate to achieve that and are necessary in order to do so, the mere fact that the legislative provision affects far more women workers than men cannot be regarded as a breach of Article 119.

However, it was noted that legislation as that at issue is likely to deter workers in the part-time category, in which the proportion of women is undeniably preponderant, from performing staff council functions or acquiring the knowledge necessary for performing them, thus making it more difficult for that category of workers to be represented by qualified staff council members.

In the light of all those considerations and taking into account the possibility of achieving the social policy aim in question by other means, the difference in treatment could be justified from the point of view of Article 119 and of the directive only if it appeared to be suitable and necessary for achieving that aim.

This reasoning brought the Court to the conclusion that:

> 'Where the category of part-time workers includes a much higher number of women than men, the prohibition of indirect discrimination in the matter of pay precludes national legislation which, not being suitable and necessary for achieving a legitimate social policy aim, has the effect of limiting to their individual working hours the compensation which staff council members employed on a part-time basis are to receive from their employer for attending training courses which impart the knowledge necessary for serving on staff councils and are held during the full-time working hours applicable in the undertaking but which exceed their individual part-time working hours, when staff council members employed on a full-time basis receive compensation for attendance at the same courses on the basis of their full-time working hours.'

It must also be added that Council Directive 76/207/EEC of 9 February 1976 precludes national legislation which requires that, for the purposes of calculating the length of service of public servants, periods of employment during which the hours worked are between one-half and two-thirds of normal working hours are counted only as two-thirds of normal working hours, save where such legislation is justified by objective criteria unrelated to any discrimination on grounds of sex.[2]

1. COJ, 6 February 1996, *Kuratorium für Dialyse und-Nierentransplantation eV* v. *Johanna Lewark*, Case C-457/93, *Jur.*, 1996, 243. *See also*: COJ, 7 March 1996, *Edith Freers, Hannelore Speckman* v. *Deutsche Bundespost*, Case C-278/93, *Jur.*, 1996, 1165.
2. COJ, 2 October 1997, *Hellen Gerster* v. *Freistaat Bayern*, C-1/195, not yet published; *see also:* COJ, 2 October 1997, *Brigitte Kording* v. *Senator für Finanzen*, not yet published.

373.   Indirect discrimination was also discussed in *Luisia Sabbatini* v. *European Parliament*. Sabbatini, an EC official, had lost her expatriation allowance following her marriage. Under the EC staff regulations, an official

> 'who marries a person who at the date of the marriage does not qualify for the allowance shall forfeit the right to expatriation allowance unless that official thereby becomes a head of household.'

Head of household refers normally to a married male official, whereas a married female official is considered to be head of household only in particular circumstances, for instance in cases of invalidity or serious illness of the husband. The Court ruled that the withdrawal of the expatriation allowance following the marriage of the recipient might be justified in cases in which this change in the family situation is such as to bring an end to the state of expatriation, which is the justification for the benefit in question. In this respect, however, officials cannot be treated differently according to whether they are male or female, since the termination of the status of expatriate must be dependent for both male and female officials on uniform criteria, irrespective of sex. Consequently, by rendering the retention of the allowance subject to the status of head of the household, an arbitrary difference of treatment was created between officials.[1] A similar problem was raised in *Jeanne Airola* v. *Commission*. Jeanne, working for Euratom in Italy, married an Italian and became Italian with the consequent loss of her expatriation allowance. The Court ruled that the concept of the term 'nationals' contained in the Staff Regulation must be interpreted in such a way as to avoid any unwarranted difference of treatment between male and female officials who are, in fact, placed in comparable situations. Such an unwarranted difference of treatment results from an interpretation of concepts of nationals as also embracing the nationality which was imposed by law on an official of the female sex by virtue of her marriage, and which she was unable to renounce.[2]

1. 7 June 1972, No. 20/71, IELL, *Case Law*, No. 5.
2. 20 February 1975, No. 21/74, IELL, *Case Law*, No. 15.

III. Exceptions

374. One finds exceptions to the rule of equal treatment in Article 2, §3, 4 of the 1976 directive. As derogations from the fundamental principle of equal treatment they must be interpreted restrictively.[1]

1. COJ, 15 May 1986, *M. Johnston* v. *Chief Constable of the Royal Ulster Constabulary*, No. 222/84, IELL, *Case Law*, No. 94.

A. *Nature of the Activity*

375. Article 2 of the directive is

'without prejudice to the right of the Member State to exclude from its field of application those occupational activities and, where appropriate, the training leading thereto, for which, by reason of the nature or the context in which they are carried out, the sex of the worker constitutes a determining factor.'

It should be pointed out that Article 2, §2 constitutes a possibility and not an obligation. It does not have as its object or as its effect to require the Member States to exercise that power of derogation in a particular manner. However, Article 9, §2 requires the Member States to compile a complete and verifiable list, in whatever form, of the occupations and activities excluded from the application of the principle of equal treatment and to notify the Commission of the results. The Commission must then verify the application of that provision.[1] In *Commission* v. *UK of Great Britain and Northern Ireland*, the Commission claimed that the prohibition of discrimination applied to employment in a private household or where the number of persons employed did not exceed five persons or in the case of midwives, all three cases being retained as exceptions to the equality principle. The UK was of the opinion that these exceptions were justified:

'because they involve close personal relationships between employees and employers, so that it would not be legally possible to prevent the latter from employing persons of a particular sex.'[2]

As far as households are concerned, the Court ruled that it is undeniable that this consideration might be decisive for certain kinds of employment, but certainly not for all kinds of employment in question. With regard to small undertakings, the Court found that the United Kingdom had not put forward any argument to show that in any undertaking of that size the sex of the worker would be a determining factor by reason of the nature of his activities or the context in which they are carried out. The midwife exception was however an acceptable one. The Court recognised that at the present time personal sensitivities may play an important role in relations between midwife and patient.

1. COJ, 21 May 1985, *Commission* v. *Germany*, No. 248/83, IELL, *Case Law*, No. 73.
2. *Op. cit.*

376. In the case *Johnston* v. *Chief Constable of Ulster, Northern Ireland*[1] the problem was that Ms. Johnston did not receive a contract as a full-time officer since the decision had been made that general police duties, frequently involving operations requiring the carrying of fire arms, should no longer be assigned to women. She consequently had to accept a job as a part-time communications assistant with lower pay. The Court was of the opinion that a Member State may take into consideration requirements of public safety in order to restrict general policing duties, in an internal situation characterised by frequent assassinations, to men equipped with fire-arms.

1. *Op. cit.*

377. As indicated above, the Member States are obliged to examine the exceptions of Article 2, §2 at regular intervals to see whether, in the light of social developments, they are still justified and should be retained. They are to inform the Commission of the results of their inquiry.

B. *Protection of Women*

378. Article 2, §3 of the 1976 directive on equal treatment provides that it is 'without prejudice to provisions concerning the protection of women, particularly as regards pregnancy and maternity.' Moreover, this exception is, according to the Commission, to be interpreted restrictively.[1] The Court however ruled that the directive leaves the Member States with the discretion as to the social measures they adopt in order to guarantee the protection of women in connection with pregnancy and maternity in regard both to the nature of the protective measures and to the detailed arrangements for their implementation. In *Johnston* v. *Chief Constable*, the Court held that:

'it is clear from the express reference to pregnancy and maternity that the directive is intended to protect a woman's biological condition and the special relationship which exists between a woman and her child.'

In *Ulrich Hofmann*, the question concerned a father who obtained unpaid leave from his employer for the period between the expiry of the statutory protective period of eight weeks which was available to the mother and the day on which the child reached the age of six months; during that time he took care of the child while the mother continued her employment.Ulrich claimed the pay for maternity leave, arguing that the maternity leave introduced by the *Mutterschutzgesetz* was in fact not designed to give social protection to the mother on biological and medical grounds but rather to protect the child, which follows from the fact that the leave is withdrawn in the event of the child's death, which demonstrates that the leave was created in the interests of the child and not of the mother. The Court did not follow these arguments. It ruled that the directive is not designed to settle questions concerned with the organisation of the family, or alter the division of the responsibility between parents. The directive recognises the legitimacy, in terms of the principle of equal treatment, of protecting a woman's needs in two respects. First, it is legitimate to ensure the protection of a woman's biological condition during pregnancy and thereafter until such time as her physiological and mental functions have returned to normal after childbirth; secondly, it is legitimate to protect the special relationship between a woman and her child over the period which follows pregnancy and childbirth, by preventing that relationship from being disturbed by the multiple burdens which would result from the simultaneous pursuit of employment. In principle, therefore, a measure such as maternity leave granted to a woman on the expiry of the statutory protective period falls within the scope of Art. 2, §3 of Directive 76/207, inasmuch as it seeks to protect a woman in connection with the effects of pregnancy and motherhood. That being so, such leave may legitimately be reserved to the mother to the exclusion of any other person, in view of the fact that it is only the mother who may find herself subject to undesirable pressures to return to work prematurely. The directive does not impose on Member States a requirement that they shall, as an alternative, allow such leave to be granted to fathers, even where the parents so decide.[2]

1. COJ, 12 July 1984, *Ulrich Hofmann* v. *Barmer Ersatzkasse*, No. 184/83, IELL. *Case Law*, No. 60.
2. *Idem.*

C. Positive Discrimination

379. This is accepted in Article 2, §4 of the 1976 Directive. Positive discrimination refers to measures to promote equal opportunity for men and women, in particular by removing existing inequalities which affect women's opportunities.

380. In this area, a very controversial decision was taken by the Court of Justice in the case between *Kalanke* and *Freie Hansestadt Bremen* (*City of Bremen*)[1] in which the Court rejected the automatic nature of quotas. The case was as follows.

At the final stage of recruitment to a post of Section Manager in the Bremen Parks Department, two candidates were shortlisted: Mr. Eckhard Kalanke, the plaintiff in the main proceedings, holder of a diploma in horticulture and landscape gardening, who had worked since 1973 as a horticultural employee in the Parks Department and acted as permanent assistant to the Section Manager; and Ms. Glißmann, holder of a diploma in landscape gardening since 1983 and also employed, since 1975, as a horticultural employee in the Parks Department. The Staff Committee refused to give its consent to Kalanke's promotion.

Reference to arbitration resulted in a recommendation in favour of Kalanke. The Staff Committee then stated that the arbitration had failed and appealed to the conciliation board which, in a decision binding on the employer, considered that the two candidates were equally qualified and that priority should therefore be given, in accordance with the Bremen law on equal treatment, hereinafter 'LGG,' to the woman.

Before the Labour Court, Kalanke claimed that he was better qualified than Glißmann, a fact which the conciliation board had failed to recognise. He argued that, by reason of its quota system, the LGG was incompatible among others with the Bremen Constitution and with the German Basic Law. His application was dismissed at first instance, however, and again, on appeal, by the Regional Labour Court.

The Federal Labour Court asked, essentially, whether Article 2(1) and (4) of the directive of 1976 precludes national rules such as those in the present case which, where candidates of different sexes, shortlisted for promotion, are equally qualified, automatically give priority to women in sectors where they are under-represented, under-representation being deemed to exist when women do not make up at least half of the staff in the individual pay brackets in the relevant personnel group or in the function levels provided for in the organisation chart.

The Court of Justice reasoned as follows:

> 'The purpose of the Directive is, as stated in Article 1(1), to put into effect in the Member States the principle of equal treatment for men and women as regards, *inter alia*, access to employment, including promotion. Article 2(1) states that the principle of equal treatment means that "there shall be no discrimination whatsoever on grounds of sex either directly or indirectly".
>
> A national rule that, where men and women who are candidates for the same promotion are equally qualified, women are automatically to be given priority in sectors where they are underrepresented, involves discrimination on grounds of sex.
>
> It must, however, be considered whether such a national rule is permissible under Article 2(4), which provides that the Directive "shall be without prejudice to measures to promote equal opportunity for men and women, in particular by removing existing inequalities which affect women's opportunities".
>
> That provision is specifically and exclusively designed to allow measures which, although discriminatory in appearance, are in fact intended to eliminate or reduce actual instances of inequality which may exist in the reality of social life.
>
> It thus permits national measures relating to access to employment, including promotion, which give a specific advantage to women with a view to improving

their ability to compete on the labour market and to pursue a career on an equal footing with men.

Nevertheless, as a derogation from an individual right laid down in the Directive, Article 2(4) must be interpreted strictly.

National rules which guarantee women absolute and unconditional priority for appointment or promotion go beyond promoting equal opportunities and overstep the limits of the exception in Article 2(4) of the Directive.

Furthermore, in so far as it seeks equal representation of men and women in all grades and levels within a department, such a system substitutes for equality of opportunity envisaged in Article 2(4) the result which is to be arrived at by providing such opportunity.'

Therefore the Court concluded that:

'Article 2(1) and (4) of the Directive of 1976 precludes national rules whereby candidates of different sexes shortlisted for promotion are equally qualified, automatically give priority to women in sectors where they are under-represented, under-representation being deemed to exist when women do not make up at least half of the staff in the individual pay brackets in the relevant personnel group or in the function levels provided for in the organisation chart.'

1. 17 October 1995, Case C-450/93, *Jur.* 1995, 3051.

381. The judgment by the Court has given rise to a great deal of controversy. Positive discrimination is of course legal and acceptable, but quotas seem only to be virtuous on a case by case basis, not as an automatism.

According to the Commission's interpretation, only systems of rigid quotas for the recruitment of women are declared to be unlawful; a large number of positive measures, intended to increase the number of women in certain sectors of levels of employment where they are under-represented, are not affected by this ruling. At the same time, the Commission is proposing modifying Article 2 para. 4 of Directive 76/207/EEC relating to equal treatment between men and women, in order to clearly stipulate that the measures provided for by this provision include actions in favour of recruitment and the promotion of one of the two sexes, when the latter are under-represented, on condition that the employer always has the possibility of taking account of particular circumstances in any given case.

The Commission considers that the Court simply condemned the special feature of the Bremen legislation which automatically gave women an absolute and unconditional right to appointment or promotion over men in sectors where they were under-represented provided their qualifications were the same. It is therefore of the opinion that the only type of quota system which is unlawful is one which is completely rigid and does not leave open any possibility to take account of individual circumstances: Member States and employers are therefore free to resort to any form of positive action, including flexible quotas, for example:

(i) plans for promoting women, prescribing the promotions and the time limits within which the number of women should be increased but without imposing an automatic reference rule when individual decisions on recruitment and promotion are taken;

(ii) an obligation of principle for an employer to recruit or promote by preference a person belonging to the under-represented sex; in such a case, no individual right to be preferred is conferred on any person;

(iii) reductions in social security contributions which are granted to firms when they recruit women who return to the labour market, to perform tasks in sectors where women are under-represented;

(iv) positive action measures focusing on training, professional orientation, the reorganisation of working time, child care and so on.

In the light of the outcome of the *Kalenke* case, the Commission introduced a 'Proposal for a Council Directive amending Directive 76/2071 EEC on the implementation of the principle of equal treatment for men and women as regards access to employment, vocational training and promotion, and working conditions,'[1] which replaced Article 2(4) of Directive 76/207/EEC by the following:

'4. This Directive shall be without prejudice to measures to promote equal opportunity for men and women, in particular by removing existing inequalities which affect the opportunities of the under-represented sex in the areas referred to in Article 1(1). Possible measures shall include the giving of preference, as regards access to employment or promotion, to a member of the under-represented sex, provided that such measures do not preclude the assessment of the particular circumstances of an individual case.'

In *Hellmut Marschall* v. *Land Nordrhein Westfalen*,[2] the Court qualified its position. It stated as follows:

'A national rule which, in a case where there are fewer women than men at the level of the relevant post in a sector of the public service, and both female and male candidates for the post are equally qualified in terms of their suitability, competence and professional performance requires that priority be given to the promotion of female candidates unless reasons specific to an individual male candidate tilt the balance in his favour is not precluded by Article 2(1) and (4) of the Directive, provided that:

– in each individual case the rule provides for male candidates, who are as equally qualified as the female candidates to a guarantee that the candidatures will be the subject of an objective assessment which will take account of all criteria specific to the individual candidates and will override the priority accorded to female candidates where one or more of those criteria tilts the balance in favour of the male candidate, and

– such criteria are not such as to discriminate'.

1. O.J., 22 June 1996, No. C-179/8.
2. COJ, 11 November 1997, C-409/95, not yet published. *See* further in the Annex (Treaty of Amsterdam, the amended Article 119 (Art. 147)).

§3. Object

I. Equal Pay for Equal Work or Work of Equal Value

A. Equal Work or Work of Equal Value

382.   Article 119 of the EC Treaty concerns equal work, which includes 'jobs having a high degree of similarity.'[1] Directive No. 75/117 goes further and relates to the 'same work or work to which equal value is attributed' (Art. 1). Thus it concerns jobs that are neither identical, nor similar, but to which an equal value can be attributed.

> 1. Adv. Gen. Capotorti, 28 February 1980, *Macarthys Ltd.* v. *Smith*, 27 March 1980, No. 129/79, IELL, *Case Law*, No. 35.

383.   The Court was asked to compare, in a case involving equal value, female factory workers with male stores labourers. The first were engaged in such tasks as dismantling, cleaning, oiling and reassembling telephones and other equipment. The second group was engaged in cleaning, collecting and delivering equipment and components and in lending general assistance as required. In comparison to their male colleagues, the female workers not only performed work of higher value but also they were paid less. The question then was whether the Community law principle of equal work for equal pay extends to a claim for equal pay on the basis of work of equal value in circumstances where the work of the claimant has been assessed to be of higher value than that of the person with whom the claimant sought comparison. The answer, based on Article 119, was *a fortiori* positive. To adopt a contrary interpretation would be tantamount to rendering the principle of equal pay ineffective and nugatory. In this case, the employer would indeed easily be able to circumvent the principle by assigning additional or more onerous duties to workers of a particular sex who would then be paid a lower wage.[1]

> 1. 4 February 1988, *Mary Murphy and others* v. *Bord Telecom Eirann*, No. 157/86, IELL, *Case Law*, No. 119.

384.   Article 119 and the directive apply to *piece-work pay schemes* in which pay depends entirely or in large measure on the individual output of each worker.[1]
The principle of equal pay means that the mere finding that in a piece-work pay scheme the average pay of a group of workers, consisting predominantly of women carrying out one type of work, is appreciably lower than the average pay of a group of workers consisting predominantly of men, carrying out another type of work, to which equal value is attributed does not suffice to establish that there is discrimination with regard to pay. However, where, in a piece-work pay scheme in which individual pay consists of a variable element depending on each worker's output and a fixed element depending on the group of workers concerned, it is not possible to identify the factor which determined the rates or units of measurement used to calculate the variable element in the pay, the employer may have to bear the burden of proving that the differences found are not due to sex discrimination.

For the purposes of the comparison to be made between the average pay of two groups of piece-workers, the national court must satisfy itself that the two groups each encompass all the workers who, taking account of a set of factors such as the nature of the work, the training requirements and the working conditions, can be considered to be in a comparable situation and that they cover a relatively large number of workers ensuring that the differences are not due to purely fortuitous or short-term factors or to differences in the individual output of the workers concerned.

When ascertaining whether the principle of equal pay has been observed, it is for the national court to decide whether, in the light of circumstances such as, first, the factor that the work done by one of the groups of workers in question involves machinery and requires in particular muscular strength whereas that done by the other group is manual work requiring in particular dexterity and, secondly, the fact that there are differences between the work of the two groups with regard to paid breaks, freedom to organise one's own work and work-related inconveniences, the two types of work are of equal value or whether those circumstances may be considered to be objective factors unrelated to any discrimination on grounds of sex which can justify any pay differentials.

The principle of equal pay for men and women also applies where the elements of the pay are determined by collective bargaining or by negotiation at local level. However, the national court may take that fact into account in its assessment of whether differences between the average pay of two groups of workers are due to objective factors unrelated to any discrimination on grounds of sex.

1. COJ, 31 May 1995, *Specialarbejderforbundet i Danmark* v. *Dansk Industri, originally Industriens Arbejdsgivere, acting for Royal Copenhagen A/S*, Case C-400/93, *Jur.*, 1995, 1275.

385. Article 1, §2 of the 1975 directive provides that where a job classification system is used for determining pay, it must be based on the same criteria for both men and women and thus be drawn up so as to exclude any discrimination on grounds of sex.

Job classification was discussed in the case *Gisela Rummler* v. *Dato-Druck*. Beside elements like the degree of knowledge, concentration and responsibility, the factors muscle demand and muscular efforts were involved. The Court ruled that the directive did not prohibit the use, in a job classification system for the purpose of determining rates of pay, of the criteria of muscle demand or muscular effort or that of the heaviness of the work if, in view of the nature of the tasks involved, the work to be performed does require a certain degree of physical strength, as long as the system as a whole, by taking other criteria into account, precludes any discrimination on the grounds of sex. The Court further declared that the use of values reflecting the average performance of workers of one sex as a basis for determining the extent to which work makes demands or requires effort or whether it is heavy constitutes a form of discrimination on grounds of sex, contrary to the directive. A job classification system must take into account criteria for which workers of each sex may show particular aptitude.[1]

The question arose whether the principle of equal pay for the same work is to be interpreted in relation only to a 'single workplace.' The question was not decided upon by the Court.[2] However, in the *Defrenne II* Case, the Court stated that:

'it is impossible not to recognise that the complete implementation of the aim pursued in Article 119, by means of the elimination of all discrimination, direct and indirect, between men and women workers, not only as regards individual undertakings but also entire branches of industry and even of the economic system as a whole, may in certain cases involve the elaboration of criteria whose implementation necessitates the taking of appropriate measures at Community and at national level.'[3]

In the same judgment, moreover, the Court limited the direct effect of Article 119 to work that is carried out in the same establishment or service, whether private of public. Advocate-General VerLoren van Themaat was nevertheless of the opinion that the Danish Government, in the above-mentioned Danish case, by limiting the comparison of work to the same establishment, was adding a condition which did not appear either in Article 119 or in the directive. As appears from the second sentence of Article 1 of the directive, a comparison of duties within the same fixed establishment of an undertaking or even within a single undertaking will not always be sufficient. In certain circumstances, comparison of work of equal value in other undertakings covered by the same collective agreement will be necessary. As the Commission however did not formally raise that objection, there was no reason for the Court to decide the question.[4]

In the case *Macarthys Ltd.* v. *Wendy Smith*, the question was raised whether the principle of equal pay for equal work is confined to situations in which men and women are contemporaneously doing equal work for their employer. Wendy Smith was a warehouse manageress with a weekly salary of £50. She complained of discrimination in pay because her predecessor, a man, whose post she took up after an interval of four months, received a salary of £60 per week. The Court had to acknowledge that, as the Employment Appeal Tribunal properly recognised, it cannot be ruled out that a difference in pay between two workers occupying the same post but at different periods in time may be explained by the operation of factors which are unconnected with any discrimination on grounds of sex, like the period of time between the periods of employment, a change in the general economic conditions or the adoption of a more restrictive income policy. In the absence of such justification unequal payment is contrary to Article 119. The principle enshrined in Article 119 that men and women should receive equal pay for equal work is thus not confined to situations in which men and women are contemporaneously doing equal work for the same employer. Submission was also made of the question whether a woman could claim not only the salary received by a man who previously did the same work for her employer, but also, more generally, the salary to which she would be entitled were she a man, even in the absence of any man who was concurrently performing, or had previously performed, similar work, of thus 'a hypothetical male worker.' The answer was that such a proposition requires comparative studies of entire branches of industry and therefore the elaboration by the Community and national legislative bodies of criteria of assessment. It follows from this that, in cases of actual discrimination falling within the scope of direct application of Article 119, comparisons are confined to parallels which may be drawn on the basis of concrete appraisals of the work actually performed by employees of different sex within the same establishment or service.

Finally, consecutive jobs are equal jobs in accordance to Article 119. The Court did not need the nation 'work of equal value' contained in the directive to arrive at that conclusion.

1. 1 July, 1986, No. 237/85, IELL, *Case Law*, No. 97.
2. *Commission* v. *Denmark*, 30 January 1985, No. 143/83, IELL, *Case Law*, No. 64.
3. 8 April 1976, No. 43/75, IELL, *Case Law*, No. 22.
4. *See also Macarthys Ltd*. v. *Wendy Smith*, op. cit.

B. Equal Pay

386.   Article 119 contains the notion 'equal pay.' The 1975 directive simply refers to Article 119, while the 1976 directive only talks of working conditions, without mentioning the word 'pay.' One could indeed say that pay is a condition of work and thus is covered by the 1976 directive regarding equal treatment. In fact the question boils down to the interpretation of Article 119, which contains the following definition:

> 'For the purpose of this article "pay" means the ordinary basic or minimum wage or salary and any other consideration, whether in cash or in kind, which the worker receives, directly or indirectly, in respect of his employment for his employer.'

Equal pay without discrimination based on sex means:

a. that pay for the same work at piece rates shall be calculated on the basis of the same unit of measurement;
b. that pay for work at time rates shall be the same for the same job.

The notion 'pay' has given rise to quite a number of interpretation controversies.[1] In particular, the distinction between direct and indirect wages remains a difficult one. The problem was first tackled in the case of *Gabrielle Defrenne (I)*. Defrenne was employed by Sabena as an air hostess. A Royal Decree of 3 November 1969 laid down the retirement pension scheme in respect of air crews of aviation companies. That decree however excluded air hostesses. Ms Defrenne was covered by the overall general pension scheme. However, within that scheme she could not receive full benefits since her contract of employment, adopted under the terms of the collective agreement, provided that she could not continue to perform her duties beyond the age of 40 years. So there were no possibilities for her to have a full career and moreover she could not claim any retirement pension before the age laid down by the general scheme, that is to say 60 years for women. The question consequently put to the Court was whether the retirement pension granted under the terms of the social security financed by contributions from workers, employers and by State subsidy, constitutes a consideration which the worker receives indirectly in respect of his employment from his employer.

1. A maternity benefit is pay in the meaning of Article 119. To the extent that it is calculated on the basis of pay received by a woman before the commencement of the maternity leave, the amount of benefit must include pay rises awarded between the beginning of the period and the end of the maternity leave (COJ, 13 February 1996, *Joan Gillespie and Others* v. *Northern Health and Social Services Board and Others*, Case C-342/93, *Jur.*, 1996, 475). 15 June 1978, *G. Defrenne* v. *Sabena*, No. 149/77, IELL, *Case Law*, No. 29.

387. The Court based its reasoning in 1971 (thus before the 1976 directive) in line with the opinion of the Advocate General, ascertaining that the interpretation difficulties concentrate on the sentence 'any other consideration, whether in cash or in kind, which the worker receives directly or indirectly, in respect of his employment from the employer.'

According to the Court, the following elements must be retained:

1. direct or indirect payment from the employer to the worker;
2. payment in respect of his employment.

The question then was whether 'pensions' carry both elements. Here a distinction was made between different kinds of pensions: general schemes, which benefit all workers, and special schemes, which only benefit particular groups of workers.

388. The Court ruled that, although consideration in the nature of social security benefits is not in principle alien to the concept of pay, there cannot be brought within this concept, as defined in Article 119, social security schemes or benefits, in particular retirement pensions directly governed by legislation without any element of agreement within the undertaking or the occupational branch concerned, which are obligatorily applicable to general categories of workers.[1] These schemes assure the workers the benefit of a legal scheme, to the financing of which workers, employers and possibly authorities contribute in a measure determined less by the employment relationship between the employer and the worker than by considerations of social policy. Accordingly, the part due from the employers in the financing of such schemes does not constitute a direct or an indirect payment to the worker. Moreover, the worker will normally receive the benefits legally prescribed, not by reason of the employer's contribution but solely because the worker fulfils the legal conditions for the granting of benefits. These are likewise characteristics of special schemes, which, within the framework of the general system of social security established by legislation, relate in particular to certain categories of workers. It follows that a retirement pension established within the framework of a social security scheme laid down by legislation does not constitute consideration which the employee receives indirectly in respect of his employment from his employer within the meaning of Article 119.

> 1. The Court observed that the Community legislature intended to authorise the determination of a different pensionable age according to sex for the purpose of granting old-age and retirement pensions, and also for forms of discrimination which are directly linked to that difference. COJ, 7 July 1992, *The Queen* v. *Secretary of State for Social Security Ex parte: The Equal Opportunities Commission (EOC)*, No. C-9/91, *Jur.*, 1992, 4297; *see also: Ten Oever G.C.* v. *Stichting Bedrijfspensioenfonds voor het Glazenwassersen Schoonmaakbedrijf*, 6 October 1993 No. C-109/91, not yet published.

389. In the case of special retirement schemes, different hypotheses must be considered. Pensions that are directly paid by the employer constitute direct pay in the sense of Article 119. The reason is that they are a payment in respect of employment, while in most cases wage deductions take place. Additional retirement schemes, independent from the overall general legal schemes with employer's contributions and established for a specific group of workers employed in different occupational or inter-occupational enterprises, also constitute 'pay,' although payment is made by a fund and one is thus confronted in a certain sense with a form of indirect pay. Indeed, the employer makes a contribution and there is a specific link with the employment relation. Such systems show close links with the employer.

390. Special systems of social security, which are characterised by the fact that they are, from the administrative and organisational points of view, part of the general State system and which provide for higher amounts than the general system (thus specific systems for mine workers, seamen, for the sectors of gas and electricity and so on), cannot be separated from those general systems. Here the link with the employer is too weak. There is no real relationship between the contribution and the amount of the pension; the employer does not pay either directly or indirectly.

In conclusion, one can say that general and specific retirement schemes – established within the framework of a more general social policy – are not 'pay' in the meaning of Article 119 of the EC Treaty. Pensions paid by the employer, or through employers' funds established for that purpose, on the contrary do constitute 'pay.' This means that Ms. Defrenne lost her case. I repeat the criteria: there should be a consideration:

– paid directly or indirectly by the employer;
– in respect of employment: on the grounds of a (specific) employment relation in a (specific) undertaking.

> 'On this point, it should be recalled that the Court has stated on several occasions that the only possible decisive criterion is whether the pension is paid to the worker by reason of the employment relationship between him and his former employer, that is to say, the criterion of employment based on the wording of Article 119 itself.
>
> Admittedly, the Court has recognized that the employment criterion cannot be regarded as exclusive, since pensions paid under statutory social security schemes may reflect, wholly or in part, pay in respect of work.
>
> On the other hand, considerations of social policy, of State organization, of ethics, or even budgetary concerns which influenced, or may have influenced, the establishment by the national legislature of a particular scheme cannot prevail if the pension concerns only a particular category of workers, if it is directly related to length of service and if its amount is calculated by reference to the last salary.
>
> Furthermore, a survivor's pension provided for by an occupational pension scheme is an advantage deriving from the survivor's spouse's membership of the scheme and accordingly falls within the scope of Article 119.
>
> It follows from the foregoing that a survivor's pension paid under an occupational pension scheme of the kind in issue,[1] which essentially arises from the employment of the beneficiary's spouse, is linked to the latter's pay and falls within the scope of Article 119 of the Treaty'.[2]

1. Insurance scheme of a State electricity company.
2. COJ, 17 April 1997, *Dimossia Epicheirissi Ilektrismou (DEI)* v. *Efthimios Evrenenopoulos*, C-147/95, not yet published.

391.   In *Liefting and others* v. *Direction of the Academic Hospital of Amsterdam*, pensions were again at the centre of attention. The case concerned a social security system under which:

1. the contributions are calculated on the basis of the employee's salary but may not exceed a certain limit;
2. husband and wife are treated as one person, the contributions being calculated on the basis of their combined salaries, subject once again to the upper limit;
3. the State is bound to pay, on behalf of its employee, the contributions owned by him; and
4. where both husband and wife are civil servants, the authority employing the husband is primarily responsible for paying the contributions and the authority employing the wife is required to pay the contributions only insofar as the upper limit is not reached by the contributions paid on behalf of the husband.

The contribution paid on behalf of the wife was thus smaller than the contribution on behalf of the husband. Both enjoyed the same disposable salary, but the husband's gross salary was higher than the wife's because the contribution was added to that salary. This is important since the gross salary is taken into account directly to determine the calculation of other advantages linked to the salary such as redundancy payments, unemployment benefits, family allowances and credit facilities. The Court rightly decided that such an arrangement is incompatible with the principle laid down in Article 119 of the EC Treaty insofar as the resultant differences between the gross salary of a female civil servant whose husband is also a civil servant and the gross salary of a male civil servant directly affect the calculation of other benefits dependent on the salary, such as severance pay, unemployment benefit, family allowances and loan facilities.[1]

In *D. Neath* v. *Hugh Steeper Ltd.*[2] three questions were raised on the interpretation of Article 119 and on the the effects in time of the *Barber* judgment.

The three questions were raised in the context of proceedings concerning the rules for granting a company pension and the transfer of pension rights. The point at stake was the use of actuarial factors differing according to sex in the sphere of private occupational pension schemes.

The Court stated that, in the context of a defined-benefit occupational pension scheme such as that in question in the main proceedings, the employer's commitment to his employees concerned the payment, at a given moment in time, of a periodic pension for which the determining criteria were already known at the time when the commitment was made and which constituted pay within the meaning of Article 119. However, that commitment did not necessarily have to do with the funding arrangements chosen to secure the periodic payment of the pension, which thus remained outside the scope of application of Article 119.

In contributory schemes, funding was provided through the contributions made by the employees and those made by the employers. The contributions made by the employees were an element of their pay since they were deducted directly from an employee's salary, which by definition was pay. The amount of those contributions had therefore to be the same for all employees, male and female, which was indeed so in the case before the Court. This was not so in the case of the employer's contributions which ensured the adequacy of the funds necessary to cover the cost of the pensions promised, thus securing payment in the future, that being the substance of the employer's commitment.

It followed that, unlike periodic payment of pensions, inequality of employers' contributions paid under funded defined-benefit schemes, which was due to the use of actuarial factors differing according to sex, was not struck at by Article 119.

A similar case was dealt with in *Worringham and Humphreys* v. *Lloyd's Bank Limited*. In Lloyd's all permanent staff of the Bank are, on entering employment, required to become members of a retirement benefits scheme; each member, with the exception of women under 25, is required to contribute 5 per cent of his or her salary to the fund. Contributions are deducted from a member's salary at source and paid by the Bank directly to the trustees. Here also the gross salary of the male members was higher, which led to different rules regarding other aspects not related to that pension, such as that the above-mentioned 5 per cent contribution is included to determine the amount of certain benefits and social advantages such as redundancy payments, unemployment benefits and family allowances, as well as mortgage and credit facilities. Logically, the Court concluded that a contribution to a retirement benefits scheme that is paid by an employer in the name of employees by means of an addition to the gross salary and which therefore helps to determine the amount of that salary constitutes 'pay' within the meaning of the second paragraph of Article 119 of the EC Treaty.[3]

1. 18 September 1984, No. 23/83, IELL, *Case Law*, No. 63.
2. 22 December 1993, No. Case C-152/91, not yet published.
3. 11 March 1981, No. 69/80. IELL, *Case Law*, No. 40.

392.   In *Garland* v. *British Rail*, the dispute concerned discrimination alleged to be suffered by female employees who on retirement no longer continued to enjoy travel facilities for their spouses and dependent children although male employees continued to do so. The question that, was whether such facilities constitute pay within the meaning of Article 119, especially since the employer grants them although he is not contractually bound to do so. The Court first retained the point that the special rail travel facilities granted after retirement must be considered to be an extension of the facilities granted during the period of employment. As they are granted in kind by the employer to the retired male employee or his dependents directly or indirectly in respect of his employment, they fulfil the criteria enabling them to be treated as pay within the meaning of Article 119. The Court ruled that the argument that the facilities are not related to a contractual obligation is immaterial. The legal nature of the facilities is not important for the purposes of the application of Article 119 provided they are granted in respect of employment.[1]

Another case concerned an expatriation allowance for Community officials. The purpose of such an allowance is to compensate civil servants for the special expenses and disadvantages resulting from the entry into the service of the Communities and the resulting obligation to change place of residence. Staff regulations provided that an official 'who marries a person who at the date of marriage does not qualify for the allowance shall forfeit the right to the expatriate allowance unless that official thereby becomes a head of household.' The head of a household however normally refers to a married male official, whereas a married female official is considered to be head of household only in exceptional circumstances, in particular in cases of invalidity or serious illness of the husband. This indicates that the allowance is paid to married officials not only in consideration of the personal situation of the recipient, but also of the family situation created by the marriage. Since the Staff Regulations cannot treat officials differently according to whether they are male or female, and since termination of the status of expatriate must depend on both male and female officials on uniform criteria, irrespective of sex, the Court annulled the decisions by which the applicant's expatriate allowance was withdrawn.[2] Article 119 also applies to the conditions of access to voluntary redundancy benefits paid by an employer to a worker wishing to leave his employment.[3]

By retaining legislation which excludes female workers over the age of 60 from the benefit of additional redundancy payments, a Member State equally fails to fulfil its obligations under Article 14.[4]

Finally, conditions of age, such as the age of 40 years at which the employment contract of G. Defrenne had to come to an end, have indirectly to do with remuneration, but of course do not constitute 'pay' in the sense of Article 119.

1. 2 February 1982, No. 12/81, IELL, *Case Law*, No. 43.
2. COJ, 7 June 1972, *Sabbatini* v. *European Parliament*, No. 20/71, IELL, *Case Law*, No. 5.
3. COJ, 16 February 1982, *Arthur Burton* v. *British Railways Board*, No. 19/81, IELL, *Case Law*, No. 44.
4. COJ, 17 February 1993, *Commission of the European Communities* v. *Kingdom of Belgium*, No. C-173/91, not yet published.

393.   In *Newstead* v. *Department of Transport*, the following case was discussed: the occupational pension scheme to which Newstead belonged made a provision for a widow's pension fund. That fund was financed in part by the contributions of civil servants. However, although male civil servants, whatever their marital status, were obliged to contribute 1.5 per cent of their gross salary to the fund, female civil servants were never obliged to contribute to the fund but could in certain circumstances be permitted to do so. In the case of a civil servant who was at no time married while he was covered by the occupational scheme, it was provided that his contributions to the widow's pension fund should be returned to him, with compound interest at the rate of 4 per cent *per annum*, when he would leave the Civil Service. Should he die before then, that amount would be paid to his estate. Mr. Newstead, who was unmarried, argued that the obligation to contribute to the widow's pension fund had the effect of discrimination against him in comparison with a female civil servant in an equivalent post, since she was not obliged to give up 1.5 per cent of her gross salary. The Court, in judging the case, brought to mind its earlier judgments, whereby it simply observed that Article 119 was applicable in particular where the gross pay of men was higher than that of women in order to make up for the fact that only men were required to contribute to a social security scheme. The Court emphasised that although the extra pay was subsequently deducted by the employer and paid into a pension fund on behalf of the employee, it determined the calculation of other salary-related benefits (redundancy payments, unemployment benefits, family allowances, credit facilities) and was therefore, a component of the worker's pay for the purposes of the second paragraph of Article 119. For Newstead, the Court ruled, those circumstances were not present. The deduction in question resulted in a reduction in net pay because of a contribution paid to a social security scheme and in no way affected gross pay, on the basis of which the other salary-related benefits mentioned above were normally calculated. It followed, rather surprisingly, that Article 119 was not applicable. Directive No. 76/207 of 9 February 1976 was not applicable either, as it is not intended to apply in social security matters, nor was Directive No. 79/7 of 19 December 1978, as Article 3, §2 of that directive states that it 'shall not apply to the provisions concerning survivors benefits.' It should be added that Article 9 of Directive No. 86/372 of 24 July 1986 on the implementation of the principle of equal treatment for men and women in occupational social security schemes provides that:

> 'Member States may defer compulsory application of the principle of equal treatment with regard to . . . (b) survivors' pensions until a directive requires the principle of equal treatment in statutory social schemes in that regard.'

George Noel Newstead lost his case although *prima facie* he must have been sure that this was one he could not lose. It becomes immediately clear that the notion 'pay' in the meaning of Article 119 and the equal treatment directives belongs to advanced legal technology.

394.   This was confirmed in *Douglas Harvey Barber* v. *Guardian Royal Exchange Group*, which related to Barber's right to an early retirement pension on his being made compulsory redundant. Barber's conditions provided that, in the event of redundancy, members of the pension fund established by the Guardian were entitled to an immediate pension subject to having attained the age of 55 for men and 50 for women. Staff who did not fulfil those conditions received certain cash benefits calculated on the basis of their years of service and a deferred pension payable at the normal pensionable age, which was fixed at 62 for men and 57 for women. Barber was made redundant when he was aged 52. The Guardian paid him the cash benefits provided for in the severance terms, the statutory redundancy payment and the *ex-gratia* payment. He would have been entitled to a retirement pension as from the date of his 62nd birthday. It was undisputed that a woman in the same position as Mr. Barber would have received an immediate retirement pension as well as the statutory redundancy payment and that the total value of those benefits would have been greater than the amount paid to Mr. Barber. Therefore, Barber contended that he was discriminated against.

395.   In deciding this case the Court took a number of important decisions on principle, while confirming some others:

1. the fact that certain benefits are paid after the termination of the employment relationship does not prevent them from being in the nature of pay, within the meaning of Article 119 of the EC Treaty;[1]
2. compensation in connection with redundancy constitutes a form of pay to which the worker is entitled in respect of his employment and which is paid to him upon the termination of his employment relationship, whether it is paid under a contract of employment, by virtue of legislative provisions or on a voluntary basis;

3. unlike the benefits awarded by national statutory social security schemes, a pension paid under a contracted-out scheme constitutes consideration paid by the employer to the worker in respect of his employment and therefore falls within the scope of Article 119;

4. it is contrary to Article 119 to impose an age condition which differs according to sex in respect of pensions paid under a contracted-out scheme, even if the difference between the pensionable age for men and that for women is based on the one provided for by the national statutory scheme;[2]

5. the Court emphasised the fundamental importance of transparency and, in particular, of the possibility of a review by the national courts, in order to prevent and, if necessary, eliminate any discrimination based on sex;

6. if the national courts are under the obligation to make an assessment and a comparison of all the various types of consideration granted, according to the circumstances, to men and women, juridical review would be difficult and the effectiveness of Article 119 would be diminished as a result. It follows that genuine transparency permitting an effective review is assured only if the principle of equal pay applies to each of the elements of remuneration granted to men or women;

7. the Court held that, according to its established case-law, Article 119 applies directly to all forms of discrimination which can be identified solely with the aid of the criteria of equal work and equal pay referred to by the article in question, without national or Community measures being required to define them with greater precision in order to permit their application;

8. the direct effect of Article 119 may not be relied upon to claim entitlement to a pension, with effect from a date prior to that of his judgment, except in the case of workers or those claiming for them who have before that date initiated legal proceedings or raised an equivalent claim under the then applicable law. The Court recalled indeed that it could, by way of exception, taking account of the serious difficulties which its judgment might create in regard to past events, be moved to restrict the possibility for all persons concerned to rely on the interpretation which the Court, in proceedings with reference to a preliminary ruling, gave to a provision.[3]

---

1. This was confirmed in *Commission* v. *Belgium*, 17 February 1993, No. C-173/91, IELL, *Case Law*, No. 201. 'By maintaining in force legislation which renders female workers who have attained the age of 60 ineligible for a supplementary allowance payable upon redundancy, provided for by Collective Labour Agreement No. 17, which was given the force of law by Royal Decree of 16 January 1975, the Kingdom of Belgium has failed to fulfil its obligations under Article 119 of the Treaty.'

2. *See also* COJ, 14 December 1993, *M. Moroni* v. *Finma Collo GmbH*, No. C-110/91, not yet published.

3. 17 May 1990, No. 262/88, IELL, *Case Law*, No. 146. *See also*: COJ, 6 September 1993, *G.C. Ten Oever* v. *Stichting, op. cit.*; 14 December 1993, M. Moroni, *op. cit.*, and 22 December 1993, *D. Neath* v. *Hugh Steeper Ltd.*, No. C-152/91, not yet published.

396.   The pension saga continues. In the *Bird Eye Walls Limited* v. *F.M. Robert case*,[1] the question was raised whether when judging equal treatment regarding bridging pensions reference should be made to State pensions which the woman concerned actually receives. In this case the Court held that:

1. It is not contrary to Article 119 of the EC Treaty, when calculating the amount of a bridging pension which is paid by an employer to male and female employees who have taken early retirement on grounds of ill health and which is intended to compensate, in particular, for loss of income resulting from the fact that they have not yet reached the age required for payment of the State pension, to take account of the amount of the State pension which they will subsequently receive and to reduce the amount of the bridging pension accordingly, even though, in the case of men and women aged between 60 and 65, the result is that a female ex-employee receives a smaller bridging pension than that paid to her male counterpart, the difference being equal to the amount of the State pension to which she is entitled as from the age of 60 in respect of the periods of service completed with that employer.
2. It is not contrary to Article 119 of the EC Treaty, when calculating the bridging pension, to take account of the full State pension which a married woman would have received if she had not opted in favour of paying contributions at a reduced rate, entitling her to a reduced pension only, or not entitling her to a pension, or of the widow's pension which may be drawn by the woman concerned and which is equivalent to a full State pension.

   1. COJ, *Bird Eye Walls Limited* v. *F.M. Robert*, 9 November 1993, No. C-132/92, not yet published.

397.   On 28 September 1994, the Court of Justice decided in not less than 6 cases relating to the implications of the *Barber* case.[1] The harvest of these judgments can be summarised as follows:

1. By virtue of the *Barber* judgment, the direct effect of Article 119 of the Treaty may be relied upon, for the purpose of claiming equal treatment in the matter of occupational pensions, only in relation to benefits payable in respect of periods of service subsequent to 17 May 1990, subject to the exception in favour of workers or those claiming under them who have, before that date, initiated legal proceedings or raised an equivalent claim under the applicable national law.
2. The limitation of the effects in time of the *Barber* judgment applies to survivor's pensions and consequently equal treatment in this matter may be claimed only in relation to periods of service subsequent to 17 May 1990.

   The limitation of the effects in time of the *Barber* judgment is applicable to benefits not linked to the length of actual service only where the operative events occurred before 17 May 1990.
3. The principles laid down in the *Barber* judgment, and more particularly the limitation of its effects in time, concern not only contracted-out but also non-contracted-out occupational schemes.
4. The use of actuarial factors varying according to sex in funded defined-benefit occupational pension schemes does not fall within the scope of Article 119 of the Treaty. Consequently, inequalities in the amounts of capital benefits or substitute benefits, whose value can be determined only on the basis of the arrangements chosen for funding the scheme, are likewise not struck at by Article 19.
5. The principle of equal treatment, laid down in Article 119, applies to all pension benefits paid by occupational schemes, without any need to distinguish

according to the kind of contributions to which these benefits are attributed, namely employers' contributions or employees' contributions. However, in so far as an occupational pension scheme does no more than provide the membership with the necessary arrangements for management, additional benefits stemming from contributions paid by employees on a purely voluntary basis, are not covered by Article 119.

6. In the event of the transfer of pension rights from one occupational scheme to another owing to a worker's change of job, the second scheme is obliged, on the worker's reaching retirement age, to increase the benefits it undertook to pay him when accepting the transfer so as to eliminate the effects, contrary to Article 119, suffered by the worker in consequence of the inadequacy of the capital transferred, this being due in turn to the discriminatory treatment suffered under the first scheme, and it must do so in relation to benefits payable in respect of periods of service subsequent to 17 May 1990.

7. Article 119 is not applicable to schemes which have at all times had members of only one sex.

8. Article 119 precludes an occupational scheme from retrospectively raising the retirement age for women in relation to periods of service completed between 17 May 1990 and the date of entry into force of the measures by which equality is achieved in the scheme in question.

9. Article 119 does not allow a situation of equality to be achieved otherwise than by applying to male employees the same arrangements as those enjoyed by female employees.

10. Benefits paid under a pension scheme for public servants must be regarded as pay within the meaning of Article 119.

11. Married men placed at disadvantage by discrimination must be treated in the same way and have the same rules applied to them as married women.

1. COJ, 28 September 1994, *Coloroll Pension Trustees Ltd* v. *James Richard Russel and Others*, C-200/91, *Jur.*, 1994, 4389; *Constance Christina Ellen Smith and Others* v. *Avdel Systems Ltd.*, Case C-408/92, *Jur.*, 1994, 4435; *Maria Nelleke Gerda van den Akker and Others* v. *Stichting Shell Pensioenfonds*, Case C-28/93, *Jur.*, 1994, 4527; *Bestuur van het Algemeen burgerlijk pensioenfonds* v. *G.A. Beune*, Case C-7/93, *Jur.*, 1994, 4471; *Anna Adriaantje Vroege* v. *NCIV Instituut voor Volkshuisvesting BV and Stichting Pensioenfonds NCIV*, Case C-57/93, *Jur.*, 1994, 4541; *Geertruida Catharina Fisscher* v. *Voorhuis Hengelo BV and Stichting Bedrijfspensioenfonds voor de Detailhandel*, Case C-128/93, *Jur.*, 1994, 4583.

398.   The right to join an occupational pension scheme falls within the scope of Article 119 and is therefore covered by the prohibition of discrimination. The limitation of the effects in time of the *Barber* judgment does not apply to the right to join an occupational pension scheme or to the right of the payment of a retirement pension. The fact that a worker can claim retroactive membership of an occupational pension scheme does not enable him to avoid paying contributions for the period of membership concerned.[1]

1. COJ, 24 October 1996, *Francina Johanna Maria Dietz* v. *Stichting Thuiszorg Rotterdam*, Case C-435/93, not yet published.

398bis.   It should be noted that Directive 86/378 of 24 July 1986 on the implementation of the principle of equal treatment for men and women in occupational social security schemes was amended by Directive 96/97 adopted on 2 December 1996.[1] This Directive brings the 1986 Directive into line with the judgments of the Court of Justice in Barber and subsequent cases.

    1. O.J., L 046, 17 February 1997.

II. Access to Employment, Promotion, Vocational Training

399.   Directive No. 76/207 of 9 February 1976 aims at the implementation of the principle of equal treatment as regards access to employment, vocational training and promotion, and working conditions. This includes selection criteria for access to all jobs or posts, whatever the sector or branch of activity, and to all levels of the occupational hierarchy (Art. 3, §1), as well as to vocational guidance, vocational training, advanced vocational training and retraining; these must be accessible on the basis of the same criteria and at the same levels without any discrimination on grounds of sex (Art. 4). It is interesting to note that offers of employment do not fall within the scope of the directive.[1]

The Court of Justice ruled in a Dutch case that an employer is in direct contravention of the principle of equal treatment if he refuses to enter into a contract of employment with a candidate whom he had decided was suitable for the post in question where such refusal is based on the possible adverse consequences for him of employing a *pregnant woman* as a result of rules adopted by the public authorities on unfitness for work which treat inability to work because of pregnancy and confinement in the same way as inability to work because of illness.[2]

However, Directive 76/207 is to be interpreted as not applying to a social security scheme, such as a supplementary allowance or income support, simply because the conditions of entitlement for receipt of the benefits may be such as to affect the ability of a single parent to take up access to vocational training or part-time employment.[3]

    1. COJ, 21 May 1985, *Commission* v. *Germany*, No. 248/83, IELL, *Case Law*. No. 73.
    2. 8 November 1990, *E.J.P. Dekker* v. *Stichting Vormingscentrum voor Jonge Volwassenen (VIV-Centrum) Plus*, No. C-177/88, IELL, *Case Law*, No. 153.
    3. COJ, 16 July 1992, *S. Jackson and P. Cresswell* v. *Chief Adjudication Officer*, Joined Cases Nos. C-63/91 and C-64/91. IELL, *Case Law*, No. 192.

III. Working Conditions

400.   Equal treatment concerning working conditions is provided for in Article 1 of the 1976 directive on equal treatment, while conditions governing dismissals are retained in Article 5, §1.[1] The term working conditions is not defined.

In Italy a law of 1977 provides that women who have adopted children or who have obtained custody thereof prior to adoption may claim maternity leave following the entry of the child into the adoptive family and the financial benefits relating thereto. The adoptive father does not have that right. That distinction, the Court ruled, is justified by the legitimate concern to assimilate as far as possible the conditions of entry of the child into the adoptive family to those of the arrival of a newborn child into the family during the very delicate initial period.[2]

More and more attention is paid to unwanted conduct of a sexual nature at work. Sexual harassment is sex discrimination because the gender of the recipient is the determining factor in who is harassed. The Commission adopted on 27 November 1991 a Recommendation on the Protection of the Dignity of Women and Men at Work.[3] The Commission recommends Member States to take action to promote awareness that conduct of a sexual nature, or other conduct based on sex affecting the dignity of women and men at work, including conduct of superiors and colleagues, is unacceptable and that such a conduct may, in certain circumstances, be contrary to the principle of equal treatment within the meaning of the Articles 3, 4 and 5 of the directive of 1976.

This is the case when:

(a) such a conduct is unwanted, unreasonable and offensive to the recipient;
(b) a person's rejection of, or submission to, such conduct on the part of employers or workers (including superiors or colleagues) is used explicitly or implicitly as a basis for a decision which affects that person's access to vocational training, access to employment, continued employment, promotion, salary or any other employment decisions: and/or
(c) such conduct creates an intimidating hostile or humiliating working environment for the recipient.

Member States are recommended to take action in the public sector and to encourage employers and employee representatives to develop measures. These actions and measures are specified in *A Code of Practice on measures to combat sexual harassment*, issued by the Commission.[4]

It is important to note that since sexual harassment often entails the abuse of power, employers may have a responsibility for the misuse of the authority they delegate.

The majority of the recommendations contained in the Code are for action by the employers. They should formulate policy statements and communicate them to the workers, including clear and precise procedures, informal resolution of problems, advice and assistance, investigations, disciplinary rules for the offenders and the prohibition of retaliation against an employee for bringing a complaint of sexual harassment in good faith. Collective agreements may be a vehicle for introducing such policies.

Also important for its practical implications is the ruling in the case of *Marshall v. Southampton Health Authority*.[5] Ms. Marshall was dismissed when she was aged 62. Had she been a man, she could have worked until 65 years of age. Following the Court, the term 'dismissal' contained in Article 5, §1 of Directive No. 76/207 must be given a wide meaning: an age limit for the compulsory dismissal of workers pursuant to an employer's general policy concerning retirement falls within the term dismissal construed in that manner, even if the dismissal involves the grant of a retirement pension. Article 5, §1 must be interpreted as meaning that a general policy concerning dismissal involving the dismissal of a woman solely because she has attained the age limit for a State pension, which age is different for men and women, constitutes discrimination on grounds of sex. Article 5, §1 may be relied upon as against a State authority acting in its capacity as employer, in order to avoid the application of any national provision which does not conform to Article 5, §1. In doing so, the directive has a direct binding effect against public (State) authorities.

In the case between Mrs. Hertz and her former employer, Aldi Market, the question was raised whether equal treatment allows dismissal because of repeated absences due to illness, which originated in her pregnancy and confinement. The Court stated that the 1976 directive did not provide for the case in which an illness originated in pregnancy or confinement. It permitted, however, national provisions guaranteeing women specific rights on the ground of pregnancy and confinement, such as maternity leave. In the case of an illness which developed after maternity leave, it was unnecessary to distinguish an illness which originated in pregnancy or confinement from any other illness. A pathological condition of that kind was therefore covered by the general rules applicable to illness. The Court stated that women and men were both liable to be ill. Although certain problems were peculiar to one or other sex, the only question was therefore whether a woman was dismissed on the grounds of absence due to illness under the same condition as a man; if so, there was no direct discrimination on grounds of sex. The Court consequently concluded that the directive does not preclude dismissals resulting from absences due to an illness which originated in pregnancy or confinement.[6]

The Court ruled that the termination of a contract without a fixed term on account of a woman's pregnancy, whether by annulment or avoidance, cannot be justified on the ground that statutory prohibition, imposed because of pregnancy, temporarily prevents an employee from performing night-time work.[7]

1. *See* concerning night work: Part I, Chapter 7, §3.
2. 26 October 1983, *Commission* v. *Italy*, No. 163/82, IELL, *Case Law*, No. 53.
3. O.J., 4 February 1992, No. C-27/4.
4. *Idem.*
5. COJ, 26 February 1986, No. 152/84, IELL, *Case Law*, No. 86, *See also Burton* (1982), *op. cit.*
6. 8 November 1990, *Handels- og Kontorfunktionaerernes Forbund i Danmark* v. *Dansk Arbejdsgiverforening*, No. C-179/88, IELL, *Case Law*, No. 154.
7. COJ, 5 May 1994, *G. Habermann-Beltermann* v. *Arbeiterwohlfart, Bezirkverband Ndb./Opf. eV.*, No. C-421/92, *Jur.*, 1994, 1657.

401. In another case[1] the Court was asked to decide whether the Equal Treatment Directive prohibits the dismissal of a *transsexual* because of his/her decision to undergo gender reassignment.

P. who had been born with the physical attributes of a man, used to work as a manager in an educational establishment operated by Cornwall County Council. In April 1992 P.'s employer was informed that P. had decided to undergo gender reassignment which meant that, following a period of time during which P. would dress and behave as a woman, P. would have surgery to be given the physical attributes of a woman. P. was subsequently dismissed with effect from December 1992 and, although the Council maintained that the reason for the dismissal was redundancy, the Industrial Tribunal (UK) found that the real reason for the dismissal was P.'s proposal to undergo gender reassignment.

The Court referred first to jurisprudence of the European Court of Human Rights which states that 'Transsexuals who have been operated upon . . . form a fairly well-defined and identifiable group.' It then observed that the stated aim of the directive is to ensure that there is 'no discrimination whatsoever on grounds of sex' and pointed out that the right not to be discriminated against on grounds of sex is one of the fundamental human rights whose observance the Courts has a duty to ensure.

The Court continued:

> 'Accordingly, the scope of the directive cannot be confined simply to discrimination based on the fact that a person is of one or other sex. In view of its purpose and the nature of the rights which it seeks to safeguard, the scope of the directive is also such as to apply to discrimination arising, as in this case, from the gender reassignment of the person concerned.
>
> Such discrimination is based, essentially if not exclusively, on the sex of the person concerned. Where a person is dismissed on the ground that he or she intends to undergo, or has undergone, gender reassignment, he or she is treated unfavourably by comparison with persons of the sex to which he or she was deemed to belong before undergoing gender reassignment.
>
> To tolerate such discrimination would be tantamount, as regards such a person, to a failure to respect the dignity and freedom to which he or she is entitled, and which the Court has a duty to safeguard.'

The Court concluded that the dismissal of such a person was contrary to Article 5(1) of the directive, unless the dismissal could be justified under Article 2(2). There was, however, no material before the Court to suggest that there was a defence for the dismissal in this case.

1. COJ, 30 April 1996, *P. v. S. and Cornwall County Council*, Case C-13/94, not yet published.

IV. Social Security, Pensions

402. The directive of 1976 does not apply to matters of social security. Article 1, §2 provides that the Council would act on this later and this was done through Directive No. 79/7 of 19 December 1978 on the progressive implementation of the principle of equal treatment for men and women in matters of social security. This directive concerns, for example, schemes which provide protection for old age. Article 7, §1A, of the directive provides however that the directive shall be without prejudice to the rights of Member States to exclude: 'the determination of pensionable age for the purposes of granting old-age and retirement benefits and the possible consequences thereof for other benefits.' The exception must be interpreted restrictively and must be distinguished from the qualifying age as a condition for dismissal, which, as indicated earlier, must be equal for men and women. It follows that the exception contained in Article 7, §1A applies only to the determination of pensionable age for the purposes of granting old-age and retirement pensions and the possible consequences thereof for other benefits.[1]

In one case the European Court of Justice furthermore held that once a Member State decides to introduce the same pensionable age for men and women and thus to abolish the different age requirement, both men and women have to be treated equally with regard to the calculation of pension benefits. A difference in calculation can not be justified by an in the meantime abolished difference in age requirements.[2]

1. COJ, 26 February 1986, *Joan Roberts v. Tate & Tyle Industries Ltd.*, Case No. 151/84, IELL, *Case Law*, No. 85; 26 February 1986, *Vera Mia Beets-Proper* v. *F. van Lanschot Bankiers NV*, No. 262/84, IELL, *Case Law*, No. 87.
2. COJ, 1 July 1993, *R. Van Cant* v. *Rijksdienst voor Pensioenen*, No. C-154/92, not yet published.

§4. Proof

403. Regarding proof of discrimination, it is business as usual: *actori imcumbit probatio*. The appellant must prove his or her point. Exceptionally that rule is reversed. This is the case where an undertaking applies a system of pay that is totally lacking in transparency. Then it is up to the employer to prove that his practice in the matter of wages is not discriminatory, if a female worker establishes, in relation to a relative large number of employees, that the average pay of women is less than that for men. Criteria such as mobility, vocational training or the length of service of the employee are acceptable to justify a different pay provided that the employer can prove that such criteria are of importance for the performance of the specific tasks which are entrusted to the employee.[1]

Where, in a *piece-work pay scheme* in which individual pay consists of a variable element depending on each worker's output and a fixed element according to the group of workers concerned, it is not possible to identify the factor which determined the rates or units of measurement used to calculate the variable element in the pay, the employer may have to bear the burden of proving that the differences found are not due to sex discrimination.[2]

1. COJ, 17 October 1989, *Handels- of Kontorfunktionaernes Forbund i Danmark* v. *Dansk Arbejdsgiverforening (for Danfoss)*, No. 109/88, IELL, *Case Law*, No. 138.
2. COJ, 31 May 1995, *Specialarbejderforbundet i Danmark* v. *Dansk Industri, originally Industriens Arbejdsgivere, acting for Royal Copenhagen A/S*, Case C-400/93, not yet published.

404. On 15 December 1997 the Council adopted a Directive on the burden of proof in cases of discrimination based on sex.[1] 'The aim of the Directive is to ensure that the measures taken by the Member States to implement the principle of equal treatment are made more effective, in order to enable all persons who consider themselves wronged because the principle has not been applied to them to have their rights asserted by judicial process after possible recourse to other competent bodies' (Art. 1).

The key provisions of the Directive are as follows:

i) *Definitions*:
   - Equal treatment shall mean that there shall be no discrimination whatsoever, either directly or indirectly;
   - Indirect discrimination shall exist where an apparently neutral provision, criterion or practice disadvantages a substantially higher proportion of the members of one sex unless that provision, criterion or practice is appropriate and necessary and can be justified by objective factors unrelated to sex (Art. 2).
ii) *Scope*: the situations covered by:
   - Article 119 of the Treaty (equal pay for equal work);
   - The directives on:
     – Principle of equal pay (1975);
     – Access to employment, vocational training and working conditions (1976);
     – Pregnant workers and breast feeding (1992);
     – Parental leave (1996);

- Any civil or administrative procedure concerning the public or private sector which provides for means of redress under national law pursuant to the measures referred to above with the exception of out-of-court procedures of a voluntary nature or provided for in national law (Art. 3).[2]

iii) *Burden of proof:*
- Member States shall take measures to ensure that, when persons who consider themselves wronged because the principle of equal treatment has not been applied to them, establish, before a court or other competent authority, facts from which it may be presumed that there has been direct or indirect discrimination, it shall be for the respondent to prove that there has been no breach of the principle of equal treatment.[3]

    Member States are allowed to introduce rules of evidence which are more favourable to plaintiffs (Art. 4).

iv) *Information – non regression:*
- Member States shall ensure that measures taken to implement the Directive are brought to the attention of all the persons concerned (Art. 5).
- Implementation of the Directive may not lead to a reduction of the level of protection of workers in the areas in which it applies (Art. 6).

v) *Implementation:*
Member States have to comply by 1 January 2001.

1. O.J., 20 January 1998, L 14/6.
2. '*Judicial process*' and '*court*' cover mechanisms by means of which disputes may be submitted for examination and decision to independent bodies which may hand down decisions that are binding on the parties to those disputes. 'Out-of-court procedures mean in particular procedures such as conciliation and mediation.'
3. Member States need not to apply this obligation to proceedings in which it is for the court or competent body to investigate the facts of the case.

§5. IMPLEMENTATION

405.   Both the 1975 and the 1976 directives contain quite a number of measures to implement the principle of equal treatment:

- Member States must adapt their national legislation;
- Member States shall abolish all discrimination between men and women arising from laws, regulations or administrative provisions that is contrary to the principle of equal pay (Art. 3, 1975);
- any laws, regulations and administrative provisions contrary to the principle of equal treatment shall be abolished (Art. 3, §2,a and 4, §2,a, 1976);
- laws, regulations and administrative provisions contrary to the principle of equal treatment when the concern for protection which originally inspired them is no longer well founded must be revised (Art. 3, §2,c, 1976);
- Member States must take all necessary measures to ensure that provisions appearing in collective agreements, wage scales, wage agreements or individual contracts of employment that are contrary to the principal of equal pay shall be, or may be, declared null and void or may be amended (Art. 4, 1975; 3, §2B, §4B and §5B, 1976).

Directive No. 76/207 covers all collective agreements without distinction as to the nature of the legal effects that they do or do not produce. The need to ensure that the directive is completely effective requires that any clause is covered, even if the agreements have only *de facto* consequences, for the employment relationship.[1] Nullity means that the wages which are null are automatically replaced by the higher wages.[2]

1. COJ, 8 November 1983, *Commission* v. *United Kingdom*, No. 165/82, IELL, *Case Law*, No. 54.
2. Adv. Gen. in *Defrenne II, op. cit.*

§6. ANNOUNCEMENT, ENFORCEMENT, DIRECT EFFECT

I. Announcement

406.   The directives (respectively in Articles 7 and 8) of 1975 and 1976 both provide that the Member States shall take care that the relevant provisions adopted pursuant to the directives, together with the relevant provisions already in force, are brought to the attention of employees by all appropriate means, for example at their place of employment.

II. Protection against Dismissal

407.   Articles 5 and 7 of the 1975 and 1976 directives respectively provide that the Member States shall take the necessary measures to protect employees against dismissal by the employer as a reaction to a complaint within the undertaking or to any legal proceedings aimed at enforcing compliance with the principle of equal pay.

III. Legal Proceedings

408.   Both directives provide, respectively in Articles 2 and 6, that the Member States shall introduce into their national legal systems such measures as are necessary to enable all persons, who consider themselves wronged by failure to apply to them the principle of equal treatment, to pursue their claims by judicial process after possible recourse to other competent authorities. The principle of effective judicial control is a principle that underlines the constitutional traditions common to the Member States as laid down in Articles 6 and 13 of the European Convention for the Protection of Human Rights.[1]

1. COJ, 15 May 1986, *Johnston, op. cit.*

IV. Sanctions

409.   The directives do not contain sanctions. Yet Article 6 of the 1975 directive states that the Member States shall take the measures necessary to ensure that the principle of equal pay is applied. The need for sanctions follows not only from Article 6, but also from Article 6 of the 1976 directive, which guarantees measures to pursue claims by judicial process after possible recourse to other competent authorities. This problem was dealt with in *Sabine von Colson and Elizabeth Kamann*

v. *Land Nordrhein-Westfalen*,[1] in which two qualified social workers (Sabine and Elizabeth) were refused to be hired, for reasons related to their sex, by a prison which caters exclusively for male prisoners and which is administered by the Land. Since under German law the only sanction for discrimination is compensation, the German Labour Court found that it could only order the reimbursement of the travel expenses incurred by the plaintiff in pursuing her application for the post and that it could not allow the plaintiff's other claims. The question was then whether these claims were possible under Community law. The European Court gave the following answers:

> '1. Directive No. 76/207 does not require discrimination on grounds of sex regarding access to employment to be made the subject of a sanction by way of an obligation imposed on the employer, who is the author of the discrimination, to conclude a contract of employment with the candidate discriminated against;
> 2. as regards sanctions for any discrimination which may occur, the directive does not include any unconditional and sufficiently precise obligation which, in the absence of implementing measures adopted within the prescribed time limits, may be relied on by an individual in order to obtain specific compensation under the directive, where it is not provided for or permitted under national law;
> 3. although the 1976 directive, for the purpose of imposing a sanction for the breach of the prohibition of discrimination, leaves the Member States free to choose between the different solutions suitable for achieving its objective, it nevertheless requires that if a Member State chooses to penalise breaches of that prohibition by the award of compensation, then in order to ensure that it is effective and that it has a deterrent effect, that compensation must in any event be adequate in relation to the damage sustained and must therefore amount to more than purely nominal compensation such as, for example, the reimbursement only of the expenses incurred in connection with the application. It is for the national court to interpret and apply the legislation adopted for the implementation of the directive in conformity with the requirement of Community law, insofar as it is given discretion to do so under national law.'

1. COJ, 10 April 1984, No. 14/83, IELL, *Case Law*, No. 57.

410. The question was equally addressed in the very important case *Marshall II* concerning the amount of compensation recoverable by a victim of discrimination. It was raised in connection with a dispute between Ms. Marshall and her former employer concerning a claim for compensation for damages sustained by Marshall as a result of her dismissal by the authority Southampton.

That claim was based on the illegality of that dismissal (Judgment of 26 February 1986) since Article 5(1) of the directive was to be interpreted as meaning that a general policy concerning dismissal involving the dismissal of a woman solely because she had attained or passed the qualifying age for a State pension, which age was different under national legislation for men and for woman, constituted discrimination on grounds of sex, contrary to the directive. The Court observed that according to the Sex Discrimination Act 1975, where an Industrial Tribunal finds that a complaint of unlawful sex discrimination in relation to employment is well founded, it may order the defendant to pay the complainant compensation. However, the amount of the compensation may not exceed a specified limit.

Furthermore, at the time of the facts, an Industrial Tribunal had no power, or at least the relevant to provisions were ambiguous as to whether it had such power, to award interest on compensation.

Article 6 of the directive, the Court said, puts Member States under a duty to take the necessary measures to enable all persons who consider themselves wronged by discrimination to pursue their claims by judicial process. Such obligation implies that the measure in question should be sufficiently effective to achieve the objective of the directive and should be capable of being effectively relied upon by the persons concerned before national courts.

However, Article 6 does not prescribe a specific measure to be taken in the event of a breach of the prohibition of discrimination, but leaves Member States free to choose between the different solutions suitable for achieving the objective of the directive, depending on the different situations which might arise.

So, the objective was to arrive at real equality of opportunity and could not therefore be attained in the absence of measures appropriate to restore such equality when it had not been observed.

In the event of discriminatory dismissal contrary to the directive, a situation of equality could not be restored without either reinstating the victim of discrimination or, in the alternative, granting financial compensation for the damage sustained.

Where financial compensation was the measure adopted in order to achieve the objective indicated above, it had to be adequate, in that it had to enable the damage actually sustained as a result of the discriminatory dismissal to be made good in full in accordance with the applicable national rules.

A first question is whether it is contrary to Article 6 of the directive for national provisions to lay down an upper limit on the amount of compensation recoverable by a victim of discrimination.

A second question is whether Article 6 requires that (a) the compensation for damage sustained as a result of the illegal discrimination should be full and (b) that it should include an award of interest on the principal amount from the date of the unlawful discrimination to the date when compensation was paid.

The Court held that the interpretation of Article 6, as set out above, provided a direct reply to the first part of the second question relating to the level of compensation required by the provision.

It also followed from that interpretation that the fixing of an upper limit of the kind at issue in the main proceedings could not, by definition, constitute proper implementation of Article 6 of the directive, since it limited the amount of compensation *a priori* to a level which was not necessarily consistent with the requirement of ensuring real equality of opportunity through adequate compensation for the damage sustained as a result of discriminatory dismissal.

With regard to the second part of the second question relating to the award of interest, it sufficed to say that full compensation for the damage sustained as a result of a discriminatory dismissal could not leave out of account factors, such as the effluxion of time, which might in fact reduce its value. The award of interest, in accordance with the applicable national rules, had therefore to be regarded as an essential component of compensation for the purposes of restoring real equality of treatment.

In a third question it was sought to establish whether a person who had been injured as a result of discriminatory dismissal might rely, as against an authority of the State acting in its capacity as employer, on Article 6 of the directive in order to oppose the application of national rules which imposed limits on the amount of damages which might be obtained by way of compensation.

The Court held that the combined provisions of Article 5 and Article 6 of the directive gave rise to no rights on the part of a person who had been injured as a result of discriminatory dismissal, on which that person could rely before the national courts as against the State and authorities which were an emanation of the State.

The fact that Member States might choose among different solutions in order to achieve the objective pursued by the directive depending on the situations which might arise, could not result in an individual's being prevented from relying on Article 6 in a situation like the one in the main proceedings in which the national authorities had no degree of discretion of applying the chosen solution.

The Court pointed out in that connection that the right of a State to choose among several possible means of achieving the objectives of a directive did not exclude the possibility for individuals of enforcing before the national courts rights whose content could be determined sufficiently precisely on the basis of the provision of the directive alone.

Therefore the Court ruled as follows:

1. The interpretation of Article 6 of Council Directive 76/207/EC of 9 February 1976 on the implementation of the principle of equal treatment for men and women as regards access to employment, vocational training and promotion, and working conditions must be that reparation of the damage sustained by a person injured as a result of discriminatory dismissal may not be limited to an upper limit fixed *a priori* and by the absence of interest intended to compensate for the loss sustained by the recipient of the compensation as a result of the effluxion of time until the capital sum awarded is actually paid.

2. A person who has been injured as a result of discriminatory dismissal may rely on provisions of Article 6 of the directive as against an authority of the State acting in its capacity as an employer in order to set aside a national provision which imposes limits on the amount of damages recoverable by way of compensation.

    1. COJ, *Marshall M.H.* v. *Southampton and South West Hampshire Area Health Authority*, No. C-271/91, 2 August 1993, not yet published.

410bis. This was confirmed in *Draehmpaehl Nils* v. *Urania Immobilienreserve OHG* (1997).[1] The Court stated as follows:

'In this regard, it must be pointed out that, even though the Directive does not impose a specific sanction on the Member States, nevertheless Article 6 obliges them to adopt measures which are sufficiently effective for achieving the aim of the Directive and to ensure that those measures may be effectively relied on before the national courts by the persons concerned.

Moreover, the Directive requires that, if a Member State chooses to penalize a breach of the prohibition of discrimination by the award of compensation, that compensation must be such as to guarantee real and effective judicial protection, have a real deterrent effect on the employer and must in any event be adequate in relation to the damage sustained. Purely nominal compensation would not satisfy the requirements of an effective transposition of the Directive.

In choosing the appropriate solution for guaranteeing that the objective of the Directive is attained, the Member States must ensure that infringements of Community law are penalized under conditions, both procedural and substantive, which are analogous to those applicable to infringements of domestic law of a similar nature and importance.

It follows from the foregoing that provisions of domestic law which, unlike other provisions of domestic civil law and labour law, prescribe *an upper limit of three months' salary for the compensation which may be obtained in the event of discrimination on grounds of sex in the making of an appointment do not fulfill those conditions'*.

Regarding the question 'whether the Directive precludes provisions of domestic law imposing a ceiling on the aggregate amount of compensation payable to several applicants discriminated against on the grounds of their sex in the making of an appointment' the Court stated:

'As the Court held in its judgment in *Von Colson and Kamann*, the Directive entails that the sanction chosen by the Member States must have a real dissuasive effect on the employer and must be adequate in relation to the damage sustained in order to ensure real and effective judicial protection.

It is clear that a provision which places *a ceiling of six months' salary on the aggregate amount of compensation for all applicants harmed by discrimination* on grounds of sex in the making of an appointment, where several applicants claim compensation, may lead to the award of reduced compensation and may have the effect of dissuading applicants so harmed from asserting their rights. Such a consequence *would not represent real and effective judicial protection* and would have no really dissuasive effect on the employer, as required by the Directive.

Moreover, such a ceiling on the aggregate compensation is not prescribed by other provisions of domestic civil law or labour law.

However, as the Court has already held, the procedures and conditions governing a right to reparation based on Community law must not be less favourable than those laid down by comparable national rules'.

1. Case No. C-180/95, 22 April 1997, not yet published.

V. Direct Effect

411. Article 119 of the EC Treaty is directly applicable and may thus give rise to individual rights which the courts must protect.[1] Indeed, the article is clear and sufficiently precise in its content, does not contain any reservation and is complete in itself in the sense that its application by national courts does not require the adoption of any subsequent measure of implementation either by the States or by the Community.

Article 5, §1 of Directive No. 76/207 may be relied upon in a claim for damages against a body, whatever its legal form, which has been made responsible for providing a public service under the control of the State and has for that purpose special powers beyond those which result from the normal rules applicable in relations between individuals.[2]

In this context it must be remembered that the Court has repeatedly stated the Member States' obligation to achieve the result envisaged by the directive and that their duty under Article 5 of the EC Treaty to take all appropriate measures, whether general or particular, to ensure the fulfilment of that obligation, is binding on all the authorities of Member States including, for matters within their jurisdiction, the courts. It follows that, in applying national law, and in particular the provisions of national legislation specifically introduced in order to implement Directive No. 76/207, national courts are required to interpret their national law in the light of the wording and the purpose of the directive in order to achieve the result referred to in the third paragraph of Article 189 of the EC Treaty.[3] The Court found it necessary to recall in *Marshall II* that wherever the provisions of a directive appear, as far as their subject-matter is concerned, to be unconditional and sufficiently precise, those provisions may be relied upon by an individual against the State where that State, either in its capacity as authority or as employer, fails to implement the directive in national law by the end of the prescribed period or where it fails to implement the directive correctly. Article 5, §1 of Directive No. 76/207 may be considered as unconditional and sufficiently precise to be relied upon by an individual versus the State.[4]

1. COJ, *Defrenne II*.
2. COJ, 12 July 1990, *A. Foster and Others* v. *British Gas*, No. C-188/89, IELL, *Case Law*, No. 149.
3. *Johnston, op. cit.*
4. *Marshall II, op. cit.*

VI. Code of Conduct

412. On 17 July 1996, the European Commission adopted a code of practice concerning the application of equal pay for women and men for work of equal value. The aim of this code is:

(i) to provide concrete advice to employers and partners in the collective bargaining carried out at the level of the enterprise (sectoral and intersectoral) to ensure application of the principle 'equal pay for equal work' in all its elements;
(ii) elimination of discrimination based on sex when the remuneration structures are based on systems of classification and evaluation of employment.

Designed in close collaboration with social partners, this code reflects as much as possible the approach proposed by them, i.e., a short code intended to be applied:

(i) in a voluntary and effective fashion and able to be used during the different phases of the collective negotiation;
(ii) at the work place in the public and private sector.

Employers are encouraged to follow the recommendations contained therein by adapting them to the dimension and structure of their companies.

Chapter 6. Protection of Motherhood

413.   In its Action Programme implementing the Community Charter, the Commission has included among its aims the adoption by the Council of a Directive on the protection of pregnant women at work. The Directive of 19 October 1992 (No. 92/85) is based on Article 118A of the EC Treaty, and constitutes the tenth individual directive within the meaning of Article 16(1) of Directive 89/391 of 12 June 1989 on the introduction of measures to encourage improvements in safety and heath of workers at work.[1] It follows that the articles of the aforementioned framework directive are applicable, in particular Article 10 (worker information), 11 (consultation and participation of workers) and 12 (training of workers). It should be recalled that in the definition of the framework directive, the meaning of worker is 'any person employed by an employer, including trainees and apprentices' and the meaning of employer is 'any natural or legal person who has an employment relationship with the worker and has responsibility for the undertaking and/or establishment.'

   1. Article 15 of the latter directive provides that particularly sensitive groups must be protected against dangers which specifically affect them (O.J. 29 June 1989, No. L 183/1).

414.   The purpose of the directive is to implement measures to encourage improvements in the safety and health at work of pregnant workers and workers who have recently given birth or who are breast feeding.[1]
   The directive provides the following protective measures:

1. For all activities liable to involve a specific risk of exposure to the agents, processes or working conditions involving risks to the safety or health and any possible effect on the pregnancies or breast feeding, the employer shall assess the nature, degree and duration of exposure in order to decide what measures should be taken. The employer shall take the necessary measures to ensure that, by temporarily *adjusting the working conditions* of the worker concerned, the exposure of that worker to such risks is avoided. If this is not possible, the employer shall take the necessary measures to move the worker to another job. If moving to another job is not technically and/or objectively feasible or cannot reasonably be required on duly substantiated grounds, the worker concerned shall be granted leave in accordance with national legislation and/or national practice (Art. 5). This includes the maintenance of a payment to, and/or entitlement to an adequate allowance (Art. 11,1). Article 11,3 indicates what an adequate allowance should look like.
2. An *alternative to night work*. This may simply mean a transfer of daytime work, leave from work or extension of maternity leave (Art. 7).

3. A *continuous period of maternity leave of at least 14 weeks* allocated before and/or after confinement. (Art. 8,1) This maternity leave must include a compulsory leave of least two weeks, allocated before and/or after confinement (Art. 8,2).
4. The *prohibition of dismissal* of the workers concerned during the period from the beginning of their pregnancy to the end of the maternity leave. If a worker is dismissed during this period, the employer must cite duly substantiated grounds for her dismissal in writing (Art. 10,1 and 2).

The directive explicitly mentions 'that it may not have the effect of reducing the level of protection afforded to pregnant workers, workers who have recently given birth or who are breastfeeding as compared with the situation which exists in each Member State on the date on which this Directive is adopted.' (Art. 1,3).

The social partners are allowed by way of collective bargaining agreement to take the necessary measures for the implementation of the directive at national level (Art. 14).

1. Council Directive 92/91/EC of 19 October 1992 on the introduction of measures to encourage improvements in the safety and health at work of pregnant workers and workers who have recently given birth or are breastfeeding (tench individual directive within the meaning of Article 16(1) of Directive 89/391/EC), O.J., 28 November 1992, No. L 348/1.

Chapter 7. Working Time, Sunday Rest, Nightwork and Parental Leave

§1. Working Time

I. In General

415. Regarding working time, two recommendations must be mentioned. The first dates from 22 July 1975 and concerns the principle of the 40 hour work week and the principle of four weeks' annual paid holidays;[1] these principles were to be applied throughout the Community in all sectors by 31 December 1978 at the latest and as far as possible before that date. Needless to say, this recommendation has at present only a historical, symbolic value and has been overtaken by events.

A second recommendation, namely of 10 December 1982, relates to retirement age.[2] With this recommendation the Council invites the Member States to acknowledge flexible retirement, i.e., the right to choose when employed people will take their retirement pension, as one of the aims of social policy. Employed workers receiving a retirement pension cannot be excluded from any form of paid employment. The recommendation states further that retirement preparation programmes should be started during the years preceding the end of the working life with the participation of organisations representing employers and employed persons and other interested bodies.

1. O.J., 30 July 1975, No. L 199.
2. O.J., 18 December 1982, No. L 357.

416. On 3 August 1990, a proposal for a directive concerning certain aspects of the organisation of working time was made by the Commission with the aim of implementing points 7 and 8 of the Community Charter for fundamental social rights. The proposal is made on the basis of Article 118A of the EC Treaty, which allows for a decision in the Council with a qualified majority, and concerns basic rules providing for:

– daily, weekly and yearly rest;
– night work, shift work;
– the protection of the health and safety of employees in the event of changes in working patterns resulting from adjustments to working time.

The Commission departs from the fact that in recent years the disassociation of individual working time and plant operation hours has been becoming increasingly important in most of the Member States: individual hours are becoming shorter and operation hours longer. Exceptionally, individual working time may become longer such as in the case of week-end work, during which the employee works, for example, 2×12 hours. This tendency has helped enterprises to become more flexible, to increase their capacity utilisation, to adapt smoothly to new circumstances, to achieve productivity gains and to enhance competitiveness. Furthermore, the increase in plant operating hours is often conducive to investment in modernisation and, in any case, enables undertakings to make savings in relation to the fixed productive capital for a given output. These tendencies also seem to match more closely with the aspiration of employees to combine occupational and family responsibilities more successfully. In addition, the increased flexibility of working time arrangements helps to integrate more people into the labour market and to enhance employment opportunities.

In this context, however, the Commission indicates that one must consider the extent to which workers can rely on minimum rules concerning certain rest periods to protect themselves against excessively long hours, which may be detrimental to the health and the safety of the workers at their workplace. There is no doubt that work fatigue (depending of course on the type of work and the conditions under which it is exercised) is increased by the duration of working hours. The physical and mental effort in work exceeding eight hours becomes increasingly strenuous as fatigue sets in, even in the case of light work. These effects are exacerbated considerably by jobs requiring static or strained postures, or involving repetitive movements or heavy complicated tasks. In the context of application of modern technologies in particular, long hours tend to increase the numbers of errors and mistakes. Greater probability of accidents at work – especially serious accidents – and increased stress often occurs in the final hours of work. The same is true for weekly working time: a weekly working time of more than 50 hours can, in the long run, be harmful to the health and the safety of workers (fatigue, disturbed sleep, problems revealed during medicals). The same considerations can be made in the case of night work and shift work. Hence the proposals of the Commission.

For the purposes of the directive the following definitions apply:

- *working time*: hours of work during which the employee is at the disposal of the employer at the work site;
- *rest period*: any period after the normal daily or weekly performance of work during which the employee is not at the disposal of the employer;
- *night service*: all work performed during a period of not less than seven consecutive hours comprised between 08.00 pm and 09.00 am;
- *shift work*: a method of work organisation whereby workers succeed each other in accordance with a certain time schedule: this may involve rotating or successive crews and be discontinuous or continuous;
- *night worker*: an employee who performs night work, whether through shift work or otherwise on a regular basis;
- *shift worker*: an employer rostered into a shift work schedule.

II. The Directive of 23 November 1993

417. Council Directive 93/104/EC concerning certain aspects of the organisation of working time was adopted on 23 November 1993.[1] The directive was adopted on the basis of Article 118A, thus with a qualified majority vote. No general consensus could be reached. The majority of the Member States have gone far to meet as much as possible the demands of the UK which remained opposed to the directive. The consequence was that the directive has become a rather tortuous and difficult instrument, not always very progressive, containing a lot of exceptions and possibilities for derogations. The UK does not accept the Article 118A basis and indicated it would fight the directive before the Court of Justice. The Court of Justice, however, ruled that Article 118A has to be interpreted in a broad way.[2]

The main principles are:

1. minimum rest period of eleven consecutive hours for every 24 hours;
2. a break when daily working time is more than six hours;
3. a minimum uninterrupted rest period of 24 hours for every seven-day week (added, except in some circumstances, to the eleven hours of daily rest), which in principle includes Sunday;
4. average work for each seven day period not surpassing 48 hours, including overtime;
5. annual paid leave of at least four weeks; this minimum period theoretically cannot be replaced by financial compensation;
6. night work: a) normal working hours of no more than an average of 8 hours per 24-hour period b) for work involving particular strain leading to major physical or mental tension, 8 hours maximum per 24 hours.

1. O.J., 13 December 1993, No. L 307/18.
2. COJ, 12 November 1996, *UK* v. *Council of the European Union*, Case C-84/94. *See further*, Chapter 8, §2.

A. The Considerans: Legitimation, Goals and Objectives

418. The considerans refers to Article 118A of the Treaty which provides that the Council shall adopt, by means of directives, minimum requirements for encouraging improvements, especially in the working environment, to ensure a better level of protection of the safety and health of workers.

Those directives are to avoid imposing administrative, financial and legal constraints in a way which would hold back the creation and development of small and medium-sized undertakings. The provisions of Council Directive 89/391/EC of 12 June 1989 on the introduction of measures to encourage improvements in the safety and health of workers at work, the considerans continues, are fully applicable to the areas covered by this directive without prejudice to more stringent and/or specific provisions contained therein.

The completion of the internal market must lead to an improvement in the living and working conditions of workers in the European Community. This process must result from an approximation of these conditions while the improvement is being maintained, as regards in particular the duration and organisation of working time and forms of employment other than open-ended contracts, such as fixed-term contracts, part-time working, temporary work and seasonal work.

This means that

'– every worker must have a right to a weekly rest period and to annual paid leave, the duration of which must be progressively harmonised in accordance with national practices;
– every worker must enjoy satisfactory health and safety conditions in his working environment;
– in order to ensure the safety and health of workers, the latter must be granted minimum daily, weekly and annual periods of rest and adequate breaks;
– it is also necessary to place a maximum limit on weekly working hours;
– there is a need to limit the duration of periods of night work, including overtime, and to provide for employers who regularly use night workers to bring this information to the attention of the competent authorities if they so request;
– night workers should be entitled to a free health assessment prior to their assignment and thereafter at regular intervals and that whenever possible they should be transferred to day work for which they are suited if they suffer form health problems;
– the situation of night and shift workers requires that the level of safety and health protection should be adapted to the nature of their work and that the organisation and functioning of protection and prevention services and resources should be efficient;
– specific working conditions may have detrimental effects on the safety and health of workers; whereas the organisation of work according to a certain pattern must take account of the general principle of adapting work to the worker;
– there is a need to limit the duration of periods of night work, including overtime, and to provide for employers who regularly use night workers to bring this information to the attention of the competent authorities if they so request;
– that night workers should be entitled to a free health assessment prior to their assignment and thereafter at regular intervals and that whenever possible they should be transferred to day work for which they are suited if they suffer from health problems.'

The considerans also gives due attention to the ILO conventions and recommendations concerning working time, the diversity in the Member States, flexibility, subsidiarity and social dialogue.

B. Scope and Definitions

1. Scope

419. The directive lays down minimum safety and health requirements[1] for the organisation of working time and applies to:

a. minimum periods of daily rest, weekly rest and annual leave, to breaks and maximum weekly working time; and
b. certain aspects of night work, shift work and patterns of work.

It applies to all sectors of activity, both public and private,[2] with the exception of air, rail, road, sea, inland waterway and lake transport, sea fishing, other work at sea and the activities of doctors in training.

1. The provisions of Directive 89/391/EC are fully applicable to the matters referred to in paragraph 2, without prejudice to more stringent and/or specific provisions contained in this directive (Art. 1,4).
2. Within the meaning of Article 2 of Directive 89/391/EC, without prejudice to Article 17 of this directive (Art. 1,2).

2. Definitions

420. For the purposes of the directive, the following definitions apply:

1. *working time*: any period during which the worker is working, at the employer's disposal and carrying out his activity or duties, in accordance with national laws and/or practice;
2. *rest period*: any period which is not working time;
3. *night time*: any period of not less than seven hours, as defined by national law, and which must include in any case the period between midnight and 05.00 a.m.;
4. *night worker*:
   a. on the one hand, any worker, who, during night time, works at least three hours of his daily working time as a normal course; and
   b. on the other hand, any worker who is likely during night time to work a certain proportion of his annual working time, as defined at the choice of the Member State concerned:
      i. by national legislation, following consultation with the two sides of industry; or
      ii. by collective agreements or agreements concluded between the two sides of industry at national or regional level;
5. *shift work*: any method of organising work in shifts whereby workers succeed each other at the same work stations according to a certain pattern, including a rotating pattern, and which may be continuous or discontinuous, entailing the need for workers to work at different times over a given period of days or weeks;
6. *shift worker*: any worker whose work schedule is part of shift work.

C. Minimum Rest Periods, Other Aspects of the Organisation of Working Time

1. Daily Rest

421. Every worker is entitled to a minimum daily rest period of 11 consecutive hours per 24-hour period (Art. 3).

2. Breaks

422. Where the working day is longer than six hours, every worker is entitled to a rest break, the details of which, including duration and the terms on which it is granted, shall be laid down in collective agreement or agreements between the two sides of industry or, failing that, by national legislation (Art. 4).

3. Weekly Rest Period

423.   Per each seven-day period, every worker is entitled to a minimum uninterrupted rest period of 24 hours plus the 11 hours' daily rest referred to in Article 3. The minimum rest period in principle includes Sunday.[1]

If objective, technical or work organisation conditions so justify, a minimum rest period of 24 hours may be applied (Art. 5).

> 1. The European Court annulled the section stating that the minimum weekly rest should in principle include Sunday (second sentence of Article 5). The Court stated that 'the Council had failed to explain why Sunday, as a weekly rest day, is more closely connected with the health and safety of workers than any other day of the week' *UK* v. *Commission*, 12 November 1996.

4. Maximum Weekly Working Time

424.   The period of weekly working time is limited by means of laws, regulations or administrative provisions or by collective agreements or agreements between the two sides of industry.

The average working time for each seven-day period, including overtime, does not exceed 48 hours (Art. 6).

5. Annual Leave

425.   Every worker is entitled to paid annual leave of at least four weeks in accordance with the conditions for entitlement to, and granting of, such leave laid down by national legislation and/or practice.

The minimum period of paid annual leave may not be replaced by an allowance in lieu, except where the employment relationship is terminated (Art. 7).

D. Night Work/Shift Work, Pattern of Work

1. Length of Night Work

426.   Normal hours of work for night workers do not exceed an average of eight hours in any 24-hour period.

Night workers whose work involves special hazards or heavy physical or mental strain do not work more than eight hours in any period of 24 hours during which they perform night work.

Work involving special hazards or heavy physical or mental strain shall be defined by national legislation and/or practice or by collective agreements concluded between the two sides of industry, taking account of specific effects and hazards of night work (Art. 8).

2. Health Assessment and Transfer of Night Workers to Day Work

427.   Night workers:

a. are entitled to a free health assessment before their assignment and thereafter at regular intervals;
b. suffering from health problems recognised as being connected with the fact that they perform night work are transferred whenever possible to day work to which they are suited.

The free health assessment must comply with medical confidentiality and may be conducted within the national health system (Art. 9).

3. Guarantees for Night-Time Working

428.   The work of certain categories of night workers may be subject to certain guarantees, under conditions laid down by national legislation and/or practice, in the case of workers who incur risks to their safety or health linked to night-time working (Art. 10).

4. Notification of Regular Use of Night Workers

429.   An employer who regularly uses night workers brings this information to the attention of the competent authorities if they so request (Art. 11).

5. Safety and Health Protection

430.   Member States shall take the measure necessary to ensure that:

1. night workers and shift workers have safety and health protection appropriate to the nature of their work;
2. appropriate protection and prevention services or facilities with regard to the safety and health of night workers and shift workers are equivalent to those applicable to other workers and are available at all times (Art. 12).

6. Pattern of Work

431.   An employer who intends to organise work according to a certain pattern takes account of the general principle of adapting work to the worker, within a view, in particular, must taker the necessary measures to alleviate monotonous work and work at a predetermined work-rate, depending on the type of activity, and of safety and health requirements, especially as regards breaks during working time (Art. 13).

E. Miscellaneous Provisions

1. More Specific Community Provisions

432. The provisions of this directive do not apply where other Community instruments contain more specific requirements concerning certain occupations or occupational activities (Art. 13).

2. More Favourable Provisions

433. This directive does not affect Member States' right to apply or introduce laws, regulations or administrative provisions more favourable to the protection of the safety and health of workers or to facilitate or permit the application of collective agreements or agreements concluded between the two sides of industry which are more favourable to the protection of the safety and health of workers (Art. 15).

3. Reference Periods

434. Member States may lay down:

1. for the application of Article 5 (weekly rest period), a reference period not exceeding 14 days;
2. for the application of Article 6 (maximum weekly working time), a reference period not exceeding four months. The periods of paid annual leave and the periods of sick leave shall not be included or shall be neutral in the calculation of the average;
3. for the application of Article 8 (length of night work), a reference period defined after consultation of the two sides of industry or by collective agreements or agreements concluded between the two sides of industry at national or regional level. If the minimum weekly rest period of 24 hours required by Article 5 falls within that reference period, it shall not be included in the calculation of the average (Art. 16).

4. Derogations

435. With due regard for the general principles of the protection of the safety and health of workers, Member States may derogate from Articles 3, 4, 5, 6, 8 or 16 when, on account of the specific characteristics of the activity concerned, the duration of the working time is not measured and/or predetermined or can be determined the workers themselves, and particularly in the case of:

a. managing executives or other persons with autonomous decision-taking powers;
b. family workers; or
c. workers officiating at religious ceremonies in churches and religious communities.

Derogations may be adopted by means of laws, regulations or administrative provisions or by means of collective agreements or agreements between the two sides of industry provided that the workers concerned are afforded equivalent periods of compensatory rest or that, in exceptional cases in which it is not possible, afforded appropriate protection.

Derogation from Articles 3 (daily rest), 4 (breaks), 5 (weekly rest period), 8 (length of night work) and 16 (reference periods):

a. in the case of activities where the worker's place of work and his place of residence are distant from one another or where the worker's different places of work are distant from one another;
b. in the case of security and surveillance activities requiring a permanent presence in order to protect property and persons, particularly security guards and caretakers or security firms;
c. in the case of activities involving the need for continuity of service or production, particularly:
   i. services relating to the reception, treatment and/or care provided by hospitals or similar establishments, residential institutions and prisons;
   ii. dock or airport workers;
   iii. press, radio, television, cinematographic production, postal and telecommunications services, ambulance, fire and civil protection services;
   iv. gas, water and electricity production, transmission and distribution, household refuse collection and incineration plants;
   v. industries in which work cannot be interrupted on technical grounds;
   vi. research and development activities;
   vii. agriculture;
d. where there is a foreseeable surge of activity, particularly in:
   i. agriculture;
   ii. tourism;
   iii. postal services.

Derogation from Articles 3 (daily rest), 4 (breaks), 5 (weekly rest period), 8 (length of night work) and 16 (reference periods) is allowed:

a. in the circumstances described in Article 5 (4) Directive 89/391/EEC of 12 June 1989 concerning the introduction of measures to encourage improvements in the safety and health of workers at work;
b. in cases of accident or imminent risk of accident.

Derogation from Article 3 (daily rest) and 5 (weekly rest period) is allowed:

a. in the case of shift work activities, each time the worker changes shift and cannot take daily and/or weekly rest periods between the end of one shift and the start of the next one;
b. in the case of activities involving periods of work split up over the day, particularly those of cleaning staff.

Derogations may be made from Articles 3 (daily rest), 4 (breaks), 5 (weekly rest period), 8 (length of night work) and 16 (reference periods) by means of collective agreements or agreements concluded between the two sides of industry at national or regional level or, in conformity with the rules laid down by them, by means of collective agreements or agreements concluded between the two sides of industry at a lower level.

Member States in which there is no statutory system ensuring the conclusion of collective agreements or agreements concluded between the two sides of industry at national or regional level, on the matters covered by this directive, or those Member States in which there is a specific legislative framework for this purpose and within the limits thereof, may, in accordance with national legislation and/or practice, allow derogations from Articles 3, 4, 5, 8 and 16 by way of collective agreements or agreements concluded between the two sides of industry at the appropriate collective level.

The derogations[1] shall be allowed on condition that equivalent compensating rest periods are granted to the workers concerned or, in exceptional cases where it is not possible for objective reasons to grant such periods, the workers concerned are afforded appropriate protection.

Member States may lay down rules:

– for the application of this paragraph by two sides of industry, and
– for the extension of the provisions of collective agreements or agreements concluded in conformity with this paragraph to other workers in accordance with national legislation and/or practice.

The option to derogate from the reference periods (Art. 16) may not result in the establishment of a reference period exceeding six months.

However, Member States shall have the option, subject to compliance with the general principles relating to the protection of the safety and health of workers, of allowing, for objective or technical reasons or reasons concerning the organisation of work, collective agreements or agreements concluded between the two sides of industry to set reference periods in no event exceeding 12 months.

Before the expiry of a period of seven years from the date referred to in Article 18(1)(a), the Council shall, on the basis of a Commission proposal accompanied by an appraisal report, re-examine the provisions of this paragraph and decide what action to take (Art. 17).

1. Provided for in the first and second subparagraphs of Article 17.3.

5. Final Provisions (Art. 18)

a. DATE OF IMPLEMENTATION

436. Member States shall adopt the laws, regulations and administrative provisions necessary to comply with this directive by 23 November 1996 or shall ensure by that date that the two sides of industry establish the necessary measures by agreement, with Member States being obliged to take any necessary steps to enable them to guarantee at all times that the provisions laid down by this directive are fulfilled.

b. MAXIMUM WEEKLY WORKING TIME

437. A Member State shall have the option not to apply Article 6, while respecting the general principles of the protection of the safety and health of workers, and provided it takes the necessary measures to ensure that:

- no employer requires a worker to work more than 48 hours over a seven-day period, calculated as an average for the reference period referred to in point 2 of Article 16, unless he has first obtained the worker's agreement to perform such work;
- no worker is subjected to any detriment by his employer because he is not willing to give his agreement to perform such work;
- the employer keeps up-to-date records of all workers who carry out such work;
- the records are placed at the disposal of the competent authorities, which may, for reasons connected with the safety and/or health of workers, prohibit or restrict the possibility of exceeding the maximum weekly working hours;
- the employer provides the competent authorities at their request with information on cases in which agreement has been given by workers to perform work exceeding 48 hours over a period of seven days, calculated as an average for the reference period referred to in point 2 of Article 16.

Before the expiry of a period of seven years from the date referred to in (a), the Council shall, on the basis of a Commission proposal accompanied by an appraisal report, re-examine the provisions of this point (i) and decide on what action to take.

c. TRANSITIONAL PERIOD: ANNUAL LEAVE

438. Member States shall have the option, as regards the application of Article 7, of making use of a transitional period of not more than three years from the date referred to in (a), provided during that transitional period:

- every worker receives three weeks' paid annual leave in accordance with the conditions for the entitlement to, and granting of, such leave laid down by national legislation and/or practice; and
- the three-week period of paid annual leave may not be replaced by an allowance in lieu, except where the employment relationship is terminated.

Member States shall forthwith inform the Commission thereof.

When Member States adopt these measures they shall contain a reference to this directive or shall be accompanied by such reference on the occasion of their official publication. The methods of making such a reference shall be laid down by the Member States.

d. GENERAL LEVEL OF PROTECTION

439. Without prejudice to the right of Member States to develop, in the light of changing circumstances, different legislative, regulatory or contractual provisions in the field of working time, as long as the minimum requirements provided for in this directive are complied with, implementation of this directive shall not constitute valid grounds for reducing the general level of protection afforded to workers.

e. COMMUNICATION OF TEXTS-REPORTS-INFORMATION

440. Member States shall communicate to the Commission the texts of the provisions of national law already adopted or being adopted in the field governed by this directive.

Member States shall report to the Commission every five years on the practical implementation of the provisions of this directive, indicating the viewpoints of the two sides of industry.

The Commission shall inform the European Parliament, the Council, the Economic and Social Committee and the Advisory Committee on Safety, Hygiene and Health Protection at Work thereof.

Every five years the Commission shall submit to the European Parliament, the Council and the Economic and Social Committee a report on the application of this directive.

§2. SUNDAY REST

441. Sunday rest was dealt with by the Court at different occasions.[1] More specifically the question was raised whether rules, prohibiting retailers from opening their premises on Sunday are compatible with Community law and more especially whether such a prohibition is a measure having equivalent effect to a quantitative restriction on imports in the meaning of Article 30 of the EC Treaty. In the case against Marchandise and Cie criminal proceedings were launched against them because they repeatedly employed workers in retail shops on Sundays after 12.00 noon in contravention with the Belgian Labour Act of 16 March 1971.

The first point which must be made, the Court stated, is that national rules prohibiting retailers from opening their premises on Sunday apply to imported and domestic products alike. In principle, the marketing of products imported from other Member States is not therefore made more difficult than the marketing of domestic products. Next it must be recalled that such a prohibition is not compatible with the free movement of goods provided for in the Treaty unless any obstacle to Community trade thereby created did not exceed what was necessary in order to ensure the attainment of the objective in view and unless that objective was justified with regard to Community law. In those circumstances, the Court continued, it is therefore necessary that rules such as those at issue pursue an aim which is justified with regard to Community law. As far as that question is concerned, the Court has already stated in its judgment of 14 July 1981[2] that national rules governing the hours of work, delivery and sale in the bread and confectionery industry constitute a legitimate part of economic and social policy, consistent with the objectives of public interest pursued by the Treaty. The same consideration must apply as regards national rules governing the opening hours of retail premises. Such rules reflect certain political and economic choices insofar as their purpose is to ensure that working and non-working hours are so arranged as to accord with national and regional socio-cultural characteristics, and that, in the present state of Community law, is a matter for the Member States. Furthermore, such rules are not designed to govern the patterns of trade between the Member States.

Therefore, Article 30 of the Treaty must be interpreted as meaning that the prohibition which is laid down does not apply to national rules prohibiting retailers from opening their premises on Sunday where the restrictive effects on Community trade which may result therefrom do not exceed the effects intrinsic to rules of that kind.

1. COJ, 23 November 1989, *Torfean Borough Council* v. *B & Q plc*, No. C-145/88, IELL, *Case Law*, No. 138*bis*; COJ, 28 February 1991, *Union Départementale des Syndicats CGT de l'Aisne* v. *Sidef Conforama and Others*, No. C-312/89, IELL, *Case Law*, No. 160 and *Criminal proceedings against A. Marchandise and Others*, No. C-332/89, IELL, *Case Law*, No. 161. *See also*: COJ, 16 December 1992, *Reading Borough Council* v. *Payless Diy Limited and Others*, No. C-304/90, not yet published; COJ, 16 December 1992, *Council of the City of Stoke-on-Trent and Norwich City Councils* v. *B & Q plc*, No. C–169/91, not yet published.
2. *Oebel* (1981) ECR 1993, No. 155/80.

§3. NIGHT WORK AND EQUAL TREATMENT

442. The Community has tackled the problem of night work for women indirectly from the angle of equal treatment, namely on the basis of Article 5 of the Directive (76/207) of 9 February 1976. Indeed, by judgment of 4 October 1989, the *Tribunal de Police* (local criminal court), Illkirch (France) referred a question on the interpretation of Article 5 of the 1976 directive to the Court for a preliminary ruling. The question arose in the course of criminal proceedings brought against Mr. Stoeckel, the manager of SUMA SA, who was charged with having employed 77 women on night work contrary to Article L-23 of the French *Code du Travail*. This question was even more delicate due to the fact that French legislation on night work resulted from the ratification of ILO Convention No. 89, containing a prohibition of night work for women in industry.[1] The decision of the Court necessitated France, as well as Belgium, to denounce Convention No. 89.

The resolution of the problem of conflicting international instruments, namely emanating from the ILO from the one hand and the supranational norms, emanating from the Community, on the other hand, concerning night work for women and equal treatment of men and women, lies in Article 234(2) of the EC Treaty. Pursuant to this article, the Member States concerned shall to the extent that international agreements are not compatible with the Treaty 'take all appropriate steps to eliminate the incompatibilities.'

In the case under review a restructuration of the concerned enterprise had been negotiated between the employer and the trade unions and an agreement had been concluded to introduce shift and night work, in order to prevent the redundancy of some 200 employees. The agreement concerning night work applied also to female workers.

In the proceedings before the *Tribunal de Police* Mr. Stoeckel had maintained that Article L-213 of the *Code du Travail* contravened Article 5 of the 1976 directive concerning equal treatment between men and women.

The French Government argued that the prohibition of night work for women, qualified by numerous derogations, was in keeping with the general aims of protecting female employees and with special considerations of a social nature, such as the risk of assault and the greater burden of household work borne by women.

1. *See*: M.A. Moreau, 'Travail de nuit des femmes, observations sur l'arrêt de la CJCE du 25 juillet 1991,' *Droit Social*, 1992, 174–185.

443. Turning to the aims of protecting female employees, the Court held that it was not evident that, except in cases of pregnancy and maternity, the risks incurred by women in such work were broadly different in kind from the risks incurred by men. As far as the risks of assault were concerned, the Court ruled that, on the assumption that they were greater at night than by day, suitable measures could be adopted to deal with them without jeopardising the fundamental principle of equal treatment of men and women.

With regard to family responsibilities, the Court reiterated that the directive did not seek to settle questions as to the organisation of the family or alter the allocation of the responsibilities between the partners. Turning to the numerous derogations from the prohibition of night work to which the French Government had referred, the Court held that they were inadequate to give effect to Directive 76/207, since that directive did not allow any general principle excluding women from night work; the derogations could, indeed, be a source of discrimination. Therefore, the Court ruled as follows: Article 5 of the 1976 directive is sufficiently precise to impose on the Member States the obligation not to lay down by legislation the principle that night work by women is prohibited, even if that obligation is subject to exceptions, where night work for men is not prohibited.[1]

1. COJ, 25 July 1991, *Ministère Public* v. *A. Stoeckel*, No. C-345/89, IELL, *Case Law*, No. 167. For some critical background information on night work *see*: Singleton & Dirikx, *Ergonomics, Health and Safety*, Leuven, 1991.

444. A question to the Court for a preliminary ruling on the interpretation of Articles 1 to 5 of Council Directive 76/207/EC was raised in criminal proceedings brought by the French Ministère Public and the Direction du Travail et de l'Emploi against Jean-Claude Levy, who was summoned for having employed 23 women on night work contrary to Article L213-1 of the French Code du Travail.

That provision was adopted to implement Convention No. 89 of the International Labour Organisation of 9 July 1948 on night work for women in industry.

In its judgment of 25 July 1991 in the *Stoeckel* Case the Court held that Article 5 of the directive was sufficiently precise to impose on the Member States the obligation not to lay down by legislation the principle that night work by women was prohibited, even if that is subject to exceptions, where night work by men is not prohibited. It followed that in principle the national court had to ensure the full effect of that rule and not apply any contrary national provision.

In the present case the question for a preliminary ruling was basically whether the national court had the same obligation where the national provision which was incompatible with the Community rule was intended to implement a convention such as the ILO Convention which was concluded by the Member State concerned with other Member States and non-Member States prior to the entry into force of the EC Treaty.

In determining whether a Community rule could be frustrated by a prior international convention it was necessary to consider whether the convention imposed on the Member State concerned obligations compliance with which might still be insisted on by non-Member States who were parties to the convention.

In that respect the Court held that although it was true that equality of treatment for men and women constituted a fundamental right recognised by the Community legal system, its implementation even at Community level had been progressive requiring the intervention of the Council by means of directives and those directives recognised temporarily certain derogations from the principle of equality of treatment.

In those circumstances it was not sufficient to cite the principle of equality of treatment to prevent compliance with obligations of a Member State in that field under a prior international convention where observance of the obligations was protected by the first paragraph of Article 234 of the Treaty.

In the present case if it appeared from the development of international law that the prohibition of night work for women provided for by the ILO Convention was repealed by subsequent conventions binding the same parties, the provisions of the first paragraph of Article 234 of the Treaty would not be applicable. There would then be nothing to prevent the national court from applying Article 5 of the directive and disregarding contrary national provisions.

However, it was not for the Court in proceedings for a preliminary ruling but for the national court to determine the obligations under a prior international convention of the Member State concerned and to define the limits in order to determine to what extent those obligations precluded the application of Article 5 of the directive.

The Court ruled as follows:

'The national court must ensure full respect of Article 5 of Council Directive 76/207/EEC of 9 February 1976 on the implementation of the principle of equal treatment for men and women as regards access to employment, vocational training and promotion, and working conditions and not apply any contrary provision of national law unless application of such a provision is necessary to ensure compliance by the Member State concerned with obligations resulting from a convention concluded prior to the entry into force of the EC Treaty with non-Member States.'[1]

1. COJ, *Ministère Public* v. *J.C. Levy*, 2 August 1993, No. C-158/91, not yet published.

§4. Parental Leave

445. Parental leave was introduced by Directive 96/34/EC of 3 June 1996 on the framework agreement on parental leave concluded by UNICE, CEEP and the ETUC, 14 December 1995.[1] The agreement referred to is the first European collective labour agreement concluded by the recognised social partners under the Maastricht Agreement on Social Policy (1991).[2]

The cross-industry organisations indeed concluded, on 14 December 1995, a framework agreement on parental leave and forwarded to the Commission their joint request to implement this framework agreement by a Council Decision on a proposal from the Commission.

At the occasion of the Madrid summit, the members of the European Council (except for the UK) welcomed the conclusion of this framework agreement. The text, before being implemented by way of a directive, was forwarded to the EP and ESC.

1. O.J., 19 June 1996, No. L 145/4.
2. *See further* Part II, Chapter 1.

I. Objectives and Principles

A. *Objectives*

446.   The framework agreement sets out minimum requirements on parental leave and time off from work on grounds of *force majeure*, as an important means of reconciling work and family life and promoting equal opportunities and treatment between men and women.

B. *Values*

1. Family Life

447.   The agreement aims to reconcile work and family life by encouraging the introduction of new flexible ways of organising work and time which are better suited to the changing needs of society and which should take the needs of both undertakings and workers into account. Family policy should be looked at in the context of demographic changes, the effects of the ageing population, closing the generation gap and promoting women's participation in the labour force. Moreover, men should be encouraged to assume an equal share of family responsibilities, for example, they should be encouraged through means such as awareness programmes to take parental leave.

2. Equal Treatment

448.   At the same time the agreement wants to promote equal opportunities and treatment between men and women. For that reason parental leave is granted on a non-transferable basis (Clause 2,2).

C. *Subsidiarity and Proportionality*

449.   In keeping with the principles of subsidiarity and proportionality, the directive is confined to the minimum required to achieve the objectives and does not go beyond what is necessary to achieve that purpose. Therefore, the agreement

is only a framework agreement setting out minimum requirements and provisions for parental leave, distinct from maternity leave, and for time off from work on grounds of *force majeure*, and refers back to Member States and social partners for the establishment of the conditions of access and detailed rules of application in order to take account of the situation in each Member States.

Consequently, Member States should:

– provide for the maintenance of entitlements to benefits in kind under sickness insurance during the minimum period of parental leave;
– where appropriate under national conditions and taking into account the budgetary situation, consider the maintenance of entitlements to relevant social security benefits as they stand during the minimum period of parental leave.

The contracting parties agree that management and labour are best placed to find solutions that correspond to the needs of both employers and workers and must therefore have conferred on them a special role in the implementation and application of the present agreement, which is another application of the subsidiarity principle.

D. Competitiveness – SME's

450. The agreement takes not only into consideration the need to improve social policy requirements, but also to enhance the competitiveness of the Community economy and to avoid imposing administrative, financial and legal constraints in a way which would impede the creation and development of small and medium-sized undertakings.

II. Scope

451. The agreement lays down minimum requirements designed to facilitate the reconciliation of parental and professional responsibilities for working parents (Clause 1,1).

It 'applies to all workers, men and women, who have an employment contract or employment relationship as defined by the law, collective agreements or practices in force in each Member State' (Clause 1,2). It thus applies as well to the public as to the private sector.

III. Content

A. Parental leave

1. Notion

452. The agreement grants men and women workers an individual right to parental leave on the grounds of the birth or adoption of a child, to enable them to take care of that child, for at least three months, until a given age up to 8 years to be defined by Member States and/or management and labour (Clause 2,1).

The right to parental leave is, in principle, granted on a non-transferable basis (Clause 2,2).

2. Conditions of Access and Detail

453.   The conditions of access and detailed rules for applying parental leave shall be defined by law and/or collective agreement in the Member States, as long as the minimum requirements of this agreement are respected (Clause 2,3).

Member States and/or management and labour may, in particular:

(a) decide whether parental leave is granted on a full-time or part-time basis, in a piecemeal way or in the form of a time-credit system;
(b) make entitlement to parental leave subject to a period of work qualification and/or a length of service qualification which shall not exceed one year;
(c) adjust conditions of access and detailed rules for applying parental leave to the special circumstances of adoption;
(d) establish notice periods to be given by the worker to the employer when exercising the right to parental leave, specifying the beginning and the end of the period of leave;
(e) define the circumstances in which an employer, following consultation in accordance with national law, collective agreements and practices, is allowed to postpone the granting of parental leave for justifiable reasons related to the operation of the undertaking (e.g., where work is of a seasonal nature, where a replacement cannot be found within the notice period, where a significant proportion of the workforce applies for parental leave at the same time, where a specific function is of strategic importance). Any problem arising from the application of this provision should be dealt with in accordance with national law, collective agreements and practices;
(f) in addition to (e), authorise special arrangements to meet the operational and organisational requirements of small undertakings.

3. Protection against Dismissal – Return

454.   In order to ensure that workers can exercise their right to parental leave, Member States and/or management and labour shall take the necessary measures to protect workers against dismissal on the grounds of an application for, or the taking of, parental leave in accordance with national law, collective agreements or practices (Clause 2,4).

At the end of parental leave, workers shall have the right to return to the same job or, if that is not possible, to an equivalent or similar job consistent with their employment contract or employment relationship (Clause 2,5).

4. Acquired Rights – Status of Employment

455.   Rights acquired or in the process of being acquired by the worker on the date on which parental leave starts shall be maintained as they stand until the end of parental leave. At the end of parental leave, these rights, including any changes arising from national law, collective agreements or practice, shall apply.

Member States and/or management and labour shall define the status of the employment contract or employment relationship for the period of parental leave (Clause 2,5–6).

5. Social Security

456.   All matters relating to social security in relation to this agreement are for consideration and determination by Member States according to national law, taking into account the importance of the continuity of the entitlements to social security cover under the different schemes, in particular health care.

B. *Time off from Work on Grounds of Force Majeure*

457.   Member States and/or management and labour shall take the necessary measures to entitle workers to time off from work, in accordance with national legislation, collective agreements and/or practice, on grounds of *force majeure* for urgent family reasons in case of sickness or accident making the immediate presence of the worker indispensable.

Member States and/or management and labour may specify the conditions of access and detailed rules and limit this entitlement to a certain amount of time per year and/or per case (Clause 3).

IV. Final Provisions

A. *General*

458.   Member States may apply or introduce more favourable provisions than those set out in this agreement.

Implementation of the provisions of this agreement shall not constitute valid grounds for reducing the general level of protection afforded to workers in the field covered by this agreement. This shall not prejudice the right of Member States and/ or management and labour to develop different legislative, regulatory or contractual provisions, in the light of changing circumstances (including the introduction of non-transferability), as long as the minimum requirements provided for in the present agreement are complied with.

The present agreement shall not prejudice the right of management and labour to conclude, at the appropriate level including European level, agreements adapting and/or complementing the provisions of this agreement in order to take into account particular circumstances.

B. *Implementation*

459.   Member States shall adopt the laws, regulations and administrative provisions necessary to comply with the Council decision within a period of two years from its adoption or shall ensure that management and labour[1] introduce the necessary measures by way of agreement by the end of this period. Member States may, if necessary to take account of particular difficulties or implementation by collective agreement, have up to a maximum of one additional year to comply with this decision.

1. Within the meaning of Article 2(4) of the Agreement on social policy.

C. Disputes and Interpretation

460.   The prevention and settlement of disputes and grievances arising from the application of this agreement shall be dealt with in accordance with national law, collective agreements and practices.

Without prejudice to the respective role of the Commission, national courts and the Court of Justice, any matter relating to the interpretation of this agreement at European level should, in the first instance, be referred by the Commission to the signatory parties who will give an opinion.

D. Review

461.   The signatory parties shall review the application of this agreement five years after the date of the Council decision if requested by one of the parties to this agreement.

V. Directive of 3 June 1996: Implementation

462.   The proper instrument for implementing the framework agreement, the considerans to the directive indicates, 'is a Directive within the meaning of Article 189 of the Treaty, whereas it is therefore binding on the Member States as the results to be achieved, but leaves them the choice of form and methods.'

According to Article 2 of the directive, the Member States shall bring into force the laws, regulations and administrative provisions necessary to comply with this directive by 3 June 1998 at the latest or shall ensure by that date at the latest that management and labour have introduced the necessary measures by agreement, the Member States being required to take any necessary measure enabling them at any time to be in a position to guarantee the results imposed by the directive. They shall forthwith inform the Commission thereof.

The Member States may have a maximum additional period of one year, if this is necessary to take account of special difficulties or implementation by a collective agreement. They must forthwith inform the Commission of such circumstances.

When Member States adopt these measures, they shall contain a reference to this directive or be accompanied by such reference on the occasion of their official publication. The methods of making such reference shall be laid down by Member States.

Chapter 8. Safety and Health

§1. First Measures

I. Euratom

463. Initially, the Treaties did not bestow on the Communities important competences regarding health and safety. It was only the Euratom Treaty that contained some explicit provisions regarding this issue: Chapter III of Title II of the Euratom Treaty is indeed devoted to 'health and safety.' Articles 30 and 31 obliges the Community to lay down basic standards for the protection of the health of workers and the general public against the dangers arising from ionising radiations. The expression basic standards means:

a. maximum permissible doses compatible with adequate safety;
b. the maximum permissible levels of exposure and contamination;
c. the fundamental principles governing the health surveillance of workers (Art. 30).

Each Member State had to lay down the appropriate provisions to ensure compliance with the basic standards established and were obliged to take the necessary measure with regard to teaching, education and vocational training (Art. 33).[1]

  1. *See* Directive No. 80/836 of 15 July 1980 amending the directives laying down the basic safety standards for the health protection of the general public and workers against the dangers of ionising radiation (O.J., 17 December 1980, No. L 246, amended by Directive No. 84/467, O.J., 5 October 1984, No. L 265).

II. EC: Transport

464. The Commission was obliged, in order to justify action regarding safety matters in the EC, to give a rather extensive interpretation to the general competence conferred on the Community by Article 75C of the EC Treaty regarding transport, namely: to lay down 'any appropriate measures.' On the basis of this (very implicit) competence, quite a number of important regulations and directives were adopted, of which we retain only those which are still valid at present:

– Regulation No. 3820/85 of 20 December 1985 on the harmonisation of certain social legislation relating to road transport;[1]

- Regulation No. 3821/85 of 20 December 1985 on recording equipment in road transport;[2]
- Directive No. 88/599 of 23 November 1988 on standard checking procedures on recording equipment in road transport;[3]
- Directive No. 89/684 of 21 December 1989 on vocational training for certain drivers of vehicles carrying dangerous goods by road.[4]

1. O.J., 31 December 1985, No. L. 370.
2. O.J., 31 December 1985, No. L. 371.
3. O.J., 29 November 1988, No. L. 325.
4. O.J., 30 December 1989, No. L. 398.

III. Other Actions

465.   Notwithstanding the fact that Community institutions had only limited competence in the area of health and safety, quite a number of important initiatives were taken in the framework of Article 100 of the EC Treaty regarding the approximation of laws. In its resolution of 21 January 1974 concerning a social action programme, the Council confirmed the necessity to establish an action programme for workers aimed at the humanisation of their living and working conditions with particular reference to improvement in safety and health conditions at work. It was pointed out that protective measures differed from country to country and that those national measures, which have a direct influence on the functioning of the common market, had to be harmonised and improved upon in view of an harmonious economic and social development in the Community. This set of ideas prompted the adoption of quite an important number of measures of which we retain only the most important:

- Directive No. 77/576 of 25 July 1977 on the provision of safety signs at places of work;[1]
- Directive No. 78/610 of 29 June 1978 on the protection of health of workers exposed to vinyl chloride monomer;[2]
- Directive No. 80/1107 of 27 November 1980 on the protection of workers from the risks related to exposure to chemical, physical and biological agents at work;[3]
- Directive No. 82/501 of 24 June 1982 on the major accident hazards of certain industrial activities;[4]
- Directive No. 82/605 of 28 July 1982 on the protection of workers from the risks related to exposure to metallic lead and its ionic compounds at work;[5]
- Directive No. 83/477 of 19 September 1983 on the protection of workers from the risks of exposure to asbestos at work;[6]
- Directive No. 86/188 of 12 May 1986 on the protection of workers from the risks related to exposure to noise at work;[7]
- Directive No. 88/364 of 9 June 1988 on the protection of workers by the banning of certain specified agents and/or certain work activities;[8]
- Directive No. 91/322 of 29 May 1991, establishing indicative limit values by implementing Council Directive 80/1107/EC on the protection of workers from the risks related to exposure to chemical, physical and biological agents at work;[9]

– Directive No. 92/29/EEC of 31 March 1992 concerning the minimum safety and
health requirements for improved medical treatment on board vessels.[10]

1. O.J., 7 September 1977, No. L 299 amended by Directive No. 79/640, O.J., 19 July 1979, No.
   L 183.
2. O.J., 22 July 1978, No. L 197.
3. O.J., 3 December 1980, No. L 327, amended by Directive No. 88/642 of 16 December 1988,
   O.J. 24 December 1988, No. L 358.
4. O.J., 5 August 1982, No. L 230, amended by Directive No. 87/216, O.J., 28 March 1987, No.
   L 85 and Directive No. 88/610, O.J., 7 December 1988, No. L 336.
5. O.J., 23 August 1982, No. L 247.
6. O.J., 24 September 1983, No. L 263..
7. O.J., 24 May 1986, No. L 137.
8. O.J., 9 July 1988, No. L 179. This directive is based on Article 118A. As the proposal dates
   from 1984 and that directive was part of a series of directives we still include it under this
   period.
9. O.J., 5 May 1991, No. L 177.
10. O.J., 30 April 1992, No. L 113/19.

§2. 1987: THE SINGLE EUROPEAN ACT AND ARTICLE 118A

466. The Single Act of 1986 introduced Article 118A into the EC Treaty and
thus clearly affirmed the competence of the Community in relation to health and
safety for workers. Pursuant to Article 118A §1:

> 'Member States shall pay particular attention to encouraging improvements,
> especially in the working environment, as regards the health and safety of
> workers, and shall set as their objective the harmonisation of conditions in this
> area, while maintaining the improvements made.'

Within the framework of cooperation among the Community institutions and in
order to achieve the objective laid down in the first paragraph of Article 118A, the
Council, acting by a qualified majority on a proposal from the Commission, in
cooperation with the EP and after consulting the ESC, adopted, by means of a
directive, minimum requirements for gradual implementation, with regard to the
conditions and technical rules existing in each of the Member States (Art. 118A,
§2 first sentence). Such directives shall avoid imposing administrative, financial
and legal constraints in a way that would hold back the creation and development
of small and medium-sized undertakings (Art. 118A, §2, second sentence). Finally,
the provisions adopted pursuant to Article 118A will not prevent any Member State
from maintaining or introducing more stringent measures for the protection of
working conditions compatible with the Treaty (§3). These are thus far the basic
legal provisions.

467. It follows from the drafting and wording of Article 118A that this text is
the result of difficult and complex negotiations, which will undoubtedly lead to a
number of interpretative difficulties, even more so as the directives involved can be
adopted by a qualified majority in the Council and consequently no State enjoys a

right of veto, as is the case concerning 'the rights and interests' of employed persons (Art. 100A, §2 of the EC Treaty). A great deal must thus be said in order to start to clarify this text. First, we must point out that health and safety is a shared responsibility: both the Member States and the Community are competent for the improvement of health and safety. Secondly, the Community institutions lay down minimum requirements, upon which the Member States can improve, not derogate to the detriment of the workers. These requirements will gradually be implemented over a certain period of time. Furthermore, one should avoid imposing administrative, financial and legal constraints that would hinder the development of small and medium-sized enterprises. Thus, there should be no unnecessary 'red tape.' Whether this last requirement is legally enforceable remains to be seen. We are here, once again, confronted with a more programmatic policy obligation than with a legally enforceable text of the Treaty.

468.   The interpretation difficulties, in which the Court will obviously play a decisive role, relate especially to the words in paragraph 1 of Article 118A, namely: 'the working environment,' 'health and safety of workers,' and the conditions and technical rules' in relation to the expression 'working conditions' in paragraph 3.

469.   The Court has had an occasion to do so in the *UK* v. *Council of the European Union*,[1] in which the UK tried to obtain the annulment of the directive on the organisation of working time (1993). The UK contended that the directive was illegal, because it was based on Article 118A of the Treaty, which allows for qualified majority voting. Article 118A, according to the UK, has to be strictly interpreted and could thus not constitute an appropriate legal basis for a directive on working time. That directive should have been based on articles of the Treaty, like 100 or 235, which however require unanimity in the Council of Ministers.

The Court of Justice, however, ruled in favour of a broad interpretation. It stated:

> 'Article 118A confers upon the Community internal legislative competence in the area of social policy. The existence of other provisions in the Treaty does not have the effect of restricting the scope of Article 118A. Appearing as it does in the chapter of the Treaty which deals with "Social Provisions", Article 118A relates only to measures concerning the protection of the health and safety of workers. It therefore constitutes a more specific rule than Articles 100 and 100a. That interpretation is confirmed by the actual wording of 100 Article 100a(1) itself, which states that its provisions are to apply save where otherwise provided in this Treaty. The applicant's argument cannot therefore be accepted.
>
> There is nothing in the wording of Article 118A to indicate that the concepts of "working environment", "safety" and "health" as used in that provision should, in the absence of other indications, be interpreted restrictively, and not as embracing all factors, physical or otherwise, capable of affecting the health and safety of the worker in his working environment, including in particular certain aspects of the organisation of working time. On the contrary, the words "especially in the working environment" militate in favour of a broad interpretation of the powers which Article 118A confers upon the Council

for the protection of the health and safety of workers. Moreover, such an interpretation of the words "safety" and "health" derives support in particular from the preamble to the Constitution of the World Health Organisation to which all the Member States belong. Health is there defined as a state of complete physical, mental and social well-being that does not consist only in the absence of illness or infirmity.

In conferring on the Council power to lay down minimum requirements, Article 118A does not prejudge the extent of the action which that institution may consider necessary in order to carry out the task which the provision in question expressly assigns to it – namely, to work in favour of improved conditions, as regards the health and safety of workers, while maintaining the improvements made. The significance of the expression "minimum require-ments" in Article 118A is simply, as indeed Article 118A(3) confirms, that the provision authorises Member States to adopt more stringent measures than those which form the subject-matter of Community action.

Furthermore, there is no support in the wording of Article 118A for the argument that Community action should be restricted to specific measures applicable to given groups of workers in particular situations, whilst measures for wider purposes should be adopted on the basis of Article 100 of the Treaty. Article 118A refers to "workers" generally and states that the objective which it pursues is to be achieved by the harmonisation of "conditions" in general existing in the area of the health and safety of those workers.

In addition, the delimitation of the respective fields of application of Arti-cles 100 and 100a, on the one hand, and Article 118A, on the other, rests not upon a distinction between the possibility of adopting general measures in the former case and particular measures in the latter, but upon the principal aim of the measure envisaged.

It follows that, where the principal aim of the measure in question is the protection of the health and safety of workers, Article 118A must be used, albeit such a measure may have ancillary effects on the establishment and functioning of the internal market.'

In his opinion the Advocate General found confirmation of the view favouring a broad interpretation in the proposal made by Denmark at the Inter-Governmental Conference on the Single Act. According to the Advocate General.

'the concept of "working environment" in Danish law is a very broad one, covering the performance of work and conditions at the workplace, as well as technical equipment and the substances and materials used. Accordingly, the relevant Danish legislation is not limited to classic measures relating to safety and health at work in the strict sense, but also includes measures concerning working hours, psychological factors, the way work is performed, training in hygiene and safety, and the protection of young workers and worker represen-tation with regard to security against dismissal or any other attempt to under-mine their working conditions. The concept of "working environment" is not immutable, but reflects the social and technical evolution of society . . .

Ultimately, the only limits on the definition of the concept of "working environment" which I have proposed are to be found in the term *workers*, which
it underlies. That rules out the possibility of using Article 118A as a basis for
a measure whose subject-matter is the safety and health of the population *in
general*, perhaps by reference to a risk which is not peculiar to workers.

In my view, the terms "*safety and health*" should in their turn be given a broad
interpretation, having regard to that conception of the working environment.

... the origin of Article 118A militates against a strict interpretation of the
terms "safety and health". It is far removed from an approach confined to the
protection of workers against the influence of physical or chemical factors
alone. Secondly, it seems to me that a restrictive approach would run counter
to the trend in our society. The Council and the interveners have referred in
that regard, very pertinently, to the principle adopted by the World Health
Organization – to which, I would note in passing, all the Member States of the
European Union belong – to the effect that "health is a state of complete
physical, mental and social well-being and does not consist only in the absence of illness or infirmity".

... there is nothing in the wording of Article 118A which suggests that any
aspect of the well-being or safety – broadly speaking – of workers should be
excluded; on the contrary, that provision expressly refers to "improvements"
and to harmonisation "while maintaining the improvements made".

In any event, such a wide interpretation of the concept of health in particular, which is consistent with that advocated by the WHO, has already been
accepted by the Community institutions for the adoption of directives on the
basis of Article 118A. For instance, in Directive 92/85/FEC (concerning pregnant women), the maintenance of income during maternity leave (whether in
the form of remuneration or of an "adequate" allowance) is regarded as
indissociable from a pregnant woman's health.'

In conclusion, Article 118A gives a broad mandate to the EU to proceed in this
area.

1. COJ, 12 November 1996, Case C-84/94, not yet published.

I. Health and Safety in the Working Environment

470. The question remains what the terms, employed in Article 118A, mean.
It is obvious that they need to be employed in their normal significance. Indeed,
words mean what they mean. This is our second basic rule. With these two basic
rules in mind we propose the following definitions.

471. The term '*working environment*' relates to the place where the work is to
be done. This is not only the facilities in the undertaking to which the employee
has access. The notion is broader than that. It concerns the undertaking as well as
the home, in the case of homework; it also relates to the construction site in the

case of a construction worker, to the class room for the teacher, to mines in the case of a miner, the soccer stadium for a professional soccer player, the racing circuit for the professional cyclist and so on.

472. The terms safety and health are complementary. Both aim at the promotion of human integrity: the physical and mental status of the employee. The purpose is indeed not only the prevention of damages (stress, work accidents, professional diseases) but also , in a positive way (agreeable, comforting, refreshing), the promotion of health and safety of the employees. Article 118A aims not only at the elimination of the risks that endanger the health and safety of workers, but also at the establishment of those measures which promote them in a positive way.

473. Thus the terms health and safety relate to:

– machines and installations, and to the introduction of new technologies, products and materials;
– lighting, temperature, radiation, electricity, gas;
– the situation at the workplace, the construction site;
– the organisation of work and the work rhythm;
– transport of and from the enterprise and within the undertaking;
– the organisation of catering and the cafeteria;
– the use of alcohol and drugs, as well as smoking;
– sport and leisure activities.

This enumeration is certainly not exhaustive, but exemplary. In any case it indicates that, notwithstanding a restrictive interpretation, which we defend – for legal, not political reasons – we are dealing with an important and wide ranging issue.

474. To this we should add that Article 118A, to our mind, also concerns the policy organisations relating to health and safety in the undertaking. As such, this included the eventual organisation, mission and working of a service for safety in the undertaking, an eventual service for industrial medicine, as well as possible medical, nursing or pharmaceutical services. Under the scope of this organisation, the following can also be added: the information and training of workers regarding the prevention of work accidents and occupational diseases. One must see to it that information on safety instruction is given in a language that the workers can effectively understand. In Belgium, for example, we well remember the catastrophe in Marcinelle, more than 30 years ago, when several dozen Italian workers died because they were not fully familiar with the safety instructions, which were written in French. The drafting of a safety plan, the organisation of a fire-brigade, specific measures of protection for handicapped workers and other measures are also needed.

475. It is also evident that *workers' participation* is a concern here. Information to and the consultation of workers, as well as their involvement in decisions relating to policies are a few points that can be dealt with by Community law on the basis of Article 118A. It is equally clear that, when decisions are made at the distant headquarters of, say, a multinational group, the necessary measures should be taken so that local management as well as workers at the subsidiaries receive enough information beforehand so that they are able to exert sufficient influence on the decision-making process. Finally, one must remark that health and safety belong to the nucleus of the unalienable rights or workers. These rights must in principle be equal whatever the size of the enterprise in which these workers are employed. There is no room for deregulation within this subject.

II. Application

476. The Community seems to use its competence regarding health and safety in a very dynamic way. Pursuant to Article 118A of the EC Treaty, a framework directive of 12 June 1989 has been adopted, as well as more individual directives, with the intention to cover all risks relating to health and safety at work, concerning *inter alia*: the workplace, work equipment, personal protective equipment, work with visual display units, the handling of heavy loads involving risks of back injury, temporary or mobile work sites, fisheries and agriculture (Art. 16, §1 of the framework directive), prohibition of certain agents and activities, the improvement of health and safety at work of workers with a fixed duration or temporary employment relationship, and improved medical treatment on board vessels. For the proposals concerning atypical work and the protection of motherhood, which are based on Article 118A, we refer to Part I, Chapters 3 and 5.

A. The Framework Directive of 12 June 1989

477. This framework Directive No. 89/391 concerns the introduction of measures to encourage improvements in the safety and health of workers at work.[1] It embraces general principles concerning the preventing of occupational risks, the protection of safety and health, the elimination of risk and accident factors, information, consultation, balanced participation and training of workers and their representatives, as well as general guidelines for the implementation of said principles (Art. 1, §2).

1. O.J., 29 June 1989, No. L 183.

1. Scope and Definitions

478. The directive applies to all sectors of activity, both public and private (industrial, agriculture, commercial, administrative, service, educational, cultural, leisure, etc.) with the exception of certain specific activities in the civil protection services, such as the armed forces and the police. In any event, the safety and health of workers must be ensured as far as possible in the light of the objectives of the directive.

479. For the purposes of the directive, the following terms have the following meanings:

a. *worker*: any person employed by an employer, including trainees and apprentices, but excluding domestic servants;
b. *employer*: any natural or legal person who has an employment relationship with the worker and who has responsibility for the undertaking and/or establishment;
c. *workers' representative* with specific responsibility for the safety and health of workers: any person elected, chosen or designated in accordance with national laws and/or practices to represent workers where problems arise relating to the safety and health protection of workers at work;
d. *prevention*: all the steps or measures taken or planned at all stages of work in the undertaking to reduce occupational risks (Art. 3).

2. Employer's Obligations

480. The employer has the duty to ensure the safety and the health of workers in every aspect related to the work. Member States can exclude or limit the employer's responsibility for reasons of *force majeure* (Art. 5, §1 and §4).

The employer must take the necessary measures, including the prevention of occupational risks and the provision of information and training (Art. 6, §1). The employer of course carries the full financial burden: measures related to safety, hygiene and health at work may in no circumstances involve the workers in the financial cost (Art. 6, §5).

The employer must implement the measures on the basis of the following general principles of prevention:

a. avoid risks;
b. evaluate the risks that cannot be avoided;
c. combat the risks at source;
d. adapt the work to the individual, especially as regards the design of work places, the choice of work equipment and the choice of working and production methods, with a view, in particular, to alleviating monotonous work and work at a predetermined work-rate and to reducing their effect on health;
e. adapt to technical progress;
f. replace the dangerous by the non-dangerous or the less dangerous;
g. develop a coherent overall prevention policy to cover technology, the organisation of work, working conditions, social relationships and the influence of factors relating to the working environment;
h. give collective protective measures priority over individual protective measures;
i. give appropriate instructions to the workers (Art. 6, §2).

481. The employer is furthermore obliged, taking into account the nature of the activities of the enterprise and/or establishment, to:

a. evaluate the risks to the safety and health of workers, *inter alia* in the choice of work equipment, the chemical substances or preparations used, and the fitting-out of work places;

b. where he entrusts tasks to a worker, take into consideration the worker's capabilities as regards health and safety;
c. ensure that the planning and introduction of new technologies are the subject of consultation with the workers and/or their representatives, as regards the consequences and the choice of equipment, the working conditions and the working environment for the safety and the health of workers;
d. take appropriate steps to ensure that only workers who have received adequate instructions have access to areas where there is serious and specific danger (Art. 6, §3).

Where several employers share a work place, the employers shall cooperate in implementing safety and health provisions (Art. 6, §4).

The employer designates one or more qualified workers to carry out activities related to the protection and prevention of occupational risks; eventually the employer enlists competent external services or persons (Art. 7). Measures must be taken regarding first aid, fire fighting and evacuation of workers, etc. (Art. 8).

3. Information, Consultation and Participation of Workers

482. Workers should receive all the necessary information concerning the safety and health risks, and the protective and preventive measures and activities in respect of both the undertaking and/or establishment in general and each type of workstation and/or job. The employees' representatives must have access, in order to carry out their functions, to the risk assessment and protective measures and the list and reports which have been established to that end, etc. (Art. 10). *Consultation* and *participation* are provided for in Article 11. This presupposes:

– the consultation of workers;
– the rights of workers and/or their representative to make proposals;
– balanced participation in accordance with national laws or practices. This means that reference is made, regarding workers' participation, to national law and practice and that there are no Community rules relating to that matter.

Workers' representatives may not be placed at a disadvantage because of their activities. They should enjoy adequate time off work, without loss of pay, and provided with the necessary means to exercise their functions. When they have grievances, workers and their representatives are entitled to appeal to the responsible authorities; representatives must be given the opportunity to submit observations during inspection visits by the competent authority (Art. 11).

4. Miscellaneous

483. The framework directive finally contains stipulations relating to the adequate safety and health training of workers; worker's obligations (namely, to take care as far as possible of his own safety and health and that of other persons) as well as health surveillance: each worker, if he so wishes, should receive health surveillance at regular intervals (Arts. 12–14).

B. The Individual Directives

484. Pursuant to the framework directive, different individual directives were adopted:

- Directive No. 89/654 of 30 November 1989 concerning the minimum safety and health requirements;[1]
- Directive No. 89/655 of 30 November 1989 concerning the use of work equipment by workers at work.[2] 'Work equipment' means any machine, apparatus, tool or installation used at work;
- Directive No. 89/656 of 30 November 1989 on the use of by workers of personal protective equipment at the workplace;[3]
- Directive No. 90/269 on the manual handling of loads where there is a particular risk of back injury;[4]
- Directive No. 90/270 of 29 May 1990 on work with display screen equipment;[5]
- Directive No. 90/394 of 28 June 1990 related to exposure to carcinogens at work;[6]
- Directive No. 90/679 of 26 November 1990 related to exposure to biological agents at work;[7]
- Directive No. 92/47/EC of 24 June 1992, on the implementation of minimum safety and health requirements at temporary or mobile construction sites;[8]
- Directive No. 92/58/EC of 24 June 1992, on the minimum requirements for the provision of safety and/or health signs at work;[9]
- Directive No. 92/85/EC of 19 October 1992, on the introduction of measures to encourage improvements in the safety and health at work of pregnant workers and workers who have recently given birth or are breastfeeding;[10]
- Directive No. 92/91/EC of 3 November 1992, concerning the minimum requirements for improving the safety and health protection of workers in the mineral-extracting industries through drilling;[11]
- Directive No. 92/104/EC of 3 December 1992, on the minimum requirements for improving the safety and health protection of workers in surface and underground mineral-extracting industries;[12]
- Directive No. 92/57 of 24 June 1992 on the implementation of minimum safety and health requirements at temporary or mobile construction sites;[13]
- Directive No. 92/58 of 24 June 1992 on the minimum requirements of safety and health signs at work;[14]
- Directive No. 92/85 of 19 October 1992 concerning the introduction of measures to encourage improvements in the safety and health at work of pregnant workers who have recently given birth or are breastfeeding;[15]
- Directive No. 93/103 of 23 November 1993 concerning the minimum safety and health requirements for work on board fishing vessel.[16]

Many of these directives have been amended.

In these different directives we find stipulations concerning the information, training, consultation and participation of workers, whereby reference is made to the relevant rules in the framework directive.

1. O.J., 30 December 1989, No. L 393.
2. O.J., 30 December 1989, No. L 393.
3. O.J., 30 December 1989, No. L 393.
4. O.J., 21 June 1990, No. L 156.
5. O.J., 21 June 1990, No. L 156.
6. O.J., 26 July 1990, No. L 196.
7. O.J., 31 December 1990, No. L 374.
8. O.J., 26 August 1992, No. L 245.
9. O.J., 26 August 1992, No. L 245.
10. O.J., 28 November 1992, No. L 348.
11. O.J., 28 November 1992, No. L 348.
12. O.J., 31 December 1992, No. L 404.
13. O.J., 26 August 1992, No. L 245/6.
14. O.J., 26 August 1992, No. L 245/23.
15. O.J., 28 November1992, No. L 348/1.
16. O.J., 13 December 1993, No. L 307/1.

Chapter 9. Employee Participation in Profits and Enterprise Results

485.   The Member States of the Community are in favour of encouraging financial participation by employees in profits and enterprise results, as indicated in the Recommendation approved by the Council of Ministers on 27 July 1992.[1]

In the Recommendation the argument is made that participation by employees is an effective means of helping them to become more involved in their firm's future, while at the same time reconciling the role of employees within the firm, their aspiration for a better remuneration and the financial equilibrium of the firm. Even though financial participation schemes are currently applied with varying degrees of success in the Member States, this point of view has finally been accepted by all.

Of course, all sources of prejudice have not vanished overnight. The Recommendation points out that 'empirical research into the effects of such schemes in practice does not yet provide overwhelming evidence of strong overall advantages.' The researchers nevertheless conclude that 'there are sufficient indications that such schemes produce a number of positive effects, particularly on the motivation and productivity of employed persons and on competitiveness,' and that they should be promoted within the Community.

1. O.J., No. 92/443, 26 August 1992, No. L 245/53.

486.   The Recommendation thus invites the Member States to acknowledge the potential benefits of a wider use of a broad variety of schemes to increase the participation of employed persons in profits and enterprise results by means of profit-sharing, employee share-ownership or a combination of both. The Recommendation calls on the Member States to ensure that their legal structures are adequate to allow the effective introduction of financial participation schemes and consider the possibility of encouraging them by means of fiscal or other financial incentives. The Member States are also asked to encourage the use of such schemes by supplying adequate information and, before deciding on which schemes to promote, to take account of experience gained in other Member States. The Recommendation goes on to propose that the social partners should have a wide range of options or arrangements available, so as to ensure that their choice can be made as close as possible to the employees and the enterprise.

487.   Finally, the Recommendation sets out, in an annex, the promotion of participation by employed persons in profits and a number of points to be taken into consideration by Member States when they prepare new participation schemes or review existing ones. These are as follows:

1. *Regularity*: the application of participation schemes on a regular basis and the granting of 'bonuses' at least once a year.
2. *Pre-determined formula*: the definition, in a clear way and before the beginning of each reference period, of the formula for calculating the amounts allocated to employed persons.
3. *Maintaining wage negotiations*: the existence of financial participation schemes should not stand in the way of normal negotiations dealing with wages and conditions of employment or of setting wages and working conditions through such negotiations. The question of the agreement on new provisions in the field of the financial participation of employed persons may be taken up in the normal negotiations dealing with wage-setting and working conditions, without replacing them.
4. *Voluntary participation*: the opportunity for both enterprises and employed persons to express a choice, within the framework of any laws, regulations or agreements which may exist in the Member States, on the adoption of a participation scheme or on the financial participation scheme or arrangements in which they wish to participate.
5. *Calculation of amounts allocated to employed persons*: the amount of bonuses should not generally be fixed in advance, but determined on the basis of a predetermined formula reflecting the enterprise's performance during a certain period (expressed in terms of profits or any other indicator) the criteria chosen to measure the performances being clearly specified.
6. *Amounts*: the formula for calculating bonuses should be such that it will produce the expected incentive, although it should not exceed a specific ceiling (in relative or absolute terms) in order to avoid wide fluctuations in income.
7. *Risks*: employees should be made aware of the risks inherent in financial participation schemes; apart from the risks of income fluctuation inherent in participation schemes, employed persons may be exposed to additional risk if their participation takes the form of investments that are relatively undiversified; in this context, the possibility of providing for mechanisms to protect against the risk of depreciation in the value of assets merits consideration.
8. *Beneficiaries*: beneficiaries are primarily employed persons, i.e., wage-earners covered by employment contracts; as far as possible, access to participation schemes should be open to all persons employed by the enterprise. More generally, workers in similar objective situations should have equal rights with regard to access to participation schemes.
9. *Enterprise type*: participation schemes may be instituted by both privately-owned firms and public enterprises, as long as suitable indicators of enterprise results or profits are, or can be, made available.
10. *Size of enterprises*:
    a. small and medium-sized enterprises should have adequate opportunities to be able to implement financial participation schemes; in particular, it is important to ensure that administrative constraints are few in number and that, if needed at all, minimum financial requirements are not too high;
    b. in larger enterprises, especially multinational companies, it may be useful to link all or part of employee benefits to the performance of a separate profit unit rather than to overall enterprise results;

    c. the size of enterprises may also affect the choice of the most appropriate scheme.

11. *Complexity*: complex participation schemes should be avoided.

12. *Information and training*: to ensure the success of any type of participation scheme, substantial efforts will be required to provide relevant information and, if need be, training for all employed persons concerned.

Chapter 10. Restructuring of Enterprises

488.   During the 1970s, called by some the golden years for European labour law, three directives were adopted which were intended to protect the workers against the functioning of the common market. I remember from the discussions we had in the group of experts on labour law from the different Member States that the reasoning underlying those directives was the following: there is a larger market with an increase in scale to which the undertakings will have to adapt themselves; this means: restructuring, mergers, takeovers, collective dismissals and bankruptcies. Indeed, it was said, the worker should not have to pay the price for the establishment of a common, bigger market; rather the worker should be protected against the social consequences of this restructuring. On the basis of this reasoning, three directives were proposed and, also due to the then political composition of the Council, adopted. These directives relate respectively to collective redundancies (1975), the transfer of undertakings or parts thereof (1977) and the insolvency of the employer (1980). One will notice, when analyzing these directives, that the managerial prerogative concerning economic decisions remains intact. There were at some times proposals regarding collective redundancies to prohibit dismissals, in conformity with the then prevalent French legislation, but these proposals were not retained, as will be made clear later. In short, the directives only address the social consequences of restructuring.

§1. Collective Redundancies

489.   Directive No. 75/129 of 17 February 1975 on the approximation of laws of the Member States relating to collective redundancies[1] finds its origin in the AKZO Case. In 1973 AKZO, a Dutch-German multinational enterprise, was engaged in a process of restructuring and wanted to make some 5,000 workers redundant. As AKZO had a number of subsidiaries in different European EC Member States, it could in a sense compare the costs of dismissal in those countries and choose to dismiss in that country where the cost was the lowest. When this strategy became apparent, there was somewhat of an outrage in some European quarters and a demand for a European rule to make such strategies impossible in the future and to lay down a European wide minimum floor of protection in the case of collective dismissals. This led to a proviso in the Council Resolution of 21 January 1974 concerning a social action programme and consequently to a directive concerning collective redundancies.

1. O.J., 22 February 1975, No. L 48.

490. Directive No. 75/129 is based on Article 100 of the EC Treaty which relates to the approximation of laws, regulations or administrative rules of the Member States that directly affect the establishment or the funding of the Common Market. In the 'whereas' to the directive we can read that:

> 'it is important that greater protection should be afforded to workers in the event of collective redundancies while taking into account the need for balanced economic and social development within the Community';

> 'that despite increasing convergence' (one wonders which convergence?) 'differences are still maintained between the provisions in force in the Member States of the Community concerning the practical arrangements and procedures for such redundancies and the measures designed to alleviate the consequences of redundancy for workers, that these differences can have a direct effect on the functioning of the market.'

Consequently, this approximation must be promoted while improvement is being maintained within the meaning of Article 117 of the EC Treaty. The provisions of the directive are thus intended to serve to establish a common body of rules applicable in all Member States, whilst leaving it up to the Member States to apply or introduce provisions that are more favourable to workers.[1] The directive provides for the information and consultation of the workers in the case of collective redundancies, as well as for a notification of the competent public authority. At the same time, periods are introduced during which no notice of termination may be given.

Council Directive No. 92/56 of 24 June 1992 amended the Directive No. 75/129. Several reasons inspired the amendments: other forms of termination of employment contracts on the initiative of the employer should be equated to redundancies, and the provisions of the original directive should be clarified and supplemented as regards the employer's obligations regarding informing and consulting of worker's representatives.

The amended directive explicitly states that it can be left to the social partners to take the appropriate measures by way of collective bargaining agreement to implement the amendments (Art. 2).[2]

1. COJ, 8 June 1982, *Commission* v. *Italy*, No. 91/81, IELL, *Case Law*, No. 47*bis*.
2. Directive No. 92/56, O.J., 26 August 1992, No. L 245.

I. Definitions and Scope

491. Article 1 of the directive contains a definition of both 'collective redundancies' and 'workers' representatives.' The directive applies in the case of (1) a dismissal, which is (2) collective. The first requirement thus is that there is an employer who dismisses employees.

> 'The termination by workers of their contract of employment following an announcement by the employer that he is suspending payment of his debts cannot be treated as dismissal by the employer for the purposes of the directive.'[1]

The dismissal must be effected by an employer for one or more reasons not related to the individual workers concerned. The dismissals further need to be collective; this means that, according to the choice of the Member States, the number of redundancies is:

– either, over a period of 30 days:
    (1) at least 10 in establishments normally employing more than 20 and less than 100 workers;
    (2) at least 10 per cent of the number of workers in establishments normally employing at least 100 but less than 300 workers;
    (3) at least 30 in establishments normally employing 300 workers or more:
– or, over a period of 90 days, at least 20, whatever the number of workers normally employed in the establishments in question.

Although the Directive primarily deals with collective dismissal of workers, the 1992 amendment holds that 'for the purpose of calculating the number of redundancies ... termination of an employment contract which occur to the individual workers concerned shall be assimilated to redundancies, provided that there are at least five redundancies.'

The directive in principle also applies to collective redundancies where the establishment's activities are terminated as a result of a judicial decision.

    1. COJ, 12 February 1985, *Metalarbejderforbund and Specialarbejderforbund i Danmark* v. *H. Nielsen & Son, Maskinfabrik A/S, in liquidation*, No. 284/83, IELL, *Case Law*, No. 69.

    492.   The question of the meaning of the notion of establishment arose in proceedings between the company *Rockfon A/S* and the *Specialarbejderforbundet i Danmark*[1] (the Danish trade union for semi-skilled workers, hereinafter the 'SID') concerning the dismissal of a number of employees alleged to have been carried out without observance of the consultation and notification procedures laid down by the directive. Rockfon is part of the Rockwool multinational group.

Questions were, first, whether Article 1(1)(a) of the directive precludes two or more undertakings in a group from establishing a joint recruitment and dismissal department so that dismissals in one of the undertakings may take place only with the approval of that department; and, secondly, whether, in such circumstances, the term 'establishment' in Article 1(1)(a) is to be taken to mean all the undertakings using that recruitment and dismissal department, or whether each undertaking in which the employees made redundant normally work must be counted as an 'establishment.'

As regards the first part of the question, the Court stated that:

> 'it is sufficient to state that the sole purpose of the Directive is the partial harmonisation of collective redundancy procedures and that its aim is not to restrict the freedom of undertakings to organise their activities and arrange their personnel departments in the way which they think best suits their needs.'

The term 'establishment' is not defined in the directive. Rockfon maintained that it was not an establishment since it had no management which could independently effect large scale dismissals.

The Court observed that the term 'establishment' is a term of Community law and cannot be defined by reference to the laws of the Member States. The various language versions of the directive use somewhat different terms to convey the concept in question. A comparison of the terms used show that they have different connotations signifying, according to the version in question, establishment, undertaking, work centre, local unit or place of work.

As was held in *Bouchereau*, the different language versions of a Community text must be given a uniform interpretation and in the case of divergence between the versions the provision in question must therefore be interpreted by reference to the purpose and general scheme of the rules of which it forms part.

The directive was adopted on the basis of Articles 100 and 117 of the Treaty, the latter provision concerning the need for the Member States to promote improved working conditions and an improved standard of living for workers, so as to make possible their harmonisation while the improvement is being maintained. It is apparent from the first recital in its preamble that the directive is indeed intended to afford greater protection to workers in the event of collective redundancies.

Two observations may be made in that respect. First, an interpretation of the term 'establishment,' like that proposed by Rockfon, would allow companies belonging to the same group to try to make it more difficult for the directive to apply to them by conferring on a separate decision-making body the power to take decisions concerning redundancies. By this means, they would be able to escape the obligation to follow certain procedures for the protection of workers and large groups of workers could be denied the right to be informed and consulted which they have as a matter of course under the directive. Such an interpretation therefore appears to be incompatible with the aim of the directive.

Secondly, the Court has held that an employment relationship is essentially characterised by the link existing between the employee and the part of the undertaking or business to which he is assigned to carry out his duties.

Therefore the Court concluded:

> 'the term establishment, appearing in Article (1)(a) of the 1980 directive must be understood as meaning, depending on the circumstances, the unit to which the workers made redundant are assigned to carry out their duties. It is not essential, in order for there to be an establishment, for the unit in question to be endowed with a management which can independently effect collective redundancies.'

1. COJ, 7 December 1995, Case C-449/93, *Jur.*, 1995, 4291.

493.   The directive is not applicable to:

a. collective redundancies effected under contracts of employment concluded for limited periods of time or for specific tasks except where such redundancies take place prior to the date of expiry or the completion of such contracts;
b. workers employed by public administrative bodies or by establishments governed by public law (or, in Member States where this concept is unknown, by equivalent bodies);
c. the crews of sea-going vessels.

II. Information and Consultation of Workers' Representatives

494. Information concerning the collective redundancies must be given before-hand. This means before the decision is taken. The text of Article 2, §1 is clear on this point: it concerns an employer who is *contemplating* collective redundancies. The amended directive explicitly mentions that the employer has to inform the workers' representatives in *good time*. The directive only applies when the employer projects collective redundancies. Such a project is necessary if the employer contemplates dismissals and wants to notify the competent authority (Art. 3, §1).

> 'The directive applies only where the employer has in fact contemplated collective redundancies or has drawn up a plan for collective redundancies. It does not apply in the case where, because of the financial state of the undertaking, the employer ought to have contemplated collective redundancies but did not do so.'[1]

1. COJ, 7 December 1995, Case C-449/93, *Jur.*, 1995, 4291.

495. The purpose of the information is to enable the workers' representatives to make constructive proposals. The employer shall at least notify them of: the reasons of the projected redundancies, the number of categories of workers to be made redundant; the number or categories of workers normally employed; the period over which the projected redundancies are to be effected; the criteria proposed for the selection of the workers and the method for calculating any redundancy payment (other than those arising out of national legislation and/or practice). The employer is obliged to forward to the competent authority a copy of the information given to the workers with the exception of the information on the method of calculating redundancy payments (Art. 2, §3). The workers' representatives are also entitled to a copy of the information which the employer must forward to the authorities. The worker's representatives may send any comments they may have to the competent authority (Art. 3, §2).

496. The 1992 amendment holds irrespective whether the decision regarding collective redundancies is being taken by the employer or by an undertaking controlling the employer (Art. 2,4). In considering alleged breaches of the information and consultation duties account shall not be taken of any defence on the part of the employer that the necessary information has not been provided to him by the undertaking which took the decision leading to collective redundancies. The employer is obliged to consult the worker's representatives with a view to reaching an agreement (Art. 2, §1). This is a very strong form of consultation, which is very close to collective bargaining. The consultations must cover ways and means of avoiding collective redundancies or reducing the number of workers affected, and of mitigating the consequences (Art. 2, §2).

The amended Article 2, §2 specifies that this concerns accompanying social measures aimed, *inter alia*, at aid for redeploying or retraining workers made redundant.

497. Workers' representatives are those provided for by the laws or the practices of the Member States. Since the judgment of the Court of Justice of 8 June

1994[1] it is no longer possible that there are no worker's representatives in the case where a Member State would not have an overall system of worker's representation. According to the Court of Justice – condemning the UK – 'employers face a statutory obligation to inform and consult with employees when they are planning collective redundancies, or if they transfer employees from one business to another. This means that even non-unionised companies will have to establish machinery for consultation even if it does not already exist.'

Thus, the European Court of Justice ruled that UK rules on the protection of employees' rights in the event of companies changing hands or when collective redundancies take place, breached EC law. The Court said the UK had failed to implement fully binding EC directives. The directives relate, as said, to the safeguarding of employees' rights in the event of the transfer of a business or collective redundancies. Both place a duty on employers to inform and consult representatives of workers affected by a transfer or redundancies.

The UK was taken to court by the Commission for failure to implement these directive properly by not providing for the designation of employees' representatives in firms where the employer refused to recognise trade unions.

The UK argued that employers who did not recognise trade unions were not covered by the obligations in the directives because union recognition in companies was traditionally based on voluntary recognition.

The Court did not accept that argument. It said the aim of the directives was to ensure comparable protection for employees' rights in all Member States and to harmonise the costs of such provisions for companies in the EC. To that end, the directives laid down compulsory obligations on employers regarding informing and consulting employees' representatives.

The Court found Member States had no opportunities under the directives to limit the rights of employees to those companies which under national laws were obliged to have union representation. Although one of the directives specifically provided for situations in which companies did not have employees' representatives, the Court said this provision should not be read in isolation and that its effect was to allow employees without such representation to be properly informed. The Court said it was not the intention of the Community legislature to allow the different legal systems within the EC to accept a situation in which no employees' representatives were designated since designation was necessary to ensure compliance with the obligations laid down in the directive.

The Court was not concerned either by the fact that the directives did not contain specific provisions requiring Member States to designate workers' representatives if there were none.

The directives required Member States to take all the measures necessary to ensure employees were informed and consulted through their representatives in the event of either a transfer or collective redundancies. That obligation did not require there to be specific provisions on the designation of employees' representatives.

Two further claims were made by the Commission. The first was that UK rules only required the employer to consult with the employees' representatives, to take into consideration what was said, to reply and giver reasons if the representations were rejected. The obligation under the directives was to consult representatives with a view to seeking agreement. The UK conceded its rules did not provide for this.

The second claim was that the sanctions provided for in the national rules for failure to comply with the obligations to consult and inform were not a sufficient deterrent for employers.

The Court said where a Community directive did not specifically provide and penalty for an infringement, or where it referred for that purpose to national laws, the obligations of the Member States under the Rome Treaty were to require them to ensure that infringements of EC law were penalised under conditions, both procedural and substantive, which were analogous to those applicable to infringements of national law of a similar nature and importance and which, in any event, made the penalty effective, proportionate and dissuasive.

1. *Commission* v. *UK*, C-382/92 and 383/92, *Jur.*, 1994, 2435.

III. The Role of the Government

498. The role of the competent public authority is limited to information, the laying down of a period during which dismissals have no effect and to seeking solutions in the problems raised by the projected collective redundancies. Once the workers' representatives are duly informed and consulted, the authority is notified. The employer must notify the authority in writing of any projected collective redundancies. This notification must contain the reasons for the redundancies, the number of the workers to be made redundant, the number of the workers normally employed and the period over which the redundancies are to be effected. *De facto* this is the same information that has already been forwarded to the workers. However, the Member States may provide that in the case of planned collective redundancies arising from termination of the establishment's activities as a result of a judicial decision, the employer shall be obliged to notify the competent authority in writing only if the latter so requests.

499. The collective redundancies take effect not earlier than 30 days after the notification of the competent authority without prejudice to any provisions governing individual rights with regard to the notice of dismissal. This period must be used by the competent public authority to seek solutions to the problems raised by the projected collective redundancies (Art. 4, §§1–2). Which solutions ought to be sought is not indicated in the directive, but one might think of placement of workers, retraining, outplacement and others. Once more we must deal with a stipulation of a programmatic nature.

500. The Member States can grant the competent authority the power to reduce the period of 30 days or to extend it. Where the initial period provided for is shorter than 60 days. Member States can grant the power to extend the period to 60 days following notification, or even longer, where the problems raised by the projected collective redundancies are not likely to be solved within the initial period. The employer must be informed of the extension and the grounds for it before the expiry of the initial period of 30 days (Art. 4, §3).

The amended directive allows Member States not to apply Article 4 to collective redundancies arising from termination of the establishment's activities where this is a result of a judicial decision (Art. 4, §4).

§2. Transfer of Undertakings, Mergers and Divisions of Public Limited Liability Companies

I. Transfer of Undertakings

501. Directive No. 77/187 relates to the safeguarding of employees' rights in the event of transfers of undertakings, businesses or parts of businesses.[1] It is based on Article 100 of the EC Treaty concerning the approximation of laws. The justification of this directive goes along the same lines as the one relating to collective redundancies, as can be deduced from the 'whereas' in which is said that economic trends are bringing in their wake, at both national and Community level, changes in the structure of undertakings, through transfer of undertakings, business or parts of business to other employers as a result of legal transfers or mergers. It is thus necessary to provide for the protection of employees in the event of a change of employer, in particular, in that their rights are safeguarded. There are, however, so the 'whereas' continues, still differences between the Member States in regard to the extent of the protection of employees in this respect and these differences should be reduced. As there differences have a direct effect on the functioning of the common market, it is therefore necessary to promote the approximation of laws in this field while maintaining the improvement prescribed in Article 117 of the EC Treaty. The purpose of the directive is to ensure that the rights of employees are safeguarded in the event of a change of employer by enabling them to remain in employment with the new employer on the terms and conditions agreed at the transfer.[2] The purpose of the directive is therefore to ensure that the restructuring of undertakings within the common market does not adversely affect the workers in the undertakings concerned.[3]

1. O.J., 5 March 1977, No. L 61.
2. O.J., 15 June 1988, *P. Bork International A/S in liquidation and others* v. *Foreningen of Arbejds-ledere i Danmark, acting on behalf of Birger E. Peterson, and Junckers Industries A/S*, No. 101/87, IELL, *Case Law*, No. 123.
3. COJ, 7 February 1985, *H.B.M. Abels* v. *The Administrative Board of the Bedrijfsvereniging voor de Metaal Industrie en de Electronische Industrie*, No. 135/83, IELL, *Case Law*, No. 66.

A. Definitions and Scope

502. Different actors operate within the framework of this directive: the transferor, the transferee, and the representative of the employees. The *transferor* is any natural or legal person who, by reason of a transfer of an undertaking, ceases to be the employer. The *transferee* is any natural or legal person who, by reason of the transfer of an undertaking, becomes the employer of the undertaking (Art. 2A and B). The term 'worker's representatives' means the representatives provided for by the laws and practice of the Member States, with the exception of members of administrative, governing or supervisory bodies of companies who represent employees on such bodies in certain Member States (Art. 2C) such as, for example, Germany.

503. It is common knowledge that the directive does not contain an express definition of the term 'employee.' In order, so the Court reasons, to establish its meaning, it is necessary to apply generally recognised principles of interpretation by referring in the first place to the ordinary meaning attributed to that term in its context and by obtaining such guidance as may be derived from Community texts and from concepts common to the legal system of the Member States. Considering that the directive is intended to ensure that the employees' rights are safeguarded in the event of a change of employer by guaranteeing acquired rights and protection against dismissal solely by the fact of the transfer, the Court concludes that there is no need for a Community definition. Indeed it is clear from the provisions of Articles 3 and 4 that the directive is intended to achieve only partial harmonisation, essentially by extending the protection guaranteed to workers independently of the laws of the individual Member States to cover the case where an undertaking is transferred. Its aim is therefore to ensure, as far as possible, that the contract of employment or the employment relationship continues unchanged with the transferee so that the employees affected by the transfer of the undertaking are not placed in a less favourable position solely as a result of the transfer. It is however not intended to establish a uniform level of protection throughout the Community on the basis of common criteria. It follows that Directive No. 77/187 may be relied upon only by persons who are, in one way or another, protected as employees under the law of the Member State concerned. If they are so protected, the directive ensures that their rights arising from a contract of employment or an employment relationship are not diminished as a result of the transfer. It must therefore be held that the term 'employee' within the meaning of Directive No. 77/187 must be interpreted as covering any person who, in the Member State concerned, is protected as an employee under national employment law. It is for the national court to establish whether that is the case.

504. The directive applies to the transfer of an undertaking, business or part of a business – situated within the territorial scope of the Treaty – to another employer as a result of a legal transfer or a merger (Art. 1, §§1–2). The key element of the definition lies in the fact whether the employees are, as a consequence of the transfer of the undertaking, confronted with a new, legal employer; in other words, the selling of a number of shares with the consequence that there is a new economic owner is not relevant.

> 'The directive is applicable where, following a legal transfer or merger, there is a change in the legal or natural person who is responsible for carrying on the business and who, by virtue of that fact, incurs the obligations of an employer *vis-à-vis* the employees of the undertaking, regardless of whether or not ownership of the undertaking is transferred.'[1]

Thus any agreement by which the capacity of employer is transferred, is covered. This is the case where there is a transfer of an undertaking pursuant to a lease-purchase agreement of the kind available under Dutch law (a purchase and sale on deferred payment, by which the parties agree that the object sold shall not become the property of the purchaser by mere transfer) and to the retransfer of the undertaking upon the termination of the lease-purchaser agreement by judicial decisions;[2] also in the case where the owner of a leased undertaking takes over its operation following a breach of the lease by the lessee;[3] the directive applies as well where, after notice is given to bring the lease to an end or upon termination thereof, the owner of an undertaking retakes the possession of the lease and thereafter sells it to a third party who shortly afterwards brings back into operation the undertaking, which has ceased upon termination of the lease, with just over half the staff that was employed in the undertaking by the former lessee, provided that the undertaking in question retains its identity.[4]

On 19 May 1992, the European Court of Justice determined that the directive also applies in a 'situation in which a public body decides to terminate the subsidy paid to one legal person, as the result of which the activities of that legal person are fully and definitively terminated and to transfer it to another legal person with similar aims.'[5]

The directive 'is to be interpreted as covering a situation in which an undertaking entrusts by contract to another undertaking the responsibility for carrying out cleaning operations which it previously performed itself, even though, prior to the transfer, such work was carried out by a single employee.'[6]

The Court of Justice, however, ruled rightly that the reorganisation of structures of the public administration or the transfer of administrative functions between public administrative authorities does not constitute a transfer of an undertaking within the meaning of the directive.[7]

1. COJ, 5 May 1988, *H. Berg and J.T.M. Busschers* v. *I.M. Besselen*, Joined Cases Nos. 144 and 145,87, IELL, *Case Law*, No. 122.
2. *Idem.*
3. COJ, 17 December 1987, *Landesorganisationen i Danmark for Tjenerforbunket i Danmark* v. *Molle Kro*, No. 276/86, IELL, *Case Law*, No. 113.
4. COJ, *Bork International A/S, op. cit.*
5. COJ, 19 May 1992, *S. Redmond Stichting* V. *H. Bartol and Others*, No. C-29/91, IELL, *Case Law*, No. 186.
6. COJ, 14 April 1994, *Schmidt C.* v. *Spar und Leihasse*, No. C-392/92, *Jur.*, 1994, 1311.
7. COJ, 15 October 1996, *Annette Henke* v. *Gemeinde Schierke and Verwaltungs-gemeinschaft 'Brocken'*, Case C-298/94, not yet published.

505. The directive applies provided that the undertaking in question retains its identity, as it does if it is a going concern whose operation is actually continued or resumed by the new employer, with the same or similar activities. In order to determine whether those conditions are met, it is necessary to consider all the circumstances surrounding the transaction in question, including, in particular, whether or not the undertakings' tangible and intangible assets and the majority of its employees are taken over, the degree of similarity between the activities carried on before and after the transfer of the period, if any, for which those activities ceased in connection with the transfer.[1]

It is therefore 'necessary to determine, having regard to all the circumstances of the facts surrounding the transaction in question, whether the functions performed are in fact carried out or resumed by the new legal person with the same activities or similar activities, it being understood that activities of a special nature which pursue independent aims may, if necessary, be treated as a business or part of a business within the meaning of the directive.'[2]

The directive may thus apply in a situation in which an undertaking entrusts another undertaking by contract with the responsibility for running a service for employees, previously managed directed, for a fee and various benefits the terms of which are determined by agreement between them.[3]

1. COJ, *Bork International A/S, op. cit.*
2. COJ, 19 May 1992, *S. Redmond Stichting* v. *H. Bartol and Others*, No. C-29/91, *op. cit.*
3. COJ, 12 November 1992, *A. Watson Rask and K. Christensen* v. *ISS Kantineservice A/S*, No. C-209/91, IELL, *Case Law*, No. 195.

506.   The same problem was dealt with in the case *Spijkers.*[1] Mr. Spijkers was employed as an assistant-manager by Gebroeders Colaris Abattoir at Ulbach over Worm (Netherlands). On 27 December 1982, by which date the business activities of Colaris 'had entirely ceased and there was no longer any goodwill in the business,' the entire slaughterhouse with various rooms and offices, the land and certain specific goods were purchased by Benedik Abattoir. Since that date, although in fact only since 3 February 1983, Benedik Abattoir operated a slaughterhouse under the joint account of Alfred Benedik and itself. All the employees of Colaris were taken over by Benedik Abattoir, apart from Mr. Spijkers and one other employee. The business activity which Benedik Abattoir carries on in the buildings is of the same kind as the activity previously carried on by Colaris; the transfer of the business assets enabled Benedik Abattoir to continue the activities of Colaris, although Benedik Abattoir did not take over Colaris' customers. On 3 March 1983, Colaris was declared insolvent. By a writ of 9 March 1983, Mr. Spijkers summoned Benedik Abattoir and Alfred Benedik to appear in proceedings for interim relief and sought an order that they should pay him his salary from 27 December 1982, or at least from such a date as the President thought fit, and should provide him with work within two days of the order. In support of his claims he contended that there had been a transfer of an undertaking in the meaning of the directive and that this entailed, by operation of law, a transfer to Benedik Abattoir of the rights and obligations arising from his contract of employment with Colaris. After being dismissed in first instance and on appeal, Mr. Spijkers appealed in Cassation to the *Hoge Raad der Nederlanden*, which stayed the proceedings and referred the question to the Court of Justice whether this case fell under the application of the directive, namely whether a transfer of an undertaking had taken place.

1. COJ, 18 March 1986, *J.M.A. Spijkers* v. *Gebroeders Benedik Abattoir CV and Alfred Benedik en Zonen BV*, No. 24/85, IELL, *Case Law*, No. 88.

507.   In the course of the proceedings before the Court, the United Kingdom Government and the Commission suggested that the essential criterion is whether the transferee is put in possession of a going concern and is able to continue its activities or at least activities of the same kind. The Netherlands Government emphasised that, in regard to the social objective of the directive, it was clear that the term 'transfer' implied that the transferee actually carried on the activities of the transferor as part of the same business. The Court accepted that view. It is clear from the scheme of Directive No. 77/187 and from the terms of Article 1, §1 thereof that the directive is intended to ensure the continuity of employment relationships existing within a business, irrespective of any change of ownership. It follows that the decisive criterion for establishing whether there is a transfer for the purpose of the directive is whether the business in question retains its identify. Consequently, a transfer of an undertaking does not occur merely because its assets are disposed of. Instead it is necessary to consider, in the case such as the present, whether the business was disposed of as a going concern, as would be indicated, *inter alia*, by the fact that its operation was actually continued or resumed by the new employer, with the same or similar activities.

508. In order to determine whether these conditions were met, it is necessary to consider all the facts characterising the transaction in question, including the type of undertaking or business, whether or not the tangible assets of the business, such as buildings and movable property, were transferred, the value of its tangible assets at the time of the transfer, whether or not the majority of its employees were taken over by the new employer, whether or not its customers were transferred and the degree of similarity between the activities carried on before or after the transfer and the period, if any, for which those activities were suspended. It should be noted, however, that all these circumstances are merely single factors in the overall assessment to be made and cannot be considered in isolation. It is for the national court to make the necessary factual appraisal, in the light of the criteria for the interpretation set out above, in order to establish whether there was a transfer in the sense indicated above. In conclusion, it is necessary to consider whether, with regard to all the facts characterising the transaction, the business was disposed of as a going concern, as would be indicated *inter alia* by the fact that the operation was actually continued or resumed by the new employer, with the same or similar activities.

509. The issue was again addressed in *Albert Merckx and Patrick Neuhuys* v. *Ford Motors Company Belgium SA*,[1] in proceedings brought by Merckx and Neuhuys against Ford concerning the effects on the contracts of employment concluded by Merckx and Neuhuys with Anfo Motors SA of the discontinuance of Anfo Motors' business and the assumption by Novarobel SA of the dealership held by Anfo Motors. The judgment underlines again that the notion of transfer has to be evaluated on a case by case basis and that the Court of Justice is giving a very broad interpretation. This is extremely important becauce of the increase of outsourcing in our growing information and networking society.

At the time, Merckx and Neuhuys were salesmen with Anfo Motors. Anfo Motors sold motor vehicles as a Ford dealer in a number of municipalities in the Brussels conurbation, Ford also being its main shareholder.

On 8 October 1987 Anfo Motors informed Merckx and Neuhuys that it would discontinue all its activities on 31 December 1987 and that with effect from 1 November 1987 Ford would be working with an independent dealer, Novarobel, in the municipalities covered by the Anfo Motors dealership. It stated that Novarobel would take on 14 of the 64 employees of Anfo Motors, who would retain their duties, seniority and all other contractual rights.

Anfo Motors also sent a letter to its customers in order to inform them of the discontinuance of its activities and to recommend to them the services of the new dealer.

By letter of 27 October 1987, Merckx and Neuhuys refused to accept the proposed transfer, claiming that Anfo Motors could not require them to work for another company, in another place and under different working conditions, without any guarantee as to whether the client base would be retained or a particular turnover achieved.

The question was first, whether Article 1(1) of the directive must be interpreted as applying where an undertaking holding a motor vehicle dealership for a particular territory discontinues its business and the dealership is then transferred to another undertaking which takes on part of its staff and is recommended to customers, without any transfer of assets. Secondly, having regard to the facts in the main proceedings and in order to provide a helpful response to the national court, it is necessary to establish whether Article 3(1) of the directive precludes an employee of the transferor at the date of transfer of the undertaking from objecting to the transfer of his contract of employment or employment relationship to the transferee.

The Court stated again that:

> 'it is settled case-law that the decisive criterion for establishing whether there is a transfer for the purposes of the Directive is whether the entity in question retains its economic identity, as indicated *inter alia* by the fact that its operation is actually continued or resumed. In order to determine whether that condition is met, it is necessary to consider all the facts characterising the transaction in question, including the type of undertaking or business, whether or not the business's tangible assets, such as buildings and movable property, are transferred, the value of its intangible assets at the time of the transfer, whether or not the majority of its employees is taken over by the new employer, whether or not its customers are transferred and the degree of similarity between the activities carried on before and after the transfer and the period, if any, for which those activities were suspended.
>
> All those factors, taken as a whole, support the view that the transfer of the dealership in the circumstances of the main proceedings is capable of falling within the scope of the Directive. It must be ascertained, however, whether certain factors relied on by Merckx and Neuhuys may rebut that finding.
>
> The purpose of an exclusive dealership for the sale of motor vehicles of a particular make in a certain sector remains the same even if it is carried on under a different name, from different premises and with different facilities. It is also irrelevant that the principal place of business is situated in a different area of the same conurbation, provided that the contract territory remains the same.
>
> In that regard, if the Directive's aim of protecting workers is not to be undermined, its application cannot be excluded merely because the transferor discontinues its activities when the transfer is made and is then put into liquidation.

Article 4(1) of the Directive provides that the transfer of an undertaking, business or part of the business does not in itself constitute grounds for dismissal. However, that provision is not to stand in the way of dismissals that may take place for economic, technical or organisational reasons entailing changes in the workforce.

Accordingly, the fact that the majority of the staff was dismissed when the transfer took place is not sufficient to preclude the application of the Directive.

It is clear from that case-law that, for the Directive to apply, it is not necessary for there to be a direct contractual relationship between the transferor and the transferee. Consequently, where a motor vehicle dealership concluded with one undertaking is terminated and a new dealership is awarded to another undertaking pursuing the same activities, the transfer of undertaking is the result of a legal transfer for the purposes of the Directive, as interpreted by the Court.'

Thus, the Court ruled, 'Article 1(1) of the Directive of 14 February 1977 must be interpreted as applying where an undertaking holding a motor vehicle dealership for a particular territory discontinues its activities and the dealership is then transferred to another undertaking which takes on part of the staff and is recommended to customers, without any transfer of assets.'

In *Süzen* v. *Zehnacker*[2] the question was raised whether the directive applies to a situation in which a person who had entrusted the cleaning of his premises to a first undertaking terminates his contract with the latter and, for the performance of similar work, enters into a new contract with a second undertaking without any concomitant transfer of tangible or intangible business assets from one undertaking to the other.

A cleaning lady, Mrs. Süzen, whose job it was to clean a school, had been dismissed with seven other persons after the school had terminated the contract that bound it to their employer (the cleaning company, Zehnacker). Out of the eight persons, seven were re-employed by the cleaning company Leforth, which had signed the new contract with the school. Mrs. Süzen, who had not been taken on again, felt she was part of the same economic entity which had been moved to the new cleaning company.

The Court stated as follows:

'The mere fact that the service provided by the old and the new awardees of a contract is similar does not support the conclusion that an economic entity has been transferred. An entity cannot be reduced to the activity entrusted to it. Its identity also emerges from other factors, such as its workforce, its management staff, the way in which its work is organized, its operating methods or indeed, where appropriate, the operational resources available to it.

The mere loss of a service contract to a competitor cannot therefore by itself indicate the existence of a transfer within the meaning of the directive. In those circumstances, the service undertaking previously entrusted with the contract does not, on losing a customer, thereby cease fully to exist, and a business or part of a business belonging to it cannot be considered to have been transferred to the new awardee of the contract.

It must also be noted that, although the transfer of assets is one of the criteria to be taken into account by the national court in deciding whether an undertaking has in fact been transferred, the absence of such assets does not necessarily preclude the existence of such a transfer.

The national court, in assessing the facts characterizing the transaction in question, must take into account among other things the type of undertaking or business concerned. It follows that the degree of importance to be attached to each criterion for determining whether or not there has been a transfer within the meaning of the directive will necessarily vary according to the activity carried on, or indeed the production or operating methods employed in the relevant undertaking, business or part of a business. Where in particular an economic entity is able, in certain sectors, to function without any significant tangible or intangible assets, the maintenance of its identity following the transaction affecting it cannot, logically, depend on the transfer of such assets.

Since in certain labour-intensive sectors a group of workers engaged in a joint activity on a permanent basis may constitute an economic entity, it must be recognized that such an entity is capable of maintaining its identity after it has been transferred where the new employer does not merely pursue the activity in question but also takes over a major part, in terms of their numbers and skills, of the employees specially assigned by his predecessor to that task. In those circumstances, the new employer takes over a body of assets enabling him to carry on the activities or certain activities of the transferor undertaking on a regular basis.

It is for the national court to establish, in the light of the foregoing interpretative guidance, whether a transfer has occurred in this case'.

One conclusion is certain. A mere change of sub contractors is in itself not a transfer of an enterprise. The transfer must relate to a stable economic activity. The term entity refers to an organized grouping of persons and assets facilitating the exercise of an economic activity which pursues a specific objective.

1. COJ, 7 March 1996, Joined Cases C-171/94 and C-172/94, *Jur.*, 1996, 1253.
2. COJ, 11 March 1997, *Ayse Süzen* v. *Zehnacker Gebäudereinigung GmbH Krankenhausservice*, C-13/95.

510.   The question was raised whether the directive also applies if the undertaking is temporarily closed and consequently has no employees. In this case a seasonal business, such as a hotel, was meant. The Court ruled that, in order to decide this case, account must be taken of all the factual circumstances surrounding the transaction in question, including where appropriate, the temporary closure of the undertakings and the fact that there were no employees at the time of the transfer, although these facts alone do not preclude the applicability of the directive in the case of a seasonal business.[1]

1. COJ, 17 December 1987, *Landesorganisationen i Danmark* v. *Ny Molle Kro, op. cit.*

511. The problem of whether the directive is applicable in the case of the transfer of an undertaking where the transferor has been adjudged insolvent came up in the *Abels* Case. Abels was employed since 1961 by the private limited company Thole BV, Enschede, the Netherlands, when, by successive decisions of the Arrondissementsrechtbank, Thole was granted a *'surséance van betaling'* (judicial leave to suspend payment of debts), first provisionally on 2 September 1981 and then definitively on 17 March 1982, before being put into liquidation on 9 June 1982. It was during the liquidation proceedings that, pursuant to an agreement concluded by the liquidator, Thole's business was transferred with effect from 10 June 1982 to the private TTP BV, Enschede, which continued to operate the undertaking and took over most of its work-force, including Mr. Abels. Abels, however, did not receive wages for the period from 1 to 9 June 1982. Consequently, the question was put to the Court whether the scope of the directive extends to a situation in which the transferor of an undertaking is adjudged insolvent or is granted a *'surséance van betaling.'*

512. According to the plaintiffs in the main proceedings, the Netherlands Government and the Commission, the term *'overdracht krachtens overeenkomst'* in the Dutch-language version of the directive indicates that its scope is confined to transfers effected on the basis of agreements entered into voluntarily, to the exclusion of any transfer resulting from legal proceedings whose purpose is the collective and compulsory liquidation of the debtor's assets or the overcoming of the debtor's financial difficulties in order to prevent such liquidation. Those procedures are excluded, even in cases of sales by private agreement since the essential factor of contractual autonomy is lacking by virtue of the fact that the transfer involves the intervention of the court and that the form and the subject-matter of the same are determined by weighing up the various interests involved in such procedures.

513. A comparison of the various language versions of the provision in question shows that there are terminological divergences among them as regards the transfers of undertakings. Whilst the German (*'vertragliche Übertragung'*). French (*'cession conventionnelle'*), Greek (*'sumbatkij exphoorijsij'*), Italian (*'cessione contrattuale'*) and Dutch (*'overdracht krachtens overeenkomst'*) versions clearly refer only to transfers resulting from a contract, from which it may be concluded that other types of transfer such as those resulting from an administrative measure or judicial decision are excluded, the English (*'legal transfer'*) and Danish (*'overdragelse'*) versions appear to indicate that the scope is wider. Moreover, the Court continues, it should be noted that the concept of contractual transfer is different in the insolvency laws of the various Member States, as has become apparent in these proceedings. Whilst certain Member States consider that in certain circumstances a sale effected in the context of liquidation procedures is a normal contractual sale, even if the judicial intervention is a preliminary requirement for the conclusion of such a contract, under other legal systems the sale is in certain circumstances regarded as taking place by virtue of a measure adopted by a public authority. In view of these divergences, the scope of the provision at issue cannot be appraised solely on the basis of textual interpretation. Its meaning must therefore be clarified in the light of the scheme of the directive, its place in the system of Community law in relation to the rules of insolvency, and its purpose.

514. Insolvency law is characterised by special procedures intended to weigh the various interests involved, in particular those of the various classes of creditors; consequently in all the Member States there are specific rules, which may derogate, at least partially, from other provisions of a general nature, including provisions of social law. The specificity of insolvency law is confirmed in Community law. Thus the 1975 directive on collective redundancies expressly excludes from its scope workers affected by the termination of an establishment's activities 'where it is the result of a judicial decision' (Art. 1, §2, d). Moreover, the specificity of insolvency law was also reflected in the adoption of the 1980 directive on the insolvency of the employer. This directive creates a system to ensure the payment of outstanding claims relating to pay which applies equally to undertakings that have been adjudged insolvent. In view of the fact that insolvency law is the subject of specific rules both in the legal systems of the Member States and in the Community legal order, the Court concludes that if the directive had been intended to apply also to transfers of undertakings in the context of such proceedings, an express provision would have been included for that purpose.

515. That interpretation, the Court indicates, also follows necessarily from a consideration of the purpose of the directive. The preamble to the directive indicates that the directive's aim of affording protection to workers in the event of transfers of undertakings is to be seen against the background of economic trends and the need referred to in Article 117 of the EC Treaty. The question then is whether, if the directive were held to be applicable to liquidation or similar proceedings, the resulting social and economic effects would be favourable or prejudicial to the interests of employees. The Commission and the Court are of the opinion that the effects would be prejudicial to the interests of the workers. Such an extension of the scope of the directive might persuade a potential transferee from acquiring an undertaking on conditions acceptable to the creditors thereof, who, in such a case, would prefer to sell the assets of the undertaking separately. This would entail the loss of all jobs in the undertaking, and detract from the usefulness of the directive. It is apparent, the Court says, that a serious risk of general deterioration in working and living conditions, contrary to the social objectives of the Treaty, cannot be ruled out. It can therefore not be concluded that Directive No. 77/187 imposes on the Member States the obligation to extend the rules laid down therein to transfers of undertakings, businesses or parts of business taking place in the context of insolvency proceedings instituted with a view to the liquidation of the assets of the transferor under the supervision of the competent judicial authority.

516. The Court, however, held another opinion regarding the question of '*surséance van betaling*' (judicial leave to suspend payments of debts). It is to be noted that proceedings such as those relating to a '*surséance van betaling*' have certain features in common with liquidation procedures, in particular inasmuch as the proceedings are, in both cases, of a judicial nature. They are, however, different from liquidation proceedings insofar as the supervision exercised by the Court over the commencement and the course of such proceedings is more limited. Moreover, the object of such proceedings is primarily to safeguard the assets of the insolvent undertaking and, where possible, to continue the business of the undertakings by means of a collective suspension of the payment of debts with a view to reaching a settlement that will ensure that the undertaking is able to continue operation in the future. If no such settlement is reached, proceedings of this kind may, as in the present case, lead to the debtor being put into liquidation. It follows that the reasons for not applying the directive to transfers of undertakings taking place in liquidation proceedings are not applicable to proceedings of this kind taking place at an earlier stage.[1] Article 1, §1 of the directive does not apply to transfers of undertakings made as part of a creditor's settlement of the kind provided for in an Italian legislation of compulsory administrative liquidation as referred to in the Law of 3 April 1979 on special administration for large undertakings in difficulties. However, that paragraph does apply when, in accordance with a body of legislation such as that governing special administration, it has been decided that the undertaking is to continue trading and for as long as that decision remains in effect.[2] The Member States are however at liberty to apply the principles to a transfer of an undertaking where the transferor has been adjudged insolvent on their own initiative.[3]

1. COJ, 7 February 1985, *Abels, op. cit.*
2. 25 July 1991, *G. d'Urso and Others* v. *Ercole Marelli Ellettromeccanica (EMG), Nuova Emg and Others*, No. C-362/89, IELL, *Case Law*, No. 168.
3. COJ, *A. Botzen, op. cit.*

B. Acquired Rights

1. Individual Rights

517. The rule of thumb is that the rights and obligations of the employee arising from his contract of employment in the case of a transfer are *automatically* transferred. In other words, the employees who are employed on the date of transfers are automatically transferred to the new employer with all their acquired rights, whether they or the new employer want it or not. Therefore, the terms of the contract work or of the working relationship may not be altered with regard to the salary, in particular its day of payment and composition, notwithstanding that the total amount is unchanged. The directive does not preclude, however, an alteration of the working relationship with the new head of the undertaking in so far as the national law allows such an alteration independently of a transfer of the undertaking.[1]

As the Court has repeatedly held, 'the Directive is intended to safeguard the rights of workers in the event of a change of employer by making it possible for them to continue to work for the new employer under the same conditions as those agreed with the transferor.

It is likewise settled case-law that the rules of the Directive, in particular those concerning the protection of workers against dismissal by reason of the transfer, must be considered to be mandatory, so that it is not possible to derogate from them in a manner unfavourable to employees.

It follows that in the event of the transfer of an undertaking the contract of employment or employment relationship between the staff employed by the undertaking transferred may not be maintained with the transferor and is automatically continued with the transferee.

It must, however, be stated that, according to the second subparagraph of Article 3(1), the automatic transfer of employment relationships to the transferee does not prevent the Member States from providing for joint liability of the transferor and transferee.

By reason of the mandatory nature of the protection afforded by the Directive, and in order not to deprive workers of that protection in practice, the transfer of the contracts of employment may not be made subject to the intention of the transferor or the transferee, and more particularly, that the transferee may not obstruct the transfer by refusing to fulfill his obligations'.[2]

It is, for the safeguarding of the employee's rights, only of importance whether the part of the undertaking for which the employees were working, is transferred or not. This is to say that the directive does not cover the transferor's rights and obligations arising from a contract of employment or an employment relationship with employees who, although not employed in the transferred part of the undertaking, performed certain duties which involved the use of assets assigned to the part transferred or who, whilst being employed in an administrative department of the undertaking, which has not itself been transferred, carried out certain duties for the benefit of the part transferred. An employment relationship, the Court argued, is essentially characterised by the link existing between the employee and the part of the undertaking or the business to which he is assigned to carry out his duties. In order to decide whether the rights and obligations under an employment relationship are transferred, it is therefore sufficient to establish to which part of the undertaking or business the employee was assigned.[3] Whether or not such a contract or a relationship exists at that time must be assessed on the basis of national law, subject, however, to compliance with the mandatory provisions of the directive concerning the protection of employees from dismissal as a result of the transfer.[4]

1. COJ, 12 November 1992, *A. Watson Rask and K. Christensen* v. *ISS Kantineservice A/S*, No. C-209/91, *op. cit.*
2. COJ, 14 November 1996, *Claude Rotsaett de Hertaing* v. *J. Benoidt SA*, in liquidation and others, C-305/94, not yet published.
3. *Idem.*
4. *Bork, op. cit.*

518.   The acquired rights are not only those that exist on the date of the transfer (Art. 3, §1), but also those arising before the date of the transfer.[1] This means that the transferor, after the date of the transfer and by virtue of the transfer alone, is discharged from all obligations arising under the contract of employment or the employment relationship, even if the workers employed in the undertaking do not consent or if they object.[2] Article 3, §1, 2nd subparagraph stipulates, indeed, that the Member States may provide for joint responsibility of the transferor and the transferee following the transfer. It follows that, unless the Member States avail themselves of this possibility, the transferor is released from his obligations as an employer solely by the reason of the transfer and that this legal consequence is not conditional on the consent of the employees concerned. Similarly, the argument based on the principle of the law of obligations which, it is claimed, is generally recognised in the legal systems of the Member States, namely that a debt may be transferred only with the creditor's consent, cannot be accepted in the light of the

clear language of the directive which provides for the automatic transfer of obligations arising from employment contracts to the transferee.[3] It should be added that
an employee cannot waive the rights conferred upon him by mandatory provisions
of Directive No. 77/187 even if the disadvantages resulting from his waiver are
offset by such benefits that, taking the matter as a whole, he is not placed in a worse
position.[4] The directive refers only to the rights and obligations of workers whose
contract of employment or employment relationship is in force at the date of the
transfer and not to those who have ceased to be employed by the undertaking in
question at the time of the transfer. The transferee of an undertaking is not liable
in respect of obligations concerning holiday pay and compensation to employees
who were not employed in the undertaking on the date of the transfer.[5] We must
also add that Directive No. 77/184 does not cover the transfer of the rights and
obligations of persons who were employed by the transferor at the date of the
transfer, but who, by their own decision do not continue to work as employees of
the transferee.[6]

The question arises 'whether the transfer of the contracts of employment and
employment relationships pursuant to Article 3(1) of the Directive necessarily takes
place on the date of the transfer of the undertaking, or whether it may be postponed
to another date at the will of the transferor or the transferee.

From the actual wording of the Directive follows that the transfer of the contracts
of employment and employment relationships takes place on the date of the transfer
of the undertaking.

Article 3(1) is to be interpreted as meaning that after the date of transfer the transferor is in principle discharged, by virtue of the transfer alone, from all obligations
arising under the contract of employment or in the employment relationship. Given
the Directive's objective of protecting workers, that can only be done if the obligations in question are transferred to the transferee as from the date of transfer.

To allow the transferor or transferee the possibility of choosing the date from
which the contract of employment or employment relationship is transferred would
amount to allowing employers to derogate, at least temporarily, from the provisions
of the Directive. However, those provisions are mandatory.[7]

The directive does, in view of the fundamental freedom of labour the employee
enjoys, require Member States to provide that the contract of employment or the
employment relationship should be maintained with the transferor, in the event of
the employee freely deciding not to continue the contract of employment or the
employment relationship with the transferee. Neither does the directive preclude it.
In such a case, it is for the Member States to determine the fate of the contract of
employment or the employment relationship with the transferor.[8] This means that,
in cases that national law does not provide otherwise, the employee deciding not
to continue the employment relationship with the transferee may still be bound by
an employment contract with the transferor. This reasoning of the European Court
may lead to bizarre consequences and calls for great caution in case of transfer of
an enterprise.

1. *Abels, op. cit.*
2. *Berg, op. cit.*
3. *Idem.*

4. COJ, 10 February 1988, *Foreningen af Arbejdsledere I Danmark* v. *Daddy's Dance Hall AS No. 324/86*, IELL, *Case Law*, No. 120.
5. COJ, 7 February 1985, *Knud Wendelboe and others* v. *L.J. Musie A/S, in liquidation*, No. 19/83, IELL, *Case Law*, No. 65.
6. *Foreningen*, No. 105/84, *op. cit.*
7. *Idem.*
8. COJ, 16 December 1992, *G. Katsikas and Others* v. *A Konstantinidis and Others*, Joined Cases Nos. C 132/91, C 138/91, IELL, *Case Law*, No. 198.

2. Collective Agreements

519. Pursuant to Article 3, §2 of the directive the transferee shall, following the transfer, continue to observe the terms and conditions agreed in any collective agreement on the same terms applicable to the transferor under that agreement, until the date of termination or expiry of the collective agreement or the entry into force or application of another collective agreement.[1] The directive does not oblige the transferee to continue to observe the terms and conditions agreed in any collective agreement in respect of workers who are not employed by the undertaking at the time of the transfer.[2] Member States may limit the period of observing such terms and conditions, with the proviso that it shall not be less that one year (Art. 3, §2, 2nd subparagraph).

1. *See also*: COJ, 12 November 1992, *A. Watson Rask and K. Christensen* v. *ISS Kantineservice A/S*, No. C-209/91, IELL, *Case Law*, No. 195.
2. *Landesorganisationen* v. *Ny Molle Kro*, 17 December 1978, No. 287/86, IELL, *Case Law*, No. 113.

3. Social Security

520. The provisions regarding acquired rights do not cover employees' rights to old age, invalidity or survivor's benefits under supplementary company or inter-company pension schemes outside the statutory social security schemes in Member States. Member States have, however, to adopt the measures necessary to protect the interests of employees and of persons no longer employed in the transferor's business at the time of the transfer in respect of the rights conferring on them immediate or prospective entitlements to old-age benefits, including survivors' benefits, under the supplementary schemes (Art. 3, §3).

4. Protection Against Dismissal

521. Article 4, §1 of the directive protects the concerned employees in the case of a transfer against dismissal by the transferor or the transferee on the grounds of the transfer, except for economic, technical or organisational reasons entailing changes in the work-force. In order to ascertain whether the employees were dismissed solely as a result of the transfer, it is necessary to take into consideration the objective circumstances in which the dismissal took place such as, in particular, the fact that it took effect on a date close to that of the transfer and that the employees in question were taken on again by the transferee. Accordingly, the employees whose contract of employment or employment relationship was terminated with effect from a date prior to that of the transfer, contrary to Article 4, §1 must be regarded as still in the employment of the transferor, with the result, in particular, that the employer's obligations toward them are automatically transferred from the transferor to the transferee.[1]

1. P. Bork, *op. cit.*

522.   In *Merckx and Neuhuys* v. *Ford Motors Company Belgium SA*[1] the issue of the employee's power to prevent the transfer of his contract or the employment relationship was raised. Here, the Court held, as in *Foreningen af Arbejdsledere i Danmark* v. *Danmols Inventar*[2] that the protection which the directive is intended to guarantee is redundant where the person concerned decides of his own accord not to continue the employment relationship with the new employer after the transfer.

It also follows, the Court said, from the judgment in *Katsikas and Others* v. *Konstandinidis*[3] that, whilst the directive allows the employee to remain in the employ of his new employer on the same conditions as were agreed with the transferor, it cannot be interpreted as obliging the employee to continue his employment relationship with the transferee. Such an obligation would jeopardise the fundamental rights of the employee, who must be free to choose his employer and cannot be obliged to work for an employer whom he has not freely chosen.

It follows that, in the event of the employee deciding of his own accord not to continue with the contract of employment or employment relationship with the transferee, it is for the Member States to determine what the fate of the contract of employment or employment relationship should be. In the light of that submission, it should be noted that Article 4(2) provides that if the contract of employment or the employment relationship is terminated because the transfer within the meaning of Article 1(1) involves a substantial change in working conditions to the detriment of the employee, the employer is to be regarded as having been responsible for termination. Consequently, if, as Merckx and Neuhuys pretend, Novarobel (the transferee) refused to guarantee to maintain their former level of remuneration, it must be regarded as responsible for the termination of the employment relationship.

1. *Op. cit.*
2. *Op. cit.*
3. *Op. cit.*

523.   Pursuant to the second paragraph of the same paragraph, the Member States may provide that this protection against dismissal does not apply to certain specific categories of employees who are not covered by the laws or practices of the Member States in respect of protection against dismissal. This exception must be interpreted restrictively.

'It is clear from the wording of Article 4, §1 and from the scheme of the directive that the provision in question is designed to ensure that employees rights are maintained by extending the protection against dismissal by the employer afforded by national law to cover the case in which a change in employer occurs upon the transfer of an undertaking.'

Consequently, that provision applies to any situation in which employees affected by the transfer enjoy some, albeit limited – in the case of the trial period – protection against dismissal under national law, with the result that, under the directive, that protection may not be taken away from them or curtailed solely because of the transfer.[1]

1. COJ, 15 April 1986, *Commission* v. *Belgium*, No. 237/84, IELL, *Case Law*, No. 89.

524. If the contract of employment or the employment relationship is terminated because the transfer involves a substantial change in working conditions to the detriment of the employee, the employer shall be regarded as having been responsible for termination of the contract of employment or the employment relationship (Art. 4, §2).

5. Workers' Representation

525. If the business preserved its autonomy, the status and function of the representatives or of the representations of the employees affected by the transfer shall be preserved, unless the conditions necessary for the re-appointment of the representatives of the employees or for the reconstituting of the representation of the employees are fulfilled. If the term of office of the representatives of those employees affected by the transfer expires as a result of the transfer, the representatives shall continue to enjoy the protection provided by national law or practice (Art. 5).

C. Information and Consultation

526. The directive provides that the transferor and the transferee shall be required to inform the representatives of their respective employees affected by the transfer with the following information:

– the reasons for the transfer;
– the legal, economic and social implications of the transfer for the employees;
– the measures envisaged in relation to the employees.

The transferor must give such information in good time before the transfer is carried out. The transferee must give such information in good time, and in any event before his employees are directly affected by the transfer as regards their conditions of work and employment (Art. 6, §1). If the transferor or the transferee contemplates measures in relation to his employees, he shall consult his workers' representatives in good time or on such measures with a view to seeking agreement (Art. 6, §2).

527. If national rules provide that workers' representatives may have recourse to an arbitration board to obtain a decision on the measures to be taken in relation to employees, the Member States may limit the information and consultation to cases where the transfer carried out gives rise to a change in the business likely to entail serious disadvantages for a considerable number of the employees. The information and consultations shall at least cover the measures envisaged in relation to the employees and take place in good time before the change in the business (Art. 6, §3). Member States may limit the obligations to undertakings or businesses which, in respect of the number of employees fulfil the conditions for the election or designation of a collegiate body representing the employees (Art. 6, §4). They may also provide that where there are no workers' representatives in an undertaking or a business, the employees must be informed in advance when a transfer is about to take place (Art. 6, §5).

II. Mergers and Divisions of Public Limited Liability Companies

528. The (third and sixth) directives concerning the mergers and divisions of public limited liability companies of 9 October 1978 and 17 December 1982[1] respectively provide that Directive No. 77/187 concerning acquired rights regulates the protection rights of the employees of each of the merging companies (Art. 12) or of the companies involved in a decision (Art. 10). These directives were taken in view of the coordination of national legislation regarding public limited liability companies, provided for in Article 54, §3G of the EC Treaty.

> 1. Based on Article 54, §3G of the EC Treaty, No. 78/855 (O.J., 20 October 1978, No. L 295) and No. 82/891 O.J., 31 December 1982, No. L 287.

529. For the purpose of these directives, *merger* (by acquisition or by the formation of a new company) means the operation whereby one or more companies are wound up without going into liquidation and transfer to another all their assets and liabilities in exchange for the issue to the shareholders of the company or companies being acquired of shares in the acquiring company and cash payments, if any, not exceeding 10 per cent of the nominal value of the shares so issued or, where they have no nominal value, of their accounting par value (Art. 3, §1 and 4, §1).

530. For the purpose of the directive, *division* (by acquisition or by formation of new companies) means the operation whereby, after being wound up without going into liquidation, a company transfers to more than one company all its assets and liabilities in exchange for the allocation to the shareholders of the company being divided of shares in the companies receiving contributions as result of the division (hereinafter referred to as 'recipient companies') and possibly a cash payment not exceeding 10 per cent of the nominal value of the shares allocated, or where they have no nominal value, of their accounting *par value* (Art. 2, §1 and 21, §1).

§3. Insolvency of the Employer

531. The protection of employees in the event of the insolvency of their employer is regulated by Directive No. 80/987 of 20 October 1980.[1] This directive is based on Article 100 of the EC Treaty regarding the approximation of national legislations. The 'whereas' to the directive indicates that it is necessary to provide for the protection of employees in the event of the insolvency of their employer, in particular in order to guarantee payment of their outstanding claims, while taking account of the need for balanced economies and social developments in the Community. The underlying idea is of course that the restructuring which will be brought about by the functioning of the common market may lead to bankruptcies and insolvencies. Considering that differences still remain between the Member States as regards the extent of the protection of employees in their respect, the 'whereas' states that efforts should be directed towards reducing these differences, which can have a direct effect on the functioning of the common market. Therefore the approximation of laws should be promoted while the improvement within the meaning of Article 117 of the EC Treaty is maintained.

1. O.J., 28 October 1980, L 283, amended by Directive No. 87/164, 2 March 1987, O.J., 11 March 1987, No. L 66.

532.   In a very important case the Court ruled that interested parties may not assert the rights laid down in the directive against the State in proceedings before the national courts in the absence of implementing measures adopted within the prescribed period.[1] The Court accepted however the principle of liability of the State. Indeed the full effectiveness of Community law would be undermined and the rights deriving from it would be less safeguarded if individuals were unable to obtain reparation when their rights were undermined by the infringement of Community law imputable to a Member State. It follows that Community law lays down the principle according to which the Member States are obliged to compensate individuals for damage caused to them by infringements of Community law imputable to the Member State.

The Court expanded at length on the principle of State liability. First, the Court said, it was important to bear in mind that the Treaty created the Community's own legal order, which was integrated into the legal systems of the Member States, was binding on their courts and covered not only the Member States but also their nationals, and, just as it imposed burdens on individuals, Community law also gave rise to rights forming part of their legal heritage; such rights arose not only where they were expressly provided for by the Treaty but also by virtue of obligations which the Treaty imposed in clear terms both on individuals and Member States and on Community institutions.

Furthermore, as the Court had consistently held, it was incumbent on the national courts responsible for applying Community law in the areas within their purview to ensure that those provisions took full effect and to safeguard the rights which they conferred on individuals.

The full effectiveness of Community law would bee undermined and the rights deriving from it would be less safeguarded if individuals were unable to obtain reparation when their rights were undermined by an infringement of Community law imputable to a Member State.

The possibility of obtaining reparation from Member States was particularly necessary where, as in the present case, the full effectiveness of Community provisions was conditional upon action being taken by a Member State and where, consequently, individuals were unable, in the absence of such action, to enforce before the national courts the rights granted to them by Community law.

It followed that the principle whereby a State was liable for damage caused to individuals as a result of infringements of Community law attributable to it was inherent in the system of the Treaty. The Member States' obligation to make reparation for such damage was also based on Article 5 of the Treaty, pursuant to which the Member States were required to take all appropriate measures, whether general or particular, to ensure fulfilment of the obligations incumbent on them under Community law. Those obligations included the duty of neutralising the unlawful consequences of infringements of Community law.

It followed from the foregoing considerations that Community law laid down the principle according to which the Member State were obliged to compensate individuals for damage caused to them by infringements of Community law imputable to the Member States. Where, as in the present case, a Member State failed to fulfil the obligation incumbent on it under the third paragraph of Article 189 of the Treaty to take all necessary measures to achieve the result pursued by a directive, the full effectiveness of that provision of Community law created a right to compensation provided that three conditions were fulfilled. The first such condition was that the result to be achieved by the directive involved the attribution of rights attaching to individuals. The second condition was that the subject-matter of those rights could be identified by reference to provisions of the directive. Finally, the third condition was the existence of a causaal link between the infringement of the obligation incumbent upon the Member State and the damage suffered by the persons aggrieved.

Those conditions were sufficient to confer on individuals entitlement to obtain compensation, based directly on Community law. Subject to that reservation, it was on the basis of national law concerning liability that the Member State concerned was required to compensate for the damage caused. In the absence of Community rules, it was for the legal system of each Member State to designate the competent courts and lay down the procedures for legal proceedings intended fully to safeguard the rights of individuals under Community law.

The Court also stated that the substantive and formal conditions laid down by the legislation of the Member States concerning compensation for damage could not be less favourable than those applicable to similar claims of an internal nature and could not be so arranged as to make it virtually impossible or excessively difficult to obtain compensation.

In those circumstances, it was the responsibility of the national court to give effect, in the context of national law on liability, to the right of workers to obtain compensation for damage suffered by them as a result of failure to transpose the directive.

In Federica Maso and others,[2] the Court decided that: 'In making good the loss or damage sustained by employees as a result of the belated transposition of the Directive on the insolvency of their employer, a Member State is entitled to apply retroactively to such employees belatedly adapted implementing measures, including rules against aggregation or other limitations on the liability of the guarantee institution, provided that the Directive has been properly transposed. However, it is for the national court to ensure that reparation of the loss or damage sustained by the beneficiaries is adequate. Retroactive and proper application in full of the measures implementing the Directive will suffice for that purpose unless the beneficiaries establish the existence of complementary loss sustained on account of the fact that they were unable to benefit at the appropriate time from the financial advantages guaranteed by the Directive with the result that, loss must also be made good'.

1. 19 November 1991, *A. Francovich and Others* v. *Italian Republic*, Joined Cases Nos. C 6/90 and C 9/90, IELL, *Case Law*, No. 175. *See also*: COJ, 3 December 1992, *M. Suffritti and Others* v. *Instituto Nazionle Della Previdernze Sociale (INPS)*, Joined Cases Nos. C 140/01, 141/91, 278/91 and 279/91, IELL, *Case Law*, No. 197.
2. COJ, 10 July 1997, C 295/2, not yet published.

533. In summary, one can say that the purpose of the directive is to approximate the laws of the Member States relating to the protection of the employees in the event of the insolvency of their employer and for that purpose it provides specific safeguards to ensure the payment of their outstanding claims. The directive provides in particular:

– for the insurance of the payment of employees' outstanding claims resulting from contracts of employment by guarantee institutions, the assets of which are independent from the employer's operating capital and inaccessible to proceedings for insolvency;
– that the non-payment of compulsory contributions due from the employer within the framework of national statutory social security schemes does not adversely affect the employee's benefit entitlements;
– that the employees' entitlement to old-age and survivors' benefit under supplementary company or inter-company pension schemes outside the statutory social security schemes is protected.

I. Definitions and Scope

534. The directive applies to employees' claims arising from contracts of employment or employment relationships and existing against employers who are in a state of insolvency (Art. 1, §1). For the definition of the terms 'employee,' 'employer,' 'pay,' 'right conferring immediate entitlement' and 'right conferring prospective entitlement,' the directive refers to national law (Art. 2, §2).[1] Member States, may, by way of exception, exclude claims by certain categories of employees from the scope of the directive, by virtue of the special nature of the employee's contract of employment or employment relationship or of the existence of other forms of guarantee offering the employee protection equivalent to that resulting from the directive (Art. 1, §2). In *Wagner Miret* v. *Fondo de garantia salarial*,[2] the national court (Spain) asked whether members of higher management staff could be excluded from the scope of the directive on insolvency of employers since they were not included in Section 1 of the annex to the directive. The Court observed that the directive on insolvency of employers was intended to apply to all classes of employees defined as such by the national law of a Member State apart from those listed in the annex thereto and thus also to higher management.

The directive confers upon the Member States the power to exclude from it scope, by way of exception, the claims of certain categories of employees. When the exclusion is authorised, by virtue of the special nature of the contract of employment or employment relationship, that exclusion is not conditional on the existence of a form of guarantee other than the one resulting from the directive, offering equivalent protection. However, when the exclusion is authorised precisely because there is such a guarantee, it is possible only if the employee enjoys protection which, while being based on a scheme whose detailed rules differ from those laid down by the directive, affords employee the essential guarantees set out therein.[3]

It follows both from the aim of the directive, which is to provide a minimum protection for all employees, and from the exceptional nature of the possibility of exclusion allowed for by Article 1, §2, that this provision cannot be interpreted broadly. Therefore it is limited to the categories expressly mentioned in the list annexed to the directive.[4]

1. *See also*: COJ, 3 December 1992, *M. Suffritti and Others* v. *Instituto Natzionale della Previdenze Sociale (INPS)*, Joined Cases Nos. C 140/91, 141/91, 278/91 and 279/91, IELL, *Case Law*, No. 197: 'Employees may not rely on the provisions of the Council Directive 80/987/EEC of 20 October 1980, . . . in proceedings before the national courts in order to obtain payment from the guarantee fund established under Italian Law No. 297/82 of the severance grant provided for by that Law without taking into account the temporal requirement which it lays down, namely that the benefits provided for by the fund are to be granted only if the employment relationship ceased and the insolvency or implementation procedure took place after the entry into force of that Law.'
2. COJ, 16 December 1993, No. C-334/92, not yet published.
3. COJ, 8 November 1990, *Commission of the European Communities* v. *Hellenic Republic*, No. C-53/88, IELL, *Case Law*, No. 152.
4. COJ, 2 February 1989, *Commission* v. *Italy*, No. 22/87, IELL, *Case Law*, No. 132.

535. The Court, however, in an Italian case,[1] had to consider the question whether the directive, to the extent that it protects only employees whose employers are subject to proceedings involving their assets in order to satisfy collectively the claims of creditors, is valid in the light of the principle of equal treatment.

The directive, the Court stated, was adopted on the basis of Article 100 of the Treaty and its aim is to promote the approximation of national laws while maintaining improvement within the meaning of Article 117 of the Treaty.

In the exercise of the powers conferred on them by Article 100 of the Treaty, the Community institutions have a discretion in particular with regard to the possibility of proceeding towards harmonisation only in stages, given the specific nature of the field in which co-ordination is sought and the fact that the implementation of harmonising provisions of that kind is generally difficult.

Prior to the adoption of the directive, institutions to guarantee the claims of employees in the event of the insolvency of their employer had already been set up in several Member States, albeit under widely differing terms, whilst there were no such institutions in some other Member States.

In view of that situation, it undoubtedly constitutes a further step towards providing improved working conditions and an improved standard of living for workers throughout the Community and towards the gradual harmonisation of laws in the field for the obligation to set up institutions to guarantee the claims of employees in the event of the insolvency of their employers, as defined in Article 2(1) of the directive, to be extended to all the Member States.

In those circumstances and in the light of the difficulty of finding a concept of insolvency capable of unambiguous application in the different Member States, the distinction drawn between employees according to whether or not their employer is subject to proceedings to satisfy collectively the claims of creditors, derives from a concept of insolvency based on a criterion which is in itself objective and is justified by reason of the aforesaid difficulties of harmonisation.

> 1. COJ, 9 November 1995, *Andrea Francovich* v. *Italian Republic*, Case C-479/93, *Jur.*, 1995, 3843.

536.   An employer is deemed to be in a state of insolvency:

– where a request has been made for the opening of proceedings involving the employer's assets to satisfy collectively the claims of creditors;
– where the competent authority has either decided to open the proceedings or established that the employee's undertaking or business has been definitively closed down and the available assets are insufficient to warrant the opening of the proceedings (Art. 2, §1).

II. Guaranteed Pay

537.   The directive guarantees pay for the period prior to a given date, which is, at the choice of the Member States:

– choice (1): at the onset of the employer's insolvency;
– choice (2): at the onset of the notice of dismissal issued to the employee concerned on the account of the employer's insolvency;
– choice (3): at the onset of the employer's insolvency[1] or the date on which the contract of employment was discontinued on account of the employer's insolvency.

The Member States have the option to limit the liability of guarantee institutions; there must however always be a minimum protection, which varies according to the choice of the protected period the Member States have made:

– choice (1): the payment of outstanding claims relating to pay for the last three months of the contract of employment occurring within a period of six months preceding the date of the onset of the insolvency;
– choice (2): the payment relating to pay for the last three months of the contract of employment preceding the date of the notice of dismissal;

– choice (3): the payment relating to pay for the last 18 months of the contract of employment preceding the date of the onset of the insolvency or the date on which the contract of employment with the employee was discontinued on account of the insolvency. In this case, Member States may limit the liability to make payment to pay corresponding to a period of eight weeks or to several shorter periods totalling eight weeks (Art. 4, §§1–2).[2]

However, in order to avoid the payment of sums going beyond the social objective of the directive, Member States may set a ceiling on the liability for employees' outstanding claims. When Member States exercise this option, they shall inform the Commission of the methods used to set the ceiling (Art. 4, §3). Moreover, the directive does not affect the option of Member States (a) to take the necessary measures to avoid abuses; (b) to refuse or reduce the liability if it appears that the fulfilment of the obligation is unjustifiable because of the existence of special links between the employee and the employer and of common interests resulting in collusion between them (Art. 10).

1. The 'onset of the employer's insolvency', corresponds to the date of the request that proceed to satisfy collectively the claims of creditors opened, since the guarantee cannot be provided prior to a decision to open such proceedings or to a finding that the business has been definitively closed down where the assets are insufficient (*idem*).
2. The phrase 'the last three months of the contract employment or employment relationship must interpreted as meaning three rolling months (*idem*) . . .'.

III. Guarantee Institutions

538. The payment of the employees' outstanding claims is guaranteed by guarantee institutions (Art. 3, §1). Member States lay down detailed rules for the organisation, financing and operation of guarantee institutions, complying with the following principles in particular.

a. the assets of the institutions shall be independent of the employer's operating capital and inaccessible to proceedings for insolvency;
b. employers shall contribute to financing, unless it is fully recovered by the public authorities;
c. the institutions' liabilities shall not depend on whether or not obligations to contribute to financing have been fulfilled (Art. 5).

The directive on the insolvency of employers does not require Member States to create a single guarantee institution for all classes of employees and consequently to make management staff dependent on the guarantee institution set up for other classes of employees. From the discretion given to Member States it has to be concluded that management staff could not rely on the directive to claim payment of arrears of salary from the guarantee institution set up for classes of employees.

When it interprets and applies national law every national court must assume that 'the State intended fully to implement the obligations under the directive in question.'

The Member State concerned is required to make good the damage suffered by the management staff by reason of the failure to comply with the directive in relation thereto.[1]

1. COJ, 16 December 1993, *T. Wagner Miret* v. *Fondo de garantia salarial*, No. C-334/92, not yet published.

538bis.   Where the employer is established in a Member State other than that in which the employee resides and was employed, the guarantee institution responsible in the event of the insolvency of their employer, for the payment of that employee's claims in the event of the employer's insolvency is the institution of the State in which either it is decided to open the proceedings for the collective satisfaction of creditors' claims or it has been established that the employer's undertaking or business has been closed down.[1]

1. COJ., 17 September 1997, *Carina Mosbaeck* v. *Lonmodtagernes Garantifond*, C-97 331/13, not yet published.

IV. Social Security

539.   Member States may stipulate that the guarantee funds are not obliged to pay contributions due under national statutory schemes or under supplementary company or inter-company schemes outside the national statutory social security schemes (Art. 6). An interpretation of Article 6, which would in effect allow the Member States unilaterally to limit the scope of obligations deriving from the directive, cannot be upheld. It is apparent from the mere wording of Article 6 that it merely authorises the Member States not to impose upon the guarantee institutions, provided for in Articles 3 and 5, responsibility for the contributions not paid by the insolvent employer, by allowing them to choose for that purpose another system for guaranteeing employees' entitlement to social security benefits.[1]

Member States must take the necessary measures to ensure that non-payment of compulsory contributions due from the employer under national statutory social security does not adversely affect the employees' benefit entitlement in respect of those insurance institutions inasmuch, as the employees' contributions were deducted at source from the remuneration paid (Art. 7); this provision does not however affect the option of Member States or refuse or reduce this guarantee if it appears that the fulfilment of the obligation is unjustifiable because of the existence of special links between the employee and the employer and of common interests resulting in collusion between them (Art. 10B). Member States shall equally ensure that the necessary measures are taken to protect the interests of employee and of persons having already left the employer's undertaking or business at the date of the onset of the insolvency in respect of rights conferring on them immediate or prospective entitlements to old-age benefits, including survivors' benefits, under supplementary company or inter-company pension schemes outside the national statutory social security schemes (Art. 8).

1. COJ, 2 February 1989, *Commission* v. *Italy*, No. 22/87, IELL, *Case Law*, No. 132.

Part II. Collective Labour Law

540. Traditionally, collective labour law embraces the body of rules that govern the relations between the collectivity of employees and the employer of a group of employers. The following rights come to mind: the right to trade union freedom, the right of employers and employees to set up organisations at their own choosing in view of the promotion of their professional interests, the right to workers' participation in the company in decisions that affect their interests, including the right to free and autonomous collective bargaining and the right to conclude collective agreements. The rules concerning economic warfare, namely regarding strikes and lockouts as well as the set of measures aimed at the prevention of the settlement of collective labour conflicts belong equally to collective labour law. One can say without any hesitation that these issues have remained within the *national jurisdiction* and that the collective measures that are proposed at European level, are mostly so controversial that a consensus between both sides of industry and among the Member States seems to be impossible; this state of affairs will remain so in the near future.

541. There is no doubt that the Community Charter on the Fundamental Social Rights of Workers (December 1989) contains quite a number of points that belong to the field of collective labour law. Thus the right of association for employers and employees, including positive and the negative trade union freedom (point 11), the right to negotiate and conclude collective agreement, eventually, if the parties deem to desirable, at European level (point 12). The right to resort to collective action, including the right to strike, is explicitly recognised, while recourse to conciliation, mediation and arbitration in order to facilitate the settlement of industrial disputes is encouraged (point 13). Information, consultation and participation of workers shall especially be developed in companies or groups of companies having subsidiaries in various Member States. These must be implemented in due time, particularly in the following cases: technological change, restructuring and mergers of undertakings, collective redundancy procedures, and when transfrontier workers in particular are affected by employment policies pursued by the undertaking where they are employed (points 17–18).

542. One cannot but underline again that the Charter refers for most of the collective labour law rights to existing national legislation of practice, which suggests a very definite division of competence between the Member States and the Community in terms of the subsidiarity principle. The wording of the Charter is not accidental, but rather very deliberate. I must add that when one analyses the information and consultation rights that workers' representatives have under the directives concerning collective redundancies (1975), transfer of undertakings (1977) and the different health and safety directives, one must ascertain time and again that the notion of 'workers' representatives' must be seen in the national context. The social action programme (1990) limited its proposals concerning collective labour law aspects, beside existing initiatives (the Vth directive and the SE), which we will discuss later, to a community instrument regarding information, consultation and participation of employees in undertakings with a European dimension. Here a distinction has to be made between the 15 Member States of the EU and the 14 (minus the UK). Indeed, as already explained before, in Maastricht (1991) a far-reaching Agreement on Social Policy was reached allowing legally binding collective agreement *erga omnes*, which opens new possibilities if the social partners want to engage on that road.

In Part II of this book on European Labour Law and Industrial Relations, we will first examine the likelihood of European collective bargaining (Chapter 1); secondly, we deal with the proposals concerning workers' participation (Chapter 2), namely: information and consultation (§1) the proposed Vth directive (§2) the European SE (§3) and the European Works Councils (§4). Especially the last item, the EWC, opens new perspectives, again for the 14, since the adoption of a directive on EWCs and/or a procedure for the purpose of informing and consulting the employees. The directive concerns some 2,000 European-scale enterprises.

Chapter 1. Collective Bargaining

§1. FOR THE 15

543. Pursuant to Article 118B of the EC Treaty, introduced by the Single Act of 1986, the Commission 'shall endeavour to develop the dialogue between management and labour at a European level which could, if the two sides consider it desirable, lead to relations based on agreement.' The cautious wording of Article 118B clearly indicates that bargaining at a European level is not self-evident. It nevertheless means that collective bargaining is recognised as a full-fledged instrument to regulate, beside regulations and directives, working conditions at a European level. One has however to ascertain that there are, up to now, practically no collective agreements at a European level, that most employers' representatives especially abhor the idea and that both European sides of industry lack an effective mandate to carry them out at a European level.

544. On the other hand, one must recognise that the Commission does its utmost to develop and sustain a bilateral *'social dialogue'* at a European level, in addition to the numerous meetings which take place between the European social partners and parties in the ESC and other consultative bodies. Over and over again the Commission has expressed the desire to have a constructive dialogue, especially since 1985, around themes like 'employment and the introduction of new technologies,' which could possibly lead to European framework agreements, to which national sectorial and inter-industry wide bargaining could refer. These talks which are more or less regularly held, at the initiative of the Commission, between the social partners have led to agreement on texts, which were made public under the name 'common orientations' Partners in this dialogue are UNICE, CEEP and ETUC. The agreements took the form of joint opinions concerning training and motivation, information and consultation (6 March 1987) and on setting of a European area of occupational and geographical mobility, improvement of the labour market in Europe (13 February 1990), on Education and Training (19 June 1990), on the Transition from School to Adult and Working Life (6 November 1990), on New Technologies, Work Organisation and Adaptability to the Labour Market (10 January 1991), on Ways of Facilitating the Broadest Possible Effective Access to Training Opportunities (20 December 1991), on Vocational Qualifications and Certification (13 October 1992), Guidelines for Turning Recovery into a Sustained and Job-Creating Growth Process (16 May 1995) and a joint declaration called: action for employment in Europe: a Pact of Confidence (14 November 1996).[1] Finally, one can mention the sectorial and joint committees and informal groups, which operate at sectorial level and are a forum for the exchange of information and ideas, rather than a setting in which collective bargaining takes place.[2]

1. The text of these joint opinions is published in the *Codex European Labour Law*, which is a part of the IELL.
2. *See* General Introduction, §1, III, H.

§2. AFTER MAASTRICHT: FOR THE 14

545. In this section we want to raise some problems which accompany the possibility to conclude European collective agreements, pursuant to the Maastricht Protocol on Social Policy and the consecutive agreement between the Member States. In order to do so a number of introductory remarks are called for since collective bargaining constitutes a complex and delicate set of relationships, which are not self-explanatory. Collective bargaining within national boundaries already is not an easy subject, neither politically, sociologically, nor legally; *a fortiori* it is even more complex if undertaken at European or at a wider international level. We also put the first European Collective Agreement on Parental Leave (14 December 1995) into perspective.[1]

1. *See* Part I, Chapter 7, §4.

I. Introductory Remarks

A. Broad and Narrow

546. There are at least two meanings of the term 'collective bargaining'[1]: a broad one and a narrow one. In a broad sense collective bargaining embraces 'all sorts of bipartite or tripartite *discussions* concerning labour problems' involving both sides of industry and governmental authorities aimed at wider understanding, resolutions, preparing or implementing policies, trying eventually to reach compromises, without necessarily resulting in a binding agreement. Self-evidently this broad meaning of bargaining comprises all forms of consultation, co-operation and concertation.

A narrower meaning of collective bargaining focuses on discussions leading to binding agreements, either *de facto*, moral or legal and usually confined to both sides of industry. Collective bargaining in this sense involves a process of negotiations between employers and representatives of the employees as well as an agreement containing binding rules. It is in this latter and thus narrower sense which we use the term throughout this chapter.

1. E. Cordoba, 'Collective Bargaining' in: *Comparative Labour Law and Industrial Relations in Industrialised Market Economies* (ed. R. Blanpain), 4th ed., Vol. 2, Chapter 22, p. 151.

B. A Multifaceted Role

547. As E. Cordoba[1] rightly indicates, collective bargaining serves various functions, namely: determining wages and working conditions, settlement of disputes and the regulation of relations between the collective parties, and it is *de facto* also a form of employee participation.

1. *Op. cit.*

C. Agreement with a Double Content

548. Given its complex nature the collective agreement is like a double-yolked egg: it has a double content.

1. The Normative Part

549. On the one hand the collective agreement contains stipulations about wages and working conditions which regulate the labour relations between the employer(s) and the employees. These wages and working conditions have a *normative nature*; they are the norms which regulate the working conditions of those which fall within the territorial, personal and occupational scope of the collective agreement.

550. The normative part of the collective agreement contains *individual normative stipulations*, comprising the conditions of the individual employees (wages, benefits, cost of living clauses, job classification, working time, holidays, vacations and so on). They also comprise *collective normative stipulations* in the enterprise or the branch of activity. They are norms which generate obligations neither for the contracting parties nor for the employer in relation to individual employees. They are a sort of in-between rules (between individual normative and obligatory), which regulate 'collective' labour relations. Examples of collective normative rules are the provisions in e.g., sectorial collective agreements covering: 1) the establishment, competence and functioning of the works council in the enterprise; 2) procedures for the settlement of industrial disputes; 3) establishment of certain funds and the like.

2. The Obligatory Part

551. The collective agreement, like any other agreement, generates obligations between the contracting parties which have to be clearly distinguished from the normative rules. These obligations can be explicit (e.g., concerning the interpretation of the agreement) or implicit. To the implicit obligations, in certain EC countries, belong among other the peace obligation (abstention of industrial action as long as the agreement is in force), which can be relative or absolute. Some also accept that there is an implicit duty for the contracting parties to implement the collective agreement (exercise influence on their members to live up to the agreement). A peace obligation can, self-evidently, also be dealt with *explicit verbis.*

D. Free Collective Bargaining: Pluralist Democracy

552. It is not superfluous to recall in this context that free collective bargaining and the autonomy of the parties have always been regarded as fundamental aspects of the freedom of association.[1] Indeed, freedom of association, collective bargaining and the right to strike go, like we said earlier, hand in hand. Employees, and eventually employers, associate in order to bargain collectively and bargaining without the right to strike amounts to collective begging. Autonomous collective bargaining constitutes a prerequisite for a pluralist democratic society, namely that '*plures*,' this means more institutions and persons than one group, e.g., a given political party, participate in social decision and rule making. Needless to say, collective bargaining (point 12) as well as the right to strike (point 13) belong to the fundamental social rights of workers as expressed in the Community Charter of 1989.

1. B. Creighton, 'Freedom of Association' in: *Comparative Labour Law and Industrial Relations in Industrialised Market Economies* (ed. R. Blanpain), 4th ed., Vol. 2, Chapter 17, p. 38.

E. Subsidiarity

553. The subsidiarity rule, pointing out that problems must be settled at the most suitable level, addresses not only the relation between the European and national or regional levels, as far as European or national governmental authorities are concerned, but also whether problems can be dealt with either by governmental intervention or by agreements between the parties concerned, which in the social arena means the social partners. So the subsidiarity rule also points out that there is room for collective bargaining at European level when this is the best way of doing things.

F. Abstention from an International (Legal) Framework

554. There is no doubt that international legal instruments have always been almost mute as far as collective bargaining at international or European level between management and labour is concerned, as bargaining at that level is bedeviled by strategic considerations by the parties involved. Even the Guidelines for Multinational Enterprises, like those promulgated by the OECD Member States (1976, as amended) or the ILO Tripartite Declaration on Social Policy of Multinational Enterprises (1977) do neither explicitly nor implicitly refer to transnational bargaining, given the conflicting views of the governments and the social partners involved. Thus, the Maastricht Agreement on Social Policy is a break-through in this area, but it self-evidently does not contain precisely formulated rules, legally organising and monitoring the different juridical questions which accompany European collective agreements.

G. Specific Legislation

555. In the absence of specific European legal rules, the question arises as to which legal rules should apply in case a collective agreement is concluded at European level. There is no doubt that there are insufficient European general

principles of law to deal satisfactorily with the legal problems which accompany a European collective agreement. In order to do so one will have to look to national law for a solution. Here one must distinguish between two possibilities: either the parties choose the national law which will apply to their agreement or they do not. In the latter case the national legal system with which the agreement is most closely connected, may apply. Reference in this framework could be made to the Convention on the Law applicable to Contractual Obligations of 19 June 1980, although the drafters of that Convention did certainly not have collective European agreements in their minds when they elaborated the Convention. In any case, unless European law ultimately would prevail, national law will be applied by the local courts in case of a dispute concerning the application of the terms and conditions, laid down by a European collective agreement, of e.g., an individual employment contract.

556.   In the present legal state of affairs, the European Court does not seem to be competent to handle any preliminary question regarding the validity or the interpretation of a European agreement, giving the wording of Article 177 of the EC Treaty, whereby preliminary questions are limited to actions of the Community institutions.

II. Parties to the Agreement

557.   A collective agreement is an agreement between one or more employers or employers' association(s) and one or more trade unions, including other *bona fide* representatives of employees, concerning the terms and conditions of employment and the rights and the obligations of the contracting parties.
Agreements at European level can be either a:

1. European company agreement;
2. European industry agreement;
3. European multi-industry wide agreement;
4. European multi-regional agreement.

A. *The European Company Agreement*

558.   In the case of a European company agreement the *employers' side* is composed of either a European company, having non-incorporated subsidiaries in various EC Member States or the representatives of various legally incorporated subsidiaries, located in Member States, which are part of a European or a multinational group. It is clearly not necessary that there are subsidiaries in all EC countries. One could, moreover, envisage that some subsidiaries are not situated in the EC and yet nevertheless are involved in the bargaining and the consequent agreement; equally that agreements are only concluded with some of the subsidiaries.

559.   The labour side could be composed of representatives of the *trade unions*, which represent employees working in the different subsidiaries, or (theoretically

at least) of *a European company trade union*, which may have been established and which has competence and thus a mandate to bargain over and conclude an agreement concerning wages and conditions in the company.

One can also envisage that an EWC could be party to a European collective company agreement, depending on the composition and the competences of the council. The EWC could be composed of representatives of employees, who are directly elected to that end, e.g., at national level, or who are delegates of national councils or similar bodies, such as shop stewards, committees of hygiene and others. These (direct and indirect) representatives should have a mandate to bargain and to agree at a European level. There should be at best an explicit mandate in both cases. In the case of direct representation, this is self-evident; in the case of indirect representation, there should be an explicit mandate certainly for those representatives who do not enjoy that competence at home, which is the case for many works councils, since in a number of countries the (legal) right to bargain is reserved to the trade unions. The problems which ensue are discussed in the light of the structure of EWCs, below.[1]

1. *See.* Chapter 2, §4, IV.

560. The possibility of *multi-company agreements* cannot be excluded *a priori*.

B. The European Industry Agreement

561. Parties to the European industry agreement are self-evidently employers' associations and trade unions.

The (national) trade unions, representative of the employees in that branch of industry and competent to bargain, could either form one or more European sectorial trade unions, which have a mandate to negotiate and conclude agreements or be represented as such around the negotiation table and become parties to the collective agreement, or could mandate a *negotiating committee*.

The same goes *ceteris paribus* for the employers' side.

C. The European Multi-Industry Agreement

562. The European multi-industry agreement could either cover the European private sector (profit – socio profit)[1] as a whole or more than one branch of industry. Again one can conceive that one or more *European confederal trade unions*, grouping national confederations, could be party to a collective agreement provided that they have a mandate to that end. There may be a difficulty, resulting from the fact that some *national confederations* may not themselves have the competence to conclude collective agreements and therefore could not delegate that competence to a European body. One could also imagine that national confederations would be party to the agreement.

1. Public companies, affecting the functioning of the common market included.

563.   In the case of an inter-industry wide agreement, covering only some sectors of industry, one might imagine that *national unions*, representing those sectors, could be party to the collective agreement.

564.   On the part of the employers one or more *European confederations of employers' associations* may be a party, maybe the national confederations themselves. The same thing can be said regarding competence and agreement covering only some sectors, as is the case with the unions.

D. The European Multi-Regional Agreement

565.   An agreement could also be concluded covering different regions of the European Community, situated in different Member States. These agreements could be industry or multi-industry agreements.

Here European regional *employers'* association(s) could be a party to the agreement as well as the (national) regional employers' organisations or national employers' organisations.

From the *trade union side*, there could be European regional trade unions, (national) regional trade unions or national trade unions at the negotiation table.

III. The Competence to Conclude Collective Agreements

566.   In order to be able to conclude collective agreements the parties must have the necessary competence. Here we have to distinguish between the power to negotiate, the power to conclude and the power to ratify the agreement.

In the case of organisations there must be a mandate to this end, given by employer or employee members to their organisation or conferred by law. In the case of a European organisation, the composing organisations must have the competence to give such a mandate to their European organisation.

Such a mandate can be explicit or implicit.

Of course there is the possibility for e.g., national organisations to constitute a bargaining team, which would conduct negotiations on behalf of the organisations and conclude the agreement while retaining the power of ratification.

IV. The Maastricht Deal: Specific Legal Problems

567.   As has already been indicated, very intricate problems arise regarding European collective agreements under the Maastricht Agreement, both for those which will be implemented by a decision of the Council as well as for those agreements, which will have to stand on their own (legal) feet.

A. Implementation in Accordance with National Practice

1. Contracting Parties

568.   The first question which rises is: who can be a party to a European collective agreement? A party may be an employer, let us say a European company, or a European employer's organisation, or a European trade union of employees organised at either regional, sectorial, or confederal level. As indicated earlier, parties must have the necessary competence to conclude a collective agreement. In order to do so they should have a (explicit) mandate from their members. Members of UNICE, who do not have the practice of bargaining at a national level like e.g., the *Deutsche Arbeitgebersbund* or the Confederation of British Industries, may be in a difficult position to give such a mandate, unless the constituent members of the latter organisations would agree to do so. This may eventually involve an amendment of the by-laws of those organisations.

Contracting parties in the Agreement on Parental Leave are the 'cross-industry organisations,' UNICE, CEEP for the employers' side and ETUC for the employees' side. In the considerans (13) to the directive it is noted that the Commission has 'taken into account the representative status of the signatory parties ...'. *See,* however, regarding this point our earlier remarks on the representativity of the European social partners.[1]

  1. General Introduction, §3, IV, C1b.

2. Content of the Agreement

569. Parties can conclude agreements on wages and working conditions, in the broadest sense of the word. The parties are autonomous and are not bound by the areas which are excluded in Article 2,6, although one must recognise that agreements on issues like the right to strike or the right to impose lock-outs at a European level are hardly likely, although theoretically possible.

The Collective Agreement of 14 December 1995 deals with parental leave, which is a working condition in the sense of Article 2 of the Agreement on Social Policy (1991).

3. Form and Language

570. The European collective agreement will probably have to be drafted in writing in the various official languages of the Member States in which the agreement is intended to have an effect, although it does not seem that this would condition its validity, except when national legislation, applicable to the agreement, would contain certain linguistic requirements, as is the case in Belgium.

The *territorial* scope of the Collective Agreement on Parental Leave is the 14 Member States of the EU (minus the UK) and, according to the applicable procedure, the EEA Member States. The personal scope relates to: 'all workers, men and women, who have an employment contract or employment relationship as defined by the law, collective agreements or practices in force in each Member State' (Clause 1,2). It thus applies as well to the public as to the private sector.

4. Scope

571. The *territorial* scope of the agreement will not necessarily be limited to the 14 Member States and the EEA Members as some of the possible contracting parties, e.g., UNICE and the ETUC, have membership outside the Community (of the 14 Member States and the EEA Members). It is theoretically possible that e.g., the CBI and the TUC would agree to implement a European collective agreement in the United Kingdom; the same could e.g., be true for Switzerland. The personal scope of application of the agreement will depend on the content of the agreement itself, namely the kind of employers and employees which are meant to be covered: in principle all employers and employees, who fall within the territorial and *professional* scope of the collective agreement. The professional scope is determined by the sectors of activity for which the contracting social partners are competent. The agreement can apply to all undertakings which operate in the common market. It is in this context not relevant whether they are private or public (owned by the Government or other public authorities or operating under their control). The only important factor is whether they effect the functioning of the common market. The agreement can however not apply to the public sector *sensu stricto*, i.e., those institutions which involve direct or indirect participation in the exercise of powers conferred by public law in the discharge of functions whose purpose is to safeguard the general interests of the State or of other public authorities.[1]

1. *Cfr. Lawrie-Blum* v. *Land Baden-Würtemberg*, 3 July 1986, No. 66/85, IELL. *Case Law*, No. 98.

5. Binding Effect

572. As far as the binding effect of the agreement is concerned we must distinguish between the obligatory and the normative part of the agreement. The binding effect of the *obligatory part* will depend on the law applicable to the contract. If this is Belgian, as e.g., the agreement was concluded in Brussels and parties did not choose another legal system, the relations between the contracting parties might be governed by the Belgian Act of 5 December 1968 on joint committees and collective agreements, with all the problems this involves.

573. The binding effect of the agreement on *the members of the contracting parties*, e.g., on the national confederations of employers as far as UNICE is concerned, will depend on the by-laws of UNICE. The obligations resulting from those by-laws may eventually be sanctioned by disciplinary measures in case of non-compliance. At any rate, there is on the basis of Article 4 of the Protocol no legal obligation whatsoever for any national association to put a European collective agreement on the national negotiation table, nor is there an obligation of result, namely that there should be a collective agreement at national level. Mandatory bargaining does indeed not belong to a widespread European tradition.[1]

1. A legal obligation for some forms of mandatory bargaining does, however, exist in France, Luxemburg, Portugal and Spain and for some issues in Denmark and the Netherlands.

574. The only obligation which exists for members of contracting parties, like employers' associations or trade unions, may follow, as indicated earlier, from the by-laws of their respective European organisations and may oblige them to engage in collective bargaining at national or lower levels. It is questionable however whether e.g., an individual employee could sue either a national employers' organisation or a trade union, which does not start to bargain on the issues, laid down in the European agreement. Much will depend here on the status of national law and the rights of third parties relating to contractual or other obligations others may have.

575. Implementation of the *normative part* of the European collective agreement will consist, as the declaration in the final act of the Maastricht Conference indicates, in developing collective bargaining according to the rules of each Member State. Here problems arise as certain Member States do not have procedures to provide for an *erga omnes* effect of collective agreements, while at the same time, the binding effect of the collective agreements, as far the hierarchy of legal sources (legislation, work rules, individual agreements, custom . . .) is concerned, differs considerably from country to country. Some Member States have procedures of extension of agreements to the private sector as a whole, others do not. In certain countries, the non-compliance with a collective agreement, thus extended, is penally sanctioned, while in other countries no penal sanctions apply.

Thus, there are no real guarantees that the agreements will be fully and *erga omnes* implemented through normal (national) collective bargaining structures or mechanisms. In order to obtain an *erga omnes* effect with a comparable legal outcome, consequently one is, in attendance of further legislative Community developments in this area, *de facto* bound to turn to the Council for a decision.

6. Interpretation

576. As has already been indicated, the European Court does not seem to be competent to handle any preliminary question regarding the interpretation of a European collective agreement, given the wording of Article 177 of the EC Treaty, whereby preliminary questions are limited to actions of the Community Institutions. Interpretation mechanisms may however be provided for by the contracting parties themselves in the collective agreement, either by way of conciliation or even arbitration mechanisms. National courts could also be called upon to rule on the meaning of the language of European collective agreements. As a general rule, the party, seeking interpretation, will, in order to qualify as a litigating party, have to give evidence of a manifest interest.

The first Collective Agreement, namely on Parental Leave provides, in its final provisions (6), that 'without prejudice to the respective role of the Commission, national courts and the Court of Justice, any matter relating to the interpretation of this agreement at European level should, in the first instance, be referred by the Commission to the signatory parties who will give an opinion.' That opinion, obviously, has only an indicative nature and is not binding. Final binding decisions on the interpretation of the agreement will be made by the Court of Justice.

Parties could obviously conclude an interpretative agreement that could be rendered binding by a Council decision, but that is another matter.

7. Duration

577.   Parties will have to lay down in their agreements, rules concerning the duration and termination of the agreement: as a general rule, agreements are either for an indefinite or a fixed duration. In case of an indefinite duration a period of notice and certain formalities might be provided for. The national law, applying to the agreement, will then have to be followed.

The Agreement on Parental Leave is for an indefinite period. It does not contain provisions to denounce the agreement partly or totally. It has, however, a clause that parties will review the application of the agreement after the date of the Council decision if requested by one of the parties. This does not take away that either party has the right to denounce the agreement at any time. In that case, the directive might become an empty shell.

B. Implementation by Council Decision

578.   Much of what has been said about the implementation by national procedures is also relevant to the implementation of a European collective agreement by way of a Council decision. We limit ourselves to a number of specific points.

As indicated earlier, the first Inter-Industry wide European Collective Agreement on Parental Leave, was implemented by a directive of 4 June 1996.

1. Which Agreements?

579.   It is evident that the collective agreements which qualify the first to be implemented by a Council decision are the European multi-industry agreements, which cover all employers and all employees. It is indeed these agreements which are meant to replace Council directives, which apply in principle to all employers and employees of the Community. One can however not exclude *a priori* the possibility of implementing by way of a Council decision sectorial, regional or even European company agreements. First, the text of the Maastricht Agreement is fairly general and not limited to exclusively inter-industry wide collective agreements. Secondly, one has to respect and to promote, also in view of full implementing the subsidiarity principle, the dynamism and the autonomy of collective bargaining. In other words a decision by the Council implementing collective agreements, other than inter-industry-wide is not only *de jure* but also *de facto* a viable possibility.

2. Content

580.   The content of the agreement has to be limited to matters covered by Article 2, paragraphs 1 and 3, which were enumerated above. It seems to me that the Council has to accept or reject the text of the agreement as a whole and that it cannot change the content or retain only a part of the agreement, unless the contracting parties and the Commission agree. The Council decision will only implement the normative part of the agreement. Actually, it does not seem necessary that the decision should cover the contractual relations (obligatory part of the collective agreement) between the parties as well.

3. Scope

581.   The *territorial scope* of the agreement will, self-evidently, be limited to the territory of the 14 Member States. The decision will effect the EFTA countries in the framework of the EEA Agreement.

4. Binding Effect

582.   The binding effect of the decision will depend on the instrument which the Council decides to use: a regulation, a directive or a decision. Here the Council is the guardian of the *erga omnes* effect. This means that the European agreement, in case of a regulation or a directive, will supersede national legislation and national collective agreements, work rules, individual agreements and the like. Such a Council decision could also, it seems to me, amend or abolish previous regulations, directives or recommendations.

One may ask whether multi-industry Community agreements, implemented by a Council decision, would also supersede sectorial agreements or regional or company agreements, which are also implemented by a Council decision. The answer seems, in the present state of affairs, to be positive, in the sense that the higher collective agreement contains minimum standards which agreements at a lower level have to respect and can expand. As indicated earlier the Council always has the last word and can at all times withdraw its decision implementing the agreement or adopt another instrument, which simply amends or abolishes the collective agreement completely or partially.

The Collective Agreement on Parental Leave was, as indicated earlier, implemented by way of a directive. This seems to be the logical path, since it is a framework agreement leaving much to be filled in at national level, either by the Member States or by the competent social partners. The directive is binding on the Member States as to the results to be achieved, but leaves them the choice of form and method.

5. Interpretation

583.   In case of a Council decision the agreement is self-evidently up for eventual interpretation by the European Court pursuant to the relevant Treaty provisions concerning preliminary questions.

Again, the contacting parties may elaborate their proper arrangements to settle interpretation problems, e.g., by way of conciliation or arbitration.

Regarding the Collective Agreement on Parental Leave, we refer to A.6 of this section.

6. Master or Slave

584.   The relation between the (European collective) agreement and the Council decision implementing the agreement is of the utmost importance. The question arises indeed whether the collective agreement will through the implementation procedure become incorporated in the Council decision and thus *de jure* disappear, as being absorbed by the Council decision, cease to exist or whether the agreement will continue to live its own life and the decision is thus only giving an *erga omnes* effect to an agreement, which remains in a sense in the hands of the contracting parties. Much will depend on how the Council decision will be constructed: whether the decision will simply absorb the text of the agreement or whether the decision will state that the (following) agreement has become implemented by a Council decision. In the latter case, the agreement remains the property of the social partners, which can denounce the agreement at their will or following the provisions of the agreement, if they want to do so, which otherwise would not be possible. In that case the Council decision would become an empty shell. It is appropriate, in order to respect to a maximum the autonomy of the social partners, not to follow the road of incorporation of the agreement into the Council decision.

The directive of 3 June 1996, implementing the Collective Agreement on Parental Leave, respected the autonomy of the social partners by giving binding force to the agreement, which was published as an annex to the Directive. The text of the agreement was thus not amended in any way. The European Parliament, however, complained that it was not really involved and could only come in, after the text was agreed upon by the social partners and the Commission had taken the steps for implementation by a Council decision.

Chapter 2. Workers' Participation

§1. INFORMATION AND CONSULTATION

585. Under this heading we pay special attention to the so-called Vredeling proposal,[1] named after the then social Commissioner H. Vredeling, which was adopted by the Commission on 24 October 1980 concerning the information and consultation of employees employed in undertakings with a complex structure, especially *multinational enterprises.*[2] The target of the proposal was both the national enterprise and the group as a whole, so that local management would be in a position to give the employees of the subsidiary a clear picture of the activities of the undertaking as a whole, when this undertaking operates in various' countries. Secondly, the proposal intended to provide for the local workers' representatives to have access to top management when information at a local level would be insufficient. Finally its purpose was that local management would be able to provide the workers' representatives with adequate information at a local level and with consultation opportunities regarding important decisions affecting local conditions that would be taken at distant headquarters.

1. One should also mention the following proposals, which provide for a certain role to be played by workers (participation, or if not possible, at least information and consultation):
   – Proposal for a Council Directive supplementing the statute for a European association with regard to the involvement of employees, O.J., 21 April 1992, No. C-99;
   – Proposal for a Council Directive supplementing the statute for a European cooperative society with regard to the involvement of employees, O.J., 21 April 1992, No. C-99;
   – Proposal for a Council Directive supplementing the statute for a European mutual society with regard to the involvement of employees, O.J., 21 April 1992, No. C-99.
2. *See further* for a more detailed study: R. Blanpain, F. Blanquet and others, *The Vredeling Proposal, Information and Consultation of Employees in Multinational Enterprises*, Kluwer, 1983, 219 p.

586. According to the proposal, at least every six months the management of the parent company would forward to the local management information concerning the group as a whole and relating in particular to:

a. structure and manning;
b. the economic and financial situation;
c. the situation and probable development of business and production and sales;
d. the employment situation and probably trends;
e. production and investment programmes;

f. rationalisation plans;
g. manufacturing and working methods, in particular the introduction of new work methods;
h. all procedures and plans able to have a substantial effect on employees' interests.

The management of the subsidiary will forward this information to the workers' representatives. If the information is not available, then the representatives are allowed to request that information from top management (the famous by-pass of local management by the employees).

587. Where the management of a dominant undertaking proposes to take a decision concerning the whole or a major part of the dominant undertaking or one of its subsidiaries which is liable to have substantial effects on the interests of its employees, it is required to forward precise information to the management of each of its subsidiaries within the Community not later than 40 days before the adoption of the decision, giving details of:

– the grounds for the proposed decision;
– the legal, economic and social consequences of such a decision for the employees concerned;
– the measures planned in respect to the employees.

This information must be given in the case of decisions relating to:

a. the closure or transfer of an establishment or a major part thereof;
b. restrictions, extensions or substantial modifications to the activities of the under-taking;
c. major modifications with regard to organisation;
d. the introduction of long-term cooperation with other undertakings or the cessation of such cooperation.

The management of the subsidiary is required to communicate this information without delay to the workers' representatives and to ask for their opinion within a period of not less than 30 days. In the case of decisions likely to have a direct effect on the employees' terms of employment and conditions, the management of the subsidiary is required to hold consultations with the workers' representatives with a view to reaching agreement on the measures planned in respect of the employees. Where the information is not communicated or consultations do not take place as required, another access to top management is possible (another by-pass of local management).

588. Few proposals have aroused such heated debate as the Vredeling proposal. Both camps entrenched themselves. Everybody proclaimed that employees were entitled to information and consultation. The way in which this had to be organised

and the dimension involved were other matters. A consensus between the social partners seemed impossible and moreover the governments were deeply divided. An amended proposal for a directive on procedures for informing and consulting employees of 13 July 1983 was equally unsuccessful and the Vredeling proposal was buried. The problem was postponed and was to be discussed in 1989, but nothing happened and Vredeling belongs to history. As indicated above, the Commission would within the framework of the social action programme of 1990, prepare an 'instrument concerning the information and consultation of employees.' This took the form of a proposal for a directive on the establishment of a *European Works Council* in Community-scale undertakings or groups of undertakings for the purpose of informing and consulting employees (*see further* §4).

§2. PARTICIPATION IN THE PUBLIC LIMITED LIABILITY COMPANIES

589.   Pursuant to its coordinating mission, contained in Article 54, §3G of the EEC Treaty, the Council and the Commission have, within the framework of the freedom of establishment, elaborated many directives aiming at the coordination of national legislation relating to public limited liability companies, e.g., the aforementioned directives concerning the mergers and divisions of public limited liability companies. For many years, there has been a proposal on the table concerning the structure of public limited companies. The first proposal dates from 1972. It was amended in 1983: for a fifth directive concerning the structure of public limited liability companies and the powers and obligations of their organs.[1] One of the reasons why this initiative, after 20 years, has not been successful is the fact that it contains provisions relating to workers' participation. The 'whereas' underlines that whereas the laws of certain Member States provide for employee participation within the supervisory board or administrative organ and no such provision exists in other Member States, the Commission is of the opinion that the provision should be made for such participation in all Member States. In order to respect the different national systems as much as possible and to reach some degree of worker participation, the Commission proposals allow Member States to choose different models of workers' participation within the framework of a one-tier system or a two-tier system of companies. These proposals concerning workers' participation, which we will analyze further on, met with unconditional resistance from the employers and from certain Member States, which evidently underlined that they are in favour of workers' participation, but contend that this is a matter of national concern in conformity with the subsidiarity rule; that no legislative intervention is needed, certainly not at a Community level, and that the matter must be left to spontaneous relationships between both sides of industry. The ETUC, from its side, is disappointed that the proposals of the Commission do not go further since none of the proposed models gives the workers sufficient influence on management decision-making. Part of the controversy is whether this question can be dealt with by means of qualified majority voting in the Council, or whether unanimity is needed.

1. 19 August 1983, O.J., 9 September 1983, No. C-240.

590.   The proposal departs from the fact that there are in the Community at present two different sets of arrangements concerning the organisation of the administration of this type of company. One of these provides for one administration organ only (one-tier) while the other provides for two, namely a management organ responsible for managing the business of the company and an organ responsible for controlling the management body (two-tier). In practice, the Commission remarks in the 'whereas,' even under those arrangements which provide for only one administrative organ, a *de facto* distinction is often made between executive members who manage the business of the company and the non-executive members who confine themselves to supervision. In both systems a clear demarcation is desirable between the responsibilities of the persons charged with one or other of these duties; the general introduction of such a distinction will facilitate the formation of public limited companies by members or groups of members from different Member States and, thereby, the interpenetration of undertakings within the Community. Furthermore, the Commission indicates, the general introduction of the two-tier system on a compulsory basis is for the time being impracticable though such systems should be made generally available at least as an option for public limited companies; one-tier systems may therefore be maintained provided they are endowed with certain characteristics designed to harmonise their functioning with that of two-tier structures. Consequently, the Member States shall provide that the company shall be organised according to a two-tier system (management organ and supervisory organ); they may however permit the company to have a choice between a two-tier system and a one-tier system (administrative organ) (Art. 2 §1).

I. The Structure of the Company

A. *The Two-Tier System*

591.   In a dualistic or two-tier system the company is managed by a management organ under the supervision of a supervisory organ. Where the management organ has several members, a member will be appointed who is more particularly responsible for the questions of personnel and employee relations (Art. 3). The members of the supervisory board are appointed by the general meeting of shareholders (Art. 4, §1).

592.   The supervisory organ has wide-ranging informative powers: the management organ shall, not less than every three months, send to the supervisory organ a written report on the progress of the company affairs; this will present the draft annual accounts and a draft annual report; the supervisory organ receives on request a special report on the affairs of the company or on certain aspects thereof (Art. 11). Moreover, the authorisation of the supervisory organ must be obtained for decisions of the management organ relating to:

a. the closure or transfer of the undertaking or of substantial parts thereof;
b. substantial curtailment or extension of the activities of the undertaking;

c. substantial organisational changes within the undertaking;
d. establishment of long-term cooperation with other undertakings on the termination thereof (Art. 12).

B. The One-Tier System

593.   In the one-tier system the company is managed by the executive members of an administrative organ under the supervision of the non-executive members of that organ. The executive members of the administrative organ are appointed by the non-executive members. Where the administrative organ has more than one executive member, one of them will be more particularly responsible for questions of personnel and employee relations (Art. 21, §2).

594.   The competences of the members of the administrative organ are *grosso modo* the same as those of the members of the two-tier system. The executive members of the administrative board present, not less than every three months, to the non-executive members a written report on the progress of the company's affairs; the executive members present them with the draft annual accounts and the draft annual report; the non-executive members receive, at their request, a special report on the affairs of the company or on certain aspects thereof (Art. 21R). The administrative organ is not able to delegate power to decide on the following operations:

a. the closure or the transfer of the undertaking or substantial parts thereof;
b. substantial curtailment or extension of the activities of the undertaking;
c. substantial organisational changes within the undertaking;
d. establishment of long-term operation with other undertakings or the termination thereof (Art. 21S).

II. Models of Participation

595.   In elaborating the different models of workers' participation, the Commission has inspired itself on various ways in which participation is organised in the Member States. Four models were retained:

– the German model;
– the Dutch Model;
– employee participation through a body representing company employees;
– participation through collectively agreed systems.

596.   Member States may however provide that employee participation shall not be implemented in respect of a company when a majority of employees has expressed its opposition to such participation (Art. 4, §2 and 21B §2).

597. In the *German (two-tier) system*, elected employees or trade-unionists are members of the supervisory organ of the company. They constitute one third of the members in companies which employ from 500 to 2,000 employees. If one third is more than three, trade-unionists can have a seat in the board. In companies that employ 2,000 employee or more, a system of quasi-parity prevails in the supervisory organ. There are namely as many members representing the shareholders as there are members representing the employees. The chairperson of the supervisory organ, however, is always a representative of the shareholders and has a casting vote in he case of deadlock. It should be mentioned that this latter German model provides for a specific place in the supervisory organ of a representative of the (higher) middle-management, namely of the so-called '*leitende Angestellten.*' This representative is chosen out of a list of two, nominated by the '*leitende Angestellten,*' by all the white-collar workers, '*leitende Angestellten*' included.

598. The *Dutch (two-tier) model* starts from the reasoning that there is no room in the supervisory organ either for employees or for trade-union representatives. In order to avoid unnecessary confrontation and to guarantee a smooth decision-making process a system of co-option has been set up. Under this model, whenever a vacancy in the board comes up, the remaining members of the board will co-opt candidates from a list of candidates, nominated separately by shareholders, management and the works council, which is composed of employees only in the Netherlands. Out of these nominees, the remaining members of the board will choose a new member. That new member can neither be an employee or a trade-unionist, as indicated, but should be an independent and socially accepted person. If one of the groups (shareholders, management or works council) is of the opinion that the co-opted nominee does not qualify, it can pronounce a veto against him or her in which situation the case can be brought before the 'Enterprise Chamber' (Court) of Amsterdam, which will decide whether to sustain or not sustain the veto. It is self-evident that trade unions have lists of social commissionaires candidates, which they provide to the works council, and that there is a *de facto* concertation among the groups involved in order to arrive at a consensus.

599. Employee participation *through a body representing company employees* means that a kind of workers' council is established at the level of the enterprise which has the right, in relation to the company's management organ, to regular information and consultation on the administration, situation, progress and prospects of the company, its competitive position, credit situation and investment plans. It also has the same rights to information as those conferred on the members of the supervisory organ or the non-executive members of the administrative organ. The workers' representatives need furthermore to be consulted in cases in which the supervisory organ needs to grant authorisation (closure, transfer, etc.). If the opinion of the employees' representatives is not followed by management, the reasons for this decision must be communicated.

600. The last system, proposed by the Commission, is *employee participation through collectively agreed systems*. In this model, employee participation is regulated in accordance with collective agreements concluded between the company and organisations representing its employees. These collective agreements will provide for comparable rights to information and consultation as in the other models.

A. The Two-Tier System

601.   In the two-tier system, Member States can choose (for companies of 1,000 or more) between:

– the German system: the members of the supervisory organ shall be appointed by the general meeting with, as far as the shareholders' representatives are concerned, a maximum of two-thirds and, as far as the workers' representatives are concerned, by a minimum of one-third but subject to a maximum of one-half; in any case voting procedures must ensure that the shareholders' representatives have the last word (quasi-parity) (Art. 4B);
– the Dutch system: the members of the supervisory board are appointed by that organ. However, the shareholders or the workers' representatives may object to the appointment of a proposed candidate on the grounds that either he lacks the ability to carry out the duties or, if he were appointed, the supervisory organ would be improperly constituted. In that case the appointment shall not be made unless the objection is declared unfounded by an independent body existing under public law (Art. 4C);
– employee participation through a body representing company employees (Art. 4D);
– employee participation through collectively agreed systems (Art. 4E).

Netherlands

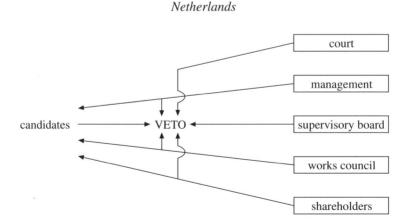

Germany

Supervisory Board: companies 500 < employees ≤ 2,000

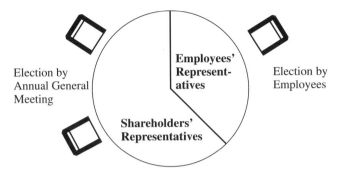

At least 3 members, for limited companies and corporations
(≤ 2,000 employees)

Germany

≥ 2,000 employees

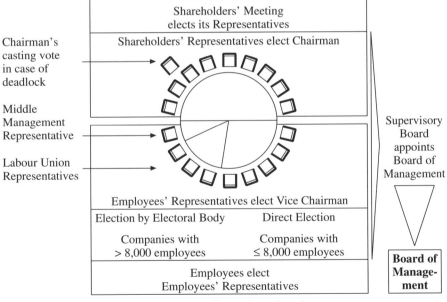

Election to Supervisory Board

602.   The proposed directive contains a number of guarantees with the aim of safeguarding a number of fundamental democratic rights. Member States must ensure that the following principles are observed:

a. the relevant members of the supervisory organ and workers' representatives shall be elected in accordance with systems of proportional representation ensuring that minors are protected;
b. all employees must be able to participate in the election;
c. all elections shall be by secret ballot;
d. free expression of opinion shall be guaranteed (Art. 4I).

B. The One-Tier System

603.   In the one-tier system, the following three systems are retained:

– the non-executive members of the administrative organ are appointed by the general meeting of shareholders by a maximum of two-thirds and by employees of the company by a minimum of one-third but subject to a maximum of one-half; in any event voting procedures should ensure that the representatives of the shareholders have the last word (Art. 21D);
– employee participation through a body representing company employees (Art. 21E);
– employee participation through collectively agreed systems (Art. 21F).

§3. THE SOCIETAS EUROPAEA (SE)

I. More than 20 Years of Discussion

604.   The first proposal for a regulation on the statute for a European company (Societas Europaea, SE) dates from 1970; the proposal was amended in 1975. Recently, the idea was revitalised with a proposal for a Council regulation on the statute for a European Company, on the one hand, and a directive complementing the statute for a European Company with regard to the involvement of employees in the European Company, on the other, both of 25 August 1989.[1] In 1991, amended proposals were made.[2] The proposal remains, after more than 20 years, as controversial as it was in 1970.

    1. O.J., 16 October 1989, No. C-263.
    2. O.J., 29 May 1991, No. C-138 and 8 July 1991, Nos. C-178/1.

605.   In the reformulation of its proposals, the Commission took account of the new dimension by the Single Act of 1986, on the one hand, and of the dynamics of the 1992 project, on the other. The completion of the internal market and the improvement it must bring about in the economic and the social situation throughout the Community, mean not only that barriers to trade must be removed, but also that the structures of production must be adapted to the Community dimensions.

For this purpose it is essential that companies whose business is not limited to satisfying purely local needs should be able to plan and carry out the reorganisation of their business on a Community-wide scale. In the actual state of affairs companies still have to choose a form of company governed by a particular national law. The legal framework within which business must still be carried on in Europe, as it is still based entirely on national laws, no longer applies to the creation of groups consisting of companies from different Member States. It is thus essential to ensure as far as possible that the economic unit and the legal unit of business in Europe coincide.

606.   The essential objective of the legal rules governing a European company is to make it possible for companies from different Member States to merge or to create a holding company, and to enable companies or other legal bodies carrying on economic activities and governed by the law of different Member States, to form a joint subsidiary. Companies may be formed throughout the Community under the form of a European public limited company (SE). The capital of the SE shall be divided into shares. The liability of the shareholders for the debts and obligations of the company shall be limited to the amount subscribed by them. The SE is a commercial company whatever the object of its undertaking. It shall have legal personality (Art. 1 regulation). The capital of the SE amounts to no less than ECU 1,000,000 (Art. 4). It should be pointed out that the statute is not legally binding, but voluntary: the companies are free to choose it or not.

607.   The proposed statute is legally based upon Article 100A of the EEC Treaty. This is of course important, since proposals based on Article 100A can be adopted by qualified majority. This is obviously a controversial point, certainly as regards taxes. It is also remarkable that workers' participation is the subject of a separate instrument, namely, a directive based upon Article 54 of the EEC Treaty, within the framework of freedom of establishment in which different directives aiming at the approximating of national legislation regarding limited liability companies have been enacted. We should also point out that the proposed directive retains the one-tier system as well as the two-tier system, similar to the proposed Vth directive, to which we basically refer as far as organs of the company and their competences are concerned. In a nutshell: the Vth directive aims at the coordination of national legalisations; the SE has a uniform European system as its target. Both proposals are inspired by the same principles regarding workers' participation.

II. Models of Participation

608.   Workers' participation in the SE is regulated by the proposed directive of 25 August 1989, with the exception of Article 33 of the regulation of the same date, pursuant to which:

> 'the administrative or management of each of the founder companies shall discuss with its workers' representatives the legal economic and employment implications of the formation of a SE holding company for the employees and any measures proposed to deal with them.'

The 'whereas' to the proposed directive indicates that in order to promote the economic and social objectives of the Community, arrangements should be made for employees to participate in the supervision and strategic development of the SE. The great diversity of rules and practices existing in the Member States regarding the manner in which employees' representatives participate make it possible to lay down uniform rules on the involvement of employees in the SE. This means that account should be taken of the specific characteristics of the laws of the Member States by establishing for the SE a framework comprising several models of participation, and authorising first Member States to choose the model best corresponding to their national traditions, and secondly, the management or administrative board, as the case may be, and the workers' representatives of the SE or of its founder companies to choose the model most suited to their social environment. The directive forms an indispensable complement to the provisions of the regulation and it is therefore necessary to ensure that the two sets of provisions are applied concomitantly. An SE may not be formed unless one of the systems of the workers' participation has been chosen (Art. 3, §2).

609. The involvement of employees means the participation 'in the supervision and strategic development of the SE' (Art. 2). A distinction must however be made between the registered office and the establishments of the SE. The status and duties of the workers' representatives in the establishment is determined by national law. Regarding the registered office, Member States can choose between four models, just as for the Vth directive. Each Member State determines the manner in which the participation models shall be applied for a SE having its registered office in its territory (Art. 3, §4). Each Member State may retain all models or restrict its choice to one or more models (Art. 3, §5).

610. The models retained by the Commission are the following:

– the *German model*: the members of the supervisory board or the administrative board are at least by one-third and not more than one-half appointed by the employees or their representatives (model 1) (Art. 4, 1st indent);
– the *Dutch model*: co-option by the board. However, the general meeting of shareholders or the workers' representatives may, on specific grounds, object to the appointment of a particular candidate. In such cases, the appointment may not be made until an independent body established under public law has declared the objection inadmissible (model 2) (Art. 4, 2nd indent);
– a separate body shall represent the employees of the SE. The number of members of that body and the detailed rules governing their election or appointment shall be laid down in the statutes in consultation with the workers' representatives of the founder companies in accordance with the law or practices of the Member States (Art. 5, §1). These representative have rights to information and consultation comparable to those provided for in the proposed Vth directive (model 3);
– another model may be established by means of an agreement concluded between the management boards and the administrative boards of the founder companies and the employees or their representatives in those companies. The parties to the negotiation may be assisted by experts of their choice at the expense of the

founder companies. The agreement may be concluded for a fixed period and renegotiated at the expiry of that period. However, the agreement concluded shall remain in force until the entry into force of the new agreement. Where the two parties to the agreement so decide, or where no such agreement can be reached, a standard model provided by the law of the State shall apply. This model shall ensure, for the employees, at least the rights of information and consultation as mentioned (Art. 6) (model 4).

611. The model to be applied shall be determined by an agreement concluded between the management board and the administrative boards of the founder companies and the workers' representatives of those companies, as provided by the laws and practices of the Member States. Where no agreement can be reached, the management and the administrative boards shall choose the model applicable to the SE (Art. 3, §1). A chosen model may always be replaced by another by means of an agreement. The workers' representatives of the SE shall be elected in accordance with systems which appropriately take into account the number of staff they represent. All the employees must be able to participate in the vote (Art. 7). The first time, the workers' representatives of the SE shall be appointed by the workers' representatives of the founder companies in proportion to the number of employees they represent (Art. 8). The workers' representatives receive such financial material resources as enable them to meet and perform their duties in an appropriate manner (Art. 9).

Employee participation in the capital or in the profits or losses or the SE may be organised by means of a collective agreement (Art. 11).

612. In a *Communication on worker information and consultation* of 14 November 1995,[1] the Commission relaunched the debate on workers' participation and indicated possible directions for Community action:

'Various options are possible.

Option 1: maintain the status quo
This option would mean continuing the discussions in the Council on the basis of the existing proposals and maintaining the fragmented approach to Community action on employee information, consultation and involvement. The main disadvantage of this option is that as things stand, it seems to offer little hope of progress.

Option 2: global approach
This option involves a change in the way of looking at the whole question. Instead of attempting to establish, at Community level, sets of specific rules for each entity to be covered by Community rules on company law, attempts would be made to establish a general framework at European level on informing and consulting employees. This would make it possible to withdraw the proposals for directives annexed to the proposals for regulations on the statute for a European company, a European association, a European co-operative society and a European mutual society. The same would apply to the social provisions in the proposal for the "*fifth directive*" and the "*Vredeling proposal*".

Given that the European Community already has a legal framework for employee information and consultation at transnational level, this global approach would mean quite simply that a Community instrument on information and consultation at national level would have to be adopted. Before taking this approach, a number of questions need to be answered: Would it be in keeping with the principles of subsidiarity and proportionality? What would be the nature of the proposal (approximation of legislation or establishment of minimum requirements)? and, lastly, Which legal basis should be used (Treaty or Maastricht Social Agreement)?

The main advantage of this option is that it is a step towards simplifying Community law and European social policy. It could also make it easier – and, in fact, might even be necessary – to achieve progress with the above-mentioned proposals, since the businesses concerned which are of purely national scale would then be covered by this general framework.

Option 3: immediate action on the proposals concerning the statute for a European company, a European association, a European co-operative society and a European mutual society
If the global approach set out above is adopted, immediate steps could be taken to unlock these proposals, especially the proposal on the statute for a European company, the adoption of which is particularly urgent. This would be justified by the importance of this instrument for the organisation of companies at European level and by the urgent need to find a legal vehicle which meets the needs of major trans-European transport infrastructure projects (the Member States have indicated that they will need two years to introduce the implementing provisions for the Statute, in spite of its immediate legal effect).

This could be done in two ways:

The above-mentioned proposals for directives would be withdrawn on the same condition, *mutatis mutandis*, as that set out in Article 136 of the proposal for a regulation on the statute for a European company, which stipulates that no European company, European association, European co-operative society or European mutual society could be set up in a Member State which had not transposed the "*European Works-Councils*" Directive.

This solution would have the advantage of maintaining the compulsory link between the establishment of these organisations and their application of the procedures for employee information and consultation, which has always been a key element in these proposals. It would also prevent discrimination between these organisations depending on the Member State in which they decided to locate their registered office.

No conditions would be attached to the withdrawal of these proposals. In this case, only the Community provisions in force (the "*European Works Councils*", "*collective redundancies*" and "*business transfers*" Directives) would be applicable to the organisations concerned, as appropriate.

The disadvantage of this sub-option is that one Member State is not covered by the "*European Works Councils*" Directive. This would mean that the European companies, European associations, European co-operative societies and European mutual societies which are of multinational scale and have their registered offices in this Member State would not be subject to the same obligations in the area of transnational information and consultation of employees, as would be the case for organisations with their registered office in another Member State.

The arguments set out above are provided as a contribution to the discussion which the Commission would like to see developed among the Member States, in the EP and the ESC and between the social partners at Community level. The Commission reaffirms that it is open to any way of achieving the objectives at the heart of this debate. These are, first, to put an end to the unacceptable situation of never-ending institutional discussion of the above-mentioned proposals and, second, to supplement the Community legal framework in the area of employee information and consultation and to make it more coherent and effective.

The Commission would like to receive the comments and views of the Member States, the EP, the ESC and the social partners at European level on these matters. It is particularly interested in knowing their views on the options set out in this communication.'

612bis.   The discussion got a new lease of life, thanks to the expert group, presided over by Mr. E. Davignon, a leading industrialist and former vice-president of the European Commission. The group of experts on 'European systems of worker involvement' was set up in November 1996.

The group was given as its main task the following by the Commission: to examine the type of involvement rules to be applied to the European Company. It delivered its final report in May 1997.

The proposals of the Davignon group (1997)[2] can be summarized as follows. The group decided to limit its discussions to three of the four ways of setting up a European Company set out in the draft ECS:

– the merger of existing companies;
– the creation of a joint holding company; and
– the creation of a joint subsidiary.

The conversion of existing national public limited liability companies was not retained, in order to avoid the possibility of becoming a European Company in order to escape national systems.

All European Companies, whatever their number of employees, would have a system of worker involvement.[3] It follows the route of the EWC since it recommends that negotiation should be the primary method of establishing the worker involvement system. Only if these negotiations fail would a set of statutory 'reference rules' apply.

The report provides for detailed recommendations on the negotiating procedure for the European Company's worker involvement arrangements.

The employees would be represented by a negotiating body, made up of workers' representatives appointed 'in accordance with national practices and procedures'. Workers' representatives are entitled to the services of experts.

The content of the agreement would be flexible, but the report gives an indicative list of what the content of the agreement might be. Again, there is a parallel with the EWC.

If no agreement is reached, a set of reference rules will apply.

There are two forms of involvement:

– information and consultation through a group of employee representatives;
– the representation of employees on the European Company's board.

Workers' representatives would be members of the management board or supervisory board. Workers' representatives would make up one-fifth of the total members of the board in question, with a minimum of two members.

The employee representatives on the board would be full members.

The report was welcomed by the Council, by the EP, and the social partners.

612ter.   In the meantime, the Commission is continuing its consultations on its 1995 Communication. This may lead either to legislative proposals by the Commission, but probably also to an European collective agreement, if the social partners want to take that route.

1. COM(95)547 final.
2. 'European Company Statute revisited, European Works Council Bulletin', 1997, 10, 8–13.
3. 'All arrangements allowing workers' representatives to take part in company decision-making processes with a view to ensuring the collective expression and permanent consideration of their interests in the context of decisions concerning the management and economic and financial development of the company'.

§4. Information and Consultation: The Directive on European Works Councils or Procedures[1]

I. The Genesis of the Directive – A Spirit of Cooperation

A. Genesis

613.   Information and consultation of employees has always been part of the European social agenda, practically since the beginning of the 1960s. However, few issues have aroused such a heated debate. Now, after so many years, the adoption of a European Directive of 22 September 1994 on the establishment of an EWC or a procedure in Community-scale undertakings and Community-scale Groups of Undertakings for the purposes of informing and consulting employees is a fact. Within some years – at the latest by the year 2000 – Community-scale undertakings will be legally obliged to have an EWC or an information and consultation procedure. The directive will apply to enterprises which occupy at least 1,000 employees and have at least two subsidiaries in two Member States of the European Union (excluding the UK) and/or of the EEA-EFTA Countries with each at least 150 employees. It is estimated that some 2,000 companies will have to comply.

By no latter than 15 December 1999 the Directive will also apply to the UK.[2]

1. (94/95 EC) O.J., 30 September 1994, No. L254/65.
2. Council Directive 97/74 of 15 December 1997 extending to the UK Directive 94/45 (O.J., 16 January 1998, L 10/22).

614. The mandatory character of the directive has been widely criticised, especially from the employer's side. With this criticism in mind, the European Union wanted to promote as much as possible 'voluntarism' and encouraged the voluntary conclusion of agreements on information and consultation between the central management of the companies and the representatives of the employees even before the directive entered into force on 23 September 1996. Agreement prior to that date will continue to be valid even after 1997 and can be prolonged by the parties.

615. Thus, Community-scale undertakings and the representatives of the employees have a choice to make: whether they want to wait until the directive enters into force or whether they want to conclude a so-called preexisting agreement – in force – (Art. 13). Such an agreement leaves quite some flexibility to the parties, although a number of minimum requirements have to be lived up to.

616. On 5 December 1990, the Commission adopted a 'Proposal for a Council Directive on the Establishment of an EWC in Community-scale Undertakings or Groups of Undertakings for the Purposes of Informing and Consulting Employees.'
It has to be noted that the Commission's proposal (of 5 December 1990) has not yet been withdrawn by the Commission. This means that if the UK would 'want to adhere' to that directive, this could be done by a decision of the Council without any new procedure or proposals being necessary.

617. At none of its meetings did the Council reach unanimous agreement on the Commission's proposal, as required by the legal basis for the proposal (Article 100 of the EC Treaty). The Council did, however, establish, at its meeting on 12 October 1993, a broad consensus among the great majority of delegations on a text submitted by the Belgian Presidency. The Commission informed the Council of its intention to initiate, on entry into force of the Treaty on the European Union on 1 November 1993, the procedures provided for in the Agreement on Social Policy annexed to the Protocol on Social Policy on the basis of the text submitted by the Belgian Presidency and the views expressed in the course of the Council's discussions.

618. The Commission decided to set these procedures in motion. 18 November 1993 saw the commencement of a six-week period of consultation of the social partners at European level, in accordance with Article 3(2) of the Agreement on Social Policy, with the dispatch of a first consultative document on the possible direction of Commission's action in the field of information and consultation of workers in Community-scale undertakings or groups of undertakings. The employers' associations, federations and confederations and the trade unions submitted a general opinion to the Commission on the questions put to them.

619. On 8 February 1994, in accordance with Article 3(3) of the Agreement on Social Policy, the Commission decided to consult the social partners at Community level on the content of the proposal, including the possible legal basis for such a proposal.

620.   Indeed, on 8 February 1994 the Commission introduced a new proposal with a view to consultation with management and labour at European level on the content of the proposal envisaged by the Commission.

The proposal was only addressed to the 11 Member States which were signatories of the Agreement on Social Policy. The UK was therefore excluded.

The main body of the Flynn proposal was intended to provide for a legal framework within which an agreement can be concluded between central management and representatives of employees. The parties are free to set up the information and consultation mechanism most suited to their needs.

621.   By the deadline for this second phase of consultation (30 March 1994), the social partners sent to the Commission their views on the consultation document. Despite all the efforts made, the social partners failed to reach agreement on setting in motion the procedure provided for in Article 4 of the Agreement on Social Policy.

622.   On 13 April 1994 the Commission, taking the view that a Community initiative on the information and consultation of workers in Community-scale undertakings and groups of undertakings was still warranted, decided to adopt the present proposal, with a view to presenting it to the Council on the basis of Article 2(2) of the Agreement on Social Policy.

This proposal took over again most of the elements of the Belgian compromise, whilst reintroducing some greater elements of flexibility of the Flynn proposal. The opt-out of the UK from the Social Agreement was completely respected. The directive was adopted in first reading by the Council of Ministers on 22 June 1994.

623.   The directive was adopted in second reading on 22 September 1994, giving companies almost until the year 2000 to try to negotiate an information and consultation agreement with their employees.

623bis.   In accordance with the Amsterdam European Council of 16–17 June 1997, whereby the agreement was noted of the IGC to incorporate the Agreement of Social Policy in the Treaty, Directive 94/45EC was extended to the United Kingdom. This was done by Council Directive 97/74 of 15 December 1997.[1] The Directive will apply from 15 December 1999 onwards.

  1. O.J., 16 January 1998, L 10/22.

B. A Spirit of Cooperation

624.   Article 9 of the directive, concerning the operation of EWCs and information and consultation procedures for workers, orders parties, namely central management and the EWC 'to work in a spirit of cooperation with due regard to their reciprocal rights and obligations.' The same applies 'to cooperation between central management and employees' representatives in the framework of an information and consultation procedure for workers.' A similar obligation is also retained in Article 6(1) of the directive in relation to the negotiation of an agreement, which should take place 'in a spirit of cooperation with a view to reaching an agreement.'

625.   This deliberate choice for cooperation has many important consequences. It clearly:

1. aims at integrating the employees and their representatives in the undertaking as a going concern, at promoting their understanding and involvement in full respect of managerial prerogatives, thus backing the free market economy, but in a constructive, socially corrected way;
2. and consequently contains a rejection of the class-conflict model of IR at the same time furthering the model of harmony between management and labour.

626.   Another extremely important consequence is the fact that the directive contains in no way whatsoever a European mandate to engage in industrial warfare in whatever form. The directive gives no right to bargain on wages and conditions, nor to call for industrial action at European level. Neither the EWC nor the procedure can, legally speaking, be vehicles for international solidarity action between the various undertakings/establishments in the European enterprises.

The fact is that the Maastricht Agreement on Social Policy expressly excludes matters like the right to strike or the right to impose lock-outs, with the consequence that there is no legal basis for the establishment of such rights under the Maastricht Protocol and Agreement.

II. Objective and Scope of the Directive

A. *Objective*

627.   The purpose of the directive is to improve the right to information and to consultation of employees in Community-scale undertakings and groups of undertakings. To this end, appropriate mechanisms for transnational information and consultation (i.e., one or more EWCs or one or more procedures with the purpose of informing and consulting employees) have to be established in every Community-scale undertaking and every Community-scale group of undertakings, where this is requested (Art. 1,1).

B. *Scope*

1. Territorial

a. THE FOURTEEN EU MEMBER STATES (AND THE UK?)

628.   As the directive has been adopted under the Maastricht Agreement, its territorial application only relates to the 14 Member States, not to the UK, which has, as said, opted out of the Social Chapter.

So undertakings within the UK and their employees do not fall under the scope of the directive; the same goes for undertakings established outside the 14 Member States, taking into account what we will say about the EEA-EFTA countries later.

Community-scale undertakings and groups of undertakings with their central management in the UK will, of course, be subject to the same obligations as are imposed on undertakings and groups of undertakings from non-Community countries, insofar they fall under the conditions laid down in the directive: 1000 employees and 2 × 150 employees in two Member States and/or EEA-EFTA countries.

In accordance with the Amsterdam European Council of 16–17 June 1997, whereby the agreement was noted of the IGC to incorporate the Agreement of Social Policy in the Treaty, Directive 94/45EC was extended to the United Kingdom. This was done by Council Directive 97/74 of 15 December 1997.[1] The Directive will apply from 15 December 1999 onwards.

1. O.J., 16 January 1998, L 10/22.

b. THE EUROPEAN ECONOMIC AREA (14+2)
629. The EEA-EFTA countries are involved in the decision-making process leading to European legislation but have no voting rights. After a Community instrument is adopted by the Council of Ministers it then goes to the Joint Committee of the EEA which will decide whether the instrument will be translated in the national laws of the EEA-EFTA countries. Every EFTA country has to agree. So formally there is a kind of opting in the EU legislation by those Member States. If they opt in, the annexes to the EEA Treaty, which contains the list of applicable Community texts, is amended. The annexes contain a list of the applicable Community legislation. Whenever a new instrument is adopted, a corresponding amendment will be made to the annexes of the EEA Agreement.

630. This applies also to European measures taken in conformity with the Maastricht Agreement on Social Policy. Therefore, the directive on information and consultation of employees will have to be formally inserted in the law of the EEA-EFTA countries and theoretically at least, the opting in can be rejected. In practical terms however one is talking about an opting out since the EEA-EFTA countries are involved in the negotiations of the directive. The text which comes thus on the desk of the Council of Ministers is also the result of their input. Indeed, from the beginning it has been the intention that there should be one legal-economic-social area (with some exceptions) among the EEA Members. So the normal course of action is that the directive will also apply to such countries as Iceland and Norway.

c. COMPANIES WITH HEADQUARTERS OUTSIDE THE EEA
631. The directive also covers cases where undertakings or groups of undertakings have their headquarters outside the territory of the Member States. Where this is the case, such businesses should be treated in a similar way as Community-scale undertakings based on either a representative of the undertaking or group of undertakings or the undertaking with the highest number of employees in the territory of one of the Member States.

2. Personal: Which Companies?

632. The directive applies to private as well as to public undertakings, irrespective of whether they belong to the private or to the public (economic) sphere. The notion undertaking covers any legal form of undertaking. This notion, not explicitly defined in the directive, may be a parent company, a subsidiary, an establishment, a branch or any other form of economic entity.

An 'undertaking' may also consist of a group of subsidiaries, establishments and the like.

a. Numbers

633. According to the directive an EWC or a procedure for informing and consulting employees has to be established in every Community-scale undertaking and in every Community-scale group of undertakings (Art. 1,2).

(1) Community-scale Undertaking

634. A 'Community-scale undertaking' means an undertaking with at least 1,000 employees within the Member States and at least 150 employees in each of at least two of the addressed Member States.

Unless a broader scope is provided for by the agreement, the powers and competence of EWC(s) and the scope of information and consultation procedures cover, in the case of a Community-scale undertaking, all the establishments located within the Member States (Art. 1,4).

The prescribed workforce size thresholds is to be based on the average number of employees, including part-time employees, employed during the previous two years, calculated (*pro rata*) according to national legislation and/or practice (Art. 2,2).

635. The directive does not contain an express definition of the term employee. Considering that the directive intends to achieve only partial harmonisation of information and consultation processes in the EU, the term employee should be interpreted as covering any person who, in the Member State concerned, is considered to be an employee under national employment law. The same goes for the notion part-time worker, as is clearly indicated in Article 2,2.

636. The employees concerned must be employed by a Community-scale undertaking or establishment thereof. This means that temporary workers, working for the benefit of a Community-scale undertaking user and subcontracted or posted workers will not count as employees of that undertaking, unless national law and/or practice would indicate otherwise.

It seems that it is of no interest whether the employee is engaged as a blue-collar worker, a white-collar worker, a manager or an official (*fonctionnaire*) or even whether the terms on which he is employed come under public or private law.

637. The directive applies equally to employees engaged for an indefinite period as for those engaged for a fixed term contract, contracts for replacement and the like. The same normally goes for employees whose contract of employment is suspended for reason of sickness leave, military service and the like, again unless national law or practice would say otherwise.

638. Member States must ensure that information on the average number of employees is made available at the request of the parties concerned by the application of the directive (Art. 11,2).

(2) Group of Undertakings

639. A 'group of undertakings' comprises, according to Article 2(b), 1 of the directive, a controlling undertaking and its controlled undertakings.

640. The terms 'controlled undertaking' and 'controlling undertaking' are based on Council Directive 89/440/EEC of 18 July 1989, amending Directive 71/305 EEC concerning the coordination of procedures for the award of public works contracts.

641. For the purposes of the directive, a 'controlling undertaking' means an undertaking which can exercise a dominant influence over another undertaking ('the controlled undertaking') by virtue of, for example, ownership, financial participation or the rules which govern it (Art. 3,1).

Article 3,1 aims at covering all possible 'controlling undertakings.'

All undertakings, which may exercise a dominant influence can be deemed to fulfil the duties under the directive (Art. 4) and they themselves will have to decide which of them will be the 'controlling undertaking.' This can equally occur if employee representatives would differ on which company should be looked upon as the 'controlling undertaking.'

The ability to exercise a dominant influence shall be presumed, without prejudice to proof to the contrary, when, in relation to another undertaking, an undertaking directly or indirectly:

a. holds a majority of the undertaking's subscribed capital, or
b. controls a majority of the votes attached to that undertaking's issued share capital, or
c. can appoint more than half the members of the undertaking's administrative, managerial or supervisory body (Art. 3,2).

The controlling undertaking's rights as regards voting and appointment shall include the rights of any other controlled undertaking and those of any person or body acting in his or its own name but on behalf of the controlling undertaking or of any other controlled undertaking (Art. 3,3).

A dominant influence shall not be presumed to be exercised solely by virtue of the fact that an office holder is exercising his functions, according to the law of a Member State relating to liquidation, winding up, insolvency, cessation of payments, compositions or analogous proceedings (Art. 3,5).

642. The law applicable in order to determine whether an undertaking is a 'controlling undertaking' shall be the law of the Member State which governs that undertaking (Art. 3,6 para. 1).

As the possibility of exercising a dominant influence can be indicated by the central management, who can equally reverse the presumption of Article 3,2 central management seems to have a certain flexibility to choose the applicable law. The same applies in case of conflict of laws.

Where the law governing that undertaking is not that of a Member State, the law applicable shall be the law of the Member State within whose territory the representative of the undertaking or, in the absence of such a representative, the central management of the group undertaking which employs the highest number of employees in any one Member State is situated (Art. 3.6, para. 2).

In this case, central management can freely, without possible intervention of the employees, indicate which undertaking or person shall act as 'representative,' thereby choosing at the same time the law it wants to apply.

643. A 'Community-scale group of undertakings' means a group of undertakings with the following characteristics:

– at least 1,000 employees within the Member States; at least two group undertakings in different Member States; and
– at least one group undertaking having at least 150 employees in one Member State and at least one other group undertaking with at least 150 employees in another Member State (Art. 3,1(c)).

Where a Community-scale group of undertakings comprises one or more undertakings which are Community-scale undertakings, the EWC will be established at the level of the group, unless the agreement(s) provide(s) otherwise (Art. 1,3).

Unless a wider scope is provided for by the agreements, the powers and competence of EWCs and the scope of information and consultation procedures cover, in the case of a Community-scale undertaking all the establishments located within the Member State and in the case of a Community-scale group of undertakings, all group undertakings located within the Member States (Art. 1,4).

b. Central Management
644. 'Central management' means the central management of a Community-scale undertaking or, in the case of a Community-scale group of undertakings, of the controlling undertaking (Art. 2,1(e)).

c. Merchant Navy Crews
645. Member States may provide that this directive shall not apply to merchant navy crews (Art. 1,5).

III. Definitions and Notions

A. Information and Consultation

646. The directive does not contain a definition of the word 'information.' So we have to refer to the ordinary meaning attributed to that term in its context and by obtaining such guidance as may be derived from Community texts and from concepts common to the legal system of the Member States.

647. The meaning of the word '*information*' seems rather simple: it is the communication of knowledge. Disclosure of information to the representatives of employees means that the employer provides information of which explanation may be sought and questions can be raised.

648. *Consultation* has been defined by the directive on EWCs or procedures as 'the exchange of views and establishment of dialogue between employees' representatives and central management or any other more appropriate level of management' (Art. 2,1(f)).

649. Article 2,1(f) of the directive on the establishment of EWC or a procedure addresses these questions only in very broad terms when it states that exchange of views and dialogue will take place between the representatives of the employees and central management or any other appropriate level of management. First, this leaves the parties to the agreement free to decide which level of management would be more appropriate. Moreover, other questions will have to be worked out between the parties themselves, within the guidelines laid down in the directive, unless the parties would conclude a preexisting agreement.

B. Representation of Employees

650. The concept of 'employees' representatives' has to be seen in the light of Council Directives 75/129 EC on collective redundancies and 77/187/EC on transfer of undertakings. According to Article 2,1(d) of the directive on EWCs or procedures, 'employees' representatives' means the representatives of the employees as provided by national law and/or practice of the Member States. In contrast to the directive on transfer of undertakings, this directive does not exclude members of administrative, governing or supervisory bodies of companies, who represent employees on such bodies in certain Member States.

Unlike the above-mentioned directives on collective redundancies and transfer of undertakings, this directive on EWCs or procedures contains the very important provision that Member States must provide that employees in undertakings and/or establishments in which there are no employees' representatives through no fault of their own, have the right to elect or appoint members of the special negotiating body (Art. 5,2(a), second para.); this without prejudice to national legislation and/or practice laying down thresholds for the establishment of employee representation bodies (Art. 5,2(a), para. 3). This means among others that Member States may provide that only establishments with, e.g., at least 50 employees will participate in the election or appointment of members of the special negotiating body.

As the notion 'employees' representatives' refers to the laws or practice of the Member States, this implies that it might be possible for 'non-employees' (e.g., permanent trade union business agents) to be elected or appointed provided national law and/or practice would foresee this possibility.

IV. Establishment of an EWC or a Procedure

651. The establishment of an EWC or procedure by way of agreement between the parties takes different steps which have to be accomplished within a given period of time, at the latest within a period of three years after the initial request by the employees to initiate negotiations has been launched. So, if neither party moves, nothing will happen; the process can also be terminated by the special negotiating body, which may decide not to open negotiations or to cancel negotiations already opened, by a 2/3 majority of the members of the special negotiating body.

652. So the steps are:

– the request to initiate negotiations, either on the initiative of the employees' representatives or of the central management;
– the establishment of the negotiating body;
– the convening of a negotiating meeting;
– the conclusion of an agreement.

All this has to be accomplished within a time span of three years after the request to initiate negotiations. If not, the subsidiary requirements will apply. These rules can be evaded if parties conclude an agreement before the date of entry into force of the directive.

The same applies *ceteris paribus* in case of renegotiation of the agreement with this understanding that the existing EWC (or its members employees) will constitute the negotiating body (*see* Annex – subsidiary requirements 1,f, 2nd para.).

653. In case the subsidiary requirements apply and an EWC has been established, that EWC shall examine, four years after its establishment, whether to open negotiations for the conclusion of the agreement referred to in Article 6 or to continue to apply the subsidiary requirements adopted in accordance with the annex (Annex 1(f), para. 1). This brings us somewhere near the year 2004.

A. The Obligation to Negotiate in a Spirit of Cooperation

654. The directive contains a mandatory duty for the parties to negotiate, namely 'in a spirit of cooperation with a view to reaching an agreement on the detailed arrangements for implementing the information and consultation of employees' (Art. 6,1). This mandatory requirement is self-evidently important and has many implications.

655. The obligation to negotiate in a spirit of cooperation, and thus certainly not in a spirit of confrontation, is *de facto* not much more than a mere policy guideline, an expectation on the part of the European authorities and hardly a legally enforceable rule. Self-evidently, in case of rude refusal or obstructions to negotiate, measures and procedures should be available (Art. 11,3) and the subsidiary requirements (Art. 7,1) will apply. But one cannot dictate love, especially to those who still believe in class war.

656. However, the point is important. It underlines the need for a spirit of trust and good faith on which employee relations should be founded. But such a state of mind and soul is not necessarily present and depends a lot on the ideology of those involved. The truth of the matter is that trust can be built even between parties who have opposing interests. Building of trust and fostering a spirit of cooperation is not spontaneous, but requires continuous and conscientious efforts from all sides and should be cherished and nourished constantly.

B. Responsibility and Initiation of Negotiations

1. Responsibility of Central Management

657. The central management of the Community-scale undertaking or group of undertakings is responsible for creating the conditions and the means necessary for the setting up of an EWC or procedure for transnational information and consultation upon the terms and in the manner laid down by this directive (Art. 4,1).

Where the central management is not situated in a Member State, a central management's representative in a Member State, to be designated if necessary, shall take on the responsibility for the setting up of an EWC or a procedure. In the absence of such a representative, the above-mentioned responsibility will lie with the management of the establishment or the central management of the group undertaking employing the highest number of employees in any one Member State (Art. 4,2). The term employee should be interpreted as covering any person who, in the Member State concerned, is considered to be an employee; the calculation will take place according to national legislation and/or practice. What we said earlier concerning the notion employee in relation to the Community-scale undertaking or group of undertakings applies accordingly.

658. For the purposes of the directive, the representative of management, as provided for in Article 4,2 shall be regarded as central management (Art. 4, para. 3).

2. Initiation of the Negotiation

659. The procedure designed to ensure the right to transnational information and consultation of employees shall be initiated either: on the initiative of the central management, or at the written request of at least 100 employees in total or their representatives in at least two undertakings or establishments in at least two different Member States (Art. 5,1). One hundred employees in total are sufficient. There is no need to have 100 employees or their representatives in each of the two undertakings or establishments in the different Member States.

3. One or More EWC-Procedures

660. The directive only provides for the obligation of setting up one (negotiated or standard) EWC or one alternative procedure, even if a Community-scale undertaking or group of undertakings, would be composed of Community-scale undertakings or groups which on their own would also qualify for the establishment of an EWC or an alternative procedure (Art. 1, paras. 2 and 3). In this case, the directive obliges to establish an EWC or an alternative procedure at the 'highest' level only.

C. The Negotiation of the Agreement

661. The negotiation for the establishment of an EWC or a procedure will take place between central management and a special negotiation body, composed of representatives of the employees (Art. 5,2). With a view to the conclusion of such an agreement the central management has to convene a meeting with the special negotiating body. It has to inform the local management accordingly (Art. 5,4).

1. Parties to the Agreement and the Special Negotiating Body

662.   Parties to the agreement are thus the Community-scale undertaking or group of undertakings, represented by the central management on the one hand and the representatives of the employees (as defined in every Member State) which will constitute a special negotiating body, according to Article 5 of the directive. The special negotiating body has in a sense a specific legal personality, with the necessary competence to conclude and eventually to terminate an agreement establishing an EWC or a procedure. By the same token the special negotiation body should have the legal competence to introduce actions before the courts in case of a dispute relating to the matters covered by the directive. For the purposes of concluding an agreement, the special negotiating body acts by a majority of its members (Art. 6,5).

a. Composition of the Negotiating Body

663.   The special negotiating body shall be established in accordance with the following guidelines:

a. The Member States shall determine the method to be used for the election or appointment of the members of the special negotiating body who are to be elected or appointed in their territories (Art. 5,2(a), para. 1).

   The election or appointment of the members within each Member State shall be organised according to the legislation of those Member States (*see* Declaration No. 2 of Council and Commission). The Member States will have to pay special attention to whom can elect and be elected. It comes to mind that managers – at local as well as at central levels – although they may legally be considered to be employees, would not qualify, neither as possible candidates for election nor as electors; but is seems reasonable to limit that group of managers to those who really run the local or central undertaking (senior management) and thus to interpret this notion restrictively. This means that blue-collars, white-collars and 'cadres' (middle and higher management) would qualify as well as electors as elected or appointed members of the special negotiating body. To become a member, employees self-evidently need to agree to be a candidate to that end.

   This means also that, e.g., trade unions could represent the employees, according to national law/practice. As indicated, Member States shall 'provide that employees in undertakings and/or establishments in which there are no employees' representatives through no fault of their own, have the right to elect or appoint members of the special negotiating body' (Art. 5,2 (a) para. 2). Member States have the right to lay down thresholds for the establishment of employee representation bodies (Art. 5,2 (a) para. 3). As said above, this means that member States may provide that only employees of establishments/undertakings with, e.g., at least 50 employees will be qualified to participate in the election or appointment of the members of the special negotiating body.

b. The special negotiating body shall have a minimum of three members and a maximum of seventeen members. (Art. 5,2(b)).

According to Declaration No. 2 of the Commission and the Council, the maximum number of seventeen members should not necessarily be reached.

From 15 December 1997 onwards, the number 17 will be replaced by 18, from that moment on the Directive will also apply to the UK.

c. In these elections or appointments it must be ensured: firstly, that 'each Member State in which the Community-scale undertaking has one or more establishments or in which the Community-scale group of undertakings has the controlling undertaking or one or more controlled undertakings is represented by one member' (Art. 5,2(c) indent 1). It also stands to reason, that the Member States and the contracting parties should, as much as possible and where appropriate, look for ways and means to have the different groups of employees adequately represented in the negotiating body, namely younger and senior employees, men and women, blue- and white-collar workers and (junior) managers.

Secondly, that there are supplementary members in proportion to the number of employees working in the establishments, the controlling undertaking or the controlled undertakings, as laid down in the legislation of the Member State within the territory of which the central management is situated (Art. 5,2(c) indent 2).

d. The central management and local managements shall be informed of the composition of the special negotiating body (Art. 5,2 para. (d)), supposedly by local managements and/or the representatives themselves on an individual or on a collective basis. This last way seems the most indicated one and might be combined with the possibility for the representatives of employees to launch a written request to initiate negotiations, according to Article 5,1 of the directive.

b. Task of the Negotiating Parties

664. The special negotiating body and the central management of the Community-scale undertaking or group of undertakings have the task, without prejudice to the autonomy of the parties, of determining, by means of a written agreement on the detailed arrangements for implementing the transnational information and consultation of employees:

– the scope (undertakings or establishments) of the EWC;
– the composition of the EWC, the number of members, the allocation of seats and the term of office;
– the functions and the procedure for information and consultation of the EWC; the venue, frequency and duration of meetings of the EWC;
– the financial and material resources to be allocated to the EWC; the duration of the agreement and the procedure for its renegotiation or for establishing one or more information and consultation procedures instead of an EWC (Art. 6,3).

2. Refusal or Cancellation of the Negotiations

665. The special negotiating body may decide, by at least 2/3 of the votes, not to open negotiations or to terminate the negotiations already opened. Such a decision stops the procedure to conclude an agreement. Where such a decision has been taken, the provisions (subsidiary requirements) in the Annex do not apply. A new request to convene the special negotiating body may be made at the earliest two years after the above-mentioned decision, unless the parties concerned lay down a shorter period (Art. 5,5).

3. Experts and Costs

666.   For the purpose of the negotiation, the special negotiating body may be assisted by experts of its choice (Art. 5,4, para. 2). These experts can be employees or non-employees, for example, trade union representatives. There is no doubt that the trade unions consider this to be their role and want to assist the representatives of the employees to that end. This point is however also negotiable.

Any expenses relating to the negotiations have to be borne by the central management so as to enable the special negotiating body to carry out its tasks in an appropriate manner (Art. 5,6 para. 1). In compliance with this principle, Member States may lay down budgetary rules regarding the operation of the special negotiating body. They may in particular limit the funding to cover one expert only (Art. 5,6 para. 2).

4. Role of the Trade Unions and of the Employers' Associations

667.   Although trade unions and employer's associations are, according to the directive, not directly involved as parties to the agreement to be concluded concerning information and consultation, they may play an active role in practice. Undoubtedly, the European trade union secretariats (European sectoral level) and the ETUC (European inter-industry-wide level) are strongly behind the moves for a European social dialogue, but the choice by the European Union that the agreements should be concluded by the representatives of the employees and not necessarily by the trade unions has been a deliberate one. This leaves in a sense all options open. Trade unions can however play a role, e.g., in the training of members of the EWCs, by acting as experts, even as contracting parties and the like. The same goes for UNICE as well as for the (national) employer's associations, which can help to monitor and guide undertakings-members. National trade unions may play a role in the election or appointment of the (national) representatives in the special negotiating body if national law or practice provides them with such a role, as, e.g., might be the case in Belgium or France.

D. Nature, Binding Effect, Form and Language of the Agreement

1. Nature and Binding Effect of the Agreement

668.   The agreement can be looked upon as a special kind of collective labour agreement concluded between representatives of European management on the one hand and the European representatives of the employees under the form of a

negotiating body, establishing an EWC or an information or consultation procedure on the other hand. One can qualify the agreement as, like the French say, a 'contract-institution,' namely a contract which creates an institution, a framework for information and consultation between management and labour, which will lead its own life once it has been created. The agreement has, like any other collective labour agreement, an obligatory part and a normative part. The obligatory part relates to the rights and obligations of the contracting parties, the normative part being the information and consultation institution-procedure which has been set up, with its scope, composition, competence and the like. The contracting parties not only create, but also control the very existence of the EWC or the procedure since they will always have the right, taking agreed upon formalities and/or terms of notice into account, to denounce the agreement.

669. The binding effect of both (obligatory and normative) parts of the agreement thus will depend on the law applicable to the contract. If this is Belgian, because, e.g., the agreement was concluded in Brussels or because the venue of the meeting of the European committee or in the framework of a procedure as well as the central management's location are in Brussels, and parties did not choose another legal system, the relations between the contracting parties might be governed by Belgian law. This would then be the general principles of Belgian contractual law, since the Belgian Act of 5 December 1968 on joint committees and collective labour agreements would not apply, because in order to qualify for a binding legal collective agreement (in the sense of the 1968 Act), parties need to be, from the employee's side, representative (Belgian) trade unions, which is not the case for the special negotiating body operating in the framework of the directive.

2. Form and Language of the Agreement

670. It stands to reason that the agreement establishing an EWC or a procedure has to be drawn up in writing, and that it has to be signed by the representatives of management and by the majority of the individual representatives of the employees, assembled in the negotiating body. The negotiating body is, as said, a full fledged legal party, and not only a forum, an instrument, or a vehicle of communication between the involved actors. More formal aspects of the agreement regarding its legality, the number of copies to be signed and so on will be governed by the requirements of the applicable law.

671. The agreement could be drafted in various official languages of the Member States, depending on the (national) composition of the negotiating parties. One language is also possible, coupled to translations or without translations, provided the signing parties would understand what they sign. Special attention will have to paid to the national legislation which is applicable to the agreement, especially if this legislation would contain certain linguistic requirements as is, e.g., the case in Belgium and France.

E. Content of the Agreement

672.   The content of the agreement is self-evidently the business of the contracting parties: they decide autonomously what they want to put in the agreement and what not. Article 6 of the directive contains however a list in case of the establishment of an EWC. That list is a mandatory list of subjects, but parties are autonomous in deciding upon the concrete content to be given to the listed points.

According to the directive, a distinction must be made between the setting up of an EWC and the elaboration of a procedure. It is not so easy to see the difference between an EWC and a procedure, especially since Article 6,3, second para. provides in case of a procedure also for the right for the employee representatives to meet to discuss the information conveyed to them. Indeed 'the agreement must stipulate by what method the employees' representatives shall have the right to meet to discuss the information conveyed to them. This information shall in particular relate to transnational questions which significantly affect workers' interests.' It would therefore seem logical that an EWC is a more institutionalised form of communication and dialogue, while the procedure is a much looser one. But, as said, it is not clear where the procedure ends and the EWC begins and *vice versa*. One might say that an agreement which does not lay out in detail all the points covered by Article 6,2 may preferably qualify for a procedure instead of for an EWC. Parties could, however, make their intentions clear and indicate in the agreement whether they opt for an EWC or for a procedure.

For a procedure one could imagine *inter alia*: written reports forwarded by management, information and consultation at local level by any means; within or outside existing proceedings at national level – such as a visit of a European or national human resources manager to the employee representatives at plant or national level, provided the information and consultation relates to transnational issues. This procedure must not necessarily be the same in all undertakings, but may differ from one Member State to another, between different businesses of the group and the like.

In any case, parties are free to decide on these matters and can qualify their arrangement as they see fit, taking into account the right of the employees' representatives to discuss the information conveyed to them and engage in a dialogue.

The agreement is not, unless it provides otherwise, subject to the subsidiary requirements referred to in the Annex (Art. 6,4 para. 1).

1. Scope

673.   The agreement has to indicate '*the member undertakings of the Community-scale undertakings or the establishments of the Community-scale undertaking which are covered by the agreement*' (Art. 6,2a).

The agreement will have to indicate the territorial and personal scope (establishments/undertakings) covered by the agreement, possibly addressed by various EWCs in case of a group. The scope may also contain undertakings outside the EU and the EEA-EFTA countries.

2. The Setting up of an EWC

674.   Article 6,2(b) concerns *the composition of the EWC and the number of members, the allocation of seats and the term of office.*

The agreement can provide that the EWC may be composed of representatives of employees only, or also of representatives of management, whilst parties could also agree that the EWC is (consecutively) chaired by a representative of either group (management, employees). Parties should reflect, as we indicated earlier, on an appropriate representation of the different groups of employees, like blue-white collars, managerial employees, female workers and the like. Parties can also agree on other members, e.g., trade union business agents, who may also participate either as full fledged members or as pure observer members, advisers or as experts and the like. Complete freedom exists for the parties to the agreement regarding these matters. Parties may also agree whether there will be a select committee for the workers' group or of the EWC itself, if the EWC would be composed of employees only.

Major problems could arise in case of mergers or other restructurations of undertakings/establishments which might affect the composition of the EWC (especially, e.g., in case of a merger of two groups which have their own EWC).

As the directive is silent on this matter, the matter should be addressed according to the law applicable. If the applicable law does not regulate the problem, parties will have to renegotiate their agreement. So long as a new agreement is not reached, the existing agreement(s) continue(s) to have their effect. In case no new agreement is reached within the terms foreseen in Article 7, subsidiary requirements will apply.

Allocation of seats in the EWC will usually take the numerical strength of the employees in the undertaking(s) and establishments into account. Regarding elections or appointments parties would be well advised to stick as closely as possible to the national law and/or practice and follow, e.g., the same way as for the election of the representatives to the special negotiating body. Candidates should ideally have a given seniority (e.g., of one year) in the establishment undertaking as an employee in order to be able to represent their colleagues with a certain degree of insight and competence. The term of office should cover a number of years, not too long and not too short. Two to three years seems a minimum; five years a maximum.

675.   Article 6,2(c) concerns the functions and the procedure for information and consultation of the EWC.

The agreement might specify the competencies of the EWC more precisely as far as the nature of the consultation is concerned and among others indicate that the prerogatives of management shall not be affected. The agreement should also clearly indicate the subject matter of the information and consultation exercise; for this, a source of inspiration may be the subjects enumerated in the subsidiary requirements. In enumerating the subject matters one should take into account that the employees are especially entitled to information and consultation regarding transnational questions which significantly affect their interests, such as jobs, working conditions in the broad sense of the word, etc. Employees are in particular interested in the mitigation of social consequences of some managerial decisions.

Here come especially to mind information about future developments and prospects: indeed, employees are more interested in the future of the business than in the social-economic history of the company.

676. The agreement should equally contain something on the 'when' (yearly or/and *ad hoc*?) of the information and consultation (before decisions are taken or as soon as possible in case of *ad hoc* cases?); the organisation of the exchange of views and/or the dialogue and of possible feedback; as well on confidential and/or prejudicial information, on the role of experts, on accountants to check the exactitude of the information and the like. Others points may concern: voting majorities, the drafting of the agenda, the drafting of reports, the organisation of working parties, eventual training of the delegates, communication of information and consultation results to the rank and file and to the trade unions; contacts with the press etc.

Points here are also: written and/or oral procedure and timing. Regarding information: will documents be sent beforehand and how long before the meeting takes place? One might equally agree on the timing between information and consultation; on tabling of motions and voting; on interpretation and translation (languages); on the role of experts etc.

677. Article 6,2(d) concerns the venue, frequency and duration of meetings.

The agreement may say something about invitations to and the place of the meetings, make a difference between general, let us say yearly information, and *ad hoc* information meetings, when special important events take place, such as closures, collective dismissals and the like. The agreement may also provide for preliminary meetings; meetings of working parties, of the select committee of the workers' group and the like, and determine the length of such meetings etc.

678. Article 6,2(e) concerns the financial and material resources to be allocated to the EWC.

Central management will have to provide the necessary financial resources to pay for the functioning of the EWC (secretariat, catering, housing . . .); while the agreement has to cover payment of travel expenses, loss of wages of the employees' representatives and the like. Experts will normally be paid by the party they assist, or by the organisation they represent, which may be subsidised to this end by the EU, but the agreement could provide otherwise and eventually indicate that the costs of the experts will be borne by central management.

679. Article 6,2(f) concerns the duration of the agreement and the procedure for its renegotiation.

The agreement may be open-ended, with a term of notice, and contain certain forms (e.g., a registered letter) and also proposals for renegotiation, to be respected in case of denouncement of the agreement and the like. The agreement could be denounced, totally or partially, by either central management or the (majority of the members of) the negotiating body. Both parties may also agree to terminate the agreement.

The agreement can also be concluded for a fixed period, after which it comes automatically to an end. Parties can also foresee a fixed period with a prolongation for (a similar) period unless one of the parties would have terminated the agreement before a certain date (e.g., one year before the term ends).

In any case, there must be a procedure for its renegotiation. The renegotiation would normally take place between the central management and a negotiating body. However, according to the Annex (point 1(f), para. 2) this is the (employee representatives of) the EWC. If no new agreement is reached before the old one expires, the subsidiary requirements will apply.

680. The agreement could also expand on the law applicable to the agreement, on the settlement of interpretation or application difficulties, either by way of conciliation or arbitration, on the competent court and the like.

For the purposes of concluding the agreement the special negotiating body shall act by majority of its members (Art. 6,5).

3. The Setting up of a Procedure

681.   Article 6,3 of the directive states

> 'that the central management and the special negotiating body may decide, in writing, to establish one or more information and consultation procedures instead of an EWC. The agreement must stipulate by what method the employees' representatives have the right to meet to discuss the information conveyed to them. This information shall relate in particular to transnational questions which significantly affect the interests of the employees.'

Parties should amongst others focus, and *ceteris paribus*, on

a. the scope of the procedure;
b. the mode of operation, including 'the right to meet to discuss the information';
c. the matters subject to information and consultation;
d. the financial and material resources to be allocated for the functioning of the procedure;
e. the duration of the agreement and the procedure for its renegotiation;
f. the law applicable to the agreement.

V. Prejudicial and Confidential Information. Ideological Guidance

682.   According to Article 8,2, para. 1 of the directive, Member States may, in specific cases under the conditions and limits laid down by national legislation, provide that the central management situated in its territory is not obliged to transmit information when its nature is such that it would seriously harm the functioning of the undertakings concerned or would be prejudicial to them.

A Member State may make such dispensation subject to prior administrative or judicial authorisation (Art. 8,2, para. 2).

Member States shall, according to Article 8,1 of the directive, also provide that members of special negotiating bodies or of EWCs and any experts who assist them are not authorised to reveal any information which has expressly been provided to them in confidence. The same applies to the employees' representatives in the framework of an information and consultation procedure. This obligation continues to apply wherever these persons are, even after the expiry of their terms of office.

683. One has to add that Article 8,3 of the directive contains the possibility for Member States to lay down particular provisions for the central management of undertakings and establishments in its territory which pursue directly and essentially the aim of ideological guidance with respect to information and the expression of opinions, on condition that, at the date of adoption of the directive, such particular provisions already existed in the national legislation.

In this regard the Council and the Commission stated: 'this means undertakings and establishments which directly and essentially pursue: political, professional organisation, religious, charitable, educational, scientific or artistic aims, aims involving information and the expression of opinions.'

684. Where Member States apply Article 8 of the directive concerning confidential (and prejudicial) information, they have to provide for administrative or judicial appeal procedures which the employees' representatives may initiate when the central management requires confidentiality or does not give information in accordance with Article 8 (Art. 11,4). 'Such procedures may include procedures designed to protect the confidentiality of the information in question' (Art. 11,4, para. 2).

VI. Protection of Employees' Representatives

685. The employee representatives have the same protection as their national colleagues. Indeed, Article 10 of the directive provides that members of special negotiating bodies, members of EWCs and employees' representatives exercising their functions within an information and consultation procedure, enjoy in the exercise of their functions the same protection and guarantees provided for employees' representatives by the national legislation and/or practice in force in the country of employment, especially as regards attendance at meetings of special negotiation bodies or EWCs or any other meetings within the framework of the agreement establishing a procedure; this also relates to payment of wages of members who are on the staff of the Community-scale undertaking or group of Community-scale undertakings for the period of absence necessary for the performance of their duties.

686. Additionally, one may have to resort to international private labour law rules in order to determine which national system is applicable in case an employee representative would, e.g., be employed in more than one country, e.g., in the capacity of commercial traveller.

VII. Compliance with the Directive – Links – Final Provisions

A. *Compliance with the Directive*

687. Each Member State has to ensure that the management of establishments which form part of a Community-scale group of undertakings which are situated within its territory and their employees' representatives or, as the case may be, employees abide by the obligations laid down by the directive, regardless of whether or not the central management is situated in its territory (Art. 11,1).

Member States must ensure that the information on the average number of employees is made available by undertakings at the request of the parties concerned by the application of the directive (Art. 11,2).

688. Member States have to provide for appropriate measures in the event of failure to comply with this directive. In particular, they shall ensure that administrative or judicial procedures are available to enable the obligations deriving from this directive to be enforced (Art. 11,3).

As already indicated earlier, Member States provide for administrative or judicial procedures which the employees' representatives may initiate when the management requires confidentiality or does not give information for reasons of confidentiality. Such procedures may include procedures designed to protect the confidentiality of the information in question (Art. 11,4).

Member States are thus entitled to maintain or introduce more stringent protective measures compatible with the Treaty, limited however to their territory. It seems to us less likely that Member States will impose more stringent measures, since they will, for obvious reasons, look carefully at what kind of protective measures are provided for in other Member States.

B. *Links*

689. Article 12 of the directive concerns the links between this directive and other provisions, both European and national. It says that this directive shall apply without prejudice to measures taken pursuant to the directives on collective redundancies (1975) as amended and on the transfer of undertakings (1977). Regarding national provisions it indicates that 'this Directive shall be without prejudice to existing rights to information and consultation of employees under national law.'

C. *Final Provisions*

690.

> 'Member States shall bring into force the laws, regulations and administrative provisions necessary to comply with this Directive not later than two years after the adoption of this Directive, or shall ensure by that date at the latest that management and labour introduce the required provisions by way of agreement,

the Member States being obliged to take necessary steps enabling them at all times to guarantee the results imposed by this Directive. They shall forthwith inform the Commission thereof.'

This means that Article 14,1 of the directive gives Member States the option to give the national social partners (in conjunction with national legislation if necessary) the possibility to conclude collective agreements implementing the Directive. These collective agreements must be binding in law and cover all undertakings and employees concerned. This is, in particular, the case where national provisions contain extension procedures which may make collective agreements binding *erga omnes*. This is, e.g., the case in Belgium, France, Germany and the Netherlands and not (necessarily) in such States as the Scandinavian countries, where this presents a special problem.

691. The question arises whether a collective agreement, even when extended by governmental decree and thus generally binding, is an appropriate vehicle for implementing the directive into national law. The reason is simple and will (partly) depend on the national law, applicable to the agreement. Indeed, contrary to other labour law directives, the EWC directive fundamentally transcends national borders; this goes as well for the EWC as for an information/consultation procedure. The national collective agreement transposing the directive, out of necessity, has to partially or totally regulate labour relations of which the participants (enterprises, establishments, representatives of employees and the like) operate in other countries. A (national) collective agreement will, e.g., thus have to indicate under what conditions an Article 13 agreement is valid and indicate the number of supplementary members for the EWC to represent employees of certain addressed Member States, which are out of necessity situated in other Member States. One could give many more examples of extraterritorial realities, which have to be regulated by the national collective agreement implementing the directive. Now, normally a collective agreement is legally only equipped to regulate labour relations and conditions which fall within national borders, except when national law would provide otherwise; and even the latter is questionable. So, it will depend on national law whether collective agreements are the appropriate base for implementing a directive which transcends, so to speak, national boundaries. One thing is for sure: the Belgian legislation on collective bargaining does not provide for such a legal base. Consequently, the Belgian collective agreement. No. 62 of 6 February 1996, cannot be seen as an appropriate way of implementing the EWC directive. The EWC directive itself cannot change Belgian law concerning collective agreements. Belgian law allows for legally binding agreements regarding Belgian labour relations, not regarding those relations which transcend Belgian boundaries.

692.

'When Member States adopt these measures, they shall contain a reference to this Directive or shall be accompanied by such reference on the occasion of their official publication. The methods of making such reference shall be laid down by Member States' (Art. 14,2).

VIII. Subsidiary Requirements: a Mandatory EWC

693.   If the central management and the special negotiating body so decide or if the central management refuses to commence negotiations within six months of the request by the representatives of the employees to initiate negotiations or if, after three years from the date of this request, they are unable to conclude an agreement providing for an EWC or a procedure for informing and consulting employees, the subsidiary requirements, laid down by the legislation of the Member State in which the central management is situated, apple (Art. 7,1).

The subsidiary requirements as adopted in the legislation of the Member State must satisfy the provisions set out in the Annex to the directive (Art. 7,2).

The subsidiary requirements thus constitute in a sense the mandatory core regarding information and consultation rights, which the European legislator wants European undertakings to live up to, if the parties do not follow the voluntary road by concluding an agreement setting up an EWC or by establishing an information and consultation procedure. Indeed, the subsidiary requirements provide, as indicated, for a mandatory establishment of an EWC.

A. Composition of the EWC

694.   The EWC is to be composed of employees of the Community-scale undertaking or Community-scale group of undertakings, elected or appointed from their midst by the employees' representatives or, in the absence thereof, by the entire body of employees (Annex 1(b), para 1).

The election or appointment of members of an EWC shall be carried out in accordance with national legislation and/or practice (Annex 1(b), para. 2).

The EWC has a minimum of 3 members and a maximum of 30. Where its size so warrants, it shall elect a select committee from among its members comprising at the most three members. It shall adopt its own rules of procedure.

The maximum of 30 need not necessarily be reached. A lower number may be provided by the applicable law (national law of the Member State in which the central management is situated) (Council and Commission Declaration No. 2).

695.

'In the election or appointment of members of the EWC, it must be ensured:
firstly, that each Member State in which the Community-scale undertaking has one or more establishments or in which the Community-scale group of undertakings has the controlling undertaking or one or more controlled undertakings, is represented by one Member;
secondly, that there are supplementary members in proportion to number of employees working in the establishments, the controlling undertakings or the controlled undertakings as laid down by the legislation of the Member State within the territory of which the central management is situated' (Annex 1(d)).

'The central management and any other more appropriate level of management shall be informed of the composition of the EWC' (Annex 1(e)).

B. Competence

696.   The competence of the European Committee is limited to information and consultation on the matters which concern the Community-scale undertaking or Community-scale group of undertakings as a whole or at least two of its establishments or group undertakings situated in different Member States (Annex 1(a), para. 1).

In the case of undertakings or groups of undertakings, the competence of the European committee shall be limited to those matters concerning all their establishments or group undertakings situated within the Member States or concerning at least two of their establishments or group undertakings situated in different Member States (Annex 1(a) para. 2).

1. General Information (Annual)

697.   The EWC has the right to meet with the central management once a year, to be informed and consulted, on the basis of a report drawn up by the central management, on the progress of the business of the Community-scale undertaking or Community-scale group of undertakings and its prospects. The local management shall be informed accordingly (Annex 2, para. 1).

698.   The meeting has to relate in particular to the structure, economic and financial situation, the probable development of the business and of production and sales, the situation and probable trends of employment, investments, and substantial changes concerning organisation, introduction of new working methods or production processes, transfers of production, mergers, cutbacks or closures of undertakings, establishments or important parts thereof, or collective redundancies (Annex 2, para. 2).

2. *Ad hoc* Information

699.   Where there are exceptional circumstances affecting the employees' interests to a considerable extent, particularly in the event of relocations, the closure of establishments or undertakings or collective redundancies, the select committee or, where no such committee exists, the EWC shall have the right to be informed. It shall have the right to meet, at its request, the central management, or any other more appropriate level of management within the Community-scale undertaking or group of undertakings having its own powers of decision, so as to be informed and consulted on measures significantly affecting employees' interests.

Those members of the EWC who have been elected or appointed by the establishments and/or undertakings which are directly concerned by the measures in question shall also have the right to participate in the meeting organised with the select committee (Annex 3, para. 2).

C. Procedure

700.   The EWC shall have the right to meet with the central management once a year and if there are exceptional circumstances, particularly affecting considerably the interests, as indicated above.

The yearly meeting takes place on the basis of written report.

The special *ad hoc* information and consultation meeting has to take place as soon as possible on the basis of a report drawn up by the central management or any other appropriate level of the management of the Community-scale group of undertakings, on which an opinion may be delivered at the end of the meeting or within a reasonable time, One may assume that this report should also be in writing, unless great urgency would prevent this and an oral report would have to be made.

This meeting shall not affect the prerogatives of the central management (Annex 3, para. 4).

Member States may provide for rules concerning the chairing of the information and consultation meetings (Annex 4, para. 1). This means that the applicable law may, e.g., provide for management to preside the meeting, as this is a common practice in most Member States.

Before any meeting with the central management, the EWC or the select committee, where necessary enlarged in accordance with the second paragraph of point 3 of the Annex (*see* previous para.), shall be entitled to meet without the management concerned being present (Annex 4, para. 2).

The members of the EWC shall inform the representatives of the employees of the establishments or of the undertakings of Community-scale group of undertakings or, in the absence of representatives, the workforce as a whole, of the content and outcome of the information and consultation procedure, carried out in accordance with his annex, without prejudice to Article 8 of the directive, relating to confidential information (Annex 5).

701.   The EWC shall adopt its own rules of procedure. (Annex 1, para.).

D. Role of Experts

702.   The EWC or the select committee may be assisted by experts of its choice in so far as this is necessary for it to carry out its tasks (Annex 6). These experts can be employees as well as non-employees and thus, e.g., also trade union representatives. There is no doubt that the trade unions consider this to be a role for them and are eager to assist the representatives of the employees towards that end.

E. Expenses

703.   The operating expenses of the EWC are, according to Annex 7 to the directive, borne by the central management. The central management concerned has to provide the members of the EWC with such financial and material resources as to enable them to meet and perform their duties in an appropriate manner.

F. Future Developments

704. Four years after the EWC is established it shall examine whether to open negotiations for the conclusion of the agreement referred to in Article 6 or to continue to apply the subsidiary requirements adopted in accordance with this annex.

Articles 6 and 7 will apply, *mutatis mutandis*, if a decision has been taken to negotiate an agreement according to Article 6 and the 'special negotiating body' shall be replaced by 'EWC' (Annex 1(f)).

IX. Pre-existing Agreements – in Force

705. As already indicated earlier, the EU wants to favour voluntarism in the setting up of an EWC or of an information and consultation procedure by encouraging the conclusion of agreements to that end even before the directive enters into force.

With this objective in mind, Article 13 of the directive declares as follows:

'the obligations arising from this Directive shall not apply to Community-scale undertakings and groups of undertakings in which, on the date of the implementation of this Directive according to Article 14,1 (22 September 1996) or the date of its earlier transposition into the law of the Member State in question, there is already an agreement, providing for the transnational information and consultation, covering the entire workforce. When the agreements referred to expire, the parties to such agreements may jointly decide to renew them. Where this is not the case, the provisions of this Directive shall apply.'

A. Timing, Form, Language and Format of the Agreement

1. Timing, Form and Language

706. The agreement has to be concluded before the implementation of the directive into national law, that is 22 September 1996 or the date of its transposition in the Member State in question, where this is earlier than the above-mentioned date.

707. Although Article 13 of the directive does not indicate that the agreement should be in writing, it seems absolutely indicated that it should, since the existing agreement will be up for examining whether it qualifies as an agreement in force, escaping the obligations under the directive on the establishment of an EWC or a procedure for the purposes of informing and consulting employees.

708. The agreement could be drafted in various official languages, depending on the composition of the negotiating parties. One language is also possible, coupled to translations or without translations, provided the signing parties would understand what they sign. Special attention will have to paid to the national legislation which is applicable to the agreement, especially if this legislation would contain certain linguistic requirements as is, e.g., the case in Belgium and France.

2. Format: Detail or Permanent Negotiation?

709. Parties will have to choose the format of the agreement: whether they want it detailed, more or less as a bible, or whether they see the agreement as one containing the essential principles regarding an evolving relationship, whereby problems are solved as parties go along. It is, however, crystal clear that the directive itself and the subsidiary requirements are a good yardstick of what parties are entitled to expect from each other and of what could be done.

B. Nature, Binding Effect and Applicable Law

710. For these questions we can refer to §4, IV.D of this chapter.

C. Scope and Parties to the Agreement

711. Special attention has to be given to the (personal) scope of the agreement. Indeed, Article 13 stipulates that the agreement should cover the entire workforce.

The parties to the agreement are self-evidently the representatives of the Community-scale undertaking or groups of undertakings, let us say central management on the one hand and the representatives of the employees at the other hand.

D. Content of the Agreement

1. An EWC, a Procedure or Another Mechanism

712. Parties have to decide whether they want to establish an EWC, a procedure or another mechanism for the purposes of information and consultation. They will also have to agree on the number of members.

There is also the possibility to create a select or executive committee, representing the employees-members or the EWC as a whole, which could steer the EWC and/or be available for *ad hoc* interventions. Pre-meetings, the role of experts and the like are other issues which must be decided.

In case of a procedure instead of an EWC-committee, similar questions arise: who will be involved, get informed and consulted and how will parties relate to each other? Again, maximum flexibility is allowed but at a given point employees' representatives and those of management should meet and engage in a dialogue, and all of this has to be laid down in writing.

2. Competence: Information and Consultation

713. Article 7 of the directive and the subsidiary requirements are obvious reference points to determine the content of the information and consultation obligations between the parties. Information and consultation have, in particular, to relate to transnational issues, involving undertakings-establishments of at least two Member States (Art. 13,1).

3. Functioning

714. Parties have to decide when the representatives of the (central) management and of the employees will meet: annually and/or *ad hoc* at the occasion of important events affecting the interests of the employees; on meeting(s) of the select-executive committee, on possible preliminary meetings before meeting with central management and the like. Other points concern the drafting of the agenda (e.g., every party has the right to put points on the agenda), documents to be submitted, meeting rules, ways of formulation opinions, exchange of views, dialogue, reporting (minutes of the meetings), feedback, etc.

715. Employees' representatives may need the help of some form of secretariat and perhaps the benefit of some facilities, like a room, access to modern information technology, telecommunications and the like. This could also be subject of the agreement.

The agreement might also contain wording concerning the languages and interpretation facilities to be used for the implementation of the information and consultation exercise. It is self-evident that languages must be used which employees' and management's representatives effectively understand. This will thus entirely depend on the composition of the EWC-committee or of those involved in the procedure and on their respective linguistic skills.

4. Role of Experts – Expenses

716. The role of experts is essential for the functioning of the EWC-committee or the successful conduct of a procedure. Employees' representatives should be free to choose their experts. These may be other employees, trade union representatives or even outside independent persons. The agreement may lay down rules on who can be an expert, their numbers, whether they have access to which documents, whether they can assist in preliminary meetings or meetings of an EWC-procedure and the like. It is normal that the expenses of the experts would be paid by the undertaking, unless trade unions would benefit from EU subsidies towards that end. Expenses for the functioning of the EWC-procedure should be borne by the undertaking.

E. Prejudicial and Confidential Information

717. These points could be addressed in the agreement along the lines of what the directive contains: which information will and can be given, which information is prejudicial/confidential and which information can be passed on to the employees and others.

F. Status of the Employee Representatives

718.   Also the status of employee representatives may be addressed in the agreement. Parties could consider adopting language indicating that employees cannot be discriminated against for reasons of defending opinions regarding their office and/ or conferring upon them the same protection as under national law. We refer to what has been said earlier (§4. VI).

G. Duration of the Agreement

719.   The agreement should indicate its duration. The agreement may be open-ended, with a term of notice and certain forms (e.g., a registered letter) and also proposals for renegotiation, to be respected in case of denouncement of the agreement. The agreement could be denounced, totally or partially, by either management or the representatives of the employees taking the requirements of the applicable provisions into account. Both parties may also agree to terminate the agreement.

The agreement can also be for a fixed period, after which it comes automatically to an end. Parties can also foresee a fixed period with a prolongation for the same period unless one of the parties has terminated the agreement before a certain date (e.g., one year before the term ends).

Parties might also agree upon a procedure for its renegotiation. In case of renewal the agreement will continue to escape the obligations which arise under the directive. If no new agreement is reached before the old one expires the directive will apply.

H. Overview of Past Experience

1. The First Councils (1985–1994)

720.   EWCs (1985–1994) exist in one form or another in some 30 enterprises. The first was established in Thomson Consumer Electronics (1985). Since then a number of them were set up: in Bull, Volkswagen, Europipe, Pechiney, Nestle, BSN Group, Allianz, Rhone-Poulenc, Elf-Aquitaine, Saint Gobain, Scansped Group AB, Continental Car Europe, Airbus Industry, Eurocopter and others.[1] An analysis of the agreements between the involved multinational groups and the European sectorial trade unions clearly shows that the competences of the councils are limited to information and in fewer cases to consultation. Europipe forms an exception, having equal representation of German and French workers in the supervisory board, which has to consent before a number of important economic-financial decisions can be taken. For a better insight into the significance of the councils we give two examples: Thomson Consumer Electronics and Volkswagen.[2]

---

1. *See* 'Information and consultation in European multinationals' – part one and two, *European Industrial Relations Review*, Nos. 228 and 229 (January and February 1993).
2. *See*: Hutsebaut M., *The Social Dimension of the Internal Market*, Second Part: 'Workers' Rights in European Companies,' European Trade Union Institute, Brussels, Info 26, 1988; European

Trade Union Institute, *The Social Dimension of the Internal Market. Part IV. EWCs*, Brussels, 1991; European Foundation for the Improvement of Living and Working Conditions, *Report on European-level Information and Consultation in Multinational Companies – An Evaluation of Practice*, Dublin, 1992, by M. Gold and M. Hall.

721. Thomson Consumer Electronics is a multinational enterprise producing household electrical appliances, with subsidiaries in France, Germany, Italy, Spain, and the UK. On 7 October 1985 two protocol agreements were signed between Thomson and the European Metal Workers' Federation (EMF), setting up, on the one hand, a TGP-EMF Liaison Committee and, on the other hand, a TGP European Branch Commission. These agreements, concluded on an experimental basis for a period of 2 years, were renewed in December 1987, this time for an open-ended period. The Liaison Committee is composed of representatives of the trade unions who are members of the EMF. The Branch Commission is composed of representatives of the workers from the different subsidiaries.

722. The Liaison Committee is to meet once a year on either Thomson or EMF initiative. With the agreement of both parties, the Committee may meet on an *ad hoc* basis, even in a restricted form. The Committee is composed of 13 members representing the trade unions and one member representing the EMF. Costs of the meeting are paid by Thomson. The competences of the Committee are mainly of an informative nature, covering economic and financial aspects, research and development. The Committee will be informed, prior to implementation, of major structural, industrial and trading modifications and changes in the economic and legal organisation of Thomson. It will be informed of the measures taken and planned for adapting the organisation and the work force to technological change as well as adapting employees' skills in the light of employment problems. The members of the Liaison Committee may express opinions on all defined areas. The EMF is to have access to the documents transmitted to the European Branch Committee. It undertakes to respect the confidential or secret nature of these documents, as the case may be, *vis-à-vis* third parties.

723. The Branch Commission will be convened by Thomson once a year. It exists of 26 representatives of the workers. Expenses of the meeting are paid by Thomson. Salaries of staff delegates will continue to be paid throughout the period of the meeting. Their terms of office in the Commission is 2 years. The European Branch Commission will be informed of the financial, industrial commercial and research activity of Thomson. It will be notified of measures taken or considered for adapting the personnel of subsidiaries of the countries involved to technological developments and of personnel qualification in regard to employment problems. The Commission will also be informed, before implementation, of any significant structural or industrial modifications, if the decision is to be made at the level of Thomson. The Commission will equally be informed of any modifications to the economic or legal organisation of Thomson (acquisitions or sales or subsidiaries).

724. On 7 February 1992 an agreement on cooperation was concluded between the management of the Volkswagen Group and the Volkswagen European Group Works Council, which was set up on 30 August 1990. This Council is composed of

17 members: 8 members Volkswagen AG: 2 members Audi AG (thus 10 Germans); 5 members Seat SA (Spain) and 2 members Volkswagen Brussels SA (Belgium).

With this agreement the parties wish to establish a social dialogue at European level. They seek in this way 'to make an active contribution to future understanding and structuring within the framework of the development of Europe into a political union of European states with a single market.' With its European brands of Volkswagen, Audi, Seat and Skoda, and the setting up of new European production facilities, the Volkswagen group has accepted responsibility in the development of Europe which includes the social obligation towards the workforces and locations on the basis of active collaboration with employee representatives and unions. Parties agreed 'that a successful social development is dependent on international competitiveness achieved through a high level of productivity and flexibility, making constantly increasing demands in respect of the quality and environmental acceptability of the products.' 'Both parties regard this agreements as a basis within the Volkswagen Group for working together at European level in the spirit of constructive dialogue and cooperative surmounting of economic, social and ecological challenges and for jointly solving any conflicts which may arise.'

725.   The representatives of management and of the workers shall meet at least once a year. The topics to be dealt with at the meetings, to the extent that they are of general importance for the European production plants, shall relate primarily to the following areas:

– securing of jobs and plants, and plant structures;
– development of Group structures;
– productivity and cost structures;
– development of working conditions (e.g., working hours, wages and salaries, job design); new production technologies;
– new forms of work organisation; work safety, including plant and environment protection; the effects of political developments and decisions of the Volkswagen Group.

726.   Discussion of these topics should at the same time serve an exchange of information on development trends and strategies and promote progress to the benefit of all concerned.

The Council shall in due time be informed regarding planned cross-border transfers of production (main investment emphasis, production scope, essential company functions). This applies to transfers which may have a substantial adverse effect on the interests of employees at production plants of the Volkswagen Group in Europe. The Council 'has the right to comment within an appropriate period which shall be agreed upon by both parties in each case immediately on receipt of the information. In its comments the Council can require explanation of the planned transfer in the framework of consultations jointly laid down. These consultations shall take place early enough for the views of the Council to be taken into account of in the decision making process.' 'The rights and duties of the responsible company bodies in each case remain unaffected,' indicating that managerial prerogative remains intact. Volkswagen undertakes to bear the costs of the works council.

727. Needless to say, the experience up to now shows a great diversity. Some agreements are formal and in writing, others informal; in others still there are agreed practices. Most are strictly informative. Unions do play a role in the composition of the councils, either as members or in appointing the employee-members of the councils. Many times the arrangement will involve a joint employee forum; while the size varies from 12 (BSN) to 75 (Elf Acquitaine), although in most cases the number rarely exceeds 30. Meetings are most of the time annual, with sometimes preliminary meetings or *ad hoc* meetings. The agreements are at first concluded for a short period, e.g., of two years, and then are prolonged indefinitely. Finally, costs are taken care of by the companies.

728. The following benefits to management are reported:

– explain corporate strategy;
– facilitate company restructuring;
– foster international contacts and exchange views;
– create a sense of belonging to an international company.

729. Benefits to employee representatives were recorded as follows:

– gather information directly from group headquarters;
– use information for national collective bargaining;
– improve international contacts;
– exchange information on best practice;
– set an example for other multinationals;
– develop a joint international policy.

730. It seems that a number of existing arrangement would be either too informal or to sketchy to qualify as valid preexisting agreements, as envisaged by Article 13 of the directive.[1]

1. For more details, *see* Gold and Hall, *op. cit.*, 48–51.

2. Pre-directive Agreements (1994–1996)

731. The possibility to conclude agreements to which the obligations of the directive would not apply, undoubtedly spurred negotiations and the conclusion of now more than some 140 agreements. Almost every day new agreements are reported. So, the picture is changing daily. Fifty-one agreements, up to May 1995, were analysed in the 'Review of Current Agreements on Information and Consultation in European Multinationals' (1996).[1] This overview gives us an idea of what is going on. Let us have a closer look at some of the items.

1. *A Report for the European Commission (DG V) by* P. Bonneton, M. Carley, M. Hall and H. Krieger, European Foundation, Dublin, 1996. 175 p.

a. Countries of Headquarters-Coverage

732.   It is interesting to note that (in May 1995) the bulk of undertakings or group of undertakings with pre-directive agreements are headquartered in France (22) and Germany (15). Then follow Sweden (5), the UK (4), Finland, Italy, Norway (2), Austria, Japan, Spain and the USA (1).

Most agreements concern the addressed Member States and the UK, which is included notwithstanding the British opt-out. In a few instances Central and Eastern European countries, like Hungary, are included. Exceptionally, there are worldwide works councils as in the case of SKF and Nat West.

For undertakings or groups of undertakings, which, due to the extension of the Directive to the UK, fall within the scope of the agreement, the date for concluding an Article 13 agreement is no later than 15 December 1999.[1]

1. Article 4 of Council Directive 97/74 of 15 December 1997 extending to the UK Directive 94/
   45 EC (O.J., 16 January 1998, L 10/22).

b. Parties to the Agreements

733.   Parties to the agreements are representatives of management, which in itself causes no significant problems, on the one hand, and representatives of employees, on the other hand.

Regarding the latter, a great variety can be noticed, as various participants intervene:

– international or European trade secretariats (e.g., IMF-IUF-EMF);
– national trade unions;
– works council representatives or other employee representatives.

c. EWC or Procedure

734.   As a general rule, an institution or a body of one form or another is established. So a 'procedure,' allowing for even more flexibility, seems not to be a favoured formula. Most agreements do not use the name European Works Council, but have a variety of names such as forum, structure for dialogue, group committee, consultative council, dialogue, etc.

d. Composition of the EWC

735.   In most of the cases, the EWCs are joint bodies of which both management representatives and employee representatives are members.

The number of employee representatives varies widely from 70 members (Saint-Gobain) to 20 (BP Oil) and 8 (Grundig). The vast majority have 10–40 members. Mostly, representatives are employees of the group who already have a representative function in the undertaking (shop steward, member of a national works' council, etc.). So the representativeness of the employee representatives is in a sense guaranteed by the mandate they hold within their own country.

In a number of cases officials of national or international trade unions participate in the activities of the works council either as member or as an invitee.

The members are either appointed or elected at national level or nominated by trade unions. Direct elections are rather rare.

Management is represented by high level-senior managers like CEO's (20 agreements) and group/general managers (22). In some agreements, it is specified that national management may attend or that guests can be invited.

e. Select Committee
736. In quite a number of agreements (19) a kind of executive, like a select committee, comprising a few key members, has been set up, sometimes bipartite, sometimes only employee-composed, performing a variety of functions: coordination, contact, preparing the EWC meetings and so on.

f. Duration of the Mandate
737. Where the duration of the mandate is specified (18 agreements), the term ranges from two to four years.

g. Competence
738. The competence of the EWC relates self-evidently to information and consultation. Topics include:[1]

- corporate strategy;
- the economic and financial situation of the undertaking;
- the situation regarding sales and turnover:
- production programmes;
- rationalisation, reorganisation and restructuring;
- production and working methods;
- closures of establishments;
- partial closures of establishments;
- take-overs and mergers at the level of the undertaking;
- the policy regarding technology;
- market trends;
- reductions in capacity;
- the relocation of production;
- the employment situation;
- developments at branch level;
- investment policy, both at the level of the undertaking and for each production line;
- training;
- safety and health protection; and
- working conditions.

Information and consultation is usually confined to transnational issues.

1. Buschak W., *European Works Councils. The EC-Directive: ETUC analysis and comments*, 2nd enlarged edition, s.d., Brussels, p. 29.

h. Meetings
739. The majority of agreements provide for annual meetings, often one-day meetings.

Many agreements foresee in the organisation of preliminary meetings, which precede the (annual) meeting of the EWC.

Agenda's, where dealt with in the agreements, are in most cases subject to a joint input in their drafting. The same goes for the minutes of the meeting. In a number of cases, the minutes are forwarded to other interested parties (managers and national representatives of employees).

i. Experts

740. Of the 51 agreements examined in the above-mentioned review, 22 contain a clause allowing under one form or another access to experts' advice. Different formulas are used.

j. Confidentiality

741. A clause concerning confidentiality is contained in no less that 25 agreements. In most instances agreements provide 'that EWC members are covered by an obligation to treat as confidential any information presented as such by management or on any company secrets.'[1]

> 1. *Review, op. cit.*, p. 35.

k. Costs

742. According to most agreements, the costs relating to the organisation of the preliminary meetings and the meetings of the EWC are borne by the undertakings. In general, headquarters will pay for the meetings (location, interpretation, catering . . .) while the subsidiaries will cover the expenses related to the participation of their respective representatives-employees, travel expenses, accommodation, eventually pay. Exceptionally, expenses related to the participation of union business agents are also covered. The same goes for the meetings of the select committees. In some cases EWCs or committees will have their own budget, allocated by the undertaking.

Usually representatives will get time off with pay while attending meetings, while in a number of cases extra time off is provided.[1]

> 1. For more details *see: Review, op. cit.*, 37–38.

l. Languages and Training

743. The agreement is usually drafted in the native language of the company, while in a large number of cases translations have been made in other languages.

In a majority of agreements, simultaneous translation is provided, from time to time on request, into a number of languages. Sometimes, there is one major language, e.g., English, German or French, and translation will be provided for as appropriate. The same goes for the drafting of the minutes.

Of the 51 examined agreements, 11 provide for some training on languages, finance and economics. At times, specific courses are offered.

m. Duration of the Agreements

744.   Here also, a great variety can be noticed in the pre-directive agreements and only some general points can be brought forward. Thus, agreements are:

– for an indefinite duration;
– for a minimum period of, e.g., up to five years;
– for a fixed term (one, two, four or six years).

A majority of agreements provides for a term of notice, e.g., of six months. Sometimes, a review process is provided for. In one (project) agreement there is a clause providing that management, if the agreement would be challenged by legal recourse, has the right to terminate the agreement.

n. Applicable Law

745.   In a number of cases (mostly French), agreements indicate applicable law, meaning that the agreement will be governed by that law. The case of National Westminster (a British multinational) is interesting as the agreement not only applies worldwide, including the USA, but also provides that the seat of the Works Council will be in London and that English law is applicable to the agreement.

3. Analysis of Pre-existing Agreements

746.   The European Foundation for Living and Working Conditions analyses on a regular basis the agreements establishing EWC's. The latest study[1] involves 111 agreements and contains a wealth of information. Some of the more important figures are reproduced below:

Nationality of the home country of the company:

Germany:	27%
France:	22%
UK:	14%
Nordic Countries:	13%
USA:	8%
Outside EU:[2]	7%

Sector of activity

Metalworking:	30%
Chemicals:	28%
Food:	10%
Construction:	9%

Signatories

Trade unions:	55%[3]
Central Works Councils:	26%

Coverage

15 Member States:	40%
Europe:	33%
EEA:	10%
Worldwide:	2%
Outside Europe:	33%
Group as a whole:	80%
Divisional:	15%

Composition

Employees only:	25%
+ management:	75%

Employee representatives:

0–10	7%
11–20	31%
21–30	42%
31–40	8%
41–50	7%
51 +	5%

Nomination:

by trade unions:	64%
by works councils:	55%
direct elections:	19%.

External members:

trade unions:	22%

Select Committee:	46%
agenda:	67%
preparing:	53%
coordination:	50%
minutes:	28%
time-place:	23%.
specific:	42%
extra-ordinary meeting:	7%

Competence (information and consultation)

Economic and financial situation:	87%
Employment/social issue:	85%
Business, production, sales:	65%
Investment:	50%
Structure:	47%
Transfer, mergers, redundancies:	40%

Organization: 38%
Health and Safety: 33%
Environment: 30%
Training: 23%

Meetings
Yearly: 88%
Twice a year: 9%
Extraordinary: 74%

Chair:
  Management: 54%
  Employee: 18%
  Joint/rotating: 6%

Feedback
Overall: 55%

Joint communiqué:
  workforce: 30%
  representatives: 6%
  managers: 3%

Distribution of minutes
  workforce: 7%
  managers: 8%
  representatives: 9%

Expert
Overall: 84%

Preparatory meetings: 41%
Meetings: 66%
Select committee: 5%
Agreement of management: 58%

Confidentiality
Overall: 77%

Protection
Overall: 43%

1. Mark Carley, Sabine Geissler and Hubert Krieger, *The contents of voluntary agreements on European-level information and consultation: preliminary findings of an analysis of 111 agreements*, September 1996, 14 p.
2. Japan, Switzerland and Australia.
3. 41 per cent European Federations.

X. Review of the Directive by the Commission

747. 'Not later than five years after the adoption of this Directive, the Commission shall, in consultation with the Member States and with management and labour at European level, review its operation and, in particular, examine whether the workforce size thresholds are appropriate with a view to proposing suitable amendments to the Council, where necessary' (Art. 15).

This will bring us well into the 21st century. The information and consultation directive may then, provided it survives the review, apply to more than 20 Member States with more than 500 million inhabitants.

Epilogue: In Search of . . .

We Need More (Good) Jobs

748. Everyone will agree that Europe needs more jobs and jobs which are well paid and with decent working conditions. Those jobs are increasingly lacking. Millions of Europeans are out of a job and the numbers are increasing. No one knows the exact figure – as those responsible for the figures have different ways of calculation and keeping them down – but we talk about millions. More than half of the work force in Europe lives under social harassment: is afraid of losing its employment. Employment in Europe is under pressure of *new technologies* wiping out certain jobs, creating others but not necessarily for those who were pushed out of the job market, of relocation to developing and other countries where conditions are offered no one can match: where workers work at 10 per cent of the European hourly labour costs with very minimal rights. Jobs are *re-engineered* away, restructured as costs have to go down and the work can be done more rationally, also in teams of permanent workers, motivated by new *human resources management* techniques with the aid of increasing numbers of flexible workers.

There is no doubt that *unemployment is one of the greatest social disasters* hitting our modern societies. Indeed, for many people, work is the best path to a meaningful life, opening the way to the market of goods and services and offering the possibility for a positive contribution to one's own family and for society at large. Working usually leads to enriching human contacts. Surely, work contributes to the development of the human personality and of human objective and subjective culture. Unemployment on the contrary leads to marginalisation and exclusion.

Given its societal importance, it is the duty of all of us to maximise the possibilities so that everyone can have the opportunity to exercise a meaningful job. All paths must be explored so that more fellow-citizens will benefit from doing suitable work.

Balance

749. Many might agree that when formulating proposals to promote job opportunities from the angle of labour law, one should look for measures which, without

– imposing more obligations on companies, either financially or organisationally;
– undermining the fundamental rights of workers and employment seekers;
– endangering the social security system; or
– entailing additional burdens on the public finances,

would:

1. materialise each possibility for employment by better matching supply and demand on the labour market;
2. encourage hiring of employees;
3. optimise the competitiveness of the enterprises and future employment opportunities;
4. prevent exclusion and marginalisation by safeguarding a better integration of employment seekers in the world of work; and
5. better answer the existing needs in society, especially in the non-profit sector.

No (Easy) Answer(s)

750. The drama is that Europe is split right down the middle about what to do about employment, job creation, wages and conditions. To put it bluntly and too over-simplified: some want to leave it to the invisible hand of the market and let the market play; others want to socially correct the market by introducing labour law, providing minimum protection against the blind market: regulation v. deregulation.

Subsidiarity

751. Here the principle of subsidiarity comes in. It is less innocent than it looks, but is seen by some as a way of limiting Community intervention also in the area of social policies. In any case, defining subsidiarity for the first time and giving it at the same time the central position it deserves in the Treaty as a guide to the development of Community law, Article 3B of the EC Treaty states that the Community shall in the areas which do not fall within its exclusive competence take action 'only and insofar as the objectives of the proposed action cannot be sufficiently achieved by the Member States and can therefore, by reason of scale or effects of proposed action, be better achieved by the Community.'

Subsidiarity not only relates to the question at which level, European or national, decisions should be taken, but also whether this should be done either through the avenue of legislation or through collective bargaining.

Subsidiarity concerns *de facto* the interpretation of the competences of the Community and those areas, where both the Community and the Member States are competent, which is self-evident in (most) labour law and some industrial relations matters, namely in the framework of the Maastricht Protocol on Social Policy and the consecutive agreement. As far as the EC is concerned, it has a restrictive meaning, which is also true for the implied and external competence of the EC. In order to constitute the appropriate level the EC will have to deliver *better results* than other levels, having regard to the objectives and the scale or effects of the proposed action.

Subsidiarity is, it seems, less a legal than a political notion when gauging the 'better results' one is looking for. The role of the Court of Justice concerning the interpretation and application of the subsidiarity principle constitutes at present a completely open question.

Anyway, subsidiarity should be used in its full (and original) sense: that the (European) centre as well as the constituent parts see to it that the ideals of freedom and social rights, as laid down in the Community Charter, are realised at different and appropriate levels in a Europe of peoples and regions, in a house, where there are many rooms.

Strategies

752. Not only different philosophies in all shades and colours of the rainbow divide political tendencies and consequently Member States, as well as employers' associations and trade unions, but also varying strategies are involved.

A point of departure is self-evidently the enormous variety between the labour law systems which has even been enhanced within the framework of the EEA, as now 17 countries are Members; the traditions regarding the role of legislation versus collective bargaining and/or *laissez faire* and/or managerial unilateralism; the power relations between trade unions/representatives of workers and management, legal or *de facto* and so many others, which make it extremely difficult to find common ground. Some see a competitive advantage in their way of attracting new investment and hopefully jobs.

A Two Track Social Europe?

753. Indeed, there are for labour law purposes now to Europe's: the 15 and the 14+2 (the 15 minus the UK but plus 2 EFTA countries: Iceland and Norway).

The 15

Unanimity

754. For the 15 the Single European Act prevails. Although the Single European Act does allow a qualified majority for the adoption of measures 'which have as their objective the establishment and functioning of the internal market,' the Act requires *unanimity* for measures relating to 'the rights and interests of employed persons' (Art. 100 A2). This means that every country in the Council of Ministers enjoys a veto power when voting on such issues. The chances that at least one employment minister will veto a labour law proposal are great indeed.

Qualified Majority

755.   Despite the general rule of unanimity, Article 118A of the Treaty allows the Council of Ministers to adopt laws governing *health and safety matters in the workplace by a qualified majority*. One of the most debated questions concerns the parameters of health and safety. Some argue for a broad Article 118A interpretation, which would go beyond the normal meaning of words and provide the European authorities with expanded ability in order to engage in progressive social policy making. I would argue that correct interpretation begins with the general rule of Article 100A, that rights and interests of employed persons should be decided on a unanimous basis. Article 118A, which allows a qualified majority only for health and safety matters in the workplace, constitutes an exception to the general rule. Therefore, Article 118A should be interpreted in a restrictive manner. Still, to the extent health and safety issues in the work place include a wide range of matters, the rule would encompass a large number of labour problems.

Ultimately, both the general rule and its exception complement each other. Both promote a worker's integrity in addition to his or her physical and psychological well-being. Safety and health concerns include the prevention of stress, work accidents and professional diseases.

Social Dialogue

756.   Although Article 118B of the EC Treaty requires the Commission to endeavour 'to develop the dialogue between management and labour at the European level which could, if the two sides consider it desirable, lead to relations based on agreement,' prospects for European *collective bargaining* are almost non-existent. Trade unions do not have enough power at the European level to force the employers' associations or multinational groups to meet around the bargaining table.

A '*social dialogue*' between employers and trade unions at the European level has taken place for a number of years at Val Duchesse, near Brussels, and has led to informal agreements on such issues as motivation and vocational training, information and consultation with respect to the introduction of new technologies, adaptability and flexibility on professional and geographic mobility and the improvement of the functioning of the Common Market in Europe. However, the outcomes of these talks are labelled 'common orientations,'[1] and do not even constitute informal guidelines. No real effort has been made to implement these 'common orientations' at national or sectorial levels. Undoubtedly, a number of sectorial talks do take place in various joint committees, but those talks mostly concern the sharing of information or consultation, not bargaining. At present more than 140 European Works Councils have already been established with information and some consultation rights.

They will undoubtedly receive an important impetus by the implementation of the directive on the establishment of EWC or procedures for informing and consulting employees. Surely, the directive is limited to European Community-scale enterprises which operate on the continent, but will also have an impact on companies with British headquarters, which have subsidiaries in the other Member States or in the EEA areas.

1. The social dialogue is the exercise whereby representatives of the European employers' organisations and of the European trade unions meet, under the guidance of the European Commission, in order to explore possibilities of common understanding regarding social matters.

Marginal and Fundamental

757.   The impact of the Social Chapter of the EC Treaty on the national labour law systems has been both *marginal and fundamental*. Marginal, as labour law has remained basically a national affair, due to the wording and limits as provided for in Article 100A2 of the EC Treaty, requiring unanimity. Fundamental as quite a number of fundamental principles and labour laws have been affirmed and/or acted upon: thus equal treatment as well in the area of free movement of labour, with all it involves, as in the area of sexual equality where Community law and its imple-mentation by the European Court has been of the highest importance. Important labour laws concern collective dismissals, acquired rights in case of transfer of enterprises, working time and above all health and safety.

However, there is not yet a common social market and social policies, also in the area of equal treatment, are undermined by the crisis rather than enhanced. It is like taking an umbrella away when it's raining.

The 14+2

Social Charter

758.   In December 1989, at their summit in Strasbourg under the French Presid-ency, the heads of government of 11 countries adopted a *Charter of Fundamental Social Rights*; only the United Kingdom refused to sign. The declaration has no binding force as it is purely an expression of political goals. It identifies twelve fundamental social rights as the objectives of the signatories:

1. freedom of movement;
2. freedom to choose and engage in an occupation and to be fairly remunerated;
3. improvement of living and working conditions;
4. social protection;
5. freedom of association and collective bargaining;
6. vocational training;
7. gender-equal treatment;
8. information, consultation and participation;
9. protection of health and safety at the workplace;
10. protection of children and young persons;
11. protection of the elderly and
12. the protection of the disabled.

By adopting the Charter, the Member States committed themselves to take the necessary steps to realise these rights. Progress however has been slow and has led to the Maastricht Protocol and Agreement on Social Policies for the 11.

Community Law

759.   Indeed, at Maastricht a separate Protocol on Social Policy was concluded, followed by an Agreement on Social Policy between the then 12 Member States minus the United Kingdom: the Community and the 11 Member States committed themselves to the promotion of employment, improved living and working conditions, proper social protection, dialogue between management and labour, the development of human resources with a view to lasting employment and the combating of exclusion. The agreement includes an extension of the social competence of the Community as well as of qualified majority voting and the possibility for collective labour agreements to be concluded at Community level with, under certain conditions, binding effect *erga omnes*.

760.   There can be no doubt that the Protocol and the Agreement on Social Policy which has been concluded on the basis of the Protocol form an integral part of the Treaty and are therefore a primary source of Community law with all the consequences this entails.

All this means that there will be a two-track social Europe: one for the Community as a whole and one for the Community and the EEA Members minus the United Kingdom. One and another signifies also that there are two possible avenues for the 14 Member States along which to develop their social policies: one within the framework of the EC Treaty (for the 15 Member States), which remains largely unchanged after Maastricht, and one within the framework of the agreement between the 14 Member States. If a proposal is vetoed by the United Kingdom, under the EC Treaty procedures, the 14 might take it up again under the social umbrella of the Protocol on Social Policy and their agreement.

A new social *acquis communautaire* may be developed by the 14 Member States, which the United Kingdom will have to implement in due time, when the political majority changes in Britain and the government in power decides to rejoin the Community as far as social policy is concerned. The difference will be that this new *acquis communautaire* will have been developed without decisive British input. The European employers were moreover not too happy with the British position: a more conciliatory stand by the United Kingdom may have paved the way to an agreement by the 15 Member States in the framework of which the United Kingdom might have played a, for the benefit of the employers, moderating role, which is at present to a lesser degree possible under the Maastricht Agreement. At any rate the new social dimension will apply to subsidiaries of British companies, operating in Europe.

A New Social Dimension

761.   The Community (of the 14) thus received a broad mandate in the social sphere: these competences do not fall within the ambit of Article 100A2 of the EC

Treaty, which allowed for a veto right of Member States regarding rights and interests of workers. The Community's social competence under the Maastricht Agreement will be interpreted on its own merits and not restrictively, as is the case with the social policy provisions under the *acquis communautaire*.

Accessorium Sequitur Principale

762.   The social policy issues will be dealt with by the Council either by qualified majority (e.g., information and consultation of workers) or by unanimity (e.g., representation of workers). There is a delicate relationship between these issues, when a Community proposal contains elements of both groups, one belonging to the basket of majority competences, the other to be voted upon by unanimity. Here the adagium: *accessorium sequitur principale* should be invoked to determine whether an issue, *in toto*, will be decided upon by qualified majority or by way of unanimity.

An Enhanced Role for the Commission and the Social Partners

763.   The task of the Commission has been enhanced as well as the role of the social partners, providing an excellent example of the application of the principle of subsidiarity. The role of the social partners goes from consultation with the Community, also on Community legislation, to implementation of Council directives and to European-wide collective bargaining. Thus the autonomy of the social partners in relation to the government has been considerably enhanced.

European Collective Bargaining

764.   In this field there has been a real legal breakthrough: an historic agreement between the European social partners on 31 October 1991 in Brussels paved the way for genuine acceptance of European bargaining and for agreeing to a mechanism to provide a binding effect of the collective agreements *erga omnes* throughout the Community by the 14 Member States.

Those European collective agreements, which can be concluded at different levels (enterprise, sector, multi-industry, the Community as a whole) will either be implemented in accordance with national practices regarding collective bargaining or by way of a Council decision. The latter will beyond doubt give the agreement effect *erga omnes*. It shall be noted that such a Council decision is taken at the request of the social partners and on the proposal of the Commission.

One has however at the same time to take into account that the collective agreement is a very complex legal institution and the possible conclusion of agreements at a European level makes it even more complex. There is no doubt that further down the road specific European legislation will be needed in order to see to it that European collective agreements have the full effect they intend to have. European framework legislation is obviously needed because the solution of falling back on the legislation of one of the Member States is not adequate, neither for the obligatory part nor for the normative part of the collective agreement. There should be a possibility to approach the Court of Justice regarding disputes concerning the interpretation of European collective agreements, as one envisages that it is to have a uniform Community-wide interpretation of agreements. This is certainly not possible at present for those agreements, which do not get the Community blessing by way of a Council decision.

765.   Here the first European collective agreement, concluded under the Maastricht Agreement on Social Policy, can be reported, namely the one on Parental Leave, concluded on 14 December 1995. The agreement was implemented by a Council Directive of 4 June 1996. Earlier attempts to reach agreements on information and consultation and on the burden of proof regarding equal treatment had failed. A new agreement was concluded on Part-time work on 6 June 1997, and other agreements may be expected as the social partners may be called upon to consider, in the framework of consultations with the Commission and of the social dialogue, other issues regarding the flexibility of the labour market, information and consultation of employees and sexual harassment.

766.   It may well be that the number of social partners will increase and that other organisations join UNICE, CEEP and the ETUC in the social dialogue, as the present interpretation of the notion social partners by the Commission is inappropriate and inadequate.

Informing and Consulting Employees: the EWC or a Procedure

767.   Information and consultation of employees has always been part of the European social agenda, practically since the beginning of the 1960s. However, few issues have aroused a more heated debate. Now, after so many years, the adoption of a European directive on the establishment of a EWC or a procedure in Community-scale undertakings and Community-scale Groups of Undertakings for the purposes of informing and consulting employees is a fact. Within some years – at the latest by the year 2000 – Community-scale undertakings will be legally obliged to have a EWC or an information and consultation procedure. The directive will apply to enterprises which occupy at least 1,000 employees and have at least two subsidiaries in two Member States of the European Union (excluding the UK) and/or of the EEA-EFTA countries with each at least 150 employees. It is estimated that some 2,000 companies will have to comply.

768.   The mandatory character of the directive has been widely criticised, especially from the employer's side. With this criticism in mind, the European Union wants to promote as much as possible 'voluntarism' and encourages the voluntary conclusion of agreements on information and consultation between the central management of the companies and the representatives of the employees even before the directive enters into force, which at the earliest will be 1997. Agreements existing prior to that date will continue to be valid even after 1997 and can be prolonged by the parties.

Thus, Community-scale undertakings and the representatives of the employees had a choice to make: whether they wanted to wait until the directive would enter into force or whether they wanted to conclude a so-called pre-existing agreement. Such an agreement leaves quite some flexibility to the parties, although a number of minimum requirements have to be lived up to.

The Battle Goes On

769.   The directive on the establishment of EWCs or procedures in Community-scale undertakings and Community-scale groups of undertakings for the purposes of informing and consulting employees is the outcome of a long and protracted battle demonstrating fundamentally opposed views concerning the way our market economies should function, and which kind of capitalism to pursue. That basic conflict has not come to an end; on the contrary. As already stated above, the battle goes on between regulation and deregulation, between pure marketeers and those who advocate social corrections of the market economy, including minimum standards and overall rules of conduct for enterprises. The same tension can be seen in the present discussions concerning the social clause in international trade.

770.   So in a sense there is nothing new. However, as events go by, one wonders whether this directive may be one of the last important Community instruments in the European labour law area as the momentum for more deregulation and flexibility takes full swing, more countries join the Common Market and consequently more diversity characterises the European Union, making agreements between so many divergent Member States and social partners on what kind of social policies to pursue at European level more difficult to reach.

771.   The debate regarding information and consultation of employees was not so much about the principle of informing and consulting the employees itself. Indeed, the European social partners, UNICE and the ETUC recognise its merits, as their Joint Opinion on Information and Consultation of 1987 clearly demonstrates, and the right to information and consultation is enshrined in many international instruments like the European Social Charter of the Council of Europe (1988) and the Community Charter of the fundamental Social Rights of Workers (1989). The point of contention was how the implement the principle.

772.   Employers stress diversity, flexibility, voluntarism, informality; trade unions insist on minimum rules, on some formalism, on binding objectives and on an effective follow up.

Power Relations

773.   The debate should also be seen in the framework of the power relations between management and labour which have been dramatically affected, especially in a period in which the economic world becomes more and more international and

almost totally escapes the grip of European actors, i.e., politicians, trade unions and also employers and their organisations. It is quite clear that the social partners, the employers' associations as well as the trade unions lose influence and members, both at national as at European level, and even more so at world level. Trade unions are also losing power on the market place. Undertakings have become the main participants on the markets; they have their own specific strategies in which trade unions play less and less a role or no role at all. Decentralisation, empowerment, individualisation coupled with teamwork, driven by re-engineering and bench marking are the main characteristics shaping the industrial relations and human resources management policies of the enterprises today. In this 'new brave world,' collectively cooked up 'information and consultation schemes' seem to many of the protagonists more than outdated. No wonder, then, that many enterprises, and consequently their organisations, vehemently oppose not so much the idea of in-forming and consulting employees, but the thought of having trade unions back on their playing fields through the back door of EWCs. Many, especially US based undertakings, do not like that the power the trade unions lost in the market place is conquered back in political arenas.

774.   These are some of the fundamental reasons why the UK opted out of the Maastricht Agreement on Social Policy and why the European social partners failed in their attempt to conclude a European collective agreement on the issue of infor-mation and consultation, although they tried very hard as their credibility as 'social partners' was and is at stake. UNICE had to back out of the negotiations, as the CBI (a curious partner) withdrew its support when minimum mandatory requirements regarding transnational information and consultation were put on the table by the trade unions.

The directive constitutes a kiss of life to the social dialogue at European level. It first recognises, almost officially and without any conditions, the pre-existing agreements regarding information and consultation of employees and reinforces by the same token the idea of the autonomy of the social partners, in itself an expres-sion of the subsidiarity principle. It secondly lays down in a flexible but firm way, structures of social dialogue and democracy at European levels; flexible as the parties are entitled – on a foot of equality – to determine their own methods; firm, as minimum mandatory requirements come into play where voluntarism fails. By doing so, the EU has strengthened the role and the powers of the European social partners.

775.   The directive does not, however, basically affect managerial prerogative, which remains in full; neither does the directive establish a right for the employees' representatives to bargain on wages and conditions at European level or to call for industrial action: neither the EWC not the procedure can, legally speaking, be vehicles for international solidarity action. However, the directive leaves the exist-ing bargaining and industrial action rights intact. The truth of the matter is that the employers see the directive as already a bridge too far, while the trade unions consider the EWC as an important stepping stone on the road to European bargain-ing. Such an ambiguity seems unavoidable.

776.   That EC legal requirements can have some teeth is clearly shown by the landmark judgments of the Court of Justice of 8 June 1994,[1] interpreting the information and consultation requirements of the directives on Collective Redundancies (1975) and on Transfers of Undertakings (1977), leading to the conclusion that the British system of employee relations failed to implement fully the EC directives. These directives impose compulsory obligations on employers. The directive on informing and consulting also will have an impact on the UK notwithstanding its opt-out of the Maastricht Agreement on Social Policy: the fact is that many UK headquartered undertakings with businesses on the European continent will also be obliged to set up an EWC or procedure, as will many overseas multinationals which are present in Europe.

    1. *Commission* v. *U.K.*, C-382/92 and 383/92, *Jur.*, 1994, 2435.

Voluntarism

777.   The employers' criticism about too many rigidities in European labour markets has inspired the directive on the establishment of an EWC or a procedure for the purposes of informing and consulting employees, in a very large degree. Indeed, 'voluntarism' is the directive's main vehicle for the establishment of an EWC or an information or consultation procedure. The European parties in the Community-scale undertakings or groups of undertakings are free to do their own thing; they can conclude their own agreements as they see fit. All the options are open and they are plenty: indeed, the directive leaves wide-ranging flexibility. What is needed is a spirit of cooperation, leading to the conclusion of an agreement between central management and the employees' representatives on transnational (= European) information and consultation. That's all.

Cooperation

778.   The only obligation parties have is to negotiate and to agree; and this the directive expects to be done in 'a spirit of cooperation.' There is a challenge and a choice to be made. In particular, undertakings have to decide which way to go: wait and see or to be pro-active, taking the specifics of each situation into account, such as the presence of trade unions insisting on the conclusion of an agreement. Concluding an agreement earlier, before the directive enters into force, provides room for more flexibility, may contribute to a spirit of cooperation, improve corporate image and enhance integrated IR and HRM policies. Indeed, Article 9 of the directive stresses the need for central management and the EWC to work in a spirit of cooperation with due regard to their reciprocal rights and obligations. The same applies to the cooperation in the framework of an information and consultation procedure for workers.

Balance

779.   Given the social history and developments in the majority of EU-EEA Member States, where information and consultation constitute well-established principles and practices, a measure of the kind of a European directive on information and consultation of employees was, in the long term, unavoidable. It has taken several decades to have a European instrument of this nature. It reflects a certain balance between the interests of both sides. The fact that several enterprises are already voluntary engaged in developing their own schemes, adapting to what their management and employees see as their specific needs and interests, gives hope that the directive will contribute to the economic as well as to the social efficiency all enterprises need.

The Path is Clear: Time to Dream

780. Indeed, there is, after Maastricht, a new horizon, a 'new frontier,' there are growing possibilities for a fair social Europe, based on more solidarity than before as the economic and social cohesion were equally strengthened, with a fuller participation of the social partners in the elaboration of European social policies. Likewise the powers of the EP were strengthened. Again, there are novel opportunities. We all know that the road to the well-being of all in Europe, Western as well as Central and Eastern Europe, is long, narrow and difficult. But let us take up the challenge: we know that we are on the right track of fundamental human freedoms and social rights, of liberty of speech and expression, of respect for privacy and that there is adequate room for private initiative. There are more challenges than answers. The wider the Community becomes, the more it will be difficult for politicians and social partners, wherever the last still operate as such, to foster the necessary will to elaborate an adequate social dimension for the Europeans. It is again time for vision and bold decisions. It is never too late to dream, even after the Treaty of Amsterdam of 16–17 June 1997, which we will look at in the annex.

Appendices

Appendix 1. Community Charter on the Fundamental Social Rights of Workers (1989)

THE HEADS OF STATE OR THE GOVERNMENT OF MEMBER STATES OF THE EUROPEAN COMMUNITY MEETING AT STRASBOURG ON 9 DECEMBER 1989[1]

WHEREAS under the terms of Article 117 of the EEC Treaty, the Member States have agreed on the need to promote improved living and working conditions for workers so as to make possible their harmonisation while the improvement is being maintained;

WHEREAS following on from the conclusions of the European Councils of Hanover and Rhodes the European Council of Madrid considered that, in the context of the establishment of the single European market, the same importance must be attached to the social aspects as to the economic aspects and whereas, therefore, they must be developed in a balanced manner;

HAVING REGARD to the Resolutions of the European Parliament of 1 March 1989, 14 September 1989 and 22 November 1989, and to the Opinion of the Economic and Social Committee of 22 February 1989;

WHEREAS the completion of the internal market is the most effective means of creating employment and ensuring maximum well-being in the Community; whereas employment development and creation must be given first priority in the completion of the internal market; whereas it is for the Community to take up the challenges of the future with regard to economic competitiveness, taking into account, in particular, regional imbalances;

WHEREAS the social consensus contributes to the strengthening of the competitiveness of undertakings, of the economy as a whole and to the creation of employment; whereas in this respect it is an essential condition for ensuring sustained economic development;

WHEREAS the completion of the internal market must favour the approximation of improvements in living and working conditions, as well as economic and social cohesion within the European Community while avoiding distortions of competition;

1. Text adopted by the Heads of State or Government of 11 Member States.

Appendix 1

WHEREAS the completion of the internal market must offer improvements in the social field for workers of the European Community, especially in terms of freedom of movement, living and working conditions, health and safety at work, social protection, education and training;

WHEREAS in order to ensure equal treatment, it is important to combat every form of discrimination, including discrimination on grounds of sex, colour, race, opinions and beliefs, and whereas, in a spirit of solidarity, it is important to combat social exclusion;

WHEREAS it is for Member States to guarantee that workers from non-member countries and members of their families who are legally resident in a Member State of the European Community are able to enjoy, as regards their living and working conditions, treatment comparable to that enjoyed by workers who are nationals of the Member State concerned;

WHEREAS inspiration should be drawn from the Conventions of the International Labour Organisation and from the European Social Charter of the Council of Europe;

WHEREAS the Treaty, as amended by the Single European Act, contains provisions laying down the powers of the Community relating *inter alia* to the freedom of movement of workers (Articles 7, 48 to 51), the right of establishment (Articles 52 to 58), the social field under the conditions laid down in Articles 117 to 122 in particular as regards the improvement of health and safety in the working environment (Article 118a), the development of the dialogue between management and labour at European level (Article 118b), equal pay for men and women for equal work (Article 119) the general principles for implementing a common vocational training policy (Article 128), economic and social cohesion (Article 130a to 130e) and, more generally, the approximation of legislation (Articles 100, 100a and 235); whereas the implementation of the Charter must not entail an extension of the Community's powers as defined by the Treaties;

WHEREAS the aim of the present Charter is on the one hand to consolidate the progress made in the social field, through action by the Member States, the two sides of industry and the Community;

WHEREAS its aim is on the other hand to declare solemnly that the implementation of the Single European Act must take full account of the social dimension of the Community and that it is necessary in this context to ensure at appropriate levels the development of the social rights of workers of the European Community, especially employed workers and self-employed persons;

WHEREAS, in accordance with the conclusions of the Madrid European Council, the respective Community rules, national legislation and collective agreements must be clearly established;

WHEREAS, by virtue of the principle of subsidiarity, responsibility for the initiatives to be taken with regard to the implementation of these social rights lies with the

442

Member States or their constituent parts and, within the limits of its powers, with the European Community; whereas such implementation may take the form of laws, collective agreements or existing practises at the various appropriate levels and whereas it requires in many spheres the active involvement of the two sides of industry;

WHEREAS the solemn proclamation of fundamental social rights at European Community level may not, when implemented, provide grounds for any retrogression compared with the situation currently existing in each Member State,

HAVE ADOPTED THE FOLLOWING DECLARATION CONSTITUTING THE 'COMMUNITY CHARTER OF THE FUNDAMENTAL SOCIAL RIGHTS OF WORKERS':

TITLE I. FUNDAMENTAL SOCIAL RIGHTS OF WORKERS

Freedom of movement

1. Every worker of the European Community shall have the right to freedom of movement throughout the territory of the Community, subject to restrictions justified on grounds of public order, public safety or public health.

2. The right to freedom of movement shall enable any worker to engage in any occupation or profession in the Community in accordance with the principles of equal treatment as regards access to employment, working conditions and social protection in the host country.

3. The right of freedom of movement shall also imply:

  (i) harmonisation of conditions of residence in all Member States, particularly those concerning family reunification;
 (ii) elimination of obstacles arising from the non-recognition of diplomas or equivalent occupational qualifications;
(iii) improvement of the living and working conditions of frontier workers.

Employment and remuneration

4. Every individual shall be free to choose and engage in a occupation according to the regulations governing each occupation.

5. All employment shall be fairly remunerated. To this end, in accordance with arrangements applying in each country:

  (i) workers shall be assured of an equitable wage, i.e., a wage sufficient to enable them to have a decent standard of living;
 (ii) workers subject to terms of employment other than an open-ended full-time contract shall benefit from an equitable reference wage;

(iii) wages may be withheld, seized or transferred only in accordance with national law; such provisions should entail measures enabling the worker concerned to continue to enjoy the necessary means of subsistence for him or herself and his or her family.

6. Every individual must be able to have access to public placement services free of charge.

Improvement of living and working conditions

7. The completion of the internal market must lead to an improvement in the living and working conditions of workers in the European Community. This process must result from an approximation of these conditions while the improvement is being maintained, as regards in particular duration and organisation of working time and forms of employment other than open-ended contracts, such as fixed-term contracts, part-time working, temporary work and seasonal work.

The improvement must cover, where necessary, the development of certain aspects of employment regulations such as procedures for collective redundancies and those regarding bankruptcies.

8. Every worker of the European Community shall have a right to a weekly rest period and to annual paid leave, the duration of which must be progressively harmonised in accordance with national practises.

9. The conditions of employment of every worker of the European Community shall be stipulated in laws, a collective agreement or a contract of employment, according to arrangements applying in each country.

Social protection

According to the arrangements applying in each country:

10. Every worker of the European Community shall have a right to adequate social protection and shall, whatever his status and whatever the size of the undertaking in which he is employed, enjoy an adequate level of social security benefits.

Persons who have been unable either to enter or re-enter the labour market and have no means of subsistence must be able to receive sufficient resources and social assistance in keeping with their particular situation.

Freedom of association and collective bargaining

11. Employers and workers of the European Community shall have the right of association in order to constitute professional organisations or trade unions of their choice for the defence of their economic and social interests.

Every employer and every worker shall have the freedom to join or not to join such organisations without any personal or occupational damage being thereby suffered by him.

12. Employers or employers' organisations, on the one hand, and workers' organisations, on the other, shall have the right to negotiate and conclude collective agreements under the conditions laid down by national legislation and practice.

The dialogue between the two sides of industry at European level which must be developed, may, if the parties deem it desirable, result in contractual relations in particular at inter-occupational and sectoral level.

13. The right to resort to collective action in the event of a conflict of interests shall include the right to strike, subject to the obligations arising under national regulations and collective agreements.

In order to facilitate the settlement of industrial disputes the establishment and utilisation at the appropriate levels of conciliation, mediation and arbitration procedures should be encouraged in accordance with national practice.

14. The internal legal order of the Member States shall determine under which conditions and to what extent the rights provided for in Articles 11 to 13 apply to the armed forces, the police and the civil service.

Vocational training

15. Every worker of the European Community must be able to have access to vocational training and to benefit therefrom throughout his working life. In the conditions governing access to such training there may be no discrimination on grounds of nationality.

The competent public authorities, undertakings or the two sides of industry, each within their own sphere of competence, should set up continuing and permanent training systems enabling every person to undergo retraining more especially through leave for training purposes, to improve his skills or to acquire new skills, particularly in the light of technical developments.

Equal treatment for men and women

16. Equal treatment for men and women must be assured. Equal opportunities for men and women must be developed.

To this end, action should be intensified to ensure the implementation of the principle of equality between men and women as regards in particular access to employment, remuneration, working conditions, social protection, education, vocational training and career development.

Measures should also be developed enabling men and women to reconcile their occupational and family obligations.

Appendix 1

Information, consultation and participation for workers

17. Information, consultation and participation for workers must be developed along appropriate lines, taking account of the practises in force in the various Member States.

This shall apply especially in companies or groups of companies having establishments or companies in two or more Member States of the European Community.

18. Such information, consultation and participation must be implemented in due time, particularly in the following cases:

- (i) when technological changes which, from the point of view of working conditions and work organisation, have major implications for the workforce, are introduced into undertakings;
- (ii) in connection with restructuring operations in undertakings or in cases of mergers having an impact on the employment of workers;
- (iii) in cases of collective redundancy procedures;
- (iv) when transfrontier workers in particular are affected by employment policies pursued by the undertaking where they are employed.

Health protection and safety at the workplace

19. Every worker must enjoy satisfactory health and safety conditions in his working environment. Appropriate measures must be taken in order to achieve further harmonisation of conditions in this area while maintaining the improvements made.

These measures shall take account, in particular, of the need for training, information, consultation and balanced participation of workers as regards the risks incurred and the steps taken to eliminate or reduce them.

The provisions regarding implementation of the internal market shall help to ensure such protection.

Protection of children and adolescents

20. Without prejudice to such rules as may be more favourable to young people, in particular those ensuring their preparation for work through vocational training, and subject to derogations limited to certain light work, the minimum employment age must not be lower than the minimum school-leaving age and, in any case, not lower than 15 years.

21. Young people who are in gainful employment must receive equitable remuneration in accordance with national practice.

22. Appropriate measures must be taken to adjust labour regulations applicable to young workers so that their specific development and vocational training and access to employment needs are met.

The duration of work must, in particular, be limited without it being possible to circumvent this limitation through recourse to overtime and night work prohibited in the case of workers of under 18 years of age, save in the case of certain job laid down in national legislation or regulations.

23.   Following the end of compulsory education, young people must be entitled to receive initial vocational training of a sufficient duration to enable them to adapt to the requirements of their working life; for young workers, such training should take place during working hours.

Elderly persons

According to the arrangements applying in each country:

24.   Every worker of the European Community must, at the time of retirement, be able to enjoy resources affording him or her a decent standard of living.

25.   Any person who has reached retirement age but who is not entitled to a pension or who does not have other means of subsistence, must be entitled to sufficient resources and to medical and social assistance specifically suited to his needs.

Disabled persons

26.   All disabled persons, whatever the origin and nature of their disablement, must be entitled to additional concrete measures aimed at improving their social and professional integration.

These measures must concern, in particular, according to the capacities of the beneficiaries, vocational training, ergonomics, accessibility, mobility, means of transport and housing.

TITLE II. IMPLEMENTATION OF THE CHARTER

27.   It is more particularly the responsibility of the Member States, in accordance with national practices, notably through legislative measures or collective agreements, to guarantee the fundamental social rights in this Charter and to implement the social measures indispensable to the smooth operation of the internal market as part of a strategy of economic and social cohesion.

28.   The European Council invites the Commission to submit as soon as possible initiatives which fall within its powers, as provided for in the Treaties, with a view to the adoption of legal instruments for the effective implementation, as and when the internal market is completed, of those rights which come within the Community's area of competence.

Appendix 1

29. The Commission shall establish each year, during the last three months, a report on the application of the Charter by the Member States and by the European Community.

30. The report of the Commission shall be forwarded to the European Council, the European Parliament and the Economic and Social Committee.

Appendix 2. Protocol on Economic and Social Cohesion (1991)

The High Contracting Parties

Recalling that the Union has set itself the objective of promoting economic and social progress, *inter alia*, through the strengthening of economic and social cohesion;

Recalling that Article 2 of the Treaty establishing the European Community includes the task of promoting economic and social cohesion and solidarity between Member States and that the strengthening of economic and social cohesion figures among the activities of the Community listed in Article 3;

Recalling that the provisions of Part Three, Title XIV, on economic and social cohesion as a whole, provide the legal basis for consolidating and further developing the Community's action in the field of economic and social cohesion, including the creation of a new fund;

Recalling that the provisions of Part Three, Title XII on trans-European networks and Title XVI on environment envisage a Cohesion Fund to be set up before 31 December 1993;

Stating their belief that progress towards Economic and Monetary Union will contribute to the economic growth of all Member States;

Noting that the Community's Structural Funds are being doubled in real terms between 1987 and 1993, implying large transfers, especially as a proportion of GDP of the less prosperous Member States;

Noting that the European Investment Bank is lending large and increasing amounts for the benefit of the poorer regions;

Noting the desire for greater flexibility in the arrangements for allocations from the Structural Funds;

Noting the desire for modulation of the levels of Community participation in programmes and projects in certain countries;

Noting the proposal to take greater account of the relative prosperity of Member States in the system of own resources;

Appendix 2

REAFFIRM that the promotion of economic and social cohesion is vital to the full development and enduring success of the Community, and underline the importance of the inclusion of economic and social cohesion in Articles 2 and 3 of this Treaty;

REAFFIRM their conviction that the Structural Funds should continue to play a considerable part in the achievement of Community objectives in the field of cohesion;

REAFFIRM their conviction that the European Investment Bank should continue to devote the majority of its resources to the promotion of economic and social cohesion, and declare their willingness to review the capital needs of the European Investment Bank as soon as this is necessary for that purpose;

REAFFIRM the need for a thorough evaluation of the operation and effectiveness of the Structural funds in 1992, and the need to review, on that occasion, the appropriate size of these Funds in the light of the tasks of the Community in the area of economic and social cohesion;

AGREE that the Cohesion Fund to be set up before 31 December 1993 will provide Community financial contributions to projects in the fields of environment and trans-European networks in Member States with a per capita GNP of less than 90 per cent of the Community average which have a programme leading to the fulfilment of the conditions of economic convergence as set out in Article 104c;

DECLARE their intention of allowing a greater margin of flexibility in allocating financing from the Structural Funds to specific needs not covered under the present Structural Funds regulations;

DECLARE their willingness to modulate the levels of Community participation in the context of programmes and projects of the Structural Funds, with a view to avoiding excessive increases in budgetary expenditure in the less prosperous Member States;

RECOGNISE the need to monitor regularly the progress made towards achieving economic and social cohesion and state their willingness to study all necessary measures in this respect;

DECLARE their intention of taking greater account of the contributive capacity of individual Member States in the system of own resources, and of examining means of correcting, for the less prosperous Member States, regressive elements existing in the present own resources system;

AGREE to annex this Protocol to the Treaty establishing the European Community.

Appendix 3. UNICE, the ETUC and CEEP Joint Proposal of the Draft Treaty for European Political Union (1991)

Article 118

(4) A Member State may entrust management and labour at their joint request with the implementation of the directive adopted in accordance with paragraphs 2 and 3.

In that event, it shall see it that (no later than the date of entry into force of directive) management and labour have established the requisite measures by agreement between themselves, but the Member State concerned shall take such action as is needed to enable it at all times to secure the results to be achieved by virtue of the directive.

Article 118A

(1) The Commission's task is to promote the consultation of the social partners at Community-level and take any measure, useful to facilitate their dialogue, ensuring a balanced support of the parties.
(2) For this purpose, before presenting its proposals in the field of social policy, the Commission will consult the social partners on the possible guidelines for a Community action.
(3) If, after this consultation, the Commission considers that a Community action is desirable, it will consult the social partners regarding the content of the envisaged proposals. The social partners will transmit to the Commissions an opinion or, if appropriate, a recommendation.
(4) In the course of this consultation the social partners may inform the Commission of their desire to engage the process provided for in Article 118.b, paragraphs 1 and 2. This procedure may not exceed 9 months duration, unless an extension is jointly agreed by the social partners concerned.

Article 118B

(1) The dialogue between the social partners at Community level can lead, if the latter so desire, to relations based on agreements.
(2) Those agreements concluded at Community level may be realised either – according to the procedures and practises appropriate to the social partner and to the Member States or – in matters covered by Article 118, at the joint request of the signatories, on the basis of a decision of the Council on a proposal from the Commission, with regard to the agreements as they have been concluded. This decision will follow the voting procedures of Article 118.

Appendix 4. Protocol on Social Policy (1991)

Noting that eleven Member States, that is to say the Kingdom of Belgium, the Kingdom of Denmark, the Federal Republic of Germany, the Hellenic Republic, the Kingdom of Spain, the French Republic, Ireland, the Italian Republic, the Grand Duchy of Luxembourg, the Kingdom of the Netherlands, and the Portuguese Republic, wish to continue along the path laid down in the 1989 Social Charter; that they have adopted among themselves an Agreement to this end; that this Agreement is annexed to this Protocol; that this Protocol and the said Agreement are without prejudice to the provisions of this Treaty, particularly those relating to social policy which constitute an integral part of the *acquis communautaire*:

1. Agree to authorize those eleven Member States to have recourse to the institutions, procedures and mechanisms of the Treaty for the purpose of taking among themselves and applying as far as they are concerned the acts and decisions required for giving effect to the above-mentioned Agreement.
2. The United Kingdom of Great Britain and Northern Ireland shall not take part in the deliberations and the adoption by the Council of Commission proposals made on the basis of this Protocol and the basis of this Protocol and the above-mentioned Agreement.

   By way of derogation from Article 148(2) of the Treaty, acts of the Council which are made pursuant to this Protocol and which must be adopted by a qualified majority shall be deemed to be so adopted if they have received at least forty-four votes in favour. The unanimity of the members of the Council, with the exception of the United Kingdom of Great Britain and Northern Ireland, shall be necessary for acts of the Council which must be adopted unanimously and for those amending the Commission proposal.

   Acts adopted by the Council and any financial consequences other than administrative costs entailed for the institutions shall not be applicable to the United Kingdom of Great Britain and Northern Ireland.
3. This Protocol shall be annexed to the Treaty establishing the European Community.

Appendix 5. Agreement on Social Policy Concluded Between the Member States of the European Community With the Exception of the United Kingdom of Great Britain and Northern Ireland (1991)

The undersigned eleven HIGH CONTRACTING PARTIES, that is to say the Kingdom of Belgium, the Kingdom of Denmark, the Federal Republic of Germany, the Hellenic Republic, the Kingdom of Spain, the French Republic, Ireland, the Italian Republic, the Grand Duchy of Luxembourg, the Kingdom of the Netherlands and the Portuguese Republic (hereinafter referred to as 'the Member States').

WISHING to implement the 1989 Social Charter on the basis of the 'acquis communautaire'.

CONSIDERING the Protocol on social policy,

HAVE AGREED as follows:

Article 1

The Community and the Member States shall have as their objectives the promotion of employment, improved living and working conditions, proper social protection, dialogue between management and labour, the development of human resources with a view to lasting high employment and the combatting of exclusion. To this end the Community and the Member States shall implement measures which take account of the diverse forms of national practices, in particular in the field of contractual relations, and the need to maintain the competitiveness of the Community economy.

Article 2

1. With a view to achieving the objectives of Article 1, the Community shall support and complement the activities of the Member States in the following fields:

- improvement in particular of the working environment to protect workers' health and safety;
- working conditions;
- the information and consultation of workers;
- equality between men and women with regard to labour market opportunities and treatment at work;
- the integration of persons excluded from the labour market, without prejudice to Article 127 of the Treaty establishing the European Community (hereinafter referred to as 'the Treaty').

453

2. To this end, the Council may adopt, by means of directives, minimum requirements for gradual implementation, having regard to the conditions and technical rules obtaining in each of the Member States. Such directives shall avoid imposing administrative, financial and legal constraints in a way which would hold back the creation and development of small and medium-sized undertakings.

The Council shall act in accordance with the procedure referred to in Article 189c of the Treaty after consulting the Economic and Social Committee.

3. However, the Council shall act unanimously on a proposal from the Commission, after consulting the European Parliament and the Economic and Social Committee, in the following areas:

- social security and social protection of workers;
- protection of workers where their employment contract is terminated;
- representation and collective defence of the interests of workers and employers, including co-determination, subject to paragraph 6;
- conditions of employment for third-country nationals legally residing in Community territory;
- financial contributions for promotion of employment and job-creation, without prejudice to the provisions relating to the Social Fund.

4. A Member State may entrust management and labour, at their joint request, with the implementation of directives adopted pursuant to paragraphs 2 and 3.

In this case, it shall ensure that, no later than the date on which a directive must be transposed in accordance with Article 189, management and labour have introduced the necessary measures by agreement, the Member State concerned being required to take any necessary measure enabling it at any time to be in a position to guarantee the results imposed by that directive.

5. The provisions adopted pursuant to this article shall not prevent any Member State from maintaining or introducing more stringent protective measures compatible with the Treaty.

6. The provisions of this article shall not apply to pay, the right of association, the right to strike or the right to impose lock-outs.

Article 3

1. The Commission shall have the task of promoting the consultation of management and labour at Community level and shall take any relevant measure to facilitate their dialogue by ensuring balanced support for the parties.

2. To this end, before submitting proposals in the social policy field, the Commission shall consult management and labour on the possible direction of Community action.

3. If, after such consultation, the Commission considers Community action advisable, it shall consult management and labour on the content of the envisaged proposal. Management and labour shall forward to the commission an opinion or, where appropriate, a recommendation.

4. On the occasion of such consultation, management and labour may inform the Commission of their wish to initiate the process provided for in Article 4. The duration of the procedure shall not exceed nine months, unless the management and labour concerned and the Commission decide jointly to extend it.

Article 4

1. Should management and labour so desire, the dialogue between them at Community level may lead to contractual relations, including agreements.

2. Agreements concluded at Community level shall be implemented either in accordance with the procedures and practises specific to management and labour and the Member States or, in matters covered by Article 2, at the joint request of the signatory parities, by a Council decision on a proposal from the Commission.

The Council shall act by qualified majority, except where the agreement in question contains one or more provisions relating to one of the areas referred to in Article 2(3), in which case it shall act unanimously.

Article 5

With a view to achieving the objectives of Article 1 and without prejudice to the other provisions of the Treaty, the Commission shall encourage cooperation between the Member States and facilitate the coordination of their action in all social policy fields under this Agreement.

Article 6

1. Each member State shall ensure that the principle of equal pay for male and female workers for equal work is applied.

2. For the purpose of this article, 'pay' means the ordinary basic or minimum wage or salary and any other consideration, whether in cash or in kind, which the worker receives directly or indirectly, in respect of his employment, from his employer.

Equal pay without discrimination based on sex means:

(a) that pay for the same work at piece rates shall be calculated on the basis of the same unit of measurement;
(b) that pay for work at time rates shall be the same for the same job.

3. This article shall not prevent any Member State from maintaining or adopting measures providing for specific advantages in order to make it easier for women to pursue a vocational activity or to prevent or compensate for disadvantages in their professional careers.

Appendix 5

Article 7

The Commission shall draw up a report each year on progress in achieving the objectives of Article 1, including the demographic situation in the Community. It shall forward the report to the European Parliament, the Council and the Economic and Social Committee.

The European Parliament may invite the Commission to draw up reports on particular problems concerning the social situation.

Appendix 6. Declarations

1. Declaration on Article 2(2)

The eleven High Contracting Parties note that in the discussion on Article 2(2) of the Agreement it was agreed that the Community does not intend, in laying down minimum requirements for the protection of the safety and health of employees, to discriminate in a manner unjustified by the circumstances against employees in small and medium-sized undertakings.

2. Declaration on Article 4(2)

The eleven High Contracting Parties declare that the first of the arrangements for application of the agreements between management and labour at Community level – referred to in Article 4(2) – will consist in developing, by collective bargaining according to the rules of each Member State, the content of the agreements, and that consequently this arrangement implies no obligation on the Member States to apply the agreements directly or to work out rules for their transposition, nor any obligation to amend national legislation in force to facilitate their implementation.

Appendix 7. Protocol concerning Article 119 of the Treaty Establishing the European Community (1991)

HAVE AGREED UPON the following provision, which shall be annexed to the Treaty establishing the European Community:

For the purposes of Article 119 of this Treaty, benefits under occupational social security schemes shall not be considered as remuneration if and in so far as they are attributable to periods of employment prior to 17 May 1990, except in the case of workers or those claiming under them who have before tat date initiated legal proceedings or introduced an equivalent claim under the applicable national law.

Appendix 8. Overall Approach to the Application by the Council of the Subsidiarity Principle and Article 3b of the Treaty on European Union (1992)[1]

I. Basic Principles

The European Union rests on the principle of subsidiarity, as is made clear in Articles A and B of Title I of the Treaty on European Union. This principle contributes to the respect for the national identities of Member States and safeguards their powers. It aims at decisions within the European Union being taken as closely as possible to the citizen.

1. Article 3b of the EC Treaty[2] covers three main elements:

- a strict limit on Community action (first paragraph);
- a rule (second paragraph) to answer the question 'Should the Community act?'. This applies to areas which do not fall within the Community's exclusive competence;
- a rule (third paragraph) to answer the question: 'What should be the intensity or nature of the Community's action?'. This applies whether or not the action is within the Community's exclusive competence.

2. The three paragraphs cover three distinct legal concepts which have historical antecedents in existing Community Treaties or in the case-law of the Court of Justice:

(i) The principle that the Community can only act where given the power to do so – implying that national powers are the rule and the Community's the exception – has always been a basic feature of the Community legal order. (The principle of attribution of powers).

(ii) The principle that the Community should only take action where an objective can better be attained at the level of the Community than at the level of the

---

1. Conclusions of the Presidency, Edinburgh, 12 December 1992.
2. Article 3b, as introduced in the EC Treaty by the Treaty on European Union, reads as follows:
   'The Community shall act within the limits of the powers conferred upon it by this Treaty and of the objectives assigned to it therein.
   In areas which do not fall within its exclusive competence, the Community shall take action, in accordance with the principle of subsidiarity, only if and in so far as the objectives of the proposed action cannot be sufficiently achieved by the Member States and can therefore, by reason of the scale of effects of the proposed action, be better achieved by the Community.
   Any action by the Community shall not go beyond what is necessary to achieve the objectives of this Treaty.'

individual Member States is present in embryonic or implicit form in some provisions of the ECSC Treaty and the EEC Treaty; the Single European Act spelled out the principle in the environment field. (The principle of subsidiarity in the strict legal sense).

(iii) The principle that the means to be employed by the Community should be proportional to the objective pursued is the subject of a well-established case-law of the Court of Justice which, however, has been limited in scope and developed without the support of a specific article in the Treaty. (The principle of proportionality or intensity).

3. The Treaty on European Union defines these principles in explicit terms and gives them a new legal significance:

- by setting them out in Article 3b as general principles of Community law;
- by setting out the principle of subsidiarity as a basic principle of the European Union;[1]
- by reflecting the idea of subsidiarity in the drafting of several new Treaty articles.[2]

4. The implementation of Article 3b should respect the following basic principles:

- Making the principle of subsidiarity and Article 3b work is an obligation for all the Community institutions, without affecting the balance between them. An agreement shall be sought to this effect between the European Parliament, the Council and the Commission, in the framework of the interinstitutional dialogue which is taking place among these Institutions.
- The principle of subsidiarity does not relate to and cannot call into question the powers conferred on the European Community by the Treaty as interpreted by the Court. It provides a guide as to how those powers are to be exercised at the Community level, including in the application of Article 235. The application of the principle shall respect the general provisions of the Maastricht Treaty, including the 'maintaining in full of the acquis communautaire', and it shall not affect the primacy of Community law nor shall it call into question the principle set out in Article F(3) of the Treaty on European Union, according to which the Union shall provide itself with the means necessary to attain its objectives and carry through its policies.
- Subsidiarity is a dynamic concept and should be applied in the light of the objectives set out in the Treaty. It allows Community action to be expanded where circumstances so require, and conversely, to be restricted or discontinued where it is no longer justified.
- Where the application of the subsidiarity test excludes Community action, Member States would still be required in their action to comply with the general rules laid down in Article 5 of the Treaty, by taking all appropriate measures to ensure

1. *See* Articles A and B of the Treaty on European Union.
2. Articles 118a, 126, 127, 128, 129, 129a, 129b, 130 and 130g of the EC Treaty Article 2 of the Agreement on social policy. Furthermore, Article K.3(2)b directly incorporates the principle of subsidiarity.

fulfilment of their obligations under the Treaty and by abstaining from any measure which could jeopardize the attainment of the objectives of the Treaty.
- The principle of subsidiarity cannot be regarded as having direct effect; however, interpretation of this principle, as well as review of compliance with it by the Community institutions are subject to control by the Court of Justice, as far as matters falling within the Treaty establishing the European Community are concerned.
- Paragraphs 2 and 3 of Article 3b apply only to the extent that the Treaty gives to the institution concerned the choice whether to act and/or a choice as to the nature and extent of the action. The more specific the nature of a Treaty requirement, the less scope exists for applying subsidiarity. The Treaty imposes a number of specific obligations upon the Community institutions, for example concerning the implementation and enforcement of Community law, competition policy and the protection of Community funds. These obligations are not affected by Article 3b: in particular the principle of subsidiarity cannot reduce the need for Community measures to contain adequate provision for the Commission and the Member States to ensure that Community law is properly enforced and to fulfil their obligations to safeguard Community expenditures.
- Where the Community acts in an area falling under shared powers the type of measures to apply has to be decided on a case by case basis in the light of the relevant provisions of the Treaty.[1]

II. Guidelines

In compliance with the basic principles set out above, the following guidelines – specific to each paragraph of Article 3b – should be used in examining whether a proposal for a Community measure conforms to the provisions of Article 3b.

First paragraph (Limit on Community action)

Compliance with the criteria laid down in this paragraph is a condition for any Community action.

In order to apply this paragraph correctly the institutions need to be satisfied that the proposed action is within the limits of the powers conferred by the Treaty and is aimed at meeting one or more of its objectives. The examination of the draft measure should establish the objective to be achieved and whether it can be justified in relation to an objective of the Treaty and that the necessary legal basis for its adoption exists.

---

1. The new Articles 126 to 129 of EC Treaty in the area of education, vocational training and youth, culture and public health will explicitly rule out harmonisation of laws and regulations of Member States. It follows that the use of Article 235 for harmonisation measures in pursuit of the specific objectives laid down in Articles 126 to 129 will be ruled out. This does not mean that the pursuit of other Community objectives through Treaty articles other than 126 to 129 might not produce effects in these areas. Where Articles 126, 128 and 129 refer to 'incentive measures,' the Council considers that this expression refers to Community measures designed to encourage cooperation between Member States or to support or supplement their action in the areas concerned, including where appropriate through financial support for Community programmes or national or cooperative measures designed to achieve the objectives of these articles.

Appendix 8

Second paragraph (Should the Community act?)

(i) This paragraph does not apply to matters falling within the Community's exclusive competence.

For Community action to be justified the Council must be satisfied that both aspects of the subsidiarity criterion are met: the objectives of the proposed action cannot be sufficiently achieved by Member States' action and they can therefore be better achieved by action on the part of the Community.

(ii) The following guidelines should be used in examining whether the above-mentioned condition is fulfilled:

– the issue under consideration has transnational aspects which cannot be satisfactorily regulated by action by Member States; and/or

– actions by Member States alone or lack of Community action would conflict with the requirements of the Treaty (such as the need to correct distortion of competition or avoid disguised restrictions on trade or strengthen economic and social cohesion) or would otherwise significantly damage Member States' interests; and/or

– the Council must be satisfied that action at Community level would produce clear benefits by reason of its scale or effects compared with action at the level of the Member States.

(iii) The Community should only take action involving harmonisation of national legislation, norms or standards where this is necessary to achieve the objectives of the Treaty.

(iv) The objective of presenting a single position of the Member States *vis-à-vis* third countries is not in itself a justification for internal Community action in the area concerned.

(v) The reasons for concluding that a Community objective cannot be sufficiently achieved by the Member States but can be better achieved by the Community must be substantiated by qualitative or, wherever possible, quantitative indicators.

Third paragraph (Nature and extent of Community action)

(i) This paragraph applies to all Community action, whether or not within exclusive competence.

(ii) Any burdens, whether financial or administrative, falling upon the Community, national governments, local authorities, economic operators and citizens, should be minimised and should be proportionate to the objective to be achieved;

(iii) Community measures should leave as much scope for national decision as possible, consistent with securing the aim of the measure and observing the requirements of the Treaty. While respecting Community law, care should be taken to respect well established national arrangements and the organisation and working of Member States' legal systems. Where appropriate and subject to the need for proper enforcement, Community measures should provide Member States with alternative ways to achieve the objectives of the measures.

(iv) Where it is necessary to set standards at Community level, consideration should be given to setting minimum standards, with freedom for Member States to set higher national standards, not only in the areas where the treaty so requires (118a, 130t) but also in other areas where this would not conflict with the objectives of the proposed measure or with the Treaty.

(v) The form of action should be as simple as possible, consistent with satisfactory achievement of the objective of the measure and the need for effective enforcement. The Community should legislate only to the extent necessary. Other things being equal, directives should be preferred to regulations and framework directives to detailed measures. Non-binding measures such as recommendations should be preferred where appropriate. Consideration should also be given where appropriate to the use of voluntary codes of conduct.

(vi) Where appropriate under the Treaty, and provided this is sufficient to achieve its objectives, preference in choosing the type of Community action should be given to encouraging cooperation between Member States, coordinating national action or to complementing, supplementing or supporting such action.

(vii) Where difficulties are localised and only certain Member States are affected, any necessary Community action should not be extended to other Member States unless this is necessary to achieve an objective of the Treaty.

III. Procedures and Practices

The Treaty on European Union obliges all institution to consider, when examining a Community measure, whether the provision of Article 3b are observed.

For this purpose, the following procedures and practices will be applied in the framework of the basic principles set out under paragraph II and without prejudice to a future inter-institutional agreement.

a. **Commission**

The Commission has a crucial role to play in the effective implementation of Article 3b, given its right of initiative under the Treaty, which is not called into question by the application of this article.

The Commission has indicated that it will consult more widely before proposing legislation, which could include consultation with all the Member States and a more systematic use of consultation documents (Green Papers). Consultation could include the subsidiarity aspects of a proposal. The Commission has also made it clear that, from now on and according to the procedure it already established in accordance with the commitment taken at the European Council in Lisbon, it will justify in a recital the relevance of its initiative with regard to the principle of subsidiarity. Whenever necessary, the explanatory memorandum accompanying the proposal will give details on the considerations of the Commission in the context of Article 3b.

The overall monitoring by the Commission of the observance of the provisions of Article 3b in all its activities is essential and measures have been taken by the Commission in this respect. The Commission will submit an annual report to the European Council and the European Parliament through the General Affairs Council on the application of the Treaty in this area. This report will be of value in the debate on the annual report which the European Council has to submit to the European Parliament on progress achieved by the Union (*see* Article D in the Treaty on European Union).

b. Council

The following procedure will be applied by the Council from the entry into force of the Treaty. In the meantime they will guide the work of the Council.

The examination of the compliance of a measure with the provisions of Article 3b should be undertaken on a regular basis; it should become an integral part of the overall examination of any Commission proposal and be based on the substance of the proposal. The relevant existing Council rules, including those on voting, apply to such examination.[1] This examination includes the Council's own evaluation of whether the Commission proposal is totally or partially in conformity with the provisions of Article 3b (taking as a starting point for the examination the Commission's recital and explanatory memorandum) and whether any change in the proposal envisaged by the Council is in conformity with those provisions. The Council decision on the subsidiarity aspects shall be taken at the same time as the decision on substance and according to the voting requirements set out in the Treaty. Care should be taken not to impede decision-making in the Council and to avoid a system of preliminary or parallel decision-making.

The Article 3b examination and debate will take place in the Council responsible for dealing with the matter. The General Affairs Council will have responsibility for general questions relating to the application of Article 3b. In this context the General Affairs Council will accompany the annual report from the Commission (*see* 2 a) *above*) with any appropriate considerations on the application of this Article by the Council.

Various practical steps to ensure the effectiveness of the Article 3b examination will be put into effect including:

- working group reports and COREPER reports on a given proposal will, where appropriate, describe how Article 3b has been applied,
- in all cases of implementation of the Articles 189b and 189c procedure, the European Parliament will be fully informed of the Council's position concerning the observance of Article 3b, in the explanatory memorandum which the Council has to produce according to the provisions of the Treaty.

The Council will likewise inform the Parliament if it partially or totally rejects a Commission proposal on the ground that it does not comply with the principle of Article 3b.

---

1. In the course of this examination, any Member State has the right to require that the examination of a proposal which raises Article 3b issues be inscribed on the provisional agenda of a Council in accordance with Article 2 of the Council's rules of procedure. If such examination, which will include all relevant points of substance covered by the Commission proposal, shows that the majority required for the adoption of the act does not exist, the possible outcomes include amendment of the proposal by the Commission, continued examination by the Council with a view to putting it into conformity with Article 3b or a provisional suspension of discussion of the proposal. This does not prejudice Member States or Commission rights under Article 2 of the Council's rules of procedure nor the Council obligation to consider the opinion of the European Parliament.

Selected Bibliography

Amoroso, B., 'A Danish Perspective; the Impact of the Internal Market on the Labour Unions and the Welfare State,' *Comparative Labour Law Journal*, 1990, 438–497.

Barnard, C., 'A Social Policy for Europe: Politicians 1, Lawyers 0,' *The International Journal of Comparative Labour Law and Industrial Relations*, 1992, 15–31.

Bercusson, B. & van Dijk, J.J., 'The Implementation of the Protocol and Agreement on Social Policy of the Treaty on European Union,' *Idem*, 1995, 3–30.

Bercusson, B., *European Labour Law*, London, Butterworths, 1996.

Betten, L., *International Labour Law, Selected Issues*, Kluwer, Deventer, 1993.

Betten, L. (ed.), *The Future of European Social Policy*, Kluwer, Deventer, 1989.

Blanpain R., 'Equal Treatment in Employment,' in *International Encyclopaedia for Comparative Law*, Volume XVI, Chapter XV (1990).

Blanpain, R. (ed.), *Temporary Work and Labour Law in the European Community and Member States*, Kluwer, Deventer, 1993.

Blanpain, R., 'Representation of Employees at Plant and Enterprise Level,' in *International Encyclopaedia for Comparative Law*, Chapter XIII, 1993.

Blanpain, R., *Will I still have a Job Tomorrow? Reflections on a new Strategy. From Routine Jobs to Creativity*, Peeters, Leuven, 1994.

Blanpain, R., Blanquet, F. *et al.*, *The Vredeling Proposal. Information and Consultation of Employees in Multinational Enterprises*, Deventer, 1983.

Blanpain, R. & Engels, C., *Codex European Labour Law*, IELL.

Blanpain, R. & Engels, C. (eds.), *Comparative Labour Law and Industrial Relations in Industrialized Market Economies*, 6th ed., Kluwer Law International, The Hague, 1997.

Blanpain, R., Engels, C. & Pellegrini, C. (eds.), *Contractual Policies Concerning Continued Vocational Training in the European Community Member States*, Peeters, Leuven, 1994.

Blanpain, R., Köhler, E., & Rojot J. (eds.), *Legal and Contractual Limitations to Working Time*, Peeters, Leuven, 1997.

Blanpain, R. & Weiss, M. (eds.), *The Changing Face of Labour Law and Industrial Relations*, Liber Amicorum for Clyde W. Summers, Nomos Verlagsgesellschaft, Baden-Baden, 1993.

Blanpain, R. & Windey, P., *The European Directive on European Works Councils. Information and Consultation of Employees in Multinational Enterprises in Europe.*, Second and revised ed., Peeters, 1996.

Selected Bibliography

Blanpain, R. & Hanami, T. (eds.), *European Works Council. The Implementation of the European Directive. Views from Overseas: Japan and UK*, Leuven, Peeters, 1995.

Blanpain, R., *The Bosman Case: The End of the Transfer System?*, Leuven, Peeters, 1996.

Blanpain, R., Hepple, B., Sciarra, S. & Weiss, M., *Fundamental Social Rights: Proposals for the European Union*, Leuven, Peeters, 1996.

Byre, A., *Leading Cases and Materials on the Social Policy of the EEC*, Kluwer, Deventer, 1989.

Bovis, Ch. & Cnossen, Ch., 'Stereotyped Assumptions versus Sex Equality: A Socio-legal Analysis of Equality Laws in the European Union,' *The International Journal of Comparative Labour Law and Industrial Relations*, 1996, 7–23.

Brewster, C. & Teague, P., *European Community Social Policy*, London, Institute of Personnel Management, 1989.

Campbell, J. (ed.), *European Labour Unions*, Greenwood Press London, 1992.

Dowling, D.C., 'EC Employment Law After Maastricht: "Continental Social Europe"?,' in *The International Lawyer*, 1993, No. 1, 26 p.

EC, *European Social Policy,* Luxembourg, 1996.

European Trade Union Institute, *The European Industry Committees and the Social Dialogue, Experiences at Sectoral Level and in Multinational Companies*, Brussels, 1993.

European Trade Union Institute, *The Social Dimension of the Internal Market*, Part IV, 'European Works Councils,' Brussels, 1991.

Evju, S., 'European Labour Law from a Norwegian Perspective,' *International Journal of Comparative Labour Law and Industrial Relations*, 1995, 327–339.

Ferner, A. & Hyman, R. (eds.), *Industrial Relations in the New Europe*, Blackwell, Oxford, 1992, 640.

Fitzpatrick, B., 'Community Social Law after Maastricht,' *Industrial Law Journal*, 1992, 199–213.

Gamillscheg, F., 'Conflict of Laws in Employment Contracts and Industrial Relations,' *Comparative Labour Law and Industrial Relations*, 4th ed., Deventer, 1990, 353–370.

Gold, M. (ed.), *The Social Dimension. Employment Policy in the European Community*, Mackays of Chatham PLC, London, 1993.

Hepple, B.A., *European Social Dialogue – Alibi or Opportunity? The Institute of Employment Rights*, London, 1993.

Hepple, B.A., 'The Crisis in EEC Labour Law,' *The Industrial Law Journal*, 1987, 77–87.

Hepple, B.A. & Byre, A., 'EEC Labour Law in the United Kingdom – A New Approach,' *Industrial Law Journal*, 1989, 129–143.

Hepple, B.A., 'Social rights in the European Economic Community: a British Perspective,' *Comparative Labour Law Journal*, 1990, 425–440.

Jacobs, A.T.J.M., 'The Netherlands and the Social Dimension of the Single European Market,' *Comparative Labour Law Journal*, 1990, 462–470.

Jacobs, A. & Zeijen, H., *European Labour Law and Social Policy*, Tilburg, 1993.

Lenaerts, K., 'Fundamental Rights to be Included in a Community Catalogue,' *European Law Review*, 1991, 367–390.

Lenaerts, K., 'Some Thoughts about the Interaction Between Judges and Politicians,' *The University of Chicago Legal Forum*, 1992, 93–133.

Loenen, T. & Veldman, A., 'Preferential Treatment in the Labour Market after Kalanke: Some Comparative Perspectives,' *International Journal of Comparative Labour Law and Industrial Relations*, 1996, 43–53.

Nazerali, J. & Plumbey-Jones, K., 'New Draft Acquired Rights Directive – A Step in the Dark,' *European Business Law Review*, 1995, 31–36.

Nielsen, R. & Swyszczak, E., *The social Dimension of the European Community*, Handelshojskolens Forlag, Copenhagen, 1993.

Outram, S., *European Social Policy*, Oxford, Blackwell, 1996.

Sadowski, D. & Jacobi, O., *Employers Associations in Europe: Policy and Organisation*, Baden-Baden, 1991.

Toth, A.G., 'The Principle of Subsidiarity in the Maastricht Treaty,' *Common Market Law Review*, 1992, 1079–1105.

Treu, T., 'European unification and Italian labour relations,' *Comparative Labour Law Journal*, 1990, 441–461.

Valticos, N. & Van Potobsky, G., 'International Labour Law,' in *IELL*, I, Deventer, 1995.

van Doorne-Huiskes, A. (ed.), *Women and the European Labour Markets*, London, Chapman, 1995.

Veneziani, B. (ed.), *Law, Collective Bargaining and Labour Flexibility in E.C. Countries*, Asap, Rome, 1992.

Vogel-Polsky, E. & Vogel, J., *L'Europe Sociale 1993: Illusion, Alibi ou Réalité?*, Bruxelles, 1991.

Von Prondzynski, F., 'Irish Labour Law and the European Community,' *Comparative Labour Law Journal*, 1990, 498–510.

Watson, P., 'Social Policy after Maastricht,' *Common Market Law Review*, 1993, 481–513.

Weatherill, S. & Beaumont, P., *EC Law: the Essential Guide to the Legal Working of the European Community*, Penguin Books, London, 1993.

Weiss, M., 'Labour Law and Industrial Relations in Europe 1992: a German Perspective,' *Comparative Labour Law Journal*, 1990, 411–424.

Weiss, M., 'The Significance of Maastricht for European Community Social Policy,' *The International Journal of Comparative Labour Law and Industrial Relations*, 1992, 3–14.

Wilke, M. & Wallace, H., *Subsidiarity: Approaches to Power-sharing in the European Community*, The Royal Institute of International Affairs, London, 1990.

Wyatt, D. & Dashwood, A., *European Community Law*, Sweet & Maxwell, London, 1993.

Selected Bibliography

Alphabetical List of Cited Cases of the European Court of Justice

Abels H.B.M. v. *The Administrative Board of the Bedrijfsvereniging voor de Metaalindustrie en de Electrotechnische Industrie*, 7 February 1985, No. 135/83: *IELL*, 1, A, b, 66; *Jur.*, 1985, 469.

Adoui Rezguia v. *Belgian State and City of Liège*; *Dominique Cornuaille* v. *Belgian State*, 18 May 1982, Joined Cases Nos. 115 and 116/81: *IELL*, 1, A, b, 46; *Jur.*, 1982, 1665.

Airola Jeanne v. *Commission of the European Communities*, 20 February 1975, No. 21/74: *IELL*, 1, A, b, 15; *Jur.*, 1975, 221.

Alaimo Angelo v. *Préfet du Rhône*, 29 January 1975, No. 68/74: *IELL*, 1, A, b, 14; *Jur.*, 1975, 109.

Allué P. and Mary C. Coonan v. *Università degli Studi di Venzia*, 30 May 1989, No. 33/88: *IELL*, 1, A, b, 136; *Jur.*, 1989, 1591.

Allué P. and Others v. *Universita degli Studi di Venezia and Others*, 2 August 1993, Joined Cases No. C-259/91, C-331/91 and C-332/91, not yet published.

Aranitis Georgios v. *Land Berlin*, Case C-164/94, *Jur.*, 1996, 135.

Arbeitswohfart des Stadt Berlin e.V. (ASWB) v. *M. Böttel*, 4 June 1992, No. C-360/90, *IELL*, 1, A, b, 188.

Association de soutien aux travailleurs immigrés (ASTI) v. *Chambre des Employés Privés*, 4 July 1991, No. C-213/90, *IELL*, 1, A, b, 166; *Jur.*, 1991, 3507.

Barber Douglas Harvey v. *Guardian Royal Exchange Assurance Group*, 17 May 1990, No. 262/88, *IELL*, 146; *Jur.*, 1990, 1889.

Barra Bruno v. *Belgian State and City of Liège*, 2 February 1988, No. 309/85: *IELL*, 1, A, b, 117; *Jur.*, 1988, 355.

Beets-Proper Vera Mia v. *F. van Lanschot Bankiers N.V.*, 26 February 1986, No. 262/84: *IELL*, 1, A, b, 87; *Jur.*, 1986, 773.

Belgian State v. *René Humbel and Marie-Thérèse Humbel née Edel*, 27 September 1988, No. 263/86: *IELL*, 1, A, b, 130; *Jur.*, 1988, 5365.

Berg Harry and Jonannes Theodorus Maria Busschers v. *Ivo Martens Busselsen*, 5 May 1988, Joined Cases Nos. 144 and 145/87: *IELL*, 1, A, b, 122; *Jur.*, 1988, 2559.

Bernini M.J.E. v. *Netherlands Ministry of Education and Science*, 26 February 1992, No. C-3/90, *IELL*, 1, A, b, 185.

Bestuur van het Algemeen Burgerlijk Pensioenfonds v. *G.A. Beune*, 28 September 1994, Case C-7/93, *Jur.*, 1994, 4471.

Bettray I. v. *Staatssecretaris van Justitie*, 31 May 1989, No. 344/87: *IELL* 135; *Jur.*, 1989, 1621.

List of Cited Cases

Bilka-Kaufhaus GmbH v. *K. Weber von Hartz*, 13 May 1986, No. 187/84: *IELL*, 1, A, b, 93; *Jur.*, 1986, 1607.

Bird Eye Walls Limited v. *F.M. Robert*, 9 November 1991, No. C-132/92, not yet published.

Blaizot Vincent v. *University of Liège and others*, 2 February 1988, No. 24/86: *IELL*, 1, A, b, 118; *Jur.*, 1988, 379.

Bleis A. v. *Ministère de l'Education Nationale*, 27 November 1991, No. C-4/91, *IELL*, 1, A, b, 177; *Jur.*, 1991, 5627.

Bonino Anna v. *Commission of the European Communities*, 12 February 1987, No. 233/85: *IELL*, 1, A, b, 102; *Jur.*, 1987, 739.

Bonsignore C.A. v. *Oberstadtdirektor der Stadt Köln*, 26 February 1975, No. 67/74: *IELL*, 1, A, b, 17; *Jur.*, 1975, 297.

Botzen Arie and Others v. *Rotterdamsche Droogdok Maatschappij BV*, 7 February 1985, No. 186/83: *IELL*, 1, A, b, 68; *Jur.*, 1985, 519.

Brown Malcolm Steven v. *Secretary of State for Scotland*, 21 June 1988, No. 197/86: *IELL*, 1, A, b, 124; *Jur.*, 1988, 3205.

Burton Arthur v. *British Railway Board*, 16 February 1982, No. 19/81: *IELL*, 1, A, b, 44; *Jur.*, 1982, 555.

Caisse d'Allocations Familiales de la Région Parisienne v. *Mr. and Mrs. Richard Meade*, 5 July 1984, No. 238/83: *IELL*, 1, A, b, 59; *Jur.*, 1984, 2631.

Campana Angelo v. *Bundesanstalt für Arbeit*, 4 June 1987, No. 375/85: *IELL*, 1, A, b, 103; *Jur.*, 1987, 2387.

Castelli Carmela v. *Office National des Pensions pour Travailleurs Salariés (ONTPS)*, 12 July 1984, No. 261/83: *IELL*, 1, A, b, 62; *Jur.*, 1984, 3199.

Centre public d' aide sociale de Courcelles v. *Marie-Christine Lebon*, 18 June 1987, No. 316/85: *IELL*, 1, A, b, 105; *Jur.*, 1987, 2811.

Chollet Monique (née Bauduin) v. *Commission of the European Communities*, 7 June 1972, No. 32/71: *IELL*, 1, A, b, 6; *Jur.*, 1972, 363.

Coloroll Pension Trustees Ltd v. *James Richard Russel and Others*, 28 September 1994, C-200/91; *Jur.*, 1994, 4389.

Commission v. *Belgium*, 2 July 1996 (distribution of water, gas and electricity), Case C-173/94, not yet published.

Commission v. *Belgium*, 12 September 1996, Case C-278/98, not yet published.

Commission of the European Communities v. *Council of the European Communities*, 30 May 1989, No. 242/87: *IELL*, 1, A, b, 135bis; *Jur.*, 1989, 1425.

Commission of the European Communities v. *Council of the European Communities*, 30 May 1989, No. 355/87; *Jur.*, 1989, 1517.

Commission of the European Communities v. *Federal Republic of Germany*, 21 May 1985, No. 248/83: *IELL*, 1, A, b, 73; *Jur.*, 1985, 1459.

Commission of the European Communities v. *Federal Republic of Germany*, 23 May 1985, No. 29/84: *IELL*, 1, A, b, 74; *Jur.*, 1985, 1661.

Commission of the European Communities v. *Federal Republic of Germany*, 18 May 1989, No. 249/86: *IELL*, 1, A, b, 134bis; *Jur.*, 1989, 1263.

Commission of the European Communities v. *French Republic*, 4 April 1974, No. 167/73: *IELL*, 1, A, b, 10; *Jur.*, 1974, 359.

Commission of the European Communities v. *French Republic*, 30 April 1986, No. 96/85: *IELL*, 1, A, b, 91; *Jur.*, 1986, 1475.
Commission of the European Communities v. *French Republic*, 3 June 1986, No. 312/86: *IELL*, 1, A, b, 130; *Jur.*, 1988, 6315.
Commission of the European Communities v. *French Republic*, 25 October 1988, No. 307/84: *IELL*, 1, A, b, 95; *Jur.*, 1986, 1725.
Commission of the European Communities v. *French Republic*, 30 June 1988, No. 318/86: *IELL*, 1, A, b, 126; *Jur.*, 1988, 3559.
Commission of the European Communities v. *Grand Duchy of Luxembourg*, 9 June 1982, No. 58/81: *IELL*, 1, A, b, 48; *Jur.*, 1982, 2175.
Commission of the European Communities v. *Grand Duchy of Luxembourg*, 19 March 1993, No. C-111/91, *IELL*, 1, A, b, 202.
Commission v. *Hellas*, 2 July 1996, Case C-290/94, not yet published.
Commission of the European Communities v. *Hellenic Republic*, 15 March 1988, No. 147/86: *IELL*, 1, A, b, 121; *Jur.*, 1988, 1637.
Commission of the European Communities v. *Hellenic Republic*, 30 May 1989, No. 305/87: *IELL*, 1, A, b, 13ter; *Jur.*, 1989, 1461.
Commission of the European Communities v. *Hellenic Republic*, 8 November 1990, No. 53/88, *Jur.*, 1990, 3971.
Commission of the European Communities v. *Italian Republic*, 8 June 1982, No. 91/81: *IELL*, 1, A, b, 47*bis*; *Jur.*, 1982, 2133.
Commission of the European Communities v. *Italian Republic*, 6 November 1985, No. 131/84: *IELL*, 1, A, b, 82; *Jur.*, 1985, 3531.
Commission of the European Communities v. *Italian Republic*, 10 July 1986, No. 235/84: *IELL*, 1, A, b, 99; *Jur.*, 1986, 2291.
Commission of the European Communities v. *Italian Republic*, 15 October 1986, No. 168/85: *IELL*, 1, A, b, 100; *Jur.*, 1986, 2945.
Commission of he European Communities v. *Italian Republic*, 15 November 1986, No. 160/85: *IELL*, 1, A, b, 101; *Jur.*, 1986, 3245.
Commission of the European Communities v. *Italian Republic*, 16 June 1986, No. 225/85: *IELL*, 1, A, b, 104; *Jur.*, 1987, 2625.
Commission of the European Communities v. *Italian Republic*, 2 February 1989, No. 22/87: *IELL*, 1, A, b, 132; *Jur.*, 1989, 143.
Commission of the European Communities v. *Italian Republic*, 30 May 1989, No. 340/87: *Jur.*, 1989, 1483.
Commission of the European Communities v. *Italian Republic*, 26 October 1983, No. 163/82: *IELL*, 1, A, b, 53; *Jur.*, 1983, 3273.
Commission of the European Communities v. *Jean-Louis Tourdeur and Others*, 3 October 1985, No. 232/84: *IELL*, 1, A, b, 80; *Jur.*, 1985, 3223.
Commission v. *Luxembourg*, 2 July 1996, Case C-473/93, not yet published.
Commission of the European Communities v. *Kingdom of Belgium*, 28 March 1985, No. 215/83: *IELL*, 1, A, b, 72; *Jur.*, 1985, 1039.
Commission of the European Communities v. *Kingdom of Belgium*, 17 December 1980, No. 149/79: *IELL*, 1, A, b, 39; *Jur.*, 1982, 3881.
Commission of the European Communities v. *Kingdom of Belgium*, 26 May 1982, No. 149/79: *IELL*, 1, A, b, 47; *Jur.*, 1982, 1845.

Dansk Metalarbejderforbund and Specialarbejderforbundet i Danmark v. *H. Nielsen & Son, Maskinfabrik A/S, in liquidation,* 12 February 1985, No. 284/83: *IELL,* 1, A, b, 69; *Jur.,* 1985, 553.

Dansmark Aktive Handelrejsende acting for Carina Mosbaeck v. *Lonmodtagernes Garantifond,* 17 September 1997, C-117/96, not yet published.

Defrenne Gabrielle v. *Belgian State,* 25 May 1971, No. 80/70: *IELL,* 1, A, b, 4; *Jur.,* 1971, 445.

Defrenne Gabrielle v. *Société Anonyme Belge de Navigation Aérienne Sabena,* 8 April 1976, No. 43/75: *IELL,* 1, A, b, 22; *Jur.,* 1976, 455.

Defrenne Gabrielle v. *Société Anonyme Belge de Navigation Aérienne Sabena,* 15 June 1978, No. 149/77: *IELL,* 1, A, b, 29; *Jur.,* 1978, 1365.

Dekker E.J.P. v. *Stichting Vormingscentrum voor Jong Volwassenen (VJV-centrum) Plus,* 8 November 1990, *IELL,* Case Law, No. 153; *Jur.,* 1990, 3941.

Demirel Meryem v. *Stadt Schwäbisch Gmünd,* 30 September 1987, No. 12/86: *IELL,* 1, A, b, 109; *Jur.,* 1987, 3719.

de Vos Peter v. *Stadt Bielefeld,* 14 March 1996, Case C-315/94, not yet published.

Diatta Aissatou v. *Land Berlin,* 13 February 1985, No. 267/83: *IELL,* 1, A, b, 70; *Jur.,* 1985, 567.

Dietz Francina Johanna Maria v. *Stichting Thuiszorg Rotterdam,* 24 October 1996, Case C-435/93, not yet published.

di Leo C. v. *Land Berlin,* 13 November 1990, No. C-308/89, *IELL,* Case Law, No. 155; *Jur.,* 1990, 4185.

Dimossia Epicheirissi Ilektrismou (DEI) v. *Efthimios Evrenenopoulos,* 17 April 1997, C-147/95, not yet published.

Directeur régional de la sécurité sociale de Nancy v. *Auguste Hirardin and Caisse régionale d'assurance maladie du Nord-Est,* 8 April 1976, No. 112/75: *IELL,* 1, A, b, 21; *Jur.,* 1976, 553.

Dona Gaetano v. *Mario Mantero,* 14 July 1976, No. 13/76: *IELL,* 1, A, b, 25; *Jur.,* 1976, 1333.

Donato Casagrande v. *Landeshauptstadt München,* 3 July 1974, No. 9/74: *IELL,* 1, A, b, 11; *Jur.,* 1974, 773.

Draehmpaehl Nils v. *Urania Immobilienreserve OHG,* 22 April 1997, C-180/95, not yet published.

Dzodzi M. v. *Belgian State,* 18 October 1990, Joined Cases Nos. 297/88 and 197/89; *IELL,* Case Law, No. 151; *Jur.,* 1990, 3763.

Echternach G.B.C. and A. Moritz v. *the Netherlands Minister for Education and Science,* 15 March 1989, Joined Cases Nos. 389 and 390/87: *IELL,* 1, A, b, 133; *Jur.,* 1989, 723.

Elefanten Schuh GmbH v. *Pierre Jacqmain,* 24 June 1981, No. 150/80: *IELL,* 1, A, b, 41bis; *Jur.,* 1981, 1671.

F. (Mr. and Mrs.) v. *Belgian State,* 17 June 1975, No. 7/75; *IELL,* 1, A, b, 18; *Jur.,* 1975, 1171.

Federal Republic of Germany and Others v. *Commission of the European Communities,* 9 July 1987, Joined Cases Nos. 281, 283 and 287/85: *IELL,* 1, A, b, 107; *Jur.,* 1987, 3203.

List of Cited Cases

Fisscher Geertruida Catharina v. *Voorhuis Hengelo BV and Stichting Bedrijfs-pensioenfonds voor de Detailhandel*, 28 September 1994, Case, C-128/93, *Jur.*, 1994, 4583.

John O'Flynn v. *Adjudication Officer*, 23 May 1996, C-237/94, not yet published.

Foreningen af Arbejdsledere i Danmark v. *A/S Danmols Inventar, in liquidation*, 11 July 1985, No. 105/84: *IELL*, 1, A, b, 77; *Jur.*, 1985, 2639.

Foreningen af Arbejdsledere i Danmark v. *Daddy's Dance Hall A/S*, 10 February 1988, No. 324/86: *IELL*, 1, A, b, 120; *Jur.*, 1988, 739.

Foster A. and Others v. *British Gas plc*, 12 July 1990, No. 188/89: *IELL*, 1, A, b, 149, *Jur.*, 1990, 3313.

Franchovich A. and Others v. *Italian Republic*, 19 November 1991, Nos. C-6/90 and C-9/90; *IELL*, 1, A, b, 175; *Jur.*, 1991, 5357.

Francovich Andrea v. *Italian Republic*, 9 November 1995, Case C-479/93, *Jur.*, 1995, 3843.

Frascogna Maria v. *Caisse des dépôts et consignations*, 9 July 1987, No. 256/86: *IELL*, 1, A, b, 106; *Jur.*, 1987, 3431.

Freers Edith, Hannelore Speckman v. *Deutsche Bundespost*, 7 March 1996, Case C-278/93, *Jur.*, 1996, 1165.

Garland Eileen v. *British Rail Engineering Limited*, 9 February 1982, No. 12/81: *IELL*, 1, A, b, 43; *Jur.*, 1982, 359.

Gerster Hellen v. *Freistaat Bayern*, 2 October 1997, C-1/95, not yet published.

Giagounidis P. v. *Stadt Reutlingen*, 5 March 1991, *IELL*, Case Law, No. 162; *Jur.*, 1991, 1069.

Gillespie Joan and Others v. *Northern Health and Social Services Board and Others*, 13 February 1996, Case, C-342/93, *Jur.*, 1996, 475.

Giménez Zaera Fernando Roberto v. *Instituto Nacional de la Seguridad Social y Tesoreria General de la Seguridad Social*, 29 September 1987, No. 126/86: *IELL*, 1, A, b, 108; *Jur.*, 1987, 3697.

Giovanni Maria Sotgiu v. *Deutsche Bundespost*, 12 February 1974, No. 172/73: *IELL*, 1, A, b, 9; *Jur.*, 1974, 153.

Gravier Françoise v. *City of Liège*, 13 February 1985, No. 293/83: *IELL*, 1, A, b, 71; *Jur.*, 1985, 593.

Groener A. v. *Minister for Education and the City of Dublin Vocational Education Committee (CDVEC)*, 28 November 1989, No. 379/87: *IELL*, 1, A, b, 139; *Jur.*, 1989, 3967.

Grimaldi S. v. *Fonds des Maladies Professionnelles*, 13 December 1989, No. C-332/88, *Jur.*, 1989, 4407.

Guiot Michel v. *Climatec SA*, Case C-272/94, not yet published.

Gül E. v. *Regierungspräsident Dusseldorf*, 7 May 1986, No. 131/85: *IELL*, 1, A, b, 92; *Jur.*, 1986, 1573.

Habermann-Beltermann G. v. *Arbeiterwohlfarht, Bezirksverband Ndb./Opf. e.V.*, 5 May 1994, No. C-421/92, *Jur.*, 1994, 1657.

Haim S. v. *Kassenzahnärztliche Vereinigung Nordrhein (KVN)*, 9 February 1994, No. C-319/92, not yet published.

Handels- og Kontorfunktionaerernes Forbund i Danmark v. *Dansk Arbejdsgiver-forening (for Danfoss)*, 17 October 1989, No. 109/88: *IELL*, 1, A, b, 138; *Jur.*, 1989, 3979.

Handels- og Kontorfunktionaerernes Forbund i Danmark v. *Dansk Arbejdsgiver-forening*, 8 November 1990, No. C-179/88, *IELL*, Case Law, No. 154; *Jur.*, 1990, 3979.

Harz Dorit v. *Deutsche Tradax GmbH*, 10 April 1984, No. 79/83: *IELL*, 1, A, b, 58; *Jur.*, 1984, 1921.

Henke Annette v. *Gemeinde Schierke and Verwaltungsgemeinschaft 'Brocken'*, 15 October 1996, Case C-298/94, not yet published.

Hoekstra M.K.M. (née Unger) v. *Bestuur der Bedrijfsvereniging voor Detaihandel en Ambachten (Administration of the Industrial Board for Retail Trades and Businesses)*, 19 March 1964, No. 75/63: *IELL*, 1, A, b, 1; *Jur.*, 1964, 369.

Höfner K. and F. Elser v. *Macrotron GmbH*, 23 April 1991, *IELL*, Case Law, No. 164; *Jur.*, 1991, 1979.

Hofmann Ulrich v. *Barmer Ersatzkasse*, 12 July 1984, No. 184/83: *IELL*, 1, A, b, 60; *Jur.*, 1984, 3047.

Industriebond FNV and Federatie Nederlandse Vakbeweging (FNV) v. *The Nether-lands State*, 7 February 1985: *IELL*, 1, A, b, 67; *Jur.*, 1985, 511.

Institut national d'assurances sociales pour travailleurs independents v. *Nicola Cantisani*, 11 July 1985, No. 111/84: *IELL*, 1, A, b, 78; *Jur.*, 1985, 2671.

Inzirillo Vito v. *Caisse d'Allocations Familiales de l'Arrondissement de Lyon*, 16 December 1976, No. 63/76: *IELL*, 1, A, b, 26; *Jur.*, 1976, 2057.

Iorio Paolo v. *Azienda autonoma delle Ferrovie dello Stato*, 23 January 1986, No. 298/84: *IELL*, 1, A, b, 83; *Jur.*, 1986, 247.

Ivenel Roger v. *Helmut Schwab*, 8 June 1982, No. 133/81: *IELL*, 1, A, b, 46*bis*; *Jur.*, 1982, 1891.

Jackson S. and P. Cresswell v. *Chief Adjudication Officer*, 16 July 1992, Joined Cases Nos. C-63/91 and C-64/91, *IELL*, 1, A, b, 192.

Jenkins J.P. v. *Kingsgate (Clothing Productions) Ltd.*, 31 March 1981, No. 96/80: *IELL*, 1, A, b, 41; *Jur.*, 1981, 911.

Job Centre Coop. ar 1, Case No. C-55/96.

John O'Flynn v. *Adjudication Officer*, 23 May 1996, C-237/94, not yet published.

Johnston M. v. *Chief Constable of the Royal Ulster Constabulary*, 15 May 1986, No. 222/84: *IELL*, 1, A, b, 94; *Jur.*, 1986, 1651.

Kalanke v. *Freie Hansestadt Bremen (City of Bremen)*, 17 October 1995, Case C-450/93, *Jur.*, 1995, 3051.

Katsikas G. and Others v. *A. Konstantinidis and Others*, 16 December 1992, Joined Cases Nos. C-132/91, C-138/91 and C-139/91, *IELL*, 1, A, b, 193.

Kempf R.H. v. *Staatssecretaris van Justitie*, 3 June 1986, No. 139/85: *IELL*, 1, A, b, 96; *Jur.*, 1986, 1741.

Klein Steffen v. *Comission of the European Communities*, 20 June 1985, No. 29/84: *IELL*, 1, A, b, 75; *Jur.*, 1985, 1907.

List of Cited Cases

Knud Wendelboe and others v. *K.J. Music ApS in liquidation*, 7 February 1985, No. 19/83: *IELL*, 1, A, b, 65; *Jur.*, 1985, 457.

Koks G.F. v. *Raad van Arbeid*, 23 September 1982, No. 275/81: *IELL*, 1, A, b, 50; *Jur.*, 1982, 3013.

Kording Brigitte v. *Senator für Finanzen*, 2 October 1997, C-100/95, not yet published.

Kowalska Maria v. *Freie und Hansestadt Hamburg*, 27 June 1990, No. 33/89: *IELL*, 1, A, b, 147; *Jur.*, 1990, 2591.

Kraus Dieter v. *Land Baden-Württenberg*, 31 March 1993, No. C-19/92, not yet published.

Kuratorium für Dialyse und- Nierentransplantation v. *Johanna Lewark*, 6 February 1996, *Jur.*, 1996, 243.

Lair Sylvie v. *Universität Hannover*, 21 June 1988, No. 39/86: *IELL*, 1, A, b, 124; *Jur.*, 1988, 3161.

Landesambt für Ausbildungsförderung Nordrhein-Westfalen v. *Lubor Gaal*, C-7/94, *Jur.*, *Jur.*, 1995, 1031.

Land Nordrhein Westfalen v. *Uecker Kari; Jacquet Vera* v. *Land Nordrhein Westfalen*, 5 June 1997, Joined Cases C-64/96 and C-65/96, not yet published.

Landsorganisationen i Danmark for tjenerforbundet i Danmark v. *Ny Molle Kro*, 17 December 1987, No. 287/86: *IELL*, 1, A, b, 113 *Jur.*, 1987, 5465.

Lawrie-Blum Deborah v. *Land Baden-Württemberg*, 3 July 1986, No. 66/85: *IELL*, 1, A, b, 98; *Jur.*, 1986, 2121.

Levin D.M. v. *Staatssecretaris van Justitie*, 23 March 1982, No. 53/81: *IELL*, 1, A, b, 45; *Jur.*, 1982, 1035.

Tribunal de Police de Metz v. *J.-C. Levy*, 2 Augustus 1993, No. C-158/91, not yet published.

Liefting W.G.M. and Others v. *Directie van het Academisch Ziekenhuis Amsterdam*, 18 September 1984, No. 23/83: *IELL*, 1, A, b, 63; *Jur.*, 1984, 3225.

Maag H. v. *Commission of the European Communities*, 11 July 1985, No. 43/84: *IELL*, 1, A, b, 76; *Jur.*, 1985, 2581.

Macarthys Ltd. v. *Wendy Smith*, 27 March 1980, No. 129/79: *IELL*, 1, A, b, 35; *Jur.*, 1980, 1275.

Hellmut Marschall v. *Land Nordrhein-Westfalen*, 11 November 1997, C-409/95, not yet published.

Marshall M.H. v. *Southampton and South-West Hampshire Area Health Authority (Teaching)*, 26 February 1986, No. 152/84: *IELL*, 1, A, b, 86; *Jur.*, 1986, 723.

Marshall M.H. v. *Southampton and South West Area Health Authority*, 2 August 1993, No. C-271/91, not yet published.

Marsman Pieter v. *M. Roskamp*, 13 December 1972, No. 44/72: *IELL*, 1, A, b, 7; *Jur.*, 1972, 1243.

Frederico Maso and others v. *Italian Republic*, 10 July 1997, C-373/95, not yet published.

Matteuci Annunziata v. *Communauté française of Belgium and Commissariat général aux relations internationales of the Communauté française of Belgium*, 27 September 1988, No. 235/87: *IELL*, 1, A, b, 129; *Jur.*, 1988, 5589.

Maxwell Middleburgh D. v. *Chief Adjudication Officer*, 4 October 1991, No. C-15/ 90, *IELL*, 1, A, b, 173; *Jur.*, 1991, 4655.

Merckx Albert and Patrick Neuhuys v. *Ford Motor Company Belgium*, 7 March 1996, Joined Cases C-171/94 and C-172/94, *Jur.*, 1996, 1253.

Meyers Jennifer v. *UK*, 13 July 1995, *Jur.*, 1995, 2131.

Ministère Public v. *Gilbert Even and Office National des Pensions pour Travailleurs Salariés*, 31 May 1979, No. 207/78; *IELL*, 1, A, b, 32; *Jur.*, 1979, 2019.

Ministère Publique v. *J.C. Levy*, 2 August 1993, No. C-158/91, not yet published.

Ministère Public v. *Robert Heinrich Maria Mutsch*, 11 July 1985: *IELL*, 1, A, b, 79; *Jur.*, 1985, 2781.

Ministère Public v. *A Stoeckel*, 25 July 1991, No. C-345/89, *IELL*, 1, A, b, 167; *Jur.*, 1991, 4047.

Ministère Public v. *Robert Heinrich Maria Mutsch*, 11 July 1985: *IELL*, 1, A, b, 79; *Jur.*, 1985, 2781.

Moroni M. v. *Firma Collo GmbH*, 14 December 1993, No. C-110/91, not yet published.

Morson Elestina Esselina Christina v. *State of the Netherlands and Head of the Plaatselijke Politie within the meaning of the Vreemdelingenwet; Sewradjie Jhanjan* v. *State of the Netherlands*, 27 October 1982, Joined Cases Nos. 35 and 36/82: *IELL*, 1, A, b, 51; *Jur.*, 1982, 3723.

Moser Hans v. *Land Baden-Württemberg*, 28 June 1984, No. 180/83: *IELL*, 1, A, b, 56; *Jur.*, 1984, 2539.

Mulox IBC Limited v. *H. Geels*, 13 July 1993, No. C-125/92, not yet published.

Murphy Mary and Others v. *Board Telecom Eireann*, 4 February 1988, No. 157/ 86: *IELL*, 1, A, b, 119; *Jur.*, 1988, 673.

Merci Convenzionali porto di Genova v. *Siderurgica Gabrielli SpA*, 10 December 1991, No. C-179/90 *IELL*, 1, A, b, 178, *Jur.*, 1991, 5889.

Neath D. v. *Hugh Steeper Ltd.*, 22 December 1993, No. C-152/91, not yet published.

Newstead George Noel v. *Department of Transport of Her Majesty's Treasury*, 3 December 1987, No. 192/85: *IELL*, 1, A, b, 112, *Jur.*, 1987, 4753.

Nimz H. v. *Freie Hansestadt Hamburg*, 7 February 1991, *IELL*, Case Law, No. 158; *Jur.*, 1991, 297.

Nonnenmacher, widow of H.E. Moebs v. *Bestuur der Sociale Verzekeringsbank*, 9 June 1964, No. 92/63: *IELL*, 1, A, b, 2; *Jur.*, 1964, 583.

P. v. *S. and Cornwall County Council*, 30 April 1996, Case C-13/94, not yet published.

P. Bork International A/S, in liquidation, and Others v. *Foreningen of Arbejdsledere i Danmark, acting on behalf of Birger E Petersen and Junckers Industrier A/S*, 15 June 1988, No. 101/87: *IELL*, 1, A, b, 123; *Jur.*, 1988, 3057.

Pecastaing Josette v. *Belgian State*, 5 March 1980, No. 98/79: *IELL*, 1, A, b, 34; *Jur.*, 1980, 691.

Pesca Valencia Limited v. *Minister for Fisheries and Forestry, Ireland and the Attorney General*, 19 January 1988, No. 233/86: *IELL*, 1, A, b, 115; *Jur.*, 1988, 83.

List of Cited Cases

Peskeloglou Anstasia v. *Bundesanstalt für Arbeit*, 23 March 1983, No. 77/82: *IELL*, 1, A, b, 52; *Jur.*, 1983, 1085.

Petit C. v. *Office National des pensions (ONP)*, 22 July 1992, No. C-153/91, *IELL*, 1, A, b, 193.

Raulin V.J.M. v. *Netherlands Ministry of Education and Science*, 26 February 1992, No. C-357/89, *IELL*, 1, A, b, 184.

Razzouk C. and A. Beydoun v. *Commission of the European Communities*, 20 March 1984, Joined Cases Nos. 75 and 117/82,: *IELL*, 1, A, b, 55; *Jur.*, 1984, 1509.

Reading Borough Council v. *Payless DIY Limited and Others*, 16 December 1992, No. C-304/90, not yet published.

Redmond Stichting v. *H. Bartol and Others*, 19 May 1992, No. C-29/91, *IELL*, 1, A, b, 186.

Regina v. *Pierre Bouchereau*, 27 October 1977, No. 30/77: *IELL*, 1, A, b, 28; *Jur.*, 1976, 2057.

Regina v. *Secretary of State for Home Affairs ex parte Mario Santillo*, 22 May 1980, No. 131/79: *IELL*, 1, A, b, 37; *Jur.*, 1980, 1585.

Regina v. *Stanislaus Pieck*, 3 July 1980, No. 157/79: *IELL*, 1, A, b, 38; *Jur.*, 1980, 2171.

Regina v. *Vera Ann Saunders*, 28 March 1979, No. 175/78: *IELL*, 1, A, b, 31; *Jur.*, 1979, 1129.

Reina Francesco and Letizia Reina v. *Landeskreditbank Baden-Württemberg*, 14 January 1982, No. 65/81: *IELL*, 1, A, b, 42; *Jur.*, 1982, 33.

Rinner-Kühn Ingrid v. *FWW Spezial-Gebäudereinigung GmbH & Co. KG*, 13 July 1989, No. 171/88: *IELL*, 1, A, b, 136 ter; *Jur.*, 1989, 2743.

Roberts Joan v. *Tate & Lyle Industries Limited*, 26 February 1986, No. 151/84: *IELL*, 1, A, b, 85; *Jur.*, 1986, 703.

Rockfon A/S v. *Specialarbejderforbundet i Danmark*, 7 December 1995, Case C-449/93, *Jur.*, 1995, 4291.

Claude Rotsaert de Hertaing v. *J. Benoidt SA*, in liquidation and Others, 14 November 1996, C-305/94, not yet published.

Roux D. v. *Belgian State*, 5 February 1991, No. C-363/89, *IELL*, *Case Law*, No. 157; *Jur.*, 1991, 273.

Royer Jean Noël, 8 April 1976, No. 48/75: *IELL*, 1, A, b, 23, *Jur.*, 1976, 497.

Rummler Gisela v. *Dato-Druck GmbH*, 1 July 1986, No. 237/85: *IELL*, 1, A, b, 97; *Jur.*, 1986, 2101.

Rush Portuguesa Lda v. *Office National d'Immigration*, 27 March 1990, No. 113/89: *IELL*, 1, A, b, 143; *Jur.*, 1990, 1417.

Rutili Roland v. *Minister for the Interior*, 22 October 1975, No. 36/75: *IELL*, 1, A, b, 19; *Jur.*, 1975, 1219.

Wilhelmus Rutten Petrus v. *Cross Medical Ltd*, 9 January 1997, C-383/95, not yet published.

S. Michel v. *Fonds national de reclassement social des handicapés*, 11 April 1973, No. 76/72: *IELL*, 1, A, b, 8; *Jur.*, 1973, 457.

478

Sabbatini Luisa (née Bertoni) v. *European Parliament*, 7 June 1972, No. 20/71: *IELL*, 1, A, b, 5; *Jur.*, 1972, 345.

Sagulo Concetta, Gennaro Brenca and Addelmadjid Bakhouche, 14 July 1977, No. 8/77: *IELL*, 1, A, b, 27; *Jur.*, 1977, 1495.

Sanicentral GmbH v. *Réné Collin*, 13 November 1979, No. 25/79: *IELL*, 1, A, b, 33*bis*; *Jur.*, 1979, 3423.

Sàrl Prodest v. *Caisse Primaire d'Assurance Maladie de Paris*, 12 July 1984: *IELL*, 1, A, b, 61; *Jur.*, 1984, 3153.

Six Constructions Ltd. v. *Paul Humbert*, 15 February 1989, No. 32/88: *IELL*, 1, A, b, 132*bis*; *Jur.*, 1989, 341.

Sloman Neptun Schiffarts AG v. *Seebetriebsrat Bodo Ziesemer der Sloman Neptun Schiffarts AG*, 17 March 1993, Joined Cases Nos. C-72/91 and C-73/91, not yet published.

Schmid Hugo v. *Belgian State*, 27 May 1993, No. C-310/91, not yet published.

Schmidt C. v. *Spar- und Leihkasse der früheren Ämter Bordeesholm*, Kiel und Cronshagen, 14 April 1994, No. C-392/92, *Jur.*, 1994, 1311.

Scholz Ingetraut v. *Opera Universitaria di Cagliari and Others*, 23 February 1994, No. C-419/92, *Jur.*, 1994, 505.

Smith Constance Christina Ellen and Others v. *Avdel Systems Ltd*, 28 September 1994, Case C-408/92, *Jur.*, 1994, 4435.

Somafer SA v. *Saar-Ferngas AG*, 22 November 1978, No. 33/78: *IELL*, 1, A, b, 29*bis*; *Jur.*, 1978, 2183.

Specialarbjderforbundet i Danmark v. *Dansk Industri, originally Industriens Arbejds-givere, acting for Royal Copenhagen A/S*, 31 May 1995, Case C-400/93, *Jur.*, 1995, 1275.

Spijkers J.M.A. v. *Gebroeders Benedik Abattoir CV and Alfred Benedik en Zonen BV*, 18 March 1986, No. 24/85: *IELL*, 1, A, b, 88; *Jur.*, 1986, 1119.

Spotti M.C. v. *Freistaat Bayern*, 20 October 1993, No. C-272, not yet published.

Spruyt L.A. v. *Bestuur van de Sociale Verzekeringsbank*, 25 February 1986, No. 284/84: *IELL*, 1, A, b, 84; *Jur.*, 1986, 685.

Stadt Lengerich v. *Angelika Helmig*, 15 December 1994, Cases C-399/92, C-409/92, C-425/92, C-34/93, C-50/93 and C-78/93, *Jur.*, 1994, 5727.

State of the Netherlands v. *Ann Florence Reed*, 17 April 1986, No. 59/85: *IELL*, 1, A, b, 90; *Jur.*, 1986, 1283.

Steen V. v. *Deutsche Bundespost*, No. C-332/90, *IELL*, 1, A, b, 182; *Jur.*, 1992, 341.

Suffritti M. and Others v. *Instituto Natzionale della Previdenza Sociale (INPS)*, 3 December 1992, Joined Cases Nos. C-140/91, 141/91, 278/91 and 279/91, *IELL*, 1, A, b, 197.

Ayse Süzen v. *Zehnacker Gebäudereinigung GmbH Krankenhausservice*, 11 March 1997, C-13/95.

Ten Oever G.C. v. *Stichting Bedrijfspensioenfonds voor het Glazenwassers- en Schoonmaakbedrijf*, 6 October 1993, C-109/91, not yet published.

The Queen v. *Immigration Appeal Tribunal, ex parte Gustaff Desiderius Antonissen*, 26 February 1991, No. C-292/89, *IELL*, Case Law, No. 159; *Jur.*, 1991, 745.

List of Cited Cases

The Queen v. *Ministry for Agriculture, Fisheries and Food, ex parte Agegate Limited*, 14 December 1989, No. 3/87: *IELL*, 1, A, b, 141; *Jur.*, 1989, 4459.

The Queen v. *Secretary of State for Social Security ex parte The Equal Opportunities Commission (EOC)*, 7 July 1992, Case C-9/91, *Jur.*, 1992, 4297.

Torfean Borough Coucil v. *B & Q plc*, 23 November 1989, No. C-145/88, *IELL*, Case Law, No. 138*bis*; *Jur.*, 1989, 3851.

Tsiotras D. v. *Landeshauptstadt Stuttgart*, 26 May 1993, Case No. C-171/91, not yet published.

Una Coonan v. *Insurance Officer*, 24 April 1980, No. 110/79: *IELL*, 1, A, b, 36; *Jur.*, 1980, 1445.

Union Départementale des Syndicats CGT de l'Asine v. *Sidef Conforma and Others*, 28 February 1991, No. C-312/89, *IELL*, Case Law, No. 160; *Jur.*, 1991, 997.

Union nationale des entraîneurs et Cadres techniques professionels du football (Unectef) v. *Georges Heylens and Others*, 15 October 1987, No. 222/86: *IELL*, 1, A, b, 111; *Jur.*, 1987, 4097.

Union Royale Belge des Sociétés de Football Association ASBL and others v. *Jean Marc Bosman and Others*, Case C-415/93, *Jur.*, 1995, 4921.

United Kingdom of Great Britain and Northern Ireland v. *Council of European Communities*, 30 May 1989, No. 56/88: *IELL*, 1, A, b, 136*bis*; *Jur.*, 1989, 1615.

United Kingdom v. *Commission of the European Communities*, 1 October 1987, No. 84/85: *IELL*, 1, A, b, 110; *Jur.*, 1987, 3765.

United Kingdom of Great Britain And Northern Ireland v. *Council of the European Union*, 12 November 1996, Case C-84/94, not yet published.

Van Cant R. v. *Rijksdienst voor Pensioenen*, 1 July 1993, No. C-154/92, not yet published.

Van den Akker Maria Nelleke Gerda and Others v. *Stichting Shell Pensioenfonds*, 28 September 1994, Case C-28/93, *Jur.*, 1994, 4527.

Van den Broeck Chantal v. *Commission of European Communities*, 20 February 1975, No. 37/74: *IELL*, 1, A, b, 16; *Jur.*, 1975, 235.

Vander Elst R. v. *Office des Migrations Internationales*, C-43/93, *Jur.*, 1994, 3803.

Van Duyn Yvonne v. *Home Office*, 4 December 1974, No. 41/74: *IELL*, 1, A, b, 13; *Jur.*, 1974, 1337.

Von Colson Sabine and Elisabeth Kamann v. *Land Nordrhein-Westfalen*, 10 April 1984, No. 14/83: *IELL*, 1, A, b, 57; *Jur.*, 1984, 1891.

Vroege Anna Adriaantje v. *NCIV Instituut voor Volkshuisvesting BV and Stichting Pensioenfonds NCIV*, 28 September 1994, Case C-57/93, *Jur.*, 1994, 4541.

Wagner Miret T. v. *Fondo de garantia salarial*, 16 December 1993, No. C-334/92, not yet published.

Walrave B.N.O. and L.J.N. Koch v. *Association Union Cycliste Internationale, Koninklijke Nederlandsche Wielren Unie and Federación Española Ciclismo*, 12 December 1974, No. 36/74: *IELL*, 1, A, b, 12; *Jur.*, 1974, 1405.

Watson A. Rask and K. Christensen v. *ISS Kantineservice A/S*, 12 November 1992, No. C-209/91, *IELL*, 1, A, b, 195.

Watson Lynne and Allessandro Belmann, 7 July 1976, No. 118/75: *IELL*, 1, A, b, 24; *Jur.*, 1976, 2057.

Worringham Susan Jane and Margaret Humphreys v. *Lloyd's Bank Limited*, 11 March 1981, No. 69/80: *IELL*, 1, A, b, 40; *Jur.*, 1981, 767.

Wörsdorfer Marianne (née Koschniske) v. *Raad van Arbeid*, 12 July 1979, No. 9/79: *IELL*, 1, A, b, 33; *Jur.*, 1979, 2717.

Württembergische Milchverwertung-Südmilch-AG v. *Salvatore Ugliola*, 15 October 1969, No. 15/69: *IELL*, 1, A, b, 3; *Jur.*, 1969, 363.

Zaoui Saada v. *Caisse régionale d'assurance maladie de l'île de France*, 17 December 1987, No. 147/87: *IELL*, 1, A, b, 114; *Jur.*, 1987, 5511.

List of Cited Cases

Annex. The Treaty of Asterdam

1. The main outcome of European Council meeting on 16–17 June 1997, under the Presidency of the Netherlands, is the Treaty of Amsterdam, which contains no less than six sections. The new Treaty, which is still to be ratified, is significant from the point of view of European Labour Law and Industrial relations.

The Treaty, first of all, incorporates the Social Agreement of Maastricht (Title VIII).[1] This is quite important. The two track social Europe, due to the British opt-out in 1991, will come to an end. Secondly, there is a new and much acclaimed Title on Employment (Title VIa).

The Treaty deals also with:

- fundamental rights, with reference to the European Convention for the Protection of Human Rights, the European Social Charter, issues like the principle of non-discrimination, disability, equality of men and women, and the protection of data;
- positive discrimination;
- culture and non-professional sport;
- the application of the principles of subsidiarity and proportionality, clearly indicating that regarding matters of mixed competence, the EU can only intervene when there is additional (European) value and only as far as necessary, leaving maximum authority to Member States and consequently to the Social Partners.

Other points relate to:

- the European Parliament (legislative procedures, organization and composition);
- the Council (qualified majority voting);
- the Commission (appointment of President, composition and organization);
- Court of Justice (powers of the Court).

---

1. The numbers in parenthesis are the new article numbers of the integrated Treaty text, as it will stand once the Treaty of Amsterdam is ratified. *See*, Treaty of Amsterdam amending the treaty on European Unions, the treaties establishing the European Communiteis and certain related acts, O.J. C-340, 10 November 1997, p. 1.

A. CONTENTS

2. The Treaty contains VI sections and a table of contents, which reads as follows:

SECTION I – FREEDOM, SECURITY AND JUSTICE

Chapter 1. Fundamental Rights and Non-discrimination
Chapter 2. Progressive Establishment of an Area of Freedom, Security and Justice

SECTION II – THE UNION AND THE CITIZEN

Chapter 3. Employment
Chapter 4. Social Policy
Chapter 5. Environment
Chapter 6. Public Health
Chapter 7. Consumer Protection
Chapter 8. Other Community Policies
Chapter 9. Subsidiarity
Chapter 10. Transparency
Chapter 11. Quality of Legislation

SECTION III – AN EFFECTIVE AND COHERENT EXTERNAL POLICY

Chapter 12. The Common Foreign and Security Policy
Chapter 13. External Economic Relations

SECTION IV – THE UNION'S INSTITUTIONS

Chapter 14. The European Parliament
Chapter 15. The Council
Chapter 16. The Commission
Chapter 17. The Court of Justice
Chapter 18. Other Institutional Issues
Chapter 19. Role of National Parliaments

SECTION V – CLOSER CO-OPERATION – 'FLEXIBILITY'

SECTION VI – SIMPLIFICATION AND CONSOLIDATION OF THE TREATIES

B. FUNDAMENTAL RIGHTS AND NON-DISCRIMINATION

3. Here, the following points have to be retained:

• General principles underlying the Union;
• non-discrimination;
• disability;

484

- equality of men and women; and
- protection of individuals with regard to personal data.

1. Fundamental Rights

4.   Chapter 1 of the Treaty deals with 'fundamental rights and non-discrimination'. Under the heading 'General principles underlying the Union', Article F (Art. 6) of the TEU is amended as follows, of which only the first paragraph is really new:

> '1. The Union is founded on the principles of liberty, democracy, respect for human rights and fundamental freedoms, and the rule of law, principles which are common to the Member States.[1]
> 2. The Union shall respect fundamental rights, as guaranteed by the European Convention for the Protection of Human Rights and Fundamental Freedoms, signed in Rome on 4 November 1950 and as they result from the constitutional traditions common to the Member States, as general principles of Community law.[2]
> 3. The Union shall respect the national identities of its Member States.
> 4. The Union shall provide itself with the means necessary to attain its objectives and carry through its policies'.

A new fourth paragraph has been inserted in the Preamble to the TEU, which reads as follows: 'Confirming their attachment to fundamental social rights as defined in the European Social Charter signed at Turin on 18 October 1961, and in the 1989 Community Charter of the Fundamental Social Rights of Workers'.[3] The idea to include the Charter in Article F (Art. 6) of the TEU was not retained.

The general principles, being part of the TEU do not confer direct enforceable rights to European citizens, although the Court of Justice will take them into account when making its decisions.

1. 'Any European State which respects the principles set out in Article F(1) may apply to become a member of the Union'.
2. Special attention has to be drawn to Article L of the TEC concerning the role of the Court of Justice. The powers of the Court shall apply to Article (F2) with regard to action of the Institutions, insofar as the Court had jurisdiction under the Treaties establishing the European Communities and under this Treaty (Chapter 17 of the Amsterdam Treaty). In practical terms this means that any action of the Council of Ministers, the Commission and other Community Institutions, including, e.g., a given Directive, might be examined from the point of view of the Human Rights Convention by the Court.
3. This insertion is not directly legally binding, but reinforces and explains Article F(1), concerning the principles underlying the European Union, like the principles of liberty, democracy and so on.

2. Non-discrimination

5.   The idea to include legally enforceable fundamental social rights in the Treaty of the European Community was not retained at Amsterdam. This is also the case for the principle of non-discrimination. The idea is retained, but has to be worked out by the Institutions of the Community. This is what follows clearly from Article 6a TEC (Art. 13), that reads as follows:

Annex. The Treaty of Amsterdam

'Without prejudice to the other provisions of this Treaty and within the limits of the powers conferred by it upon the Community, the Council, acting unanimously on a proposal from the Commission and after consulting the European Parliament, may take appropriate action to combat discrimination based on sex, racial or ethnic origin, religion or belief, disability, age or sexual orientation'.

A number of grounds leading to discrimination were not retained; such as colour, national or social origin, culture or language, political opinion, marital status, family responsibilities and disability. One should however keep in mind that Article 6 prohibits discrimination on grounds of nationality and the declaration concerning disability, which follows.

3. Disability

6.   The Conference agrees that, in drawing up measures under Article 100a, the institutions of the Community shall take account of the needs of persons with a disability.[1]

    1. Declaration to the Final Act regarding persons with a disability.

4. Equality of Men and Women

7.   The Community shall promote a high level of employment and social protection, equality between men and women, the raising of the standard of living and quality of life, and economic and social cohesion and solidarity among Member States (Art. 2 TEC) (Art. 2).
    In all the activities referred to in this Article, the Community shall aim to eliminate inequalities, and to promote equality, between men and women (Art. 3 TEC) (Art. 3).

5. Protection of Individuals with Regard to the Processing and Free Movement of Personal Data

8.   From 1 January 1999, Community acts on the protection of individuals with regard to the processing of personal data and the free movement of such data shall apply to the institutions and bodies set up by, or on the basis of, this Treaty.

2.   Before the date referred to in paragraph 1, the Council, acting in accordance with the procedure referred to in Article 189b (Art. 251), shall establish an independent supervisory body responsible for monitoring the application of such Community acts to Community institutions and bodies and shall adopt any other relevant provisions as appropriate (Art. 213b TEC) (Art. 286).

C. Chapter 3. Employment

1. General principles

9.   Section II, on 'The Union and the Citizen' contains the new Title on Employment. That Title changes as well the TEU as the TEC. First, the goals of the TEU:

'The Union shall set itself the following objectives:

to promote economic and social progress which is balanced and sustainable and a high level of employment, in particular' (Art. B TEU) (Art. 2).

Then the TEC is amended.

'The Community shall have as its task to promote throughout the Community a harmonious and balanced development of economic activities, a high level of employment and social protection, sustainable and non-inflationary growth respecting the environment, a high degree of competitiveness and convergence of economic performance' . . . (Art. 2 TEC) (Art. 2).

- (. . .) 'the promotion of co-ordination between employment policies of the Member States with a view to enhancing their effectiveness by developing a co-ordinated strategy for employment' (Art. 3 TEC additional indent before (I)) (Art. 3). These phrases do not add so much:
- a high level of employment is now one of the objectives of the union; and
- the role of the union, regarding employment is one co-ordination of employment policies of the Member States.

2. The New Title on Employment[1]

a. An adaptable labour force and labour markets responsive to economic change

10. The Chapter contains nothing new or unexpected. It does not contain any rights for the employees or the employers. The Chapter is purely action oriented, but on the understanding that the European Union has no real competences to engage in European employment policies. We stay in the 'Eurowachter game', where the Commission will report on how Member States live up to the guidelines, which the EC has developed.

The Chapter lies in the line of the Essen strategy, which it translates into a Treaty text. Employment policies become a secondary and subordinated part of the EMU, of non-inflationary growth. Of course, inflation and debts have to be held in line, but on themselves they are insufficient to solve the unemployment problem, as experience and the millions of unemployed demonstrate abundantly.

Most important is the strategy for employment, laid down in Article 109n (Art. 125) of the Chapter, namely 'for promoting a skilled, trained and **adaptable workforce and labour markets responsive to economic change** with a view of achieving the objectives of the European Union'. The same line of reasoning goes on in Article 109o; (Art. 126): Member States, through their employment policies, shall contribute to the achievement of the objectives in a way consistent with the broad guidelines of the economic policies of the Member States and of the Community, adopted pursuant to Article 103(2) (Art. 99) of the Treaty, this is as laid down in the EMU.

Adaptable obviously stands for **flexible**. So, workers and labour markets have to become more flexible and governments and social partners have to do away with rigidities. Workers and the labour market have to be responsive to economic change. The message is clear. There will be social protection as far as non-inflationary growth, competitiveness and convergence of economic performance permit this. Let us see how this has been conceived.

1. 'To be inserted after Title VI of the TEC'.

b. Goal, framework, strategies and action

11. • **Goal**: high level of employment;
• **Framework**: the EMU;
• **Responsibility**: Member States; the Community will contribute by encouraging co-operation and by taking the objective of high level of employment in to consideration (Art. 3);
• **Strategy**: 'promoting a skilled, trained and **adaptable workforce and labour markets responsive to economic change**' (Art. 109n) (Art. 125);
• **Action**: Member States;
• annual report in the light of the EC guidelines on employment (Art. 4,3) (Art. 109q; Art. 128).

EC:
• annual report (Art. 4,1) (Art. 109q,1; Art. 128,1);
• (annual) guidelines for employment, Member States have to take into account (Art. 4,2) (Art. 109q,2; Art. 128,2);
• EC report on the basis of the national reports (Art. 4,4) (Art. 109q,2; Art. 128,2);
• 'the Council, may adopt *incentive measures* designed to encourage co-operation between Member States and to support their action in the field of employment through initiatives aimed at developing *exchanges* of information and best practices, providing comparative *analysis* and *advice* as well as promoting innovative approaches and *evaluating* experiences, in particular by recourse to *pilot projects*.

Those measures shall not include harmonization of the laws and regulations of the Member States'[1] (Art. 5) (Art. 109r; Art. 129).

12. • **Employment Committee**: the Council, after consulting the European Parliament, shall establish an **Employment Committee** with advisory status to promote co-ordination between Member States on employment and labour market policies. The tasks of the Committee shall be:

– To monitor the employment situation and employment policies in the Member States and the Community;
– without prejudice to Article 151 (Art. 207), to formulate opinions at the request of either the Council or the Commission or on its own initiative, and to contribute to the preparation of the Council proceedings referred to in Article (4) (Art. 109q; Art. 128)

In fulfilling its mandate, the Committee shall consult the social partners.

The Member States and the Commission shall each appoint two members of the Committee (Art. 6) (Art. 109s; Art. 129).

Another Committee on employment will thus be created, next to the Standing Committee on Employment, the Employment and Labour Market Committee and others.

The new Chapter is certainly not a blessing for employment, besides a lot of lip-service. What is really problematic is that this strategy of putting all the weight on adaptability and rigid labour markets is now laid down in the TEC, which will prove difficult to adapt, even when it becomes clearer and clearer that the strategy does not work and is largely insufficient.

> 1. Declaration to the Final Act on incentive measures referred to in Article (5) (Art. 109r; Art. 129) of the new Title on Employment.
>   The Conference agrees that the incentive measures referred to in Article (5) (Art. 109r; Art. 129) should always specify the following:
>   – The grounds for taking them based on an objective assessment of their need and the existence of an added value at Community level;
>   – their duration, which should not exceed five years; and
>   – the maximum amount for their financing, which should reflect the incentive nature of such measures.
>   Declaration to the Final Act on Article 5 (Art. 109r; Art. 129):
>   'It is understood that any expenditure under this Article will fall within Heading 3 of the financial perspectives.'

D. CHAPTER 4. SOCIAL POLICY[1]

1. Incorporation of the Maastricht Social Agreement. Other Texts

13. The Chapter (IV) on Social Policy, replaces Title VIII of the EC Treaty, which deals with social policy, education, vocational training and youth. The new chapter goes from Article 136 to 145. Its content reflects mainly the Agreement on Social Policy (Maastricht) to which certain sentences of the former Title VIII have been added. So, basically one can refer to what has been said in this book about the Maastricht Agreement of 1991. (Added texts are in italics.)

Article 117 (Art. 136) retains the text of Article 1 of the Agreement, but adds (in italics):

• The Community and the Member States *having in mind fundamental social rights such as those set out in the European Charter signed at Turin on 18 October 1961 and in the 1989 Community Charter of the Fundamental Social Rights of Workers,*
• *so as to make possible their harmonization while the improvement is being maintained.*

They believe that such a development will ensue not only from the functioning of the common market, which will favour the harmonization of social systems, but also from the procedures provided for in this Treaty and from the approximation of provisions laid down by law, regulation or administrative action.

Article 118 (Art. 136): (*see* Article 2 of the Agreement)[2]

1.   With a view to achieving the objectives of Article 117 (Art. 136),
2.   The Council, acting in accordance with the same procedure, may adopt measures designed to encourage co-operation between Member States through initiatives aimed at improving knowledge, developing exchanges of information and best practices, promoting innovative approaches and evaluating experiences in order to combat social exclusion.[3]

Article 118a (Art. 138) (Art. 3 of the Agreement)

Article 118b (Art. 139) (Art. 4 of the Agreement)[4]

2.   Agreements concluded at Community level shall be implemented either in accordance with the procedures and practices specific to management and labour and the Member States or, in matters covered by *Article 118*, at the joint request of the signatory parties, by a Council decision on a proposal from the Commission.
    The Council shall act by qualified majority, except where the agreement in question contains one or more provisions relating to one of the areas referred to in *Article 118(3)* (Art. 137) in which case it shall act unanimously.

Article 118c (Art. 140) (Art. 5 of the Agreement and former Art. 118 – in italics –)

With a view to achieving the objectives of *Article 117* (Art. 136) and without prejudice to the other provisions of this Treaty, the Commission shall encourage co-operation between the Member States and facilitate the co-ordination of their action in all social policy fields under this *chapter, particularly in matters relating to*:

- *Employment*;
- *labour law and working conditions*;
- *basic and advanced vocational training*;
- *social security*;
- *prevention of occupational accidents and diseases*;
- *occupational hygiene*;
- *the rights of association and collective bargaining between employers and workers.*

To this end, the Commission shall act in close contact with Member States by making studies, delivering opinions and arranging consultations both on problems arising at national level and on those of concern to international organizations.
    Before delivering the opinions provided for in this Article, the Commission shall consult the Economic and Social Committee.

Article 119 (Art. 141) (Art. 6 of the Agreement)[5]

3.   *The Council, acting in accordance with the procedure referred to in Article 189b, and after consulting the Economic and Social Committee, shall adopt measures to ensure the application of the principle of equal opportunities and equal treatment of men and women in matters of employment and occupation, including the principle of equal pay for equal work or work of equal value.*

4.   *With a view to ensuring full equality in practice between men and women in working life, the principle of equal treatment shall not prevent* any Member State from maintaining or adopting measures providing for specific advantages in order to make it easier *for the underrepresented sex* to pursue a vocational activity or to prevent or compensate for disadvantages in professional careers.

Article 119a (Art. 142) (Art. 120 of TEC)

Member States shall endeavour to maintain the existing equivalence between paid holiday schemes.

Article 120 (Art. 7 of the Agreement)

1. (1) Protocol No. 14 on social policy annexed to the TEC and the Agreement on social policy attached thereto shall be repealed.
2. Declaration to the Final Act on Article-118(2) (Art. 137):
   'The High Contracting Parties note that in the discussions on Article 118(2) (Art. 137) it was agreed that the Community does not intend, in laying down minimum requirements for the protection of the safety and health of employees, to discriminate in a manner unjustified by the circumstances against employees in small and medium-sized undertakings.'
3. Declaration to the Final Act: it is understood that any expenditure under this Article will fall within Heading 3 of the financial perspectives.
4. Declaration to the Final Act on Article 118b (Art. 137) (2).
   'The High Contracting Parties declare that the first of the arrangements for application of the agreements between management and labour at Community level – referred to in Article 118b (Art. 137) (2) – will consist in developing, by collective bargaining according to the rules of each Member State, the content of the agreements, and that consequently this arrangement implies no obligation on the Member States to apply the agreements directly or to work out rules for their transposition, nor any obligation to amend national legislation in force to facilitate their implementation.'
5. Declaration to the Final Act on Article 119 (Art. 141) (4):
   'When adopting measures referred to in Article 119 (Art. 141) (4), Member States should, in the first instance, aim at improving the situation of women in working life.'

2. Evaluation

14.   The Chapter on Social Policy basically integrates the Social Agreement of Maastricht. Fundamentally, few important changes or additions have been made. Significant is self-evidently Article 119 (3 Art. 141), which reproduces basically

the text of Article 6 of the Agreement, as an answer *in se* to the Kalanke case. (*See* Part I, Chapter 5, §2 III, C).

Most rejoicing is that there comes an end to the two-track social Europe in the EC, as the UK will ratify the Treaty, forgetting about the opt-out. A number of questions arise, e.g., concerning the directives which are or will be adopted under the Social Agreement of Maastricht, as long as the Treaty of Amsterdam is not yet ratified.

In the light of the conclusions adopted by the European Council of Amsterdam, following the United Kingdom's decision to sign up to the social provisions of the new Treaty and accept the directives already adopted – i.e., on the European Works Councils and parental leave – or that could yet be adopted on the basis of the Agreement on social policy and the Social Protocol, the Council and Commission have agreed on the following procedures to implement the Summit's conclusions:

i) Directives already adopted: their implementation will be rendered compulsory in the United Kingdom by the adoption of the directives according to Article 100 (Art. 94) of the EC Treaty. To this end, the Commission will submit proposals to the Council as soon as possible, and which: a) will comprise any necessary technical adjustments, without affecting the substance of the directives already approved; b) will provide for the adoption by London and, should it be necessary, other Member States, of the provisions for transposition into national law, at the latest, two years after adoption by Council,

ii) later directives: the same solution will be applied to any Act that could still be adopted as long as the Social Agreement remains in force, taking account of provisions contained in the aforementioned Acts.

The Member States also confirmed at the European Top of 16–17 June 1997, that, if the Treaty of Amsterdam were not to enter into force before 1 January 1998, the Council would be chaired by the Representative of the Government of the United Kingdom for matters falling under the Social Protocol of Maastricht during its Presidency in the first half of 1998.[1]

1. Presidency conclusions.

E. CHAPTER 8. OTHER COMMUNITY POLICIES

15. (a) Citizenship of the Union

New paragraph in the Preamble to the TEC, which reads as follows:
'Determined to promote the development of the highest possible level of knowledge for their peoples trough a wide access to *education* and its continuous *training*'.

(b) Culture

Amend Article 128(4) (Art. 151) of the TEC, as follows:

'The Community shall take cultural aspects into account in its action under other provisions of this Treaty, in particular in order to respect and to promote the diversity of its cultures'.

(c) Sport

Declaration to the Final Act on Sport, which reads as follows:

'The Conference emphasizes the social significance of sport, in particular its role in forging identity and bringing people together. The Conference therefore calls on the bodies of the European Union to listen to sports associations when important questions affecting sport are at issue. In this connection, special consideration should be given to the particular characteristics of amateur sport'.

F. CHAPTER 9. SUBSIDIARITY

16.   Subsidiarity goes to the hearth of the European Union. The Union should stay as close as possible to the citizens. The Union should only intervene when and as far as necessary. The Top of Amsterdam fine-tuned the principles of subsidiarity and proportionality in a Protocol. The text is so important that we reproduce him in full.

Protocol on the application of the principles of subsidiarity and proportionality[1]

The HIGH CONTRACTING PARTIES

DETERMINED to establish the conditions for the application of the principles of subsidiarity and proportionality enshrined in Article 3b of the Treaty establishing the European Community with a view to defining more precisely the criteria for applying them and to ensure their strict observance and consistent implementation by all institutions

WISHING to ensure that decisions are taken as closely as possible to the citizens of the Union

TAKING ACCOUNT of the Inter-institutional Agreement of 28 October 1993 between the European Parliament, the Council and the Commission on procedures for implementing the principle of subsidiarity

HAVE CONFIRMED that the conclusions of the Birmingham European Council on 16 October 1992 and the overall approach to the application of the subsidiarity principle agreed by the European Council meeting in Edinburgh on 11–12 December 1992, will continue to guide the action of the Union's institutions as well as the development 1992, will continue to guide the action of the Union's institutions as well as the development of the application of the principle of subsidiarity, and, for this purpose, have agreed on the following provisions which shall be annexed to the Treaty establishing the European Community:

1.   In exercising the powers conferred on it, each institution shall ensure that the principle of subsidiarity is complied with. It shall also ensure compliance with the

principle of proportionality, according to which any action by the Community shall not go beyond what is necessary to achieve the objectives of the Treaty.

2.   The application of the principles of subsidiarity and proportionality shall respect the general provisions and the objectives of the Treaty, particularly as regards the maintaining in full of the acquis communautaire and the institutional balance; it shall not affect the principles developed by the Court of Justice regarding the relationship between national and Community law, and it should take into account Article F(3) of the TEU, according to which 'the Union shall provide itself with the means necessary to attain its objectives and carry through its policies'.

3.   The principle of subsidiarity does not call into question the powers conferred on the European Community by the Treaty, as interpreted by the Court of Justice. The criteria referred to in Article 3b(2) (Art. 5) shall relate to areas for which the Community does not have exclusive competence. The principle of subsidiarity provides a guide as to how those powers are to be exercised at the Community level. Subsidiarity is a dynamic concept and should be applied in the light of the objectives set out in the Treaty. It allows Community action within the limits of its powers to be expanded where circumstances so require, and conversely, to be restricted or discontinued where it is no longer justified.

4.   For any proposed Community legislation, the reasons on which it is based shall be stated with a view to justifying that it complies with the principles of subsidiarity and proportionality; the reasons for concluding that a Community objective can be better achieved by the Community must be substantiated by qualitative or, wherever possible, quantitative indicators.

5.   For Community action to be justified, both aspects of the subsidiarity principle shall be met: the objectives of the proposed action cannot be sufficiently achieved by Member States' action in the framework of their national constitutional system and can therefore be better achieved by action on the part of the Community.

The following guidelines should be used in examining whether the above-mentioned condition is fulfilled:

– the issue under consideration has transnational aspects which cannot be satisfactorily regulated by action by Member States;
– actions by Member States alone or lack of Community action would conflict with the requirements of the Treaty (such as the need to correct distortion of competition or avoid disguised restrictions on trade or strengthen economic and social cohesion) or would otherwise significantly damage Member States' interests;
– action at Community level would produce clear benefits by reason of its scale or effects compared with action at the level of the Member States.

6.   The form of Community action shall be as simple as possible, consistent with satisfactory achievement of the objective of the measure and the need for effective enforcement. The Community shall legislate only to the extent necessary. Other

things being equal, directives should be preferred to regulations and framework directives to detailed measures. Directives as provided for in Article 189 (Art. 249), while binding upon each Member State to which they are addressed as to the result to be achieved, shall leave to the national authorities the choice of form and methods.

7.   Regarding the nature and the extent of Community action, Community measures should leave as much scope for national decision as possible, consistent with securing the aim of the measure and observing the requirements of the Treaty. While respecting Community law, care should be taken to respect well established national arrangements and the organization and working of Member States legal systems. Where appropriate and subject to the need for proper enforcement, Community measures should provide Member States with alternative ways to achieve the objectives of the measures.

8.   Where the application of the principle of subsidiarity leads to no action being taken by the Community, Member States are required in their action to comply with the general rules laid down in Article 5 (Art. 10) of the Treaty, by taking all appropriate measures to ensure fulfillment of their obligations under the Treaty and by abstaining from any measure which could jeopardize the attainment of the objectives of the Treaty.

9.   Without prejudice to its right of initiative, the Commission should:

– except in cases of particular urgency or confidentiality, consult widely before proposing legislation and, wherever appropriate, publish consultation documents;
– justify the relevance of its proposals with regard to the principle of subsidiarity; whenever necessary, the explanatory memorandum accompanying a proposal will give details in this respect. The financing of Community action in whole or in part from the Community budget shall require an explanation;
– take duly into account the need for any burden, whether financial or administrative, falling upon the Community, national governments, local authorities, economic operators and citizens, to be minimized and proportionate to the objective to be achieved;
– submit an annual report to the European Council, the Council and the European Parliament on the application of Article 3b (Art. 5) of the Treaty. This annual report shall also be sent to the Committee of the Regions and to the Economic and Social Committee.

10.   The European Council shall take account of the Commission report referred in paragraph 9, fourth indent, within the report on the progress achieved by the Union which it is required to submit to the European Parliament in accordance with Article D of the Treaty on European Union.

11.   While fully observing the procedures applicable, the European Parliament and the Council shall, as an integral part of the overall examination of Commission proposals, consider their consistency with Article 3b (Art. 5). This concerns the original Commission proposal as well as amendments which the European Parliament and the Council envisage making to the proposal.

12.   In the course of the procedures referred to in Articles 189b and 189c (Arts. 251 and 252), the European Parliament shall be informed of the Councils' position on the application of Article 3b, by way of a statement of the reasons which led the Council to adopt its common position. The Council shall inform the European Parliament of the reasons on the basis of which all or part of a Commission proposal is deemed to be inconsistent with Article 3b (Art. 5) of the Treaty.

13.   Compliance with the principle of subsidiarity shall be reviewed in accordance with the rules laid down by this Treaty'.

   1. Declaration relating to the Protocol on the application of the principles of subsidiarity and proportionality
      The High Contracting Parties confirm, on the one hand, Declaration No. 19 annexed to the Treaty establishing the European Community on the implementation of Community law and, on the other, the conclusions of the Essen European Council stating that the administrative implementation of Community law shall in principle be the responsibility of the Member States in accordance with their constitutional arrangements. This shall not affect the supervisory, monitoring and implementing powers of the Community Institutions as provided under Article 145 and 155 of the TEC (Art. 202, 211).

G. The Union's Institutions

Chapters 14 to 17 of the Amsterdam Treaty deal respectively with:

- the EP;
- the Council;
- the Commission, and
- the Court of Justice.

1. EP (Chapter 14)

18.   The *co-decision* procedure, simplified, will apply to the following new Treaty provisions, relating to European labour Law:

– Employment – Incentive measures (Art. 5-Chapter IV) (Art. 109r; Art. 129, Title VIa);
– Equal opportunities and treatment (Art. 119) (Art. 141).

The number of Members of the EP shall not exceed 700 (Art. 137 TEC) (Art. 189)

2. The Council (Chapter 15)

19.   Qualified majority voting will apply to the following new Treaty provisions, relating to European labour Law:

– Employment Guidelines (Art. 4, Chapter IV) (Art. 109q; Art. 128; Title VIa);
– Incentive measures (Art. 5, Chapter IV) (Art. 109r; Art. 129; Title VIa);

– Social exclusion (Art. 118(2)) (Art. 137);
– Equality of opportunity and equal treatment of men and women (Art. 199(3)) (Art. 268).

3. The Commission (Chapter 16)

20.   'The governments of the Member States shall nominate by common accord the person they intend to appoint as President of the Commission; the nomination shall be approved by the European Parliament.

The governments of the Member States shall, by common accord with the nominee for President, nominate the other persons whom they intend to appoint as Members of the Commission' (Art. 158(2) TEC) Art. 214).

4. The European Court (Chapter 17)

The provisions of the Treaty establishing the European Community, the Treaty establishing the European Coal and Steel Community and the Treaty establishing the European Atomic Energy Community concerning the powers of the Court of Justice of the European Communities and the exercise of those powers shall apply only to the following provisions of the Treaty:

(a) [unchanged];
(b) provisions of Title VI, under the conditions provided for by Articles K. 7 (Art. 35) and K. 12 (Art. 40);
(c) Article F(2) with regard to action of the institutions, insofar as the Court has jurisdiction under the Treaties establishing the European Communities and under this Treaty;
(d) Articles L to S (Arts. 46–53).

Point c is important as it relates to the European Convention of Human Rights of 1950.

Annex. The Treaty of Amsterdam

Index (I)

Index (I)

Index (I)

502

Index (I)

Index (II – The Treaty of Amsterdam)

Index (II – The Treaty of Amsterdam)